Tapestry in Action

Tapestry in Action

HOWARD M. LEWIS SHIP

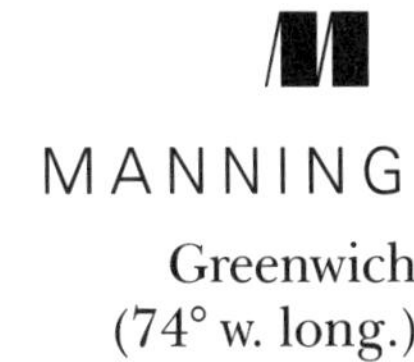

MANNING
Greenwich
(74° w. long.)

For online information and ordering of this and other Manning books, go to www.manning.com. The publisher offers discounts on this book when ordered in quantity. For more information, please contact:

Special Sales Department
Manning Publications Co.
209 Bruce Park Avenue
Greenwich, CT 06830

Fax: (203) 661-9018
email: orders@manning.com

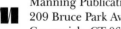

Manning Publications Co.
209 Bruce Park Avenue
Greenwich, CT 06830

Copyeditor: Liz Welch
Typesetter: Denis Dalinnik
Cover designer: Leslie Haimes

ISBN 1-932394-11-7

Printed in the United States of America
1 2 3 4 5 6 7 8 9 10 – VHG – 08 07 06 05 04

To my parents, who bought me my first computer when I was 13
and had no idea what they had started

brief contents

APPENDIXES

contents

foreword

My involvement with Tapestry began in the autumn of 2001. I read about the framework in an article in *ONJava* magazine. At the same time, our company was poised to begin several new web projects, and we were looking for a way to avoid the problems inherent in building complex web pages and forms with the standard tools. We analyzed a large number of frameworks, but Tapestry immediately attracted our attention, with its unique development method and its helpful community.

The first glance was not misleading—Tapestry proved to be a powerful and helpful instrument in practice as well. The component structure was not simply an add-on but was entrenched in the philosophy of the framework. We also discovered that Tapestry offered a number of other powerful features that proved to be critical in our work. For example, it allowed a clean separation between Java and HTML, and made it possible for the design work on the application to continue well after the code had been completed—and it could be performed by designers who never had to know anything about Tapestry. It provided internationalization capabilities well beyond simply replacing text with its translation. The framework was designed with EJBs and clustering in mind, and integrated with them effortlessly.

Today our company has libraries containing hundreds of Tapestry components. Some of these are simple, such as a Login component that manages authentication using HTTP cookies. Others are far more complex, constructed from smaller components and full of intricate JavaScript, such as a tool for dynamically defining web forms. All of these components can simply be taken off the shelf and plugged into our latest application with ease. We do not have to worry how the various components will work together—we know that they will do so by design.

During the two years we have worked with Tapestry, its development has not stood still. While the earlier versions of the framework concentrated on delivering power, version 3.0 (described in this book) concentrates on both delivering maximum ease of use for programmers and enhancing their productivity. It lowers the entry requirements, decreases the amount of developer effort needed, and makes the framework as easy to use as a scripting language for simple applications. The result is that you can achieve the same results as before but with much less coding.

The majority of these improvements have occurred and moved forward due to feedback and ideas from Tapestry users and contributors. The active community surrounding the framework helps it remain focused on resolving the problems developers encounter in the real world. A major commendation for encouraging and integrating the contributions must also go to Howard Lewis Ship, the author of this book. As the creator and original designer of Tapestry, he has made a remarkable effort to listen to users, understand their needs, and address their requirements. The other Tapestry contributors have followed his lead and have extended the framework to provide support for a variety of new functionality areas. The community has also been instrumental in the process that made Tapestry a part of the Apache Jakarta family. With this step, it became a companion project of other popular projects, including Struts, Tomcat, and log4J. All of these factors ensure that Tapestry will persist in its evolution and will continue to improve the ways in which it makes the life of web developers easier and more productive.

This book will allow you to delve into a different, better world of web development than the one you have known. It will show you an innovative approach for creating and organizing your applications, enable you to develop more robust and scalable code, and make previously difficult tasks much simpler. After you get to know Tapestry, you will start looking at web development in a very different way. Enjoy!

THEODORE TONCHEV
"MINDBRIDGE"
TECHNICAL DIRECTOR, RUSHMORE DIGITAL

preface

From the fall of 1998 through late 1999, I worked on a mix of interesting projects for my then-employer, Primix, a Boston Internet consulting firm. The first of these was a standard CRUD (Create Read Update Delete) application, and it used servlets and JavaServer Pages (JSPs). Despite the fact that we were a small team (just three or four of us at various times) working on a very modest application, it seemed like we were constantly having to reinvent the wheel. I'd had some exposure to Apple's WebObjects framework, and the difference between the two approaches was like night and day: Not only did WebObjects have better tool integration, including a WYSIWYG (What You See Is What You Get) HTML editor, it was easier to use even *without* the extra tools, just by editing the underlying template and configuration files. We were a small, smart, experienced team—but working with servlets and JSPs was always an uphill battle compared to using WebObjects.

A major part of this problem was impedance; each developer worked in his or her own corner of the application and had a particular way of working. Different developers used different naming conventions and solved similar problems in different ways—which caused extra grief when new developers cycled through the team, or when we had to venture outside our little fiefdoms to fix bugs. Remember, this was a time before J2EE servers really existed, before custom JSP tag libraries, before Sun had even started promoting the Model 2 design pattern. It was also obvious that WebObjects, with its notion of components and all the magic it did to hide URLs from the developer, was a far superior option. At the same time, steep licensing fees and lukewarm support and marketing by Apple made pitching a WebObjects solution to clients a nonstarter. We soldiered on with servlets and JSPs.

Near the end of 1999 I was left with engagements in the pipeline but no short-term responsibilities. What was to eventually become Tapestry started as a kind of mental doodle: How *does* WebObjects do it? I started drawing diagrams and sketches, puzzling out a way to gracefully connect stateless HTTP requests to stateful Java objects via Java servlets, and eventually decided to code up a little prototype to see if my ideas would work. Somewhere along the line, I came up with the name: Tapestry.

Tapestry quickly took on a life of its own; as primitive as that early code base looks compared to the Tapestry of today, it was still a solid foundation, something that would start to address the issues Primix had with servlet and JSP development. Primix was in the business of creating high-quality web sites on a regular basis, and Tapestry was a platform that would support the solid software engineering principles necessary to achieve its goals. Tapestry set up shop at SourceForge (http://sf.net) and was released under the Lesser GNU Public License.

Along the way, I realized something profound: *I could make a difference.* Interesting software didn't have to come forth directly from the Suns, IBMs, and Microsofts, or even from the Apaches; it could be homegrown, like Tapestry. With Tapestry, I really thought I could change the world…or at least, the little niche of the world that writes web applications in Java.

As fun as working on the code has been, the most fascinating part of Tapestry has been the creation of a real, online community around Tapestry. These are people for the most part I have yet to meet, who have recognized Tapestry as a Good Thing and who work as hard as I do to improve and promote it. It was on the strength of this community that Tapestry relocated from SourceForge to Apache's Jakarta project, alongside established projects such as Struts, Turbine, and Velocity.

Crafting a book about Tapestry has been more difficult and more intense an experience than anything else related to the project, but ultimately the result is worth the effort. What you are holding in your hands may open up a whole new approach to web application development for you and (I hope) will change your world for the better.

acknowledgments

Working on this book has been *the* highlight of my career to date. I've never before had the opportunity to be so focused and so self-directed for such a long time. I would never have had this opportunity without the support and friendship of Timothy Dion, the CTO of Primix, who gave me the green light to work on Tapestry in the first place, as well as the support to release it as open source. Just as instrumental was my good friend Gregory Burd, who championed Tapestry within Primix and put it into play for its first big engagement.

The Tapestry crew—Theodore Tonchev, Richard Lewis-Shell, David Solis, Neil Swinton, Harish Krishnaswamy, and Geoff Longman—have been tireless supporters of Tapestry, and good friends, many of whom I've yet to meet in person! Thanks as well to Andrew C. Oliver for sponsoring Tapestry in the Apache Jakarta project.

Writing a book is a group effort—without the tireless help from the crew at Manning, this book would never have reached your hands. Both Marilyn Smith and Liz Welch provided endless assistance with grammar and style, as well as much valuable advice. Tiffany Taylor's eagle eyes spotted an embarrassing number of typos and inconsistencies. Denis Dalinnik did a standout job of typesetting. Special thanks to Jackie Carter, for keeping me honest and keeping me focused on the reader. Thanks also to my technical reviewers, especially Bill Lear, Ryan Cox, Adam Greene, and Joel Trunick—they pushed me to create a better book than I would have thought possible. Thanks as well to

Mary Piergies for keeping it all organized, to Clay Andres for getting the whole thing started, and to publisher Marjan Bace for the vote of confidence.

Special thanks go to my wife, Suzanne, who has encouraged me every step of the way on this long process. Suzanne's support has never wavered, even as this project consumed my time, attention, energy, and the dining room table (my workspace) for months on end. Suzanne has indulged my need to talk about Tapestry and this book long past the point where anyone else would have run screaming from the room, and I love her for that, and for her boundless enthusiasm. We are stylin', baby!

about this book

Tapestry is a comprehensive web application framework for the Java programming language. Tapestry is based on components, highly reusable building blocks that can be quickly and easily combined to form pages within your application. By using and reusing components, and creating your own components, you can create richly interactive, robust applications with only a modest effort.

Tapestry's basic style is to break problems into smaller and smaller units; this complements a team development environment where different developers work on different parts of the application. The framework makes it easy for both Java and HTML-only developers to work together without accidentally undermining each other's work.

When building a web application with any technology, you will be faced with a constant stream of questions: How do I figure out what the user has requested? Where can I store this bit of information? How can I safely add this new functionality? How can I make my application scale? In too many environments, it's easy to make the wrong decision when confronted with any of these, and many other, development-time questions. It's too easy to take a quick-and-dirty detour down the wrong path, which ultimately comes back to bite you when you are least prepared to deal with it.

The central goal of Tapestry is to make the *easiest* choice the *correct* choice. Over the course of this book, we'll show you how to build applications using

Tapestry, but we will also show you the hidden traps and tangles that Tapestry helps you to avoid.

Roadmap

- Chapter 1 introduces web applications in general. We begin to describe where Tapestry fits into the overall scheme of things and expand on the basic goals achieved by the framework.
- Chapter 2 sets the stage, describing the implementation of a simple web application that plays the word game Hangman. Here we introduce many of the major concepts of Tapestry.
- Chapters 3 through 5 describe how Tapestry handles HTML form input, including the framework's sophisticated form-validation subsystem.
- Chapter 6 describes how to build basic reusable components and how to package them into component libraries.
- Chapter 7 delves into the inner implementation of Tapestry, shedding light on how the framework addresses scalability issues, localization, and the lifecycle of pages.
- Chapter 8 describes advanced components, including components that create client-side JavaScript. We also discuss integrating Tapestry with a traditional servlets-and-JSPs application.
- Chapters 9 and 10 describe the Virtual Library, a complete J2EE example application using Tapestry for the presentation layer and a mix of session and entity EJBs for the application layer. We include several real-world examples that illustrate how to build and polish a Tapestry application.

Who should read this book?

This is a book about getting things done using the Tapestry framework; as such, it will appeal to Java web developers looking for a better, easier way to build web applications. Because Tapestry is explicitly designed to support team development of web applications, this book will also be of interest to managers looking for a better way to leverage their team's efforts.

This book is targeted at people who have at least gotten their feet wet in terms of Java web application development (or perhaps have already taken the full plunge). Therefore, we assume that you are at least somewhat acquainted with a number of concepts and technologies. Obviously, an understanding of the Java programming language is a prerequisite, as well as familiarity with such key Java APIs as the collections framework. You should also be clear on the distinction between Java interfaces and Java classes.

Much of Tapestry concerns the moving of information from one object to another; this is facilitated using JavaBeans properties. The core concept of the JavaBeans framework is that an object can be treated as if it was a `Map`, as a collection of named properties that can be read or updated without knowing the actual class of the object. More information about JavaBeans is available at http://java.sun.com/products/javabeans/docs/.

You should be familiar with the basic set of HTML tags, including `<body>`, `<img>`, `<a>`, `<form>`, and `<input>`. You must also be familiar with URLs and query parameters and the difference between HTTP `GET` and HTTP `POST`.

Many of the artifacts of a Tapestry application are XML documents. You should be familiar with basic XML usage and syntax.

Some of the later examples show how to implement client-side logic. This requires an understanding of JavaScript (the scripting language that executes within a client web browser) as well as the Document Object Model, the data structure representing a web page inside a web browser.

Code conventions and downloads

This book includes copious examples, which include all the Tapestry application artifacts: Java code, HTML templates, and XML specification files. Source code in listings or in text is in a `fixed width font` to separate it from ordinary text. Additionally, Java method names, component parameters, object properties, and HTML and XML elements and attributes in text are also presented using `fixed width font`. Java method names will generally not include the signature (the list of parameter types).

Java, HTML, and XML can all be quite verbose. In many cases, the original source code (available online) has been reformatted, adding line breaks and reworking indentation, to accommodate the available page space in the book. In rare cases, even this was not enough, and listings will include line continuation markers. Additionally, comments in the source code have been removed from the listings.

Code annotations accompany many of the source code listings, highlighting important concepts. In some cases, numbered bullets link to explanations that follow the listing.

Tapestry is an open-source project, released under the very liberal Apache Software License. Directions for downloading Tapestry, in source or binary form, are available from the Tapestry home page: http://jakarta.apache.org/tapestry/. Documentation available from the home page also identifies how to download the source code via CVS so that you can build the framework locally, if you are so inclined.

The Tapestry distribution includes the Virtual Library application described in chapters 9 and 10.

The source code for all examples in this book is available from Manning's web site: www.manning.com/lewisship/. To run the examples, you need to download Tapestry and the Tomcat servlet container. Appendix B contains the details.

Author Online

The purchase of *Tapestry in Action* includes free access to a private web forum run by Manning Publications, where you can make comments about the book, ask technical questions, and receive help from the author and from other users. To access the forum and subscribe to it, point your web browser to www.manning.com/lewisship. This page provides information on how to get on the forum once you are registered, what kind of help is available, and the rules of conduct on the forum.

Manning's commitment to our readers is to provide a venue where a meaningful dialogue between individual readers and between readers and the author can take place. It is not a commitment to any specific amount of participation on the part of the author, whose contribution to the forum remains voluntary (and unpaid). We suggest you try asking the author some challenging questions, lest his interest stray! The Author Online forum and the archives of previous discussions will be accessible from the publisher's web site as long as the book is in print.

About the author

Howard Lewis Ship is the lead developer for the Tapestry project. He cut his teeth writing customer support software for Stratus Computer, but eventually traded PL/1 for Objective-C and NextStep before settling into Java. Howard is currently an independent open-source and J2EE consultant, specializing in customized Tapestry training. You can find Howard on the web at http://howardlewisship.com. In the real world, he lives in Quincy, Massachusetts, with his wife Suzanne, a novelist.

about the title

By combining introductions, overviews, and how-to examples, the *In Action* books are designed to help learning *and* remembering. According to research in cognitive science, the things people remember are things they discover during self-motivated exploration.

Although no-one at Manning is a cognitive scientist, we are convinced that for learning to become permanent it must pass through stages of exploration, play, and, interestingly, re-telling of what is being learned. People understand and remember new things, which is to say they master them, only after actively exploring them. Humans learn *in action*. An essential part of an *In Action* guide is that it is example-driven. It encourages the reader to try things out, to play with new code, and explore new ideas.

There is another, more mundane, reason for the title of this book: our readers are busy. They use books to do a job or solve a problem. They need books that allow them to jump in and jump out easily and learn just what they want just when they want it. They need books that aid them *in action*. The books in this series are designed for such readers.

about the cover illustration

The figure on the cover of *Tapestry in Action* is a "Gonaquesa Baylando," a dancing woman of the Gonaqua tribe in Africa. The Gonaquas were herders and farmers living on the southern coast of the continent near the Cape of Good Hope in what is today South Africa. The illustration is taken from a Spanish compendium of regional dress customs first published in Madrid in 1799. The book's title page states:

> *Coleccion general de los Trages que usan actualmente todas las Nacionas del Mundo desubierto, dibujados y grabados con la mayor exactitud por R.M.V.A.R. Obra muy util y en special para los que tienen la del viajero universal*

which we translate, as literally as possible, thus:

> *General collection of costumes currently used in the nations of the known world, designed and printed with great exactitude by R.M.V.A.R. This work is very useful especially for those who hold themselves to be universal travelers*

Although nothing is known of the designers, engravers, and workers who colored this illustration by hand, the "exactitude" of their execution is evident in this drawing. The "Gonaquesa Baylando" is just one of many figures in this colorful collection. Their diversity speaks vividly of the uniqueness and individuality of the world's towns and regions just 200 years ago. This was a time when the dress codes of two regions separated by a few dozen miles identified people uniquely as belonging to one or the other. The collection brings to life a sense of isolation and distance of that period—and of every other historic period except our own hyperkinetic present.

Dress codes have changed since then and the diversity by region, so rich at the time, has faded away. It is now often hard to tell the inhabitant of one continent from another. Perhaps, trying to view it optimistically, we have traded a cultural and visual diversity for a more varied personal life. Or a more varied and interesting intellectual and technical life.

We at Manning celebrate the inventiveness, the initiative, and, yes, the fun of the computer business with book covers based on the rich diversity of regional life of two centuries ago, brought back to life by the pictures from this collection.

Part 1

Getting started with Tapestry

Chapters 1 through 5 introduce you to the basic concepts of Tapestry. You'll learn how Tapestry defines an application, a page within an application, and a component within a page. These chapters gradually expose you to the more complicated challenges in developing web applications and explain how Tapestry meets these challenges.

1 Introducing Tapestry

This chapter covers

- Understanding web applications
- The goals of Tapestry
- Using the Model-View-Controller pattern
- Essential Tapestry classes and interfaces

> *"... and we're going to implement it as a web interface," your boss announces, and you start to get that sick feeling in your stomach. You had only been half-listening, daydreaming about the clever, graceful user interface you were going to create. But now you're in unknown territory; you might as well be fresh out of school! Your mental roadmap to the application starts to lose focus; you can still see the islands of code and functionality, but now you imagine a dark, churning sea between them. How are you going to get this to work as a web application?*

If you are used to creating traditional desktop applications, switching over to developing web applications can be a journey into unfamiliar territory. Web applications turn everything you know upside down—in desktop applications, your code is in the driver's seat, ultimately controlling every pixel visible to your single user, and the application is all-knowing about every mouse movement or key press. In web applications, your code is just part of an overall picture involving a variety of computers and network communications... and your code must support multiple simultaneous users. This book describes how to use the Tapestry web application framework to ease your transition into the web application development space.

The Tapestry framework is more than a crutch for new web developers; even seasoned developers and project leaders will find advantages to building their applications using it. Tapestry allows true black-box code reuse within and between applications; it addresses the concerns of large teams of developers with mixed skill sets; it has support for application internationalization as a central feature, not an afterthought. This book shows you how to leverage Tapestry to produce a more sophisticated, more robust application faster and more easily than you might suspect.

Tapestry is an open source, Java web application framework designed from the ground up to help you deliver the best web applications possible. It allows new developers to get up to speed easily, creating working applications with a surprisingly small amount of Java code. It includes numerous features that address the issues encountered during team development of large, complex, internationalized applications. Tapestry is open-ended—it doesn't shoehorn you into any one category of web application, which means you can build your own Amazon, Slashdot, Yahoo!, or eBay with it. Tapestry is designed to plug into whatever form of back-end systems you use, with a minimum of fuss.

This is a framework that lets you have it both ways: you create a web application, but you don't have to throw away everything you've previously learned about coding just because you are creating a web application instead of a traditional desktop application. The cornerstone of Tapestry is letting you write applications in terms of objects, methods, and properties—not in terms of URLs and query parameters and Java servlets.

1.1 What are web applications?

In the earliest days of the World Wide Web, the majority of web sites were entirely *static*, unchanging. Many early sites were created entirely by hand, by folks using simple text editors to directly edit the HTML of individual pages. Other sites were created in a batch mode, where a source file or database would be transformed into HTML. In fact, the original purpose of the Web was to allow physicists to easily share their publications; physics papers written using LaTeX (a special-purpose typesetting language) were translated into HTML for instant sharing.

Web sites didn't stay static for long; instead, they transformed into *web applications*. A web application is *interactive*; the end user will see links that may be clicked and HTML forms that may be filled out. These links and forms become requests sent to a server, which will respond with a new HTML page, often created (from a template) on the fly, as a personalized response to a specific request.

Figure 1.1 illustrates the general flow of a web application, which is divided into four steps:

1. A request is received by the server. Information in the request is used to dispatch control to the correct application code.
2. Application-specific code executes. This code interprets the information available to it in the URL and query parameters, and executes some application-specific logic. This includes deciding what response to send back to the client.

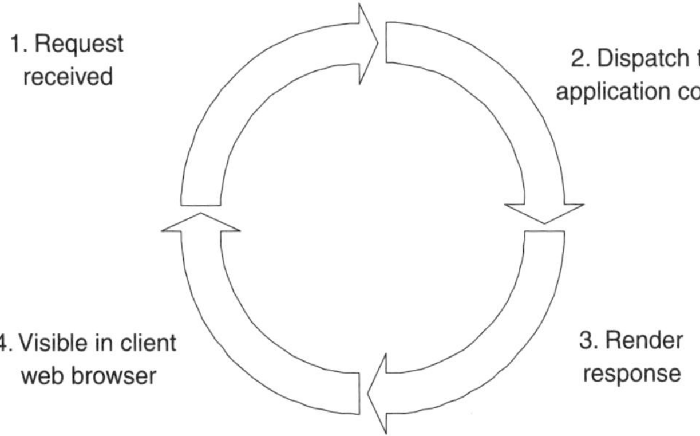

Figure 1.1 Web applications are built around a cycle; a request is received, application-specific code is executed, and a response is rendered, eventually appearing in the client's web browser.

3 A response is rendered. The response includes links and forms that will result in new request cycles.
4 The response is visible in the client web browser. Users now have a chance to see the results of the action they initiated. In addition, any client-side logic is activated.[1] The user may click links or submit forms, resulting in a new request cycle.

Web applications are written in the context of the underlying network protocol connecting the client web browser (such as Microsoft Internet Explorer or Netscape Navigator) and the web server: the Hypertext Transport Protocol (HTTP). HTTP is a stateless protocol, meaning that each request is completely independent of any requests that come before or after it. There is no explicit concept of *user identity* in HTTP or even, at the protocol level, any way to identify that a series of requests comes from a single user. The stateless nature of HTTP is an important factor in its success; a stateless protocol is much easier to implement in a web browser or a web server.

For dynamic, interactive web applications, the inherent statelessness of HTTP creates new challenges. End users are not concerned with this; they simply expect to progress from a catalog page to a shopping cart page to a checkout page. Creating a stateful application from a stateless protocol is a concern for the application developer and involves issues not present in a desktop application. By comparison, imagine writing a document by launching a text editor application, loading a file, typing a single sentence, saving the file, and then shutting down the application before repeating the whole process for the next sentence. For a web application, each request is like one sentence in that document…and part of the request had better be *which* document is being edited and *where* in the document the new sentence goes. A desktop application automatically has a kind of continuity that must be specifically engineered into a web application.

This same basic web application flow can be implemented in many different environments and languages. In the early heyday of web applications, scripting languages such as Perl were most often used to implement the application-specific code. Over time, as web applications evolved from clever novelties into critical enterprise infrastructure, the implementation choice for web applications shifted to more powerful, higher-level languages. The Java programming

[1] This takes the form of JavaScript programs embedded within the HTML that execute within the client's web browser.

language is especially well suited for web application development because of its standard web application framework, the Java Servlet API.

1.2 What are Java servlets?

The Java Servlet API is an open standard, created by Sun, for creating web applications using the Java programming language. A *servlet* is an object responsible for receiving a request from a client web browser and returning a response—an HTML page to be displayed in the browser. The Servlet API defines an interface and base class for servlets, as well as interfaces for several other supporting objects, such as the `HttpServletRequest` (which represents a request and allows the servlet to access query parameters). Vendors, both open source and proprietary, provide the actual server code and the implementations of the standard interfaces.

Servlets are most often paired with JavaServer Pages (JSPs) in order to generate a response. JSPs are a standard templating technology for servlets. A JSP is a mix of ordinary, static HTML with additional, specialized tags and directives that provide dynamic output, such as including the current user's name or the contents of an online shopping cart. Under the hood, each JSP is converted into a Java servlet that is compiled and loaded into memory. More information about servlets and JSPs is available online and in print, including *Web Development with JavaServer Pages.*[2]

A servlet operates within a *servlet container*. The servlet container serves as a bridge between HTTP and the Java servlet code that you, as the developer, will write. The servlet container is responsible for instantiating and initializing your servlets as needed. Servlet containers may be standalone, such as Apache Tomcat, or may be one part of an overall application server, such as BEA WebLogic, IBM WebSphere, or the open source JBoss application server.

The servlet container is responsible for selecting the correct servlet to invoke based on the URL of the request; a single web application will contain many servlets. The web application's *deployment descriptor* (an XML file packaged with the application) gives the name and Java class for each servlet and identifies which URLs are mapped to which servlets. For example, your application may have a registration page containing an HTML form enabling new users to register (supplying their name and email address or other data). That form will submit to the

---

[2] Duane K. Fields, Mark A. Kolb, and Shawn Bayern, *Web Development with JavaServer Pages, 2nd Edition* (Greenwich, CT: Manning Publications, 2001).

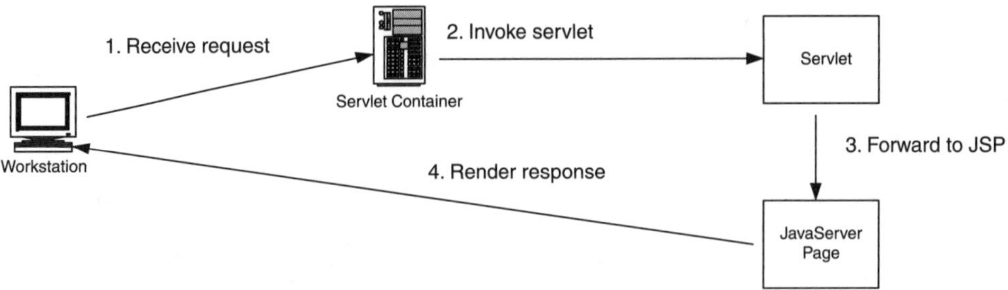

Figure 1.2 Incoming requests to the server are dispatched to a particular servlet instance. The servlet forwards to a JSP that renders the response sent back to the client web browser.

/addCustomer URL, which is mapped to the `addCustomer` servlet, which is instantiated as the `AddCustomerServlet` class. The deployment descriptor will include the following elements describing the `addCustomer` servlet's configuration:

```
<servlet>
  <servlet-name>addCustomer</servlet-name>
  <servlet-class>com.mycompany.AddCustomerServlet</servlet-class>
</servlet>

<servlet-mapping>
  <servlet-name>addCustomer</servlet-name>
  <url-pattern>/addCustomer</url-pattern>
</servlet-mapping>
```

Figure 1.2 shows how the application request cycle applies to servlets.

As can be seen from this example, each servlet represents a particular *operation* within the overall web application. The `AddCustomerServlet` class will include code that reads the query parameters submitted with the form and uses those values to create some kind of `Customer` object that can be stored into a database. Additional logic must decide what form of response to display—normally a confirmation page, but possibly the original page containing the form if an error occurred when creating the customer.

This operation-centric approach can work well for many parts of a web application. In this example, there is only one registration page, and so only one place from which the `addCustomer` servlet can be invoked. If the original registration page must be redisplayed (to present the user with an error message), there is no guesswork about what page to use; it will always be Registration.jsp.

When an operation can be associated with many different application pages, the operation-centric approach can start to become a burden. For example, many applications include pages that display long lists of information and allow users to navigate through the results one page at a time. Such pages include links to operations such as "next page of results" or "previous page of results."

Using servlets, it becomes necessary to somehow identify not just the operation, but to where the operation should be applied. Are we displaying the product catalog page, or the shopping cart page, or the related-items page? Now we need a way to identify the page; a common approach is to add a query parameter to the URL to identify that page.

Multiplexing operations onto multiple pages is just one factor a servlet developer must keep in mind. Another is dealing with the multithreaded environment in which a servlet object operates.

1.2.1 Understanding servlet multithreading

Within a servlet container each servlet is instantiated exactly once; all requests mapped to the servlet's URL pattern will be passed through to the `service()` method of a single servlet object.[3]

Servlet containers are multithreaded, which is to say they contain multiple threads of execution, allowing requests from several client web browsers to be processed simultaneously—a critical factor for building scalable web applications. Despite this, servlets are still single instances, *shared* between the threads. Servlet instances must be thread-safe; instance variables can't be used either for temporary storage during a single request or for persistent storage between requests, because any information stored in an instance variable is likely to be overwritten by other threads.

Servlets are the odd-man-out in the object-oriented world; they are technically still objects but largely fall short of the accepted definition of an object: a combination of operations and state. Servlets aren't allowed to directly store state in their own instance variables. Local variables are fine for some things, but there are specific cases where local variables are not applicable, such as forwarding to a JSP to render a response.

JSPs, like servlets, are stateless and multithreaded; therefore, there's no way that a servlet could, for example, set a property of a JSP to the current user's name. Instead, the Servlet API object `HttpServletRequest` is used to store such transient information. One aspect of the request object is that it can be used to store named attribute values. The servlet can store values into the request before forwarding to a particular JSP to render the response, as shown in figure 1.3.

---

[3] Your servlet code will be inside the `doGet()` or `doPost()` method that is invoked by the `service()` method.

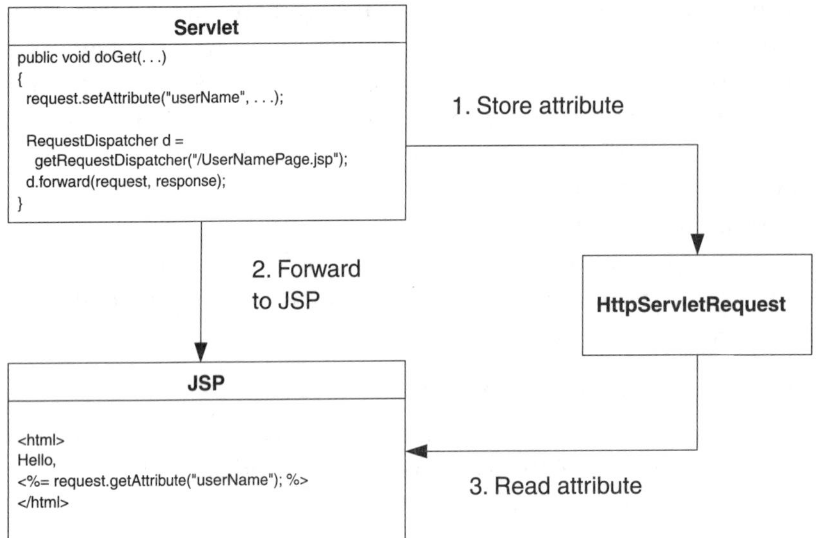

Figure 1.3 A servlet can store a request attribute before forwarding to the JSP; the JSP can then read the attribute and incorporate it into the response.

This is an example of the servlet "pushing" data into the JSP via the `HttpServletRequest`. The servlet and JSP are intimately tied together; they must agree on exactly which attributes will be stored into the request object, and there's no room for error on the naming (`username` is not the same as `userName`, for example). Overall, the `HttpServletRequest` provides a flexible solution for managing transient information; as we'll see, a similar solution addresses the more complicated problem of persistent server-side state.

1.2.2 Managing server-side state

The single attribute that most widely separates a static web site from a true web application is *server-side state*. Amazon has a shopping cart that remembers what items you've placed in it from one request to the next. Google remembers enough about your query to allow you to page through the list of results. Any application will need to identify you as a particular user and remember some amount of information about the activities you've performed while visiting the site.

For a web application to be truly interactive and personalized, it must have a way of identifying the user from one request to request, and a way to store information on the server about that particular user. This is not necessarily the same thing as authentication; the application may not be able to match the requests to a particular user account or credit card number, but that shouldn't prevent the application from tracking short-term information, such as the contents of a shopping cart in an e-commerce application—information that needs to persist from one request to the next.

So, if HTTP is stateless, how can an application store any state at all? What's needed is some form of identifier to be created on the server, sent back to the client, and returned to the server as part of subsequent requests. Fortunately, most client web browsers support HTTP cookies; a *cookie* is a small string stored within the browser. The server can invisibly include a cookie value in a response,[4] and the client browser will send the cookie value back up to the server in each subsequent request—exactly what is required to support server-side state. A series of such linked requests forms a *session*.

For servlets, server-side state is stored in the `HttpSession` object. Like the `HttpServletRequest`, the session object may store named attribute values; the difference is that such values are stored on the server *between* requests. For example, the `ShoppingCart` object created and stored in the session by the `addToShoppingCart` servlet will later be available to the checkout servlet responsible for collecting payment information, even though the user may do quite a bit of browsing around the product catalog in between those two operations.

Sessions are not created until specifically requested; the `HttpServletRequest` object includes a method, `getSession()`, for creating the session as needed. Some people or organizations do not allow HTTP cookies (most browsers allow support for cookies to be turned off, for privacy and security reasons). With a little extra effort, it is still possible to support stateful servlet applications even when the client does not support cookies.[5]

Support for servlets and JSPs is a standard feature for all popular application servers, and many developers do manage to create successful web applications using just the standard servlet technology. At the same time, there is a growing acknowledgement that servlets are just the starting point for Java web applications, as evidenced by an increasing number of popular frameworks. This goes beyond just Tapestry and includes other frameworks such as Turbine (http://jakarta.apache.org/turbine/), Maverick (http://mav.sourceforge.net/), WebWork (http://www.opensymphony.com/webwork/) and, most prominently, Struts.

---

4 The HTTP cookie is part of the HTTP "envelope" around the HTML "message"; it isn't part of the HTML and won't be visible even if the user views the HTML source of a rendered page.

5 The servlet container can encode the session ID into the application's URLs to provide session continuity.

1.2.3 Using Struts with servlets

Struts, like Tapestry, is an open source framework available from the Jakarta project, at http://jakarta.apache.org/struts/. Struts is an extension to standard servlets, rounding out rough edges and adding a few much-needed abstractions that simplify servlet coding. A comprehensive guide to Struts is available in *Struts in Action.*[6]

A Struts application uses a single servlet to represent all possible operations. The servlet uses a set of Struts-specific configuration files to dispatch incoming requests to a particular Struts `Action` object. Like servlets, Struts `Actions` are multithreaded and stateless. Struts also includes a set of JSP tag libraries that simplify and standardize the creation of dynamic web pages, especially with respect to creating URLs for links and form submissions.

Struts uses its configuration files to loosely couple `Actions` to the JSPs that render responses (and makes it easier to use another templating system, such as Velocity). JSPs are assigned logical names in the Struts configuration that can be referenced from an `Action`; if the JSP is moved or renamed, the side effects are isolated to just the Struts configuration file, not the Java code for the `Action`. The same mechanism also makes it easier to chain together a series of `Actions`; for example, the one `Action` can be used to update some server-side state and can forward to a second `Action` that stores information into the `HttpServletRequest` before forwarding to a JSP to render the response; this useful pattern is easier to accomplish in Struts than with ordinary servlets.

Struts includes a standard mechanism for converting form submissions into objects, which works by matching query parameter names against JavaBean properties of a user-defined form object. The latest release of Struts complements this with a rules-based input-validation system.

Struts standardizes some common patterns and techniques that would otherwise need to be re-invented by each developer, but it is still fundamentally similar to ordinary servlet development. Whether developing using just servlets or with servlets augmented by Struts, you will still encounter some significant limitations in the basic development model that you must overcome.

1.2.4 Understanding the limitations of servlets

There is a qualitative difference between the kind of servlet application seen in demos and tutorials and true enterprise applications. Demo applications are

[6] Ted Husted et al., *Struts in Action* (Greenwich, CT: Manning Publications, 2002).

small, focused, and limited in scope; they are often created in a short period of time by a single individual, who fills the roles of application architect, HTML developer, and Java developer simultaneously.

By contrast, development of a full-scale application entails a number of real-world concerns:

- A large number of developers (HTML and Java) may be working in parallel.
- Individual developers will have varying levels of skill and understanding.
- The HTML portions of the application may be developed by team members with little or no knowledge of Java or JSPs (or even by a completely separate, isolated team).
- Large applications (with hundreds of distinct pages) may be so complex that individual developers will understand only a small portion of the overall application.
- Successful applications will, almost by definition, grow and expand in complexity to meet new customer requirements.

These concerns manifest themselves in a number of common antipatterns, which we describe next.

Weak binding

The most fundamental issues with building, maintaining, and extending a web application using servlets surround two related problems: *weak binding* and *unwanted dependencies*. In a servlet application, the connections between pages are *weak* because those connections are expressed as URLs, not as method invocations or object properties. At the time that a JSP renders a link (or form) connecting to another page in an application, all it is doing is outputting a string as the `href` attribute of an HTML `<a>` hyperlink tag (or the `action` attribute of an HTML `<form>` tag). This is another difference between desktop applications and servlet applications: Changing a method signature in an object of a desktop application will create errors in code elsewhere in the application that uses the old method signature. The integrated development environment (IDE) will clearly show those errors, and you can find and fix all of them before running and testing your application.

In a servlet application, the connection between two servlets is reduced to a string within a JSP. The JSP must include a URL string (for the target servlet) in the response sent to the client web browser. Where does that URL string come from? The developer manually inserts it into the JSP, after consulting the web deployment descriptor (or Struts configuration file) to find the operation mapping to link to. Assuming the developer introduces no typos, the link between pages *should* be functional—but there's no way to be absolutely sure without actually running the application. This servlet-to-servlet linkage is a weak binding; the Java compiler or other tools cannot validate (at build time) that the URLs are correct and functional; validation can occur only at runtime.

Weak URL bindings don't really show their teeth until the application is altered in some way, such as a change to the signature of an application operation; for example, an operation URL may change (i.e., /addCustomer to /addRetailCustomer), or the query parameters passed in the URL may change (i.e., `productId` to `sku`). Such a change in signature will require a hunt throughout the application for references to the old operation signature, to update it to the new signature. In other words, there are unwanted dependencies between the pages that link to operations and the implementations of the operations themselves.

Team conflicts

Weak bindings can provoke one form of team conflict; another example occurs between the HTML developers and the Java developers. It is too easy for an HTML developer to make a minor change to a JSP that "breaks" the page in some way. In most environments, the entire application would need to be built, deployed, and executed in order for the offending change to be noticed. Only recently have JSP-aware HTML editors become available; when used, these editors can provide a real-time WYSIWYG view of application pages—but it is not a given that HTML developers will have access to such tools or be fully proficient using them. This can leave HTML developers in a situation where they need to build, deploy, and run the live application to see the effects of their changes—a solution that may not be practical unless the HTML developers are co-located with the Java developers.

Another form of team conflict concerns *choke points* in the application—shared files or Java classes that many Java developers will need to frequently update. A key example of this is the web deployment descriptor, the file used to define servlets and URL mappings. As each developer adds a new servlet, the file must be updated; with many developers doing similar work in parallel, the opportunity for conflicts is inevitable. Struts reduces the level of contention for the web deployment descriptor by allowing multiple configuration files to express the same kind of information, but there's still room for conflicts elsewhere.

Bad coding shortcuts

Creating servlet applications can be a *code-intensive* process; this can lead to developers taking bad coding shortcuts. A common example is merging database access code directly into a JSP. Initially this seems like a good idea, since it locates the code for database access directly with the JSP that will present the results of the query to the user.

Unfortunately, this approach leads to horrific problems in a running application. It makes the JSP very fragile in the face of any change to the underlying data model. The query will simply throw an exception at runtime if a table or column name changes. It is unlikely that shortcut code will take advantage of database connection pools, but will instead create, use, and close a connection inline. While this works fine in testing, it falls flat in the face of a high volume of concurrent users. Finally, a shortcut approach will likely not include a `try…finally` block to ensure that the connection is closed when done; this can lead to database connection leaks, another way to bring a production application to its knees.

Here are other common coding shortcuts:

- Failure to properly localize output in an internationalized application (including failure to use localized date and number formatters).
- Not using `HttpServletRequest.encodeURL()` to encode the session ID into application URLs, which breaks the application for users who do not have HTTP cookies enabled.
- Not properly filtering output to convert reserved HTML characters (such as < and >) to HTML entities; this results in visual oddities in the client web browser.
- Using short, unqualified names for `HttpServletRequest` and `HttpSession` attributes, resulting in naming conflicts and overwritten data.

Many other examples abound but require considerably more background material to fully describe. The point of this section was not to launch a diatribe against servlets—servlets are a powerful tool for creating web applications. Instead, we want to focus on the areas where servlets require too much effort or expertise on the part of the developer to be used effectively, especially in large and complex applications.

1.3 Why do we need Tapestry?

Tapestry exists to simplify Java web application development. All the features of this framework are designed to make it simpler to create robust applications that are easier to construct, debug, maintain, and extend than traditional servlet applications. Tapestry extends your reach, allowing you to create more powerful, more useful, more interactive applications faster than you would using ordinary servlets. In addition, you'll have greater confidence that your application will be free of bugs. Also, Tapestry reduces the level of contention between team members (both Java and HTML) working on a shared project.

Ultimately, Tapestry applications are still servlet applications. With enough code, and enough time to debug that code, there's nothing (from an end user's point of view) that a Tapestry application can do that a servlet application can't. Tapestry applications still follow the request cycle in figure 1.1; a request is received, some kind of server-side processing occurs, and a response is sent back to the client web browser. The difference is that Tapestry allows you to write far less code, and the code you do write is simpler and more natural because Tapestry excuses you from concerns about multithreading.

Tapestry recasts the stateless, operation-centric Servlet API into a stateful, component-centric model, the familiar coding pattern used in traditional desktop applications. The approaches you are accustomed to taking—such as combining operations and data together to form objects, using components and inheritance, storing information in instance variables, and so forth—all of these are hallmarks of Tapestry application development as well. This will not seem remarkable if you haven't done any work with servlets before; if you have, you'll be surprised by the things you don't see in a Tapestry application: the `HttpSession` and `HttpServletRequest` objects, or any thought of URLs or query parameters; all of these things are pushed down into the bowels of the Tapestry framework, where the details are handled robustly, efficiently—and invisibly.

1.3.1 What is a framework?

A *framework* is a set of cooperating classes that make up a reusable design for a specific category of software. A framework is different from a toolkit; a *toolkit* is a collection of individually reusable classes, each performing a small, isolated function that is applicable to a wide variety of uses. By contrast, a framework

> ...dictates the architecture of your application. It will define the overall structure, its partitioning into classes and objects, the key responsibilities thereof, how the classes and objects collaborate, and the thread of control. A framework predefines

> these design parameters so that you, the application designer/implementer, can concentrate on your application. The framework captures the design decisions that are common to its application domain.[7]

Frameworks are very useful; instead of your having to start with a clean slate, the design is partially filled in and the path to follow is clear. Many design decisions are already made for you, decisions that leverage the combined experience of the frameworks' authors and users. A framework also provides a significant coding head start in the form of reusable classes, utility classes, and base classes for you to extend. Ideally, you simply have to fill in the blanks, connect a few dots, and provide some application-specific subclasses. The end result is less code for you to write and more consistency between applications, not just from the developer's point of view but from the end users' perspective as well.

Many frameworks, including Tapestry, incorporate a component object model, which we will look at in the next section. This approach allows you to easily mix and match off-the-shelf objects with objects you create yourself.

1.3.2 What is a component?

A *component* is an object that fits into an overall framework; the responsibilities of the component are defined by the design and structure of the framework. A component is a component, and not simply an object, when it follows the rules of the framework. These rules can take the form of *classes* to inherit from, *naming conventions* (for classes or methods) to follow, or *interfaces* to implement. Components can be used within the context of the framework. The framework will act as a container for the component, controlling when the component is instantiated and initialized, and dictating when the methods of the component are invoked.

A component framework is a useful thing; components, more so than objects, can be easily combined to perform complex operations or to create entirely new components. The rules of the framework dictate how components can be used together. A *component object model* is the portion of the framework that defines the rules for how individual components may be combined for such purposes. The framework's component object model also dictates the responsibilities and lifecycles of *containers* (components that are constructed from other components) and contained objects.

The JavaBeans framework is a good example of a component framework—it's very general and adaptable. Following the basic naming convention for

---

[7] Erich Gamma et al., *Design Patterns: Elements of Reusable Object-Oriented Software* (Reading, MA: Addison-Wesley, 1994).

methods specified by the framework (the well-known *getters* and *setters* naming conventions) makes it possible for components created at different times and by different authors to be seamlessly combined together at runtime. The JavaBeans framework's component object model is structured around an event-notification system. Individual components may be event producers or event consumers. Another standard naming convention allows objects and components to register for event notifications in a generic fashion.

Originally, the JavaBeans framework was intended for use in developing graphical user interfaces (GUIs) for desktop applications; the components were expected to be visual objects, such as buttons and text fields, that could be manipulated in a visual GUI editor. Ultimately, the JavaBeans framework proved to be just as useful for nonvisual objects and is nowadays frequently used as the basis for other frameworks—including Tapestry.

The component approach has been widely used in many environments to support traditional GUI development, including Java's AWT and Swing. Using a component approach for web applications is less widespread but is not original to Tapestry. As far back as 1994, NeXT's WebObjects framework integrated a component object model with graphical editor tools and an object relational database layer (to handle long-term data persistence, much like entity Enterprises JavaBeans in a Java 2 Enterprise Edition application).

In WebObjects, components were responsible for both generating portions of an HTML page and responding to user requests, and the framework was responsible for hiding the details of HTTP and server-side state management. This approach to componentizing web application behavior matches the high-level design goals of Tapestry, though the overall design and implementation of the two frameworks are completely different.

1.3.3 What is Tapestry?

The Tapestry framework is a layer between a Java servlet container and a Tapestry application. Tapestry is not a standalone server; it is an extension to servlets and works within existing servlet containers (such as Tomcat) or application servers (like JBoss, WebSphere, or WebLogic), which include a servlet container. Figure 1.4 shows how Tapestry fits into the overall picture; the application consists of pages, which are themselves constructed from reusable components. The application operates within the application server. To the application server, the application is just another servlet.

Web applications are typically implemented in terms of three layers, each addressing a different concern within the overall application:

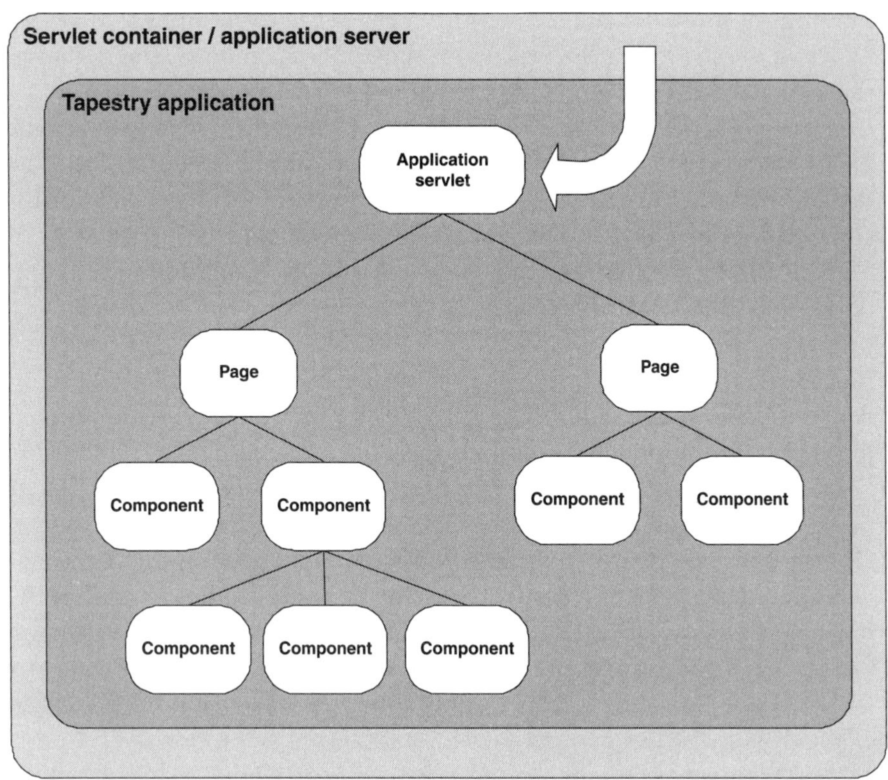

Figure 1.4 Tapestry applications run within a servlet container or application server; inside the server, the application consists of individual pages built from components. The Tapestry application servlet links the requests from the servlet container to the pages and components of the application.

- The *presentation layer* is responsible for receiving incoming HTTP requests and forming HTML responses.
- The *application layer* is responsible for all business logic; this is often implemented using Enterprise JavaBeans (EJBs).
- The *database layer* is responsible for storing data persistently.

Tapestry is only the presentation layer of an application. By this, we mean that Tapestry deals only with presenting information to an end user, as HTML,[8] and

[8] Actually, very little of Tapestry is HTML specific. Tapestry is equally at home creating Extensible Markup Language (XML), Extensible Hypertext Markup Language (XHTML), or Wireless Markup Language (WML). A suite of WML-related components is included with the framework.

handling input from the user in the form of clickable links and HTML forms. Tapestry doesn't know, or care, about the application layer, the domain logic, or the source of information. A Tapestry application can be built on top of anything from a flat-file database, to a relational database accessed via Java Database Connectivity (JDBC), all the way up to a globe-spanning network of EJBs. Tapestry doesn't mandate anything about these aspects of your application; it is concerned solely with how the presentation layer is organized.

The Tapestry framework fills a gap that is often missing in web application development: It provides a consistent structure, a *skeleton* for developers to work with. Too often, each developer is left to manage on his or her own, a freedom that is missing from other engineering disciplines and one that entails a high degree of risk. Imagine building a skyscraper by dividing the job into constructing individual floors and instructing each worker to design and build a single floor, with the intention of using a crane to stack them all up at the end. Each worker is provided with a rough sketch of the finished building and told what kind of work will be done on that floor: "We'll be putting the accounts payable department here," or "This is where the company cafeteria will go." You can imagine the kind of disaster that would result; free of any constraints, each worker would use different materials and a different layout. Elevator shafts wouldn't line up, some workers would forget to leave room for electrical wiring or plumbing…and some might even forget to put in windows!

And yet many web applications are developed under a similar kind of chaos. Specifications are incomplete; different developers approach similar problems in different ways. Some developers are unaware of important details of the project or of the many minor details of web application development. Skills sets vary, so some developers excel at writing client-side JavaScript, others are good at interacting with back-end systems—but project management may treat the developers as completely interchangeable. Too often, the success or failure of entire projects rests on the shoulders of a "SWAT team" that must glue all the bits and pieces of code together at the last minute.

Continuing with the skyscraper metaphor, Tapestry changes the picture significantly. Instead of starting with individual two-by-fours, the workers start with the empty shell of each floor, with most of the plumbing and wiring already in place. It just becomes a matter of installing those fixtures and features unique to that floor, all with the knowledge that everything will stack up properly at the end of the project. Translate *floor* to *page*, *fixture* to *component*, and *install* to *configure*, and you're well on your way to understanding what Tapestry offers you as a developer.

Tapestry is not a panacea for all development problems; however, it does provide a consistent way to describe the implementation of a web application project and the interaction between elements of the project provided by different developers. Web applications don't have elevator shafts, but they do have, for example, consistent navigation bars, or embedded search forms, or login buttons. These elements can be implemented as Tapestry components, tested separately, and reused on every page, thus guaranteeing both a consistent visual look and a consistent interactive behavior.

1.3.4 Comparing Tapestry to Swing

Tapestry represents a different way of assembling web applications, one based on combining and configuring components. Tapestry development is much closer in style to creating an application using the Swing GUI framework than traditional web application development with servlets and JSPs.

Developers who are familiar with creating desktop applications (using Swing or AWT or even toolkits for other languages and environments) are often left in the lurch when transitioning over to web applications. The familiar patterns of development don't translate well. For desktop applications, you expect to combine and configure existing components to create your application. You expect individual components to encapsulate both output (what gets drawn to the screen) and input (what happens when the user types or clicks the mouse). The components, and the framework they build upon, shield the developer from the minute details of the desktop environment: It is rare that you need to be concerned with event queues or pixel-oriented screen updates when developing a Swing application because the `JButton` component already knows how to draw on the screen and respond to user input. Traditional servlet development doesn't contain anything similar; servlets and JSPs are always custom written and tied directly to the overall application.

Tapestry restores this style of development. Tapestry pages consist of components that are configured and connected to one another. The framework allows you to create components, pages, and applications without any awareness of servlets. Like Swing developers, Tapestry developers know objects such as `HttpSession`, `HttpServletRequest`, and `HttpServlet` are present; there just isn't any pressing need to access those objects—that's Tapestry's responsibility, encapsulated within the framework and the Tapestry components. Tapestry performs all the necessary dispatching of incoming requests and uses an event-notification system to get application-specific code executed.

1.4 Understanding Tapestry's goals

At the core of Tapestry's design is a vision: It should be easier for you to do the *right* thing than the *wrong* thing—Tapestry should allow you to avoid the pitfalls and antipatterns prevalent in traditional web application development. You should end up with a robust, scalable, maintainable application not because the framework merely *allows* it, but because the framework makes that the clearest, simplest option to follow. This vision is expressed in terms of four goals that influence the design and implementation of the framework: simplicity, consistency, efficiency, and feedback.

1.4.1 Simplicity

Tapestry applications contain a surprisingly small amount of Java code. The stateless, operation-centric programming model used by normal servlet applications requires far too much Java code—code to extract and interpret query parameters from the request, code to manage data stored as session attributes, and so on—code for all the uninteresting plumbing. At the center of all this plumbing is the small amount of application-specific logic: what to *do* with the data once it has been extracted, translated, converted, and validated. In a Tapestry application, the Java code you write is just that application-specific logic (in the form of a listener method, as you'll see in chapter 2). Combining a generic component with the application-specific listener method is a simple and elegant way to structure an application. All that plumbing is no longer your responsibility; it's all buried inside the Tapestry framework.

You tell the framework what needs doing, and it takes care of the details. For example, rather than write code to build and format a URL with query parameters, you just use an existing component and configure it to execute a method you supply when it is triggered. Likewise, Tapestry's HTML form support takes care of reading object properties when a page is rendered, but also reads and interprets query parameters and updates object properties when a form is submitted (this is covered in chapters 3, 4, and 5).

1.4.2 Consistency

Consistency on a large team project can be a godsend. If you've ever been brought into an existing project, or have even filled in temporarily for another team member on a project, you've likely experienced "impedance frustration." That is, each developer names things a little differently, solves problems a little differently, puts code in different places, and so forth. Before you can be productive in another developer's code, you have to figure out that developer's style, and that causes frustration.

With Tapestry, you get a consistent environment and approach across pages, even when different pages are the responsibility of different developers. There's little or no guesswork when adding new links or forms to pages; they all work pretty much the same way because they are based on the same reusable components. Tapestry makes it easy to create new components for common functionality in an application. The application behaves consistently and is coded consistently because of reuse of both components and code.

1.4.3 Efficiency

It is important that Tapestry applications be scalable; there's no point in creating a web application if it can't handle a reasonable number of concurrent users on reasonable hardware. Internally, Tapestry uses object pools and caches to minimize the amount of processing that must occur during a request. For example, Tapestry will read each XML specification file and each HTML template exactly once and store the file's contents for later use within the application. In addition, the framework is structured so that expensive application operations (for example, performing a Java Naming and Directory Interface [JNDI] lookup to resolve an EJB's home interface) can be performed once and cached for fast access when needed again elsewhere within the application. You'll see examples of this in chapter 10.

Tapestry applications have been compared to equivalent servlet or Struts applications and found to have similar performance curves. Such results match the traditional wisdom that the presentation layer is rarely the application performance bottleneck; the time it takes to process a request and render a response is usually gated by the speed with which data can be obtained from the application's back-end database.

1.4.4 Feedback

In most web application frameworks, when something goes wrong in your code or in the framework code, you will see a stack trace in the web browser. Suddenly, you are forced to play detective, working backward from the cryptic clues provided in the stack trace to the problem. Does your code contain an error? Is there a typo in a deployment descriptor? An error communicating with your application server? A deployment problem with an EJB? You can waste large amounts of valuable developer time tracking down often-trivial problems.

The main code path into a Tapestry application has multiple layers of exception catching and reporting that ensure that a reasonable exception report is

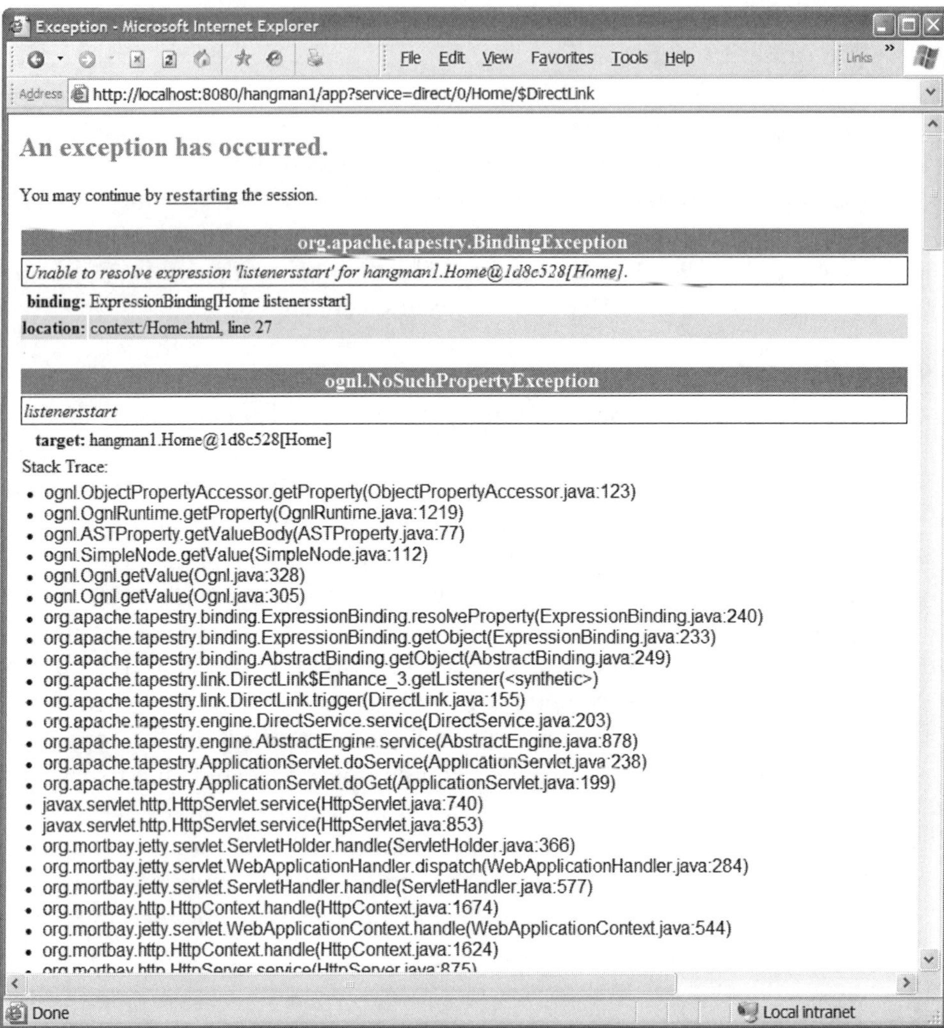

Figure 1.5 The Tapestry exception report page starts by identifying the nested exceptions, providing a stack trace for the most deeply nested exception. The exception also identifies the file and line associated with the error. In this case, line 27 of file Home.html had a typo: *listenersstart* instead of *listeners.start*.

displayed either in the client web browser or in the server's console. Figure 1.5 shows the initial portion of such an exception report (this exception was provoked by introducing a typo into the HTML template for the Hangman application, described in detail in chapter 2).

Tapestry's approach is to provide you with as much information as possible to help you rapidly fix the problem. This is represented by five factors visible in figure 1.5:

- Tapestry has worked through the stack of exceptions, starting with `org.apache.tapestry.BindingException` and digging down to `ognl.NoSuchPropertyException`.
- For each exception, it has displayed the exception message and all the properties of the exception (binding and location for the `BindingException`, and target for `NoSuchPropertyException`).
- The report identifies the exact file and line that is in error—the `location` property of the `BindingException` indicates that the error is on line 27 of file Home.html.
- The stack trace for the deepest exception, `NoSuchPropertyException`, is the most relevant, and that's the only one displayed.
- Tapestry has attempted to describe in the exception message exactly what went wrong.

Stack traces and exceptions are not always enough. Sometimes to understand a problem you need to know more about the request and general environment. As shown in figure 1.6, the exception report continues with exhaustive output about the key Servlet API objects (`HttpServletRequest`, `HttpSession`, `HttpServlet`, and `HttpServletContext`), followed by a listing of all Java Virtual Machine (JVM) system properties. Collecting this kind of information would normally require restarting the application and using the Java debugger. Tapestry saves you time by providing all this useful information immediately, at the time of the initial error, which means less time tracking down bugs and more time for everything else.

With these four central goals in mind, it's now time to start describing, at a high level, how Tapestry operates.

1.5 How does Tapestry work?

Tapestry is an extension that builds on the standard Java Servlet API. Tapestry still uses a servlet and still interacts with all the Servlet API objects: `HttpServletRequest`, `HttpSession`, and so forth. Tapestry applications are still servlet applications and can be deployed into any standard servlet container, such as Apache Tomcat, Jetty, Resin, WebLogic, or WebSphere. The framework is code compatible

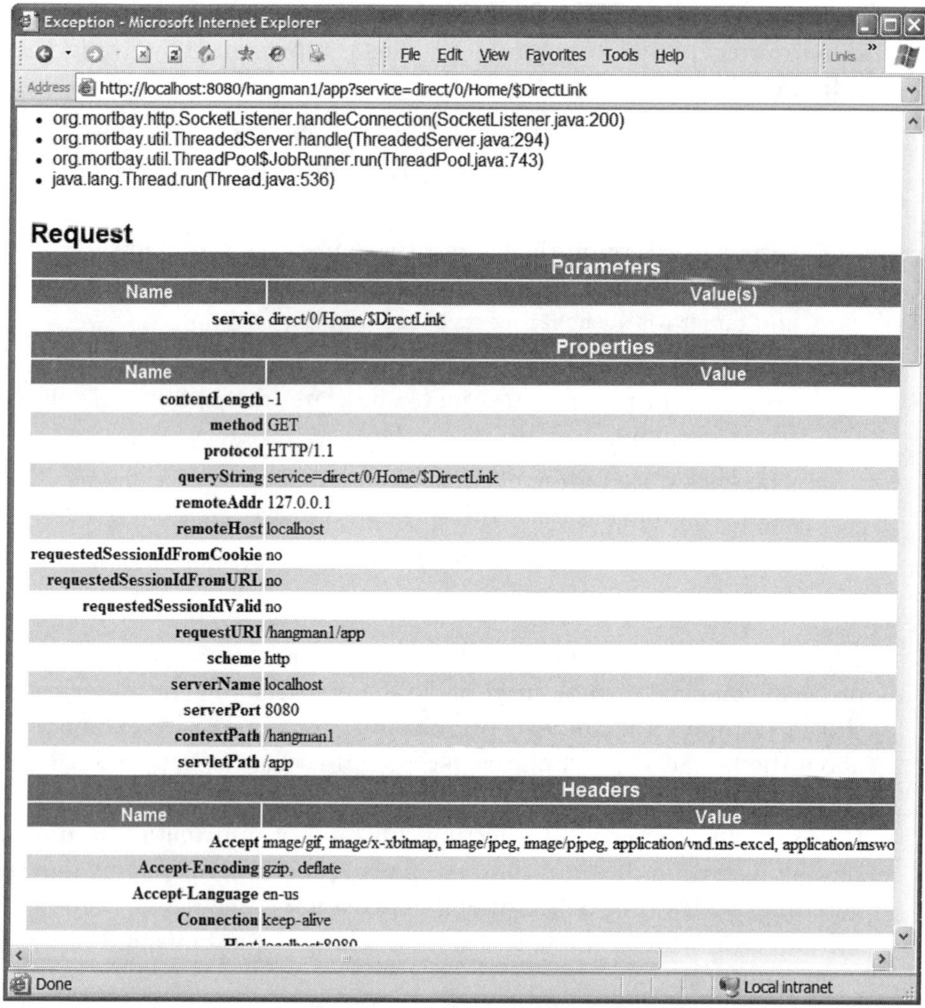

Figure 1.6 The exception report includes a vast amount of information about the Request, Session, Servlet, ServletContext, and all JVM system properties—the kind of information you would normally need to collect using the Java debugger.

with Java Development Kit (JDK) 1.2 and Servlet API 2.2,[9] which allows Tapestry to be used in virtually any recent Java application server.

---

9 Tapestry includes a servlet filter that performs a redirect of the initial application request to the Tapestry application servlet; servlet filters are a feature of Servlet API 2.3. Chapter 10 discusses the need for this filter and how to make use of it.

Tapestry applications consist of any number of pages, where the pages are each constructed from individual, reusable, configurable components. Table 1.1 defines the terms used to describe Tapestry applications.

Table 1.1 Basic terms used when describing Tapestry applications

Term	Description
Page	Applications consist of a collection of uniquely named pages; each page has a template and contains other components.
Template	An HTML template for a page (or a component). In Tapestry, a template contains ordinary HTML markup, with certain tags marked with a special attribute to indicate they are placeholders for components.
Component	A reusable object that may be used as part of a Tapestry page. Components generate HTML when a page is rendered and may also participate when a link or form in the rendered page is triggered. Components may also be used to construct new components.
Parameter	Components have parameters, which link properties of the component to properties of the page (or of domain objects accessible from the page). Components mostly read their parameters, but some components (often related to HTML forms) can update their parameters and thus update the page properties bound to the parameter.

Your Tapestry application includes templates and specifications for these elements. Those elements work together to form your GUI.

1.5.1 What's in a Tapestry application?

Like other servlet applications, Tapestry applications are most commonly distributed as Web archives (WARs). A WAR is a variation of an ordinary Java archive (JAR) file. A JAR file is used to store Java class files, but a WAR file stores a mix of files: Primarily it stores HTML files, stylesheets, and images that will be directly accessible to a client web browser using a URL. Like a JAR file, a WAR file contains many files organized into many folders within the WAR.

A deployed web application is also called a *web application context*. The default name of the context is based on the name of the WAR. Figure 1.7 diagrams a deployed web application, the Virtual Library application described in chapters 9 and 10. The Virtual Library is deployed as vlib.war, which will define a web application context URL as /vlib. Static files (those images and stylesheets) are accessible at URLs that extend from the context URL, such as http://server/vlib/images/search.png (which accesses a file stored as images/search.png inside vlib.war).

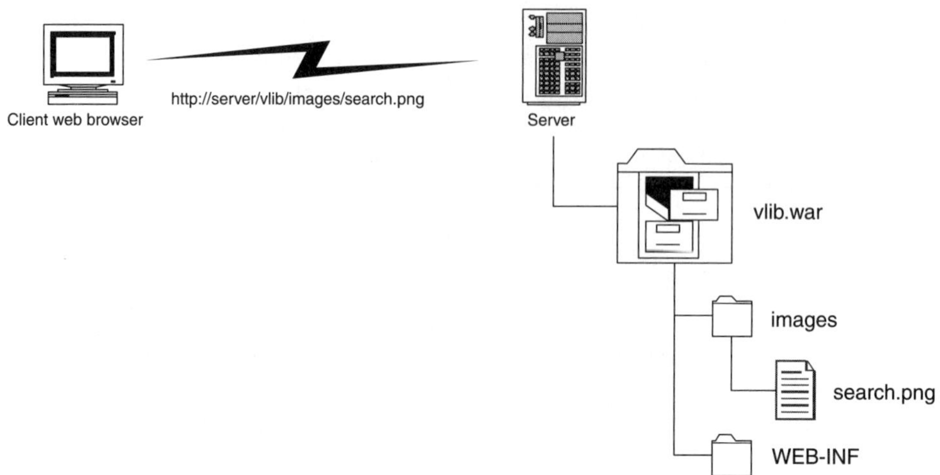

Figure 1.7 The WAR file, vlib.war, defines a context, /vlib. Resources inside the WAR file can be referenced by extending the URL for the context itself.

WARs also contain a WEB-INF folder; this includes private resources that are not made visible to clients. A servlet application will store class files and libraries inside the WEB-INF folder. Tapestry applications go further, storing additional artifacts and resources in the WEB-INF folder:

- The compiled Java classes are stored in the WEB-INF/classes folder.
- The WEB-INF/lib folder stores JAR files needed by the application's classes. In a Tapestry application, the WEB-INF/lib folder will contain the Tapestry framework JAR (e.g., tapestry-3.0.jar) as well as a number of supporting libraries needed by the framework.
- Page specifications are stored in the WEB-INF folder, with a .page extension.
- Page templates are stored in the root context folder (that is, directly within vlib.war) with an .html extension.
- Component specifications are stored in the WEB-INF folder with a .jwc extension.
- Component templates are stored in the WEB-INF folder with an .html extension.
- The WEB-INF folder also contains the web deployment descriptor, web.xml. This file defines, to the servlet container, all of the servlets and URL mappings contained in the WAR. A Tapestry application uses only a single servlet but still requires a deployment descriptor.

Appendix B discusses the example web applications for this book; it includes details on how to build and deploy the examples on your own workstation. It also goes into some detail about the directory layout for the examples, and how the Ant build tool is used to compile, package, and deploy the examples.

1.5.2 Tapestry's Model-View-Controller (MVC) pattern

Perhaps the most successful design pattern in GUI development is the Model-View-Controller pattern (MVC). Most GUI frameworks, including Swing, use some variation of MVC. The MVC pattern divides up each user interaction within the application into three categories of objects:

- **Model**—The Model object is used to store information that will ultimately be presented to the user (and possibly edited). These objects are often domain objects—objects that represent the specific application domain, such as a Customer, Order, or Product (in an e-commerce application). The Model should be completely independent of the GUI. In Java applications, the Model is often a JavaBean.
- **View**—The View object is responsible for presenting data obtained from the model in a format appropriate to the application. In a web application, a simple View may do no more than write a string into the rendered page; a very complex View may create a graphic chart based on data in the Model, and an editable View may write a text field or other form element into the response.
- **Controller**—The Controller object has two functions: First, it bridges between the Model and the View, reading data from the Model and providing it to the View. Second, it is responsible for interpreting user input and updating the Model in response; in a web application, the Controller will service incoming requests (including form submissions).

As shown in figure 1.8, the Model and View have no direct connection; instead, the Controller mediates between the two and has the added responsibility of processing user input.

The MVC pattern is useful because it emphasizes *separation of concerns*, a powerful concept that supports more flexible, more robust development. The Model and the View are kept entirely separate; they may be developed at different times, by different developers, and tested independently. The Model has no knowledge that it is part of a GUI or any type of application. The Controller is responsible for monitoring the Model and informing the View of relevant changes when the Model changes. Typically, the Model includes an

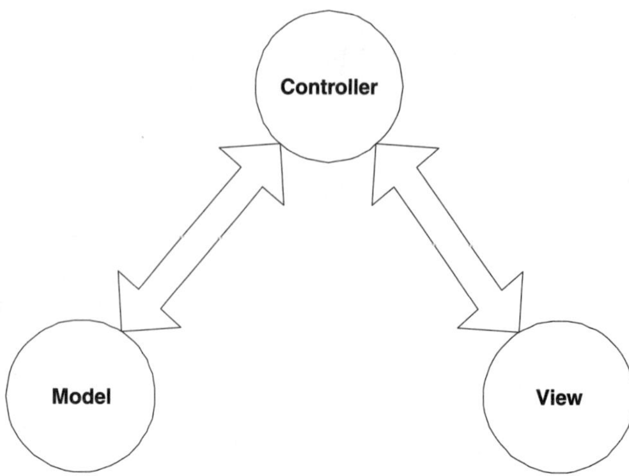

Figure 1.8 Using the Model-View-Controller pattern separates the View and the Model, which have no direct knowledge of each other. The Controller mediates between the two and handles user input.

event mechanism so that any changes will be propagated, through the Controller, to the View. A single Model may be represented by multiple Views, either as different options or simultaneously in multiple windows. A common example is to display tabular data as both a table and a chart—that's two different Views of the same Model. The MVC design pattern has been battle-tested in countless applications.

Using servlets as Controllers

Within the realm of typical servlet applications, the MVC pattern typically takes on the form shown in figure 1.9. In a servlet application, servlets play the role of Controller. A servlet will receive a request from the client and will perform an operation on the Model, the domain-specific objects for the application. For example, the request may be a form submission, and the Controller servlet will update properties of the Model domain objects and store them into a database.

The Controller servlet will then load up the `HttpServletRequest` with attributes needed by the View to render a response, in effect "pushing" information from the Model into the View. The View itself will be a JSP (or some other form of template) and can draw information from the domain objects (the Model) as it renders the response to be returned to the client.

Tapestry makes use of a common variant of MVC, where the View "pulls" information out of the Model (rather than having the Controller push information into the View). The View still has no explicit knowledge of the application; it

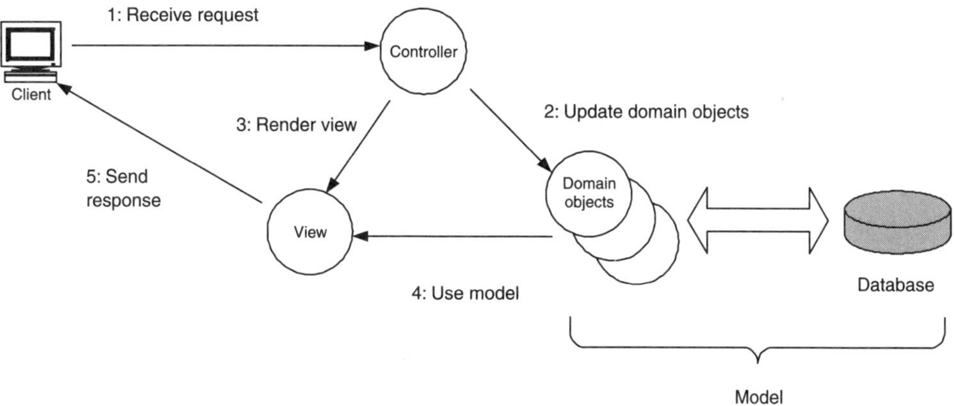

Figure 1.9 The servlet, as Controller, receives the request. It locates and updates the domain objects, possibly reading and updating database data. The Controller servlet selects a View (a JSP) to render the response. The View draws data from the domain objects as it renders, and the final response page is sent to the client.

just knows where it can read (and occasionally write) data. The Controller is still responsible for handling user input, as well as for establishing the relationships between Model and View.

The component as Controller

As shown in figure 1.10, a Tapestry component fills the role of Controller, mediating between pure-domain objects in the Model (the `LineItem` and `Product` objects, in this example) and components contained within its HTML template (TextField and Insert). Most often, this pattern applies to pages (pages are still Tapestry components), but in many cases, a component will have its own template, containing further components, and support its own interactions with the user.

The page establishes relationships between the Model and the View in terms of property expressions. *Property expressions* are implemented using another open source framework, the Object Graph Navigation Language (OGNL), a very powerful Java expression language.

The page exposes the Model objects to the View components by providing JavaBeans properties (such as the `lineItem` property in figure 1.10)—but that's just a starting point. Properties of the Model objects are bound to the components—when the page renders, the TextField component will read the `quantity` property of the `LineItem` object, and the Insert component will read the `name` property of the `Product` object. This approach of navigating the

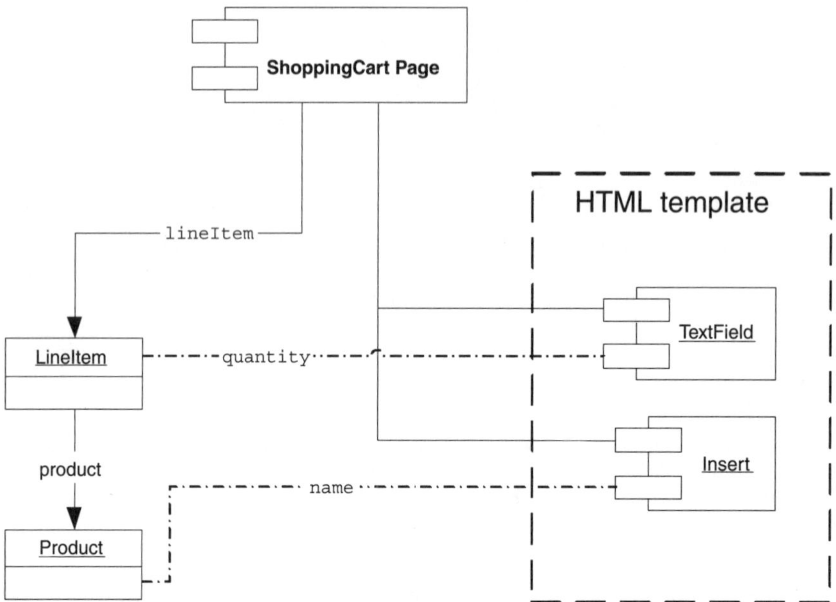

Figure 1.10 Model-View-Controller in Tapestry: The page is the Controller, `LineItem` and `Product` are domain objects forming the Model, and the TextField and Insert components are the View. The TextField component is bound to the `quantity` property of the `LineItem` object (which it both reads and updates), and the Insert component is bound to the `name` property of the `Product` object.

object graph to reach relevant properties is possible only because the page and all the components are stateful objects—JavaBeans with properties that can be read and updated. The page, in its role as Controller, is responsible for making these connections between the domain objects (the Model) and the components (the View).

OGNL OGNL is a separate open source project distributed with, and heavily utilized by, Tapestry. OGNL's primary purpose is to read and update JavaBeans properties of objects. A basic form of OGNL expression is a chain of property names, separated with periods, as in `lineItem.product.name`. This OGNL expression is roughly equivalent to the Java expression `getLineItem().getProduct().getName()` or `getLineItem().getProduct().setName()`, depending on whether the expression is being used to read or update a property. However, that's just the start of what OGNL can do. It is an extremely powerful expression language, mimicking (and in some cases exceeding) the capabilities of Java language expressions. It predates the expression language introduced with the Java Standard Tag Library (JSTL) and is both easier to use and more powerful. OGNL is the creation of Drew Davidson and Luke Blanshard. Full documentation for OGNL, as well as source and binary downloads, is available at http://www.ognl.org.

The page also fulfills its role as the Controller by providing the logic that occurs when links within the page are clicked, or when forms within the page are submitted. This logic is provided in the form of *listener methods*, short methods implemented in the page class that are invoked by the Tapestry framework.

1.5.3 Tapestry classes

The Tapestry framework consists of over 400 classes and interfaces—fortunately, when building your own applications with Tapestry, you'll most often need to be concerned only with the handful of classes, interfaces, and methods shown in figure 1.11.

At the root of the hierarchy is the `IRender` interface,[10] implemented by all objects that can render HTML. Components are the main objects that can render, but not the only ones: for example, static HTML from a page or component template is wrapped up as an object that implements the `IRender` interface.

Two key interfaces: IComponent and IPage

Two key interfaces are `IComponent` and `IPage`, which define Tapestry components and pages, respectively. All Tapestry code is coded against interfaces, not implementations; therefore, `IComponent` is consistently used throughout the framework as a parameter type or return value, never `AbstractComponent`, an implementation

[10] All Tapestry interfaces start with a leading I, as in `IRender` or `IComponent`. The only exceptions are event interfaces, such `PageDetachListener`. These are named as such for compatibility with JavaBeans naming conventions for event listener interfaces.

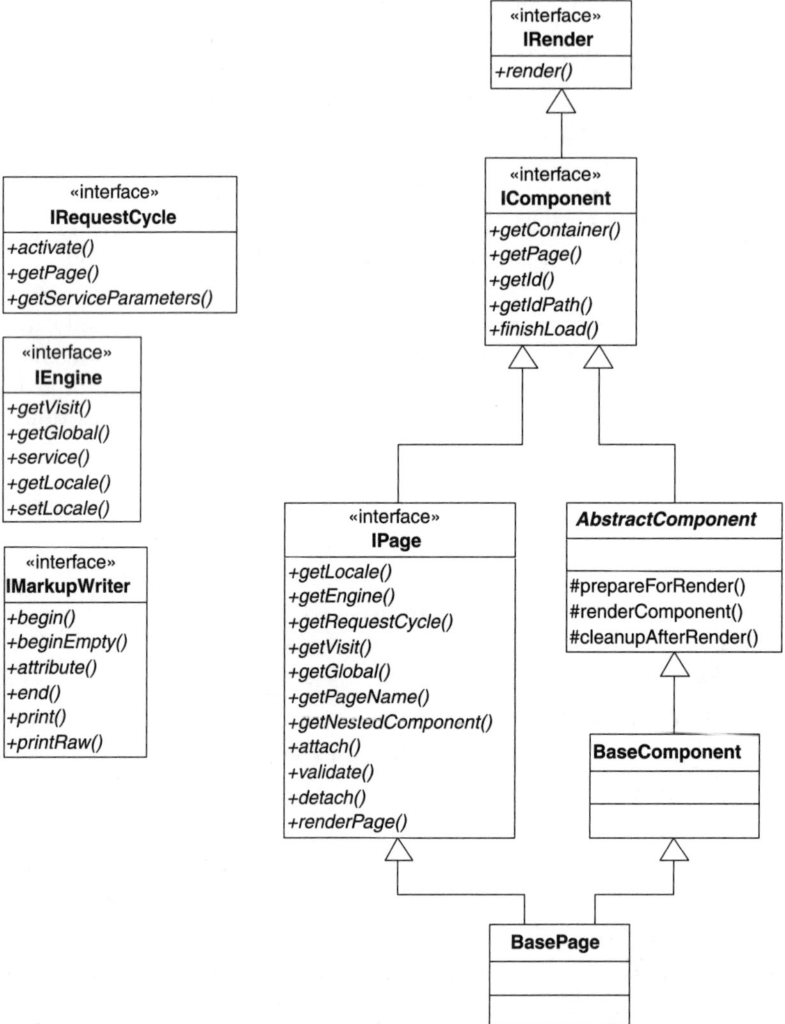

Figure 1.11 Here are the key interfaces, classes, and methods provided in the Tapestry framework.

of `IComponent`. The `AbstractComponent` class is the base class for implementing components. `AbstractComponent` is an abstract class; it defines but does not implement the `renderComponent()` method. Subclasses of `AbstractComponent` implement this method, producing all HTML output in Java code.

BaseComponent extends AbstractComponent, adding initialization logic that knows how to locate and read a template. Most components you create will subclass BaseComponent. We discuss creating components in chapters 6 and 8.

In Tapestry, pages are specialized components with additional responsibilities; this is shown by having IPage extend IComponent, and by having BasePage subclass BaseComponent. When creating new pages, you will always create subclasses of BasePage.

Three useful interfaces: IRequestCycle, IMarkupWriter, and IEngine

Most Tapestry pages and components can be coded with references to just three additional interfaces:

- IRequestCycle—A request cycle stores information about the current request. It tracks the active page involved in the request and is used to orchestrate the rendering of a response. The request cycle may also be used to access the Servlet API objects (HttpServletRequest, HttpSession, and HttpServletResponse) in the rare event that such access is necessary.
- IMarkupWriter—A markup writer is used to produce HTML output when a page is rendering a response. It operates much like a java.io.PrintWriter but includes additional methods useful for creating markup output (containing XML-style elements and attributes).
- IEngine—The engine is a central object with several related responsibilities, the core around which a Tapestry application hangs. Primarily, the engine is responsible for maintaining server-side state, but it also acts as a gateway to a number of subsystems used internally by Tapestry.

Most of the examples in the first few chapters are limited to just these interfaces; as we get under the hood in chapters 6 through 8, a few additional interfaces will be introduced.

1.6 Using Spindle

In this book, we'll be sticking close to the source with our many example Tapestry applications, presenting the different artifacts (the HTML templates, the XML specifications, and the Java code) in listings. If your development environment of choice is Eclipse (http://www.eclipse.org), you should check out Spindle, the Tapestry plug-in for Eclipse. Spindle blends customized wizards and editors for Tapestry applications into the Eclipse IDE. Spindle streamlines Tapestry application development in a number of ways:

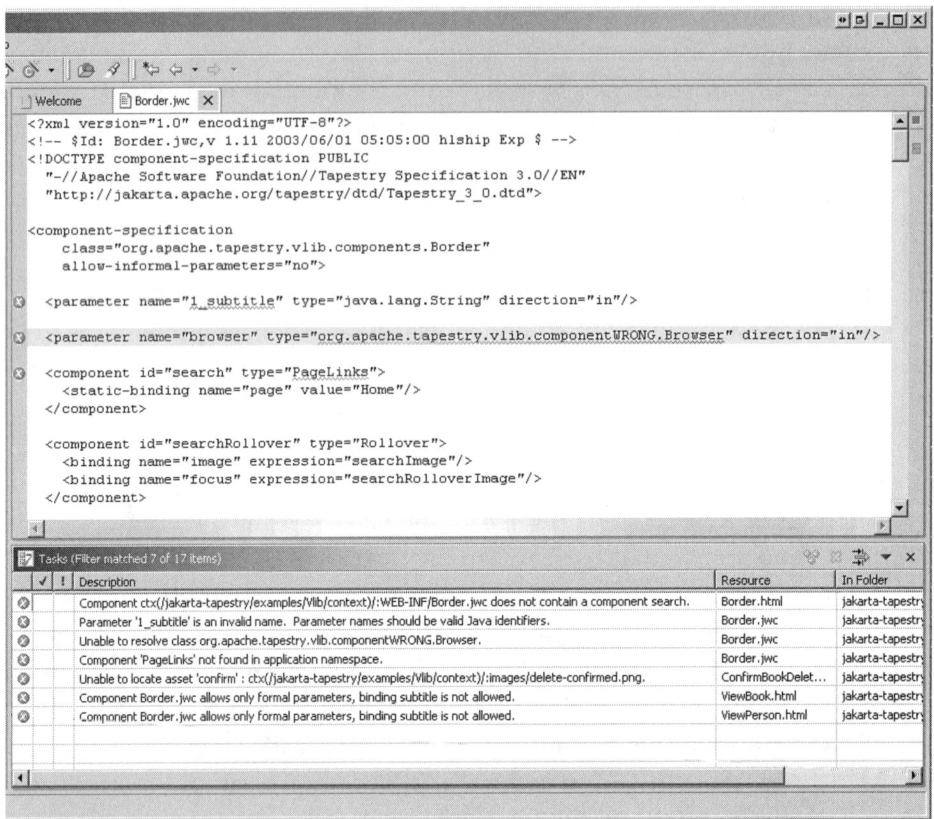

Figure 1.12 Using Spindle, errors in your templates and specifications are highlighted in the editor and listed in the Tasks view.

- Spindle scans all types of input files for a wide variety of errors, including invalid OGNL expressions, unresolvable class names, invalid or unknown component IDs, and so forth.
- Errors are identified in the Eclipse Tasks view.
- Errors are indicated with markers in the editor gutter.

Figure 1.12 shows an example, where some errors have been introduced into part of the example J2EE application described in chapters 9 and 10.

Spindle takes Tapestry to an even higher level of productivity, because it can catch errors at build time that ordinarily aren't caught until runtime. Like Tapestry, Spindle is distributed as a free, open source project. Spindle is available at http://sf.net/projects/spindle and was developed by Geoff Longman.

1.7 Summary

Ordinary Java web applications are code heavy: Adding a new interaction (such as a link or form) to a page requires creating new classes—new servlets (or new Struts `Actions`) to handle the interaction. Quite a bit of cookie-cutter code must be written just to establish the context of the interaction—which server-side objects should be affected and how. You, the developer, are responsible for making a series of small decisions: what to name the new servlet, what URL pattern to map to the servlet, what to name any query parameters, and what information to store in those parameters. Additionally, you must make coordinated changes to Java code, to the JSP, and to the web deployment descriptor. This is all unavoidable, simply an offshoot of the operation-centric approach mandated by the use of servlets, and the way in which servlets within an application are weakly bound to one another.

Tapestry applications flip this situation on its ear; a Tapestry application consists of a tiny amount of application-specific code within a web of objects, methods, and properties, and uses XML specifications and OGNL expressions, not Java code, to tie it all together. Tapestry extends your reach as a developer because of all the decisions you don't have to make and all the code you don't have to write and test. You get to concentrate on the critical aspects of your own application without having to address all the generic concerns of structuring a servlet application.

In the next chapter, we'll put together a small Tapestry application to demonstrate concretely how the framework's component-based approach to development really does simplify and accelerate application development.

2 Getting started with Tapestry

This chapter covers

- Creating HTML templates, page specifications, and page classes
- Using Tapestry components inside an HTML template
- Creating clickable links
- Encoding extra information into link URLs
- Configuring Tapestry applications for deployment

In the first chapter, we made a number of claims about what Tapestry is capable of; now it is time to start backing up those claims with hard code. Launching into a complete Java 2 Enterprise Edition (J2EE) application right here would be a bit premature; instead, we'll start with more of a toy, an application that plays the simple word game Hangman. In effect, Hangman is a "scale model" of a real Tapestry application; it demonstrates the basic capabilities of the framework and will give you an initial sense for what developing Tapestry applications is all about. Along the way, you'll see how to:

- Separate business logic from presentation logic, within the Model-View-Controller (MVC) pattern (described in chapter 1)
- Combine HTML templates, page specifications (in XML), and Java classes to form pages within the application
- Create HTML hyperlinks that activate application logic when clicked
- Encode custom application data into HTML hyperlinks
- Manage server-side state information
- Configure a Tapestry application for deployment inside a servlet container

More importantly, you'll see quite a bit about the work you *don't* have to do, because the framework takes care of it for you.

Appendix B covers how to obtain the source code for all the examples in the book, as well as how to build the examples on your own computer and deploy them into the Tomcat servlet container (Tomcat is an open source servlet container available from http://jakarta.apache.org/tomcat). Once Tomcat is running and you have downloaded the source code, you can launch the Hangman application by opening a web browser to http://localhost:8080/hangman1/app.

2.1 Introducing the Hangman application

Hangman is a simple word game for two players, played on a piece of paper or on a chalkboard. One player selects a secret target word; the other player attempts to guess the word. To start, you draw an empty gallows. The guessing player selects a letter from the alphabet; if the letter appears in the target word, the other player writes the letter in each position of the target word that the letter appears in. Each unsuccessful guess is marked by adding a line to a stick figure on the gallows: the head, torso, and then the limbs. The game is over when the word is guessed or the stick figure is completed.

The Tapestry Hangman application captures all of this functionality and, at the same time, attempts to capture the classic look of playing the game by hand

Figure 2.1 A Tapestry Hangman game in progress. The player has successfully guessed the letter A, but has also guessed E, P, and V, which are not in the target word. An important aspect of this application is the look and feel, which should resemble a game played by hand on a chalkboard.

on a chalkboard. The user interface makes use of images to represent the letters and other artifacts of the game, to provide a "hand–scrawled" look and feel. Figure 2.1 shows the middle of a game of Hangman; the player has made several wrong guesses, so parts of the stick figure are filled in, and one letter (A) has been guessed correctly so far.

At this point, all we have is a general idea for the application; before we can get to the coding stage, we must formalize this general idea into something a bit more concrete—and that begins with identifying the application flow.

2.1.1 Determining the application flow

The *application flow* is a model of how the end user will navigate through the application. Determining the flow occurs very early in the development cycle; it is driven by the specific requirements and use cases of the application. Application flow is the most abstract model of the application; it identifies the different pages in the application and how they are connected, but rarely has to precisely identify what is on any particular page. Key aspects of the application user interface are discernable from the flow diagrams, such as the need for common navigation menus or specific links between individual pages.

The flow of the Hangman application is quite simple: From the Guess page, the user makes guesses at the target word, eventually winning or losing the game. Figure 2.2 is a state diagram for this simple application; when the application is launched, the user is presented with a Start page (figure 2.4); from there, he or she can start a new game, making guesses that eventually reach either a win or a loss; from there, the player can restart the game with a new target word.

From this simple description, you can see that we'll have four distinct pages in the application:

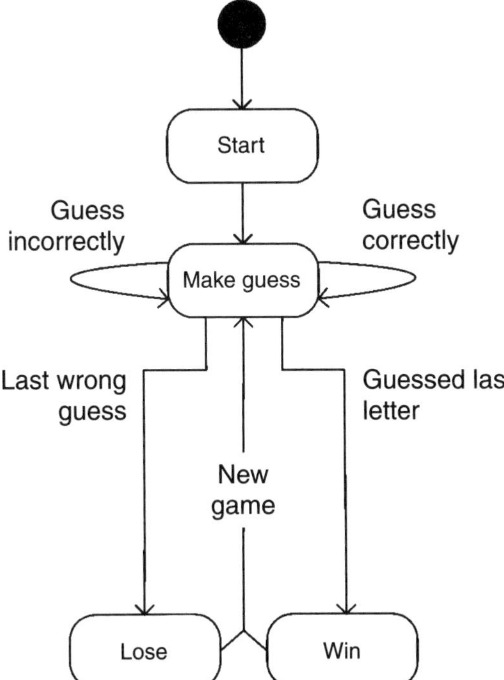

Figure 2.2
The player starts the game and makes guesses, eventually reaching the win or lose page, from which the player can start a new game (with a new word).

- **Start**—A welcome page to greet players before starting a new game
- **Make Guess**—The main page, from which players may guess letters of the target word
- **Win**—The page reached after the target word is successfully guessed
- **Lose**—The page reached after players have exhausted their guesses

Once the application flow has been determined, the next step is to prototype what the individual HTML pages will look like.

2.1.2 Creating page mockups

Page mockups are static HTML pages that represent what the active pages from the running application will look like. These are ordinary HTML pages with placeholder values representing the content that will eventually be generated dynamically by the application. The point of creating the mockups is to give the HTML developers a chance to work out the look and feel of the application, right down to fonts, colors, and graphics, without concern for how the application will be implemented.

Figure 2.3 shows the mockup for the Guess page in an HTML editor. The HTML source is shown in the upper pane, and the WYSIWYG preview appears in the lower pane. This mockup will eventually be converted for use as the Guess page's HTML template.

Page mockups should display *all* the features of the running application, especially such features as error messages that are included only conditionally. For example, a mockup may include a snippet for an error message:

```
<img src="images/error.png" width="32" height="32" align="top"/>
<span class="error-message">
  Placeholder for error message.
</span>
```

This snippet is important for two reasons: It clearly identifies how a real error message should be displayed, and it identifies exactly *where* within the page the error message should be displayed. In the Guess page mockup, the Guess and Choose sections demonstrate what the page looks like in the middle of a game, with some letters of the target word filled in and several letters from the alphabet already guessed. Having clear examples of these dynamic aspects of the page will be invaluable to the Java developer when he or she is converting the mockup into a usable HTML template.

It is not an absolute requirement that you create a mockup for every page in the application; often, mockups for only a handful of key pages will suffice, and

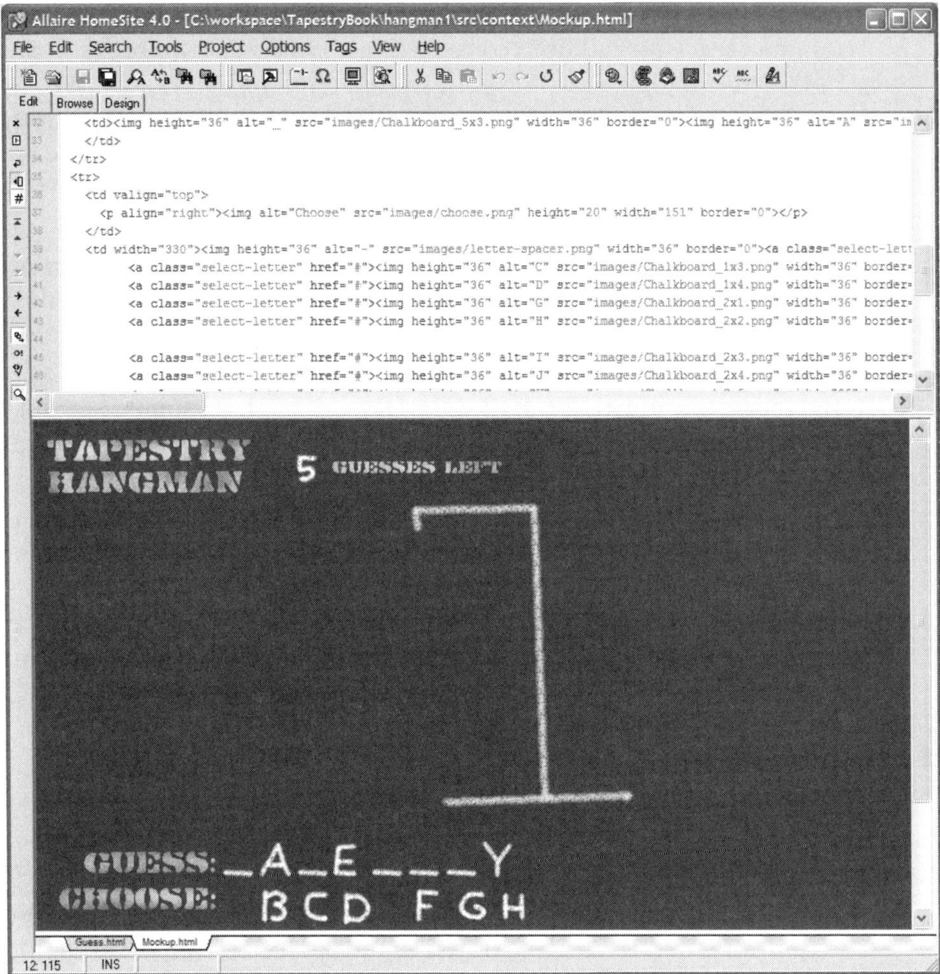

Figure 2.3 The page mockup for the Guess page in an HTML editor.

developers can use these core mockups as templates for the remaining application pages.

As you'll see shortly, converting these HTML mockup pages into usable Tapestry page templates requires a minimal number of unobtrusive changes. A mockup is converted into a page template by adding *instrumentation*: Additional tags and tag attributes are used to identify and configure Tapestry components within the template. This instrumentation is designed to be nearly invisible. Tapestry's approach stands in stark contrast to the use of JSPs, where the conversion from HTML mockup to JavaServer Page (JSP) is a one-way process. Once the HTML mockup page has been converted to a JSP, it will not preview correctly in a standard HTML editor, making all subsequent changes to the JSP that much more difficult. Within Tapestry, a page template can still be edited by an HTML developer using standard HTML editing tools; in effect, the mockups evolve into the HTML page templates yet can still be treated as mockups.[1]

This is an important aspect of Tapestry because late changes to application flow and look and feel are simply a reality when creating web applications—there's always a last-minute change: a new page to add, a background color to change, or a column width to tweak. Even in an impossibly idealized project, one where no late changes ever occurred, a subsequent release of the application would inevitably update the application flow and at least some aspect of the look and feel. Tapestry accommodates these kind of late cycle changes quite well because of how unobtrusive the instrumentation (the additional tags and tag attributes used to identify components within a template) is. Much more work can be done by an HTML developer using standard HTML editing tools, without the involvement of Java developers.

Meanwhile, even as the HTML developers are working on the mockups, the Java developers should be getting a head start on the design of the actual application, and that begins with identifying the domain objects.

2.1.3 Defining the domain objects

The architects and developers on the Java side of the team are ultimately responsible for the running application; in most applications, this becomes a question of linking a user interface to your domain objects. *Domain objects* are the objects of the middle tier, the application tier, in the overall application—they are the entity objects for data stored in a database, or objects that implement your business's specific processes. Common problems to solve involve what information is stored by these objects, how the different objects are related, and how they are read from, or stored into, a database.

Even in a simple application such as Hangman, which does not make use of a database, there are still domain objects, and still advantages (in accordance with the MVC design pattern) to keeping these objects well separated from any code directly related to the user interface.

[1] Tapestry isn't magic, and there are some limitations on maintaining full WYSIWYG previews of HTML templates once more sophisticated custom components are created and used within a page template; this subject is covered in chapter 6.

The two domain objects used in the Hangman application are `WordSource` and `Game`. The first, `WordSource`, is simply a wrapper around a list of words read from a text file and is used to dole out random words for the player to guess. `Game` is a bit more interesting; it encompasses all the logic about the game. Specifically, the `Game` object knows:

- The target word the player is attempting to guess
- Which of the 26 letters of the alphabet the player has already guessed
- Which letters of the target word have been filled in by successful guesses
- How many incorrect guesses remain
- If the player has won the game (by guessing all the letters in the target word)

As promised, the implementation of the `Game` class (in listing 2.1) knows nothing about Tapestry or any other user interface.

Listing 2.1 Game.java: domain object for the Hangman application

```
package hangman1;

public class Game
{
  private String _targetWord;
  private int _incorrectGuessesLeft;
  private char[] _letters;
  private boolean[] _guessed = new boolean[26];
  private boolean _win;

  public boolean isWin()
  {
    return _win;
  }

  public char[] getLetters()
  {
    return _letters;
  }

  public int getIncorrectGuessesLeft()
  {
    return _incorrectGuessesLeft;
  }

  public boolean[] getGuessedLetters()
  {
    return _guessed;
  }
```

Returns true once word has been guessed

Returns array of letters in the word

Returns 26 flags: letters guessed by player

```
public void start(String word)
{
  _targetWord = word;
  _incorrectGuessesLeft = 5;
  _win = false;

  int count = word.length();

  _letters = new char[count];

  for (int i = 0; i < count; i++)
    _letters[i] = '_';

  for (int i = 0; i < 26; i++)
    _guessed[i] = false;
}
```

Starts a new game

```
public boolean makeGuess(char letter)
{
  char ch = Character.toLowerCase(letter);

  if (ch < 'a' || ch > 'z')
    throw new IllegalArgumentException(
      "Must provide an alphabetic character.");

  int index = ch - 'a';

  if (_guessed[index])
    return true;

  _guessed[index] = true;

  boolean good = false;
  boolean complete = true;

  for (int i = 0; i < _letters.length; i++)
  {
    if (_letters[i] != '_')
      continue;

    if (_targetWord.charAt(i) == ch)
    {
      good = true;
      _letters[i] = ch;
      continue;
    }

    complete = false;
  }

  if (good)
```

Processes a player's guess

```
      {
        _win = complete;

        return !complete;
      }

      if (_incorrectGuessesLeft == 0)
      {
        _letters = _targetWord.toCharArray();

        return false;
      }

      _incorrectGuessesLeft--;

      return true;
    }
  }
```

Processes a player's guess

The `makeGuess()` method is invoked to process a player's guess. It updates the target word and other properties and returns true if more guesses are allowed. It returns false if the player has either won or lost the game.

The `Game` class must provide some support for the user interface, but it does so in a generic fashion without being tied to the interface; it's the Model in the MVC pattern described in chapter 1. This support takes the form of JavaBeans properties that are exposed to the user interface, such as the number of incorrect guesses remaining or the list of letters already guessed. These properties are bound to Tapestry component parameters, allowing those components to display the number of guesses remaining, the partially guessed word, or the list of remaining unguessed letters. In addition, `Game` provides methods that can be invoked by the user interface code to start a new game or to process a guess made by the player.

A second class, `WordSource`, is also used. `WordSource` is responsible for providing a random word for the player to guess. The source of the words is a small file, WordList.txt, packaged with the `WordSource` class. The `WordSource` class is provided in listing 2.2.

Listing 2.2 WordSource.java: domain object for the Hangman application

```
package hangman1;

import java.io.IOException;
import java.io.InputStream;
```

```
import java.io.InputStreamReader;
import java.io.LineNumberReader;
import java.io.Reader;
import java.util.ArrayList;
import java.util.Collections;
import java.util.List;

public class WordSource
{
  private int _nextWord;
  private List _words = new ArrayList();

  public WordSource()
  {
    readWords();
  }

  private void readWords()
  {

    try
    {
      InputStream in =
        getClass().getResourceAsStream("WordList.txt");
      Reader r = new InputStreamReader(in);
      LineNumberReader lineReader = new LineNumberReader(r);

      while (true)
      {
        String line = lineReader.readLine();

        if (line == null)
          break;

        if (line.startsWith("#"))
          continue;

        String word = line.trim().toLowerCase();

        if (word.length() == 0)
          continue;

        _words.add(word);
      }

      lineReader.close();
    }
    catch (IOException ex)
    {
      throw new RuntimeException(
        "Unable to read list of words from file WordList.txt.",
```

```
            ex);
        }

        // Randomize the word order

        Collections.shuffle(_words);

    }

    public String nextWord()
    {
        if (_nextWord >= _words.size())
        {
            _nextWord = 0;
            Collections.shuffle(_words);
        }

        return (String) _words.get(_nextWord++);
    }
}
```

When `WordSource` is instantiated, it reads the list of words. Later, the `nextWord()` method is invoked to get a new word for the player to guess. The method is designed to not repeat a target word until every word in the list has been guessed.

As with the `Game` class, this class has no direct connection to Tapestry—these objects fit firmly into the Model category within the MVC pattern. This kind of decoupling from the user interface is very important, because it means the `Game` and `WordSource` classes can be tested without having to run the Tapestry application, which in turn means the code can be fully tested inside an automated test suite. Making code testable is always a worthy goal, because no matter how simple the code is, *when you write tests, you find bugs*.

Once all the details of the domain objects are worked out, the next step is to begin work on the pages that will interact with those domain objects.

2.1.4 Defining the pages

Like any other Tapestry application, the Hangman game consists of a set number of pages, which are themselves composed of components. In a Tapestry application, each page is constructed by combining three related artifacts: an HTML template, a page specification, and a Java class.[2]

[2] Refer back to section 1.5.1 to see how to properly package these artifacts for use within a servlet container. Appendix B provides examples of how to set up your development workspace and how to use Ant to build and deploy the WAR.

Each Tapestry page has a specific, unique name. The page name is used to locate the page specification and HTML template. Part of the page specification is the name of the Java class to instantiate; this is called the *page class*, and it will include properties and methods specific to your application.

The Hangman application contains only four pages: Home, Guess, Lose, and Win, corresponding to the four pages identified in the application flow state diagram (figure 2.2). The Home page here is the same as the Start page in figure 2.2. By default, when a Tapestry application is first launched, the framework renders the page named Home. Although there are several options for changing this behavior, the simplest approach is to follow Tapestry's naming convention—by naming the first page a user will see Home.

Creating a functioning Tapestry page starts with the HTML mockup for the page. This mockup must be *instrumented* to act as an HTML template instead of a mockup. Instrumenting a mockup inserts additional attributes and tags in the mockup that tell Tapestry which parts of the template are dynamic components. Most of a template, however, is exactly the same as the mockup—simple, static HTML.

> **NOTE** In real projects, the mockups are not always available when needed by the Java developers creating the pages. In this situation, the Java developers will create simple, minimal HTML templates—just enough to wire up the functionality of the application. When the mockup is ready, some careful cut and paste from the mockup into the minimal HTML template will convert it to use the desired application look and feel.

Once the HTML template is instrumented, a *page specification* (a short XML document) can be created. The page specification has a number of responsibilities (many of which will be discussed in later chapters). Its most basic responsibility is to identify which Java class is to be instantiated as the page. In chapter 1, we described Tapestry as being a component object framework; this means that each component fits into an object hierarchy, either as a container of other components or as a containee of a specific component—or, in many cases, as both container *and* containee. Pages are still components, sitting at the root of the component object hierarchy.

As you'll see, the page class is specific to the application and contains a mixture of properties and methods that support both the rendering of the page and any user interaction in the page. Ultimately, the behavior of the page is defined by the page's properties and methods, combined with the components contained within the page—including the templates, properties, and methods of those components. This may seem a bit dizzying in theory, but in practice it all comes together simply and seamlessly. For our first example, let's start with the Home page—the simplest page in the Hangman application.

2.2 Developing the Home page

The Hangman application's Home page has only one small bit of user interaction: a link that starts a new game. This interaction is triggered by clicking the Start image, shown in figure 2.4. Like any page, the Home page is a combination of an XML page specification, an HTML template, and a Java class. Our first steps into Tapestry will be to examine how these three artifacts are combined to form a simple page.

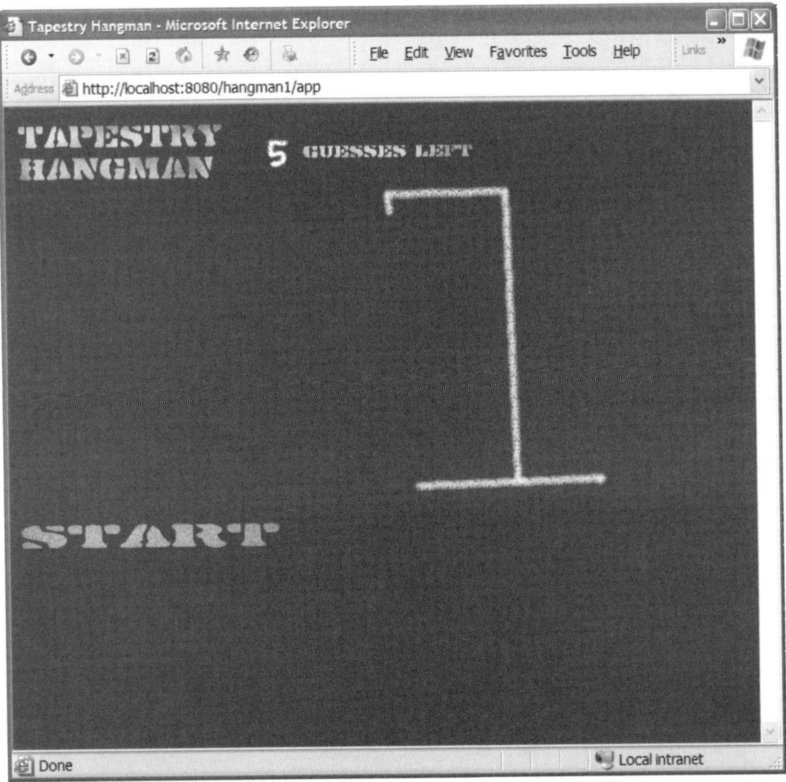

Figure 2.4 The Home page of the Tapestry Hangman application. The player may click the word *Start* to begin a game.

The Home page is displayed when the application is first launched. The Web archive (WAR) for the application must be deployed into the servlet container, and the servlet container must itself be running. This WAR will contain the Tapestry framework JARs, the page templates and specifications, the static image files (and other assets), and the compiled Java classes (this is discussed in chapter 1, section 1.5.1). When the user launches the application (by opening a web browser to http://localhost:8080/hangman1/app), the framework responds by rendering the Home page.

The first step in rendering a page is to create an instance of the page. The framework reads the Home page's specification and HTML template and uses this information to create the page instance. A Tapestry page is not a single object; the page object is the root of a tree of objects, including Tapestry components from the page's template, the contents of the HTML template, and a number of objects used to connect the individual pieces together. There's no special assembly stage for Tapestry applications, nor are there any special build steps or compilation—all that is necessary is to package the specifications, templates, and Java classes inside the WAR.

NOTE You might be concerned about performance, given all this talk of parsing specifications and templates and instantiating trees of objects—but don't be. This parsing occurs very quickly, and, unlike with JSPs, there's no time spent compiling generated Java source code (JSP compilation causes a noticeable delay the first time a JSP is used within a traditional servlet application). In line with Tapestry's efficiency goal, all the specifications and templates are read and parsed just once, and then cached for fast access when needed again in future requests. Page instances are also stored and reused in later requests.

Let's dive a little deeper and see exactly how the Home page's specification is used by the framework.

2.2.1 Understanding the Home page specification

The framework's first step toward instantiating the Home page is to locate and read the page's specification. Page specifications are validated XML files (with a .page extension) that are stored in the WEB-INF folder of the web application. The page specification's first responsibility is to identify the page class it needs to instantiate—it has other many other, optional responsibilities that we'll cover later in this chapter and in subsequent chapters. Listing 2.3 contains the complete specification for the Home page of the Hangman application.

Listing 2.3 Home.page: specification for the Home page

```
<?xml version="1.0"?>
<!DOCTYPE page-specification PUBLIC
  "-//Apache Software Foundation//Tapestry Specification 3.0//EN"
  "http://jakarta.apache.org/tapestry/dtd/Tapestry_3_0.dtd">

<page-specification class="hangman1.Home"/>
```

This is about as simple as a page specification can get; its only purpose is to identify the page class, `hangman1.Home`. This is a Java class written for the Hangman application, which will be the runtime representation of the page (see section 2.2.3 for more details). By convention, the class name for a page is the same as the page's name (though often stored inside a Java package), but of course, you are free to ignore this convention and name pages and classes differently. It's important, however, that the `<!DOCTYPE>` declaration be exactly as shown in listing 2.3.

WARNING Use the correct `<!DOCTYPE>`. Tapestry uses a validating XML parser to read specifications. Tapestry is purposely finicky about the public ID (the first string after PUBLIC), since it uses the known public ID to access a copy of the document type definition (DTD) inside the framework's JAR rather than access it over the Internet using the system ID. The public ID must exactly match the value in listing 2.3, or an `ApplicationRuntimeException` is thrown. For example, changing *Foundation* to *Floundation* will result in an exception report with this error message: *Document context:/WEB-INF/Home.page has an unexpected public id of '-//Apache Software Floundation//Tapestry Specification 3.0//EN'*. Watch out for typos; this is one area where a little cut and paste will save you some grief.

In addition, there is nothing that keeps a single page class from being used for multiple pages. Each page will have a distinct instance of the page class, just as each component in a page is a distinct instance of a component class.

2.2.2 Rendering the Home page

After parsing the page specification, Tapestry locates the HTML template for the Home page. The HTML template, which is named Home.html, is located in the root of the web application archive. This template is shown in listing 2.4.

Listing 2.4 Home.html: HTML template for the Home page

```
<html>
<head>
<title>Tapestry Hangman</title>
<link rel="stylesheet" type="text/css" href="css/hangman.css"/>
</head>
<body>
<table>
<tr>
  <td><img alt="[Tapestry Hangman]"
    src="images/tapestry-hangman.png" width="197" height="50"
    border="0"/>
  </td>
  <td width="70" align="right"><img height="36" alt="5"
    src="images/Chalkboard_3x8.png" width="36" border="0"/>
  </td>
  <td><img alt="Guesses Left" src="images/guesses-left.png"
    width="164" height="11" border="0"/>
  </td>
</tr>
<tr>
  <td>
  </td>
  <td>
  </td>
  <td><img alt="" src="images/scaffold.png" border="0"/>
  </td>
</tr>
</table>
<br/>
<a href="#" jwcid="@DirectLink"
  listener="ognl:listeners.start">
    <img src="images/start.png" width="250" height="23"
      border="0" alt="Start"/></a>
</body>
</html>
```

Dynamic portion of template

The majority of the HTML template is standard, static HTML; only a single Tapestry extension beyond ordinary HTML is used, showing up in the portion of the template that provides the link to start the game.

The `<a>` tag declares a Tapestry component within the template, giving us our first whiff of a dynamic web application rather than a static web page. The attribute `jwcid` is the indicator that Tapestry uses to identify components within the template. The name `jwcid` is simply *Java Web Component ID*. The component is type `DirectLink`, one of over 40 components provided with the Tapestry framework.

The example here is an *implicit* component, where the type of component and its configuration are declared directly in the HTML template. The `@` symbol indicates to Tapestry that the component is implicitly declared. Later in this chapter, we'll show examples of *declared* components, which have their type and configuration stored inside the page specification.

The DirectLink component is used to create a particular type of callback into the application. This component is one of the two primary ways that interaction occurs in Tapestry; the other is user-submitted forms (which are covered starting in chapter 3). The DirectLink component renders an HTML `<a>` element, supplying a URL that, when clicked by the end user, causes a specific listener method of the page to be executed (we'll discuss what a listener method is shortly, in section 2.2.3).

The position of the DirectLink component within the template is delineated by the `<a>` and `</a>` tags. Everything else in this HTML template is static HTML—text that is sent through to the client web browser unchanged. Just the portion rendered by the DirectLink component is dynamic. Figure 2.5 shows how the dynamic and static portions of the template are integrated together to form the complete response.

The Home page's HTML template is divided into five individual "chunks." Each chunk is either a block of static HTML, the start tag for a component (recognized by Tapestry because of the presence of a `jwcid` attribute), or the matching end tag for a component. Chunk ❶ is the portion of the HTML template that precedes the DirectLink component. Chunk ❷ is the component itself. Chunk ❸ is the portion of the page enclosed by the DirectLink. Chunk ❹ is the close tag for the DirectLink component. Chunk ❺ is the remainder of the template after the DirectLink.

Chunks that are enclosed directly within a component's start and end tags are part of that component's body. This is a very important part of Tapestry: Components control if and when their bodies are rendered. We'll frequently refer to the body of the component: This is the static HTML and other components that are enclosed between a component's start and end tags.

In this example, chunk ❸, containing the `<img>` tag, is the entire body of the DirectLink component. The page itself has a body, the top-level static chunks (chunks ❶ and ❺) and the components that aren't enclosed by other components

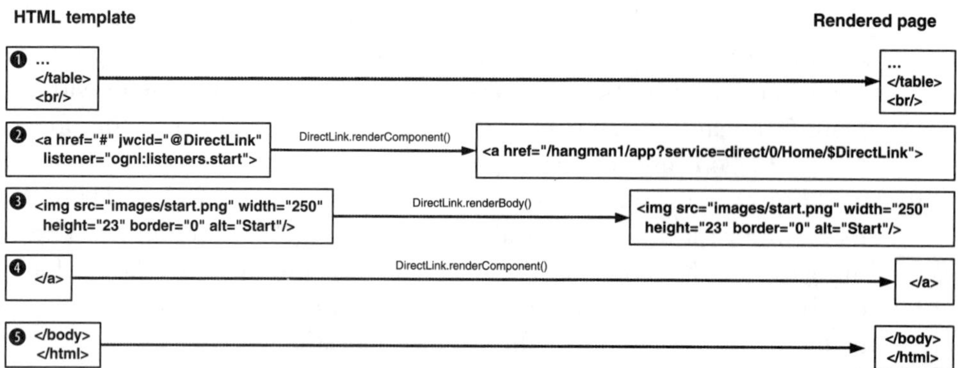

Figure 2.5 The Home page template is broken into chunks of static HTML and component tags. Static HTML chunks render as themselves; the DirectLink renders in code, in its `renderComponent()` method, and causes its body (the `<img>` tag) to render by invoking its `renderBody()` method.

(chunk ❷). When the page renders, it renders just the chunks in its body. Static HTML chunks render as themselves; they are passed on through to the client web browser unchanged. Components are responsible for rendering themselves and their body.

Figure 2.5 references two methods related to the DirectLink component: `renderComponent()` and `renderBody()`. The `renderComponent()` method is implemented by components that render in Java code (rather than using their own template). The method is invoked by the component's container, in this case the Home page itself, as part of the Home page's render.

The second method, `renderBody()`, is inherited by the DirectLink component from the `AbstractComponent` base class. The component invokes this method from its own `renderComponent()` method to render the text and components in its own body—the static `<img>` tag enclosed by the DirectLink's `<a>` and `</a>` tags.

In this case, the body of the DirectLink is simple, static HTML. That's often not the case; a component may contain a mix of static HTML and other components. Tapestry figures it all out, properly slotting each chunk of the page's template into the body of the correct component. Rendering a page is a recursive process, since components may themselves have their own templates, containing other components. Chapters 6 and 8 go into great detail about creating new components, including components that have their own template.

Tapestry's HTML template parser is very forgiving; although the examples in this book all follow Extensible HTML (XHTML) conventions, the template parser can handle the kind of HTML you'll find in the wild: unquoted attribute values, mixed uppercase and lowercase, single or double quotes, unquoted attribute values, and lots of additional whitespace. As elsewhere in Tapestry, if the parser is unable to parse a template it will throw an exception providing line-precise reporting of the problem.

The last piece of the Home page puzzle is the page class; this is where we put our application-specific logic—the code that will actually start a new game.

2.2.3 Defining the Home page class

So, what happens when the user clicks the link that was created when the page rendered? In Tapestry, that's the million-dollar question,[3] the point where all this talk of simplicity, consistency, and components starts to make a difference. Here's the short answer: You tell the component about a method in your page class to execute, and it executes the method when the link is clicked. Now, let's see what this looks like in practice. We'll start with listing 2.5, the source code for the Home page class.

Listing 2.5 Home.java: Java class for the Home page

```
package hangman1;

import org.apache.tapestry.IRequestCycle;
import org.apache.tapestry.html.BasePage;

public class Home extends BasePage
{
  public void start(IRequestCycle cycle)
  {
    Visit visit = (Visit)getVisit();

    visit.startGame(cycle);
  }
}
```

A page class has many responsibilities defined by the framework, including the ability to act as a container of other components. Fortunately, the `BasePage` class, from which the `Home` class extends, contains the code needed to fulfill all these responsibilities; for the Home page, all we need to add is the little bit of application-specific logic to be executed when the Start link is clicked. That logic shows up as a method, `start()`, implemented by the Home page class.

[3] Since Tapestry is open source, money is not the best way to gauge status. Perhaps this should be the "million download question" instead!

The `start()` method is a *listener method*, a method that will be invoked in response to a user clicking a particular link. Its implementation is to defer to the `Visit` object to actually start a new game—we'll discuss what the `Visit` object is shortly; for the moment, we'll concentrate on how it is that the `start()` method is invoked when a user clicks the link.

Listener methods are ordinary instance methods, implemented by the page's class, that have a specific method signature:

```
public void method(IRequestCycle cycle)
```

The method must always be public, return void, and take a single parameter of type `IRequestCycle`.

Tapestry components may have any number of parameters, both optional and required. The DirectLink component has several optional parameters and one that's required (`listener`). The binding for the `listener` parameter was provided in the Home page's HTML template:

```
<a href="#" jwcid="@DirectLink"
  listener="ognl:listeners.start">
  . . .
</a>
```

TIP Tapestry checks that there's a binding for each required parameter. If you remove the `listener` attribute from the HTML template for the Home page, the page will not display. Instead, you'll get an exception report with this message: *Required parameter listener of component Home/$DirectLink is not bound.* Home/$DirectLink is the name of the page and the ID of the component.

The DirectLink component's `listener` parameter is used to find the listener method it should execute when the end user clicks the link visible in his or her web browser. The `ognl:` prefix on the attribute value informs Tapestry that the value is an Object Graph Navigation Language (OGNL) expression to be evaluated, rather than a literal string constant. In Tapestry terminology, the expression `listeners.start` is *bound* to the DirectLink's `listener` parameter.

WARNING Don't forget the `ognl:` prefix. If you omit the prefix, Tapestry treats the value as a string literal. Removing the prefix from the DirectLink's `listener` parameter will result in an error like this when you click the link: *Parameter listener (listeners.start) is an instance of java.lang.String, which does not implement interface org.apache.tapestry.IActionListener.* When you see exceptions such as this, or perhaps `ClassCastExceptions` within your own code, the likely cause is a missing `ognl:` prefix.

How does the OGNL expression `listeners.start` end up executing this method? All pages and components inherit a property, `listeners`, from the `AbstractComponent` base class. The `listeners` property contains a nested property for each listener method implemented by the class. Underneath the covers, there's an interface, `IActionListener`, and a little bit of Java reflection used to connect the DirectLink component with the page's listener method; this is shown in figure 2.6.

A class may have any number of listener methods, each with a unique and individual name. Listener methods inherited from superclasses are also available through the `listeners` property.

WARNING If your OGNL expression references a listener method that doesn't exist, you'll get an exception when you click the link. For example, changing the expression to `ognl:listeners.star` results in an exception with this message: *Unable to resolve expression 'listeners.star' for hangman1.Home@19b808a[Home].* You'll also see an `ognl.NoSuchPropertyException` for the property `star`.

An invalid listener method will result in the same exception: This will occur if the method is not public or has the wrong method signature.

Sit back and think about this for a moment: We've just extended the behavior of this page within the application by writing a very short method, the `start()` listener method. The provisions we've made in the HTML template to get this

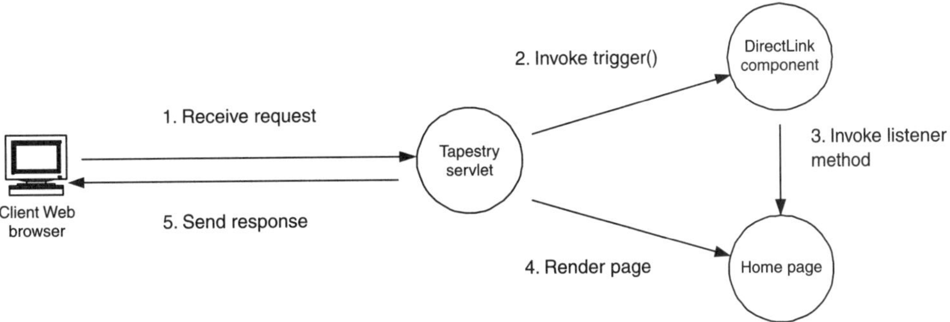

Figure 2.6 The Tapestry servlet receives and interprets the incoming request and invokes `trigger()` on the DirectLink component. The DirectLink invokes the listener method provided by the page. After the method is invoked, a page is rendered, forming the HTML response sent back to the client web browser.

listener method to execute on cue are so minor that they're barely worth considering. The Hangman application's Home page is unusual in that it has just the single bit of behavior—but you can imagine a more complicated page with many links (and, as you'll see in chapter 3, forms); adding each new bit of behavior is still just…adding another listener method.

This gets to the heart of the Tapestry goals described in chapter 1:

- **Simplicity**—Adding new operations takes minimal code and minimal changes to the HTML template.
- **Consistency**—Add as few or as many operations as you like, and the process stays the same. Look at any page in the application, and it *still* looks the same.
- **Feedback**—By working with the framework, errors in Java code, in the template, or in the specification are detected and verbosely reported by the framework.

A good practice is to keep listener methods short and focused on simply interfacing Tapestry components with business logic stored in domain objects. That's demonstrated here by having the `start()` listener method simply find the `Visit` object and let *it* do the work of actually starting a new game.

2.2.4 Examining the Visit object

The `Visit` object is an application-wide space for storing application logic and data. This object is accessible from all pages and components within the application and contains information specific to a single client of the web application. A single `Visit` object instance is shared by all pages within the application. The object fulfills much the same role as the `HttpSession` does in a typical servlet application, and in fact, the `Visit` object is ultimately stored as an `HttpSession` attribute.

All web applications eventually store some form of client-specific server-side state. The `HttpSession` acts like a map, storing named attributes. Simple as this seems, in real applications, a considerable amount of code must be written to retrieve attribute values from the `HttpSession`, cast them to the right type, create them on the fly as needed, and delete them when they are no longer needed.

Here again, Tapestry steps in to rethink this approach in terms of objects, methods, and properties. In chapter 7, we'll cover how Tapestry allows page properties to be stored persistently between requests, which is appropriate for values that are used only within a single page.

For more general data, used throughout an application, Tapestry allows for a single `Visit` object. Tapestry doesn't know or care about the type of the `Visit` object. There is no specific `Visit` class defined by the framework; each application defines its own `Visit` class. The accessor method for the `Visit` object provided by the page (defined by the interface `IPage` and implemented by the class `BasePage`) doesn't specify the type of the object:

```
public Object getVisit();
```

It then becomes a matter of casting to the application-specific type:

```
Visit visit = (Visit)getVisit();
```

The `Visit` object is automatically created by the framework the first time it is referenced; you must configure Tapestry, providing the name of the class to instantiate (this may be configured inside the web deployment descriptor; see section 2.6). Once the `Visit` object is created, it is stored in the `HttpSession` for persistent access in later requests.

Developer code never has to worry about the `HttpSession`. The `HttpSession` itself is created only as needed. A stateless application is more efficient than a stateful one, and a Tapestry application will operate in a stateless mode until there is actual server-side state to store. The framework takes care of this transition automatically, which would be very cumbersome to accomplish in ordinary servlet code because each and every servlet would need custom logic to check for the existence of the session and create it only as needed.

For our Hangman application, the `Visit` object is responsible for controlling page flow. It acts as a façade around the `WordSource` and `Game` objects, handles the process of starting a new game, and processes guesses made by the player. The `Visit` class for the Hangman application is provided in listing 2.6.

Listing 2.6 Visit.java: controller object for the Hangman application

```
package hangman1;

import org.apache.tapestry.IRequestCycle;

public class Visit
{
  private WordSource _wordSource = new WordSource();
  private Game _game = new Game();

  public void startGame(IRequestCycle cycle)        ❶ Invoked by Home page listener method
  {
    _game.start(_wordSource.nextWord());
```

```
    cycle.activate("Guess");                  ❶
  }

  public void makeGuess(IRequestCycle cycle, char ch)
  {
    if (_game.makeGuess(ch))
      return;

    cycle.activate(_game.isWin() ? "Win" : "Lose");
  }

  public Game getGame()
  {
    return _game;
  }
}
```

❷ **Invoked by Guess page listener method**

❸ **Provides game property**

❶ The `startGame()` method is invoked by a listener method on the Home page to start a new game. It is also invoked by listener methods on the Win and Lose pages.

❷ The `makeGuess()` method is invoked by a listener method on the Guess page; the listener method passes in the character to be guessed and the request cycle (so that the `Visit` object can activate the Win or Lose page, if necessary).

❸ The `Game` object is exposed as a read-only property of the `Visit` object. You'll see references to the properties of the `Game` object in the template as `ognl:visit.game.`*`property`*.

When the Home page invokes the `startGame()` method on `Visit`, `Visit` gets a random word and sets up the Game instance with it by invoking `Game`'s `start()` method. The call to `activate()` is used to change the active application page; the active page is responsible for rendering the response. Initially, the Home page is the active page, because it contains the `DirectLink` component that was triggered. Invoking the `activate()` method allows the correct page, the Guess page, to render the response.

2.3 Implementing the Home page using standard servlets

Despite the fact that the previous discussion about the DirectLink component, listener methods, and the `Visit` object was unavoidably long-winded, in the end we've shown that creating a link and getting an application-specific method to execute when the link is clicked is extremely simple.

Let's see what would be involved in accomplishing the same thing using standard servlets and JSPs. In this simple example, the JSP is very straightforward—so much so that it could as easily be an entirely static HTML page. The DirectLink component is replaced by a standard HTML link to a servlet we'll provide:

```
<a href="startGame"> <img . . . /> </a>
```

Of course, this example is not representative. Most application operations will involve quite a bit more: more servlets to implement the operation, more query parameters to fill in the details, and more code to build and interpret the URLs—all things that the Tapestry framework provides you for free.

Regardless, this example uses a very simple operation with no parameters. We still need to add a few lines to the application's web deployment descriptor, web.xml:

```
<servlet>
  <servlet-name>startGame</servlet-name>
  <servlet-class>StartGameServlet</servlet-class>
</servlet>

<servlet-mapping>
  <servlet-name>startGame</servlet-name>
  <url-pattern>/startGame</url-pattern>
</servlet-mapping>
```

Finally, we need the actual servlet, shown in listing 2.7.

Listing 2.7 StartGameServlet.java: hypothetical servlet for starting a game

```
import java.io.IOException;

import javax.servlet.ServletException;
import javax.servlet.http.HttpServlet;
import javax.servlet.http.HttpServletRequest;
import javax.servlet.http.HttpServletResponse;
import javax.servlet.http.HttpSession;

public class StartGameServlet extends HttpServlet
{
  protected void doGet(HttpServletRequest request,
    HttpServletResponse response)
    throws ServletException, IOException
  {
    HttpSession session = request.getSession(true);     <-(1) Gets or creates the session

    Visit visit = new Visit();
    session.setAttribute("visit", visit);     <-(2) Stores Visit for later
```

```
      visit.startGame();       <-3 Chooses random word to guess

      RequestDispatcher d =
        request.getRequestDispatcher("/Guess.jsp");
      d.forward(request, response);               4 Forwards to the Guess.jsp page
    }
  }
```

1. This accesses an existing `HttpSession` for the client or creates a new one if necessary.
2. We store the `Visit` object as a session attribute so that it can be accessed in later requests or by a JSP.
3. As in the Tapestry Hangman application, the hypothetical servlet `Visit` object is responsible for selecting a random word to guess.
4. The `RequestDispatcher` object is used to bridge from the servlet to a JSP that can render the response.

This servlet creates a `Visit` instance, similar in scope and implementation to the `Visit` object used in the Tapestry application. Once created, the `Visit` object is stored in the `HttpSession`, where it will be available in subsequent requests. The implementation of this `Visit` class may use the same `Game` and `WordSource` domain objects used by the real Tapestry application.

Extending this comparison from one single interaction to the innumerable interactions in a typical web application underscores the amount of developer effort needlessly wasted on most web applications. You are forced to drop out of the world of objects and methods and deal directly with aspects of the HTTP protocol and the Servlet API. You must define a URL to trigger your operation, create a new servlet class to perform that operation, and record the mapping from the URL to the servlet in the web.xml deployment descriptor. In a team environment, you will be competing with your fellow developers to update the deployment descriptor and to lay claim to the possible URLs for the application.

Certainly, as you become more experienced writing servlet-based applications, you will find shortcuts to help you streamline this effort. Unfortunately, different developers are quite likely to create their own suite of shortcuts. In a large team effort, getting the bits and pieces of the application written by different developers interoperating properly can become quite a challenge because of the impedance caused by all of the developers' individual schemes. When using Tapestry, this is rarely an issue because Tapestry defines a standard way for different parts of the application to interoperate—using objects, methods, and properties.

Now that we've seen how the Home page and the Hangman application's `Visit` object work together to start a new game, we can continue to the Guess page, the primary page in the Hangman application.

2.4 Developing the Guess page

The Guess page is the central page for the Hangman application; it allows the player to guess at letters of the target word. Figure 2.1 shows an example of the Guess page in action.

The page has a number of responsibilities:

- It displays the number of guesses remaining (as a number) as well as the number of incorrect guesses so far (as the growing stick figure).
- It displays the partially guessed target word, with lines replacing the as-yet unguessed letters.
- It displays a grid of remaining letters to guess; each letter is a clickable link.
- It supports the "hand-scrawled" look and feel, using custom images to display numbers and letters.

To accomplish all these tasks, we'll be introducing several new concepts for Tapestry specifications, HTML templates, and Java classes, as well as new Tapestry components. We'll start with the full listings for the HTML template, the page specification, and the page class, and then show how the different responsibilities we've listed are implemented—as Tapestry markup in the HTML template combined with entries in the page specification and code in the Java class. We'll begin with listing 2.8, the HTML template for the Guess page.

Listing 2.8 Guess.html: HTML template for the Guess page

```
<html>
<head>
<title>Tapestry Hangman</title>
<link rel="stylesheet" type="text/css" href="css/hangman.css"/>
</head>
<body>
<table>
<tr>
  <td><img alt="Tapestry Hangman" src="images/tapestry-hangman.png"
    width="197" height="50" border="0"/>
  </td>
```

```
    <td width="70" align="right"><img jwcid="@Image"
      alt="ognl:visit.game.incorrectGuessesLeft"
      image='ognl:getAsset("digit" +
        visit.game.incorrectGuessesLeft)'
      height="36" src="images/Chalkboard_3x8.png" width="36"
      border="0"/>
    </td>
    <td><img alt="Guesses Left" src="images/guesses-left.png"
      width="164" height="11" border="0"/>
    </td>
  </tr>
  <tr>
    <td>
    </td>
    <td>
    </td>
    <td><img jwcid="@Image"
      image='ognl:getAsset("scaffold" +
        visit.game.incorrectGuessesLeft)'
      alt="[Scaffold]" src="images/scaffold.png" border="0"/>
    </td>
  </tr>
  </table>
  <br>
  <table>
  <tr valign="center">
    <td width="160">
      <p align="right"><img alt="Current Guess"
      src="images/guess.png" align="middle" width="127" height="20"
      border="0"/></p>
    </td>
    <td><span jwcid="@Foreach" source="ognl:visit.game.letters"
      value="ognl:letter"><img jwcid="@Image"
      image="ognl:letterImage" alt="ognl:letterLabel" height="36"
      src="images/Chalkboard_5x3.png" width="36"
      border="0"/></span>

      <span jwcid="$remove$">
      <!--- Additional letters from the mockup --->
      <img height="36" alt="A" src="images/Chalkboard_1x1.png"
        width="36" border="0"/><img height="36" alt="_"
        src="images/Chalkboard_5x3.png" width="36"
        border="0"/><img height="36" alt="_"
        src="images/Chalkboard_1x5.png" width="36"
        border="0"/><img height="36" alt="_"
        src="images/Chalkboard_5x3.png" width="36"
        border="0"/><img height="36" alt="_"
        src="images/Chalkboard_5x3.png" width="36"
        border="0"/><img height="36" alt="_"
        src="images/Chalkboard_5x3.png" width="36"
        border="0"/><img height="36" alt="_"
```

❶ ❷ ❸ ❹

```
      src="images/Chalkboard_5x1.png" width="36"
      border="0"/>                                           4
    </span>
  </td>
</tr>
<tr>
  <td valign="top">
    <p align="right"><img alt="Choose" src="images/choose.png"
      height="20" width="151" border="0"/></p>
  </td>
  <td width="330"><span jwcid="selectLoop"><a href="#"
      jwcid="select" class="select-letter"><img jwcid="@Image"
      image="ognl:guessImage" alt="ognl:guessLabel" height="36"    5
      src="images/Chalkboard_5x3.png" width="36"
      border="0"/></a></span>

    <span jwcid="$remove$">
    <!-- Additional selectable letters from the mockup. --->

      <a class="select-letter" href="#"><img height="36" alt="B"
        src="images/Chalkboard_1x2.png" width="36" border="0"/></a>
      <a class="select-letter" href="#"><img height="36" alt="C"
        src="images/Chalkboard_1x3.png" width="36" border="0"/></a>
      <a class="select-letter" href="#"><img height="36" alt="D"
        src="images/Chalkboard_1x4.png" width="36" border="0"/></a>
      <img height="36" alt="-" src="images/letter-spacer.png"
        width="36" border="0"/>
      <a class="select-letter" href="#"><img height="36" alt="F"
        src="images/Chalkboard_1x6.png" width="36" border="0"/></a>
      <a class="select-letter" href="#"><img height="36" alt="G"
        src="images/Chalkboard_2x1.png" width="36" border="0"/></a>
      <a class="select-letter" href="#"><img height="36" alt="H"
        src="images/Chalkboard_2x2.png" width="36" border="0"/></a>
      <a class="select-letter" href="#"><img height="36" alt="I"     6
        src="images/Chalkboard_2x3.png" width="36" border="0"/></a>
      <a class="select-letter" href="#"><img height="36" alt="J"
        src="images/Chalkboard_2x4.png" width="36" border="0"/></a>
      <a class="select-letter" href="#"><img height="36" alt="K"
        src="images/Chalkboard_2x5.png" width="36" border="0"/></a>
      <a class="select-letter" href="#"><img height="36" alt="L"
        src="images/Chalkboard_2x6.png" width="36" border="0"/></a>
      <a class="select-letter" href="#"><img height="36" alt="M"
        src="images/Chalkboard_3x1.png" width="36" border="0"/></a>
      <a class="select-letter" href="#"><img height="36" alt="N"
        src="images/Chalkboard_3x2.png" width="36" border="0"/></a>
      <a class="select-letter" href="#"><img height="36" alt="O"
        src="images/Chalkboard_3x3.png" width="36" border="0"/></a>
      <a class="select-letter" href="#"><img height="36" alt="P"
        src="images/Chalkboard_3x4.png" width="36" border="0"/></a>
      <a class="select-letter" href="#"><img height="36" alt="Q"
        src="images/Chalkboard_3x5.png" width="36" border="0"/></a>
```

```
        <a class="select-letter" href="#"><img height="36" alt="R"
          src="images/Chalkboard_3x6.png" width="36" border="0"/></a>
        <a class="select-letter" href="#"><img height="36" alt="S"
          src="images/Chalkboard_4x1.png" width="36" border="0"/></a>
        <a class="select-letter" href="#"><img height="36" alt="T"
          src="images/Chalkboard_4x2.png" width="36" border="0"/></a>
        <a class="select-letter" href="#"><img height="36" alt="U"
          src="images/Chalkboard_4x3.png" width="36" border="0"/></a>
        <a class="select-letter" href="#"><img height="36" alt="V"
          src="images/Chalkboard_4x4.png" width="36" border="0"/></a>     6
        <a class="select-letter" href="#"><img height="36" alt="W"
          src="images/Chalkboard_4x5.png" width="36" border="0"/></a>
        <a class="select-letter" href="#"><img height="36" alt="X"
          src="images/Chalkboard_4x6.png" width="36" border="0"/></a>
        <img height="36" alt="-" src="images/letter-spacer.png"
          width="36" border="0"/>
        <a class="select-letter" href="#"><img height="36" alt="Z"
          src="images/Chalkboard_5x2.png" width="36" border="0"/></a>
      </span>
    </td>
  </tr>
  </table>
  </body>
  </html>
```

❶ This Image component selects and displays the correct image identifying the number of incorrect guesses remaining to the player.

❷ The second Image component selects and displays an image for the man on the scaffold, showing how many incorrect guesses the player has made so far.

❸ These components display the target word, with underscores marking unguessed letters within the word.

❹ This portion of the template is marked for removal (using the special `$remove$` value for the `jwcid` attribute). The `<img>` tags within the `<span>` exist for WYSIWYG preview but must be removed because they conflict with the dynamic content provided by ❸.

❺ These components provide an array of clickable letters, allowing the player to guess the next letter in the target word.

❻ This portion of the template is also marked for removal.

This page was converted directly from the HTML mockup; the bulk of the template consists of placeholder values (for the number of guesses, for the stick figure, for the partially guessed word, and for the grid of guessable letters) that will actually be discarded in favor of dynamically generated HTML. We'll go into more detail on each portion of the HTML template shortly.

Listing 2.9 is the page specification for the Guess page.

Listing 2.9 Guess.page: specification for the Guess page

```
<?xml version="1.0"?>
<!DOCTYPE page-specification PUBLIC
  "-//Apache Software Foundation//Tapestry Specification 3.0//EN"
  "http://jakarta.apache.org/tapestry/dtd/Tapestry_3_0.dtd">

<page-specification class="hangman1.Guess">

  <component id="selectLoop" type="Foreach">
    <binding name="source" expression="visit.game.guessedLetters"/>
    <binding name="value" expression="letterGuessed"/>
    <binding name="index" expression="guessIndex"/>
  </component>
                                                                    ❶
  <component id="select" type="DirectLink">
    <binding name="listener" expression="listeners.makeGuess"/>
    <binding name="parameters" expression="letterForGuessIndex"/>
    <binding name="disabled" expression="letterGuessed"/>
  </component>

  <context-asset name="digit0" path="images/Chalkboard_1x7.png"/>
  <context-asset name="digit1" path="images/Chalkboard_1x8.png"/>
  <context-asset name="digit2" path="images/Chalkboard_2x7.png"/>   ❷
  <context-asset name="digit3" path="images/Chalkboard_2x8.png"/>
  <context-asset name="digit4" path="images/Chalkboard_3x7.png"/>
  <context-asset name="digit5" path="images/Chalkboard_3x8.png"/>

  <context-asset name="scaffold5" path="images/scaffold.png"/>
  <context-asset name="scaffold4" path="images/scaffold-1.png"/>
  <context-asset name="scaffold3" path="images/scaffold-2.png"/>    ❸
  <context-asset name="scaffold2" path="images/scaffold-3.png"/>
  <context-asset name="scaffold1" path="images/scaffold-4.png"/>
  <context-asset name="scaffold0" path="images/scaffold-5.png"/>

  <context-asset name="space" path="images/letter-spacer.png"/>
  <context-asset name="dash" path="images/Chalkboard_5x3.png"/>

  <context-asset name="a" path="images/Chalkboard_1x1.png"/>
  <context-asset name="b" path="images/Chalkboard_1x2.png"/>
  <context-asset name="c" path="images/Chalkboard_1x3.png"/>
  <context-asset name="d" path="images/Chalkboard_1x4.png"/>        ❹
  <context-asset name="e" path="images/Chalkboard_1x5.png"/>
  <context-asset name="f" path="images/Chalkboard_1x6.png"/>
  <context-asset name="g" path="images/Chalkboard_2x1.png"/>
  <context-asset name="h" path="images/Chalkboard_2x2.png"/>
  <context-asset name="i" path="images/Chalkboard_2x3.png"/>
  <context-asset name="j" path="images/Chalkboard_2x4.png"/>
  <context-asset name="k" path="images/Chalkboard_2x5.png"/>
```

```
    <context-asset name="l" path="images/Chalkboard_2x6.png"/>
    <context-asset name="m" path="images/Chalkboard_3x1.png"/>
    <context-asset name="n" path="images/Chalkboard_3x2.png"/>
    <context-asset name="o" path="images/Chalkboard_3x3.png"/>
    <context-asset name="p" path="images/Chalkboard_3x4.png"/>
    <context-asset name="q" path="images/Chalkboard_3x5.png"/>
    <context-asset name="r" path="images/Chalkboard_3x6.png"/>
    <context-asset name="s" path="images/Chalkboard_4x1.png"/>   ❹
    <context-asset name="t" path="images/Chalkboard_4x2.png"/>
    <context-asset name="u" path="images/Chalkboard_4x3.png"/>
    <context-asset name="v" path="images/Chalkboard_4x4.png"/>
    <context-asset name="w" path="images/Chalkboard_4x5.png"/>
    <context-asset name="x" path="images/Chalkboard_4x6.png"/>
    <context-asset name="y" path="images/Chalkboard_5x1.png"/>
    <context-asset name="z" path="images/Chalkboard_5x2.png"/>

</page-specification>
```

❶ The `<component>` element is used to declare components. The type of component and the configuration of the component's parameters go here, in the page specification.

❷ The `<context-asset>` element defines an asset file that is stored within the web application context. This first set of assets includes the digits used to display the number of remaining incorrect guesses. These assets are given logical names that are referenced in the Java page class.

❸ The second group of `<context-asset>` elements defines the images used for the stick figure.

❹ The remaining `<context-asset>` elements define the images used for the letters of the alphabet, as well as a blank space image and the underscore image (as `dash`).

This is a much longer specification than for the Home page, and it demonstrates a couple of new features: the ability to define the type and configuration of components in the specification rather than in the HTML template, and the ability to define *assets*, which are named references to static files such as images or stylesheets. Again, we'll revisit the relevant portions of this specification shortly.

Finally, listing 2.10 is the source for the `Guess` class: the Java class for the Guess page.

Listing 2.10 Guess.java: Java class for the Guess page

```
package hangman1;

import org.apache.tapestry.IAsset;
import org.apache.tapestry.IRequestCycle;
```

```
import org.apache.tapestry.html.BasePage;

public class Guess extends BasePage
{
  private char _letter;
  private boolean _letterGuessed;
  private int _guessIndex;

  public void initialize()
  {
    _letter = 0;
    _letterGuessed = false;
    _guessIndex = 0;
  }

  public char getLetter()
  {
    return _letter;
  }

  public void setLetter(char letter)
  {
    _letter = letter;
  }

  public String getLetterLabel()
  {
    return ("" + _letter).toUpperCase();
  }

  public IAsset getLetterImage()
  {
    if (_letter == '_')
      return getAsset("dash");

    return getAsset("" + _letter);
  }

  public boolean isLetterGuessed()
  {
    return _letterGuessed;
  }

  public int getGuessIndex()
  {
    return _guessIndex;
  }

  public void setLetterGuessed(boolean letterGuessed)
  {
    _letterGuessed = letterGuessed;
  }
```

❶ **Resets page properties**

❷ **Converts letter property to an image**

```
    public void setGuessIndex(int guessIndex)
    {
      _guessIndex = guessIndex;
    }

    public IAsset getGuessImage()
    {
      if (_letterGuessed)
        return getAsset("space");

      String name = "" + getLetterForGuessIndex();

      return getAsset(name);
    }

    public char getLetterForGuessIndex()
    {
      return (char) ('a' + _guessIndex);
    }

    public String getGuessLabel()
    {
      if (_letterGuessed)
        return " ";

      char ch = Character.toUpperCase(getLetterForGuessIndex());

      return new Character(ch).toString();
    }

    public void makeGuess(IRequestCycle cycle)
    {
      Object[] parameters = cycle.getServiceParameters();
      Character guess = (Character) parameters[0];

      char ch = guess.charValue();

      Visit visit = (Visit) getVisit();

      visit.makeGuess(cycle, ch);
    }
  }
```

3 Converts guessIndex property to an image

4 Listener method invoked when a letter is clicked

1. This method is invoked when the page is created and at the end of each request, to reset any properties back to pristine values, ready for the next request.
2. This method creates a read-only, synthetic property, `letterImage`, that provides the correct image for whatever the `letter` property currently is.
3. Likewise, this `guessImage` property returns the correct image based on the `guessIndex` and `letterGuessed` properties.

❹ This listener method is invoked when a letter image is clicked; it exists to determine the correct parameters to pass to the `Visit` object's `makeGuess()` method.

`Guess` is a typical Tapestry page class; it contains properties and methods that support the rendering of the page as well as listener methods activated by links on the page.

2.4.1 Displaying the remaining guesses

The first dynamic bit is the part of the HTML template that displays the number of incorrect guesses remaining to the player:

```
<img jwcid="@Image"
   alt="ognl:visit.game.incorrectGuessesLeft"
   image='ognl:getAsset("digit" +
     visit.game.incorrectGuessesLeft)'
   height="36"
   src="images/Chalkboard_3x8.png"
   width="36" border="0"/>
```

This snippet has an array of responsibilities:

- It must render an HTML `<img>` tag and fill in a number of attributes dynamically.
- It must convert the `incorrectGuessesLeft` property of the `Game` object into a string, as the `alt` attribute.
- It must select the correct image file to display the number of guesses left and build a URL to that file (as the `src` attribute).

Earlier we saw how the DirectLink component on the Home page inserted an `<a>` tag into the response sent to the client web browser. The `Image` component, another standard Tapestry component, is actually much simpler; it inserts an `<img>` tag, generating the tag's `src` attribute from its `image` parameter. Here we want it to provide the correct image (one of the hand-drawn digits) and the corresponding `alt` value.

NOTE To support WYSIWYG editing, the HTML template uses an `<img>` tag, knowing that the component will, at runtime, render an `<img>` tag. The `Image` component will override the `src` attribute in the template, which is also here just to help with the WYSIWYG preview of the template.

In a Tapestry template, each component must have properly balanced start and end tags. An alternative, used here, is to include an XML-style empty tag, one that ends with `/>`. Tapestry is flexible about attribute quoting; because the `image` parameter's expression uses double quotes, the entire expression is enclosed in single quotes.

WARNING Match your open and close tags. You must supply a matching close tag for each component's start tag. Tapestry even checks that all the start tags and end tags on a page properly nest (it is forgiving for all tags that aren't components). Changing the end of the `<img>` tag from `/>` to just `>` will result in the following exception: *Closing tag </td> on line 13 is improperly nested with tag <img> on line 12.* Tapestry matched the `</td>` on line 13 with the `<td>` on line 12 (before the `<img>` tag) and realized that the `<img>` tag hadn't yet been closed, even though it's a component.

The first OGNL expression, `visit.game.incorrectGuessesLeft`, is very straightforward; it retrieves the `incorrectGuessesLeft` property from the `Game` object (via the `Visit` object). The `incorrectGuessesLeft` property (a number) is converted to a string and becomes the value for the `<img>` tag's `alt` attribute. In the client web browser, this value becomes the tooltip for the image and is also used for accessibility (visually impaired users may have the value read to them by their computer).

The other expression, for selecting the image is more complicated. It also obtains the `incorrectGuessesLeft` property, but then it uses that value as a parameter when invoking the `getAsset()` method on the page. This underscores why OGNL is so useful and powerful; without OGNL, this access and manipulation would have to occur in Java code. Using OGNL, we are able to assemble the complete string and invoke a Java method, `getAsset()`, on our page, all in one step. The invoked method returns the asset object representing the image to use, which is ultimately converted into a URL by the Image component and inserted in the HTML response as the `src` attribute of the `<img>` tag.

NOTE Using OGNL expressions where possible allows you to assume a rapid application development cycle, free from the normal edit/compile/deploy cycle that occurs with Java code. You can simply edit your templates and specifications in place to see changes.[4] Later, you can recode

[4] It is possible to disable the normal caching that occurs inside Tapestry so that templates and specifications are reread for each new request. This allows changes to templates and specifications to take effect immediately. Consult the Tapestry reference documentation, distributed with the framework, for the details.

OGNL expressions as Java methods for greater application efficiency. Another good option, when not prototyping, is to move nontrivial OGNL expressions into the page specification (an example of this is shown in section 2.4.3); this results in a much improved separation of the View from the Model and application logic, which ultimately yields a more maintainable application.

Tapestry allows you, as the developer, to decide how pure a separation between the View and the Model you will maintain. At one extreme, the pragmatic view, you may put as much logic (in the form of OGNL expressions) as you want directly into the HTML template. This pushes together purely presentation-oriented aspects of the application (such as layout and fonts) with the behavioral aspects of the application (shown in this example as references to page properties, including `visit` and `visit.game`). Such an approach is perfectly acceptable for prototypes, or for small projects where a strong separation between developers isn't realistic. Most of the examples in this book use this pragmatic approach simply because it puts related information side by side, making it easier to comprehend.

At the other extreme, the purist view, your HTML template contains only placeholders for components; all details about the component configuration are stored outside the template, in the page specification. This is critical on larger projects, where a division can be expected between the HTML developers responsible for page mockups and the Java developers responsible for converting the mockups into a working application. Minimizing how much of the application's implementation is exposed to the HTML developers reduces the potential for conflicts between the Java developers and the HTML developers.

Assets are any kind of file that may be distributed as part of the WAR; the most common types of assets are images and stylesheets. The Image component's `image` parameter expects an asset object (an object that implements the `IAsset` interface), not a string, and this pairs up with the `getAsset()` method, which returns just such an object. The `getAsset()` method is inherited from the `AbstractComponent` base class; it allows access to the named assets defined in the page specification.

The names of the assets come from the `<context-asset>` elements in the page specification (in listing 2.9). What's happening is a mapping from a logical name (such as x or dash) to a particular file (such as images/Chalkboard_4x6.png or images/Chalkboard_5x3.png). The assets abstraction has some other important uses related to localization and to packaging components into reusable libraries. Those uses are covered in more detail in chapters 6 and 7.

Defining assets in the page specification

The page specification for the Guess page declares assets for the letters, digits, and underscore as well as all the images of the stick figure on the gallows. The Guess page specification includes the following lines to declare the six digits used in the user interface:

```
<context-asset name="digit0" path="images/Chalkboard_1x7.png"/>
<context-asset name="digit1" path="images/Chalkboard_1x8.png"/>
<context-asset name="digit2" path="images/Chalkboard_2x7.png"/>
<context-asset name="digit3" path="images/Chalkboard_2x8.png"/>
<context-asset name="digit4" path="images/Chalkboard_3x7.png"/>
<context-asset name="digit5" path="images/Chalkboard_3x8.png"/>
```

WARNING Tapestry checks that a file matching the provided asset path exists.[5] This check occurs when the page specification is first read and takes place regardless of whether anything ever *uses* the asset. Putting a typo into one of the names in the previous snippet results in the following exception: *Unable to locate asset 'digit0' of component Guess as context:/images/Challkboard_1x7.png.*

Here, we can see how the aliasing is useful. The letters and numbers were initially drawn onto a grid, and a slicing tool was used to generate a set of individual files from the cells of the grid. The filenames provided by the slicing tool are not intuitive (they are based on the position in the grid, rather the value of the image, and so are somewhat arbitrary), but the use of assets allows the code to reference them using more friendly names. Of course, we could have simply renamed the files output by the slicing tool, but by leaving the names as is, we can change the original letter grid image and then use the same slicing tool to regenerate all the images without having to go through the painful renaming process a second time. Tapestry has provided a little bit of abstraction and flexibility that ultimately makes the build process for this application more agile, because an annoying manual step (renaming the files) is not necessary.

Assets also provide a separation of concerns, dividing the HTML developers from the Java developers. For example, an HTML developer may decide to redo the graphics for the page and use a new tool to generate the images of the digits—which would result in new filenames, possibly even new types (perhaps GIF or JPEG), but no change to the logical names of the assets. Either the HTML

[5] This applies to the context assets defined here and the private assets we'll discuss in chapter 6. A third asset type, the external asset, is not checked.

developer or the Java developer would need to update the page specification to change the filenames, but there would be no change to the HTML template or even to the Java class (if the Java class ever accessed any assets by name).

Now that we have a way of mapping from logical names to actual asset files, we still need a way to figure out which logical name, and thus, which asset, should be used when displaying the remaining guesses.

Calculating the right asset

Displaying the digit image is a matter of selecting the correct asset as the `image` parameter to the Image component. This occurs in the HTML template using an OGNL expression:

```
image='ognl:getAsset("digit" + visit.game.incorrectGuessesLeft)'
```

Here, OGNL has done something fairly complex: building up the name of the asset and invoking the page's `getAsset()` method. There are penalties, however: This chunk of text is somewhat unwieldy and forces us to use single quotes, since the expression itself contains double quotes. Putting OGNL expressions into your template, especially expressions of this complexity, is not much better than putting Java scriptlets into a JSP: Such OGNL expressions strongly tie together the presentation of the page with the implementation.

One option would be to move more of this logic into equivalent Java code. This can be easily accomplished by referencing a new, read-only property in the HTML template:

```
<IMG jwcid="@Image"
   alt="ognl:visit.game.incorrectGuessesLeft"
   image="ognl:digitImage"                  <-- Reference to the page's
   height="36"                                  digitImage property
   src="images/Chalkboard_3x8.png"
   width="36" border="0"/>
```

We would then implement an accessor method for this new `digitImage` property in the `Guess` class:[6]

```
public IAsset getDigitImage()
{
  Visit visit = (Visit)getVisit();
  int guessesLeft = visit.getGame().getIncorrectGuessesLeft();

  return getAsset("digit" + guessesLeft);
}
```

[6] Because this approach is only hypothetical, you won't see this method in the `Guess` class in listing 2.10.

Another option, which we'll explore shortly, is to move the OGNL expression into the page specification. The decision to use OGNL expressions, Java code, or some mix of the two is left to you, according to your personal taste and the particular situation. The modest runtime performance penalty for using OGNL is easily offset by increased developer productivity.

Using informal component parameters

If you check the description for the Image component in appendix C, you'll see that it defines two possible parameters: a required `image` parameter and an optional `border` parameter. However, if you run the application and view the source of the page, you'll see that the other attributes included in the `<img>` tag in the template (`alt`, `width`, and `height`) are still present in the `<img>` tag rendered by the Image component. How can this be?

The majority of Tapestry components, including Image and DirectLink, allow *informal parameters*. Informal parameters are additional parameters for the component beyond those that are formally declared by the component. These additional parameters are simply added to the rendered tag as additional attributes. Informal parameters can be unevaluated static values, such as for `width`, or expressions, such as for `alt`. Some informal parameters are discarded so that they don't conflict with attributes rendered directly by the component. For example, it doesn't matter that the template provides a value for the `src` attribute (in the `<img>` tag for the Image component); the value in the template is discarded because the Image component will itself generate an `src` attribute from the asset provided in the `image` parameter. The `src` value in the template exists to support WYSIWYG previewing of the template; its value is discarded in favor of the real, dynamic URL computed on the fly in the live application. Only components that map directly to an HTML tag will accept informal parameters; each component indicates within its own component specification whether it accepts or discards informal parameters.

So, when the Image component renders, it will mix and match the informal parameters with the HTML attributes it generates from formal parameters. This is a capability missing from JSP tags, where specifying an undeclared JSP tag attribute is simply an error. With JSP tags, you are limited to just the attributes explicitly declared for the tag, no more.

Displaying the right stick figure image

Continuing with the rest of the Guess page, the next dynamic section of the HTML template is also related to the `incorrectGuessesLeft` property; it is used to display one of several images for the gallows, showing increasing amounts of the stick figure as the `incorrectGuessesLeft` property drops toward zero.

```
<img jwcid="@Image"
  image='ognl:getImage("scaffold" +
      visit.game.incorrectGuessesLeft)'
    alt="[Scaffold]"
    src="images/scaffold.png"
      border="0"/>
```

Again, we use the same trick; we come up with a logical name for the image asset and map that logical name to an actual file by way of the `<context-asset>` elements in the page specification. This is a good, simple example of the MVC pattern in action; the Model in this case is the `Game` object and its `incorrectGuessesLeft` property, but there are two Views of the data: the first as a digit, the second as the stick figure on the gallows.

The remaining dynamic portions of the page are more complex and require using multiple components in concert to produce the desired output.

2.4.2 Generating the guessed word display

The next section of the Guess page displays the target word the player is attempting to guess, or at least as much of the target word as the player has guessed so far. Generating this portion of the page starts with the `Game` object, which has a property, `letters`, for just this purpose. The `letters` property is an array of each letter of the target word as an individual character. Each unguessed letter in the target word is replaced with an underscore character.

As with the previous examples, we can't simply output the individual letters as characters. To keep the hand-scrawled look and feel, each letter must be translated to the correct image. The template uses two different components to generate the display: a Foreach component (which performs a kind of loop) enclosing another Image component. The two components work together to display one letter after another.

```
<span jwcid="@Foreach"
   source="ognl:visit.game.letters"
   value="ognl:letter">
<img jwcid="@Image"
   image="ognl:letterImage"
   alt="ognl:letterLabel"
   height="36"
   src="images/Chalkboard_5x3.png"
   width="36"
   border="0"/>
</span>
```

Looping with the Foreach component

Foreach is a looping component; it iterates over the list of values provided by its `source` parameter[7] and *updates* its `value` parameter for each value from the source before rendering its body. This is a crucial feature of Tapestry component parameters; by binding a property to a component parameter, the component is free not only to read the value of the bound property, but also to update the property as well.

The Foreach component is represented in the template using a `<span>` tag, which is very natural: The HTML `<span>` tag is simply a container of other text and elements in a page. It doesn't normally display anything itself, but is commonly used in conjunction with a stylesheet to control how a portion of a page is rendered.

Although the Foreach's location in the template is specified using a `<span>` tag, when it renders, it does not produce any HTML directly; it simply renders the text and components in its body repeatedly. The sequence is shown in figure 2.7.

So, the Foreach component will render its body many times, but that doesn't help the Image component display the correct letter image. Just before the Foreach renders its body (on each pass through the loop), it sets a property of the page to the next letter in the word (from the array of characters provided by the `Game` object). The trick is to convert this letter into the correct image. The Guess page class includes a property, `letter`, which is bound to the Foreach component's `value` parameter so that it can be updated by the Foreach:

```
private char _letter;

public char getLetter()
{
  return _letter;
}

public void setLetter(char letter)
{
  _letter = letter;
}
```

[7] The Foreach component is flexible about how it defines "a list of values." It may be an array of objects, or a `java.util.List`, or even a single object (which is treated like an array of one object).

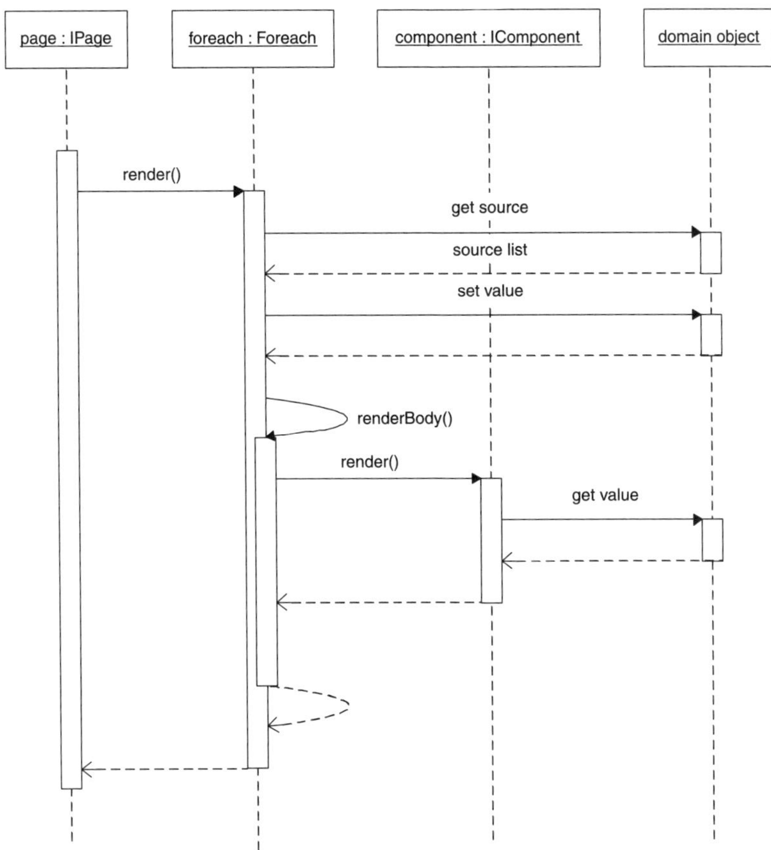

Figure 2.7 The Foreach component reads a list of values bound to its source parameter from a domain object (which is often the page that contains the component). For each item in the list, it updates a domain object property bound to its `value` parameter, and then renders its body. Components within its body can get the value from the domain object property.

NOTE In chapter 3, we'll see how Tapestry can automatically create properties at runtime (and the benefits of doing so beyond less typing). For now, we'll mechanically code these properties ourselves by supplying the instance variable and pair of accessor methods.

Translating letters to images

Once again, we are using assets to obtain the correct image to display within the page. The assets for the letters a through z are named, simply, a through z. However, there's a gotcha for the underscore character; its asset name is dash.

The Guess page class implements another method to provide the asset to display:

```
public IAsset getLetterImage()
{
  if (_letter == '_')
    return getAsset("dash");

  return getAsset("" + _letter);
}
```

This simple method captures the special rule about replacing the underscore character with the asset named dash. The Foreach component is responsible for invoking `setLetter()` with the correct letter well before `getLetterImage()` is invoked by the Image component.

> **NOTE** Because this method is public and follows the naming convention for a JavaBeans property, it can be referenced in the HTML template as `ognl:letterImage`. This is a common approach in Tapestry—creating *synthetic properties*, properties that are computed on the fly, rather than just exposing a value in an instance variable.

The letters in the list (provided by the `Game` object) are all lowercase, but the tooltip (generated from the `<img>` tag's `alt` attribute) looks better if the letter is uppercase. This is another, minor example of the Controller (the page) mediating between the Model (the `Game` object) and the View (the Image component within the HTML template). This case conversion is accomplished by binding the value for the `alt` parameter to the `letterLabel` property of the page. The `getLetterLabel()` accessor method simply converts the letter to uppercase and returns it as a string:

```
public String getLetterLabel()
{
  char upper = Character.toUpperCase(_letter);

  return new Character(upper).toString();
}
```

Removing unwanted portions of the template

If you examine the complete HTML template in listing 2.4, you'll see that just after the `</span>` tag for the Foreach component is a long chunk of additional images—images for additional letters from the target word, as dashes. These images were copied over from the original HTML mockup and are left in place so that the HTML template will still preview properly. Without these additional images, the target word will appear as a single underscore, which may not be enough to validate the layout of the page. At the same time, these extra images must not be included in a live, rendered page or the target word will appear to be six letters longer than it actually is.

Earlier, you saw that Tapestry will drop unwanted HTML attributes that are provided in HTML tags to support WYSIWYG preview. This is a larger case, where an entire section of HTML is dropped. The block to be removed is surrounded by a `<span>` tag:

```
<span jwcid="$remove$"> . . . </span>
```

The special component ID, `"$remove$"`, is the trigger for Tapestry's template parser that this portion of the HTML template should be discarded. This is a second aspect of instrumenting an HTML mockup into an HTML template: marking portions of the mockup for removal, yet leaving them in for previewing purposes.

So far on this page, we've covered just output-only behaviors: displaying the right digit image, or the right letter from the target word. The most involved part of the page comes next—the part that allows players to select letters to guess.

2.4.3 Selecting guesses

This portion of the page is a grid of letters that the player may click on to make guesses. As usual, the letters are represented as images, to keep with the hand-scrawled look and feel. As the player makes guesses, the guessed letter is erased, and one or more positions in the target word are filled in or another segment is added to the stick figure.

To accomplish this, we'll use a combination of components: another Foreach to iterate over the different letters of the alphabet, a DirectLink to create a link, and an Image to display either the image for the letter or the image for a blank space for an already guessed letter. The three components appear in the HTML template:

```
<span jwcid="selectLoop">
<a href="#"
   jwcid="select"
   class="select-letter">
   <img jwcid="@Image"
```

```
        image="ognl:guessImage"
        alt="ognl:guessLabel"
        height="36"
        src="images/Chalkboard_5x3.png"
        width="36"
        border="0"/>
</a>
</span>
```

Two of these components look a little sparse compared to previous examples; that's because we've chosen to use the declared component option for them rather than configure them in-place as implicit components. For a declared component, we just put the component ID in the HTML template. Tapestry recognizes that the value for the first `jwcid` attribute is just an ID and not a component type, because it does not contain the `@` character (as the previous usages of components have done). For a declared component, the element in the HTML template is simply a placeholder; the `jwcid` attribute provides a component ID that is used to link to a `<component>` element in the page specification. The type and configuration of the component is provided in the page specification itself:[8]

```
<component id="selectLoop" type="Foreach">
  <binding name="source" expression="visit.game.guessedLetters"/>
  <binding name="value" expression="letterGuessed"/>
  <binding name="index" expression="guessIndex"/>
</component>

<component id="select" type="DirectLink">
  <binding name="listener" expression="listeners.makeGuess"/>
  <binding name="parameters" expression="letterForGuessIndex"/>
  <binding name="disabled" expression="letterGuessed"/>
</component>
```

The information that goes into the specification is the same as what would be put directly into the HTML template, but the format is slightly different. In the HTML template, we must mark OGNL expressions with the `ognl:` prefix; but in the XML we have a specific element, `<binding>`, that is always an OGNL expression (other elements are used for literal strings and other variations). There is no difference to Tapestry whether a component is declared in the specification or in

[8] The template may still specify additional formal and informal parameters. In keeping with the goal to provide the clearest separation of presentation and logic, the informal parameters, which are most often related purely to presentation, should go in the template, and the formal parameters, which are most often related to the behavior of the component, should go in the page specification.

the HTML template; here, the sheer number of parameters for the two components indicated that specification was a better home for the component configuration than the HTML template.

WARNING Mistakenly using the `ognl:` prefix inside a page or component specification will create an OGNL expression that is invalid. You'll see an exception, such as *Unable to parse expression 'ognl:visit.game.guessedLetters'*. The fact that the `ognl:` prefix shows up in the exception message as part of the expression is the indicator that you included the prefix where it is not allowed.

Once again we are combining the behaviors of different components and using the page to mediate between them. We are also making use of new features of the Foreach and DirectLink components by binding additional parameters of the components.

Getting the images for the letters

The source of all this data is the `guessedLetters` property of the `Game` object; this is an array of 26 flags, one for each letter in the alphabet. Initially, all the flags are false, but as the player makes guesses, the corresponding flags are set to true.

The Foreach component will loop through the 26 flags and set the `letterGuessed` property of the page to true or false on each pass through the loop. In addition, binding the `index` parameter of the Foreach component directs it to set the `guessIndex` property of the page. This value starts at zero and increments with each pass through the loop. The other components simply translate from this ordinal value to a letter in the range of a to z. This functionality is implemented by additional properties and methods in the `Game` class, as shown in the following snippet:

```
private boolean _letterGuessed;
private int _guessIndex;

public boolean isLetterGuessed()
{
  return _letterGuessed;
}

public void setLetterGuessed(boolean letterGuessed)
{
  _letterGuessed = letterGuessed;
}

public int getGuessIndex()
```

```
  {
    return _guessIndex;
  }

  public void setGuessIndex(int guessIndex)
  {
    _guessIndex = guessIndex;
  }

  public char getLetterForGuessIndex()
  {
    return (char) ('a' + _guessIndex);
  }
```

Getting the right letter image for the current letter within the loop is very similar to the previous examples. Although the dash will never occur, we do have to substitute a blank image for any letter that has already been guessed:

```
  public IAsset getGuessImage()
  {
    if (_letterGuessed)
      return getAsset("space");

    String name = "" + getLetterForGuessIndex()

    return getAsset(name);
  }
```

That covers how we get the image for each letter display, but what about the link that the player uses to make a guess?

Handling the links for guesses

Were we to display the link for guesses using ordinary servlets, we'd define a query parameter whose value is the letter selected; that is, we would encode the letter into the URL. Since we're using Tapestry, we don't want to think in terms of query parameters, but instead, we want to think of objects and properties—but we still want the URL to carry this piece of information. When we render the link, we know which letter the link is for, and when the link is clicked, we need that information back. In Tapestry terms, we need to invoke a specific listener method (as before on the Home page) but also propagate along some additional data: the letter selected by the player.

We'll use a DirectLink component, as we did with the link on the Home page, but with two differences. First, we only want to display the link itself (the `<a>` and `</a>` tags) some of the time; we want to omit the link for letters that have already been guessed (the positions that show up as blank space), because letters may only be guessed a single time. Second, we need a way to know which letter has been selected. The DirectLink component includes formal parameters to satisfy both of these needs.

The `disabled` parameter is used to control whether the link renders the `<a>` and `</a>` tags. The `disabled` parameter is optional, and by default, the link is enabled. A DirectLink component will always render its body, regardless of the setting of the `disabled` parameter. The Guess page binds the `disabled` parameter to the `letterGuessed` property of the page—the same property that is set by the Foreach component and used in the `getGuessImage()` method:

```
<binding name="disabled" expression="letterGuessed"/>
```

This ensures that once a letter has been guessed, there will not be another link for that letter. Shortly, we'll see how we also ensure that the guessed letter is replaced by a blank space. Once again, we are working at the level of objects and properties, and not treating all of this HTML rendering as just a text processing problem. A common, ugly "JSP-ism" is to use embedded scriptlets to avoid writing the open and close tags, wrapping the `<a>` and `</a>` tags inside conditional blocks, which can be a messy affair.

The DirectLink embodies the Tapestry philosophy, solving a similar problem using JavaBeans properties and Tapestry component parameters. Every component decides, in its own code, whether to render; the DirectLink has a small conditional statement to control whether an `<a>` element is rendered—but that's Java code in a Java file, not cluttering up a JSP. The end result is a cleaner, simpler, easier-to-use solution.

To identify which letter is actually clicked by the player, we will use yet another component parameter, named `parameters`. We can bind a single value, or an array, or a `java.util.List` to the `parameters` parameter, which, like the `disabled` parameter, is optional (we didn't use it before with the Start link on the Home page). The collection of values provided by the `parameters` parameter is recorded into the URL constructed when the DirectLink component renders. When the link is submitted, the array of parameters is reconstructed and is available to the listener method.

For this case, we use a single value, provided by the property `letterForGuessIndex`:

```
<binding name="parameters" expression="letterForGuessIndex"/>
```

Each time the DirectLink component renders, within the Foreach component loop, the value for the `letterForGuessIndex` property will reflect the current letter in the loop and the URL written into the HTML response will be different, as a portion of the URL will be an encoding of the `letterForGuessIndex` property.

When the link is clicked, the listener method can get the parameters back:

```
public void makeGuess(IRequestCycle cycle)
{
  Object[] parameters = cycle.getServiceParmeters();
  Character guess = (Character) parameters [0];

  char ch = guess.charValue();
  Visit visit = (Visit) getVisit();

  visit.makeGuess(cycle, ch);
}
```

The parameters encoded into the URL by the DirectLink are available in the listener method as an array of object instances, which can be obtained from the `getServiceParameters()` method of the `IRequestCycle` object. Even when, as in this case, there's only a single parameter value, an array is returned. The lone character value is the first and only element in the array.

In addition, the value has been converted from a scalar type, `char`, to a wrapper object type, `Character`, but it is a simple chore to convert it back. The parameter value is not simply converted to a string; it retains its original type (which is encoded into the URL along with the value). You can see a bit of this in the web browser's Address field in figure 2.1; the URL shown contains much information used by Tapestry, but at the end is *cp*, an encoding of *character p* (the player had just clicked the letter P). Chapter 7 discusses how Tapestry encodes information into URLs.

From here, it's simply a matter of obtaining the `Visit` object and letting it do the rest of the processing of the player's guess, which may result in a win or a loss or more guessing. Because we pass the request cycle to the `Visit`, this object is fully capable of selecting which page will render the response by invoking the `activate()` method on the request cycle.

Adding this new interaction, the handling of guesses by the player, involved little more than creating the new listener method and pointing the DirectLink component at the method. Without Tapestry, this same functionality would entail not only writing a servlet and registering it into the web deployment descriptor, but also creating code to generate the hyperlink in the first place. This latter code could take the form of Java scriptlets in the JSP, or a new JSP tag in a JSP tag library. In either case, the HTML in the JSP file would deviate further from ordinary HTML, and the ability to preview the web page would be diminished. With Tapestry, the HTML template will continue to look and act like standard HTML.

Instead, we are making use of existing components, the DirectLink, and a consistent approach to encoding data into the URL. Once again, we're seeing the consistency goal: Anywhere in the application where we have a link that needs to pass along some data in the URL, we can use and reuse the same tool, the DirectLink component and its `parameters` parameter. In addition, because Tapestry properly encodes the data type with the data (rather than just converting all the parameters to strings), we can consistently pass any type of data in the URL: strings, characters, numbers, or even custom objects.

That wraps up the Guess page; we've discussed how to extract information from the `Game` domain object and present it in various ways and also figured out how to react to user input. We've kept the domain logic (in the `Game` and `WordSource` objects) separate from the presentation logic (the Guess page class, HTML template, and page specification), using listener methods and the `Visit` object as the bridge between the two aspects.

2.5 Developing the Win and Lose pages

The other two pages in the application, Win and Lose, are displayed when the player successfully guesses the word, or when the player exhausts all his or her incorrect guesses. There is nothing new on these pages; they duplicate bits and pieces of the Home and Guess pages. In fact, there's a bit of unwanted duplication in the HTML templates: the Java code and the page specifications. In chapter 6 we'll see how easy it is to create new components that encapsulate this functionality and remove this duplication. Remember: More code means more bugs!

Our Hangman application is nearly complete; all that's left is to fulfill our contract with the servlet container and create a deployment descriptor for the Hangman application WAR.

2.6 Configuring the web.xml deployment descriptor

All of these HTML templates and page specifications do not automatically become a web application. We still need a servlet to act as the bridge between the Servlet API and the Tapestry framework. Fortunately, this does not require any coding, since the framework includes the necessary servlet class. All that's necessary is to configure the web deployment descriptor, which is the file WEB-INF/web.xml. The deployment descriptor is provided in listing 2.11.

Listing 2.11 web.xml: web deployment descriptor for the Hangman application

```
<?xml version="1.0"?>
<!DOCTYPE web-app
  PUBLIC "-//Sun Microsystems, Inc.//DTD Web Application 2.2//EN"
  "http://java.sun.com/j2ee/dtds/web-app_2_2.dtd">

<web-app>
  <servlet>
    <servlet-name>hangman</servlet-name>
    <servlet-class>org.apache.tapestry.ApplicationServlet
    </servlet-class>
    <init-param>
      <param-name>org.apache.tapestry.visit-class</param-name>
      <param-value>hangman1.Visit</param-value>
    </init-param>
    <load-on-startup>1</load-on-startup>
  </servlet>

  <servlet-mapping>
    <servlet-name>hangman</servlet-name>
    <url-pattern>/app</url-pattern>
  </servlet-mapping>
</web-app>
```

The deployment descriptor maps an instance of the Tapestry `ApplicationServlet` to the path /app within the servlet context. Using /app as the servlet path is a common convention for Tapestry applications but not a requirement; Tapestry will adapt to whatever servlet mapping is actually used.

The servlet context's name is based on the name of the web application archive (the WAR file), which is hangman1.war; therefore, the complete URL of the servlet is http://localhost:8080/hangman1/app. This means that the base URL for the application is http://localhost:8080/hangman1/, which is why relative URLs (in static HTML) to assets such as images/guess.png work, both when previewing the HTML template and at runtime.

The `org.apache.tapestry.visit-class` initial parameter is used to tell Tapestry what class to instantiate as the `Visit` object.

Using the `<load-on-startup>` element in the deployment descriptor is recommended, especially during development. Loading on startup causes the application servlet to be instantiated and initialized. Often, problems in the application or deployment descriptor will be detected immediately at startup; this is an even better idea for more advanced applications that use an application specification.[9]

2.7 Summary

In this chapter, we've seen the basics of creating a web application using Tapestry. A Tapestry application is divided into individual pages; those pages are constructed by combining components, an overall HTML template, and a small amount of Java code. Tapestry leverages the Model-View-Controller pattern to isolate domain logic from the user interface. We've also begun to see the "light touch" of Tapestry, where simple properties and short Java methods are woven together to create very complex, dynamic, interactive user interfaces.

This simple application demonstrates some of the key patterns that occur when developing in Tapestry. It shows how components interact with each other by reading and setting properties. It shows how the page can act as a Controller, coordinating the domain logic and mediating between its embedded components. We've also demonstrated how easy it is to add new interactions to a page, in the form of listener methods.

We've begun to demonstrate how Tapestry, by excusing developers from mundane "plumbing" tasks, really frees up developer energies. It enables you to implement more complicated behaviors in much less time and be more confident that your code is bug free. Tapestry can give projects the one thing money truly can't buy: time—time to test and debug back-end code, time to locate and fix performance problems, even time to add new features.

[9] Application specifications are an optional file described in chapter 6. They are needed only to access some advanced feature of Tapestry, such as referencing a component library.

3 Tapestry and HTML forms

This chapter covers

- How HTML forms work
- Creating simple forms using Tapestry components
- Creating page properties using property specifications
- Creating forms containing loops

Handling links and images is a good start, but the lifeblood of any real web application is the HTML form. Individual links, as in the Hangman example from chapter 2, provide a limited form of interactivity: Users will click a link, or they won't. HTML forms provide a rich form of expression for the user—the ability to enter specific values in fields, whether by typing in a text field, clicking a check box, or selecting an option from a drop-down list.

Tapestry's approach to handling HTML forms follows its general philosophy of hiding the details of HTTP and the Servlet API and operating in terms of objects, methods, and properties. In Tapestry, a group of components work together when a form is submitted to update page properties before invoking a listener method.

In this chapter, we'll cover components for creating basic HTML form elements, including text fields, radio buttons, and check boxes. In chapter 4, we'll examine more advanced form-related components that include additional client- and server-side support. Chapter 5 discusses Tapestry components devoted to validating user input.

The source for the examples for this chapter and the following chapters is available online (see appendix B). Once you deploy the samples into Tomcat, you can access them by opening a web browser to http://localhost:8080/examples/app. You will find a listing of the examples, organized by chapter.

3.1 Understanding HTML forms

HTML forms allow us to gather complex information from users of our web applications. The use of forms is ubiquitous on the Web. Without support for forms, the Web would never have exploded; limited to just hyperlinks, it would likely have stayed as passive, static hypertext—an interesting toy, but with no possibility of creating an Amazon or an eBay. Without forms, there would be no way to build any of the interesting e-commerce, content management, or community sites.

HTML forms are significantly different from forms within a desktop application. In a desktop application, each component (text field, check box, push button) interacts with the application completely independently of the others. The user may update one field without changing the value for another field. The code for a desktop application is informed of every key press or mouse click, a luxury not possible with HTML forms. HTML forms are displayed to the user, who may use the mouse or the Tab key to move between the form controls and enter values. When the user clicks the submit button, the values for *all* of the fields and controls within the form are packaged together in a single request to the server. The server sees only the final result, not the individual mouse movements and key presses, or even the individual changes to fields.

Within an HTML form, various HTML elements work together. The outermost element, `<form>`, groups together the many other elements it encloses between its start and end tags. Other elements within `<form>` are used to create types of form controls; these are listed in table 3.1.

Table 3.1 Elements used to create form controls

HTML element	Control type
`<input type="checkbox">`	Check box (toggles on or off)
`<input type="radio">`	Radio selection (user selects one value from a list of values)
`<input type="text">`	Simple text input field
`<input type="password">`	Password field (text field where user input is obscured)
`<input type="hidden">`	Hidden field (not visible to the user)
`<input type="submit">`	Form submit button; sends the request to the server
`<input type="reset">`	Reset button; returns all fields to initial values
`<input type="image">`	Image map field; submits form and identifies where, within the image, the user clicked
`<input type="file">`	File upload
`<select>`	Drop-down list or multiple-selection list
`<textarea>`	Multiline text input field

Each of these form control elements has a `name` attribute. When the form is submitted, the value for each control is submitted as a query parameter using the control's name. Figure 3.1 shows how this comes together; when the page containing the form is rendered, a name is assigned to each element. Once the form is submitted, these values are provided in the form submission and available through the Servlet API's `HttpServletRequest` object. Figure 3.1 shows a single form; beginning at the top center, the form starts as HTML: `<form>` and `<input>` tags. The client web browser uses these to construct form controls (radio buttons, text fields, and so forth) for the user to directly interact with. When the user finishes entering information and clicks the submit button, the request includes the values for those fields as query parameter values. Within the Servlet API, those query parameters are accessible via the `HttpServletRequest` object.

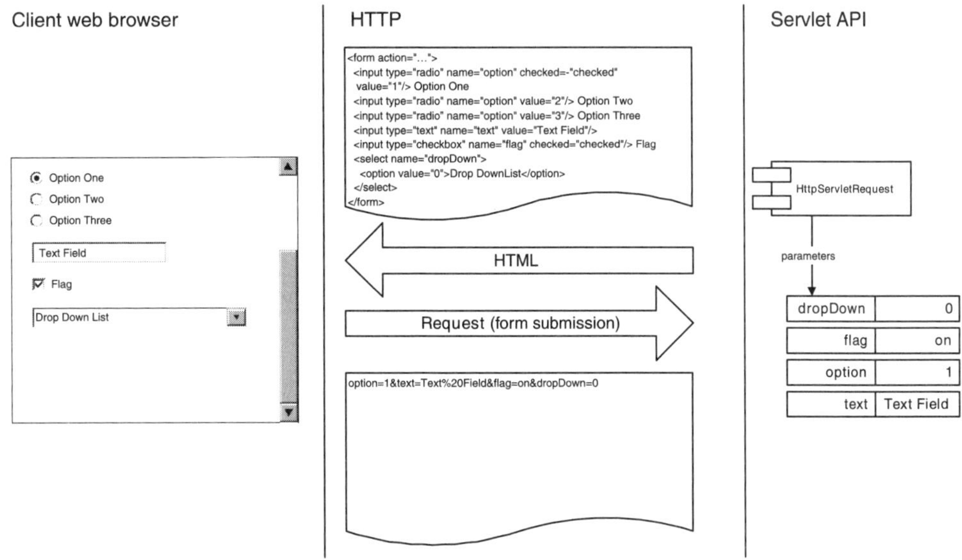

Figure 3.1 The form and the data it contains are represented in different ways at different times. The form starts as HTML sent via HTTP to the web browser. The web browser displays controls the user can interact with. The form submission contains the values entered by the user, which finally show up as Java objects.

In a servlet application, the next step is to access those query parameters and use them to update domain object properties. (This may involve some conversions, such as parsing string values into numbers.) One of the stumbling blocks when you're using servlets is ensuring that the form control names used in the JavaServer Page (JSP) match the query parameter names referenced in the servlet code. With servlets, you are responsible for coming up with appropriate names and keeping the JSP and the servlet synchronized with respect to those names. Expecting form control names in the JSP to stay synchronized with Java code in a servlet is an example of weak binding (discussed in chapter 1) between the JSP and the servlet.

Tapestry adds a layer beyond the query parameters—a layer of components. The form control components read page properties when rendering the initial HTML. The same components come back into play when the form is submitted to read the query parameters and update the page properties.

The framework takes care of all the mundane plumbing: providing names for form control elements, writing HTML, and reading query parameters. There is never a danger of the HTML template for a form getting out of synchronization with the code that handles the form submission because that logic is distributed into the very components that render the form's HTML in the first place.

All of this means that by the time your form's listener method is invoked, the components will have already updated all of your domain objects' properties to match the values entered by the user. The listener method can simply use those properties to accomplish the operation the form is intended for, whatever that may be.

To appreciate how all these concepts fit together, we'll start with a simple example before getting into the nitty-gritty of the individual Tapestry components.

3.2 Creating a simple login form

One of the most common, and basic, uses of HTML forms is to authenticate a user: collecting a username and password to identify the specific user to the application. An e-commerce application will need to know who, specifically, the user is before processing an order; most other categories of applications have a similar need to know the identity of the user. We'll start our discussion of Tapestry HTML form support with a simple version of such a form, shown in figure 3.2. The HTML template for this page is provided in listing 3.1.

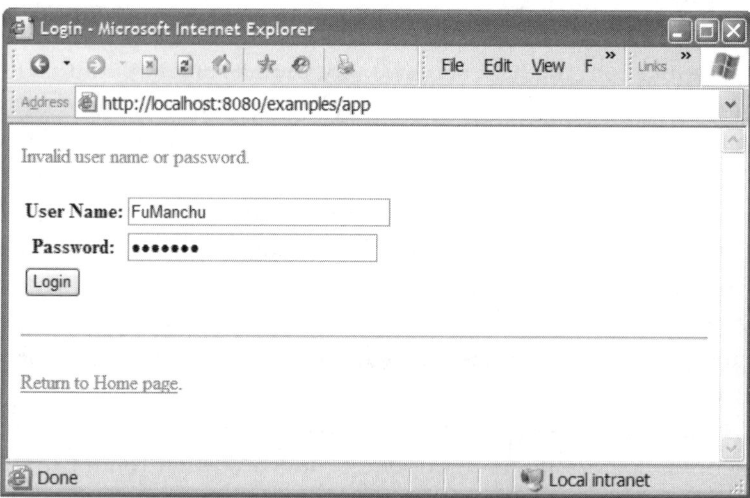

Figure 3.2 The Login page after the user has entered an incorrect username and password.

Listing 3.1 Login.html: HTML template for the Login page

```
<html jwcid="@Shell" title="Login">    <-1
<body>

<span jwcid="@Conditional" condition="ognl:message">
<font color="red">
<span jwcid="@Insert" value="ognl:message">
Error Message                                              2
</span>
</font>
</span>

<p/>

<form jwcid="@Form" listener="ognl:listeners.login">    <-3

<table>
<tr>
  <th>User Name:</th>
  <td>
    <input type="text" jwcid="@TextField"
       value="ognl:userName"                    4
       size="30"/></td>
</tr>
<tr>
  <th>Password:</th>
  <td>
    <input type="password" jwcid="@TextField"
       value="ognl:password"                        5
       hidden="ognl:true"
       size="30"/>
  </td>
</tr>
<tr>
  <td><input type="submit" value="Login"/></td>
</tr>
</table>

</form>

</body>
</html>
```

1 The Shell component is a standard Tapestry component for rendering the `<html>`, `<head>`, and `<title>` elements. It has a number of other uses, as you'll see later, such as simplifying references to Cascading Style Sheets (CSS).

❷ If there is an error, such as an unrecognized password, then the page will be redisplayed with a non-null value in its `message` property. This block of the template is used to format and display that message.

❸ A Form component, not a simple `<form>` element, must be used, and must enclose the other form control components. The component will render the URL for the form submission, in much the same way as a DirectLink component. The provided listener will be invoked when the form is submitted.

❹ The TextField component will read the `userName` property when the page renders. When the form is submitted, it will update the same property.

❺ This TextField component is configured, via its `hidden` parameter, as a password field. Tapestry uses one component, TextField, for both ordinary and password text fields.

Like the DirectLink component used in the Hangman application in chapter 2, a Form component has a `listener` parameter bound to an application-provided listener method. This particular Form component encloses some static HTML and two form control components. Both of these components are TextFields. The first TextField component edits the `userName` property of the page. The second TextField component edits the `password` property of the page and also renders as a password field (where the characters typed by the user are not visible). As in previous examples, additional attributes are provided so that the element will preview correctly in an HTML editor.

In most web application frameworks (including Jakarta Struts), you are responsible for orchestrating things so that the names of HTML form elements (and thus the names of query parameters supplied when the form is submitted) match the names of domain object properties. This kind of "engineered coincidence" creates unwanted dependencies between the text fields and the domain objects and can open up other limitations. (For example, what if there is no specific property? What if different fields update different objects?) Tapestry avoids these dependencies; the component ID, the name of the query parameter, and the Object Graph Navigation Language (OGNL) expression used to read and update the property will all be different, and the developer will be concerned only with the OGNL expression.

We've also introduced two new components that are not related to forms. The Shell component is a handy shortcut for outputting the `<html>`, `<head>`, and `<title>` elements for a page. The Conditional component evaluates a condition (an OGNL expression) and either renders its body (the portion of the page template enclosed by its start and end tags) or skips over its body. Here, the Conditional component is used to display an error message if the message is not null.

Conditional is very flexible as to what types are acceptable for its `condition` parameter. Here the parameter is bound to a string property, and the Conditional treats null or the empty string as false and a non-empty string as true.

As with the Hangman application pages in chapter 2, understanding the Login page involves more than just the HTML template; the application-specific code for the form submission is in the Java class.

3.2.1 Implementing the Login page class

Listing 3.2 shows the Java side of the form: the implementation of the Login page class and, specifically, the listener method invoked by the Form component.

Listing 3.2 Login.java: Java class for the Login page

```
package examples;

import org.apache.tapestry.IRequestCycle;
import org.apache.tapestry.html.BasePage;

public abstract class Login extends BasePage
{
  public abstract String getUserName();
  public abstract String getPassword();                    ❶
  public abstract void setMessage(String message);

  public void login(IRequestCycle cycle)     ❷
  {
    if (isValidLogin(getUserName(), getPassword()))       ❸
    {
      cycle.activate("Main");
      return;                            ❹
    }

    setMessage("Invalid user name or password.");      ❺
  }

  private boolean isValidLogin(String userName, String password)
  {
    return "tapestry".equalsIgnoreCase(userName);             ❻
  }

}
```

❶ These methods are abstract because Tapestry will create the actual properties at runtime (it will create a subclass with the necessary methods and fields). This is controlled by the page's specification.

❷ The listener method is invoked when the form is submitted, after the properties have been updated.

❸ The abstract methods are used to access the information submitted with the form.

❹ On success, the Main page is activated; a real application would do a lot more bookkeeping here.

❺ On error, the `message` property is updated. The active page is not changed, so the Login page will be redisplayed (showing the error message, and the username and password entered by the user).

❻ This is just a placeholder for the work a real application would perform; presumably, the code would use information in a database to authenticate that the username is known and that the password is valid.

By the time the Form's listener method has been invoked, the properties of the page (`userName` and `password`) will already have been updated with values provided by the user and submitted in the request as query parameters. The listener method is not responsible for extracting query parameters or any of the other plumbing normally associated with processing a form submission. In this simplified example, a valid login will result in sending the user to the Main page of the application (not shown in this example). An invalid login will present the Login page again, with a visible error message.

Here you see the simplicity and consistency goals pop up again; form submissions result in updates to properties of the page, followed by the invocation of the listener method for the Form component. There's no question about query parameter names—the information submitted in the form just shows up as properties that are accessible to the listener method. Any question of accessing the information submitted in the form becomes simple access to page properties set by the form control components. All the HTML forms in your application will be variations on this same basic pattern. Forms will always operate consistently because there's just one approach, and the normal stumbling blocks (such as what to name form controls and query parameters) just aren't your concern; they're entirely under the control of the Tapestry framework.

An additional look at listing 3.2 shows one oddity: The class itself is abstract and has abstract methods for accessing the `userName`, `message`, and `password` properties. These methods are abstract because we are letting Tapestry create the properties dynamically at runtime as *specified properties*.

3.2.2 Using specified properties

Creating JavaBean properties for a typical JavaBean object is normally straightforward. A property consists of a private instance variable and a pair of accessor methods (one to read the value, one to update the value):

```
private Type _myProperty;

public Type getMyProperty()
{
  return _myProperty;
}

public void setMyProperty(Type newValue)
{
  _myProperty = newValue;
}
```

The naming of the methods is defined by the conventions of the JavaBeans framework. In fact, the JavaBeans framework works backward from the method names (`setMyProperty()` and `getMyProperty()`) to deduce a property named `myProperty`. This is the essence of the contract between the JavaBean and the JavaBeans framework—a simple, loose, flexible contract based on this naming convention.

Using Tapestry, it is possible to create new properties on pages and components *automatically*. The page (or component) specification will define the property name and type, and Tapestry will create the property: the instance variable and the pair of accessor methods. At runtime, Tapestry actually creates a subclass of your class, which fills in these details and instantiates an instance of the subclass.

Creating new properties in this way is useful for three reasons:

- Creating properties manually is a boring, mechanical process.
- Tapestry ensures that property values are reset at the end of the request to default values automatically (this step is necessary to properly support reuse of the page object in later requests—a topic we discuss in more detail in chapter 7).
- Properties can be defined as *persistent*, meaning that they are stored on the server between request cycles. This approach to managing server-side state is introduced later in this chapter and also discussed in detail in chapter 7.

In your code, such as the Login page code in listing 3.2, you will define abstract methods to read or update the properties. You have to define only the methods you specifically need—the Tapestry-fabricated subclass will include getter and setter methods for each property you specified in the page specification. You never have to provide the implementations of these methods; Tapestry creates those implementations for you.

NOTE This approach is not unique to Tapestry. When using entity Enterprise JavaBeans (EJBs) using container-managed persistence (CMP) 2.0, you code in the same way: creating and invoking abstract accessor methods, with the expectation that the application server will provide the necessary implementations in a subclass.

The creation of new properties is triggered in the page (or component) specification. We provide the specification for the Login page in listing 3.3. Each `<property-specification>` element defines a property that we want to add to the page.

Listing 3.3 Login.page: specification for the Login page

```
<?xml version="1.0"?>
<!DOCTYPE page-specification PUBLIC
  "-//Apache Software Foundation//Tapestry Specification 3.0//EN"
  "http://jakarta.apache.org/tapestry/dtd/Tapestry_3_0.dtd">

<page-specification class="examples.Login">

  <property-specification name="message" type="java.lang.String"/>
  <property-specification name="userName" type="java.lang.String"/>
  <property-specification name="password" type="java.lang.String"/>

</page-specification>
```

In this case, all three properties are strings, but properties of all types (including primitive Java types) may be created in this way.

This Login page example is just a starting point for the kinds of forms supported by Tapestry. Tapestry has a variety of components that correspond to all the types of HTML form elements, shown in table 3.2.

Table 3.2 HTML form elements and corresponding Tapestry components

HTML element	Tapestry component	Discussed in...
`<form>`	Form	Chapter 3
`<input type="text"/>`	TextField or ValidField	Chapters 3, 5
`<textarea>`	TextArea	Chapter 3
`<input type="password"/>`	TextField	Chapter 3

Table 3.2 HTML form elements and corresponding Tapestry components *(continued)*

HTML element	Tapestry component	Discussed in...
`<select>`	Select or PropertySelection	Chapter 3, 4
`<option>`	Option	Chapter 3
`<input type="radio"/>`	Radio (and RadioGroup)	Chapter 3
`<input type="checkbox"/>`	Checkbox	Chapter 3
`<input type="submit"/>`	Submit	Chapter 3
`<input type="image"/>`	ImageSubmit	Chapter 3
`<input type="hidden"/>`	Hidden, ListEdit	Chapter 4
`<input type="file"/>`	Upload	Chapter 4

You've now seen the very basics of Tapestry's approach to HTML forms. Form control components can read properties when a page is rendered and then update the same properties when the user submits the form. To understand more, let's start with a detailed look at the Form component and how it relates to the other components.

3.3 Understanding the Form component

Central to Tapestry's approach to HTML forms support is the Form component. It is not enough to simply use a `<form>` tag in a Tapestry page; all the form control components (for creating text fields, check boxes, and such) require that they be enclosed by a Form component. The Form component's responsibilities start with the rendering of the `<form>` tag, but beyond that, the Form component orchestrates all the form control components enclosed by the Form component, both during the initial render and when the form is submitted. The Form component is combined with the other form-related components listed in table 3.2.

To appreciate what the Form component does and why it is so necessary, you may find it useful to look at the steps you would take when creating an HTML form (and a servlet to process the form submission) without using Tapestry.

3.3.1 Developing forms without Tapestry

Creating functioning HTML forms in an ordinary servlet application shifts most of the responsibility onto your shoulders. You start by identifying the purpose of the form: what business process the form will initiate, or what properties of which domain objects the form will update (or some combination of the two).

You then select which types of form controls will be used: text fields, check boxes, radio buttons, and so forth. Each of these controls is represented by a particular HTML element and configuration.

The next step is to select a unique name for each form control, typically a name with some meaning, such as `productId`, `password`, or `userName`. Most often, the name selected represents how the value will be utilized when the form is submitted; it may be the name of a property of an object, or the name of a parameter to some operation. From here, the last two steps are to create the JSP containing the `<form>` and the form control elements, and to create a servlet to process the form submission.

The end goal of the form submission is to execute some form of *business process*. Much of the time, this business process is designed to create or update data stored in a database. Other examples of business processes are more involved, such as submitting an order within an e-commerce application. In any case, these business processes are hungry for data from the user; that data arrives in the form query parameters and must be extracted from the request, converted, and validated before it can be used.

The servlet will need to know which names have been assigned to which form controls, because those names become the names of the query parameters, accessible via the `HttpServletRequest` object provided to the servlet. The servlet must extract the value for each query parameter, and then possibly convert the value from a string to an appropriate type (say, an integer or a date) and assign the value to the correct domain object property or business process parameter. There may also be some validations on individual fields or on the form as a whole. In some cases, the validations may direct that the form be redisplayed with an error message so that the user may make corrections before resubmitting the form. Validations may be on individual fields, such as checking that a numeric field contains a numeric value. Other validations may be based on comparing the values for multiple fields (for example, a form that allows a user to input a date range will check that the start date precedes the end date). Still other validations may have some external dependency; for instance, a servlet that processes an application login form must validate that the username and password are correct and will redisplay the page with an error message if they are not.

Assuming all validations pass, the next step for the servlet is to initiate a business process using all the collected parameters, and the final step is to send a response page back to the client.

Using Tapestry, nearly all of this work is eliminated.

3.3.2 Developing forms with Tapestry

Returning to the world of Tapestry, the framework's goal is once more to offload as much of this work as possible onto the framework. It is still the responsibility of the developer to handle the first stages: to identify the business process and decide which form control elements will be used. From there, the developer begins to leverage Tapestry to do the grunt work. Anything involving HTTP query parameters falls into this category.

Tapestry has a number of components that correspond to each of the standard HTML form control elements. Table 3.2 is a simple mapping between the HTML form control elements and the Tapestry form control components.

The framework supports two kinds of forms: simple and complex. The Login page is a simple form; it always renders with the same structure—a `<form>` element enclosing two text fields. In the real world, forms are not always so simple; a common example is a "shopping cart" page in an e-commerce application that shows multiple line items. It's entirely reasonable in such a form for the user to change quantities for several items within an order before submitting it. The exact set of elements in such a form is determined at runtime and will be different for different users at different times. Behind the scenes, there is some form of `Order` object and a collection of `LineItem` objects. Rendering such a page (using a JSP or a Tapestry HTML page) involves some form of loop over the available `LineItems`.

The Form component takes on the responsibility for assigning unique IDs for the form control elements. These IDs are used as the `name` attribute in the HTML element and become the name of the query parameter when the form is submitted. Having the Form component assign these IDs might seem unnecessary; after all, couldn't the components just use their component ID? In simple forms, that is exactly what happens, but not all forms are simple. What happens in a complex form, one where some components render multiple times within a loop? Each time a particular component renders, it must have a unique element ID so that the component can get a single value from a query parameter when the form is submitted. At the same time, it is desirable that complex forms with loops and conditionals be handled in the same way as simple forms. To support simplicity and consistency, this decision about what element ID to use for each component is handled by the Tapestry framework, not the developer.

As each form control component renders, it locates the Form component that encloses it. The component obtains its element ID from the Form. This element ID will be used for the `name` attribute of the element, which is later used as the name of the query parameter for the element when the form is submitted. The Form ensures that the names it provides to the components are unique. Generally, the name will match the component's ID, but if the form element component is inside a loop (such as a Foreach component), each render of the component will receive a different unique ID.

The form control components also read page properties as they render and write them as the value attribute of the element. The process continues from there through the other components enclosed by the Form. Finally, once the entire body of the Form component has been rendered, the Form component writes the </form> tag and the rendering of the rest of the page continues as normal.

The result of rendering the Form (from the Login example) is shown in figure 3.3. The output HTML is a mixture of static HTML from the template and

Form component

```
<form method="post" name="Form0" action="/examples/app">
<input type="hidden" name="service" value="direct/0/Login/$Form"/>
<input type="hidden" name="sp" value="S0"/>
<input type="hidden" name="Form0" value="$TextField,$TextField$0"/>
```

From Form's body

```
<table>
<tr>
  <th>User Name:</th>
  <td>
```

First TextField

```
<input type="text" name="$TextField" size="30"/>
```

From Form's body

```
</td>
</tr>
<tr>
  <th>Password:</th>
  <td>
```

Second TextField

```
<input type="password" name="$TextField$0" size="30"/>
```

From Form's body

```
 </td>
</tr>
<tr>
  <td><input type="submit" value="Login"/></td>
</tr>
</table>
```

Form component

```
</form>
```

Figure 3.3 The Form component writes several hidden control fields as well as rendering its body. The TextField components render themselves, with names obtained from the Form.

dynamically generated HTML produced by the Form and TextField components. The Form component writes the `<form>` and `</form>` elements, as well as several hidden form fields that store control information needed by the Form to handle the submission.

The TextField components render the `<input type="text">` elements, with the value for the `name` attribute supplied by the enclosing Form component. The names are based on the IDs of the TextField components. Since no explicit ID was assigned for either TextField component, Tapestry assigned unique component IDs for the TextFields based on their component type—`"$TextField"` and `"$TextField$0"`—and these component IDs are then used as the form element IDs. As you'll see later in the chapter, a Form incorporating any kind of loop will use even more mangled element IDs—but none of these IDs is ever visible to an application's end user or relevant to you as the application developer.

In figure 3.3, the two TextField components omitted the `value` attribute because the corresponding page properties, `userName` and `password`, were null. If the Login page was redisplayed because of an error (such as an invalid password), the page properties would be read and used for the `value` attribute.

These descriptions include a few simplifications. Tapestry forms are actually very flexible:

- A page may contain any number of Form components. They all work independently of each other, in just the same way that a page may contain any number of independent DirectLink components.
- A Form may itself be contained within another component; it doesn't have to be directly located within the page's template.
- A component enclosed by a Form may itself (in its own template) contain form control components, such as TextField or Checkbox. This is entirely valid. Tapestry dynamically finds all the components ultimately enclosed by the Form during the render, working its way through the page's template and the templates for any components within the page.
- Form control components are not limited to editing a page property; using OGNL expressions, they can edit properties of any object reachable from the page.

So far, we've only discussed what occurs when the page containing the form renders. Eventually, the user will submit the form, and then the more interesting part begins—moving values out of the query parameters and into page properties.

3.3.3 Handling form submissions

When a form is submitted, Tapestry must perform the same kind of operations that would occur in a non-Tapestry application:

- Determine the names of query parameters.
- Extract the values for query parameters.
- Perform any necessary conversions (for example, string to integer).
- Assign the converted values to the correct page properties.

Further, Tapestry needs to take into account any portions of the original form that rendered inside a loop or conditional. The difference between a traditional servlet application and a Tapestry application is that there is no single place where this mapping between query parameters and domain object properties takes place. The information is scattered across the many form control components enclosed by the Form. In a pure servlet application, this information will be present in two places: inside the JSP containing the form, and within the corresponding servlets' `doPost()` method. Within a Tapestry form, this mapping information is not "stored" anywhere but is computed on the fly during the render, and those computations must be reproduced as part of the form submission if all the data submitted in the form is to be extracted and applied to the correct objects and properties.

Tapestry takes an unusual approach to linking query parameter names (in the form submission) back to the correct components: It recovers all those names and relationships by rendering the Form *again*, as part of the form submission processing. This render is called the *rewind phase*. The rewind phase allows the Form to walk through all the components it encloses, visiting each in the same order as in the original render, even when the Form contains loops and conditionals. In this way, each form control component will be visited in the same order as in the initial render, and will obtain the exact same element ID as it did in the initial render.

During the rewind, each form control component will obtain its element ID from the Form, just as it did in the original render. Unlike the original render, where a component parameter is read and HTML is produced, during the rewind phase the component will instead read a query parameter value, convert the value as necessary, and update a domain object property.

Only the Form and its body, not the entire page, are rendered. Mixed into the Form may be other components that are not form related—if they produce HTML output during the rewind phase, it is simply discarded.

The rewind starts with the Form component itself, which renders its body. Eventually, this render will reach a form control component, such as a TextField or Checkbox. The component will acquire its element ID from the Form component, exactly as it did when it rendered. Each component can also determine, from the Form, whether a rewind is taking place. Using the element ID, the component can extract the correct query parameter from the incoming request and assign its value to a page property. The rewind then continues through any other components also contained within the Form component.

This process is flexible and allows for cases where portions of the Form's body are conditional, or where a looping component, such as a Foreach, is involved. As long as the rewind of the Form goes through the same *exact* steps as the original render, all the names and components will line up, the proper query parameters will be read by the matching components, and the values will be applied to the correct page and domain object properties. It is only after the rewind phase that the Form's listener method is invoked.

Tapestry records into the form, as a hidden field, the list of all the element IDs it allocates during the render process (this is shown in figure 3.3). It uses this information when the form is submitted to determine whether the rewind matches the render. Any deviation immediately causes an exception to be thrown detailing the cause of the mismatch.

When such a mismatch occurs, Tapestry does not display the normal Exception page; instead the StaleLink page is displayed. A *stale link* indicates that the form submission doesn't match against the current state of the application. This can happen when some bit of information stored on the server (possibly in a database) changes between the time that the page containing the form is rendered and the time the form itself is submitted. Stale links are most often provoked by a Form containing a conditional or loop based on server-side state.

Included in the output on the StaleLink page is a message identifying the point at which a mismatch occurred. On a page such as the Login form, it is impossible for a rewind mismatch to occur, because the form is simple: There are no looping or conditional components within the body of the Form component. We'll return to this subject in section 3.5, and discuss techniques for avoiding stale links in chapter 4.

3.4 Using basic form control components

Tapestry form element components fall roughly into two categories: basic and advanced. The basic components correspond more or less directly to HTML form elements such as `<input type="text">` and `<select>`. Table 3.3 describes the basic form components covered in this chapter. More advanced components are covered in chapters 4 and 5.

Table 3.3 Basic form control components

Component	Description
Checkbox	Creates a check box that edits a boolean property bound to its `selected` parameter.
Form	Creates the `<form>` element enclosing other components.
ImageSubmit	Creates a clickable image that submits the enclosing form.
Option	Creates an `<option>` element that edits a boolean property bound to the `selected` parameter.
Radio and RadioGroup	Creates a number of mutually exclusive options. A single property, bound to the RadioGroup's `selected` parameter, is edited.
Select	Creates a `<select>` element that can enclose Option components.
Submit	Creates a button that submits the enclosing form.
TextArea	Used for accepting text input larger than a single line, corresponding to a `<textarea>` form element. TextArea edits a string property bound to its `value` parameter.
TextField	Used to create a simple text-entry field, either `<input type="text">` or `<input type="password">`. TextField edits a string property bound to its `value` parameter.

Appendix D contains a complete reference to all Tapestry components.

3.4.1 Understanding the essentials

Each of the basic form control components has a similar purpose and a similar pattern of usage. These components exist to *edit* a property. When a form control component renders, it *reads* a property (bound to one of its component parameters) and uses that value to construct the HTML element and attributes it writes into the response. When the form is submitted, the same component will read a query parameter value and use that value to *update* the same property.

We've seen this already, with the TextField component, which drops quite easily into place inside an HTML template, as shown in the Login example at the beginning of this chapter. Using the TextField component is as simple as this:

- Placing the component within the HTML template, enclosed by a Form component
- Binding its `value` parameter to the page property to be edited

Each of the components is specialized to reflect the particular type of control that will be presented to the user. This specialization is not just the HTML that the component outputs, but even reflects the names and types of parameters used by the component. We'll start with the simplest component, the Checkbox, which edits a boolean property.

3.4.2 The Checkbox component

An HTML check box is created using the `<input type="checkbox">` element. A check box control appears as a small box, which may be clicked to toggle between a checked and an unchecked state—a check mark appears or disappears.

When the enclosing form is submitted, a query parameter for the check box is only sent if the check box is checked. The value for the query parameter will be the literal string `"on"` (unless the `<input>` element's `value` attribute is specified, in which case that is used as the value).

A Tapestry Checkbox component is used to edit a boolean page property. The property we want to edit is bound to the component's `selected` parameter. The property is read when the component renders, and the component will include the `selected` attribute of the `<input>` element if the property is true.

When the form is submitted, the Checkbox component will read the query parameter and update the page property to either true or false, depending on whether the check box was checked or unchecked.

For example, the following HTML template snippet is used to edit the `accepted` page property:

```
<input type="checkbox" jwcid="@Checkbox"
  selected="ognl:accepted"> I accept the terms and conditions.
```

3.4.3 Radio and RadioGroup components

In an HTML form, a radio element (`<input type="radio">`) is used to provide a number of options from which the user can select a single option. Each radio element provides a single option, and all the radio elements in a group share a single name. When the enclosing form is submitted, the value of the query parameter will match the value of the selected radio control.

In Tapestry terms, a single property will be edited by a group of related Radio components. On submission, the selected Radio component will be used to figure out the correct value to assign to the edited property.

To accomplish this, Tapestry uses a second component, RadioGroup. A RadioGroup encloses one or more Radio components. RadioGroups may not be nested, and Radio components must be enclosed by a RadioGroup—but they don't have to be *directly* enclosed by the RadioGroup; they can be spread out about the HTML template, mixed with static HTML and other components. The RadioGroup component identifies the property that is being edited by using its `selected` parameter. Each Radio component provides a particular value, bound to its `value` parameter, which will be assigned to the property if that component is selected. The value is *not* limited to a simple string value; the Radio and RadioGroup components will allow any type of object to be the value.

The RadioGroup and Radio components work together to write out the HTML element for each Radio component. The RadioGroup provides a unique option ID for each Radio that becomes the `value` attribute of the `<input>` element. The RadioGroup also tracks the current value of the property so that one and only one Radio component will be rendered as the selected element.

What's important is that the `value` attribute of each `<input>` element not match the `value` parameter of the Radio component—it must be an arbitrary option ID value instead. The `value` *parameter* may be any type: an integer, a string, or even a custom Java object. The `value` attribute can *only* be a string, and it's up to Tapestry to bridge any gap between these two representations. When the form is submitted, the RadioGroup and Radio components work backward from the selected option ID. When a particular Radio component recognizes that it was the option selected by the user, it reads its `value` parameter and provides it to the RadioGroup, which can then update the page property bound to its `selected` parameter.

For example, the following HTML template snippet is used to set the `selectedSize` property of the page to one of three values—5, 25, or 100:

```
<span jwcid="@RadioGroup" selected="ognl:selectedSize">
  <input type="radio" jwcid="@Radio" value="5"/> Small
  <br/>
  <input type="radio" jwcid="@Radio" value="25"/> Medium
  <br/>
  <input type="radio" jwcid="@Radio" value="100"/> Large
</span>
```

When the page containing this snippet renders, the `<span>` for the RadioGroup will disappear and the `name` attribute for each `<input>` element will be taken from the RadioGroup. Assuming the initial value for the `selectedSize` property is 25, the snippet will render as follows:

```
  <input type="radio" name="$RadioGroup" value="0"/> Small
  <br/>
  <input type="radio" name="$RadioGroup" value="1"
```

```
  selected="selected"/> Medium
<br/>
<input type="radio" name="$RadioGroup" value="2"/> Large
```

NOTE The names for these radio elements come from the enclosing RadioGroup component. `$RadioGroup` (in this example) is a unique ID for the particular RadioGroup component. In a page containing many RadioGroups, it will be a different value. One of the responsibilities of the Form component is to provide such unique element IDs to the form control components it encloses—but you never need to be concerned with these.

Although we've managed to automatically update a property without resorting to writing any Java code, this is still (by Tapestry standards) an unacceptably large amount of effort to update a single property. It requires one Radio component for each possible option, plus the RadioGroup component enclosing the other components. In practice, most Tapestry applications make use of the PropertySelection component instead, which is described in chapter 4. The PropertySelection can, as a single component, render itself as a drop-down list or as a table of radio buttons. In some cases, the HTML designer will want to have the radio buttons spread out within the form (not clustered together as shown here), interspersed with other components and static HTML—in that case, the combination of RadioGroup and Radio is appropriate.

3.4.4 Select and Option components

The HTML `<select>` and `<option>` elements are used together to create two types of user interface controls: drop-down lists and multiple-selection lists. A drop-down list is used to allow a single option from a list of options to be selected, much like using radio controls. Each option is displayed as a string.

A multiple-selection list allows the user to select multiple options from a list. The list of possible options appears in a box, which displays a limited number of options. If there are many options, the selection box will include a scroll bar. The user may click an option within the list or, by using a platform-specific modifier key (the Ctrl key, under Windows), select multiple options.

Each option has a *label*, which is a text string visible in the list, and a *value*, which is the value communicated in the query parameter if the option is selected when the form is submitted.

These two components are used together to support single or multiple selection from a list of items. The Select component must enclose the Option components. In effect, these components work together to act as a group of Checkbox

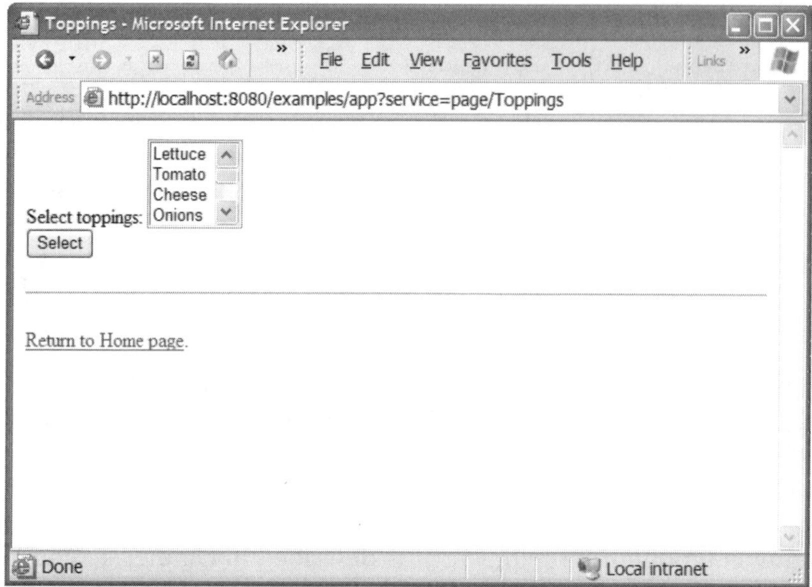

Figure 3.4 The user is provided with a multiple-selection list to choose toppings.

components. Each Option component edits an individual boolean property of the page, indicating whether that particular Option was selected or deselected when the form was submitted.

Internally, the Select and Option components work much like the Radio-Group and Radio components. The Select component is responsible for providing option IDs to the Option components during the render and informs the Option components if they were selected during the rewind.

A typical use for Select and Option is to allow the user to select several items, which are represented as a set. The following snippets show how to present a list of items and handle multiple selections of those items. In this example, it is a list of toppings that can be added to a hamburger. Figure 3.4 shows the example page.

At the core of this page's HTML template are three components: a Select component enclosing a Foreach component, which in turn encloses an Option component:

```
<select jwcid="@Select" multiple="ognl:true">
  <span jwcid="@Foreach"
    source="ognl:allToppings"
    value="ognl:topping">
    <option jwcid="@Option"
       selected="ognl:toppingSelected"
```

```
        label="ognl:topping"/>
    </span>
  </select>
```

The Select component encloses the Foreach and Option components. Its `multiple` parameter is set to true, enabling multiple selection instead of the default behavior (single selection). The Foreach component iterates through a list of possible toppings (provided by the page's `allToppings` property), updating the page's `topping` property for each one.

The Option component edits a boolean `toppingSelected` property, but what we ultimately want is a `java.util.Set` of selected toppings. This is accomplished by creating a synthetic property—a property that isn't simply a wrapper around an attribute, but is computed on the fly from other properties. The synthetic property `toppingSelected` is true when the current topping (the `topping` property) is in the set of selected toppings, and false otherwise. Updating the `toppingSelected` property adds or removes the current topping from the set. Listing 3.4 shows how easily this can be implemented.

Listing 3.4 Toppings.java: Java class for the Toppings page

```
package examples;

import java.util.HashSet;
import java.util.Iterator;
import java.util.Set;

import org.apache.tapestry.IRequestCycle;
import org.apache.tapestry.event.PageEvent;
import org.apache.tapestry.event.PageRenderListener;
import org.apache.tapestry.html.BasePage;

public abstract class Toppings extends BasePage
  implements PageRenderListener
{
  private static String[] TOPPINGS =
    { "Lettuce", "Tomato", "Cheese", "Onions", "Pickles", "Relish",
      "Mustard", "Ketchup" };

  public String[] getAllToppings()
  {
    return TOPPINGS;
  }

  public abstract String getTopping();

  public abstract void setSelectedToppings(Set toppings);
```

```
public abstract Set getSelectedToppings();

public boolean isToppingSelected()
{
  return getSelectedToppings().contains(getTopping());          ❶
}

public void setToppingSelected(boolean toppingSelected)
{
  if (toppingSelected)
    getSelectedToppings().add(getTopping());                    ❷
  else
    getSelectedToppings().remove(getTopping());
}

public void selectToppings(IRequestCycle cycle)
{
  String toppings = getToppingsList();

  ToppingsResult page =
    (ToppingsResult) cycle.getPage("ToppingsResult");
  page.setToppings(toppings);
  cycle.activate(page);
}

private String getToppingsList()
{
  if (getSelectedToppings().isEmpty())
    return "No toppings.";

  StringBuffer buffer = new StringBuffer();

  int count = getSelectedToppings().size();

  int x = 0;
  Iterator i = getSelectedToppings().iterator();

  while (i.hasNext())
  {
    if (++x > 1)
    {
      if (x == count)
        buffer.append(" and ");
      else
        buffer.append(", ");
    }

    String topping = (String) i.next();

    buffer.append(topping);
  }
```

```
    buffer.append(".");

    return buffer.toString();
  }

  public void pageBeginRender(PageEvent event)
  {
    setSelectedToppings(new HashSet());
  }

}
```

❶ The toppingSelected property is computed by seeing if the current topping (as set by the Foreach component) is in the selectedToppings set.

❷ Updating the toppingSelected property adds or removes the current topping from the selectedToppings set.

❸ This method is defined by the PageRenderListener interface, which is called as the page begins to render (or when a form within the page starts to rewind). It gives us a chance to initialize the selectedToppings property to an empty java.util.Set and thus avoid NullPointerExceptions that would occur inside getToppingSelected() and setToppingSelected().

The Toppings page specification includes specifications for two properties:

```
<property-specification name="selectedToppings"
  type="java.util.Set"/>
<property-specification name="topping" type="java.lang.String"/>
```

In addition, the class implements an interface, PageRenderListener, and a method, pageBeginRender(). Inside the setToppingSelected() method, the selectedToppings property is updated, but what is its initial value? The default initial value for properties is null, which will cause a problem unless we ensure that an instance of java.util.Set is in place in the selectedToppings property before setToppingSelected() is invoked.

That's what the PageRenderListener interface and the pageBeginRender() method do: By implementing the interface, the page instance will receive a notification as the page starts to render. This event notification takes the form of an invocation of the pageBeginRender() method defined by the interface. The implementation for the Toppings page creates a new empty java.util.HashSet and assigns it to the selectedToppings property. At the end of the request, the topping and selectedToppings properties will automatically be reset to their default value: null.

Back to the toppingSelected property. This is an example of the page acting as Controller, mediating between the Model objects and the page's components.

In this case, the Model is simply the `selectedToppings` set. The Foreach component will cycle through each of the known toppings, updating the `topping` property with a string such as `"Lettuce"` or `"Pickles"` on each pass through its loop. The `toppingSelected` property is the current topping's representation in the `selectedToppings` set. When the `toppingSelected` property is updated, it either adds or removes the current `topping` from the set (though removal is not necessary, since the set starts out empty). This all works together so that, by the time the form's listener is invoked, the `selectedToppings` set contains just the toppings that the user selected in the form.

The flexibility of the Select and Option components becomes apparent when we go beyond selecting a number of strings to selecting complex objects. For example, perhaps we are selecting from a list of `Product` objects (in an e-commerce application) or some other kind of object pulled from a database. It may not be possible to represent the entire object, or even its primary key, as a string. That doesn't affect the Select and Option components, because the `value` attribute that's recorded in the form is simply an index number, not the real value.

Option components and Checkbox components are similar from a programming model point of view. In most cases where multiple selection is not allowed, the PropertySelection component (described in chapter 4) is a better and simpler choice. In chapter 6, we introduce a more complex component, the Palette, which is suitable for handling multiple selections but requires that the client web browser execute a significant amount of client-side JavaScript.

3.4.5 Submit and ImageSubmit components

The HTML `<input type="submit">` form element creates a button control. Clicking the button submits the form for processing by the server. The button control's label matches the `value` attribute of the `<input>` tag.

A form may have any number of submit controls. When the form is submitted, the control's `value` attribute is the value for the query parameter; this makes it possible to determine *which* submit control was used to submit the form.

The weakness of the submit control is its appearance; it is always a clickable button with a text label. Most modern web applications demand precise control over the look and feel of the application and need to use an image to control the form submission. A second type of control, `<input type="image">`, creates an image that the user may click to submit the form.[1]

[1] The image control actually submits a pair of query parameters, the x and y position within the image clicked by the user. Like many technologies on the Web, the intended purpose is rarely used.

Tapestry includes two components corresponding to these two controls: Submit for a standard submit button, and ImageSubmit for a clickable image. The two components differ mostly in how they render HTML; they handle the form submissions in the same way—using one of two patterns to distinguish which component within the form was responsible for the submission.

The first pattern is to set a flag to indicate which component was clicked to submit the form. The components support two parameters for this purpose: `selected` and `tag`. The `tag` parameter is read, and the value retrieved is assigned to the `selected` parameter if and only if the component was responsible for the form submission. For example, a pair of buttons could be used to determine whether the user wishes to move an item up or down within a list:

```
<input type="submit" jwcid="@Submit"
  selected="ognl:button"
  tag="up"
  label="Move Up"/>
<input type="submit" jwcid="@Submit"
  selected="ognl:button"
  tag="down"
  label="Move Down"/>
```

If the first Submit component is clicked, the `button` property of the page will be set to the literal value `up`. If the second Submit component is clicked, the `button` property will be set to the literal value `down`. If the form is submitted otherwise, perhaps by pressing Enter within a text field, the `button` property will not be updated.

The Form's listener method can query the `button` property to decide how to accomplish the user's request. There is no limitation on the type of property to be updated (the `tag` value doesn't have to be a string; it can be any type of object), and as always, the `tag` parameter may be an expression instead of a literal value.

The second pattern involves a listener method. Submit and ImageSubmit have a `listener` parameter that may be bound to a listener method, just like a DirectLink or Form component. This allows the previous example to be rewritten more simply:

```
<input type="submit" jwcid="@Submit"
  listener="ognl:listeners.moveUp"
  label="Move Up"/>
<input type="submit" jwcid="@Submit"
  listener="ognl:listeners.moveDown"
  label="Move Down"/>
```

In this example, if the user clicks the first button, the `moveUp()` listener method will be invoked. If the user clicks the second button, the `moveDown()` listener method will be invoked. If the form is submitted otherwise, neither listener method is invoked. In either case, the form's listener is invoked last. The Submit component's listener method is invoked just as the component renders itself (during the Form's rewind phase). This means that not all properties that will be set during the form submission will have been updated yet.

It is even possible to combine the two approaches, in which case the `selected` parameter is updated before the listener method is invoked.

TIP The listener method must take care not to upset the rewind. Remember that the rewind must go through the *exact* same steps as the initial render, or the rewind will terminate with a `StaleLinkException`. A Submit component can trigger this by changing properties of the page haphazardly. The most common example is a Submit component used in a form, enclosed within a Foreach. The Submit components should not change the list used as the source parameter of the Foreach; doing so will affect the remaining iterations through the Foreach loop. Instead, the listener methods should note what operation should take place and store this information in temporary page properties. From the Form's listener, which is invoked only after the rewind completes, the desired operation can take place.

Repeatedly, we've referenced the idea that Form components can enclose Foreach components. We'll next explore an example of a complex form that combines several types of basic form control components within a Foreach.

3.5 Creating a to-do list

Now that we've introduced the basic Tapestry form components, let's do something just a little more ambitious than the login form. Let's create a simple one-page to-do list, as shown in figure 3.5.

This kind of application should be familiar to anyone who has used a personal digital assistant (PDA). There is a list of entries, which may be prioritized by the user. New entries can be created at any time, and existing entries may be marked as completed. When desired, completed entries may be removed from the list.

Figure 3.5 shows a single form, in which you could conceivably mark an item as done, change the title of another, and change the order of the items all as a single request.

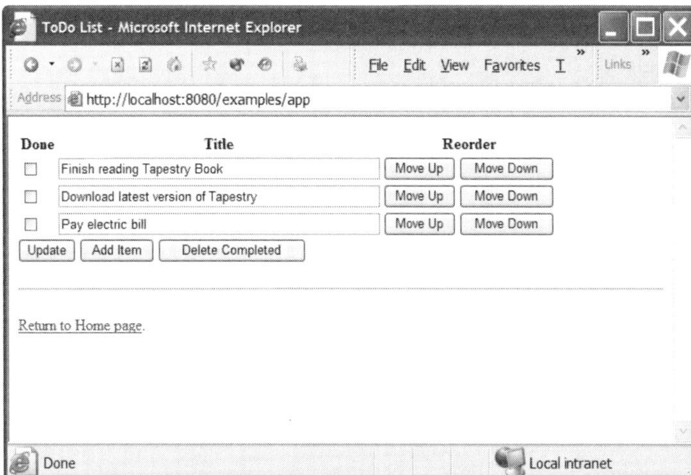

Figure 3.5 Users can create new entries, update and delete entries, and reorder the entries in the list.

We'll be making use of Checkbox, TextField, and Submit components in the application and (as promised) show how to use loops inside a Form.

3.5.1 Defining the data object

The first step is to identify how the data edited by the page will be stored. Each item in the list has three properties: a title, a completed flag, and its position in the overall list. We'll have the item store the completed flag and the title directly, and make the list responsible for item position. Listing 3.5 contains the source for this class.

Listing 3.5 ToDoItem.java: the data object used in the ToDo list page

```
package examples.todo1;

import java.io.Serializable;

public class ToDoItem implements Serializable
{
  private boolean _completed;
  private String _title;

  public ToDoItem()
  {
  }

  public ToDoItem(String title)
  {
    _title = title;
  }
```

```
    public boolean isCompleted()
    {
      return _completed;
    }

    public String getTitle()
    {
      return _title;
    }

    public void setCompleted(boolean completed)
    {
      _completed = completed;
    }

    public void setTitle(String title)
    {
      _title = title;
    }

}
```

This class is simply a property holder for two properties: `completed` and `title`. A more sophisticated application would track more data, such as priority level or due date, but this is sufficient for this example. Because instances of this class will be stored persistently (as persistent page properties ultimately stored in the `HttpSession`), the class implements the `Serializable` interface. This is necessary to allow the application server to support clustering and failover (a subject discussed in greater detail in chapter 7).

With the domain object for this application created, the next step is to define the user interface for editing a list of these items.

3.5.2 Creating the ToDo HTML template

The template for the ToDo page consists of a Form. Within the Form is a Foreach that loops over the ToDo items, and additional components for editing the properties of each item in the list. Listing 3.6 shows this template.

Listing 3.6 ToDo.html: the HTML template for the ToDo page

```
<html jwcid="@Shell" title="ToDo List">
<body>

<form jwcid="@Form" listener="ognl:listeners.formSubmit">
```

```
<table>
<tr>
  <th>Done</th>
  <th>Title</th>
  <th colspan="2">Reorder</th>
</tr>
<tr jwcid="@Foreach" element="tr"
  source="ognl:toDoList"
  value="ognl:item">                                          ❶
  <td><input type="checkbox"
        jwcid="completed@Checkbox"
        selected="ognl:item.completed"/></td>
  <td><input type="text"
        jwcid="title@TextField"
        size="50"
        value="ognl:item.title"/></td>
  <td><input type="submit" jwcid="up@Submit"
        selected="ognl:moveUpItem"
        tag="ognl:item"
        label="Move Up"/></td>                                ❷
  <td><input type="submit" jwcid="down@Submit"
        selected="ognl:moveDownItem"
        tag="ognl:item"
        label="Move Down"/></td>                              ❸
</tr>
</table>

<input type="submit" value="Update"/>
<input type="submit" jwcid="add@Submit"
  listener="ognl:listeners.addTodoItem" label="Add Item"/>
<input type="submit" jwcid="deleteCompleted@Submit"
  listener="ognl:listeners.deleteCompleted"
  label="Delete Completed"/>                                  ❹

</form>

<hr/>

<p><a href="#" jwcid="@PageLink" page="Home">Return to
Home page</a>.</p>

</body>
</html>
```

❶ This loops through the list of items supplied by the `toDoList` property, assigning each in turn to the `item` property. In addition, specifying a value for the `element` parameter causes the Foreach to render a `<tr>` element around its body for each loop, allowing the component to blend into the structure of the HTML `<table>` seamlessly and invisibly.

2. If the user clicks the Move Up button, the current `item` is assigned to the `moveUpItem` property; the actual change in ordering occurs inside the Form's listener method, `formSubmit()`.
3. Alternately, the user may click the Move Down button, and the `item` is assigned to the `moveDownItem` property.
4. These two buttons are outside the loop. Each invokes a listener method (`addTodoItem()` or `deleteCompleted()`) when clicked.

Here we're making use of another feature of the Foreach component: the `element` parameter. When a value is bound to the `element` parameter, then on each loop, the Foreach component renders the specified element around its body. In this example, the Foreach component will not only render the form element components it encloses; it will also render a `<tr>` element around each set of those form elements.

Notice that the Foreach component is positioned within the template using a `<tr>` element; in this way, the component integrates seamlessly into the overall template. Alternately, we could use a `<span>` tag as we have in the past with the Foreach component:

```
<span jwcid="@Foreach" source="ognl:toDoList"
  value="ognl:item">
  <tr>
  . . .
  </tr>
</span>
```

This alternate usage will produce virtually identical HTML output (with minor variations in whitespace) but is more intrusive; for example, it puts a `<span>` tag directly inside a `<table>` element, which is not valid HTML.

The page's HTML template shows another variation on the `jwcid` attribute: named implicit components. Putting a component ID before the `@` symbol assigns a specific ID to the component. In this example, the Checkbox component has the `jwcid` `completed@Checkbox`. This is still an implicit component (nothing more about the component goes in the page's specification); it just has the ID `completed` rather than a framework-assigned ID.[2] In a bit, we'll provoke some errors related to these components, and the error messages will be more intelligible because we used named, rather than anonymous, components.

---

[2] As you've seen in previous examples, anonymous components are assigned IDs by the framework, based on the type of component. In this case, the component ID would have been `$Checkbox`.

Much like the Hangman examples in the previous chapter, the page becomes the mediator between the components. The Foreach component gets a list of ToDoItems from the page and updates the item property for each ToDoItem within that list. Within the Foreach, the other components (the Checkbox, the TextField, and the two Submit components) are editing the current item within the loop, or other properties of the page based on the current item.

Outside the Foreach loop are additional Submit components that trigger the other two behaviors: adding a new ToDoItem, and deleting any items that are marked completed. The next step is to create the page specification, including additional properties for item and toDoList.

3.5.3 Specifying properties in the page specification

All the components in the page are fully defined in the HTML template, but a page specification (provided in listing 3.7) is still needed for two reasons: to specify the Java class for the page and to specify any properties Tapestry should create.

Listing 3.7 ToDo.page: specification for the ToDo page

```
<?xml version="1.0"?>
<!DOCTYPE page-specification PUBLIC
  "-//Apache Software Foundation//Tapestry Specification 3.0//EN"
  "http://jakarta.apache.org/tapestry/dtd/Tapestry_3_0.dtd">

<page-specification class="examples.todo1.ToDo">

  <property-specification name="toDoList"
     type="java.util.List"
     persistent="yes"/>
  <property-specification name="item"
     type="examples.todo1.ToDoItem"/>
  <property-specification name="moveUpItem"
     type="examples.todo1.ToDoItem"/>
  <property-specification name="moveDownItem"
     type="examples.todo1.ToDoItem"/>

</page-specification>
```

The first property, toDoList, is the list of ToDoItems on the page. This property is persistent; it will be stored between requests and restored in each subsequent request. Persistent page properties are covered in more detail in chapter 7.

The item property is the property set by the Foreach component on each pass through its loop. The other two properties, moveUpItem and moveDownItem, are set by the corresponding Submit components. These two components don't change the `toDoList` property, since that would upset the Form rewind. Instead, the two properties are set by the components during the rewind and are later accessed from inside the Form's listener method.

3.5.4 Initializing the toDoList property

Because the property type for `toDoList` is `java.util.List`, a collection type, it is awkward to specify its initial value in the page specification. We want to set the `toDoList` property to a reasonable value just as it is needed. Once again, we implement the `PageRenderListener` interface and provide a `pageBeginRender()` implementation to initialize the `toDoList` property the first time it is needed (just before the page renders for the first time). The ToDo page class includes the following code to perform this initialization:

```
public abstract List getToDoList();
public abstract void setToDoList(List toDoList);

public void pageBeginRender(PageEvent event)
{
  List list = getToDoList();

  if (list == null)
  {
    list = new ArrayList();
    list.add(createNewItem("Finish reading Tapestry Book"));
    list.add(createNewItem("Download latest version of Tapestry"));

    setToDoList(list);
  }
}

protected ToDoItem createNewItem(String title)
{
  return new ToDoItem(title);
}
```

When the ToDo page is first rendered, the `toDoList` property will be null. In this case, a new `ArrayList` is created, and two initial items are added to it. The property is then updated by invoking the `setToDoList()` method, and (because the page specification indicates that `toDoList` is a persistent property) behind the scenes, Tapestry stores the list into the `HttpSession` for use in later requests. This value will be used in the current request when the page renders but will also be available later, when the form within the page is submitted.

The Checkbox and TextField components do all the work of editing each `ToDoItem`'s `completed` and `title` properties. Managing the order of items inside the list requires a bit of support by the page, which we look at in the next section.

3.5.5 Handling reordering

Moving a to-do item up or down within the list requires just a bit of care. It is important that the Submit components not change the `toDoList` property while the form is still rewinding; this could lead to properties of the wrong objects getting updated. That's the first principle of Tapestry forms: The rewind phase must match the original render, object for object.

Instead, each of the two Submit components, when triggered, must note which item is to be moved up or down so that the reordering can occur later when it is safe to change the list. We've already declared two properties for this purpose in the page specification. We've also ensured that the properties are updated by making use of the `selected` and `tag` parameters of the two Submit components in the HTML template. The `item` property is set by the Foreach component before it renders the portion of the template containing the TextField, Checkbox, and Submit components. Each Submit component determines, as it rewinds, whether it was the cause of the form submission (it will see a non-null query parameter matching its element ID). If so, it updates its `selected` parameter from its `tag` parameter and then invokes its listener.[3]

The Form component's listener method is invoked after the rewind completes, when it is safe to change the `toDoList` property. This is where the items are actually moved. The `formSubmit()` listener method, from the ToDo page class, is the right place to make all these changes:

```
public void formSubmit(IRequestCycle cycle)
{
  List list = getToDoList();

  int count = list.size();
  ToDoItem moveUpItem = getMoveUpItem();
  ToDoItem moveDownItem = getMoveDownItem();

  for (int i = 0; i < count; i++)
  {
    ToDoItem item = (ToDoItem) list.get(i);

    if (item == moveUpItem)
    {
      if (i > 0)
        Collections.swap(list, i, i - 1);
```

[3] All of these parameters are optional. A Submit (or ImageSubmit) simply doesn't set its `selected` parameter if the parameter is not bound, and it doesn't invoke a listener unless one is provided.

```
          break;
        }

        if (item == moveDownItem)
        {
          if (i + 1 < count)
            Collections.swap(list, i, i + 1);

          break;
        }
      }

      setToDoList(list);
    }
```

Notice that, after modifying the list, the code invokes the method `setToDoList()` again. Tapestry relies on the developer to inform it when properties are changed by invoking the accessor method. This usually isn't an issue, because the typical types for persistent properties (numbers, booleans, and strings) are immutable. For mutable types, like `List`, Tapestry will not know to refresh the copy of the property value stored in the `HttpSession` unless the setter method is invoked. This subject is covered in greater detail in chapter 7.

3.5.6 Deleting completed items

The Submit component labeled Delete Completed is used to delete from the list all to-do items that have been marked completed. Unlike the reordering Submit components, this component's listener is invoked outside the Foreach component, so it is safe for its listener to modify the `toDoList` property directly. The listener for this component is the `deleteCompleted()` listener method of the ToDo page class:

```
public void deleteCompleted(IRequestCycle cycle)
{
  ListIterator i = getToDoList().listIterator();

  while (i.hasNext())
  {
    ToDoItem item = (ToDoItem) i.next();

    if (item.isCompleted())
      i.remove();
  }
}
```

We do take one liberty here: We should invoke `setToDoList()` at the end of the method. This can be skipped only because the Form's listener, the method `formSubmit()` listed earlier, is invoked after this listener method and always invokes `setToDoList()`.

3.5.7 Triggering stale links

There is an inherent problem in basing the dynamic portion of a form (such as the list of items in the ToDo page) on persistent properties: It is possible for the web browser and the server to get out of synchronization with each other. When the form is submitted, Tapestry will detect that the incoming form does not match the state stored on the server, a situation known as a *stale link*. When Tapestry detects a stale link, it throws a `StaleLinkException`. Having the application fail in this way is not acceptable in a production application, and we discuss how to avoid stale links in chapter 4. In the meantime, it is useful to understand the underlying causes of stale links. We can trigger a stale link for the ToDo application easily by following these steps:

1. Start the application fresh.
2. Go to the ToDo page.
3. Click the Add Item button.
4. Press the browser's back button (so that just two items are visible).
5. Click the Update button.

You should see the StaleLink page, as shown in figure 3.6. This page includes a message to help you figure out what went wrong: *Rewind of form ToDo/$Form expected allocated id #9 to be 'add', but was 'completed$1' (requested by component ToDo/completed).*

What's happened is that the form submitted with two items, but the rewind had three items to iterate over (including the new item added before you clicked the browser's back button). At the point that the completed component (a Checkbox) rendered for the third time, a mismatch occurred because when the page was originally rendered, there were only two items in that loop. The first form element after the loop is the add component (a Submit). That's where the mismatch occurs; the data recorded in the submitted form indicates that the next allocated element ID should be `add`, but the form's rewind includes a third pass through the loop and wants to allocate a third ID for the completed component.[4]

---

[4] The Form adds suffixes as necessary to form unique element IDs, starting with the element's ID as a base. So on the first pass through the loop, the completed component got the element ID `completed`, on the second pass it got the element ID `completed$0`, and on the third pass, `completed$1`.

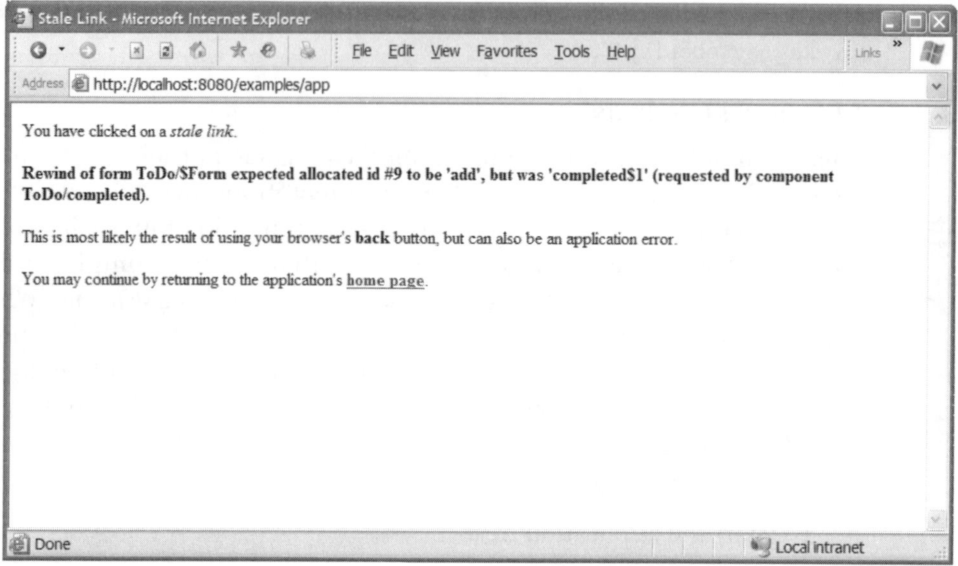

Figure 3.6 The StaleLink page is triggered by submitting a request where the client no longer matches server-side state.

> **TIP** Always give IDs to your form control components, especially if you are doing any looping or conditionals inside the Form; otherwise, the message on the StaleLink page will be much less intelligible, since the element IDs will be assigned by the framework.

Doing a view source on the page before submitting the form helps show what happened:

```
<form method="post" name="Form0" action="/examples/app">
<input type="hidden" name="service" value="direct/1/ToDo/$Form"/>
<input type="hidden" name="sp" value="S0"/>
<input type="hidden" name="Form0"
    value="completed,title,up,down,completed$0,title$0,          ❶
    ➥ up$0,down$0,add,deleteCompleted"/>

<table>
<tr>
  <th>Done</th>
  <th>Title</th>
  <th colspan="2">Reorder</th>
</tr>
<tr>
  <td><input type="checkbox" name="completed"/></td>          ❷
  <td><input type="text" name="title"
```

```
        value="Finish reading Tapestry Book" size="50"/></td>
  <td><input type="submit" name="up" value="Move Up"/></td>
  <td><input type="submit" name="down" value="Move Down"/></td>
</tr>
<tr>
  <td><input type="checkbox" name="completed$0"/></td>
  <td><input type="text" name="title$0"
        value="Download latest version of Tapestry" size="50"/>
  </td>
  <td><input type="submit" name="up$0" value="Move Up"/></td>
  <td><input type="submit" name="down$0" value="Move Down"/></td>
</tr>
</table>

<input type="submit" value="Update"/>
<input type="submit" name="add" value="Add Item"/>
<input type="submit" name="deleteCompleted"
  value="Delete Completed"/>
</form>
```

1. The Form component writes this hidden field, recording all the IDs allocated for all the enclosed components. It uses this information when the user submits the form to check that the same sequence of IDs is allocated during the rewind.
2. This portion of the output HTML is written during the first pass through the Foreach component's loop. The element IDs for the components inside the loop are `completed`, `title`, `up`, and `down`.
3. This portion of the output HTML is written during the second pass through the loop. The element IDs for the components are `completed$0`, `title$0`, `up$0`, and `down$0`. The `$0` extension is to make the element IDs unique within the Form.
4. The server-side state mandates that a third pass through the loop should take place here (because there are three to-do items), but the form was rendered when there were only two items in the list.

In the output HTML, we can see how the Form component uses hidden fields to store the list of form element IDs. This list is used during the rewind phase to ensure that the render and the rewind do, in fact, match.

Because there are three items stored in the `toDoList` property of the page, there should be a third `<tr>` within the table, containing another Checkbox, a TextField, and pair of Submit buttons. This is discovered by the Form during the rewind phase, at which point it throws the `StaleLinkException` (which results in the Stale Link page being displayed).

We've shown you how to trigger a stale link under controlled circumstances. You can be assured that if you aren't prepared for it, your users will find ways to trigger stale links under uncontrolled circumstances—typically by clicking their web browser's back button. Your end users should never see an exception page or a Stale Link page, so in chapter 4 we discuss additional components and techniques that detect and avoid stale links.

3.6 Summary

Tapestry relieves you of all the drudgery of both rendering forms and form elements and processing form submissions. A non-Tapestry servlet application will contain reams of tedious code for reading query parameters and converting string values. When you use Tapestry, this code simply disappears, leaving just higher-level code that operates directly on the properties of the domain objects. As in the examples with simple links and images, Tapestry pages with forms still look and feel like ordinary HTML pages; the Tapestry extensions fit invisibly into place. Once again we've seen where Tapestry's simplicity and consistency goals come into play: It's far easier to use the Form component and form control components to read and update properties of the page directly than it ever would be to fuss with query parameters.

Even when adding the complication of editing a list of items within a form, Tapestry performs well. Despite a few constraints placed on the developer by the framework, the effort and code required to process such complex forms is still minimal. That is far from all the framework has to offer in terms of forms support, however. In the following chapter, we pull even further ahead and describe advanced form components that do much more than simply mimic ordinary HTML elements.

4 Advanced form components

This chapter covers

- Complex components vs. simple components
- Creating drop-down lists
- Storing hidden data in forms
- Uploading files

In chapter 3, we covered the basic set of Tapestry components—components that map directly to HTML form control elements. These basic components provide a baseline for form-related functionality, but Tapestry is capable of much more. In this chapter, we'll introduce more sophisticated components that do *more*: more HTML, more client-side JavaScript, more server-side processing. Much of this chapter will focus on reworking the ToDo application from chapter 3, adding features and, ultimately, addressing the browser back button issue. In addition, we'll introduce components for uploading files and for selecting dates using a pop-up calendar. Chapter 5 will discuss the input-validation subsystem provided by Tapestry.

4.1 Introducing the advanced form components

The previous chapter covered a number of Tapestry components used for basic HTML form support. Each of the basic components maps directly to a particular HTML form control element. This chapter looks at components that break that mold by adding significant capabilities in terms of client-side or server-side processing (or both). These components, shown in table 4.1, are more *task* oriented than the *element*-oriented components of the previous chapter.

Table 4.1 Advanced form components

Component	Description
PropertySelection	Creates a drop-down list of values
Hidden	Records a property for a hidden form field and restores it on submission
ListEdit	Iterates over a list of items like Foreach, but works better within a form
Upload	Allows files to be uploaded from the client workstation
DatePicker	Uses a JavaScript pop-up window to let the user enter a date

The first of these components is the widely used PropertySelection component, which provides a streamlined approach to creating single-selection drop-down lists.

4.2 Creating drop-down lists with PropertySelection

A common feature in many web forms is a drop-down list that lets you make a selection. Whether you're asking users to choose their state of residence, a type of credit card, or some other information that has a limited set of options, it is often easiest for you, and for your users, to let them select from a list rather than prompt them to type in a value. A drop-down list makes economical use of the available screen real estate. As you'll recall, chapter 3 describes the Select and Option components, which are one approach to creating drop-down lists.

Using the Select and Option components for this purpose, however, is awkward. The Option component reads and sets a boolean property, and it requires you to implement supporting code in the page to translate between property values and a set of boolean flags. You saw this in the examples in chapter 3, where we used a synthetic boolean property to control the adding of items to or removing of items from a set. Select and Option are focused on handling multiple selection, not the more common case where only a single selection from a drop-down list is desired. Fortunately, we aren't restricted to using only Select and Option components when creating drop-down lists.

The PropertySelection component exists specifically for the purpose of allowing a user to select a single option from a drop-down list. PropertySelection will create a `<select>` element and a set of `<option>` tags when rendering, and will perform an update of a property when the form is submitted. You must provide the PropertySelection component with information about the options that are allowed. To do this, you bind the PropertySelection's `model` parameter to an object implementing the `IPropertySelectionModel` interface. The PropertySelection component uses the model when rendering and again when the form is submitted.

The model provides the following information to PropertySelection:

- The total number of options
- The property value for each option
- The label for each option (which is displayed to the user)
- The encoded value for each option, used as the `value` attribute of the `<option>` element
- The property value corresponding to an encoded value

This is an example of the Model-View-Controller pattern in action, even though it involves only a single component within a page rather than an entire page. The PropertySelection component does not have any special knowledge about the options it presents to the user; it will work with any model object provided to it. The `IPropertySelectionModel` interface is the contract between the model and the component.

The PropertySelection component is quite flexible. A simple implementation of the model supports the selection of a string value from a list (the property edited by the PropertySelection component will be a string). At the other extreme, an application may use a PropertySelection component to edit a relationship between two database objects. For example, an order-management form within an e-commerce application's account management page may allow you to select an active order from a drop-down list so that you can review the order's progress. Here, the option label will be a string identifying the `Order` object, such as a confirmation ID number. The property value will be the `Order` object itself, and the encoded option value will be the `Order` object's primary key.

In keeping with Tapestry's goal of consistency, you can use a PropertySelection component for both simple and complex models. To demonstrate how to use PropertySelection and how to create a model for it, let's look at an improved version of the ToDo application.

4.2.1 Adding priority levels to the ToDo application

In this version of the to-do list, each item stores a priority value, along with its title and completed flag. The priority can be Low, Medium, or High. Figure 4.1 shows the new version of the page.

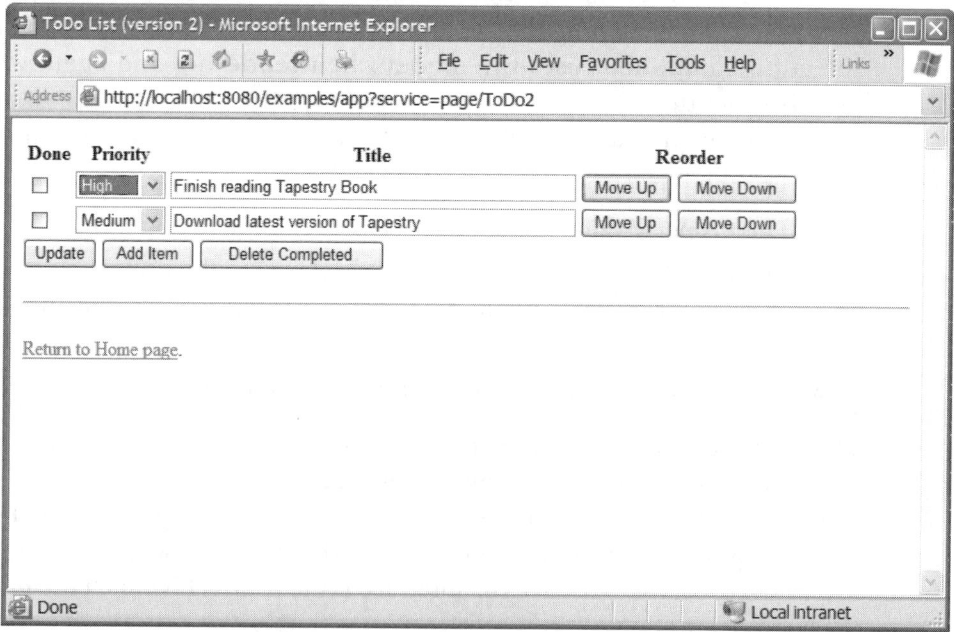

Figure 4.1 The improved ToDo page, with a PropertySelection for choosing the priority for each item.

As before, our first step is to identify how this new data will be stored. For flexibility, we'll store the priority as an integer, using 100 for Low, 200 for Medium, and 300 for High. At a later date, we can then easily add new values between these initial values (say, adding "Important" as 250). Because we'll use the other existing properties of the `ToDoItem` class, let's create a subclass that adds a new property for storing the priority value. This new subclass is shown in listing 4.1. As you can see, the `ToDoItem2` class includes public constants used to define the three priority values.

Listing 4.1 ToDoItem2.java: data object for the ToDo2 page

```
package examples.todo2;

import examples.todo1.ToDoItem;

public class ToDoItem2 extends ToDoItem
{
  public static final int LOW_PRIORITY = 100;
  public static final int MEDIUM_PRIORITY = 200;
  public static final int HIGH_PRIORITY = 300;

  private int _priority = MEDIUM_PRIORITY;

  public ToDoItem2()
  {
  }

  public ToDoItem2(String title)
  {
    super(title);
  }

  public int getPriority()
  {
    return _priority;
  }

  public void setPriority(int priority)
  {
    _priority = priority;
  }

}
```

4.2.2 Updating the HTML template

The next step is to create a new version of the ToDo page that includes a PropertySelection component for editing the `priority` properties of the to-do items. Let's start with a copy of the template from the earlier version of the ToDo list page and add new HTML and components to support the new property. The end result is the HTML template in listing 4.2.

Listing 4.2 ToDo2.html: HTML template for the ToDo2 page

```
<html jwcid="@Shell" title="ToDo List (version 2)">
<body>

<form jwcid="@Form" listener="ognl:listeners.formSubmit">

<table>
<tr>
  <th>Done</th>
  <th>Priority</th>
  <th>Title</th>
  <th colspan="2">Reorder</th>
</tr>
<tr jwcid="@Foreach"
    element="tr" source="ognl:toDoList"
    value="ognl:item">
  <td><input type="checkbox" jwcid="completed@Checkbox"
             selected="ognl:item.completed"/></td>
  <td><select jwcid="priority@PropertySelection"
              value="ognl:item.priority"
              model="ognl:priorityModel"/></td>
  <td><input type="text" jwcid="title@TextField" size="50"
             value="ognl:item.title"/></td>
  <td><input type="submit" jwcid="up@Submit"
        selected="ognl:moveUpItem"
        tag="ognl:item"
        label="Move Up"/></td>
  <td><input type="submit" jwcid="down@Submit"
        selected="ognl:moveDownItem"
        tag="ognl:item"
        label="Move Down"/></td>
</tr>
</table>

<input type="submit" value="Update"/>
<input type="submit" jwcid="add@Submit"
       listener="ognl:listeners.addTodoItem"
       label="Add Item"/>
<input type="submit" jwcid="deleteCompleted@Submit"
       listener="ognl:listeners.deleteCompleted"
       label="Delete Completed"/>
```

The PropertySelection component (annotation for the `<td><select jwcid="priority@PropertySelection" …` lines)

```
</form>

<hr/>

<p><a href="#" jwcid="@PageLink" page="Home">Return to
Home page</a>.</p>

</body>
</html>
```

The only significant change to the original HTML template is the addition of the PropertySelection component. Its `value` parameter is bound to the property we want to edit, just as with a TextField. Here, the PropertySelection component will edit the current `item`'s `priority` property. Unlike with a TextField, the property may be of any type, not just a string.

4.2.3 Implementing the page class

For the most part, the `ToDo2` class is the same as for the original page. There are two differences:

- `ToDo2` provides a read-only property, `priorityModel`, needed by the Property-Selection component.
- When adding new items, we instantiate the `ToDoItem2` class instead of `ToDoItem`.

Because they have so much in common, `ToDo2` subclasses the original class, `ToDo`, but adds one new method and overrides another. First, the `priorityModel` property (referenced in the HTML template by the PropertySelection component) is provided via the `getPriorityModel()` method. The model is needed by the Property-Selection component to create the drop-down list of priorities:

```
public IPropertySelectionModel getPriorityModel()
{
  return new PriorityModel();
}
```

New item instances are created in only one place: the `createNewItem()` method. Overriding this method in the `ToDo2` subclass allows for the creation of the `ToDoItem2` class:

```
protected ToDoItem createNewItem(String title)
{
  return new ToDoItem2(title);
}
```

All the remaining behavior from the first page applies to this page as well, and is simply inherited from the original page class.

4.2.4 Implementing the model

The PropertySelection component's model is a class that implements the `IPropertySelectionModel` interface, which consists of five methods. These methods define all the options that will be presented in the drop-down list.

When rendering, PropertySelection creates a `<select>` element, and then uses the model to obtain the number of options. The PropertySelection component interacts with the model during the render, as shown in figure 4.2. For each option provided by the model, PropertySelection obtains the option value (which may be an object type), the string value (which is the value encoded into the form as the `<option>` element's `value` attribute), and the label that will be displayed to the user. This information is used to write each `<option>` element

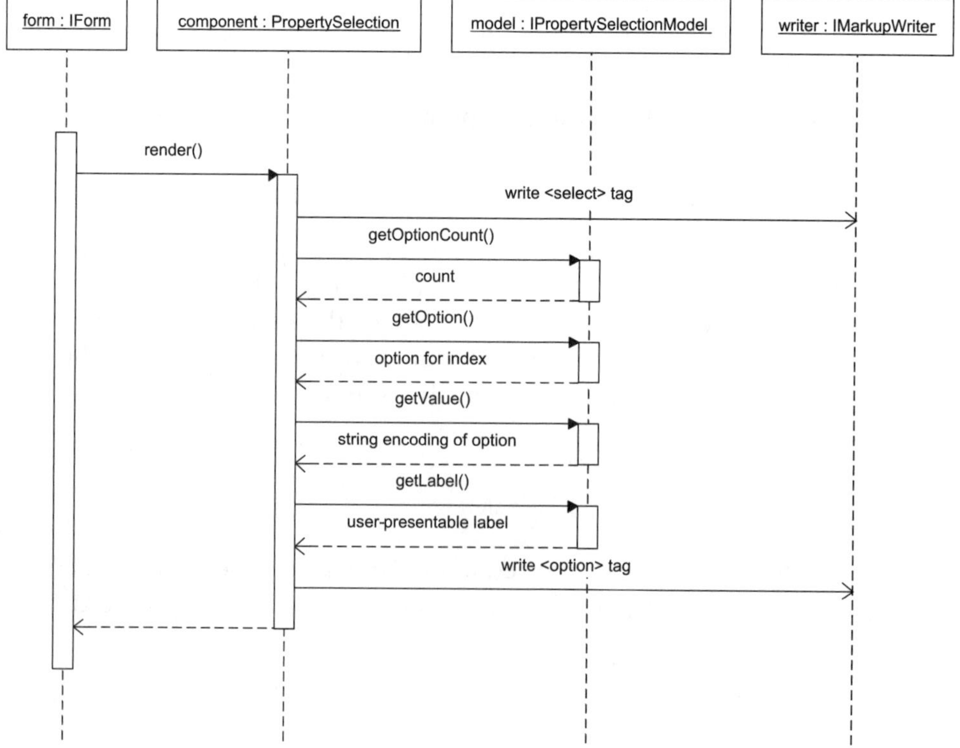

Figure 4.2 The property selection model provides the number of options as well as the information needed to render each option.

within the `<select>`. The option value is used to determine whether the `<option>` should be selected by default.

Listing 4.3 contains the PropertySelection model for selecting priority levels. It defines a class, `PriorityModel`, that implements the `IPropertySelectionModel` interface—the interface a PropertySelection model class must implement.

Listing 4.3 PropertyModel.java: PropertySelection model implementation

```
package examples.todo2;

import org.apache.tapestry.form.IPropertySelectionModel;

public class PriorityModel implements IPropertySelectionModel
{
  public int getOptionCount()
  {
    return 3;
  }

  public Object getOption(int index)
  {
    switch (index)
    {
      case 0 :
        return new Integer(ToDoItem2.HIGH_PRIORITY);

      case 1 :
        return new Integer(ToDoItem2.MEDIUM_PRIORITY);

      default :
        return new Integer(ToDoItem2.LOW_PRIORITY);
    }
  }

  public String getLabel(int index)
  {
    switch (index)
    {
      case 0 :
        return "High";

      case 1 :
        return "Medium";

      default :

        return "Low";
    }
  }
```

❶ **Converts index to property value**

```
    public String getValue(int index)
    {
      return Integer.toString(index);        ❷ Converts index
    }                                           to option value

    public Object translateValue(String value)
    {
      int index = Integer.parseInt(value);    ❸ Converts option
                                                value to property
      return getOption(index);                  value
    }
}
```

❶ The `getOptionCount()` method returns 3, because there are always exactly three options (High, Medium, and Low).

❷ The `getValue()` method returns the option value recorded into the form (as the `value` attribute of the `<option>` element). For this model, the option value is simply the index into the list of possible options—a common, efficient approach when the list of options is fixed at compile time.

❸ The `translateValue()` method is the counterpart to `getValue()`. It translates the option value back to an index number and returns the option for that index.

The first method in the `IPropertySelectionModel` interface, `getOptionCount()`, provides the number of items in the list. For this model, there are always exactly three options—High, Medium, and Low—so `getOptionCount()` always returns 3. The PropertySelection component will iterate through the possible indexes (0 through 2) and invoke the next three methods for each index.

The PropertySelection component invokes the `getOption()` method only when it is rendering (the method isn't invoked when the containing form is submitted). This method allows the PropertySelection component to determine which option, if any, should be selected initially. The first option whose value (as returned by `getOption()`) matches the value from the component's `value` parameter is selected. (The `<option>` element will include the `selected` attribute.) Keep in mind that although this example edits an integer property, PropertySelection has no knowledge of the type of property it is editing; that information is entirely contained within the model. The `value` parameter could just as easily be a double, a string, a date, or a custom application object—even an object retrieved from a database. The return value for the `getOption()` method is `Object`, and the three priority level constants are wrapped as `Integer` objects and returned.

The second method, `getLabel()`, provides the label for each option. As with `getOption()`, the parameter is the index within the loop. The returned label is presented directly to the user. In an internationalized application, the label value returned must be localized to match the page's locale.

As the PropertySelection component renders the `<option>` elements, it must have a string to use as the `value` attribute. The PropertySelection component allows the model to specify this in the `getValue()` method. A common approach, which we use here, is to encode the index as a string. The model should be able to convert this string back to an option value when the form is submitted.

In this particular model, we could have encoded the *value* for one of the three constants here. That is, we could return `100`, `200`, or `300` rather than the index.

The final model method, `translateValue()`, is used only when the form is submitted. The PropertySelection component will use this method to translate an encoded value directly to an option so that the option can be used to update the property bound to the PropertySelection's `value` parameter. The `translateValue()` method is the counterpart to the `getValue()` method. Figure 4.3 shows how this method is used by the PropertySelection component.

For this model implementation, it is convenient to simply convert the index value back to an integer and use the `getOption()` method to obtain the value to be assigned.

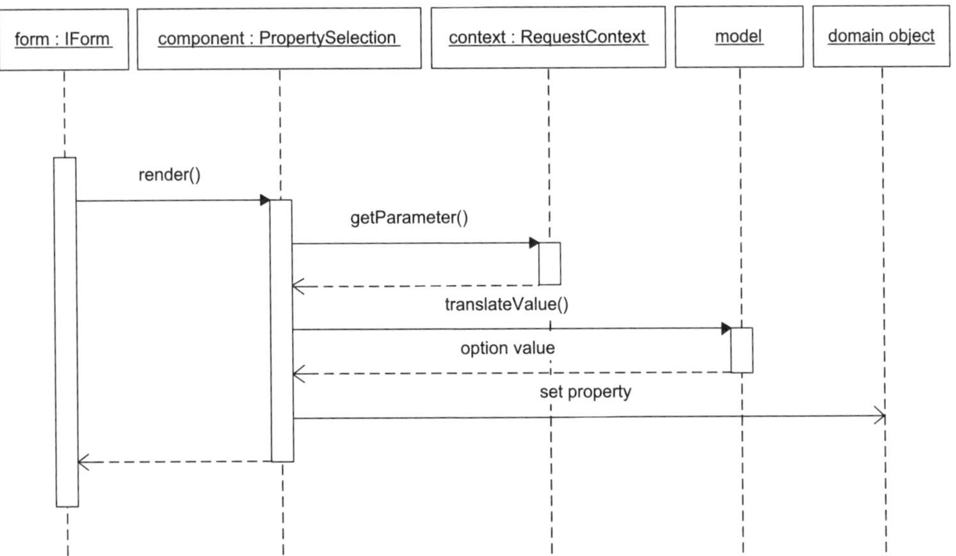

Figure 4.3 The PropertySelection rewind sequence. The value is extracted from the query parameter and the model is used to translate it to a value, which is then assigned back to the domain object property.

By combining the PropertySelection component with a custom model class, we have easily created a working drop-down list in our application with little more effort than would be required when using a TextField. With some minor changes to our Java code, we can even get rid of the custom model class and use an existing model implementation provided by the framework. We just have to replace our integer constants with enums.

4.2.5 Using enums instead of integers

Using a set of integers to represent the priority levels is somewhat of an oddity in Java coding style. In C or C++, you would almost certainly use an enum instead. Enums are preferable to integers because they limit the possible values to a finite set, which is exactly what we want here. The compiler can do much better type checking of method parameters or other expressions for enums than it can for simple integers. Java currently does not have an enum construct. Sun is expected to add support for enums in Java Development Kit (JDK) 1.5; but until that version of Java is widely available, you can simulate C enums by using Java classes.

In this take on the ToDo list application, we'll switch from representing the priority as integers and instead use an enumerated type. We'll also make use of a framework-provided model class, tailored for use with enumerated types. The final application looks identical to the previous version, ToDo2. It's simply a different way of storing data on the server side.

One of the advantages of building and using open-source software is the availability of other high-quality frameworks and libraries. Tapestry makes use of a number of such frameworks, including the OGNL library, as well as other frameworks available from the Jakarta project that hosts Tapestry. The Jakarta commons-lang library contains a number of handy utilities and classes, one of which is an `Enum` base class used for creating enumerated types. Creating a new enumerated type is as simple as creating a subclass of `Enum` and defining some public constants for the possible values. Listing 4.4 shows the implementation of the `Priority` class.

Listing 4.4 Priority.java: enum type used with the ToDo3 class

```
package examples.todo3;

import org.apache.commons.lang.enum.Enum;

public class Priority extends Enum
{
  public static final Priority HIGH = new Priority("HIGH");
```

```
  public static final Priority MEDIUM = new Priority("MEDIUM");
  public static final Priority LOW = new Priority("LOW");

  public static final Priority[] ALL_VALUES =
    { HIGH, MEDIUM, LOW };

  private Priority(String name)
  {
    super(name);
  }
}
```

The constructor for `Priority` is private; this means that the class can't be extended. There's no way to create additional instances of `Priority` beyond the three values defined here: `Priority.HIGH`, `Priority.MEDIUM`, and `Priority.LOW` (except by changing the `Priority` class to define new values). If we ever write code that needs to differentiate `ToDoItem3` instances based on priority, we can make direct comparisons to these three constant values; that is, we can use the Java equality operator, `==`, rather than invoke the `equals()` method. The `Enum` base class ensures the identity of instances, even when a `Priority` is serialized and deserialized,[1] such as when the value is directly or indirectly stored in the `HttpSession`.

From there, we again extend the `ToDoItem` class to define a `priority` property of type `Priority`. The new class, `ToDoItem3`, appears in listing 4.5.

Listing 4.5 ToDoItem3.java: data item used with the ToDo3 page

```
package examples.todo3;

import examples.todo1.ToDoItem;

public class ToDoItem3 extends ToDoItem
{
  private Priority _priority = Priority.MEDIUM;

  public ToDoItem3()
  {
  }
```

[1] Normally, when an object is serialized and then deserialized, the result is a copy of the original object—a new and separate instance. This makes sense, because (for a while) the object was just a stream of bytes. The `Enum` base class includes the necessary hooks to find the correct singleton after deserializing, which ensures that, within a JVM, there is exactly one instance of any particular `Enum` value (such as `Priority.HIGH`).

```
    public ToDoItem3(String title)
    {
      super(title);
    }

    public Priority getPriority()
    {
      return _priority;
    }

    public void setPriority(Priority priority)
    {
      _priority = priority;
    }
  }
```

The HTML template for the ToDo3 page is identical the ToDo2 HTML template (except for the page title). There's nothing to change; PropertySelection is still editing the `priority` property of the `item`, and the page still provides an instance of `IPropertySelectionModel` to handle all the translations as a `priorityModel` property. On the implementation side, the type of the `priority` property in the item class has changed from `int` to `Priority`, and the model used by the PropertySelection component has changed as well. But none of that is relevant to the interface or even to the PropertySelection component—it's all encapsulated inside the model. This is a good example of the power of the Model-View-Controller pattern: The View (the HTML template) is unchanged even when the Model (the `ToDoItem3` class) is altered considerably; the Controller (the Java page class) has modest changes to fulfill its role of bridging the two.

The ToDo3 page specification differs only in the page class we want to instantiate. The `createNewItem()` method is overridden in the `ToDo3` class to instantiate an instance of `ToDoItem3`. The only real change is related to creating a model for the PropertySelection component—this appears in the `ToDo3` page class:

```
private IPropertySelectionModel _priorityModel;

public IPropertySelectionModel getPriorityModel()
{
  if (_priorityModel == null)                           ❶ Builds and caches
    _priorityModel = buildPriorityModel();                the model

  return _priorityModel;
}

private IPropertySelectionModel buildPriorityModel()
{
```

```
  ResourceBundle bundle =
    ResourceBundle.getBundle("examples.todo3.PriorityStrings",
      getLocale());                              Constructs the model ❷

  return new EnumPropertySelectionModel(Priority.ALL_VALUES,
    bundle);                                     Uses the correct ❸
}                                                locale for the page
```

❶ The model, once constructed, is immutable. It is constructed the first time it is needed and then saved for later requests.

❷ The model is constructed using the properly localized `ResourceBundle` and the list of possible values (in the order they should appear in the drop-down list). This will be a file, PriorityStrings.properties, in the same package folder as the Java class.

❸ The page returns, in its `locale` property, the locale that should be used for any visible text.

The core of this approach is the Tapestry framework class `EnumPropertySelectionModel`. This is an implementation of `IPropertySelectionModel` geared around `Enums`. The first parameter for the constructor is an array of the `Enum` values, in the order in which they should appear in the drop-down list created by the PropertySelection component.

The second parameter is a `ResourceBundle` containing the localized labels we want to use.[2] The keys in the `ResourceBundle` are the names of the `Enum` instances, in this case `HIGH`, `MEDIUM`, and `LOW`. The PriorityStrings.properties file contains the user-presentable labels:

```
HIGH=High
MEDIUM=Medium
LOW=Low
```

Tapestry does quite a bit in terms of managing the end user's locale; we cover this topic in detail in chapter 7. For now, suffice to say that the page knows the correct locale for any localizable resources such as the PriorityStrings.properties file, and this is accessible via the `getLocale()` method inherited from the `AbstractPage` superclass.

At runtime, the PropertySelection component will use the `EnumPropertySelectionModel` to access the localized strings in the `ResourceBundle`. The model

[2] `ResourceBundle` is a utility class provided by the JDK. A `ResourceBundle` is a container of string keys and values, typically read from a set of files. `ResourceBundles` are used primarily to support localization; they allow literal strings to be moved out of Java code and into separate files, which may be edited and translated individually.

also will be responsible for creating option values and translating option values to one of the three options: `Priority.HIGH`, `Priority.MEDIUM`, or `Priority.LOW`. The end user will not see any difference in the behavior of the ToDo2 and ToDo3 pages, but internally, the implementation of the ToDo3 page is cleaner and simpler.

The PropertySelection component vastly simplifies the effort needed to create a drop-down list. This single component can be used to create lists for anything from a simple Yes or No, to a list of strings, all the way up to a list of objects read from a database. You simply provide the model listing the available options and tell the component how to store this information in the HTML form, as well as how to convert it back to application data.

In the next two sections, we describe Tapestry form components that are invisible to the end user. They allow information to be stored in the HTML form as hidden input fields and permit that information to be retrieved when the user submits the form.

4.3 Recording data in the form with Hidden

One of the more vexing problems in web application development is how to deal with the browser back button. In a traditional desktop application, the user interface displayed to the user is always in perfect synchronization with the running application, but in a web application this isn't always so. Because the user can hit the browser back button to return to a previous page (really, a previous rendering of a page stored in a cache within the web browser) and continue to click links and submit forms, it is all too easy for the user interface to be out of synch with the state of the application running on the server.

For example, consider a typical e-commerce application with a product catalog. A user may start a search for, say, digital cameras. The user eventually reaches a product details page for a particular camera, perhaps a Minolta. From there, the user clicks on a Related Items link and gets the product details for a similar Nikon camera.

Unsatisfied with the Nikon, the user hits the browser back button and returns to the page displaying the Minolta camera. This Minolta page will come out of the browser's page cache, and no interaction with the application server takes place. To the user, these are two different and distinct pages, one showing the Minolta and one showing the Nikon, exactly as if the user was thumbing through a print catalog. To the application, these are different configurations of the same page, rendered at different times. Unlike a desktop application, a web application can only guess at what is on users' screens when they submit forms.

The user then decides to purchase the Minolta and clicks the Add To Shopping Cart button to add the camera to the cart. Which camera gets added to the cart: the Minolta or the Nikon? It depends on how the application is coded.

The application may store the identity of the product displayed on the product details page on the server. Tapestry includes a facility for this (persistent page properties), but even a non-Tapestry application could do this by storing an attribute into the `HttpSession`. If the application operates this way, the user will be surprised by a Nikon camera in the shopping cart, not the Minolta the user was expecting. Because the server has no way of knowing that the user hit the browser's back button, it can only assume that the user is looking at the most recently rendered page (the one showing the Nikon details), even if the user is instead looking at the Minolta camera in a page cached within the browser.

We need a way to encode in the form the identity of the camera so that when the form is submitted, the correct camera is added to the shopping cart. In traditional web application development, this is accomplished by including a hidden field in the form. You create a hidden field by using the HTML element `<input type="hidden">`. A hidden field works like a text field, except that no user interface element is created in the web browser. The hidden field is, simply, hidden, and the value for the field is submitted along with the other fields of the form.

Tapestry includes a component, Hidden, which builds on the HTML hidden form control. The Hidden component works much like a TextField component; when it renders, it reads a domain object property bound to its `value` parameter. Unlike with TextField, the property does not have to be a string; this property type is encoded along with its value, just as you've seen before with DirectLink component parameters. Figure 4.4 shows the sequence when a Hidden component renders.

The Form component is responsible for writing the hidden field (as an `<input type="hidden">` element). In most cases, the domain object is the page object itself; as with all component parameters, it doesn't matter to the Hidden component where the value comes from. When the form is submitted, the value is extracted from the request, converted back into an object type, and used to update the domain object property, as shown in figure 4.5. A listener method may optionally be specified; if so, the listener is invoked after the property is updated. Remember that listener methods are really `IActionListener` instances. Invoking the listener method gives the page a chance to perform any additional synchronization operations related to the data stored in the hidden field.

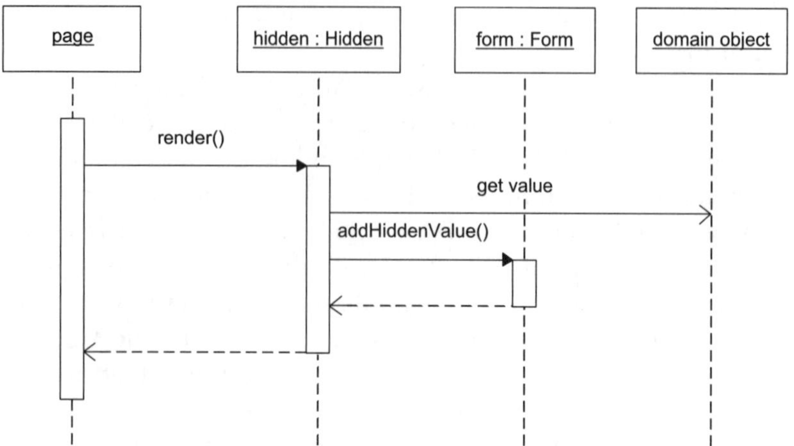

Figure 4.4 When the Hidden component renders, it extracts a property and records it in the form as a hidden field.

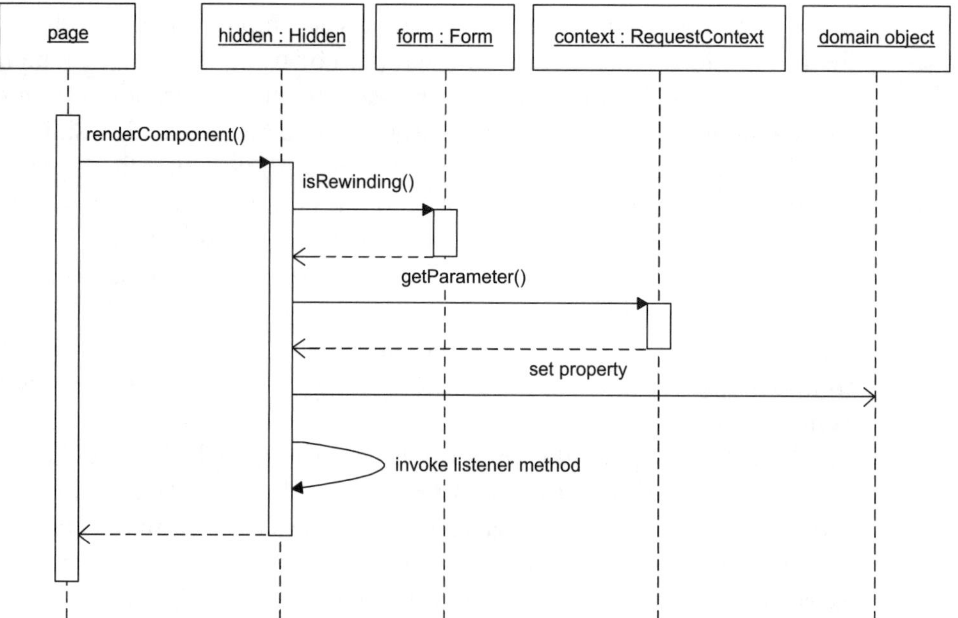

Figure 4.5 After reading and converting the query parameter, the Hidden component updates its `value` parameter and, finally, invokes its listener.

In the e-commerce example, the Hidden component would record just the identity of the `Product` entity for the camera. This might be a SKU or a database primary key. The listener method, invoked after the `id` property is restored, can then go to the database to read the `Product` entity and continue with the process of adding the camera to the shopping cart.

We provide a more complete example of using the Hidden component in chapter 10.

The Hidden component is useful for recording a single value in a form. However, there are cases where an entire list of values should be encoded. In the next section, we show you how to properly loop over such a list of values inside a form.

4.4 Looping within a form using ListEdit

Dealing with lists is a common issue related to synchronization between the client and the server. Forms may contain a Foreach component and iterate over a list of values, allowing properties of each element in the list to be edited. This is common in e-commerce applications, where a "shopping cart" page allows quantities of all the items in the shopping cart to be edited in one place. The same concept applies in many other types of applications as well.

As you saw in chapter 3, it is easy for users to trip up the Form component by using their browser's back button, triggering a `StaleLinkException`. For simple forms, without loops or conditionals, this is never an issue. However, for complex forms, which include loops and conditionals, it is possible for a Form submission to get out of sequence with the previous Form render. The simplest way for a synchronization fault to occur is when the form includes a loop that iterates over data that may change between the time the page is rendered and the time the form on the page is submitted. This often occurs when a loop works off data from a database, and rows are added to, or removed from, the database *after* the page is rendered but *before* the form is submitted (for example, if a second user is updating the database). A similar scenario is one in which the user backtracks to a page that was rendered when the application was in a different state.

So, just as the Hidden component can store a single value in a form, the ListEdit component can store a list of values in a form—and iterate over them just like a Foreach component. The interface for ListEdit resembles that of the Foreach component; it also has `source` and `value` parameters. When a ListEdit is rendering, it behaves exactly like the Foreach component, with one difference: It records a series of hidden fields in the form, one for each element in its source list. As with the Hidden component, it encodes each value, maintaining its type for later, when the form is submitted. Figure 4.6 shows how this works.

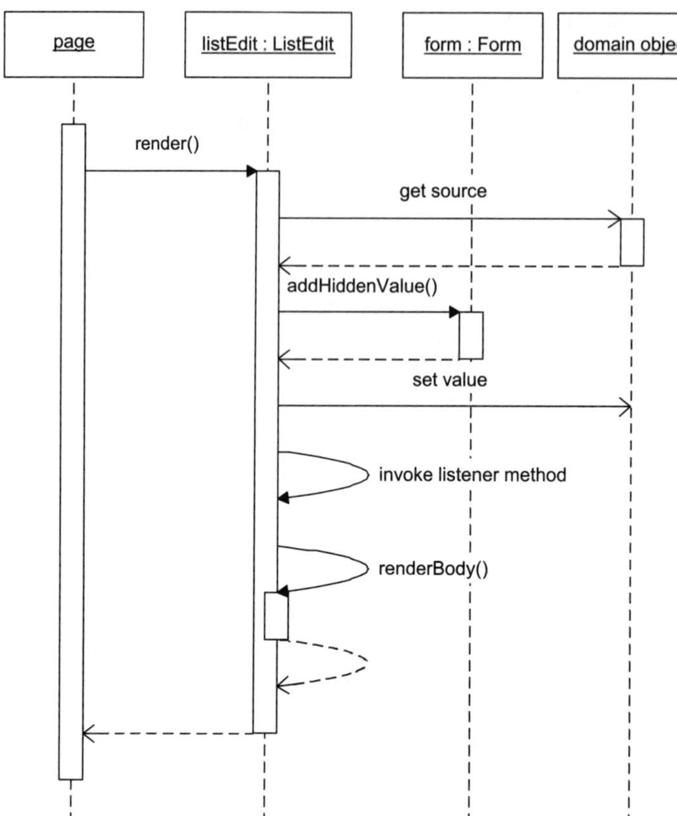

Figure 4.6 When rendering, the ListEdit component acts much like a Foreach. The listener is invoked after the value is updated on each pass through the loop.

A major departure from the Foreach component is the existence of the ListEdit's `listener` parameter. Whereas a Foreach component updates its `value` parameter and renders its body, the ListEdit component updates its `value` parameter and then invokes a listener method before rendering its body. The intent is that the successive values are some form of object ID, and the listener method is supposed to read the full object for that ID and make it available as a page property.

When the enclosing Form is rewinding, ListEdit works very differently from Foreach. During the rewinding, a ListEdit component reads the hidden fields it previously recorded (during the render); it doesn't use its `source` parameter at all when rewinding. The ListEdit component still updates the property bound to its `value` parameter, just as a Foreach component does, before rendering its body. The operation sequence for rewinding is just about the same as for rendering (except for the interaction with the Form component to record hidden field values).

While the ListEdit component provides the functionality for iterating over lists, it is commonly combined with a helper class to fill in the details, as you'll see in the next section.

4.4.1 Using the ListEditMap

The ListEdit component provides the raw structure for dealing with HTML form synchronization issues, but it requires a bit of effort to use. There's a lot of work related to supplying ListEdit with a list or collection of IDs, converting those IDs to objects, and so forth. That can turn into a bit of code, so, naturally, Tapestry offers some assistance to help you avoid unnecessary coding.

The framework includes a companion class, `ListEditMap`, which provides a server-side mapping from the object IDs that are stored in the form to the objects for those IDs, which are available on the server. A page must create a `ListEditMap` instance and load it with the object IDs and matching object values before rendering the ListEdit component, and then must reconstruct the `ListEditMap` instance when the form is submitted. The ListEdit component's `source` and `value` parameters are connected to `ListEditMap`'s `keys` and `key` properties, as shown in table 4.2.

Table 4.2 ListEditMap properties

ListEdit parameter	ListEditMap property	Usage
`source`	`keys`	The collection of keys to iterate over (render only)
`value`	`key`	A value set by ListEdit to the current key within the list of keys (render and rewind)
	`value`	The value corresponding to the current key (render and rewind)

With the ListEdit component properly configured, we can extend the ListEdit sequence diagram to show exactly how `ListEditMap` is involved, as shown in figure 4.7.

The listener method can get the current value from the `ListEditMap` instance. This listener method should always check to see if the value is null; this can occur when two users' updates overlap. If the first user deletes some objects, the second user's form submit will contain the IDs of deleted objects, which will not be present in the `ListEditMap` instance (because they have been deleted from the underlying database).

To see how ListEdit and `ListEditMap` work together, let's update our ToDo application again, replacing Foreach with a ListEdit component.

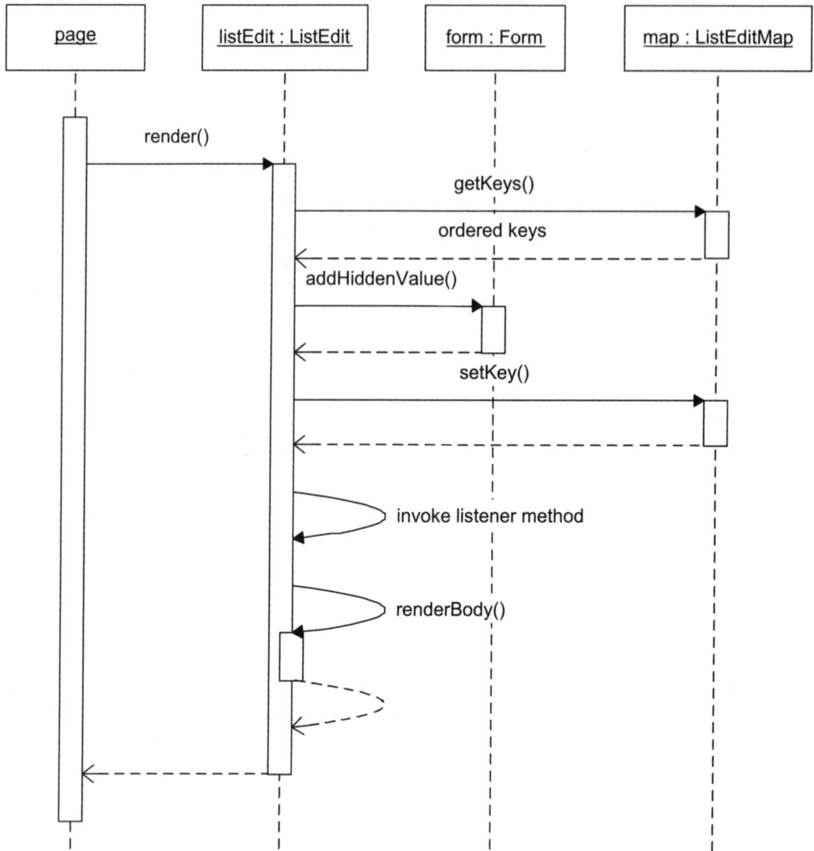

Figure 4.7 The ListEdit component is connected to the `ListEditMap` instance and keeps it informed about the current object ID (by setting the `key` property). The listener method can easily obtain the current object for that key from `ListEditMap` via the `value` property.

4.4.2 *Using ListEdit in the ToDo application*

In chapter 3, we demonstrated how easy it is to force the ToDo application (which is based on a Foreach component) to fail (with a `StaleLinkException`) by using the browser's back button. Now we'll create a fourth version of the application that doesn't have that limitation.

Creating a ToDo item with an ID

The `ListEditMap` class is built around the idea that items have some form of unique key that can be used to identify them. In a production application, these keys are likely to be some form of database primary key. The `ToDoItems` used in these example applications are not stored in a database, but we can still create a kind of unique key for the items. The first step is to extend the `ToDoItem` class yet again. Listing 4.6 shows the implementation of `ToDoItem4`, which extends from `ToDoItem3` and adds a unique immutable identifier, as an int, to each item.

Listing 4.6 ToDoItem4.java: data object for the ToDo4 page

```
package examples.todo4;

import examples.todo3.ToDoItem3;

public class ToDoItem4 extends ToDoItem3
{
  private static int _nextuid = 0;       <-1 Source of unique IDs

  private int _uid = _nextuid++;       <-2 Assigns unique ID
                                           when object created
  public ToDoItem4()
  {
    super();
  }

  public ToDoItem4(String title)
  {
    super(title);
  }

  public int getUid()
  {
    return _uid;
  }
}
```

1. A simple static variable is used to allocate unique IDs. In a real application, unique IDs would be provided by a database. This approach is acceptable only for this simple demonstration.
2. The unique ID is assigned as each instance is constructed.

Now that we have to-do items that can be identified using a unique ID, we can start updating the application to make use of the ListEdit component, starting with the page template.

Updating the page template

The template for the ToDo4 page is for the most part identical to the ToDo3 page, except for the one line concerned with the item loop:

```
<tr jwcid="listEdit" element="tr">
```

Because the ListEdit component has even more parameters than the Foreach component used in the previous examples, it makes sense to configure those parameters in the ToDo4 page specification:

```
<component id="listEdit" type="ListEdit">
  <binding name="source" expression="listEditMap.keys"/>
  <binding name="value" expression="listEditMap.key"/>
  <binding name="listener" expression="listeners.synchronizeItem"/>
</component>
```

Whereas the Foreach component in the previous to-do list examples read the `toDoList` property and directly updated the `item` property, here the ListEdit component reads and updates properties of the `ListEditMap` class. The `item` property still gets updated, but indirectly, by the `synchronizeItem()` listener method. The page is responsible for initializing the `listEditMap` property before the page renders. The `ListEditMap` is initialized with the values from the `toDoList` property (you'll see the details of this shortly) and acts as a buffer between the ListEdit component and the properties of the page.

In addition, the ToDo4 page may need to display an error message if a form submission cannot be processed; the HTML template includes a familiar pair of components for displaying the error message (if the message is non-null):

```
<span jwcid="@Conditional" condition="ognl:errorMessage">
<span style="{ font: bold; color: red }">
<span jwcid="@Insert" value="ognl:errorMessage">Error Message
</span>
<br/>
</span>
</span>
```

As in previous examples, this HTML template snippet checks to see if there is a non-null error message and, if so, displays it at the top of the page, before the form renders.

Specifying the page properties

The ToDo4 page uses the same set of specified properties as the ToDo3 page, with two additions: a `listEditMap` property (connected to the ListEdit component) and an `errorMessage` property (used to store an error message display when the form submission cannot be processed due to synchronization problems). All of these properties are defined in the ToDo4 page specification:

```
<property-specification name="toDoList"
  type="java.util.List" persistent="yes"/>
<property-specification name="item"
  type="examples.todo1.ToDoItem"/>
<property-specification name="moveUpItem"
  type="examples.todo1.ToDoItem"/>
<property-specification name="moveDownItem"
  type="examples.todo1.ToDoItem"/>
<property-specification name="listEditMap"
  type="org.apache.tapestry.form.ListEditMap"/>
<property-specification name="errorMessage"
  type="java.lang.String"/>
```

Now that we've specified the necessary properties, we need to make sure they are initialized and used properly.

Initializing the ListEditMap

Listing 4.7 contains the code for the `ToDo4` page class. It extends the `ToDo3` class, adding support for initialization and using the `ListEditMap` instance.

Listing 4.7 ToDo4.java: page class for the ToDo4 page

```
package examples.todo4;

import java.util.List;

import org.apache.tapestry.IRequestCycle;
import org.apache.tapestry.PageRedirectException;
import org.apache.tapestry.event.PageEvent;
import org.apache.tapestry.form.ListEditMap;

import examples.todo1.ToDoItem;
import examples.todo3.ToDo3;

public abstract class ToDo4 extends ToDo3
{
  public abstract void
    setErrorMessage(String message);
  public abstract void
    setListEditMap(ListEditMap listEditMap);
  public abstract ListEditMap getListEditMap();
  public abstract void setItem(ToDoItem item);

  protected ToDoItem createNewItem(String title)
  {
    return new ToDoItem4(title);
  }
```

Accessors for specified properties (annotation on the four accessor declarations)

Creates new items as instances of ToDoItem4 (annotation on `return new ToDoItem4(title);`)

```
  public void pageBeginRender(PageEvent event)          ❶ Invoked when page
  {                                                        renders or when
    super.pageBeginRender(event);                          form rewinds

    ListEditMap map = new ListEditMap();

    List items = getToDoList();                           Sets up
    int count = items.size();                             toDoList
                                                          property
    for (int i = 0; i < count; i++)
    {
      ToDoItem4 item = (ToDoItem4) items.get(i);
      int uid = item.getUid();

      map.add(new Integer(uid), item);              ❷ Adds item to the
    }                                                  ListEditMap

    setListEditMap(map);            Stores the map
  }                                 for later

  public void synchronizeItem(IRequestCycle cycle)
  {
    ListEditMap map = getListEditMap();

    ToDoItem item = (ToDoItem) map.getValue();

    if (item == null)
    {                                                              ❸
      setErrorMessage(                                             Is invoked
      ➥ "Your form submission is out of date. Please retry.");    by ListEdit
      throw new PageRedirectException(this);
    }

    setItem(item);
  }
}
```

❶ The `pageBeginRender()` method will be invoked when the page renders or when a form within the page rewinds. The super implementation must be invoked, because that ensures that the `toDoList` property is initialized.

❷ Each item is added to the `ListEditMap`, which remembers the order in which key/value pairs are added.

❸ The ListEdit component invokes this listener method after setting `ListEditMap`'s `key` property. The map's `getValue()` method returns the corresponding object, as previously stored inside `pageBeginRender()`. If the current key is not stored in the map, then null is returned—this can happen when a user submits a form after clicking the back button.

The `toDoList` property is the list of items, in the correct order (the order as manipulated by the user). `ListEditMap` remembers the order that items are added to it; its `getKeys()` method returns the keys in that order. It is safe to cast each item in the list to `ToDoItem4`, since the `createNewItem()` method has been overridden to instantiate this class.

Synchronizing the item

The second responsibility of the class is to synchronize the `item` property—the ListEdit component stores a list of to do item IDs in the form, and the page class must use these to set the `item` property to the correct instance of `ToDoItem4`. Nearly all the work for this is done by `ListEditMap` with a short listener method, `synchronizeItem()` (shown in listing 4.7), which gets the current item from the `ListEditMap` and assigns it to the page's `item` property. In addition, the `synchronizeItem()` method includes a check for a null item.

As we've described earlier, the ListEdit component will set the `key` property of the `ListEditMap` before invoking the listener method. Invoking `getValue()` on the `ListEditMap` returns the corresponding value object, as previously recorded into the map; this is an instance of `ToDoItem4`. The check for null covers race conditions between two users,[3] or one user using the browser's back button. Throwing a `PageRedirectException` aborts the form's rewind phase entirely and forces the page to render as is.

Chapter 10 describes some further functionality provided by the `ListEditMap` class—specifically, the ability to track values within the map that should be deleted. The ToDo application doesn't use this feature of `ListEditMap`, because it has its own approach for deleting completed items in the list.

The previous two sections described components, Hidden and ListEdit, that are critical to the infrastructure of an application but largely invisible to end users. Let's now return to components that users will see and interact with.

---

[3] A *race condition* is a category of software bug that is concerned with multiple users affecting the same data simultaneously. In a race condition, two (or more) users attempt the same operation at roughly the same time, and the first user to complete the operation affects the outcome of the other users. A common example of a race condition in a web application is when one user deletes an object stored in a database and another user attempts to update the same object. Whether the second user's update succeeds or fails depends on which user wins the race.

4.5 Handling file uploads

A common feature of many web applications is support for file uploads, the ability to transfer a file from the user's computer to the application server as part of a form submission. HTML includes another form control for this purpose, `<input type="file">`. When a web browser submits a request with a file upload, the normal encoding used to express the data (the Multipurpose Internet Mail Extensions [MIME] type `application/x-www-form-urlencoded`) is not used. Instead, a different encoding, `multipart/form-data`, is used for the upload.

This alternate encoding allows any number of file uploads, interspersed with normal query parameter values (from the other form controls), to be sent from the client to the server in one large binary stream. This difference in encoding should not be any more of an issue to a servlet application developer than the difference between the HTTP GET and PUT requests. Alas, the Servlet API does not include the ability to parse and interpret `multipart/form-data` content, which makes handling uploaded files an uphill battle.

Tapestry makes use of the Jakarta commons-fileupload library to seamlessly support forms that contain a mix of ordinary form elements and file uploads. When a form is submitted containing an uploaded file, Tapestry extracts the file content from the request and stores it in memory or in a temporary file (if the file content is large enough).

To the application, an uploaded file is represented by an instance of the interface `IUploadFile`. From this, an application can retrieve the following information:

- The name of the file (on the client)
- The complete path of the file (on the client)
- The MIME content type (as reported by the client)
- The content of the file, as a `java.io.InputStream`

The content of the file is deleted at the end of the request; so if the uploaded file is to be used later, it must be stored persistently either to the server's file system or in a database.

Tapestry's Upload component makes creating file upload fields as easy as creating ordinary text fields. Figure 4.8 shows a page that uses an Upload component.

It is just as easy to add an Upload component to a Tapestry Form as any other kind of component. The HTML for the Upload component from figure 4.8 is simply

```
<input type="file" jwcid="@Upload" file="ognl:file" size="100"/>
```

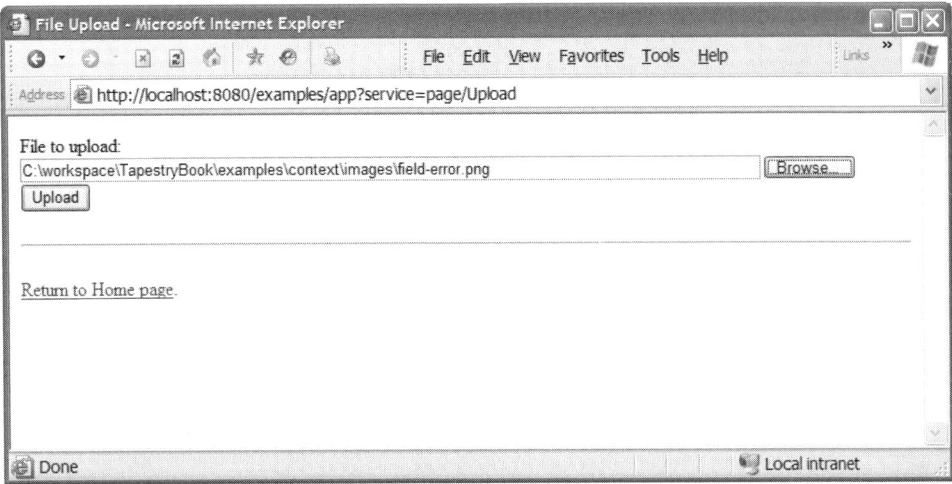

Figure 4.8 A page containing an Upload component. Clicking the Browse button will open a file selection dialog box.

Including an Upload component inside a Form *automatically* changes the encoding type of the enclosing Form to `multipart/form-data`. This is another example of the dynamic nature of Tapestry; you are not responsible for this background detail (selecting the form's encoding type)—the components automatically do the right thing.

Once the form is submitted and the file is uploaded, the file instance can be passed to another page in the same way as a simple value, such as a string or number. Inside the `Upload` page class, the listener method does just that:

```
public abstract IUploadFile getFile();

public void formSubmit(IRequestCycle cycle)
{
  IUploadFile file = getFile();

  if (file == null)
    return;

  UploadResults next =
    (UploadResults) cycle.getPage("UploadResults");
  next.setFile(file);
  cycle.activate(next);
}
```

The second page, UploadResults, displays the data available about the uploaded file, followed by a dump of the contents of the file (in hexadecimal

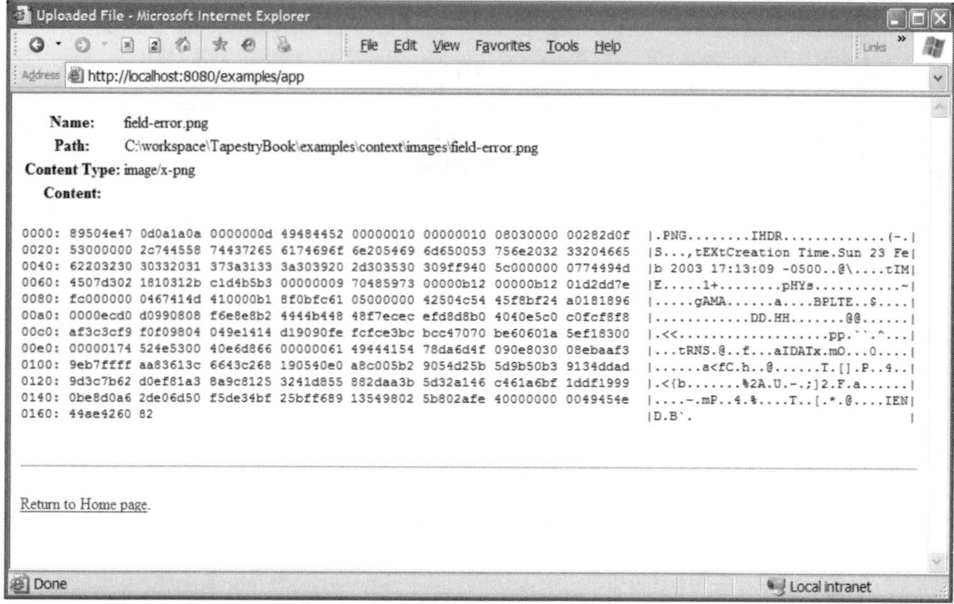

Figure 4.9 After the file is uploaded, the application displays the information available about the uploaded file.

and ASCII). Figure 4.9 shows an example of what the page looks like after uploading a small file.

Getting the output for the first three fields (name, path, and content type) is straightforward:

```
<table border="0">
<tr>
  <th>Name:</th>
  <td><span jwcid="@Insert" value="ognl:file.fileName">
    File Name</span></td>
</tr>

<tr>
  <th>Path:</th>
  <td><span jwcid="@Insert" value="ognl:file.filePath">
    File Path</span></td>
</tr>

<tr>
  <th>Content Type:</th>
  <td><span jwcid="@Insert" value="ognl:file.contentType">
    text/html</span></td>
</tr>
```

Getting the output for the binary content is a bit more involved. Tapestry doesn't have a built-in component for this kind of output, but it does include a utility class, `BinaryDumpOutputStream`. `BinaryDumpOutputStream` is a filter that takes as input a stream of bytes and produces as output the kind of text shown in figure 4.9. The trick is to get this object, which is not a component, integrated into the rendering of the page. Fortunately, as you've seen before, components aren't the only things that can render output in Tapestry. The `UploadResults` page class in listing 4.8 includes an inner class that can render the contents of an `IUploadFile`.

Listing 4.8 UploadResults.java: page class for the UploadResults page

```
package examples.upload;

import java.io.IOException;
import java.io.InputStream;
import java.io.OutputStream;
import java.io.StringWriter;

import org.apache.tapestry.ApplicationRuntimeException;
import org.apache.tapestry.IMarkupWriter;
import org.apache.tapestry.IRender;
import org.apache.tapestry.IRequestCycle;
import org.apache.tapestry.html.BasePage;
import org.apache.tapestry.request.IUploadFile;
import org.apache.tapestry.util.io.BinaryDumpOutputStream;

public abstract class UploadResults extends BasePage
{
  public abstract void setFile(IUploadFile file);
  public abstract IUploadFile getFile();

  private static class ContentRenderer           ❶ Renders binary
    implements IRender                              output
  {
    private IUploadFile _file;

    ContentRenderer(IUploadFile file)
    {
      _file = file;
    }

    public void render(IMarkupWriter writer,     ❷ Is defined by the
      IRequestCycle cycle)                          IRender interface
    {
      try
      {
        StringWriter buffer = new StringWriter();
```

```
            BinaryDumpOutputStream out =
              new BinaryDumpOutputStream(buffer);

            out.setBytesPerLine(32);
            out.setShowAscii(true);

            InputStream in = _file.getStream();       <-3 Gets content of
                                                          uploaded file
            copy(in, out);

            in.close();
            out.close();

            writer.print(buffer.getBuffer().toString());

          }
          catch (IOException ex)
          {
            throw new ApplicationRuntimeException(
              "Unable to generate binary output.", ex);
          }
        }

        private void copy(InputStream in, OutputStream out)
          throws IOException
        {
          byte[] buffer = new byte[1000];

          while (true)
          {
            int length = in.read(buffer);

            if (length < 0)
              return;

            out.write(buffer, 0, length);
          }
        }

      }

      public IRender getContentRenderer()
      {
        return new ContentRenderer(getFile());
      }
    }
```

❶ An inner class is defined to render the binary content of the file as a hexadecimal dump. The `IRender` interface is the common interface for any kind of object, component or not, that can be part of the page-rendering process.

❷ The `render()` method is the sole method defined by the `IRender` interface.

❸ The uploaded file is an instance of `IUploadFile`. The `getStream()` method provides a binary input stream of the uploaded content in the file.

To get this output, we make use of a Delegator component. Delegator delegates its rendering to another object, an object that implements the `IRender` interface. The rendering object is specified using the `delegate` parameter. The HTML template includes the Delegator component, which delegates to the `contentRenderer` property of the page:

```
<pre>
<span jwcid="@Delegator" delegate="ognl:contentRenderer"/>
</pre>
```

All that's left is to provide the `contentRenderer` property on the page:

```
public abstract IFile getFile();

public IRender getContentRenderer()
{
  return new ContentRenderer(getFile());
}
```

When the page renders, the Delegator component invokes the `render()` method on the `ContentRenderer` instance created by this method; `ContentRenderer` is responsible for reading the content of the uploaded file and outputting that content, formatted by the `BinaryDumpOutputStream` instance, into the response.

The FileUpload component shows how a Tapestry component can perform considerable server-side processing. The next component, DatePicker, shows the kind of client-side logic that can be provided by a component.

4.6 Creating pop-up date selections using DatePicker

Last but not least on our tour of advanced Tapestry form components is the DatePicker component. DatePicker allows users to enter dates using a sophisticated pop-up calendar window. The component generates client-side JavaScript that allows a pop-up window to be displayed when the user clicks an "activate" button to the right of the text field. Alternately, the user may type directly into the text field. Figure 4.10 shows a DatePicker component in action.

DatePicker allows the user to navigate easily to other months and years using the drop-down controls; it also allows the user to move forward or backward a month at a time using the two buttons in the upper-left and upper-right corners of the window. The current date may be selected by clicking the large button

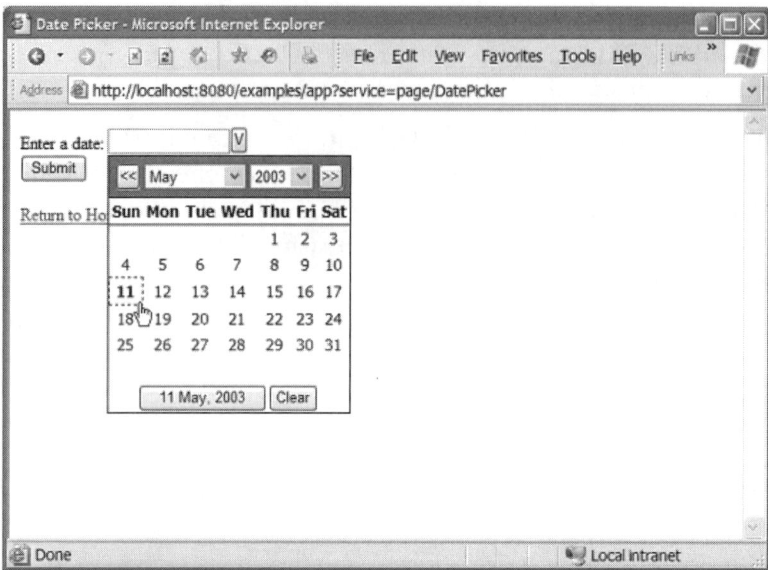

Figure 4.10 The DatePicker component uses client-side JavaScript to create a pop-up window for selecting dates.

along the bottom of the window, and clicking the Clear button closes the window with no date selected.

Using a DatePicker component is as easy as using any other Tapestry component (with one caveat, which we discuss in a moment), despite the fact that DatePicker has a considerable client-side presence. Listing 4.9 shows all that's necessary.

Listing 4.9 DatePicker.html: HTML template for DatePicker page

```
<html jwcid="@Shell" title="Date Picker">
<body jwcid="@Body">

<form jwcid="@Form" listener="ognl:listeners.formSubmit">

Enter a date: <input jwcid="@DatePicker"
                value="ognl:date"/>          DatePicker
                                             component

<br/>
<input type="submit" value="Submit"/>

</form>
```

```
<p><a href="#" jwcid="@PageLink" page="Home">
Return to Home page</a>.</p>

</body>
</html>
```

Most of this template should look familiar. The DatePicker component has a `value` parameter bound to the `date` property of the page, and the DatePicker component, being a form control component, is enclosed by a Form component. When the page is rendered, DatePicker outputs a text field and the trigger button (to the right of the text field) that displays the calendar pop-up window.

The one caveat is the use of a Body component for the `<body>` element of the template. The Body component organizes all the client-side JavaScript on the page into a single `<script>` block, just inside the `<body>` tag. Tapestry components, such as DatePicker, that use client-side JavaScript expect to be enclosed by a Body component. The Body component is also utilized to generate unique names for variables and JavaScript functions, which allows any number of DatePicker components to be used within a page. We'll discuss creating components with a client-side JavaScript aspect in more detail in chapter 8.

TIP If you fail to wrap a DatePicker component within a Body component, Tapestry will throw an exception: *DatePicker components must be contained by a Body component.* Using a Body component doesn't cost any measurable amount; you should just get in the habit of always using one.

WARNING Because of a bug in Microsoft Internet Explorer, drop-down lists will always render on top of the DatePicker pop-up; this is because the z-order of drop-down lists is fixed at the highest possible value. When creating the layout for a page using the DatePicker component, you must take this into consideration and ensure that the DatePicker component's pop-up window will display in an area free of drop-down lists.

Again, the simplicity of Tapestry is apparent here, since the DatePicker component is as easy to use, if not easier, than a TextField component. It's the same pattern: pick a component, place it in the HTML template, and configure its parameters. The fact that this component is internally complex is of no concern to the page using the component or to you as the developer when constructing the page.

4.7 Summary

Tapestry's more advanced form-related components are all built around usability: both for you, the developer, and your end users. Tapestry components not only encapsulate presentation issues, but also handle the conversions between domain properties and the string values used within HTML. The framework's component-based approach to form handling makes it possible to build forms with a much higher level of complexity without getting bogged down in the mundane details of string conversions and field naming. Once again, Tapestry lets you get more work done, better and more quickly—which leaves you more time to concentrate on the specifics of your application.

The next step is to integrate these basic form-handling concepts into an overall approach to validating user input. As you'll learn in the next chapter, Tapestry has a complete subsystem for just this purpose.

5
Form input validation

This chapter covers

- Knowing the requirements of a usable, validating interface
- Using validators and validation delegates
- Using FieldLabel and ValidField components
- Adapting output for your application's look and feel
- Performing form-level validations

Processing forms is more than creating drop-down lists and text fields; the forms are just part of an overall cycle of user input and server validation. Users will make mistakes when entering data into forms. They'll leave a required field blank, enter letters into fields clearly marked for numeric input, ignore any kind of range requirement, and type whatever they want. It isn't enough just to reject invalid input from the user as an exception case; users can be expected to find creative ways to enter invalid input on even the simplest forms. Your responsibility is to handle invalid input consistently and gracefully—that is, to create a *usable* application. Fail to take your users' needs and expectations into account by creating a slipshod, unfriendly application and you run the risk of frustrating them—and driving them away from your site. Users have some basic expectations when it comes to input validation:

- Fields with invalid data will be marked as such; whether this is with color, icons, or some other approach, it should be possible to identify fields with problems at a glance. An unfriendly application will just display an error message and expect the user to deduce the invalid field.
- Invalid input should be maintained so that it can be corrected. For example, if a user types only 15 digits of a credit card number, you should give the user a chance to enter just the 16th digit. An unfriendly application forces the user to retype the entire number from scratch.
- All errors should be visible at once, to allow the user to correct all the errors without additional server requests. An unfriendly application can recognize only one error at a time, forcing the user to submit the form multiple times.
- Client-side validations are preferable to server-side validations.

Tapestry includes an entire subsystem for validating user input, centered on its ValidField component. The subsystem allows you to easily build highly usable forms that provide useful feedback and client-side validation. We'll begin by demonstrating how to use validation for a simple user registration form, and later, we'll show you how to mix and match the validation subsystem with the DatePicker component from chapter 4.

5.1 Validating user input

The ValidField component is a variation of the TextField component described in chapter 3. For the most part, a ValidField component is used in exactly the same way as a TextField component—with some additional parameters. ValidField components are capable of editing not just string properties, but dates and numbers as well, and can be adapted to any data type with a reasonable text representation. The validations that can be used with ValidField components can apply both client-side and server-side checks on input. These checks ensure that the user provides values for required fields, or force user input to be within a specified range. In many cases, the validations are tied in with conversions, such as converting input from a string to a date or to some type of number.

An example of ValidField components in use appears in figure 5.1, which shows a page that accepts a user's name and address—the kind of page you'll see in many online applications. Initially, all the fields are blank, and the cursor is

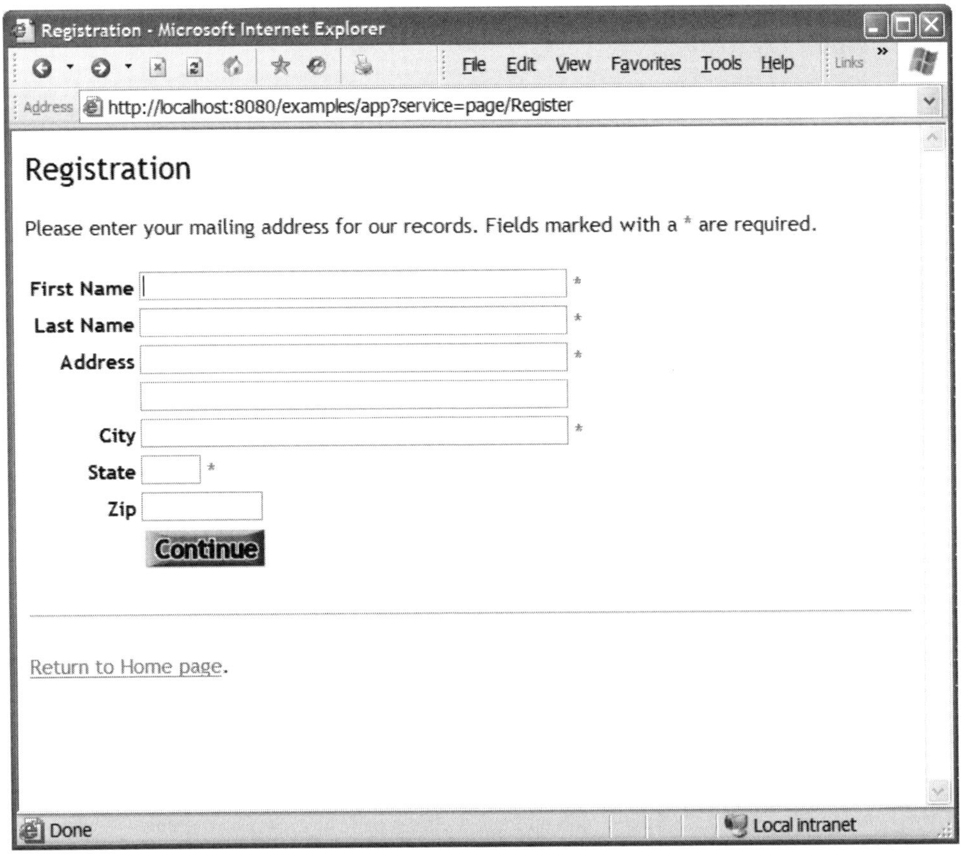

Figure 5.1 The Register page in its initial state. Each required field is marked with an asterisk, and the cursor is placed into the first required field.

automatically placed into the first required field (using a snippet of client-side JavaScript, automatically generated by the ValidField component).

If you enter values into some fields but not others and submit the form (this form does not have client-side validation enabled), you'll see a different screen (figure 5.2). The page is redisplayed so that you may make corrections. Details about the first field error appear at the top; each field that is in error is so marked in several ways: the label for the field, and the field itself, both change color, and an error marker is added to each field.[1]

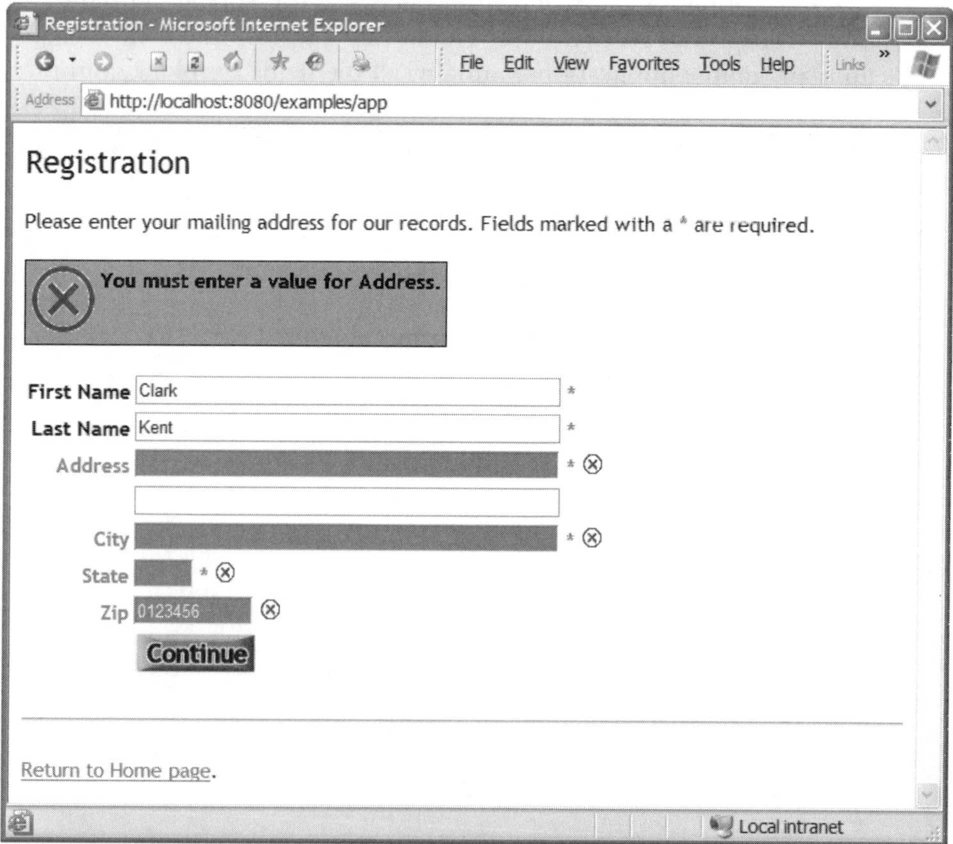

Figure 5.2 The same form partially filled out and submitted. The first error on the page is displayed prominently. All fields with errors are highlighted in three ways: the field label text is red, the field itself gets a red background, and an icon is displayed to the right of the field.

[1] As you'll see, you can easily customize the look and feel for validation to fit seamlessly into your application.

So, how does this all work? It's more than what a single component in isolation can accomplish; a component can normally affect only a small portion of the overall page, but figure 5.2 reflects changes to the output HTML scattered throughout the entire rendered page. Making this work requires one additional component (FieldLabel) and two additional objects (a validator that parses and validates the user input, and the validation delegate, which tracks fields and errors), with some subtle interactions between all four.

The next few sections give a quick overview of the various parts of the validation subsystem.

5.1.1 Using FieldLabels in conjunction with ValidFields

A FieldLabel is a companion component to a ValidField. Each FieldLabel is connected to ValidField via the FieldLabel's `field` parameter. The FieldLabel can adjust its visual look to reflect the field. If the field is in error (because of invalid user input), the FieldLabel can display itself differently. Figure 5.2 shows this; the labels on several fields have been marked red to indicate that the fields are in error.

In addition, the FieldLabel obtains the user-presentable name of the field to display from the field itself (ValidField has a `displayName` parameter used for this purpose). This ensures that the field label matches the name of the field used in any error messages, even when the name of the field is localized into the user's language, or when the field name is determined dynamically.

FieldLabels and ValidFields are largely responsible for presenting the interface to the user; the heart of input validation is provided in specialized validator objects.

5.1.2 Using validators

Validators are objects that are responsible for translating user input from strings into object types (such as numbers or dates) and performing other validation checks. Validators are not components themselves; they are objects that implement the `IValidator` interface. Validators are *used* by ValidField components, which delegate all the conversions and checks to the validator. A validator object has four responsibilities:

- Converting an object value (from a domain object property) to a string that can be used when rendering the page. The converted value is used as the `value` attribute of the `<input>` element rendered by the ValidField component.
- Converting a string value submitted with the form back into an object value so that it can be used to update a domain object property.

- Performing additional validations on the input. These validations are controlled by properties of the validator instance, which you must configure. For example, you may set the `maximum` property of a `NumberValidator` to enforce a maximum allowable value.
- Writing any client-side JavaScript needed to perform client-side validations.

Each ValidField component has a `validator` parameter, which is bound to the validator object for that field. Validator objects are meant to be shared; they don't store any information about a particular ValidField. Many ValidFields can share the same validator instance.

All validators include a `required` property of type boolean. When the `required` property is set to true, a validator will not allow an input field to be blank or to consist only of whitespace.

Tapestry provides a number of implementations of the `IValidator` interface that can be used and configured off the shelf. `StringValidator` is used for editing string properties of pages or domain objects and can apply an additional validation: a minimum number of characters that you want the field to accept.

`NumberValidator` is used for editing numeric properties of all types (`int`, `long`, `BigDecimal`, and so on). `NumberValidator` can enforce a minimum or a maximum value, or both. `DateValidator` is used for editing `Date` properties. As with `NumberValidator`, you can set a minimum or a maximum value. Later in this section, you'll see how to create a custom validator, one that enforces the format of a postal zip code (which can be seen in action in figure 5.3).

The final piece of the validation puzzle is the *validation delegate:* an object that is used to track which fields are in error within a form, and what error(s) are associated with each field.

5.1.3 Using validation delegates

The validation delegate has two distinct functions. First, it tracks the error state of each ValidField enclosed by a form. When the form is submitted, each ValidField passes the string provided by the user to the validator object for that field. The validator object may convert the string to an object type, such as `Long` or `Double`, or leave it as a string. It will also apply any validations, such as checking that the converted value fits into a specified range. If the converted value fails a validation, the validator reports the error back to the ValidField. The conversions and validations a validator can perform are flexible, and, as you'll see, it is easy to create new validators to handle new types of conversions and validations.

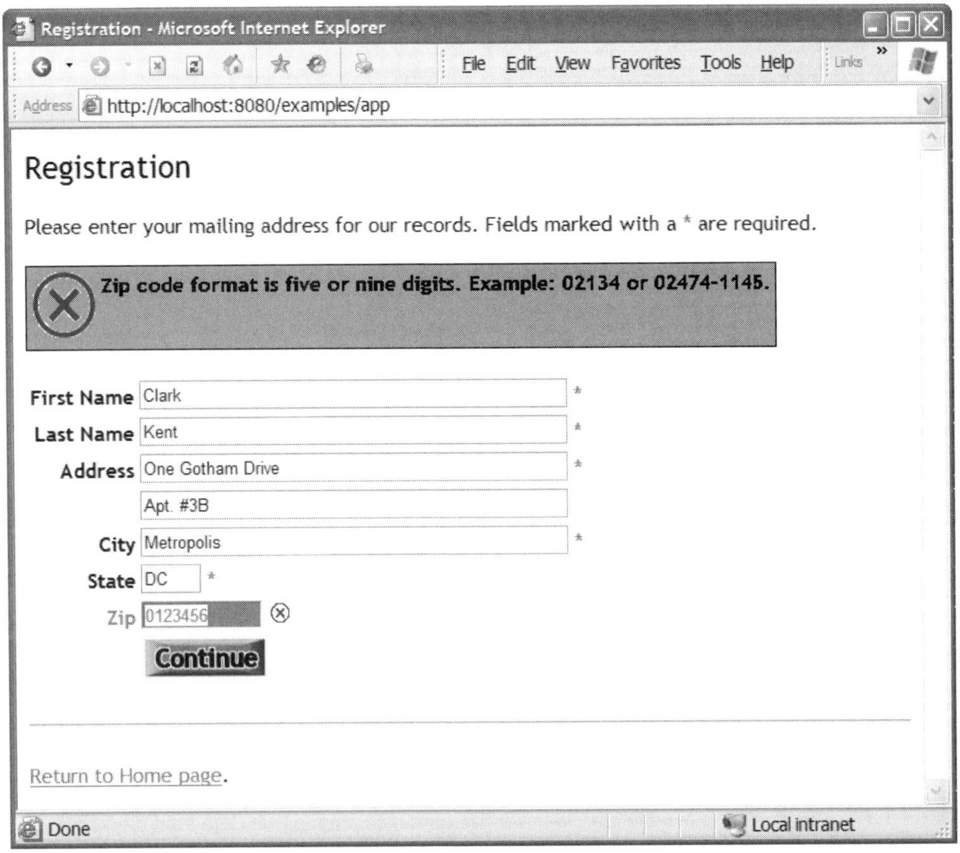

Figure 5.3 A custom validator attached to the Zip field knows the correct format for zip codes and can generate a custom error message.

Validators report these errors by throwing a `ValidationException`. The ValidField catches the exception and uses the validation delegate to record the ValidField's element ID, the exception message, and the invalid input provided by the user. The recorded exception message is the indicator that the field is in error, and will be used when the page containing the form is rendered.

Validation delegates have a second, discrete function. The delegate is responsible for *decorating* the fields and labels that are in error. The validation delegate has opportunities to render additional HTML before and after the FieldLabel renders, and before and after the ValidField renders, and can even write additional attributes into the `<input>` element rendered by the ValidField itself. The exact sequence for the FieldLabel component is shown in figure 5.4.

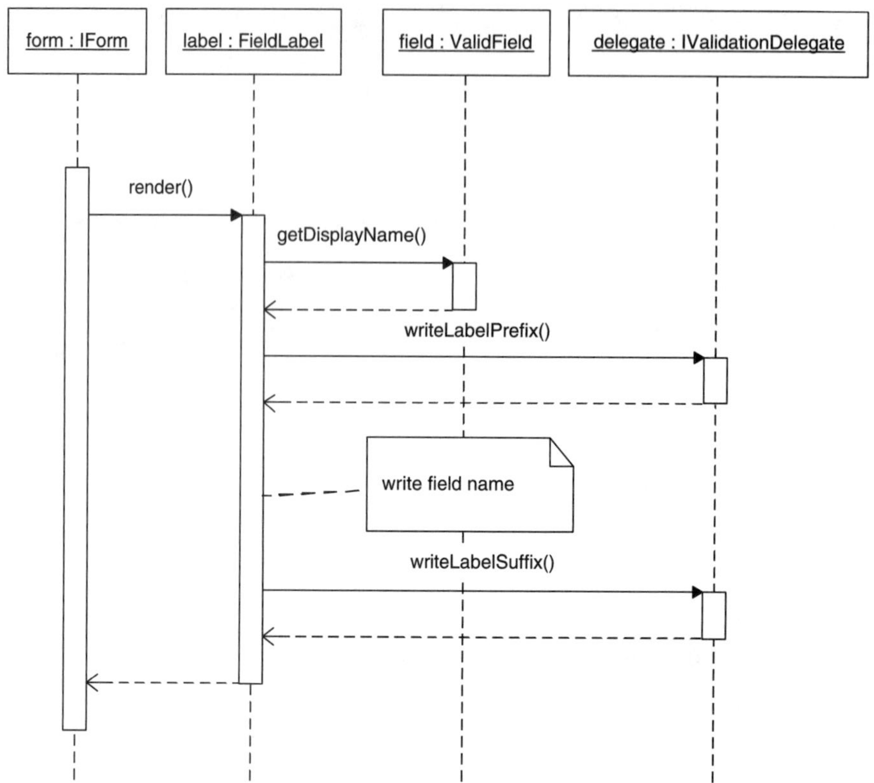

Figure 5.4 The field label gets the user-presentable name for the field from the ValidField component. It allows the delegate to render before and after it renders the field name, so that the delegate can decorate the label if the corresponding field is in error.

This additional rendering is how the labels for invalid fields, shown in figure 5.2, manage to be displayed in red. The validation delegate has a chance to wrap the FieldLabel's output in a `<span>` element, and the span references a Cascading Style Sheet (CSS) class that results in the label being displayed in red. The methods `writeLabelPrefix()` and `writeLabelSuffix()` allow the validation delegate to decorate the label by writing extra HTML around it. Likewise, both the validator and the validation delegate are integrated into the render of the ValidField, as shown in figure 5.5.

The validator's `renderValidatorContribution()` method is primarily used by the validator to write client-side JavaScript (which will perform client-side validations). The validation delegate methods (primarily, the `writeAttributes()`

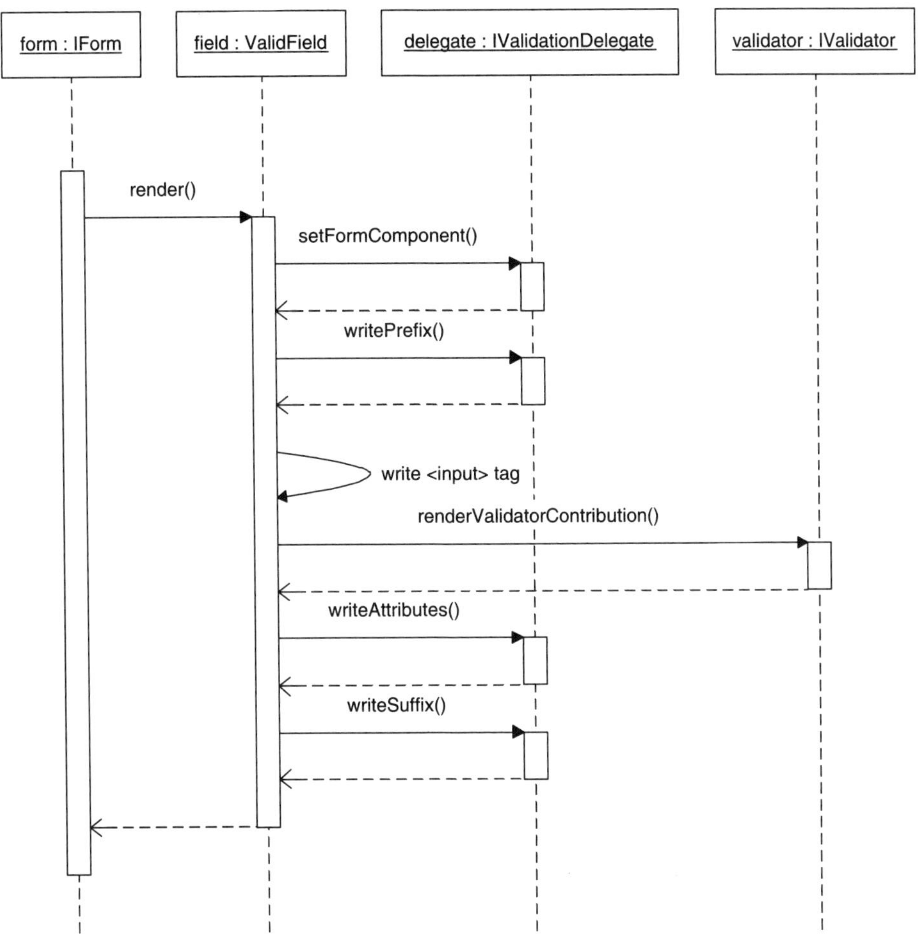

Figure 5.5 The delegate and the validator are both hooked into the rendering of the ValidField. The validator may use its hook to create client-side validation JavaScript. The delegate uses its hooks to decorate fields that are in error.

method) are used to decorate the `<input>` element (rendered by the ValidField) if the field is in error.

The primary purpose of creating a custom subclass of `ValidationDelegate` is to override these rendering methods so that an application-specific look and feel for decorating fields and labels can be created. In the examples in this chapter, we've done just that to mark the fields and labels in red, and to add an error icon after invalid fields.

The validator objects and the validation delegate object are needed by the Form and ValidField components. They are connected to the components using the components' parameters (the `delegate` parameter of the Form component, and the `validator` parameter of the ValidField component). These objects don't appear out of thin air; they must be instantiated and configured. This can be done in Java code (within your page class) or by using another feature of the page specification: helper beans.

5.1.4 Using helper beans

As we've been discussing, handling validation is about more than pages and components. It involves the participation of at least two other objects: the validator attached to each ValidField, and the validation delegate that tracks field input errors throughout a form.

Both of these objects are JavaBeans—but where and when do they get instantiated?

One possibility is to make instantiation the responsibility of the page. The page class could include fields and accessor methods, such as

```
private IValidator _required;

public IValidator getRequired()
{
  if (_required == null)
  {
    _required = new StringValidator();
    _required.setRequired(true);
  }

  return _required;
}
```

However, that kind of mechanical coding goes against the grain of Tapestry. Getting these *helper beans* instantiated and configured falls into the general "plumbing" category—the category of things that should be shifted into the framework. As you've seen before, when Tapestry provides an alternative to coding, it involves the page (or component) specification. In this case, we want to be able to control which Java class is instantiated and how it is configured. This is accomplished in the page specification using the `<bean>` element:

```
<bean name="required"
  class="org.apache.tapestry.valid.StringValidator"
  lifecycle="page">
  <set-property name="required" expression="true"/>
</bean>
```

The <bean> element shown here is equivalent to the Java code snippet. The <bean> element specifies three things:

- The Java class you want to instantiate
- The configuration of any properties of the helper bean
- The lifecycle of the bean

A helper bean may be accessed through the beans property of the page or component, using its name. For example, the OGNL expression beans.required would access the bean specified here. Helper beans are created only as needed, the first time the bean is referenced.

By default, the lifecycle of a bean is request, meaning that the bean will be released to the garbage collector at the end of the current request cycle. This is often appropriate, especially if the bean contains any state particular to the current user—such information should last only as long as the current request so that it won't be visible in a subsequent request from a different user. By using the page lifecycle, the bean is kept for as long as the page instance exists; this is appropriate for beans such as a validator that have no internal state. As you'll see in the following examples, a common use for helper beans is to define validators and validation delegates.

So far, you've seen an overview of how the various aspects of the validation subsystem (the components, the validators, and the validation delegate) operate. Next let's return to the Register page (shown in figure 5.1) and start seeing how these bits and pieces fit together to form a working, validated form.

5.2 Building the Register page

The ultimate aim of the Register page is to collect a user's name and address and store it in an Address (shown in listing 5.1).

Listing 5.1 Address.java: data object used with the Register page

```
package examples.register;

import java.io.Serializable;

public class Address implements Serializable
{
  private String _firstName;
  private String _lastName;
  private String _address1;
  private String _address2;
```

```
private String _city;
private String _state;
private String _zip;

public String getAddress1()
{
  return _address1;
}

public String getAddress2()
{
  return _address2;
}

public String getCity()
{
  return _city;
}

public String getFirstName()
{
  return _firstName;
}

public String getLastName()
{
  return _lastName;
}

public String getState()
{
  return _state;
}

public String getZip()
{
  return _zip;
}

public void setAddress1(String address1)
{
  _address1 = address1;
}

public void setAddress2(String address2)
{
  _address2 = address2;
}

public void setCity(String city)
{
```

```
      _city = city;
    }

    public void setFirstName(String firstName)
    {
      _firstName = firstName;
    }

    public void setLastName(String lastName)
    {
      _lastName = lastName;
    }

    public void setState(String state)
    {
      _state = state;
    }

    public void setZip(String zip)
    {
      _zip = zip;
    }

  }
```

Armed with this definition of what goes into an address, we can create a user interface to let users enter an address.

5.2.1 *Creating the Register HTML template*

The HTML template for the Register page is shown in listing 5.2. This template introduces a number of new concepts, so we'll take it apart one small piece at a time:

- Using the `delegate` parameter of the Form component
- Using the page's `components` property to reference other components within the page's template
- Using the FieldLabel component in conjunction with the ValidField component

Listing 5.2 Register.html: HTML template for the Register page

```
<html jwcid="@Shell" title="Registration"
  stylesheet="ognl:assets.stylesheet">
<head jwcid="$remove$">
<link rel="stylesheet" type="text/css"
  href="css/style.css"/>
</head>
<body jwcid="@Body">
```

❶ **Elements marked for removal**

```
<span class="title">Registration</span>

<p>Please enter your mailing address for our records.
Fields marked with a
<span class="required-marker">*</span>
are required.
</p>

<span jwcid="@Conditional"
  condition="ognl:beans.delegate.hasErrors">

<table class="error">
<tr valign="top">
<td>
<img height="52" alt="[Error]" src="images/form-error.png"
  width="52">
</td>
<td>
<span jwcid="@Delegator"
  delegate="ognl:beans.delegate.firstError">
  Error Message
</span>
</td>
</tr>
</table>

</span>

<form jwcid="@Form"
  listener="ognl:listeners.formSubmit"
  delegate="ognl:beans.delegate">          <-- 2 Validation delegate for the Form

<table class="form">

<tr>
<th><span jwcid="@FieldLabel"                  <-- 3 Labels connected to ValidFields
        field="ognl:components.inputFirstName">First Name
    </span></th>
<td><input type="text" jwcid="inputFirstName" size="50"/></td>   <-- 4 ValidField as a declared component
</tr>

<tr>
<th><span jwcid="@FieldLabel"
        field="ognl:components.inputLastName">Last Name
    </span></th>
<td><input type="text" jwcid="inputLastName" size="50"/></td>
</tr>

<tr>
<th><span jwcid="@FieldLabel"
     field="ognl:components.inputAddress1">Address
```

```
    </span></th>
<td><input type="text" jwcid="inputAddress1" size="50"/></td>
</tr>

<tr>
<td></td>
<td><input type="text" jwcid="@TextField"
              value="ognl:address.address2" size="50"/></td>
</tr>

<tr>
<th><span jwcid="@FieldLabel"
          field="ognl:components.inputCity">City
    </span></th>
<td><input type="text" jwcid="inputCity" size="50"/></td>
</tr>
<tr>
<th><span jwcid="@FieldLabel"
          field="ognl:components.inputState">State
    </span></th>
<td><input type="text" jwcid="inputState" size="2"/></td>
</tr>

<tr>
<th><span jwcid="@FieldLabel"
          field="ognl:components.inputZip">Zip
    </span></th>
<td><input type="text" jwcid="inputZip" size="10"/>
</tr>

<tr>
<td></td>
<td><input type="image" src="images/continue.png"
          width="100" height="32"/>
</tr>

</table>

</form>

<hr/>

<p><a href="#" jwcid="@PageLink" page="Home">
  Return to Home page</a>.</p>

</body>
</html>
```

❶ This special ID means that the element will be removed from the template. The Shell component will provide all of this, and more, in the running application. This reference to the stylesheet is useful just for WYSIWYG preview.

❷ When using validation, the Form component's `delegate` parameter is used to identify the validation delegate shared by all ValidField components enclosed by the Form.

❸ Each FieldLabel component is connected to the corresponding ValidField.

❹ Because ValidField components have even more parameters than a TextField component, it is usually best to put all that information in the page specification instead.

As is often the case with Tapestry, the HTML template is just the starting point for understanding how the page will behave when the application is running. The following sections fill in the missing details.

Defining a stylesheet for the page

The Register page makes heavy use of CSS; that's how fields and labels are highlighted in red when they are in error. To support this, the rendered page must include that stylesheet. You include stylesheets by using a `<link>` element within the `<head>` element (within the `<html>` element). Because the Shell component is writing the `<html>` and `<head>` elements, that component must write the link to the stylesheet. This is accomplished by binding its `stylesheet` parameter to an asset. A declaration for that asset will appear in the Register page's specification:

```
<html jwcid="@Shell" title="Registration"
  stylesheet="ognl:assets.stylesheet">
```

Removing portions of the template

Now comes a conundrum. We still would like the Register page to preview properly while editing, but if the template includes the `<head>` and `<link>` elements needed to include the stylesheet, then the final rendered page will include two sets of `<head>` and `<link>` elements: one from the template, and one dynamically rendered by the Shell component.

Tapestry includes a little trick to sidestep this issue:

```
<head jwcid="$remove$">
<link rel="stylesheet" type="text/css" href="css/style.css"/>
</head>
```

That special component ID, `"$remove$"`, is the key. It isn't normally a valid ID (because it contains a dollar sign). However, Tapestry allows it as a special case but doesn't define a new component. Instead, this special ID cues Tapestry to remove the element and everything enclosed by the element, as if it were never in the template in the first place. With this in place, the page previews correctly when editing, as demonstrated in figure 5.6.

The Shell component will produce the `<html>` and `<head>` element of the rendered page. To support JavaScript within the page, we must use a Body component to render the `<body>` element.

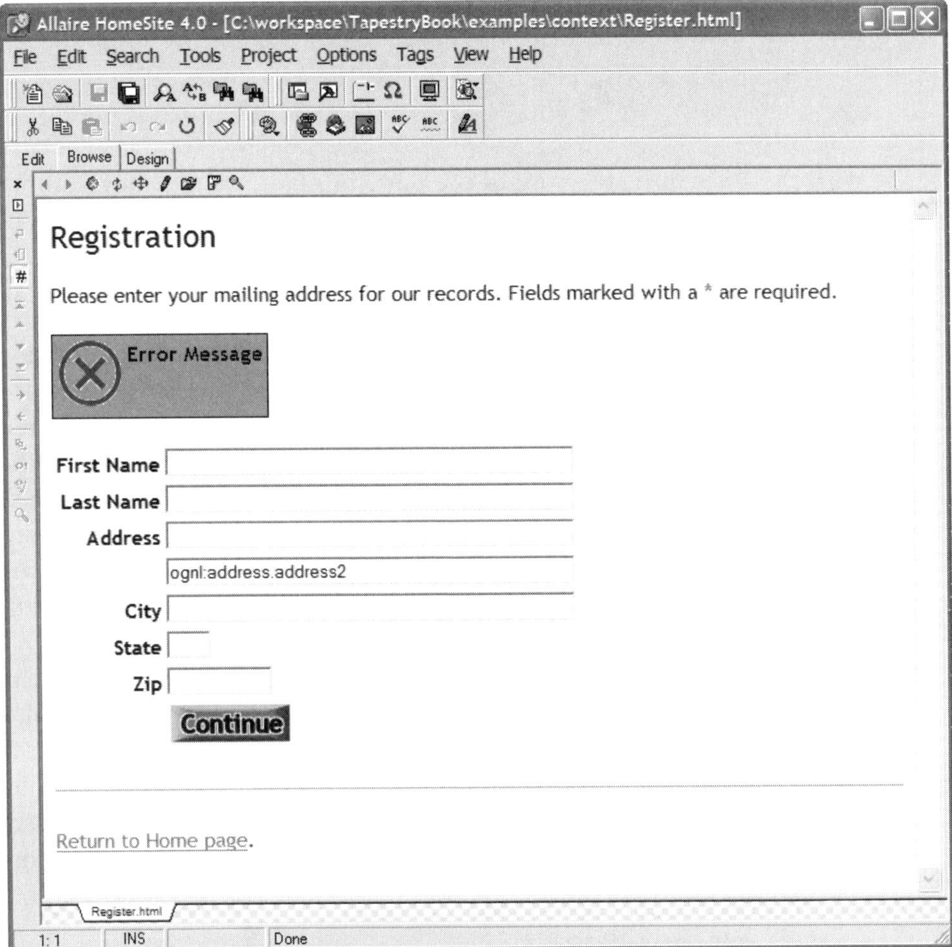

Figure 5.6 The Register page still previews properly in a WYSIWYG HTML editor.

Using a Body component

The ValidField component will almost always produce some client-side JavaScript. At the very least, initialization JavaScript is included that moves the cursor to the first field that is either required (but empty) or in error. As we discussed in chapter 4, a Body component is necessary to organize the production of client-side JavaScript. The templates for all examples in this chapter make use of a Body component:

```
<body jwcid="@Body">
. . .
</body>
```

With the basic infrastructure of the page in place, we can move on to the first dynamic section of the page: the area where any validation error messages are displayed.

Displaying validation errors

The next section of the template is concerned with displaying validation errors. The validation delegate for the page is obtained and checked to see if it contains any errors. The delegate's `hasErrors` property will always be false when a page is initially rendered. The `hasErrors` property may be set to true during the Form's rewind, when a form submission takes place. As you'll see, the Form's listener method will also query the delegate's `hasErrors` property. If the property is false, it is safe to take the validated input and move forward to the next step in the process. If `hasErrors` is true, the Register page is redisplayed to reveal the errors and decorate any fields that are in error.

Although it is possible to display all error messages for all fields that are in error, such output will be unwieldy on large forms and not very useful. Instead, the error message for the first field that is in error is displayed, but all fields throughout the form that are in error are marked. You've seen examples of this in figure 5.2, where the message refers to only the first field in error, even though several fields are marked. The HTML template makes use of Conditional and Delegator components to produce the formatted error message:

```
<span jwcid="@Conditional"
  condition="ognl:beans.delegate.hasErrors">

<table class="error">
<tr valign="top">
<td>
<img height="52" alt="[Error]" src="images/form-error.png"
  width="52"/>
```

```
</td>
<td>
<span jwcid="@Delegator"
  delegate="ognl:beans.delegate.firstError">
  Error Message
</span>
</td>
</tr>
</table>

</span>
```

In this example, the validation delegate is obtained using the OGNL expression `beans.delegate`, a reference to the delegate helper bean (which itself is declared in the page specification). The Conditional component queries the delegate's `hasErrors` property and displays the error message (formatted inside a `<table>`) only if the property is true.

The error objects that the validation delegate returns (such as the `firstError` property) are not simply strings but objects that implement the `IRender` interface. Because these are objects and not strings, we can't use an Insert component to display them. Instead, we use a Delegator component, which invokes the `render()` method on the renderable object provided to it.

The fact that these are renderable objects, rather than simple strings, opens up a whole realm of possibilities. The error objects can render all sorts of HTML, not just text: images, JavaScript pop-up windows, links, formatting—anything HTML. The intent is that customized validators for the application can provide customized error objects that are more than just a wrapper around a string. Implementations that make use of these possibilities are very application specific, which is why the validator classes provided with the framework don't use this feature.

The validation delegate, as a convenience, includes a `firstError` property that is the renderable object for the first field error. The `firstError` property is passed to the Delegator, which results in the error message being displayed.

Following the error message output is the form containing the FieldLabel and ValidField components.

Starting the Form component

The Form component is used as in examples from the previous two chapters, with one difference. An additional parameter, `delegate`, is specified to link the Form to the validation delegate. Every FieldLabel and ValidField component enclosed by the Form must use the same validation delegate—and they all will, since they all will retrieve the validation delegate through the Form:

```
<form jwcid="@Form"
  listener="ognl:listeners.formSubmit"
  delegate="ognl:beans.delegate">
```

Again, the OGNL expression `beans.delegate` resolves to a validation delegate. All the components enclosed by the Form will share this one validation delegate instance.

Using the FieldLabel component

Each ValidField will be preceded in the HTML template by a FieldLabel. The FieldLabel is connected to its partner ValidField by the FieldLabel's `field` parameter:

```
<span jwcid="@FieldLabel"
      field="ognl:components.inputFirstName">First Name
</span>
```

The OGNL expression `components.inputFirstName` is a reference to the inputFirstName component of the page. Every page provides a read-only `Map` of all the components it contains. The keys of this `Map` are the component IDs. Using OGNL, you can access the values in a `Map` just as easily as the properties of an ordinary JavaBean. Of course, to build a reference, you must know the ID of the component, which is one reason the ValidField components are given explicit IDs.

During the render, the FieldLabel discards its body (the text *First Name*) and gets, from the ValidField, the correct field name to display as a label. This may seem cumbersome, but it is useful for two reasons. First, it ensures that the label in the output HTML matches the name for the field used in any error messages generated by the ValidField's validator. Second, if the ValidField localizes the name, the FieldLabel will still match, using the locale-specific value.[2] In addition, the validation delegate will have a chance to render before and after the FieldLabel; this allows the delegate to decorate the label when the field is in error.

Using the ValidField component

In this example, each ValidField is constructed as a declared component, not an implicit component. Each ValidField appears in the HTML template, but its type and most of its parameters are declared in the page's specification. The ValidField components may not be anonymous—they must have real IDs. This is necessary so that the placeholder in the template can be linked to the entry in the page specification, but also so that the FieldLabel can be connected to the ValidField.

---

[2] Localization of Tapestry applications is discussed in chapter 7.

Each ValidField appears in the template minimally, because the bulk of the component's configuration is in the page specification:

```
<input type="text" jwcid="inputLastName" size="50"/>
```

The FieldLabel and ValidField components blend into the HTML template like any other type of Tapestry component. They are just a bit more sophisticated in terms of how they render their HTML (to allow the validators and validation delegate to decorate them) and in how they are configured. When you use Tapestry form validation, the interesting part takes place inside the page specification.

5.2.2 Creating the Register page specification

The page specification for the Register page (listing 5.3) has two main sections (beyond the elements you've seen before, such as defining the page class and declaring assets). The first section defines additional helper beans used with this page, including the validation delegate and the validators used by the ValidField components. The second section defines each of the ValidField components.

Listing 5.3 Register.page: specification for the Register page

```
<?xml version="1.0"?>
<!DOCTYPE page-specification PUBLIC
  "-//Apache Software Foundation//Tapestry Specification 3.0//EN"
  "http://jakarta.apache.org/tapestry/dtd/Tapestry_3_0.dtd">

<page-specification class="examples.register.Register">

  <bean name="delegate"
     class="examples.register.RegisterDelegate"/>        ❶ Declares validation delegate

  <bean name="required"
    class="org.apache.tapestry.valid.StringValidator"
    lifecycle="page">                                   ❷ Declares shared validator
    <set-property name="required" expression="true"/>
  </bean>

  <bean name="stateValidator"
    class="org.apache.tapestry.valid.StringValidator"
    lifecycle="page">
    <set-property name="required" expression="true"/>
    <set-property name="minimumLength" expression="2"/>
  </bean>

  <bean name="zipValidator"
    class="examples.register.PatternValidator"
    lifecycle="page">
    <set-property name="pattern">
      "\\d{5}(-\\d{4})?"
```

```
      </set-property>
      <set-property name="errorMessage">
      "Zip code format is five or nine digits.
       Example: 02134 or 02474-1145."
      </set-property>
    </bean>

    <property-specification name="address"
      type="examples.register.Address"/>

    <component id="inputFirstName" type="ValidField">
      <static-binding name="displayName"
        value="First Name"/>
      <binding name="validator"
        expression="beans.required"/>
      <binding name="value"
        expression="address.firstName"/>
    </component>

    <component id="inputLastName" type="ValidField">
      <static-binding name="displayName" value="Last Name"/>
      <binding name="validator" expression="beans.required"/>
      <binding name="value" expression="address.lastName"/>
    </component>

    <component id="inputAddress1" type="ValidField">
      <static-binding name="displayName" value="Address"/>
      <binding name="validator" expression="beans.required"/>
      <binding name="value" expression="address.address1"/>
    </component>

    <component id="inputCity" type="ValidField">
      <static-binding name="displayName" value="City"/>
      <binding name="validator" expression="beans.required"/>
      <binding name="value" expression="address.city"/>
    </component>

    <component id="inputState" type="ValidField">
      <static-binding name="displayName" value="State"/>
      <binding name="validator" expression="beans.stateValidator"/>
      <binding name="value" expression="address.state"/>
    </component>

    <component id="inputZip" type="ValidField">
      <static-binding name="displayName" value="Zip"/>
      <binding name="validator" expression="beans.zipValidator"/>
      <binding name="value" expression="address.zip"/>
    </component>

    <context-asset name="stylesheet" path="css/style.css"/>

  </page-specification>
```

3 Declares ValidField component

❶ The validation delegate is defined here, using a custom subclass, `examples.register.RegisterDelegate`. It can be referenced using the OGNL expression `beans.delegate`. The default lifecycle, "request", means that the bean will be discarded at the end of the current request.

❷ Most of the fields share a single instance of `StringValidator` as the `required` bean. Since validators don't store any internal state, the "page" lifecycle means that the bean, once created, will be kept for as long as the page instance itself.[3]

❸ Each ValidField follows this same pattern, providing a `displayName` (used by the FieldLabel and in any error messages), a `validator` (which may be shared between different fields), and a `value` to edit.

This specification includes yet another new element, `<static-binding>`. The `<static-binding>` element is used to set a component property to a fixed, literal string. Such a string is static (unchanging), in contrast to the dynamically evaluated OGNL expression used in a `<binding>` element. The `<static-binding>` element is used throughout the specification to provide the `displayName` parameter for each ValidField.

As an alternative, the value could appear in the HTML template:

```
<input type="text" jwcid="inputFirstName" size="50"
  displayName="First Name"/>
```

Either way, the `displayName` parameter will be set to a static string value. Tapestry is completely flexible as to where parameters are bound (in the specification or in the HTML template).

> **TIP** A good standard is to define formal parameters only in the page specification and informal parameters only in the HTML template. This scheme reflects that formal parameters are most often behavioral and informal parameters are more often related to presentation. Using this division keeps you from wasting time tracking down the right file when a change is needed.

This specification declares several helper beans and a number of ValidField components. The first bean defined is the validation delegate.

Defining the validation delegate and validators

The `RegisterDelegate` class is an implementation of the `IValidationDelegate` interface that customizes the rendering hooks of the delegate to reference CSS

---

3 Remember that page instances, once constructed, are cached for later reuse in subsequent requests.

styles and images specific to the Register application. We'll examine its code in detail shortly.

The majority of the fields in the form are used to edit simple string properties, and the only validation constraint applied to them is that a non-null value be supplied by the user. All such ValidField components will share a bean named `required` as their validator.

The `required` bean instantiates an instance of `StringValidator` and sets the `required` property of the `StringValidator` to true. This will force users to provide a non-empty value for the field. Like most validators, the `StringValidator` has no internal state and can therefore be retained indefinitely once created (which is what the `page` lifecycle does).

The delegate bean should not be given a lifecycle of `page` because it has a considerable amount of internal state (the error messages for fields that are in error) that is relevant only to a single request from a single user.

The ValidField for the `state` property uses a different validator, `stateValidator`. This validator is also declared as a helper bean in the page specification:

```
<bean name="stateValidator"
  class="org.apache.tapestry.valid.StringValidator"
  lifecycle="page">
  <set-property name="required" expression="true"/>
  <set-property name="minimumLength" expression="2"/>
</bean>
```

Like the `required` bean, the `stateValidator` bean sets the `required` property to true, forcing the user to provide a value. It adds a second constraint, configured through a second property, requiring the input to be at least two characters in length. The normal `size` attribute (specified as an informal parameter in the HTML template) ensures that no more than two characters are provided.

The final validator is for the zip code field. Zip codes have a pattern that is best described using a regular expression. Tapestry doesn't provide a validator along these lines, but it is easy enough to create one. Although we could create a validator that supports only the zip code pattern, it is virtually no extra work to create a flexible validator where we can configure both the regular expression pattern we want to validate against as well as the error message we want to display if the input fails to match the pattern.

In terms of maximizing usability, it is important that error messages be as helpful to the user as possible. Simply telling users that their input didn't match a regular expression would leave them frustrated and at a loss as to how to correct their input to satisfy the application. Instead, you can display a custom error message that tells users exactly what they need to do. For the zip code field, we can customize the error message to give users examples of the two zip code formats accepted. The regular expression pattern and the error message are both provided in the page specification:

```
<bean name="zipValidator"
  class="examples.register.PatternValidator"
  lifecycle="page">
  <set-property name="pattern">
    "\\d{5}(-\\d{4})?"
  </set-property>
  <set-property name="errorMessage">
    "Zip code format is five or nine digits.
     Example: 02134 or 02474-1145."
  </set-property>
</bean>
```

Here we are employing an alternate usage of the `<set-property>` element. Instead of specifying an expression attribute, as in the previous examples, we are putting the OGNL expression in the body of the `<set-property>` element. This approach is useful here, because we must enclose the literal string values (the pattern and the error message[4]) in double quotes. Putting the OGNL expression in the body is much easier when the expression is long or contains complex punctuation, such as a mix of single and double quotes.

Now that we have declared the validation delegate and the three validators, we can continue on to the ValidFields themselves.

Declaring the ValidField components

All the ValidField component declarations follow the same general template. A `displayName` for the field is provided; this is used by the FieldLabel and in any error messages created by the field's validator. Like an ordinary TextField component, the `value` parameter is bound to the property the ValidField will edit. Unlike a TextField component, however, this property can be bound to any type of property, not just string properties. Finally, a validator is specified. The validator defines the type of input acceptable in the field; similar fields can share validators. The first ValidField is used for entering the user's first name:

```
<component id="inputFirstName" type="ValidField">
  <static-binding name="displayName" value="First Name"/>
```

---

4 Alternately, we could put the message into a string properties file, and use the `<set-message-property>` element to retrieve the localized message and set the bean property from it. Appendix D has a complete description of the specification DTD.

```
    <binding name="validator" expression="beans.required"/>
    <binding name="value" expression="address.firstName"/>
  </component>
```

The inputFirstName component uses the `required` bean as its validator and edits the `firstName` property of the address.

All the remaining ValidField components follow the same pattern, providing different display names, different properties, and different page properties for editing.

Implementing the Register page

The Java code for the Register page is concerned with providing the `address` property referenced by the many ValidField components as well as handling the form submission. Listing 5.4 shows the `Register` class. We use the same lifecycle technique as before to initialize the `address` property to a non-null value before the page initially renders (and when the form is submitted). We must check for null because if the page renders again (following a form submission with an input validation error), the `pageBeginRender()` method will be invoked again (first because of the form rewind, and then again for the page render).

Listing 5.4 Register.java: Java class for the Register page

```
package examples.register;

import org.apache.tapestry.IRequestCycle;
import org.apache.tapestry.event.PageEvent;
import org.apache.tapestry.event.PageRenderListener;
import org.apache.tapestry.html.BasePage;
import org.apache.tapestry.valid.IValidationDelegate;

public abstract class Register extends BasePage
  implements PageRenderListener
{
  public abstract Address getAddress();
  public abstract void setAddress(Address address);

  public void pageBeginRender(PageEvent event)      <-❶ Initializes the
  {                                                    address property
    if (getAddress() == null)
      setAddress(new Address());
  }

  public void formSubmit(IRequestCycle cycle)
  {
    IValidationDelegate delegate =
      (IValidationDelegate) getBeans().            ❷ Accesses the
        getBean("delegate");                          delegate bean
```

```
    if (delegate.getHasErrors())
      return;

    RegisterConfirm next =
      (RegisterConfirm) cycle.getPage("RegisterConfirm");

    next.setAddress(getAddress());     <-3 Passes the Address
    cycle.activate(next);                  to the next page
  }
}
```

1. This method will be invoked when the page initially renders, when the form within the page is submitted, and again if the page is rendered after the form is submitted (because of validation errors). The ValidField components require that a non-null `Address` be available in the `address` property.
2. In Java code, accessing helper beans involves the `getBeans()` method, from which individual beans can be retrieved by name.
3. Passing along information collected in a form to another page, shown here, is a standard technique.

The listener method, `formSubmit()`, is invoked when the Form is submitted. In order to determine if there were any errors, the code accesses the validation delegate. If there are errors, the method returns, causing the Register page to redisplay with the error message shown and invalid fields highlighted.

If there are no errors, then the listener method activates the next page, which shows a confirmation. A real application would save this address information to a database before continuing, but that is beyond the scope of this example.

Most of this example is implemented using standard components and objects, but to properly validate the input provided in the zip code field, we need a custom validator class.

5.3 Validating input based on regular expressions

Sometimes, you will need to perform validations for which there is no out-of-the-box validator. In the Register example, validating that a user's zip code is properly formatted falls into that category. There's a specific regular expression that can be used, which checks if the input is a traditional five-digit zip code or an extended nine-digit zip code.

The framework doesn't include a validator that can employ regular expressions; but creating validators in Tapestry involves just two methods, so it's simple to create one of our own. Listing 5.5 is the implementation of this validator.

Listing 5.5 PatternValidator.java: validator based on regular expressions

```
package examples.register;

import org.apache.tapestry.ApplicationRuntimeException;
import org.apache.tapestry.form.IFormComponent;
import org.apache.tapestry.valid.BaseValidator;
import org.apache.tapestry.valid.ValidatorException;
import org.apache.oro.text.regex.MalformedPatternException;
import org.apache.oro.text.regex.Pattern;
import org.apache.oro.text.regex.PatternCompiler;
import org.apache.oro.text.regex.Perl5Compiler;
import org.apache.oro.text.regex.Perl5Matcher;

public class PatternValidator extends BaseValidator
{
  private String _pattern;
  private Pattern _compiledPattern;
  private String _errorMessage;
  private Perl5Matcher _matcher;

  public String toString(IFormComponent field,
    Object value)
  {
    if (value == null)
      return null;

    return value.toString();
  }

  public Object toObject(IFormComponent field,
    String input)
    throws ValidatorException
  {
    if (checkRequired(field, input))
      return null;

    if (!match(input))
      throw new ValidatorException(errorMessage, null);

    return input;
  }

  protected boolean match(String input)
  {
    if (_compiledPattern == null)
    {
      PatternCompiler compiler = new Perl5Compiler();

      try
      {
```

❶ Converts object to string

❷ Converts submitted value

❸ Returns if input blank

❹ Matches input against regular expression

❺ Compiles and caches regular expression

```
        _compiledPattern = compiler.compile(_pattern);
      }
      catch (MalformedPatternException ex)
      {
        throw new ApplicationRuntimeException(ex);
      }
    }

    if (_matcher == null)
      _matcher = new Perl5Matcher();

    return _matcher.matches(input, _compiledPattern);
  }

  public String getErrorMessage()
  {
    return _errorMessage;
  }

  public String getPattern()
  {
    return _pattern;
  }

  public void setErrorMessage(String errorMessage)
  {
    _errorMessage = errorMessage;
  }

  public void setPattern(String pattern)
  {
    _pattern = pattern;
    _compiledPattern = null;
  }
}
```

❺

❻ **Updates pattern and clears cache**

❶ The `toString()` method converts the value (obtained from the ValidField's `value` parameter) into a string, which becomes the `value` attribute of the `<input>` element.

❷ The `toObject()` method converts a string entered by the user back into an object value, throwing a `ValidatorException` if the input is improperly formed or otherwise invalid.

❸ The `checkRequired()` method checks to see if the input is blank. It throws a `ValidatorException` if the input is blank and the field is required. Otherwise, it returns true if the input is blank and false otherwise.

❹ The `match()` method does the regular expression pattern matching.

5. Converting a string into a regular expression is somewhat expensive, so it's done only the first time `match()` is invoked.
6. If the pattern changes, the cached compiled pattern should be discarded.

`PatternValidator` extends the framework class `BaseValidator`. `BaseValidator` is abstract and implements the `IValidator` interface. The `BaseValidator` class provides the boolean `required` property, plus a bit of support for client-side scripting (which allows the validator to generate client-side JavaScript to perform validations entirely within the client web browser).

The two key methods in a validator are `toString()` and `toObject()`. The `toString()` method is used to convert an object (read from the ValidField's `value` parameter) into a string. This method is used when the ValidField renders; the converted string is used as the `value` attribute of the HTML `<input>` element.

A validator should always be able to translate a null value to a string. It is acceptable to return null from `toString()` if the value passed in is null; this is what the validators provided with the framework do.

The meat of the validator is in the complementary `toObject()` method. This method is invoked when the form is submitted. The purpose of `toObject()` is to convert a string, supplied by the end user, into an object, such as an `Integer` or `Date`—whatever is appropriate for the specific type of validator. This is where all conversions and validations take place. If the string can't be converted, or the value is invalid for other reasons, the method throws a `ValidatorException` that is caught by the ValidField and used to record an error for the field.

The first step in the `PatternValidator`'s implementation of `toObject()` is to invoke the method `checkRequired()`, which is supplied by the `BaseValidator` class. This method performs two functions: It returns true if the input is null or empty (an empty string is length zero, or contains only whitespace), and it also throws a `ValidatorException` if the validator is required (and the input is null or empty). As configured in the Register page, the zip code field is optional (not required), so if the user decides not to enter a value, the field will not be in error.

Assuming a value was supplied by the user, the `toObject()` method continues by invoking the `match()` method. If the input from the user does not match the regular expression pattern configured for the validator, then a `ValidatorException` is thrown. The exception is built around the supplied error message (another configurable property of the `PatternValidator` class). This exception is caught by the validation delegate, which records the error message for later use when the page is rendered again (to display the errors to the user).

If `match()` returns true, then the input value becomes the return value for the `toObject()` method. Ultimately, this value will be assigned to the property bound to the ValidField's `value` parameter.

The `match()` method uses the Jakarta ORO framework to compile the pattern and match the compiled pattern against user input. The `PatternValidator` does a little caching, since compiling a string to a `Pattern` object is somewhat expensive; it shouldn't be done every time.

5.4 Customizing label and field decorations

In figure 5.1, all the required fields are marked with a red asterisk (to the right of the field). A glance at the HTML template for the page, in listing 5.2, shows that these markers are not in the template itself. This is an example of field decoration, one of the functions of the validation delegate. Additionally, you've seen that FieldLabels and ValidFields are also decorated when they are in error.

The base implementation of the `IValidationDelegate` interface, `ValidationDelegate`, provides all the support for tracking fields and errors, as well as simple support for decorating fields and labels. To customize the look and feel, as shown in figure 5.2, you create your own subclass, overriding several methods related to field and label decoration.

For the Register page, just such a subclass of `ValidationDelegate` is shown in listing 5.6. It overrides several methods supplied in the `ValidationDelegate` base class, supplying application-specific look and feel.

Listing 5.6 RegisterDelegate.java: validation delegate subclass for the Register page

```
package examples.register;

import org.apache.tapestry.IMarkupWriter;
import org.apache.tapestry.IRequestCycle;
import org.apache.tapestry.form.IFormComponent;
import org.apache.tapestry.valid.IValidator;
import org.apache.tapestry.valid.ValidationDelegate;

public class RegisterDelegate                  ❶ Subclasses from
  extends ValidationDelegate                     ValidationDelegate
{
  public void writeLabelPrefix(
    IFormComponent component,                  Is called before
    IMarkupWriter writer,                      FieldLabel
    IRequestCycle cycle)                       renders
  {
```

```
    if (isInError(component))
    {
      writer.begin("span");
      writer.attribute("class", "label-error");
    }
  }

  public void writeLabelSuffix(
    IFormComponent component,
    IMarkupWriter writer,
    IRequestCycle cycle)
  {
    if (isInError(component))
    {
      writer.end(); // span
    }
  }

  public void writeAttributes(
    IMarkupWriter writer,
    IRequestCycle cycle,
    IFormComponent component,
    IValidator validator)
  {
    if (isInError())
      writer.attribute("class", "field-error");
  }

  public void writeSuffix(
    IMarkupWriter writer,
    IRequestCycle cycle,
    IFormComponent component,
    IValidator validator)
  {
    if (validator != null &&
        validator.isRequired())
    {
      writer.printRaw(" ");
      writer.begin("span");
      writer.attribute("class",
        "required-marker");
      writer.print("*");
      writer.end();
    }

    if (isInError())
    {
      writer.printRaw(" ");
      writer.beginEmpty("img");
      writer.attribute("src",
        "images/field-error.png");
```

❷ Encloses label with <span>

Is called after FieldLabel renders

❸ Is called as ValidField renders

❹ Is called after ValidField renders

Marks required fields

Marks fields that are in error

```
        writer.attribute("width", 16);
        writer.attribute("height", 16);
      }
    }
  }
```

Marks fields that are in error

❶ The framework class `ValidationDelegate` provides the majority of the behavior for a validation delegate. Generally, a subclass is needed only as in this example: to override the methods used for decorating fields and labels.

❷ If the field for the label is in error, then an HTML `<span>` is wrapped around it, with a class of `label-error`. The stylesheet for the page modifies the enclosed text to make it red.

❸ `writeAttributes()` is invoked as the ValidField writes the `<input>` tag and allows the validation delegate to write additional attributes if the field is in error. Here, the CSS class `field-error` is written into the `<input>` tag if the field is in error, resulting in the white-on-red display.

❹ `writeSuffix()` is invoked after the ValidField renders the `<input>` tag. The `IValidationDelegate` interface defines an additional method, `writePrefix()`, which is invoked before the ValidField renders; and the `ValidationDelegate` base class provides a do-nothing implementation of that method.

The first two methods in the class, `writeLabelPrefix()` and `writeLabelSuffix()`, are related to decoration of field labels. The FieldLabel component invokes these methods, passing the ValidField it is connected to as the `component` parameter. These two methods rely on the `isInError()` method, which returns true if a validation error has been recorded for a component. When `isInError()` returns true, the delegate renders a `<span>` tag and writes the `class` attribute for it (as `label-error`). The `IMarkupWriter` interface is provided by Tapestry; it is much like a `java.io.PrintWriter`, but with additional methods for streamlining the output of elements and attributes, as shown in listing 5.6. Chapter 7 includes more information about `IMarkupWriter`.

The `<span>` tag started in `writeLabelPrefix()` is ended inside the `writeLabelSuffix()` method when it invokes `end()` on the writer. In between the two methods, the FieldLabel gets the `displayName` from the ValidField and writes that to the writer. For example, if the First Name field is in error (because the user submitted the form without filling in a value), then the FieldLabel, combined with the validation delegate, will render the following:

```
<span class="label-error">First Name</span>
```

Just as the FieldLabel delegates part of its rendering to the validation delegate, so does the ValidField. Three methods of the validation delegate are used to decorate fields: `writePrefix()`, `writeSuffix()`, and `writeAttributes()`. `RegisterDelegate` implements the latter two methods; the default `writePrefix()` method, inherited from the `ValidationDelegate` base class, does nothing. The `writePrefix()` method is invoked by the ValidField before it renders the `<input>` tag.

The `writeAttributes()` method is called by the ValidField after it has written the `<input>` tag and all of its attributes, but before it closes the tag. This gives the validation delegate a chance to add attributes to the tag. In this case, the delegate checks if the current component is in error; if so, a `class` attribute is added to the `<input>` tag. This CSS class is combined with the page's stylesheet to display offending fields as white text against a red background.

The `writeSuffix()` method is invoked by the ValidField after it closes the `<input>` tag. `RegisterDelegate` queries the ValidField's validator (which is passed in to the method as a parameter) to see if the validator requires a value. If so, the delegate writes HTML to display the required marker. Likewise, if the field is in error, HTML is written that marks the field using a specific image.

NOTE Normally, it is not necessary for your implementation of the `writeSuffix()` method to check that the validator parameter is not null. A ValidField component will always have a validator and will pass it into this method. This check is necessary because, in chapter 8, we create a new type of component that uses a validation delegate but does not have a validator.

As you can see, the methods defined by the `IValidationDelegate` interface are designed to be completely open-ended. With a minimal amount of effort, you can customize the look and feel of your application's labels and fields by creating and using your own subclass of the `ValidationDelegate` base class.

So far, we've covered how the validation subsystem extends normal form processing (both when rendering a page and when the form is submitted). That's only part of the story, however, since the validation framework can also contribute to the client side.

5.5 Enabling client-side validation

Performing validations when the form is submitted is a powerful approach, but an even better solution is to not submit the form until the fields are valid within the client web browser. Using a client-side solution gives users more immediate feedback (as soon as they click the submit button) because no additional round-trip to the server is required. Server-side validation will still occur when the form is submitted, since the client can't be counted on to have JavaScript enabled. In addition, for basic security and data integrity reasons, you must never rely on the client web browser to enforce any rules (in fact, you can't even count on the software at the other end of the HTTP connection to be a web browser; it could be a web spider, a screen scraper, or some kind of script).

Using Tapestry and the ValidField component, you can integrate this kind of client-side validation seamlessly into your applications. The ValidField's validator is responsible for generating this client-side JavaScript. When enabled, JavaScript event handlers are created and hooked into the form submission to perform validations within the client web browser similar to those that occur in the server.

The examples include a second version of the Register page, Register2. It is virtually identical to the first page, except that in the page specification, client scripting is enabled. If users attempt to submit the form with missing or invalid data, a client-side pop-up window advises them of the error. Figure 5.7 demon-

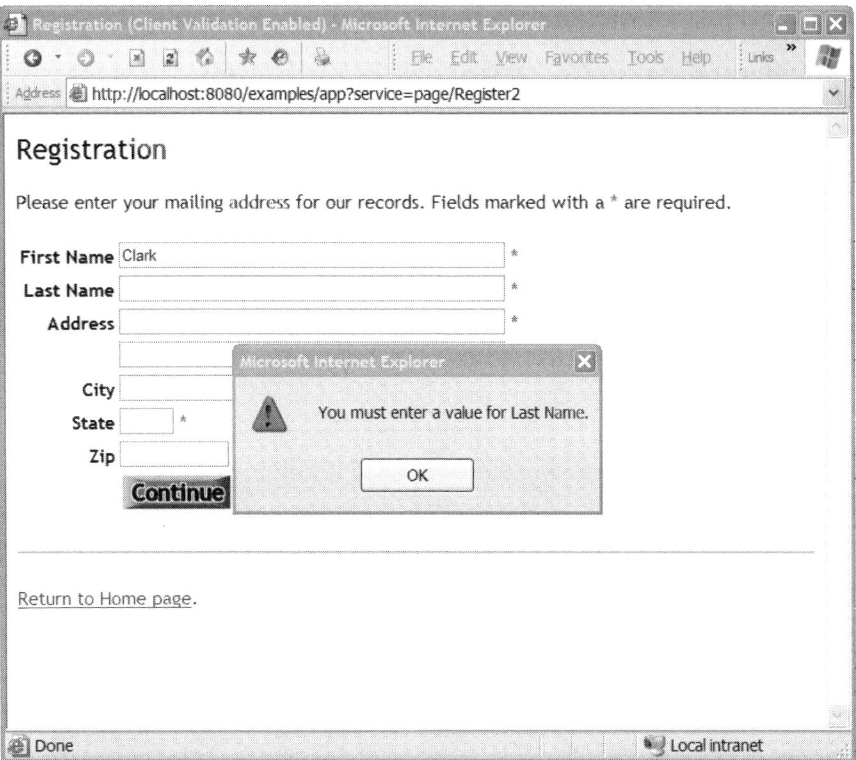

Figure 5.7 With client validation enabled, submitting the form causes validations to occur. After the user clicks the OK button, the cursor will be moved to the Last Name field.

strates what happens if you submit the form without providing a value for the Last Name field, which is required.

Enabling this support requires a small change to the page specification. The bean property `clientScriptingEnabled` must be set to true for each of the validators:

```
<bean name="required"
  class="org.apache.tapestry.valid.StringValidator"
  lifecycle="page">
  <set-property name="required" expression="true"/>
  <set-property name="clientScriptingEnabled" expression="true"/>
</bean>

<bean name="stateValidator"
  class="org.apache.tapestry.valid.StringValidator"
  lifecycle="page">
  <set-property name="required" expression="true"/>
  <set-property name="minimumLength" expression="2"/>
  <set-property name="clientScriptingEnabled" expression="true"/>
</bean>
```

To support browsers where JavaScript does not exist or is disabled, all validations still occur on the server when the form is submitted. Some validations may not be possible on the client side; they may be too complex to express in JavaScript or require access to data that isn't available in the client, such as information from a database.

You've already seen how to create new validators that perform server-side validations. Adding client-side validations for a new validator is more involved; Tapestry includes the necessary tools for dynamically generating the JavaScript (this is covered in chapter 8), and the `IValidator` interface includes a method for this purpose, `renderValidatorContribution()`. Nevertheless, getting validations to work still requires a fairly deep understanding of both Tapestry and JavaScript.

To accomplish client-side validation, each validator must

- Create a JavaScript function that accesses the field value and performs the validations; if invalid, the function must display an error window and return false
- Adapt the function to Tapestry-generated IDs for the form and the text field
- Register the script function with the Form component as a client-side submit event handler

The `BaseValidator` class, a base class implementing `IValidator` from which most validator classes extend, includes several methods for supporting client-side scripting. The key challenge is the correct generation of the JavaScript needed in the client, which uses techniques discussed in chapter 8.

In addition to adding client-side scripting support to new validators, you can change the client-side scripting support for the existing validators. The existing validators provide reasonable client-side scripting support. As shown in figure 5.7, invalid input will cause a pop-up window to appear that indicates the problem and names the field; clicking the OK button will set input focus to the field in error and select all text in the field. A demanding application may want to do more—for example, change the CSS class for fields that are in error to visually highlight such fields for the user, or display the error messages for fields on the page itself, rather than in a pop-up window. Such application-specific functionality will require application-specific client-side JavaScript, which can be supplied by configuring the validators' instances with the custom scripts (again, using techniques described in chapter 8).

So far, all discussion of validation has concerned individual fields in isolation. In many cases, there are dependencies between fields that must also be validated—form-level validations that involve two or more fields.

5.6 Handling form-level validations

Validations that involve more than one field occur inside the Form's listener method. For example, a form-level validation may check that two input dates are in ascending order, and display an error message if they are not. This is demonstrated in figure 5.8.

There's no need to throw away the rest of the validation subsystem to handle these kinds of cases; it's possible for a Form's listener method to mark fields in error, just as easily as a validator can. This is accomplished by putting additional validation logic in the Form's listener method.

The example shown in figure 5.8 is for the Dates page. This page uses two ValidField components, inputStart and inputEnd, to edit two page properties (`startDate` and `endDate`, respectively). Listing 5.7 shows the page class for the Dates page.

Listing 5.7 Dates.java: Java class for the Dates page

```
package examples.dates;

import java.util.Date;

import org.apache.tapestry.IRequestCycle;
import org.apache.tapestry.form.IFormComponent;
import org.apache.tapestry.html.BasePage;
import org.apache.tapestry.valid.IValidationDelegate;
```

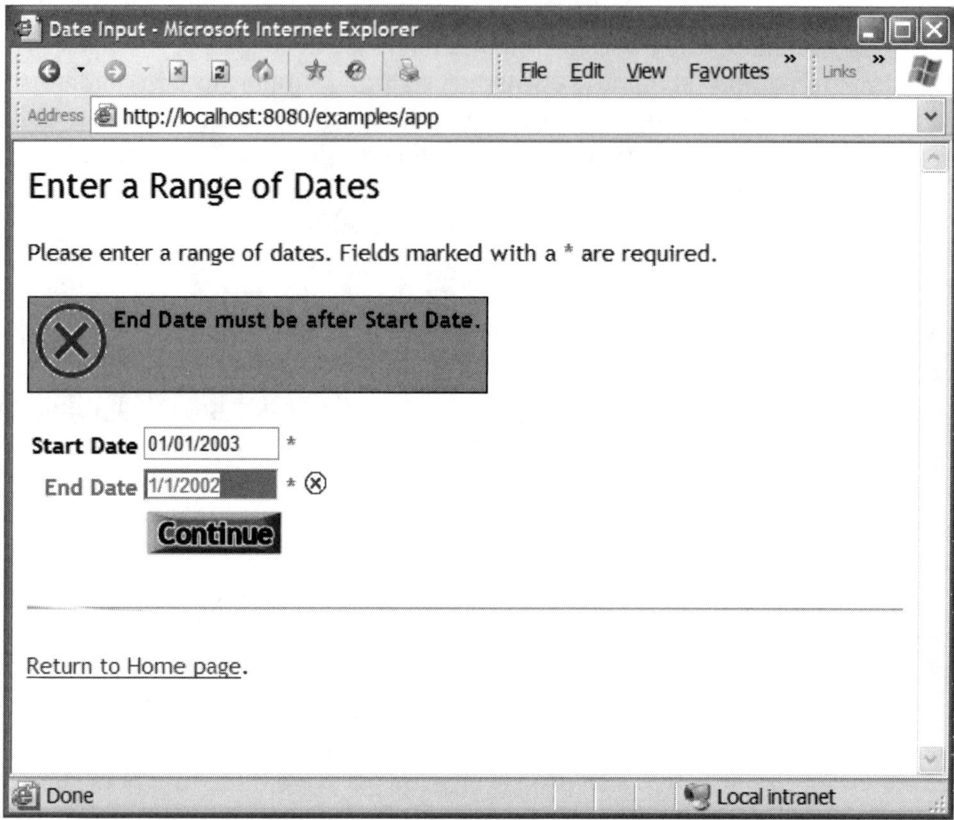

Figure 5.8 Although the input values are valid dates, the end date precedes the start date and is rejected with an error message.

```
import org.apache.tapestry.valid.ValidationConstraint;

public abstract class Dates extends BasePage
{
  public abstract Date getStartDate();
  public abstract Date getEndDate();

  public void formSubmit(IRequestCycle cycle)
  {
    IValidationDelegate delegate =
     (IValidationDelegate) getBeans().
       getBean("delegate");                    // Obtains validation delegate helper bean

    if (delegate.getHasErrors())
      return;                                  // Returns if ordinary validation errors occurred
```

```
        Date startDate = getStartDate();
        Date endDate = getEndDate();

        if (startDate.after(endDate))
        {
          IFormComponent inputEnd =
            (IFormComponent) getComponent("inputEnd");
          delegate.setFormComponent(inputEnd);
          delegate.record(
            "End Date must be after Start Date.",
            ValidationConstraint.CONSISTENCY);
          return;
        }

        DatesConfirm next =
          (DatesConfirm)cycle.getPage("DatesConfirm");
        next.setStartDate(startDate);
        next.setEndDate(endDate);
        cycle.activate(next);
      }
    }
```

1 Records a form-level validation error

1 The error is attributed to the second ValidField, the one that gets the end date. The call to `setFormComponent()` identifies the field to be assigned the error. The call to `record()` provides the error message.

This listener method starts in much the same way as in the previous example; it gets the validation delegate and simply returns if the delegate already has errors. Validation errors at this point are formatting errors in the user input, or are the result of the user omitting one of the fields (both of which are required). The remaining code in the method is executed only if there are no fundamental input errors, in which case both the `startDate` and `endDate` properties will have been supplied by the respective ValidField components (inputStart and inputEnd).

If the start date occurs after the end date, then a form-level validation error occurs. The first step is to identify the field to be associated with the error. This isn't strictly necessary; it is acceptable to not invoke the `setFormComponent()` method, in which case the error is recorded but will not be associated with any specific field within the form.

In this example, we identify the end date as the error field (we could just as easily mark the start date). The validation delegate's `record()` method lets us assign an error to the field. When the page is re-rendered, the inputEnd field will be marked in error. There are several implementations of the `record()`

method, each taking different parameter types for the message. The final parameter is of type `ValidationConstraint`, an `Enum` of different possible reasons the field is in error.[5] If none of the provided constraint values are appropriate, then null is an acceptable value. `CONSISTENCY` is used to indicate that a cross-field consistency error occurred.

Once the field is recorded as containing an error, the listener method returns. This action will cause a redisplay of the active page, complete with error messages and field decorations.

So far, you've seen a number of ways to mix and match FieldLabel and ValidField components with validators and validation logic inside listener methods. With some extra effort, it is possible to use much of the validation system without using the ValidField component, as you'll see in the next section.

5.7 Using validation without ValidField

There are times when you will want to mix and match, leveraging portions of the validation subsystem without necessarily using the ValidField component. For example, figure 5.9 shows a different version of the page from the previous example. This page uses DatePicker components, instead of ValidField components, to collect the start and end date from the user, yet it still uses the rest of the validation framework (FieldLabel components error display, and a validation delegate).

For the most part, the HTML template for the revised Dates page is the same as in the prior example (using ValidField), with some minor differences around the labels and fields. It is possible to use the FieldLabel component, although the HTML template is somewhat more involved:

```
<tr>
<th><span jwcid="@FieldLabel"
      displayName="Start Date"
      field="ognl:components.inputStart">
      Start Date</span></th>
<td><input type="text" jwcid="inputStart"
      size="10"/>
```

❶ **Labels the field as before**

❷ **Contains the DatePicker component**

[5] The validation constraint is not used by the default implementation of `IValidationDelegate` or by our custom subclass. It is provided in speculation that a more clever validation delegate implementation may have a need for it—such as customizing the decoration for an invalid field based on the type of constraint violated.

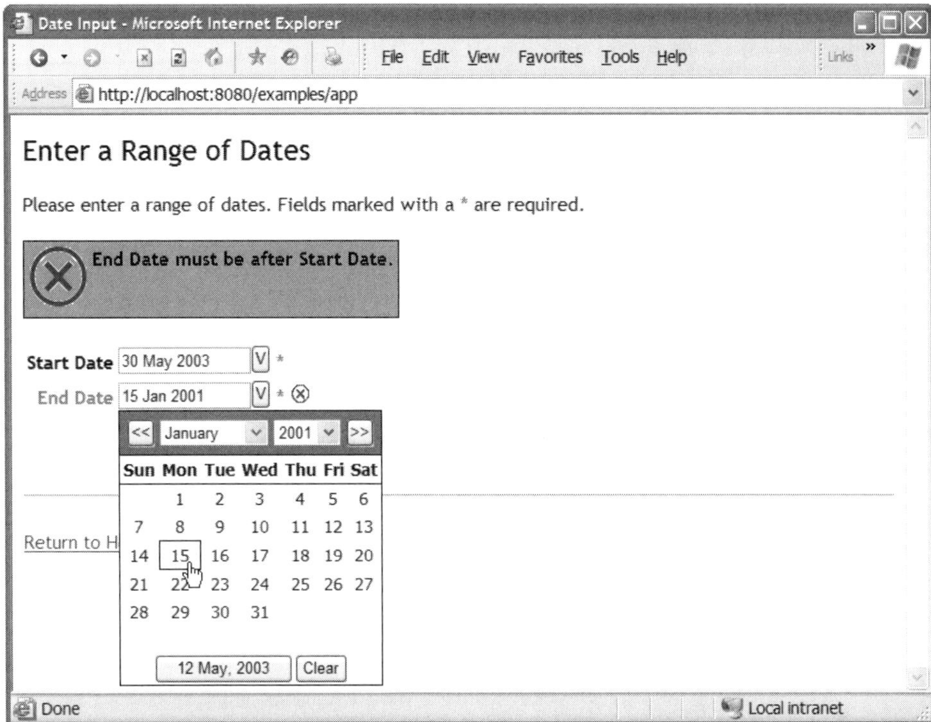

Figure 5.9 The DatePicker component can be used with the form validation framework.

```
        <span class="required-marker">*</span>
<span jwcid="@Conditional"
    condition="ognl:beans.delegate.inError">
        <img src="images/field-error.png"/>
</span>
</td>
</tr>
```

Decorates the field

❶ The FieldLabel component can still be used, but the display name must be specified as a parameter.

❷ Without a ValidField, the validation delegate is not integrated into the render. The template must include the decorations normally provided by the validation delegate: the marker for required fields and, optionally, the image used to mark error fields. The validation delegate's `inError` property is true when the current field is marked as in error.

When using a ValidField, the `displayName` (used by the FieldLabel component) is provided as a parameter of the ValidField. Without a ValidField, you must instead set the `displayName` parameter directly on the FieldLabel component.

All form-related components within a Form are tracked by the validation delegate even if they are not ValidField components. This allows errors to be attached to any kind of form control component: TextField, TextArea, PropertySelection, even DatePicker (as in this example). However, the validation delegate is *not* integrated into the rendering of these other types of components; only ValidField has all the necessary hooks. The work the validation delegate normally does, decorating invalid fields, is instead done explicitly in the template, using a Conditional component.

The validation delegate's `inError` property is true if the most recently rendered component has an error. Because the Conditional in the template follows the DatePicker component, the `inError` property will be true if there was a validation error for the DatePicker.

Because there is no ValidField, and therefore no validator, involved in form processing, even simple checks for required fields must now be done inside the Form's listener method:

```
public void formSubmit(IRequestCycle cycle)
{
  IValidationDelegate delegate =
    (IValidationDelegate) getBeans().getBean("delegate");

  Date startDate = getStartDate();
  Date endDate = getEndDate();

  if (startDate == null)
    error(delegate, "inputStart",
      "Start Date is required.",
      ValidationConstraint.REQUIRED);

  if (endDate == null)
    error(delegate, "inputEnd",
      "End Date is required.",
      ValidationConstraint.REQUIRED);

  if (delegate.getHasErrors())
    return;

  if (startDate.after(endDate))
  {
    error(
      delegate,
      "inputEnd",
      "End Date must be after Start Date.",
      ValidationConstraint.CONSISTENCY);
    return;
  }
```

Gets values set by DatePicker components

❶ Checks for missing required fields

❷ Performs form-level check

```
    DatesConfirm next =
      (DatesConfirm) cycle.getPage("DatesConfirm");
    next.setStartDate(startDate);
    next.setEndDate(endDate);
    cycle.activate(next);
  }

  private void error(
    IValidationDelegate delegate,
    String componentId,
    String message,
    ValidationConstraint constraint)
  {
    IFormComponent component =
      (IFormComponent) getComponent(componentId);

    delegate.setFormComponent(component);
    delegate.record(message, constraint);
  }
```

❶ These checks are normally done by the validator for the ValidField. Since the form uses DatePicker components instead of ValidField components, there is no validator to perform even this basic check.

❷ This form-level check is the same as in the previous example (which used ValidField components).

Despite the larger amount of code (some of which could be factored out to base classes or helper beans), the process is still straightforward: We check the properties edited by the DatePicker components, compare the values, and inform the validation delegate if there is an error.

5.8 Summary

Tapestry's validation subsystem, centered around the ValidField component, is a tremendous boon to web application usability. The validation subsystem achieves the framework's goals for simplicity and consistency, both from the end user's perspective and from your perspective as the application developer. Tapestry comes with a number of predefined validations but is completely open-ended in terms of adding new ones. With only a small amount of coding, it is possible to precisely control the look and feel of label and field decorations.

Once again, large amounts of coding disappear into the framework, and what little coding remains (in terms of new validators and validation delegates) can be easily reused within a single application, or even across multiple applications. Tapestry makes it simple to create a polished, usable user interface.

Along the way, you've also seen another technique for extending the functionality of the application with little or no coding: helper beans. Helper beans fit into the overall Tapestry framework of objects, methods, and properties, providing another dynamic way to glue custom behavior into prepackaged components such as the ValidField.

In addition, you've seen that the validation subsystem can play well with ordinary form control components, such as the DatePicker component. You are free to mix and match the pieces that best solve your particular application's issues. The ordinary form control components, the advanced components such as PropertySelection and DatePicker, and the validation subsystem can all be used together to provide a comprehensive, yet still light and agile, solution to handling all variations of form input in a Tapestry application.

Part 2

Creating Tapestry components

Chapters 6, 7, and 8 take you beyond using existing components and show you how to create your own components. Along the way, you'll see more of Tapestry's internals, including how Tapestry applications can be localized. You'll also learn how Tapestry components can generate client-side JavaScript, and how Tapestry and traditional servlet applications can interoperate.

6 Creating reusable components

This chapter covers:

- Creating component templates and specifications
- Understanding component parameters
- Working with components packaged in libraries
- Creating component libraries

So far in this book, you've seen several interesting ways of combining the components provided with the Tapestry framework to form pages, but the real fun starts when you begin creating brand-new components. Creating components with Tapestry is easy—in fact, you've been doing it all along, since pages are just a specialized type of component.

Components are the key to high levels of reuse, the Holy Grail of object-oriented development. Creating customized components for your application and then reusing them on different pages of your application, or even in entirely different applications, is a massive boost to productivity for you and your developers, because it reduces the amount of Java code and HTML templates you will have to write. It also improves the robustness of your application by cutting down on testing; you use the same component in different places, rather than duplicating templates and functionality. Remember, less code *always* translates to fewer bugs!

In this chapter, you'll learn how to create components that use their own templates and how to create components that forgo a template and produce output exclusively in Java code. You'll also see how to use components that come in a library, and how to create and package a component library for use in new applications.

6.1 Creating simple template components

The easiest components to create are those designed for a specific use within a specific application. This type of component may be used in many pages of a single application but is not applicable to other applications and, very often, exploits specific knowledge about the page or application for which it was created.

Fully reusable components must be completely free of any dependencies on a specific application. They rely heavily on the use of parameters that configure and adapt them for a particular usage within a certain application.

To some degree, an application-specific component is like a compiler macro (a concept familiar to C programmers). Simple components with templates expand when the page is loaded, adding their template and the components within it to the containing page's template.

By way of an example, we'll revisit the Hangman application from chapter 2. If you remember, it contained a lot of duplicated code related to converting numbers and characters into images (to support the "chalkboard" look and feel). Specifically, the Guess, Win, and Lose pages contained duplication, both in the page classes as well as their page specifications. Particularly onerous was the long, long list of context assets that defined the images for each letter, for each digit, and for each version of the hanged man in the gallows. Different portions of this list were duplicated in the Guess, Win, and Lose page specifications.

An obvious first step is to isolate all that image manipulation into a few reusable components, with the goal that each image asset be defined only once, within a single component specification. These components will be an example of application-specific reuse; that is, they will be completely tied to this specific application. We'll create components for displaying the numbers and the scaffold used to show the player's remaining guesses, as well as a component for displaying a particular letter. We'll then build on these, creating a component that spells out entire words. You'll also see a common type of component, known as a *border* component, which is used to provide the specific look and feel of an application (in terms of Cascading Style Sheets [CSS], basic navigation controls, and table-based layout). These are all examples of the most common types of components you'll be creating in your own applications; these components save us a bit of effort in this application, even if they won't help when we code our next one.

When we're done, the revised Hangman application will look and feel exactly the same as the original; only its internal structure will be different. When components are created and utilized properly, the result is smaller, simpler HTML templates and page specifications, less code, and, more important, less duplication of code—always a lifesaver when it comes time to fix bugs.

The source code for both the original and the revised Hangman applications is available online; appendix B discusses how to obtain the source, as well as how to build and deploy all the examples in the book. The improved Hangman described in this chapter is accessible as http://localhost:8080/hangman2/app.

Creating a template component entails creating the component specification and, optionally, the component's template, and usually involves creating a new Java class. All three together form a component. Figure 6.1 shows these artifacts. The component specification is stored in the WEB-INF folder and has a .jwc extension. The Java class is identified in the specification (defaulting to `BaseComponent` if left unspecified).

When a page template or specification references a component, Tapestry must determine how to instantiate an instance of the component's class, as a part of the overall page. The first step is to locate the component's specification, which (like a page specification) identifies the Java class Tapestry will instantiate (along with many other implementation details, such as additional embedded components). Also, most components will have their own HTML template, whose contents are integrated into the containing page's template.

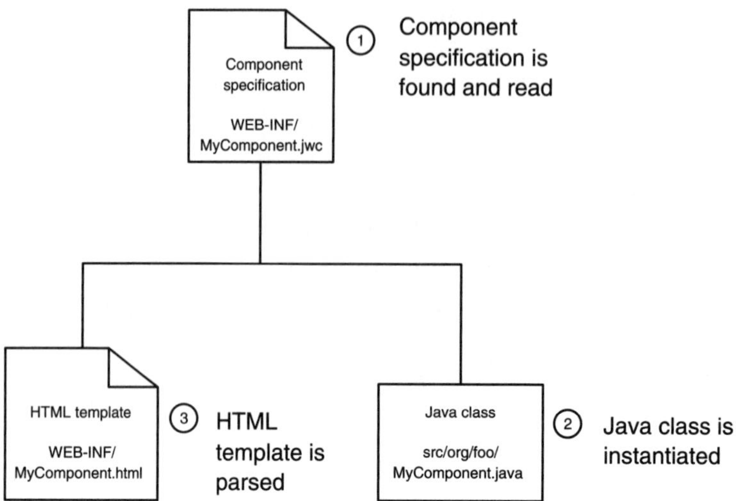

Figure 6.1 Like pages, components have a specification (with a .jwc extension) and a Java class. If they have a template, it is stored in WEB-INF with the specification.

Tapestry starts with the component type, which is used as the name of the component specification file that you want to read. These files may be built-in components bundled with the Tapestry framework, or they may come from a component library (discussed in section 6.8), or they may be application-specific components, with the specification stored in the WEB-INF folder.

After reading the specification and instantiating and configuring an instance of the component's Java class, Tapestry will then locate and parse the HTML template for the component.[1] The template for the component is stored in the WEB-INF folder, alongside the component specification (a marked difference from pages, where the template is stored one level up, in the root context folder). A template will be used only with components that inherit from `BaseComponent`—components that subclass from `AbstractComponent` work entirely in Java code, with no template.

Regardless of whether the component has a template, it must have a component specification.

[1] In fact, the component itself is responsible for locating its template; this is covered in detail in chapter 7.

6.2 Creating the component specification

A component specification tells Tapestry how to instantiate and use a component, in exactly the same way that a page specification tells Tapestry how to instantiate and use a page. A component specification includes all the same attributes and elements as a page specification:

- A `class` attribute to identify the Java class you want to instantiate
- `<property-specification>` elements to define additional properties for the component
- `<component>` elements to declare additional components contained within the component
- `<context-asset>` elements to declare assets used by the component

What a component specification adds (beyond what is available in a page specification) are additional attributes and elements to define if and how the component uses parameters, and how it fits into the overall page:

- `<parameter>` elements declare each formal parameter, providing a name and type, and indicating if the parameter is required or optional.
- `<reserved-parameter>` elements filter out unwanted informal parameters.
- The `allow-informal-parameters` attribute specifies whether informal parameters are allowed or discarded.
- The `allow-body` attribute specifies whether the body of the component (in its container's template) is kept and used, or discarded.

This chapter covers the most common aspects of the framework's component specification. Appendix D contains a complete reference to all of the Tapestry specifications.

6.2.1 Specifying the component's Java class

A component specification begins with a `<component-specification>` element. As with a page specification, the `<component-specification>` element includes a `class` attribute, which is used to specify which Java class to instantiate for the component. The attribute is optional, in which case the default class, `BaseComponent`, is used. `BaseComponent` is the base class for components that have a template.[2]

---

[2] `BaseComponent`'s superclass is `AbstractComponent`. `AbstractComponent` is for components that don't use a template. Subclasses of `AbstractComponent` must implement the `renderComponent()` method to produce their output entirely in code.

When creating new components, it is often (but not always) necessary to create a custom subclass of `BaseComponent` to contain any additional logic that can't be expressed in the specification itself. Most often, such a class will contain listener methods.

6.2.2 Discarding the component's body

Components are represented in their container's templates as a balanced pair of start and end tags.[3] The portion of the template enclosed by those tags is the component's *body*. The body is a mix of static HTML and other components. Figure 6.2 shows how a component's body is determined. Tapestry divides the page template into individual chunks, each containing static text, component start tags, or component end tags. A component's body is the static text and components it immediately encloses. Enclosed components (such as B in the diagram) themselves have a body—the static text and components they enclose.

A component may either keep or discard its body. This is controlled by the `allow-body` attribute of the `<component-specification>` element. By default, `allow-body` is set to `yes`, and the component keeps its body (though the corresponding Java class must still include code to render its body). The component will be able to integrate its body (the portion of the page template its tags enclose) with its own template (if it has one). This is appropriate for components

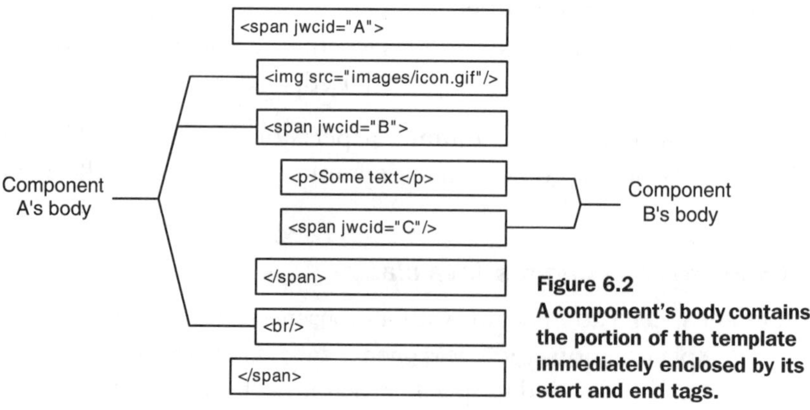

Figure 6.2 A component's body contains the portion of the template immediately enclosed by its start and end tags.

[3] So far, most of our examples have been of a page containing a component, but since components may themselves have templates, they may also be containers of other components. It is not uncommon for such nesting to go three or four levels deep, and Tapestry has no arbitrary limit on how deep such component nesting is allowed.

such as Conditional or Foreach that want to control if, when, and how often their body is rendered.

Some components discard their body, usually because the HTML element they render does not have a body. For example, the Image component discards its body because the HTML `<img>` element is always empty.

When Tapestry discards a component's body, it checks to see if the body contains other components. If so, Tapestry throws an exception (it is not allowed to define a component only to throw it away).

> **TIP** If you omit the end tag of a component, the Tapestry template parser will see an enclosed, discarded component before it sees that the tag is simply not balanced. You'll see an exception such as *Tag <input> on line 15 is a dynamic component, and may not appear inside an ignored block.*

As you'll see shortly, a component with its own template can even integrate its body (which comes from its container's template) with its own template.

6.2.3 Forbidding informal parameters

In many of our examples from previous chapters, we've used informal parameters. *Informal parameters* are additional parameters beyond those explicitly declared by the component (formal parameters are described in the next section).

Most components pass through informal parameters, adding them as attributes of the HTML element rendered by the component. This is useful in components such as DirectLink for specifying the CSS class or JavaScript event handlers. The component doesn't care about the names or values of the informal parameters; it passes them through unchanged.

In some cases, a component has no use for informal parameters. For example, the Delegator component doesn't directly render an HTML element, so it would have no use for informal parameters. Likewise, the DatePicker component renders several related HTML elements, so it disallows informal parameters as well, since it isn't clear which element would make use of them. Components that fall into this category will set the `allow-informal-parameters` attribute to `no` (the default for `allow-informal-parameters` is `yes`).

When loading a page, the framework checks to see if any informal parameters are bound to a component that does not allow them. An exception is thrown when informal parameters are used improperly.

To support WYSIWYG editing, there is one exception for components that forbid informal parameters: If an informal parameter is specified in an HTML template as a literal value, the informal parameter is silently ignored.

6.2.4 Declaring parameters

The main difference between pages and components is that components may have parameters and pages may not. Parameters are used to control and customize the behavior of a component to adapt it to the page it is used on. You've seen how common components such as Insert and DirectLink rely on the parameters you set to make them do the right thing within your pages: render the correct bit of text (the `value` parameter of Insert), or invoke the correct listener method (the `listener` parameter of DirectLink). This doesn't apply just to the built-in framework components; the components you create will also require parameters to adapt them to the specific page and situation they are needed for.

The `<parameter>` element is used to define formal parameters used by a component. This element includes six attributes, shown in table 6.1.

Table 6.1 The `<parameter>` element's attributes

Name	Description
`name`	The name used for the parameter, which must be a valid Java identifier.
`type`	The Java type of the parameter, which may be a class name or a primitive type name.
`required`	If `yes`, the parameter must be bound. Defaults to `no`.
`property-name`	Optional; specifies the name to use for a connected parameter property when the default is not allowed.
`direction`	Specifies how, if at all, you want to connect the parameter binding to a property; defaults to `custom`, which means no connected parameter property.
`default-value`	Optional OGNL expression used as a default value for the parameter if the parameter is not otherwise bound.

Component parameters are more than just JavaBean properties; parameters may represent a connection, or *binding*, between a component and some other object property. A component parameter is not just a property: It is a slot into which a binding can be plugged. Using the binding, the component can both read *and update* the bound property. As an example, consider the `value` parameter of the Foreach component. Foreach will update the property bound to the `value` parameter before rendering its body, for each item in its list (which is provided by its `source` parameter). Likewise, all the form control elements, such as TextField, both read and update their `value` parameters, reading the `value` parameter when the page is rendering but updating their `value` parameter when the containing form is submitted.

The ability to update parameters represents a fundamental difference between Tapestry component parameters and a typical JavaBean object. A Tapestry component can force a change to another object property using a parameter binding.

As you've seen in previous examples, the bindings that are plugged into component parameters run the gamut from short literal strings all the way up to complex OGNL expressions. At the code level, each parameter is a JavaBeans property into which a binding object, a class implementing the `IBinding` interface, is plugged. When a component wants to read or update the value bound to one of its parameters, the first step is to obtain the matching `IBinding` object.

Tapestry includes different implementations of `IBinding` for the three types of bindings (OGNL expressions, literal static values, and localized messages).[4] The `IBinding` interface includes methods for both reading and updating the bound value. The `getObject()` method reads the bound property value. The `setObject()` method updates the bound property's value. Only OGNL expressions can be updated; any attempt to update parameters bound to a static value or localized message results in a runtime exception.

Figure 6.3 shows how a hypothetical component can access its parameters via its binding object. The `getObject()` method retrieves a value through the binding, which can be incorporated into the rendered output of the component. The binding's `setObject()` method is used (on form submission) to update the bound property.

Before your code can access the bound property value, it needs access to the binding object itself.

Accessing bindings

For each formal parameter, Tapestry creates a binding property. A *binding property* is always of type `IBinding`, and the property name is the same as the parameter name, with `Binding` appended. As with a property specification, the framework will use existing accessor methods, but it is easiest to let Tapestry construct a subclass with the accessor methods and the underlying field. To access the binding, declare and use an abstract accessor:

```
public abstract IBinding getParameterBinding();
```

4 A special type of binding is used to access localized messages for pages and components. The details about this are provided in chapter 7.

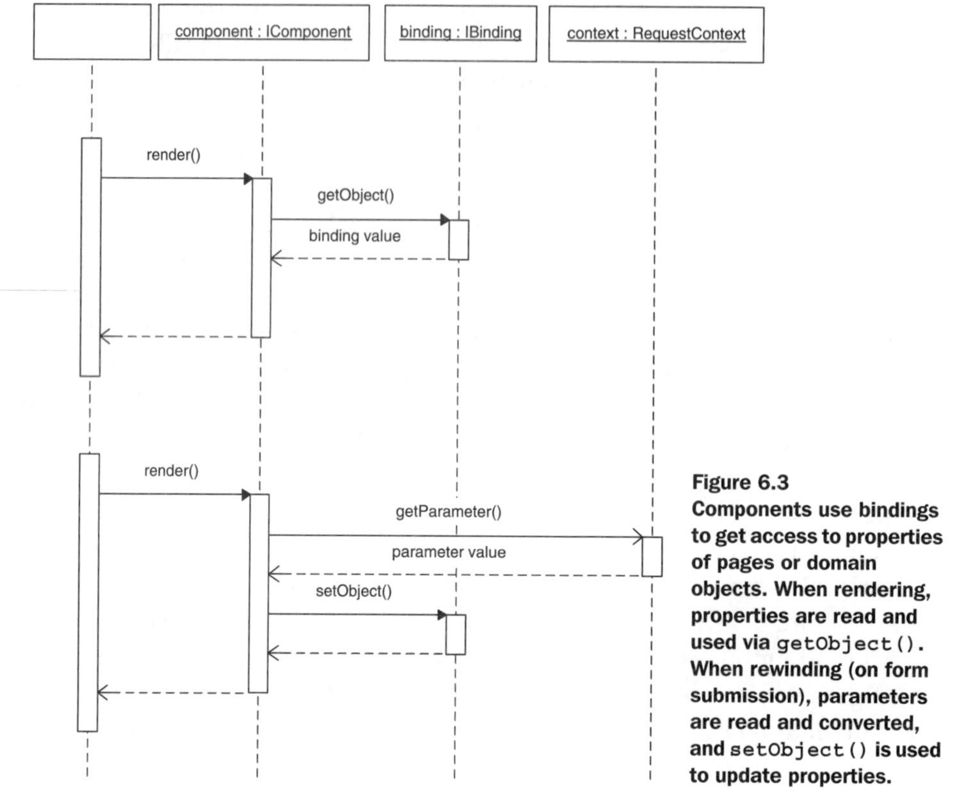

Figure 6.3 Components use bindings to get access to properties of pages or domain objects. When rendering, properties are read and used via `getObject()`. When rewinding (on form submission), parameters are read and converted, and `setObject()` is used to update properties.

Most components do not need to know about bindings, however. Tapestry has the ability to perform all the interactions with the binding object for you, behind the scenes, and represent the parameter as a JavaBean property instead. This is a much easier, more intuitive approach.

Directions for value movements

The `direction` attribute of the `<parameter>` element is used to tell Tapestry how values move between the binding and the component.[5] It can be set to one of four values: `in`, `form`, `auto`, or `custom`. The majority of component parameters will use the value `in` for this attribute. This tells Tapestry to create a *connected parameter*

---

[5] This is one of the odder naming snafus in the framework. The original intent was based on established names for parameter directions in languages that allow pass-by-reference: in, out, and in-out. What the `direction` attribute has evolved into would better be called "processing" or "connection," but names (even bad names) take on a life of their own.

property with the same name as the parameter and to manage that property, setting its value at the appropriate time, just before the component renders. As with specified properties, Tapestry will use existing accessor methods, or create new accessor methods with this signature:

```
public Type getParameter();
public void setParameter(Type parameter);
```

As with specified properties, there is no reason to create your own accessor methods; it is easier to let Tapestry create the accessor methods and underlying fields. Your code should just declare abstract accessor methods to read, and possibly update, the parameter property.

If the parameter has a name that conflicts with an existing property (perhaps one inherited from a base class), you may override the default parameter property name and use another. For example, the PageLink component has a `page` parameter, but `AbstractComponent` already defines a `page` property, so the parameter is connected to a different property, `targetPage`:

```
<parameter name="page"
  type="java.lang.String"
  required="yes"
  property-name="targetPage"
  direction="in"/>
```

Here, the name of the parameter is still `page`, but the connected parameter property is named `targetPage`. The component can access the value bound to the parameter by defining and using the method `getTargetPage()`. In addition, a second property, `targetPageBinding`, is created to store the binding object for the parameter (but since the parameter is connected to a property, there's no need to access the binding object directly).

The majority of parameters specify `in`. The processing for such parameters consists of setting the parameter property from the binding value just before the component renders, and then resetting the parameter property back to a default value just after the component renders. Figure 6.4 illustrates the steps taken by the component to set and clear the properties as part of the component's render.

In a component, the `render()` method does three things:

- It invokes `prepareForRender()` to prepare the component for rendering. This sets the value of the `direction` attribute's `in` and `form` parameters (reading the value bound to the parameter and updating the connected property with that value).
- It invokes `renderComponent()` to perform the creation of output.

- It invokes `cleanupAfterRender()` (from within a `finally` block) to clean up the component after the render. This reads the `direction` attribute's `form` parameters and updates the binding value; it also resets the attribute's `in` and `form` parameters to their default values.

Each component has its own instance of `ParameterManager`, whose job is to analyze the direction of each parameter and set and reset the connected parameter properties on the component. This is shown in figure 6.4, where the component invokes `setParameters()` on the `ParameterManager`, which then turns around and sets the value of connected parameter properties on the component. After connected parameters are set, the component invokes `renderComponent()` on itself. Once the component finishes rendering, the properties are reset back to their initial values by invoking `resetParameters()` on the `ParameterManager`—which again analyzes the parameters for the component and sets the values of the connected parameters back to their initial values.

In some cases, the parameter values, obtained from some domain object, may represent a large object (or collection of objects) that should be garbage collected. Resetting the parameter value back to null (or whatever the initial value is) ensures that dangling references to such objects are eliminated and that the garbage collector can do its work. It also ensures that, for instance, values entered by one user are not made visible to a different user (in a later request that uses the same page instance).

The first time `ParameterManager`'s `setParameters()` method is invoked, it will first read each parameter property before setting it from the binding; this value is saved for later use when the `resetParameters()` method is invoked. This means that whatever value is assigned to the property when the component is rendered the first time will be the reset value used thereafter. A component's `finishLoad()` method can be overridden to set initial values for parameter properties, which will be used as defaults for the parameters when the parameter is not bound.

Tapestry also tries to optimize the number of properties it sets from parameters. The `ParameterManager` checks to see if the binding object for each parameter is *invariant*. Bindings that are either literal values or localized messages are invariant; that is, unlike bindings based on OGNL expressions, their value will never change. In these cases, the framework sets the parameter property only once, just before the component renders the first time. In addition, there is no need to reset the property after the component renders.

Although most component parameters use `in`, the other three directions have their uses:

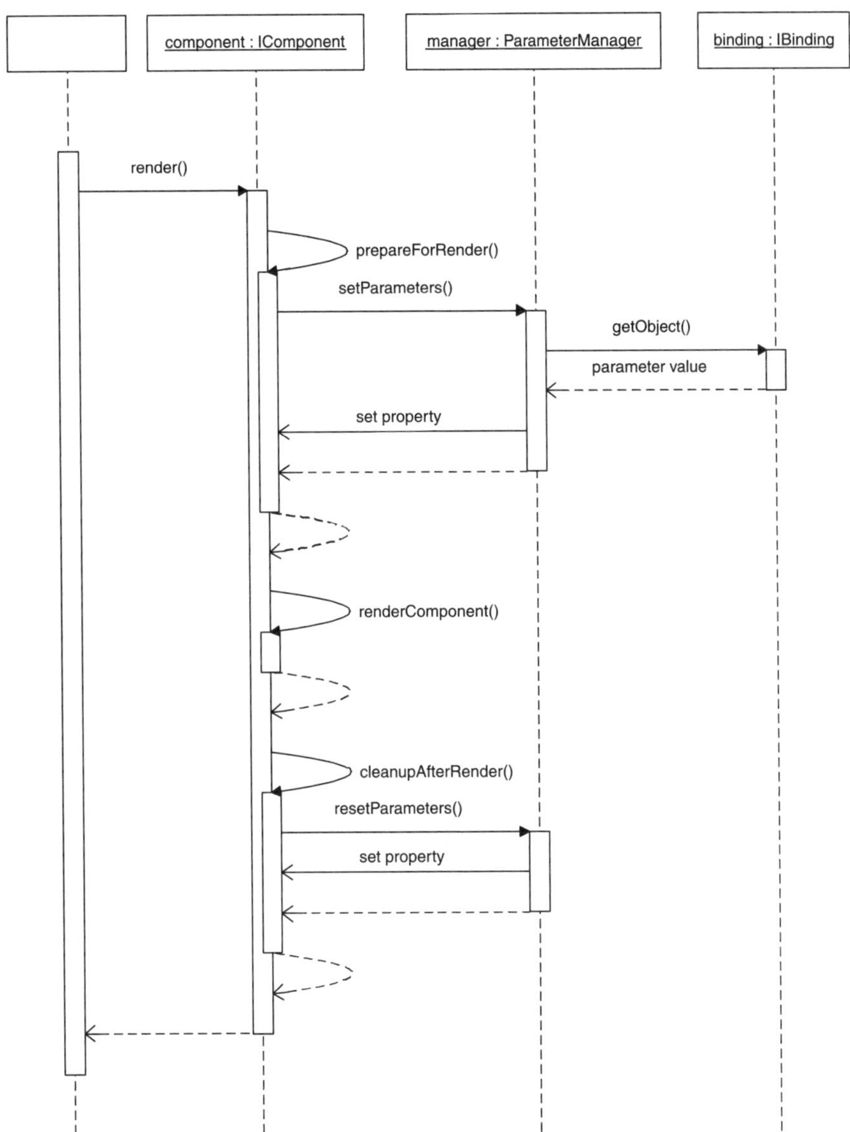

Figure 6.4 Each component's `ParameterManager` is responsible for connected parameters. For `direction="in"`, the parameter binding is read and the property set before the component's `renderComponent()` method is invoked. After rendering, the `ParameterManager` resets the property back to its initial value.

- form—The direction attribute's form value is closely related to in. It implements the flow appropriate to a form control (such as the value parameter on a TextField). On render, the property bound to the parameter is read and used to set the connected parameter property value, just like in. Once the component rewinds, the connected parameter property is read and the value is used to update the property bound to the parameter, which in does not do. This direction is used with a component parameter that is updated from a query parameter upon form submission.

CAUTION Both in and form have a weakness: The parameter property is valid only while the component is rendering—that is, while the renderComponent() method is active (or in methods invoked from the renderComponent() method). There are times when this is insufficient, when the parameter binding's value is needed outside the confines of rendering (or rewinding), in which case the value auto is typically used.

- custom—The value custom leaves control in your hands. Tapestry creates the property to store the binding object and nothing else. Your code can access the binding object and invoke the getObject() and setObject() methods on it.
- auto—The auto value is much like custom, but it implements a connected parameter property that appears the same as in. The implementation of the accessor methods obtains the matching binding object and invokes the appropriate method upon it, much like this:

```
public Type getParameter()
{
  return (Type)getParameterBinding().getObject("parameter",
    Type.class);
}

public void setParameter(Type parameter)
{
  getParameterBinding().setObject(parameter);
}
```

The value auto has some other limitations. The parameter must be required; it may not be optional. Of the primitive Java types, only boolean, int, and double are supported.[6] (byte, char, float, long, and short are not supported.) In addition, array types are not supported.

---

[6] For types boolean, int, double, and String, the synthetic getter methods use the getBoolean(), getInt(), getDouble(), and getString() methods of IBinding, respectively. The setter methods use setBoolean(), setInt(), setDouble(), and setString().

Choosing a parameter direction

As the component author, you are responsible for deciding the direction to use with your parameters, based on how the component and the parameter are utilized. Table 6.2 provides basic rules for choosing the direction.

Table 6.2 Rules for choosing the `direction` attribute

Direction	Use
`in`	The parameter is used only when the component is rendering, and the component doesn't update the parameter, ever.
`form`	The component is a form-element component; the parameter is read only when the component is rendering and is updated only when the containing form is submitted. Most of the form element components include a `value` parameter with the `direction` attribute set to `form`.
`auto`	The parameter value may be read or updated even when the component is not rendering (or rewinding), such as the `listener` parameter of the DirectLink component.
`custom`	You'd rather use `auto`, but you can't because the parameter type is not valid for `auto`, or the parameter is not required.

The vast majority of component parameters are read-only and used only when a component is actively rendering; in those situations, the value `in` for the `direction` attribute is appropriate. Choosing a parameter direction comes down to identifying when `in` can't be used; each direction in table 6.2 should be considered, in order, until a match is found.

It may turn out that a parameter is needed when the component is not rendering. For example, the `listener` parameter of a DirectLink component is needed when the DirectLink is triggered; this is an interaction between the direct service and the DirectLink component that occurs entirely outside the render process (it is shown in chapter 7, figure 7.11).

NOTE In Tapestry, engine services, such as the direct service, are used to dispatch incoming requests. You can think of them as a kind of servlet inside the Tapestry servlet. Tapestry servlets, engines, and engine services are described in detail in chapter 7.

The DirectLink component specifies the direction for the `listener` parameter as `auto`, which dynamically accesses the listener via the listener binding. This *is* a valid operation even when the DirectLink is not rendering.

NOTE Parameter directions have been identified as an area of Tapestry that requires work. See appendix A for some notes on how parameters may be changed and simplified in Tapestry release 3.1.

6.2.5 Reserving names

A potential conflict occurs when a component allows informal parameters: What happens when the component generates a particular attribute, and the informal parameter provides a value for the same attribute? For example, the Image component generates an `src` attribute from its `image` parameter; but most templates using an Image component include an `src` attribute of some kind, to support WYSIWYG preview. You could end up with the `src` attribute appearing twice (with two different values) in the rendered tag, and no clue what the client web browser will due with this extra attribute.

The solution is to forbid certain names as informal parameters. Each formal parameter name is automatically added to the list of reserved names that may not be used as informal parameters. In addition, the `<reserved-parameter>` element is used to reserve additional names:

```
<reserved-parameter name="name"/>
```

Informal parameters that match any reserved name are dropped. The comparison is case insensitive, so the informal parameter `Src`, `SRC`, or `src` would be dropped from an Image component, which reserves the parameter name `src`.

When creating components, you should identify which attributes are written out by your implementation of `renderComponent()` and reserve each such attribute as a reserved parameter. All of this applies only to components that allow informal parameters.

So, now that we have basic tools for specifying components, let's push on to see how to combine a specification, a template, and some Java code to create a fully functional component, using the Hangman application from chapter 2.

6.3 Creating the Digit and Scaffold components

The first of these components will be the Digit component, which is used on the Guess and Win pages.[7] Its input is a numeric digit, and its output, when rendering, is a complete `<img>` element that displays the digit as an image. The Scaffold

[7] The Home and Lose pages also display a digit, but it is entirely static; so, using ordinary static HTML is appropriate on those pages.

component is similar to the Digit component, the major exception being the choice of images displayed by the component. Both of these components are codeless, meaning that they use the `BaseComponent` class rather than requiring a subclass.

We'll start by examining the specification for the Digit and Scaffold components, in listings 6.1 and 6.2.

Listing 6.1 Digit.jwc: specification for the Digit component

```
<?xml version="1.0"?>
<!DOCTYPE component-specification PUBLIC
  "-//Apache Software Foundation//Tapestry Specification 3.0//EN"
  "http://jakarta.apache.org/tapestry/dtd/Tapestry_3_0.dtd">

<component-specification
  allow-body="no"
  allow-informal-parameters="no">

  <parameter name="digit" direction="in"
    required="yes" type="int"/>

  <component id="image" type="Image">
    <binding name="image">
      getAsset("digit" + digit)
    </binding>
    <binding name="alt" expression="digit"/>
  </component>

  <context-asset name="digit0" path="images/Chalkboard_1x7.png"/>
  <context-asset name="digit1" path="images/Chalkboard_1x8.png"/>
  <context-asset name="digit2" path="images/Chalkboard_2x7.png"/>
  <context-asset name="digit3" path="images/Chalkboard_2x8.png"/>
  <context-asset name="digit4" path="images/Chalkboard_3x7.png"/>
  <context-asset name="digit5" path="images/Chalkboard_3x8.png"/>

</component-specification>
```

Listing 6.2 Scaffold.jwc: specification for the Scaffold component

```
<?xml version="1.0"?>
<!DOCTYPE component-specification PUBLIC
  "-//Apache Software Foundation//Tapestry Specification 3.0//EN"
  "http://jakarta.apache.org/tapestry/dtd/Tapestry_3_0.dtd">

<component-specification
  allow-body="no"
  allow-informal-parameters="no">

  <parameter name="digit" direction="in"
    required="yes" type="int"/>
```

```
    <component id="image" type="Image">
      <binding name="image">
        getAsset("scaffold" + digit)
      </binding>
    </component>

    <context-asset name="scaffold5" path="images/scaffold.png"/>
    <context-asset name="scaffold4" path="images/scaffold-1.png"/>
    <context-asset name="scaffold3" path="images/scaffold-2.png"/>
    <context-asset name="scaffold2" path="images/scaffold-3.png"/>
    <context-asset name="scaffold1" path="images/scaffold-4.png"/>
    <context-asset name="scaffold0" path="images/scaffold-5.png"/>

  </component-specification>
```

6.3.1 *Specifying the digit parameter*

The Digit and Scaffold components each take a single parameter, `digit`, declared in each component's specification:

```
<parameter name="digit" direction="in" required="yes" type="int"/>
```

The parameter is required; when using either component, a binding for the `digit` parameter must be provided or a runtime exception will occur. The type of the parameter is `int`, a Java primitive type. This will be the type of the parameter property created to hold the parameter value.

Since the parameter's direction is `in`, the framework will automatically set the parameter property before rendering the component. As you'll see, we can use this `digit` property in the template or as part of OGNL expressions in the specification.

6.3.2 *Using the digit parameter*

The `digit` parameter is used only in the specification. The parameter is used in two ways:

- To select the correct image asset
- As the `alt` attribute for the Image component (providing an accessible title for the image)

The Image component will be used inside the Digit component's template. It contains two parameter bindings:

```
<component id="image" type="Image">
  <binding name="image">
    getAsset("digit" + digit)
  </binding>
```

```
  <binding name="alt" expression="digit"/>
</component>
```

The first binding uses the `digit` property as part of an OGNL expression to retrieve the correct asset.[8] The `digit` property is also used with the informal `alt` parameter of the Image component. The Scaffold component includes an almost identical section in its specification:

```
<component id="image" type="Image">
  <binding name="image">
    getAsset("scaffold" + digit)
  </binding>
</component>
```

6.3.3 Creating the template

The Digit component's template is tiny, just big enough to contain an Image component:

```
<img jwcid="image" width="36" height="36"/>
```

The Scaffold component's template is similar:

```
<img jwcid="image" alt="[Scaffold]"
  src="images/scaffold.png" border="0"/>
```

6.3.4 Using the Digit component

Now that we've defined the Digit component, we can use it exactly like any of the components provided with Tapestry. In the revised Guess page's template, the Digit component is used instead of the standard Image component:

```
<img jwcid="@Digit"
  digit="ognl:visit.game.incorrectGuessesLeft"
  src="images/Chalkboard_3x8.png"/>
```

As in the previous version from chapter 2, much of the component is simply there to maintain WYSIWYG preview when using an HTML editor. In this case, the choice of HTML tag (`<img>`) and the inclusion of the `src` attribute are useful for WYSIWYG preview but are meaningless to Tapestry. Regardless of what appears in the template, the Image component will render an `<img>` tag and provide a value for the `src` attribute. The `src` informal parameter will be ignored because it is a literal value provided in the HTML template and the Digit component does not allow informal parameters.

---

[8] This is an example of using the alternate form of the `<binding>` element, where a long OGNL expression is placed in the body of the element, rather than as the value of the `expression` attribute. The form is useful when the expression contains a mixture of quotes, or if it's very long or complex.

This is a marked improvement to what was necessary in chapter 2 to display the digit. There, the equivalent section of the Guess page template was bogged down with the details that are now isolated in the Digit component:

```
<img jwcid="@Image"
   alt="ognl:visit.game.incorrectGuessesLeft"
   image='ognl:getAsset("digit" +
     visit.game.incorrectGuessesLeft)'
   height="36"
   src="images/Chalkboard_3x8.png"
   width="36" border="0"/>
```

Not only is the new version more succinct and readable, it also doesn't require that the digit assets be specified in both the Win and Guess pages' specifications. Those assets are declared just once, inside the Digit component.

6.3.5 Using the Scaffold component

Likewise, the Scaffold component plugs into both the Guess and Win pages in a similar way:

```
<img jwcid="@Scaffold"
  digit="ognl:visit.game.incorrectGuessesLeft"
  src="images/scaffold.png" border="0"/>
```

Again, the details (and assets) of the component are isolated. In both of these examples, we've seen how the original portion of the Guess page's HTML template can be extracted and refined as a new component. Our next example takes a similar approach but does so without using an HTML template of its own.

6.4 Creating the Letter component

The Letter component is used to display an image corresponding to a particular letter in the alphabet. It is used in several places: on the Guess page, it is used to display the (partially guessed) target word and to display the remaining guessable letters. The Letter component is also used in the Win and Lose pages to show the complete target word.

The previous two components (Digit and Scaffold) were codeless and used HTML templates. The implementation of the Letter component uses no HTML template; instead, it implements the `renderComponent()` method to produce the HTML output in Java code. For well-focused components that produce little HTML (the Digit, Scaffold, and Letter components each render exactly one tag), implementing in code is often a better option, especially if there are any calculations to perform as part of the render (in this case, selecting the correct image based on two different parameters).

6.4.1 Specifying the Letter component

The Letter component is similar to the Digit component, taking a `letter` parameter instead of a `digit` parameter. It also includes a second parameter, `disabled`, which when set to true, forces the component to ignore the `letter` parameter and always display a blank space. The specification for this component is provided in listing 6.3.

Listing 6.3 Letter.jwc: specification for the Letter component

```
<?xml version="1.0"?>
<!DOCTYPE component-specification PUBLIC
  "-//Apache Software Foundation//Tapestry Specification 3.0//EN"
  "http://jakarta.apache.org/tapestry/dtd/Tapestry_3_0.dtd">

<component-specification
  class="hangman2.Letter"
  allow-body="no"
  allow-informal-parameters="no">

  <parameter name="letter" direction="in"
    required="yes" type="char"/>
  <parameter name="disabled" direction="in" type="boolean"/>

  <context-asset name="space" path="images/letter-spacer.png"/>
  <context-asset name="dash" path="images/Chalkboard_5x3.png"/>

  <context-asset name="a" path="images/Chalkboard_1x1.png"/>
  <context-asset name="b" path="images/Chalkboard_1x2.png"/>
  <context-asset name="c" path="images/Chalkboard_1x3.png"/>
  <context-asset name="d" path="images/Chalkboard_1x4.png"/>
  <context-asset name="e" path="images/Chalkboard_1x5.png"/>
  <context-asset name="f" path="images/Chalkboard_1x6.png"/>
  <context-asset name="g" path="images/Chalkboard_2x1.png"/>
  <context-asset name="h" path="images/Chalkboard_2x2.png"/>
  <context-asset name="i" path="images/Chalkboard_2x3.png"/>
  <context-asset name="j" path="images/Chalkboard_2x4.png"/>
  <context-asset name="k" path="images/Chalkboard_2x5.png"/>
  <context-asset name="l" path="images/Chalkboard_2x6.png"/>
  <context-asset name="m" path="images/Chalkboard_3x1.png"/>
  <context-asset name="n" path="images/Chalkboard_3x2.png"/>
  <context-asset name="o" path="images/Chalkboard_3x3.png"/>
  <context-asset name="p" path="images/Chalkboard_3x4.png"/>
  <context-asset name="q" path="images/Chalkboard_3x5.png"/>
  <context-asset name="r" path="images/Chalkboard_3x6.png"/>
  <context-asset name="s" path="images/Chalkboard_4x1.png"/>
  <context-asset name="t" path="images/Chalkboard_4x2.png"/>
  <context-asset name="u" path="images/Chalkboard_4x3.png"/>
  <context-asset name="v" path="images/Chalkboard_4x4.png"/>
```

```
    <context-asset name="w" path="images/Chalkboard_4x5.png"/>
    <context-asset name="x" path="images/Chalkboard_4x6.png"/>
    <context-asset name="y" path="images/Chalkboard_5x1.png"/>
    <context-asset name="z" path="images/Chalkboard_5x2.png"/>

</component-specification>
```

As with the Digit component, the bulk of the Letter component specification consists of specifications for all the assets: one for each letter, plus the dash (or underscore) and a placeholder.

6.4.2 Implementing the Letter component

Much of the code for the Letter component (listing 6.4) is familiar from chapter 2, where the basic ideas were duplicated in the Guess, Win, and Lose pages. The code uses the `letter` parameter to determine the correct asset, and renders an `<img>` element, deriving the `src` attribute from the asset.

Listing 6.4 Letter.java: Java class for the Letter component

```
package hangman2;

import org.apache.tapestry.AbstractComponent;
import org.apache.tapestry.IAsset;
import org.apache.tapestry.IMarkupWriter;
import org.apache.tapestry.IRequestCycle;

public abstract class Letter extends AbstractComponent
{
  public abstract boolean isDisabled();
  public abstract char getLetter();

  protected void renderComponent(IMarkupWriter writer,
      IRequestCycle cycle)
  {
    writer.beginEmpty("img");
    writer.attribute("src",
      getLetterImage().buildURL(cycle));          <- Converts asset to URL
    writer.attribute("alt", getLetterLabel());
    writer.attribute("height", 36);
    writer.attribute("width", 36);
    writer.attribute("border", 0);
  }

  public IAsset getLetterImage()
  {
    if (isDisabled())
      return getAsset("space");
```

```
    char letter = getLetter();

    if (letter == '_')
      return getAsset("dash");

    return getAsset("" + letter);
  }

  public String getLetterLabel()
  {
    if (isDisabled())
      return " ";

    return ("" + getLetter()).toUpperCase();
  }

}
```

Converts letter to alt tag value

The main method is `renderComponent()`, whose job is to render an HTML `<img>` tag, which will display the image matching the `letter` parameter. The `IMarkupWriter` interface makes it simple to output HTML elements and attributes in an orderly manner. The `beginEmpty()` method starts an element that has no body, and the `attribute()` methods write attributes for that element, properly quoting values and converting unsafe characters to HTML entities.

The remaining methods in the `Letter` class determine the correct image asset to use based on the `letter` and `disabled` parameters, and the proper string to use as for the `<img>` tag's `alt` attribute. This code was duplicated over several pages in the original Hangman application in chapter 2, but now it is in a single place, inside the Letter component.

Previously, you've seen how Java code may define abstract accessor methods to reference specified properties. The same technique is used here to access connected parameter properties. The enhanced subclass generated at runtime by Tapestry includes the necessary fields, a get method, and a set method. The code in this class is free to use those accessor methods.

6.4.3 Using the Letter component

The Letter component is used inside the Guess page to generate the grid of images that may be guessed. As before, this involves a Foreach component (the selectLoop component) to loop through the available letters, a DirectLink component (the select component) to allow any as-yet-unguessed letter to be guessed, and an anonymous Letter component to display the actual letter (or a blank space if the letter has already been guessed):

```
<span jwcid="selectLoop">
<a href="#" jwcid="select"
  class="select-letter"><img jwcid="@Letter"
     letter="ognl:letterForGuessIndex"
     disabled="ognl:letterGuessed"
     border="0"
     src="images/Chalkboard_5x3.png"/></a>
</span>
```

As with the Digit component, using the Letter component is much simpler than accomplishing the same task using the standard Image component. The Letter component hides the logic used to select the correct image and label. If maintaining the ability to preview is not important, then the template could be simplified further by removing the `src` and `border` attributes from the `<img>` element.

This is already a simplification from chapter 2, where achieving the same result required a much more involved section to render the letter image:

```
<span jwcid="selectLoop">
<a href="#"
   jwcid="select"
   class="select-letter">
   <img jwcid="@Image"
      image="ognl:guessImage"
      alt="ognl:guessLabel"
      height="36"
      src="images/Chalkboard_5x3.png"
      width="36"
      border="0"/>
</a>
```

Once again, as with the Digit and the Scaffold components, we've consolidated duplicated logic and duplicated asset specifications, and eliminated duplicated Java code. This makes the revised Guess page even shorter and more focused on handling guesses rather than figuring out which image to display for which letter.

Just as we've built new components by combining framework components, we can also build new components from other new components.

6.5 Building the Spell component

Spelling out the target word appears on three out of four pages in the Hangman application: the Guess page displays the partially guessed word, and both the Win and Lose pages display the complete target word. In this case, rather than replace a single Image component with a Letter component, we'll simplify the page template by replacing a Foreach component and an Image component with a single Spell component.

The earlier versions of these pages used a Foreach component enclosing an Image component. These components are now the basis for the Spell component, whose HTML template is shown in listing 6.5.

Listing 6.5 Spell.html: HTML template for the Spell component

```
<span jwcid="@Foreach"
  source="ognl:page.visit.game.letters"
  value="ognl:letter">
<img jwcid="@Letter" letter="ognl:letter"/>
</span>
```

This Spell component is hard-wired to do exactly one thing: spell out the word provided by the `Game` object's `letters` property (via the OGNL expression `page.visit.game.letters`). All components have a property, `page`, which identifies the page that ultimately contains the component.[9] From there, we can access the `visit` property, as well as the `game` property of the `Visit` object.

Because this component is intended for use only within the Hangman application, it doesn't make sense to define a parameter for the word to spell out; we will always configure that parameter identically, to display the target word. Instead, the component is hard-wired to the `Game` object's `letters` property.

6.5.1 Implementing the Spell component

You've already seen several examples of page properties being used to coordinate components contained by the page, and this carries over to components as well, as seen in listing 6.6.

Listing 6.6 Spell.jwc: specification for the Spell component

```
<?xml version="1.0"?>
<!DOCTYPE component-specification PUBLIC
  "-// Apache Software Foundation//Tapestry Specification 3.0//EN"
 "http://jakarta.apache.org/tapestry/dtd/Tapestry_3_0.dtd">
```

9 As you're beginning to see, components can contain components and so forth, so the page may be several levels of containment above the component.

```
<component-specification
  allow-body="no"
  allow-informal-parameters="no">

  <property-specification name="letter" type="char"/>

</component-specification>
```

In this case, the Spell component defines a `letter` property (of type `char`), which allows the Foreach and Letter components contained by Spell to work together. The Foreach updates the `letter` property, and the Letter component uses it, binding it to the `letter` parameter.

Previously, we've discussed how the page acts as controller, mediating between the components it contains. This concept extends to components (such as Spell) that contain other components. The container (whether it is a page or just another component) still is responsible for making it possible for the components it contains to work together. Here, that mediation takes the form of a property that one component (the Foreach) can write into and another component (the Letter) can read from.

6.5.2 Using the Spell component

The Spell component is used in the Guess page's HTML template to display the target word:

```
<span jwcid="@Spell">

  <img height="36" alt="A" src="images/Chalkboard_1x1.png"
    width="36" border="0">
  <img height="36" alt="_" src="images/Chalkboard_5x3.png"
    width="36" border="0">
  <img height="36" alt="_" src="images/Chalkboard_1x5.png"
    width="36" border="0">
  <img height="36" alt="_" src="images/Chalkboard_5x3.png"
    width="36" border="0">
  <img height="36" alt="_" src="images/Chalkboard_5x3.png"
    width="36" border="0">
  <img height="36" alt="_" src="images/Chalkboard_5x3.png"
    width="36" border="0">
  <img height="36" alt="_" src="images/Chalkboard_5x1.png"
    width="36" border="0">
</span>
```

Earlier, you saw how to add attributes to tags to support previewing. Here, you see an entire chunk of HTML, the series of `<img>` elements, used for the same purpose.

The Spell component does not allow a body, so the entire stretch of HTML within the Guess page's template is discarded.

Again, as with the previous components, the new usage is much easier to deal with than the old one. Back in chapter 2, we had to include the Foreach component, the Image component, and additional methods in our page (again, on all three major pages: Guess, Win, and Lose). Even omitting the "for preview" `<img>` tags (which are ultimately discarded anyway), the old way was much longer:

```
<span jwcid="@Foreach"
   source="ognl:visit.game.letters"
   value="ognl:letter">
<img jwcid="@Image"
   image="ognl:letterImage"
   alt="ognl:letterLabel"
   height="36"
   src="images/Chalkboard_5x3.png"
   width="36"
   border="0"/>
</span>
```

Eventually, a project will hit a crossroads: How valuable is it to maintain the ability to preview the page using a WYSIWYG HTML editor? As a project hits its stride and pages start to consist of more and more components, the manual effort needed to maintain the preview (when the HTML is generated within a component) may easily outweigh the utility of doing so. For example, our earlier use of the Spell component might be replaced with just a placeholder:

```
<span jwcid="@Spell">
  [@Spell component output]
</span>
```

The page no longer will preview as it did before. Rather than a somewhat accurate snapshot of a running application, the previewed HTML will more obviously be what it is: a template. Figure 6.5 shows how the updated template will preview in a WYSIWYG HTML editor.

The result of pulling back the curtain in this way is that HTML developers will have fewer questions about what they can and cannot change. In addition, HTML developers won't be confused as to where changes must take place; there will be less of a chance that they will make changes to portions of the template that Tapestry is going to discard at runtime. The downside is, of course, that development will gradually shift to the point where the live application must be run in order to see what final pages will look like.

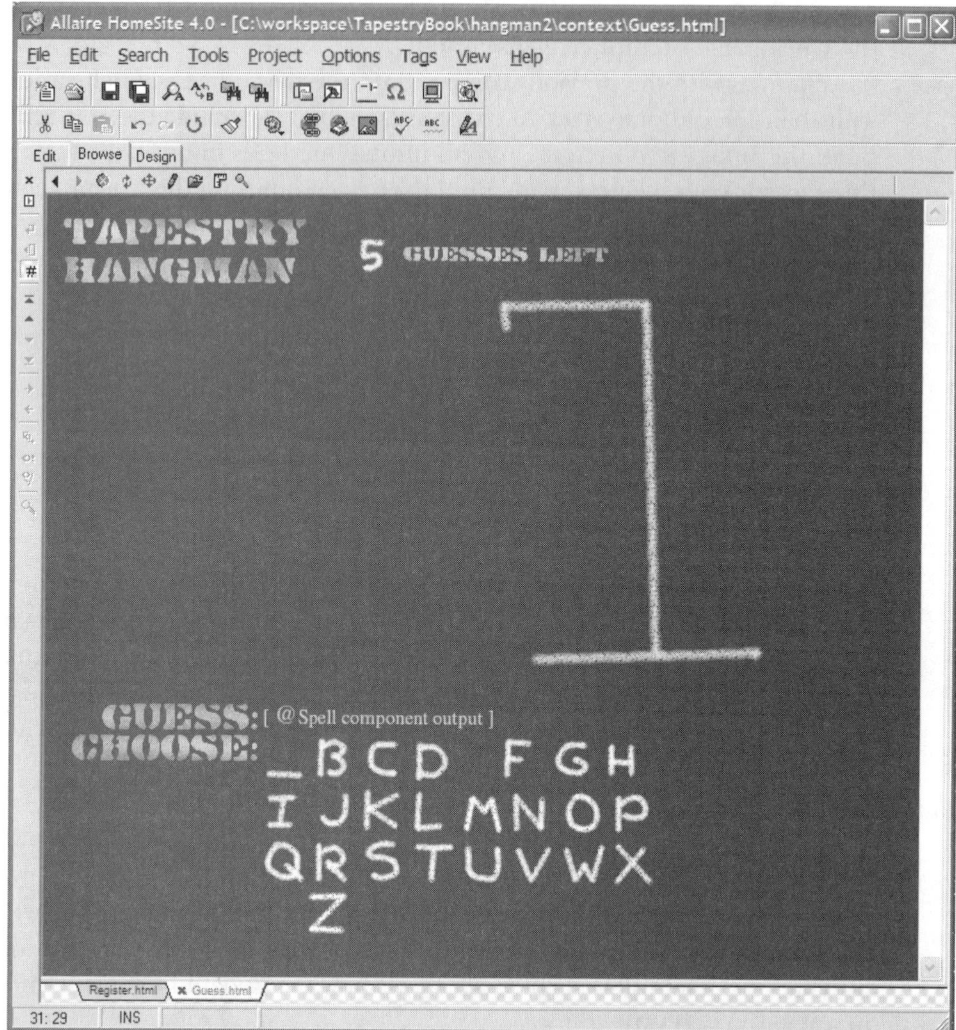

Figure 6.5 Replacing the `<img>` tags in the Spell component's body significantly changes how the template will preview.

6.6 Building the Border component

So far, all the components we've built for the Hangman application have discarded their bodies. Exciting possibilities open up when we define components that allow a body, mixing their own template with a portion of their page's template.

The revised Hangman application uses such a component, Border, to provide the Shell and Body components for each page in the application. For the Hangman application, the Border does very little; but in a more realistic Tapestry application, the same technique can be used to create more of the basic look and feel of the application: title bars up top, copyrights at the bottom, navigational controls along the top or side (as appropriate). We'll see a much more involved example of this in chapters 9 and 10, with the Border component for the Virtual Library application.

6.6.1 Creating the Border template

The HTML template for the Border component includes a Shell component and a Body component, and introduces another new component provided by the framework: RenderBody. The HTML template for the Border component is provided in listing 6.7.

Listing 6.7 Border.html: HTML template for the Border component

```
<html jwcid="@Shell" title="Tapestry Hangman"
  stylesheet="ognl:assets.stylesheet">
<body jwcid="@Body">

<span jwcid="@RenderBody">

Page specific content goes here.

</span>

</body>
</html>
```

The RenderBody component causes the component that contains it (the Border component) to render its body, which is the portion of the page's template that its start and end tags wrap around. Note the distinction between being *contained* and being *enclosed*. The RenderBody component is *enclosed* by the Body component. It is *contained* by the Border component, because it appears inside the Border component's HTML template. The Shell, Body, and RenderBody components are all contained by the Border component.

The body of the Border component may contain any mix of static HTML and components—even other components with templates (that contain more RenderBody components). RenderBody discards its body, so the note "Page specific content goes here" will not appear in the live application. Instead, the body of the Border component within its page is rendered.

6.6.2 Creating the Border specification

The Border component's specification is shown in listing 6.8.

Listing 6.8 Border.jwc: specification for the Border component

```
<?xml version="1.0"?>
<!DOCTYPE component-specification PUBLIC
  "-//Apache Software Foundation//Tapestry Specification 3.0//EN"
  "http://jakarta.apache.org/tapestry/dtd/Tapestry_3_0.dtd">

<component-specification
  allow-body="yes"
  allow-informal-parameters="no">

  <context-asset name="stylesheet" path="css/hangman.css"/>

</component-specification>
```

This specification serves two simple purposes:

- It indicates that the Border component allows, and does not discard, its body.[10]
- It allows us to specify here, and only here, the asset for the application's stylesheet.

Once again, using a component has allowed us to remove duplicate code, duplicate specifications, and duplicate assets. As usual in Tapestry, simplicity and consistency go hand in hand: Using the Border component is simpler, more consistent, and more maintainable than duplicating the Shell and Body components and the stylesheet asset.

6.6.3 Using the Border component

Using the Border component is the same as using any other component. You create a `<span>` tag in the HTML template to indicate where on the page the component belongs and to delineate the body of the component. All four pages in the application follow the same general template:

```
<html>
<head>
<title>Tapestry Hangman</title>
```

[10] This could be omitted, since the default is `yes`, but including the attribute as a reminder helps to document the purpose of the component.

```
<link rel="stylesheet" type="text/css" href="css/hangman.css"/>
</head>
<body jwcid="$content$">
<span jwcid="@Border">

  . . .

</span>
</body>
</html>
```

Back in chapter 2, we introduced the special `jwcid "$remove$"`, used to edit out a portion of the template. When using the Border component, we have a similar problem. At runtime, we want the Border component (and the Shell and Body components it contains) to render the `<html>`, `<head>`, and `<body>` elements in the page. This creates a conflict if we want to maintain the ability to preview the page in the HTML editor; we need to keep the `<link>` tag that connects the template to the stylesheet, or the page becomes virtually unreadable in the editor.

At the same time, we want to eliminate the `<html>`, `<head>`, and `<body>` elements in the page template, because they will be provided at runtime by the Border component (via the Shell component contained by the Border). If we use the `"$remove$" jwcid` on the `<html>` or `<body>` tags in the page template, the entire page will be removed! The solution is a second special `jwcid`, `"$content$"`.

The `"$remove$" jwcid` is used to remove an element and its body from the template. The `"$content$" jwcid` removes everything *but* the element's body. The `<body>` tag, everything that precedes it, the `</body>` tag, and everything that follows it are all discarded. What's left is the content inside the `<body>` tag, which is the Border component, enclosing everything else on the page. Everything then falls into place, and at runtime, the Border component properly renders the `<html>` and `<body>` tags before and around its body.

The end result of all these changes is shorter, simpler Java code and smaller, simpler templates. The code base for the entire application shrank from approximately 200 lines of code (excluding comments) to 160 lines, but, more important, virtually all redundancy in the code was removed. As much as application-specific components such as these are a modest win for an individual application, the real gains are to be made when creating fully reusable components, adaptable to many applications. The next sections describe those sorts of components.

6.7 Creating interactive, reusable components

The components described in the previous sections are output-only components: They are used when a page is rendering, but they are not themselves interactive. Adding interactivity requires using components in combinations with engine services. *Engine services*, described more fully in chapter 7, are the gateways connecting incoming requests from the client web browser with objects and code running on the server.

As an example, let's implement a clickable link for an image map. The example in this section is part of the examples application. Launch your web browser to http://localhost:8080/examples/app and click the Pets link under the chapter 6 heading.

6.7.1 Introducing the Pet Store image map

Image maps are an often-overlooked aspect of HTML. An image map is an ordinary image paired with additional HTML to define regions within the image. Each region is a rectangle or polygon within the image, defined using a series of coordinates. Each region defines a URL to trigger when that region of the image is clicked. HTML designers often use image maps because of the precision with which they can arrange buttons (or other clickable elements) inside the image.

To put this all together, the `<img>` element includes a `usemap` attribute that identifies the image map to use. A corresponding `<map>` element contains a number of `<area>` elements, and each `<area>` defines a region of the image and the URL to trigger.

A familiar example of this is part of the standard Java 2 Enterprise Edition (J2EE) demonstration application, the Java Pet Store. The first page of the Pet Store includes an image map for selecting the top-level category when shopping for a pet. Clicking the pet image brings up a catalog of that type of pet. A Tapestry version of this page is shown in figure 6.6. The utility of an image map is obvious here because the clickable regions (the small images of the different pets) are not organized into handy rows and columns.

It would be ideal to leverage the functionality of the DirectLink component (the component used so effectively in the Hangman application) but use it instead to create the `<area>` elements that define the clickable regions. We must still be able to define listener methods and pass service parameters as part of the URL. This ideal is possible, because most of the behavior of the DirectLink component is inside the direct service, and so it is easy to reuse in a new component.

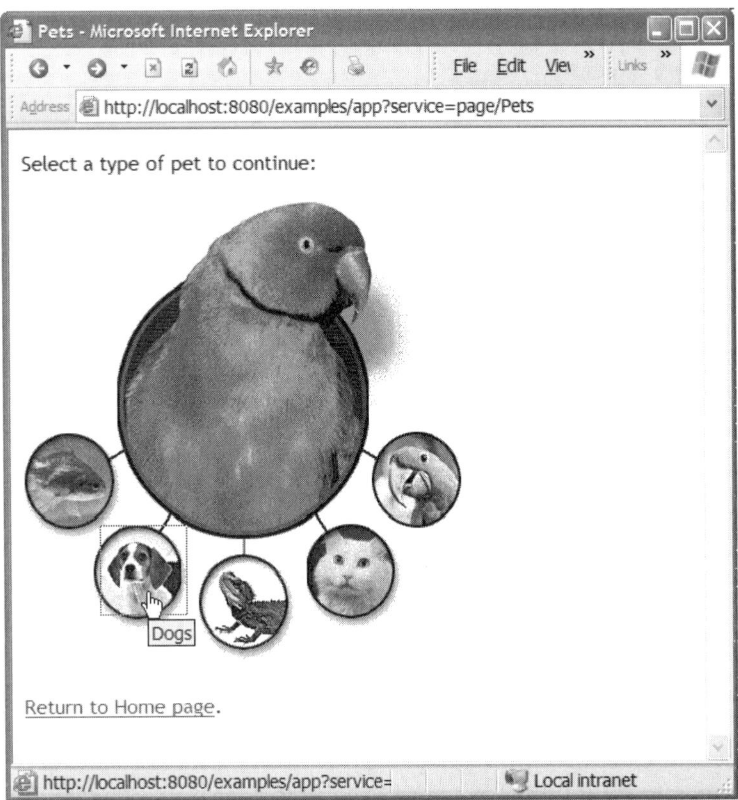

Figure 6.6 An image map allows the user to select a category of pet to shop for. Image maps allow for precise control over the layout of the active areas.

The DirectArea component can use the direct service just as easily as the DirectLink component.

6.7.2 Specifying the DirectArea component

The DirectArea component, whose specification is shown in listing 6.9, is similar to a DirectLink component; it has a required `listener` parameter and an optional `parameters` parameter. Like the DirectLink component, the DirectArea component must support informal parameters.

Listing 6.9 DirectArea.jwc: specification for the DirectArea component

```
<?xml version="1.0"?>
<!DOCTYPE component-specification PUBLIC
  "-//Apache Software Foundation//Tapestry Specification 3.0//EN"
```

```
  "http://jakarta.apache.org/tapestry/dtd/Tapestry_3_0.dtd">

<component-specification
  class="examples.DirectArea"
  allow-body="no"
  allow-informal-parameters="yes">

  <parameter name="listener" required="yes"
    direction="auto"
    type="org.apache.tapestry.IActionListener"/>        ❶
  <parameter name="parameters" type="java.lang.Object"     ❷
    direction="in"/>

</component-specification>
```

❶ Listener methods are represented as instance of the class `IActionListener`.

❷ We use `java.lang.Object` as the type since we don't know the actual type that will be provided.

The HTML `<area>` element does not allow a body, so neither does the DirectArea component. The specification defines the two parameters, `listener` and `parameters`, mimicking two of the DirectLink parameters. The `listener` parameter's direction is `auto`, not `in`. This is necessary because the listener is needed when the direct service triggers the component, and this event occurs when the component is not rendering.

In addition, the `parameters` parameter is type `java.lang.Object`; this is the correct type to use when the runtime type of the parameter is not known. As with the DirectLink component (which defines its `parameters` parameter the same way), this value may be an object, an array of objects, or a `List` of objects.

6.7.3 Implementing the DirectArea component

The DirectArea component's class, shown in listing 6.10, consists of only three methods. The `renderComponent()` method renders the `<area>` element. The `trigger()` and `isStateful()` methods are used when a request is sent by the client web browser in response to the user clicking within the image.

Listing 6.10 DirectArea.java: Java class for the DirectArea component

```
package examples;

import org.apache.tapestry.AbstractComponent;
import org.apache.tapestry.IActionListener;
import org.apache.tapestry.IDirect;
```

```
import org.apache.tapestry.IMarkupWriter;
import org.apache.tapestry.IRequestCycle;
import org.apache.tapestry.Tapestry;
import org.apache.tapestry.engine.IEngineService;
import org.apache.tapestry.engine.ILink;
import org.apache.tapestry.link.DirectLink;

public abstract class DirectArea
  extends AbstractComponent
  implements IDirect        <-- 1
{
  public abstract IActionListener getListener();
  public abstract Object getParameters();

  protected void renderComponent(IMarkupWriter writer,
      IRequestCycle cycle)
  {
    if (cycle.isRewinding())
      return;

    Object[] parameters =                                          2
      DirectLink.constructServiceParameters(getParameters());

    IEngineService service =                                       3
      cycle.getEngine().getService(Tapestry.DIRECT_SERVICE);
    ILink link = service.getLink(cycle, this, parameters);

    writer.beginEmpty("area");
    writer.attribute("href", link.getURL());      <-- 4

    renderInformalParameters(writer, cycle);      <-- 5
  }

  public void trigger(IRequestCycle cycle)      <-- 6
  {
    IActionListener listener = getListener();

    if (listener == null)                                          7
      throw Tapestry.createRequiredParameterException(this,
        "listener");

    listener.actionTriggered(this, cycle);      <-- 8
  }

  public boolean isStateful()      <-- 9
  {
    return false;
  }
```

❶ The direct service, part of the Tapestry framework, requires that the component it invokes implement the `IDirect` interface.

❷ The `DirectLink` class provides a static utility method, `constructServiceParameters()`, for converting the value bound to the `parameters` parameter into an array of objects.

❸ The `IEngineService` instance is responsible for constructing the URL, which is provided as an instance of `ILink`.

❹ The link object can provide the URL for this component.

❺ The `AbstractComponent` base class provides a method, `renderInformalParameters()`, for generating additional HTML attributes from informal parameters bound to the component.

❻ The `trigger()` method is invoked by the direct service (it is part of the `IDirect` interface).

❼ This code gets the listener object (an object implementing the `IActionListener` interface that will invoke the listener method) and checks that the object exists and is not null.

❽ The `actionTriggered()` method is defined by the `IActionListener` interface; the listener object will invoke the listener method.

❾ The `isStateful()` method is also defined by the `IDirect` interface and invoked by the direct service.

The core of this class is the `renderComponent()` method. It starts with a simple optimization; if the request cycle is rewinding (to process a form submission) instead of rendering, then there's no point in doing the rest of the work (any output will be discarded during a rewind). This scenario could occur if a Form happens to enclose the DirectArea component. When the Form is submitted, the rewind phase will pass through the DirectArea as well as all the form control components, but the DirectArea component has nothing to contribute to the Form's rewind.

The next step is to convert the `parameters` parameter into an array of objects. A static utility method in the `DirectLink` class accomplishes this for us. It will analyze the object and return an array of objects (if the value is an array or a `List`). The method will return null if there are no service parameters.

Next, we obtain the direct service from the engine and have the service construct a link back to this particular DirectArea component, including any service parameters. The next few calls to the markup writer create the `<area>` element and set the `href` attribute from the link created by the service. This component must support informal parameters; the call to `renderInformalParameters()` will convert any informal parameters into additional attributes. Components that allow a body might invoke the method `renderBody()` as well, but DirectArea doesn't allow a body (because `<area>` elements are always empty).

The flip side of the `renderComponent()` method is a pair of methods, defined by the `IDirect` interface, that are invoked when the link (encoded into the `<area>` element's `href` attribute) is triggered. As we'll discuss in chapter 7, the direct service will locate this component and start by invoking the `isStateful()` method.

The `isStateful()` method in DirectArea always returns false, indicating that the link is not stateful, and that it is okay to execute cold (when the `HttpSession` doesn't exist or has expired). That's acceptable for this example, but a truly reusable DirectArea component would, like the DirectLink component, provide a parameter for controlling the return value for this method.

The direct service then invokes the `trigger()` method. Invoking `getListener()` will retrieve the listener object from the binding for the `listener` parameter. Despite the fact that this parameter is required, it's still possible that the listener is null. The required attribute on the `<parameter>` element only ensures that the parameter was bound, not that the bound property is non-null. For example, using the value `ognl:null` would satisfy the parameter's required check, but it wouldn't give us a useful value. To be safe, we check that the listener object is not null and throw an exception in the unlikely case that it is. The `Tapestry` class (a utility class containing useful static methods) includes a method for constructing this exception.

You can also see why it was necessary to set the `listener` parameter's `direction` attribute to `auto` instead of `in`. This `trigger()` method is invoked when the DirectArea component is not rendering—the semantics of an `in` parameter would not work, since a connected property for an `in` parameter will have the correct value only while the `renderComponent()` method is executing. The direct service invokes the `trigger()` method in an entirely different request, at a different time, when the `renderComponent()` method is definitely *not* executing.

Using `auto` for the `listener` parameter's `direction` attribute is appropriate. Invoking the `getListener()` method will get the listener object from the binding, without depending on the `renderComponent()` method.

After successfully passing the required check, we know we have a non-null listener and can invoke the `actionTriggered()` method on the listener object. This will ultimately invoke the listener method provided by the application.

6.7.4 Using the DirectArea component

The Pets page uses several instances of the DirectArea component. The majority of the template, shown in listing 6.11, is simple, static HTML for the image and for the `<map>` element referenced by the image. Only the `<area>` elements are dynamic; each of these is a DirectArea component with its own listener.

Listing 6.11 Pets.html: HTML template for the Pets page

```
<span jwcid="@Border" title="Pets">

<p>Select a type of pet to continue:</p>

<img src="images/pets-image-map.gif"
     alt="Pet Selection Map"
     usemap="#petmap"
     width="350"
     height="355"
     border="0"/>

<map name="petmap">
<area jwcid="@DirectArea" listener="ognl:listeners.selectBirds"
      alt="Birds"
      coords="72,2,280,250"/>
<area jwcid="@DirectArea" listener="ognl:listeners.selectFish"
      alt="Fish"
      coords="2,180,72,250"/>
<area jwcid="@DirectArea"  listener="ognl:listeners.selectDogs"
      alt="Dogs"
      coords="60,250,130,320"/>
<area jwcid="@DirectArea" listener="ognl:listeners.selectReptiles"
      alt="Reptiles"
      coords="140,270,210,340"/>
<area jwcid="@DirectArea" listener="ognl:listeners.selectCats"
      alt="Cats"
      coords="225,240,295,310"/>
<area jwcid="@DirectArea" listener="ognl:listeners.selectBirds"
      alt="Birds"
      coords="280,180,350,250"/>
</map>

</span>
```

Inside the Java class, each listener method funnels into a single method that configures the PetCategory page and selects it as the response page:

```
private void select(String type)
{
  IRequestCycle cycle = getRequestCycle();
```

```
    PetCategory next = (PetCategory) cycle.getPage("PetCategory");

    next.setType(type);
    cycle.setPage(next);
  }

  public void selectBirds(IRequestCycle cycle)
  {
    select("birds");
  }
```

This brings us up to the PetCategory page, which now has the information it needs to display the page, customized to the user's selection. An example is shown in figure 6.7.

In a real application, there would be a product database, and the PetCategory page would perform a query and produce a listing of dogs in the inventory. For the purposes of this example, just getting to the page (and acknowledging that the user selected `dogs`) is sufficient.

Creating components with interactivity is nearly as effortless in Tapestry as creating simple output-only components. Because of the way the framework manages both the component object graph and the dispatch of incoming requests, it is easy to create links that invoke methods on component objects. From there, it is simple to call back into application-specific code using listener methods.

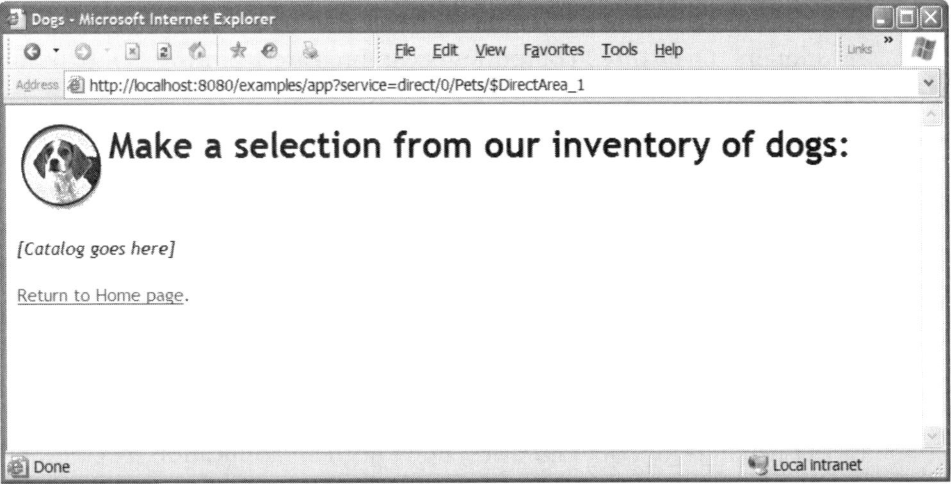

Figure 6.7 After selecting a pet using the image map, the user is brought to a page that displays an inventory of pets of the selected type.

Creating components specific to an application is an excellent way to leverage the various capabilities of members of a team. Because components are, by their nature, small and self-contained, they represent tasks that are more accessible to less-experienced team members, or to team members with specialized knowledge (of Tapestry, HTML, or client-side JavaScript).

Although we've discussed creating components that are reusable in multiple applications, we haven't covered the nuts and bolts of actually doing so. You could cut and paste the component's class, specification, and template into a new project, but then you'd be faced with all the problems of maintaining the same source code in multiple locations. Instead, Tapestry has a sophisticated way of packaging components together into libraries, as you'll see in the next section.

6.8 Using component libraries

So far, you've seen how to use components packaged with the Tapestry framework, and you've seen several techniques for creating new, application-specific components. The framework and the application are not the only places that components can come from: Components can be packaged into libraries and distributed as Java Archive (JAR) files.

The Tapestry distribution includes a secondary library, `tapestry-contrib-3.0.jar`. This contains the Contrib (short for *Contributions*) library, which includes many useful components that are not absolutely required by the framework itself. In addition, this library contains components that have been contributed by outside developers. Over time, components can migrate from the Contrib library into the main framework.

There are no special requirements for using component libraries (beyond declaring them, as described in the next section). The JAR containing the library must be on the classpath; this can be accomplished easily by copying the JAR into the WEB-INF/lib folder of the web application.

6.8.1 Declaring libraries

Before you may use a library in an application, you must first declare its use for your application. This requires that your application have an *application specification*. Application specifications are optional; applications that don't use special features (such as component libraries) don't need an application specification.

The application specification has the file extension .application and is stored in the WEB-INF folder, along with the page and component specifications. The name of the file matches the name of the servlet. For most of the examples in this book, the name of the servlet is *examples*. This is shown in the web application deployment descriptor (see listing 6.12).

Listing 6.12 web.xml: web deployment descriptor for the example application

```
<?xml version="1.0"?>
<!DOCTYPE web-app PUBLIC
  "-//Sun Microsystems, Inc.//DTD Web Application 2.2//EN"
  "http://java.sun.com/j2ee/dtds/web-app_2_2.dtd">

<web-app>

  <servlet>
    <servlet-name>examples</servlet-name>
    <servlet-class>org.apache.tapestry.ApplicationServlet
    </servlet-class>

    <init-param>
      <param-name>org.apache.tapestry.visit-class</param-name>
      <param-value>examples.Visit</param-value>
    </init-param>
    <load-on-startup>1</load-on-startup>
  </servlet>

  <servlet-mapping>
    <servlet-name>examples</servlet-name>     <-- Provides mapping to
    <url-pattern>/app</url-pattern>               servlet from URL
  </servlet-mapping>

</web-app>
```

Because the name of the servlet is *examples*, Tapestry will expect the application specification to be the file WEB-INF/examples.application. This file is shown in listing 6.13.

Listing 6.13 examples.application: application specification for the examples application

```
<?xml version="1.0"?>
<!DOCTYPE application PUBLIC
  "-//Apache Software Foundation//Tapestry Specification 3.0//EN"
  "http://jakarta.apache.org/tapestry/dtd/Tapestry_3_0.dtd">

<application name="Tapestry in Action Examples">

  <library id="contrib" specification-path=
    "/org/apache/tapestry/contrib/Contrib.library"/>

</application>
```

The root element for an application specification is `<application>`. You can optionally provide a user-presentable name for the application, which is used in some error messages. The `<library>` element defines an ID for a library and provides the path to the library's specification. The library ID must be a valid Java identifier. An application may use any number of libraries, each with a unique ID.

Application specifications can also be used to override the default locations for page and component specifications, but there's rarely a need to do so. The reference in appendix D has the details.

The specification path for a library is the complete path to the library's specification. This is a path within the Java classpath, which is appropriate because libraries are packaged as JAR files, with their resources available only through the classpath.

Now that we've given this library an ID, we can start using the components within the library.

6.8.2 Referencing library components

Components in libraries are referenced using the library ID as a prefix—for example, contrib:Table or contrib:Palette (for components Table and Palette within the component library with the ID `contrib`). This extended naming pattern will be familiar to anyone who has used XML namespaces. Prefixing is important because different libraries may define different components with the same type name. The prefix allows both you and Tapestry to tell one component from another.

Using a component from a library is as easy as using a component provided with the framework, or one particular to your application. Figure 6.8 shows an example of this. This page includes the Palette component, a sophisticated component available in the Contrib library. A Palette component is used for handling multiple selections of items from a list and (optionally) allows the user to order the selections in the list.

The Palette component represents the upper potential of fully reusable components. It combines sophisticated client-side JavaScript with images (distributed with the component inside the JAR file), and yet the look and feel of the Palette may be customized by changing the page's stylesheet or by overriding the default images used for the buttons (in the center column). Despite all this, the component is no more difficult to use than the PropertySelection component described in chapter 4.

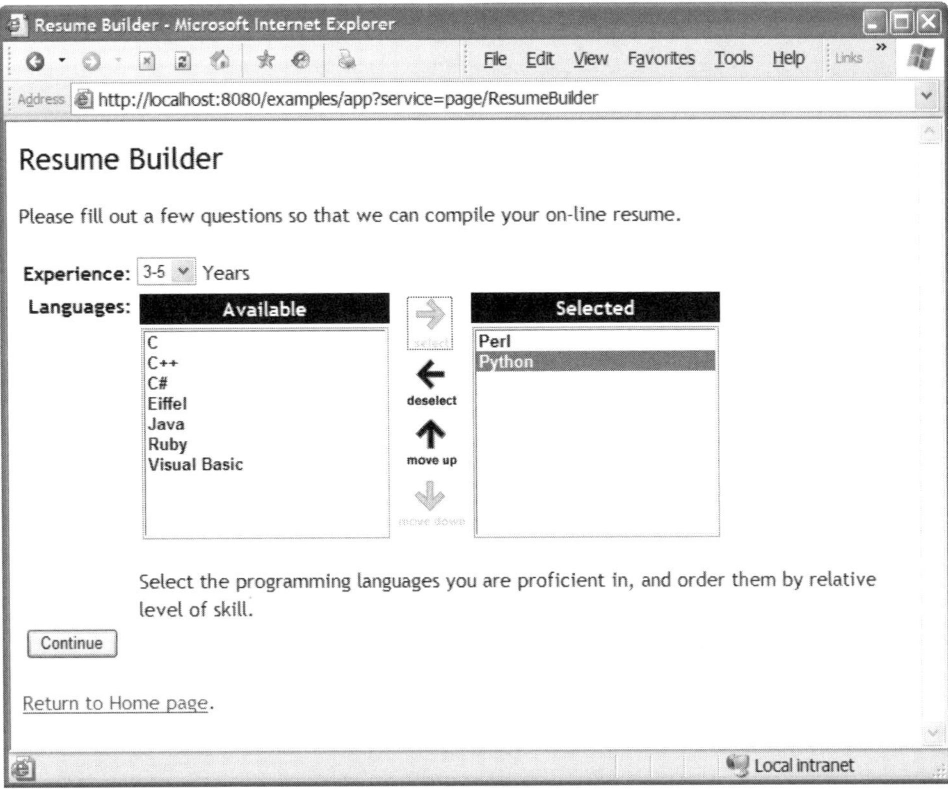

Figure 6.8 The Palette component allows multiple selection and ordering. The buttons in the center are used to move items between the two lists and to reorder items in the selected list (the right column).

Creating the Resume Builder

The example page for the Palette component is the Resume Builder, a page that could be drawn out of an online job search program. In the template (see listing 6.14), the Palette component is represented (arbitrarily) as a `<select>` element.

Listing 6.14 ResumeBuilder.html: HTML template for the Resume Builder page

```
<body jwcid="@Border" title="Resume Builder">    <-1

<span class="title">Resume Builder</span>

<p>Please fill out a few questions so that
we can compile your on-line resume.
</p>
```

```
<span jwcid="@FormError" delegate="ognl:beans.delegate"/>

<form jwcid="@Form" listener="ognl:listeners.formSubmit"
  delegate="ognl:beans.delegate">

<table class="form">

<tr>
<th>Experience:</th>
<td><select jwcid="inputExperience"/> Years</td>      <-❷
</tr>

<tr class="tall">
<th><span jwcid="labelLanguages">Languages</span>:</th>

<td><select jwcid="inputLanguages"/>     <-❸

<p>
Select the programming languages you are proficient in,
and order them by relative level of skill.
</p>

</td>
</tr>

<tr>
<td>
<input type="submit" value="Continue"/>
</td>
</tr>

</table>

</form>

</body>
```

❶ Several of the pages in the examples application make use of a Border component to deal with stylesheet issues.

❷ This `<select>` is a PropertySelection component.

❸ The Palette component is also represented by a `<select>` tag.

For comparison, the Resume Builder page includes a PropertySelection component as well as the Palette. Both are represented in the template as `<select>` tags, even though the Palette component will generate, at runtime, a considerable amount of HTML, including a `<table>` (to control layout), several links and images, and two different `<select>` elements. The downside to using sophisticated components such as Palette is that doing so unavoidably undermines the WYSIWYG preview of the page template.

Declaring components in the page specification

Both the PropertySelection and Palette components are declared components, with their type and parameters provided in the page specification. Listing 6.15 shows the specification for the Resume Builder page, which contains <component> elements for these components.

Listing 6.15 ResumeBuilder.page: specification for the Resume Builder page

```
<?xml version="1.0"?>
<!DOCTYPE page-specification PUBLIC
  "-//Apache Software Foundation//Tapestry Specification 3.0//EN"
  "http://jakarta.apache.org/tapestry/dtd/Tapestry_3_0.dtd">

<page-specification class="examples.resume.ResumeBuilder">

  <bean name="delegate"
    class="examples.register.RegisterDelegate"/>

  <property-specification name="experience"
    type="examples.resume.Experience">
    @examples.resume.Experience@JUNIOR      ❶
  </property-specification>

  <property-specification name="languages"
    type="java.util.List"/>

  <component id="inputExperience" type="PropertySelection">
    <binding name="model" expression="experienceModel"/>
    <binding name="value" expression="experience"/>
  </component>

  <component id="labelLanguages" type="FieldLabel">
    <binding name="field" expression="components.inputLanguages"/>
    <static-binding name="displayName" value="Languages"/>
  </component>

  <component id="inputLanguages" type="contrib:Palette">       ❷
    <binding name="selected" expression="languages"/>     ❸
    <binding name="model" expression="languageModel"/>         ❹
    <binding name="sort">
      @org.apache.tapestry.contrib.palette.SortMode@USER       ❺
    </binding>
  </component>

</page-specification>
```

❶ A default value can be specified for properties (as an OGNL expression). This expression references the public static field `JUNIOR` of the Java class `examples.resume.Experience`.

❷ The `contrib:` prefix references the library declared in the application specification.

❸ The `selected` parameter is a `List` of selected options.

❹ Palette uses an instance of `IPropertySelectionModel` to define the possible options, just as the PropertySelection component does.

❺ `SortMode.USER` allows for manual ordering of the selected items.

Finally, we see that library ID prefix as promised; the component type for the inputLanguages component is `contrib:Palette`, the Palette component provided in the `contrib` library. This same syntax can be used with implicit components; for example, the inputLanguages component could be declared entirely in the HTML template as

```
<select jwcid="inputLanguages@contrib:Palette"
  selected="ognl:languages"
  model="ognl:languageModel"
  sort="ognl:@org.apache.tapestry.contrib.palette.SortMode@USER"/>
```

A Palette component is configured in much the same way as a PropertySelection component. The possible values for a Palette component are defined using the same `IPropertySelectionModel` interface that is used by the PropertySelection component. Unlike PropertySelection, the Palette component is used to edit a `java.util.List` of values, bound to its `selected` parameter. In this example, we create a `languages` property on the page and have the Palette edit that property.

Part of the configuration for a Palette is the order in which items are displayed in the two columns. Items may be sorted by the label (as displayed in the user interface) or by the hidden value of each item. In this example, a third option is used, which allows manual sorting of the selected values. All of this is configured through the Palette's `sort` parameter.

Using the page stylesheet

Part of the Palette's user interface relies on the stylesheet of the page. The Palette component renders an HTML `<table>` element to lay out the two columns, the headers, and the column of buttons in the middle. This `<table>` is (by default) given the CSS class `tapestry-palette`. The stylesheet for the page includes several entries for properly displaying the Palette:

```
TABLE.tapestry-palette TH
{
  background-color: black;
```

```
    color: white;
    font-weight: bold;
    text-align: center;
  }

  TABLE.tapestry-palette SELECT
  {
    font-weight: bold;
    width: 200px;
  }

  TABLE.tapestry-palette TD.controls
  {
     text-align: center;
     vertical-align: middle;
     width: 60px;
  }
```

The HTML generated by the Palette merges with these entries in the stylesheet to produce the desired look and feel. The first block sets the headers (Available and Selected) as white text on a black background. The second block fixes the width of the `<select>` element lists. The last block sets the width of the column containing the buttons (forcing the buttons to stack vertically) and centers them horizontally and vertically. This style of CSS "hook" allows for considerable flexibility in customizing the look and feel of the Palette to fit seamlessly into the page that contains it. Without this support from the page's stylesheet, the Palette would still operate but would not look as pleasing; this is demonstrated in figure 6.9.

The remainder of the implementation of the Resume Builder page is standard form processing, as covered in chapter 4. What's important is not all the features of the Palette component, but how easily such a complex component can be incorporated into your application.

So, using components from a library is simple enough—and, as you'll see next, packaging your own components into libraries is nearly as easy.

6.9 Packaging components into libraries

The next step beyond creating a reusable component is to package that component inside a library for later reuse. Creating a component library is a very straightforward process; it just involves rethinking where some of the resources for the component (the specification, the template, and any assets) are stored. In a component library, everything is stored in the classpath, whereas application resources are stored within the web application context.

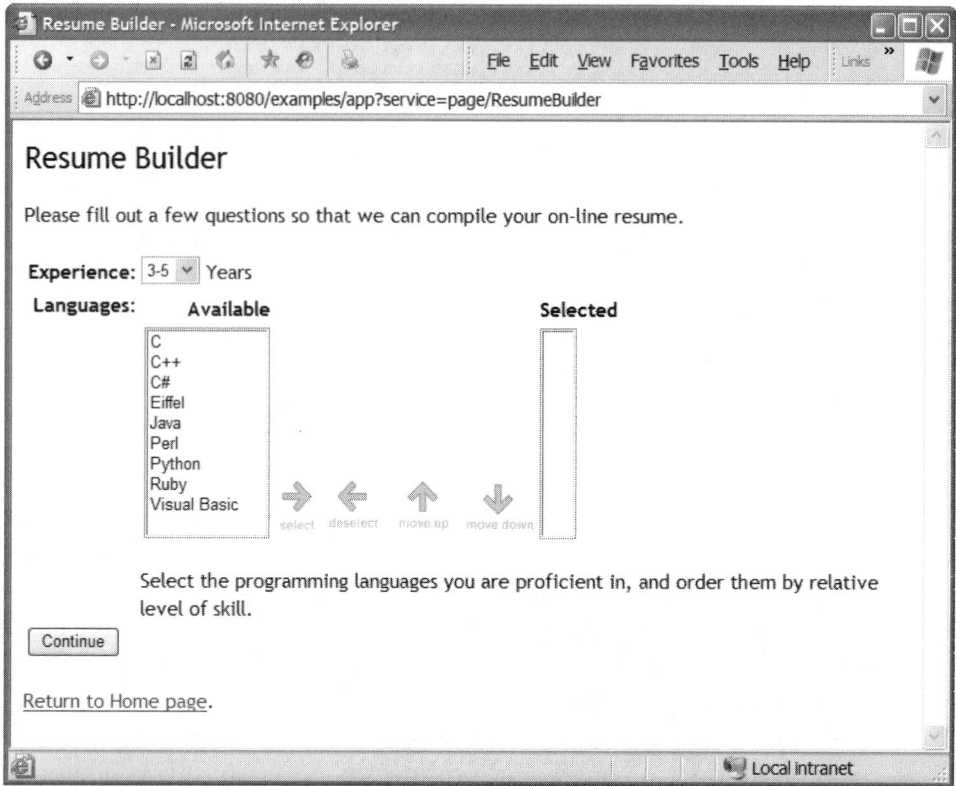

Figure 6.9 Without the support of the page's stylesheet, the Palette is functional but not as visually pleasing.

NOTE Appendix B describes the layout and process for building a Tapestry application using the Ant build tool. Building a component library as a JAR is structurally similar to building a Tapestry web application as a Web Archive (WAR) file. In the examples distribution, the `examples-library` subproject shows how to build such a library (containing the components described here and in chapter 8). The banner ads and examples subprojects show how to include the library as part of a web application.

6.9.1 *Creating the library specification*

Constructing new components to support your application is as easy as creating pages; in fact, it is largely the same process. Compartmentalizing your application in this way helps to remove redundancy in your code and specifications. It's also a good way of dividing up your team, with "big picture" developers working on pages, critical components, and back-end systems, and less-seasoned developers constructing simple components for the page developers. Tapestry's approach allows the application to be divided into small pieces that can be assigned to developers with just the right skill level.

Once you've created your own components or acquired new components in a component library, using them in your own application is as simple and natural as any of the components provided with the Tapestry framework.

To illustrate this process, we will revisit the Resume Builder example from the previous section. The Resume Builder page includes form-level validation to ensure that the user supplies at least one language proficiency. Figure 6.10 shows the page with a warning to that effect.

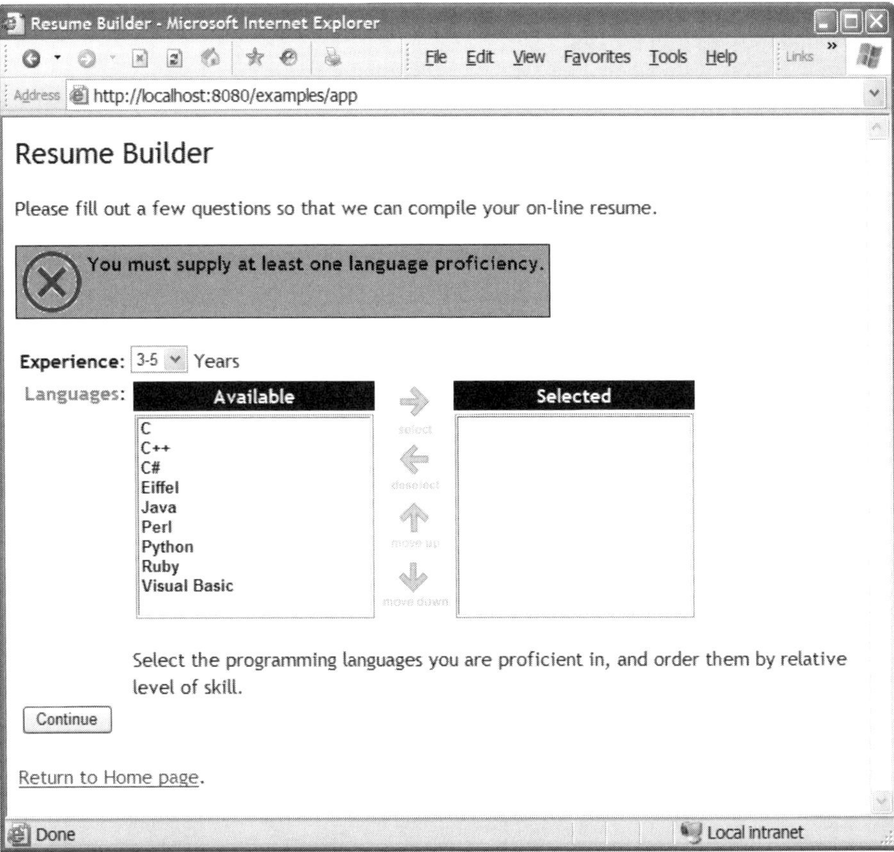

Figure 6.10 The Resume Builder page uses a FormError component (from a component library) to display the form-level validation.

In the previous section, the FormError component was an application-specific component. Let's convert it into a library component instead.

6.9.2 Creating the library specification

The first step is to select a Java package for the library and the components within the library. For this example, the Java package is `examples.library`. In this package directory, we will store the library specification, the component specification, and the component template, as well as a related asset (the X icon used by the component).

Like an application specification, the library specification can declare additional libraries used by this library. The library specification for this example library doesn't use this facility, so the specification is simply a placeholder:

```
<?xml version="1.0"?>
<!DOCTYPE library-specification PUBLIC
  "-//Apache Software Foundation//Tapestry Specification 3.0//EN"
  "http://jakarta.apache.org/tapestry/dtd/Tapestry_3_0.dtd">

<library-specification/>
```

The library specification is named Examples.library and is in the examples. library package. In the examples distribution, it is stored in the directory examples-library/src/java/examples/library. In chapter 8, we'll discuss some of the additional elements that may be put into a library specification; for now, this specification is a placeholder. By giving the library a particular location on the classpath (/examples/library), Tapestry can find any components that are included in the library, because they'll be in the same location.

6.9.3 Creating the FormError component

The FormError component is created in the same directory as the library specification. In fact, any component specifications in the directory with the library specification will be components that are part of the library.

The FormError component will take, as a parameter, an `IValidationDelegate` instance. The HTML template for the component is shown in listing 6.16.

Listing 6.16 FormError.html: HTML template for the FormError component

```
<span jwcid="@Conditional" condition="ognl:delegate.hasErrors">

<table style="{
  border-style : solid;
  color : Red;
```

```
  font-weight : bold;
  background-color : #FFFF40;
  border-width : 1px;
  border-color : Black;
  padding : 2px;
}">
<tr valign="top">
<td>
<img jwcid="@Image" height="52" alt="[Error]"
  image="ognl:assets.icon" width="52"/>
</td>
<td>
<span jwcid="@Delegator"
  delegate="ognl:delegate.firstError">Error Message</span>
</td>
</tr>
</table>

</span>
```

In order to package the FormError component as a template, some minor changes had to be made from the original page. In the original template, the outer `<table>` element referenced the CSS style for the table indirectly:

```
<table class="error">
```

The stylesheet for the page included the following in the declaration:

```
TABLE.error {
  border-style : solid;
  color : Red;
  font-weight : bold;
  background-color : #FFFF40;
  border-width : 1px;
  border-color : Black;
  padding : 2px;
}
```

For this component to be fully reusable, it may not rely on any particular information in the page's stylesheet.[11] The page may not have a stylesheet, or it may have a stylesheet that doesn't include the `TABLE.error` entry. Instead of referencing the stylesheet, the FormError component includes the necessary style information inline.

[11] Another option is to document the stylesheet requirements made by the component and force the developer to include the necessary entries in the page's stylesheet. The Palette component partially adopts this approach.

Referencing packaged images

The icon image (the X symbol) poses a similar problem: The library may be distributed as a JAR and should work with any application it is dropped into, but it also is reliant on the image asset, form-error.png. This file is packaged with the component inside the component library JAR; it is a resource on the classpath, not normally visible to the client web browser.

Normally, the client web browser may only access files (static HTML files, stylesheets, images, and so forth) that are stored in the context. Anything stored in a JAR file, or under the WEB-INF folder, is not accessible. That begs the question: How is the client web browser ever going to gain access to the file? Certainly, we don't want any solution where the files are packaged separately or must be unpackaged from the JAR files to be useful; that goes against the plug-and-play nature of Tapestry.

Tapestry includes a mechanism for serving images and other assets directly from the JAR file. You'll see how to declare such assets shortly, but the difference in the HTML template is the need to use an Image component to display the X icon rather than simple static HTML.

Creating the component specification

The component specification for the FormError defines the `delegate` parameter and the asset for the error icon. The specification is named FormError.jwc (see listing 6.17), and it is stored (with the library specification) in the /examples/library folder.

Listing 6.17 FormError.jwc: specification for the FormError component

```
<?xml version="1.0"?>
<!DOCTYPE component-specification PUBLIC
  "-//Apache Software Foundation//Tapestry Specification 3.0//EN"
   "http://jakarta.apache.org/tapestry/dtd/Tapestry_3_0.dtd">

<component-specification
  allow-body="no"
  allow-informal-parameters="no">

  <parameter name="delegate" direction="in" required="yes"
    type="org.apache.tapestry.valid.IValidationDelegate"/>

  <private-asset name="icon" resource-path="form-error.png"/>

</component-specification>
```

A new specification element, `<private-asset>`, is used (instead of `<context-asset>`) to declare assets that are stored on the classpath rather than in the web application context. Private assets are localized, just the same as ordinary context assets. Components (such as the Image component in the FormError component's template) do not know or care whether assets are context or private.

Private assets work with the asset service (one of the eight default services provided by the framework) to expose these files to the client web browser. At runtime, rather than build a URL to a static file within the web application context, the asset service builds an application URL. When the URL is triggered, the asset service will locate the asset on the classpath and send its contents, as a byte stream, back to the client web browser.

If you examine the source for the page when an error message is displayed, the Image component renders as

```
<img src="/examples/app?service=asset&amp;sp=S%2Fexamples%2Flibrary
%2Fform-error.png"
  border="0" width="52" alt="[Error]" height="52"/>
```

This URL invokes the asset service to retrieve the contents of a file stored somewhere on the classpath. In this example, the location of the file within the classpath is /examples/library/form-error.png (the `%2F` is an encoding of the slash character).

TIP Tapestry can also be configured to dynamically copy the contents of private assets to a web folder directory and build a static URL pointing to the resource. This is a better approach in production, since web servers are much faster at servicing requests for static resources than handling dynamic requests involving servlets.

6.9.4 Using the FormError component

Using the FormError component is the same as using any other component. The library containing the component must be declared in the application specification:

```
<library id="lib"
  specification-path="/examples/library/Examples.library"/>
```

This declaration identifies a second library used by the application that can be referenced with the prefix `lib:`. In the ResumeBuilder template, the FormError component is accessed using that prefix:

```
<span jwcid="@lib:FormError" delegate="ognl:beans.delegate"/>
```

Because of the prefixing system used, a single page can combine components provided by any number of libraries. The Resume Builder page, for example, still uses the contrib:Palette component later in its template.

6.10 Summary

Building reusable components in Tapestry is an extension of the techniques you've already seen for building pages. Because creating components is so easy in Tapestry, it becomes a natural problem-solving technique: divide (into components) and conquer. Building components is a great way to organize your application; it removes redundancies from your templates, specifications, and Java code.

Tapestry includes a simple and elegant way to create completely reusable components and package them as libraries. The components you create today for your current application can be instantly reused tomorrow, in your next application.

The framework even allows for libraries to build on each other; new components can be assembled by combining components provided by the framework or by other libraries.

Creating new components is just one approach to extending the basic capabilities of the Tapestry framework. In chapter 7, we'll go into more detail about the internals of the framework and then utilize that information to build even more powerful components in chapter 8.

7 Tapestry under the hood

This chapter covers

- Managing server-side state
- Understanding clustering
- Creating URLs and dispatching requests
- Rendering pages in detail
- Loading and pooling pages
- Localizing applications

Many applications can be built in Tapestry using just the techniques described in the previous chapters and an understanding of the existing components. In preparation for even more ambitious things (in chapter 8), this chapter covers a bit more about how Tapestry operates internally, describing what happens between the time a request is received by the application server and the time a listener method is invoked. We also touch on issues related to server-side state management, application localization, and how Tapestry makes use of object pools for efficiency. All of this background material lays the groundwork for understanding how to create more involved applications, as well as how to create more powerful, reusable component libraries and how to extend and change the basic behavior of the Tapestry framework.

7.1 Processing requests

In earlier chapters, we talked about offloading complexity into the framework by allowing it to control the request/response processing cycle. In this chapter, we describe how Tapestry processes the incoming request. Processing requests involves a number of overlapping concepts:

- Parsing and caching page specifications, page templates, component specifications, and component templates
- Pooling instances of pages
- Managing server-side state, including persistent page properties
- Localizing text and images on pages
- Interpreting incoming requests and dispatching to the correct objects and methods

Table 7.1 lists the key objects responsible for processing requests.

Table 7.1 Request processing framework objects used to dispatch incoming requests

Object	Description
Application servlet	Serves as a bridge between the Servlet API and Tapestry
Engine	Acts as a central hub for request processing, managing of server-side state, and accessing of Tapestry subsystems
Engine service	Builds and interprets URLs for specific Tapestry operations
Request context	Creates a façade over Servlet API objects (`HttpServletRequest`, `HttpSession`, etc.)

Table 7.1 Request processing framework objects used to dispatch incoming requests *(continued)*

Object	Description
Request cycle	Coordinates processing of a single-request, temporary cache for page instances
Page recorder	Manages persistent page properties for a single page; moves data between page properties and `HttpSession`
Page source	Manages an object pool used by the request cycle to obtain page instances
Page loader	Creates and configures new page instances as needed

7.2 Understanding the application servlet

In Tapestry, every application uses exactly one servlet: the application servlet. In traditional servlet applications there are many servlets, each representing a different operation that may occur in the application. Each of these servlets is new code for you to write, test, and debug.

One of the reasons writing servlets is more involved than writing most other kinds of Java applications is that servlets operate from within a difficult environment. Exactly one instance of each servlet is created by the servlet container. That single servlet may handle dozens of simultaneous requests, each in a separate thread. This multithreading makes instance variables on the servlet almost useless. There's no point in storing any information about the current client in an instance variable; some other thread is sure to overwrite your change almost immediately. All too frequently, subtle bugs creep in where developers violate these basic rules—bugs that show up only when the application is heavily loaded, during stress testing, or even in production, where debugging the application is most difficult, if even possible.

The `ApplicationServlet` class is provided in the framework and does not need to be subclassed to be used in an application. In Tapestry, the application servlet is just a gateway between the stateless, multithreaded world of the HTTP protocol and the Servlet API, and the normal, stateful, and single-threaded world of Java and JavaBeans.

7.2.1 Servlet request processing

You've already seen how natural it is to code in Tapestry; components can communicate with each other by setting and reading properties of their containing page. There's no awkward shuffling of values in and out of request or session attributes. Form submissions result in updates to page or domain object properties.

Global application data is stored in the `Visit` object, which persists between requests, safely stored as an `HttpSession` attribute.

All of these are examples of the kind of natural, stateful coding that the Servlet API discourages you from using. Tapestry allows you to bypass awkward, stateless coding in two ways: by shifting the coding focus away from the stateless servlet, and by using object pools.

Object pools are a well-established design pattern used to manage scarce resources. A common example is a database connection pool, where a small number of database connections are shared by a large number of potential clients. Objects are checked out of the pool for short periods, to service particular requests, and then returned to the pool for later reuse. Tapestry uses this pattern to pool instances of page objects (including all the related objects and components within a page). This ensures that, while a page (and the hierarchy of components in the page) is being used to service a request, only a single thread will access the page. The set of pages for the current request is managed by the request cycle object, which only returns the objects to the pool at the end of the request.

With Tapestry, the servlet is not the focus of request processing as it is in traditional servlet applications. The servlet is merely a gateway from the Servlet API to the Tapestry framework. The real work is done by the engine. The engine is the central hub for processing requests and is particular to a single client session. It is stored as an `HttpSession` attribute and so persists between requests. The servlet's main job is to find the engine in the `HttpSession` (or create a new instance) and invoke the `service()` method on the instance.

Figure 7.1 shows the processing that the servlet performs on a typical request (a request where the `HttpSession` already exists and the engine has already been created). All the magic in Tapestry occurs inside the engine's `service()` method. This is where the request is processed and a reply is constructed and returned to the client.

After executing the `service()` method, the application servlet stores the engine instance back in the `HttpSession`. At first glance, this may not seem necessary—getting the engine instance doesn't remove it from the `HttpSession`, so why is it necessary to store it back in the session? In a word: clustering.

7.2.2 Understanding server-side state

All web applications have some form of server-side state. It may be some transitory state information that exists during a single active request, or it may last longer, persisting from request to request or session to session. Table 7.2 lists the four types of server-side state, showing typical approaches using just the Servlet API and corresponding approaches using Tapestry.

Table 7.2 Types of server-side state

Type	Servlet API	Tapestry
Temporary variable used when rendering response (example: loop index)	• JSP bean with page or request scope • JSP local variable (using Java scriptlet) • `HttpServletRequest` attribute	• Page or component property
Client-specific data, available in later requests	• `HttpSession` attribute • HTTP cookie	• Persistent page or component property • `Visit` object, or property of `Visit` object
Non-client-specific data, available in later requests	• `ServletContext` attribute • Static variable[a]	• `Global` object, or property of `Global` object
Long-term data (outlives any single user session)	• HTTP cookie • RDBMS	• HTTP cookie • RDBMS

[a] *Because of the way class loaders work inside an application server, especially in the context of hot application redeployment, making use of static variables is not a recommended approach.*

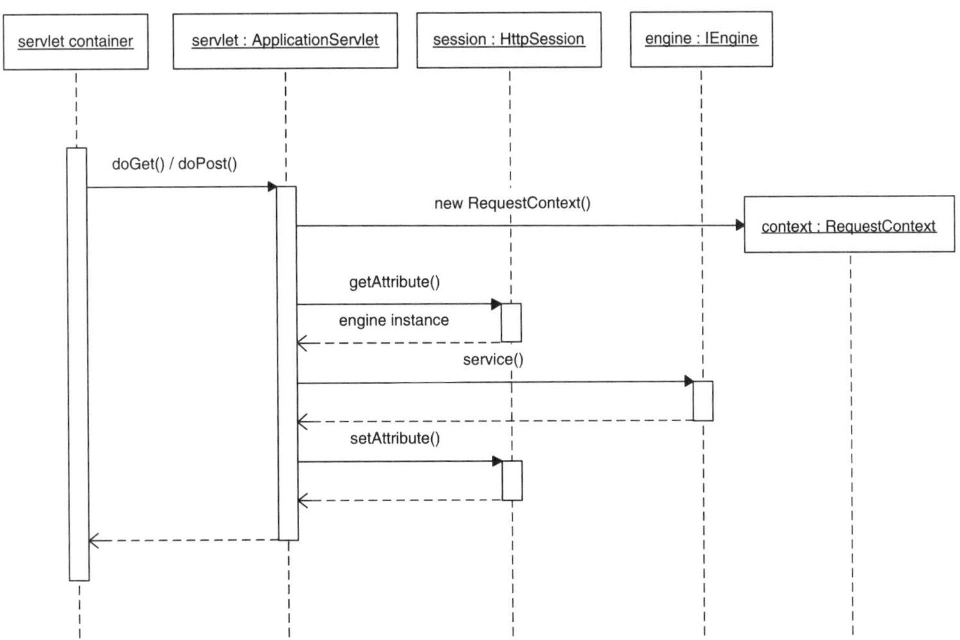

Figure 7.1 The servlet creates the `RequestContext` façade on the Servlet API objects and then locates the engine in the session. The `service()` method does all the actual work of processing the request and producing a reply. At the end of the request, the engine is stored back in the session.

As you'll see later in this chapter, Tapestry is often using the Servlet API and hiding the details. For example, persistent page properties are stored between requests as `HttpSession` attributes.

7.2.3 Managing server-side state in a cluster

The Tapestry framework is designed to support not only highly complex applications but also extremely large applications—applications with thousands of concurrent users. In the Java 2 Enterprise Edition (J2EE) world, the approach used to handle extremely high volumes is clustering: dividing the load across many servers that work together. A collection of these servers is a *cluster*. To the outside world, a server cluster appears as a single server, and maintaining this fiction requires a mix of hardware and software.

Figure 7.2 shows how this works. Clients direct their web browsers to a particular Internet address. The device at that address is not an application server, but a router or load balancer. It is a specialized server that forwards the request through a firewall to one of the cluster's application servers to process the request. The firewall prevents the client web browser from directly communicating with the application servers (or any other servers within the inner network). The router and the application server cluster work together to implement a load-balancing and fail-over strategy that determines which server each request is sent to.

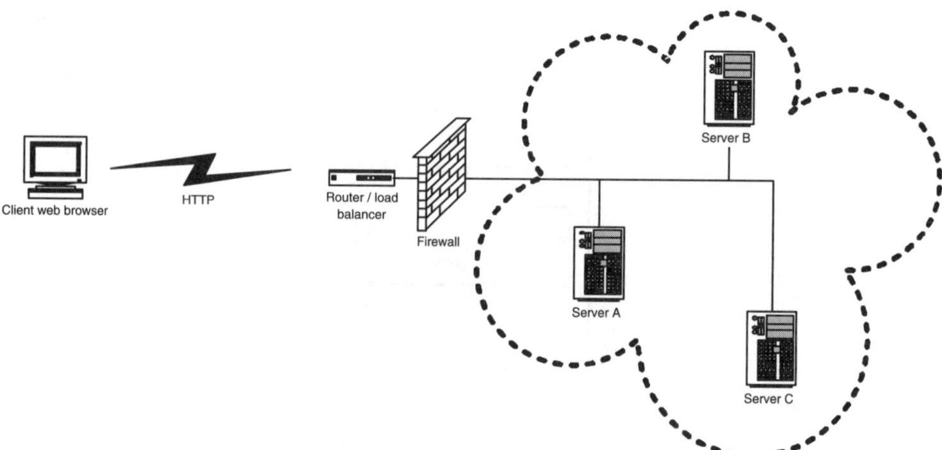

Figure 7.2 The client web browser connects to a router, which forwards the request through a firewall to one of the servers in the cluster. If one server fails or becomes overburdened, another server can take over the load. The client has no knowledge of what goes on "behind" the router.

Server clusters can be configured in many ways, according to both the specific implementations provided by various vendors and the specific needs of an application. The bottom line is that, when an application is executing in a cluster, there is no guarantee that two successive requests from the same client will be processed on the same server. Between one request and the next, any server within the cluster may be shut down, fail unexpectedly, or move processing of requests to a different server within the cluster because it is overburdened (that is, for load-balancing reasons). In some configurations, every request is processed by a different server. The client should never be made aware of any of these transitions. The client sends requests and gets responses and should have no knowledge of how those requests are satisfied.

When discussing clustering issues, it is easiest to assume that requests are handled by a primary server until the primary server either fails or deliberately shifts request processing to a second server (the backup server) due to load balancing. Although this may not match the actual configuration of a cluster, the relevant issues concerning server-side state are still accurate.

Serializing and copying attributes

One of the prerequisites for any clustering scheme to be successful is that any server-side state needed for processing the requests that was known on the primary server must be available on the new, backup server. In terms of Tapestry, the presentation layer, and the Servlet API, this means that any attributes stored into the `HttpSession` on the original server must be copied over to the backup server before it processes any requests. It also means that any server-side state in the application must be stored as `HttpSession` attributes, even though Tapestry frequently represents such state as properties on ordinary objects (which just happen to be Tapestry pages and components).

When using the Servlet API (with or without Tapestry) in a cluster, any `HttpSession` attributes are copied from the primary server and broadcast to one or more backup servers within the cluster. Different application server implementations have different strategies for clustering, all involving serializing the data (converting objects into a stream of bytes) stored in the `HttpSession` on one server and deserializing the data back into objects on one or more other servers. The serialization may occur immediately or after some delay. The deserialization may occur constantly or only just as a backup server is activated to process a request. Despite this, the common factor is that information in one server's `HttpSession` is serialized at some point and is deserialized within a different server in the cluster. Any information stored in the original `HttpSession` that can't be serialized and later deserialized is lost.

So, for a servlet application to be a good clustering citizen, it must ensure that any attributes it stores into the `HttpSession` are serializable. Because the vast majority of applications store only simple objects such as `String`, `Integer`, `Boolean`, and `Date` as their `HttpSession` attributes, this is not often an issue; all of those classes are already serializable. Tapestry does the same—the primary object it stores in the `HttpSession` is the engine itself, and the engine is serializable.

Keeping synchronized

There is still a remaining gotcha: the question of *when* the data is copied. This is left deliberately unspecified in the Servlet API specification. Although various approaches are possible, Tapestry conforms to the least common denominator approach: It expects that attributes are copied individually when the `setAttribute()` method of the `HttpSession` object is invoked. In fact, this is the exact approach taken by the popular WebLogic application server.

If the only objects stored as `HttpSession` attributes are `Strings`, `Integers`, and `Dates`, then the question of when the copy takes place is not relevant. These objects are immutable, which means they have no changeable internal state. However, if an `HttpSession` attribute is mutable (for example, a `List`, `Map`, or custom object), then the question of when serialization and copying takes place becomes relevant. Figure 7.3 shows how, with mutable `HttpSession` attribute values, it is possible for the server-side state on the primary server to get out of sync with the backup server, simply by changing an `HttpSession` attribute's internal state after storing the attribute in the `HttpSession`.

Once that internal state has been changed, the backup server's state no longer matches the actual state stored on the primary server. If the primary server fails over to the backup server, the backup server will operate with incorrect server-side state, which can lead to incorrect behavior. This class of bugs can be subtle and confusing, difficult to reproduce, and infuriating to debug in a production system. Tapestry makes every effort to ensure that this scenario never happens.

Returning to Tapestry and the `ApplicationServlet`, the last step shown in figure 7.1 is a call to `setAttribute()`.[1] Given that the engine's internal state is, in fact, quite mutable, this ensures that any changes to the engine instance are properly distributed to the other servers in the cluster.

---

[1] Actually, `setAttribute()` doesn't occur on every request; some simple optimizations are employed to avoid invoking `setAttribute()` when internal state can't have changed, such as a request that does not change a persistent page property and does not even access the `Visit` object.

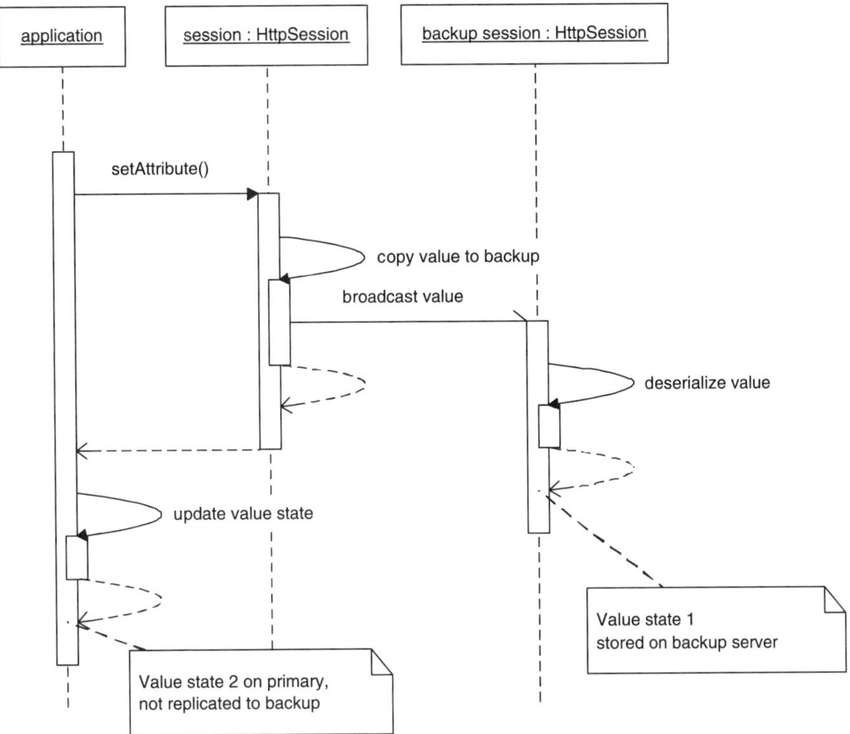

Figure 7.3 Changing a mutable object's state after storing it as an `HttpSession` attribute can lead to a lack of data synchronization between the primary and backup servers.

7.3 Understanding the Tapestry engine

At the center of every Tapestry application is an engine, which is the object that supports and organizes all aspects of the application. The engine binds together all the smaller subsystems that form a Tapestry application. Its primary concern is managing server-side state; it manages the `Visit` object described in chapter 2, which is where most application-wide state is stored. It also is integral in managing persistent page properties, which allows individual pages to have internal state that is available from one request to the next.

The most visible aspect of the engine is the `service()` method, which is the way in which incoming requests are processed and results are returned to the client web browser. The `service()` method is outlined in figure 7.4. This sequence introduces yet another layer of delegation in Tapestry: the engine service, represented

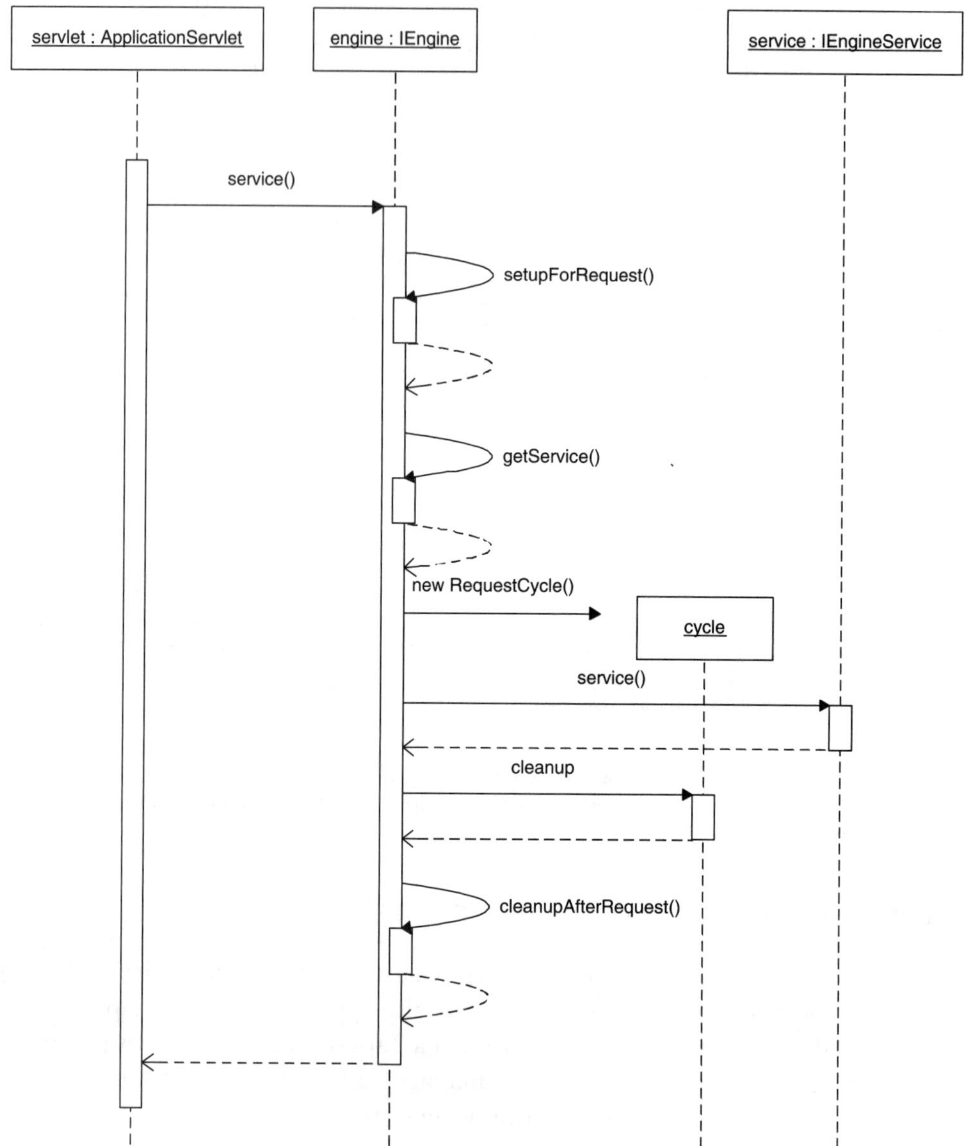

Figure 7.4 Execution of the IEngine's `service()` method. The engine initializes for the current request, locates an `IEngineService` instance for the request, and delegates to the service.

by the `IEngineService` interface. Just as the servlet delegates to the engine to perform the processing of the request and the rendering of a response, the engine delegates to an engine service. Engine services, covered in the next section, are the point at which request processing really begins.

Before invoking the engine service, the `service()` method performs many initializations, creating and configuring the subsystems within Tapestry. More important, the engine's `service()` method includes multiple levels of exception catching and reporting. Any uncaught exceptions that percolate back to this level will be reported using the Exception page, which provides a detailed report of the exception and nested exceptions as well as all the available Servlet API objects. An example exception report is shown in chapter 1, figures 1.5 and 1.6. If the application has become so unstable that even the Exception page fails, then exception output is written to the console.

7.4 Understanding engine services

In a traditional servlet application, one of the most challenging parts in managing the complexity of an application is in the generation of, and interpretation of, application URLs. Tapestry handles this problem through engine services. Engine services are the real link between requests and components.

7.4.1 What's the problem with application URLs?

Application URLs represent the various operations that can occur inside the application. The most common approach is to have an individual servlet for each operation, and to use query parameters to provide the parameters to the operations.

With small applications, or even initially with large applications, the complexity of managing URLs and query parameters isn't readily apparent. There may be some namespace conflicts (everyone on the team will want to map his or her servlet to `/add` or `/showDetail`), but with a little prefixing or suffixing (`/addCustomer`, `/addAddress`, `/showProductDetail`), these issues can be ironed out.

A larger risk is exposed as the application grows and changes. Only a tenuous relationship exists between the JavaServer Pages (JSPs) that construct and render the application URLs and the servlets that interpret those same URLs. As we've discussed before, the JSPs and the servlets are weakly bound. If a servlet's mapping changes (say, from `/add` to `/addCustomer` as new types of things that can be added are integrated into the application), every JSP that could possibly reference the servlet must be manually checked, and possibly modified, to ensure that the new correct application URL is being generated. Likewise, any change to the query parameters—anything from a change in name to a change in what kind of data is in the parameter—will have a similar ripple effect.

In a nonweb application, you would be changing specific Java methods, and a source recompile would spot the errors immediately. Modern integrated development environments (IDEs), such as Eclipse, do not even make you wait for a recompile to identify errors; modern IDEs include refactoring tools for automating many common code changes, such as adding or changing method parameters.

In the loosely coupled world of servlets and JSPs, there is no recompile stage and no built-in check. Even running the application and visiting all the pages will not necessarily uncover these mismatch errors. Remember that the servlets are not ultimately the pages of the application. Servlets are operations and serve as the transitions *between* the pages of the application. This means that the only way to verify the application is to click every link and submit every form that could possibly be affected by the original change, no matter how minor.

The core of this problem is the separation between the code that constructs the URL and the servlet code that interprets and acts on the URL. This separation can be addressed with a bit of discipline, by centralizing the URL generation code. For example, you could create public static methods on the servlet to generate application URLs. This approach ensures that the URL generation and interpretation code is all in the same place. This approach can be further improved with a custom JSP tag for each servlet (to produce the URL). However, any solution that relies on throwing custom code at the problem is suspect. Tapestry takes a different approach to organizing the application.

7.4.2 How does Tapestry handle application operations?

Tapestry is not immune from this issue, even though it contains only a single servlet. It still has to encode (into the URL) what operation to perform, what objects are involved, and any additional parameters needed by the operation. Essentially, Tapestry multitasks its single servlet to accommodate all manner of application operations, many linked to particular pages and to particular components, some global to the entire application. You've seen the three most common of these operations in the examples in previous chapters:

- Display of a page within the application
- Response to a link or form submission
- The default operation that starts an application

In Tapestry terms, these operations are provided by engine services. Engine services are objects that implement the `IEngineService` interface. This interface defines methods for both creating and servicing application URLs, all in a single object.

Engine services are much like servlets in implementation. Engine services are shared by many threads and may hold no client-specific state. Tapestry includes a default roster of nine services (shown in table 7.3), of which four (home, page, direct, and external) are commonly used. Most of the services have a corresponding component, such as the page service and the PageLink component, or the direct service and the DirectLink component.

Table 7.3 Tapestry's engine services

Service	Description
action	Invokes a listener method indirectly by rewinding the entire page, not just the contents of a form. Rarely used; the direct service is more efficient.
asset	Dynamically downloads an image or other asset file stored on the classpath (inside a JAR file). Automatically used with component assets from the framework or from a component library.
direct	Allows a component to directly respond to a request; used with most links and forms.
external	Allows "bookmarkable" links to particular pages.
home	Default service, used to display the Home page of an application.
page	Responds with a particular page within the application.
reset	Discards all cached data, including all specifications and templates. Used only during development.
restart	Discards the current session and displays the Home page.
tagsupport	Special service used by the Tapestry JSP tag library to generate URLs for inclusion in a JSP.

Services are not created equal. Some are more complicated than others, in terms of what information they encode into a URL (and, correspondingly, what information they later parse out of a URL). Let's start by looking at the simplest service: the home service.

7.4.3 Using the home service

The home service's job is to render the Home page of the application. The application's Home page is, very simply, the page named *Home*. You saw this in chapter 2, where the Home page for the Hangman application was the page displayed when the application was first accessed.

Because it does exactly one thing, the home service makes use of no query parameters. Tapestry assumes that any request with no query parameters, not even the one to specify a service, is to be processed by the home service. The home service's behavior is illustrated in figure 7.5.

In examples in earlier chapters, you saw how a listener method can make use of the `IRequestCycle`'s `activate()` method to select the active page for the current request—the page that will render the response. The home service does the same, first getting the Home page from the request cycle (using the `getPage()` method) and then activating it.

Figure 7.6 illustrates how the `activate()` method operates: It invokes the `validate()` method on the page, which is a general hook provided to pages to perform basic security validation. This validation allows for application-specific checks that a page about to be activated is acceptable for the current request and current client (in effect, the `validate()` method exists to allow for security checks—examples of this usage are shown in chapter 10). The page's `validate()` method doesn't directly implement any checks; instead, pages are allowed to

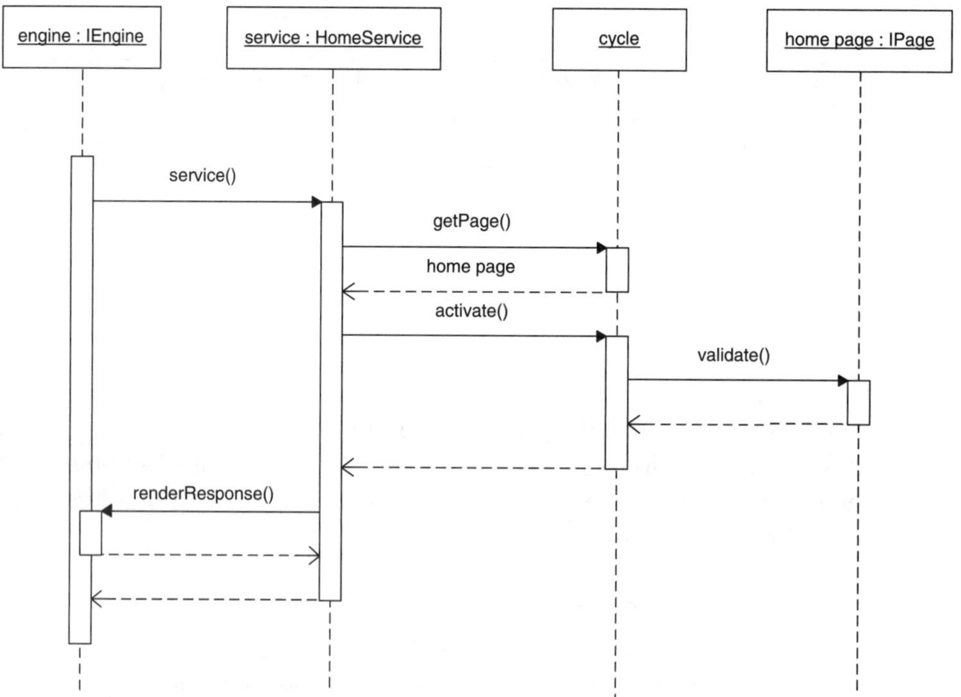

Figure 7.5 The service gets the Home page from the cycle and activates it.

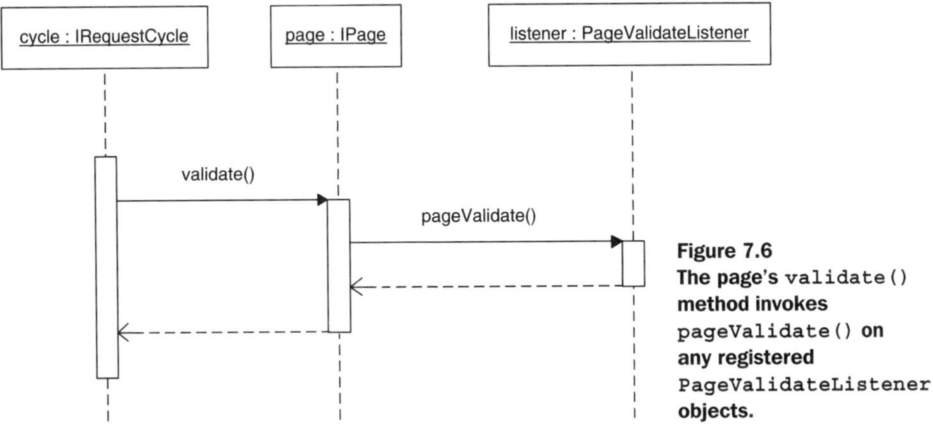

Figure 7.6 The page's `validate()` method invokes `pageValidate()` on any registered `PageValidateListener` objects.

have multiple validation listeners, objects that implement the `PageValidateListener` interface. The `validate()` method invokes the `pageValidate()` method on each of its listeners.

Most commonly, the page is its own validator. If the page implements the `PageValidateListener` interface, then it is automatically registered as its own validator. Individual components within the page may also implement the interface and be registered automatically as well.

A validator will check to see if the user is allowed to access the page. A validator may adjust the page's state or, more likely, throw a `PageRedirectException` to force a different page to be activated. When a `PageRedirectException` is thrown, the processing of the request by the service is aborted. The page specified in the exception is activated and renders a response immediately. Chapter 10 includes an example of a typical use for `pageValidate()`—to prevent users from seeing some of the pages of the application until after they have logged in to the application.

Returning to figure 7.5: after activating (and validating) the Home page, the home service invokes the engine method `renderResponse()`. This results in the active page being rendered and the response being sent back to the client web browser. Unless a validator has overridden the default behavior, it will be the Home page that renders the response.

7.4.4 Rendering pages with the page service

Next up the complexity ladder is the page service. This service is responsible for rendering a particular page, specified by name.

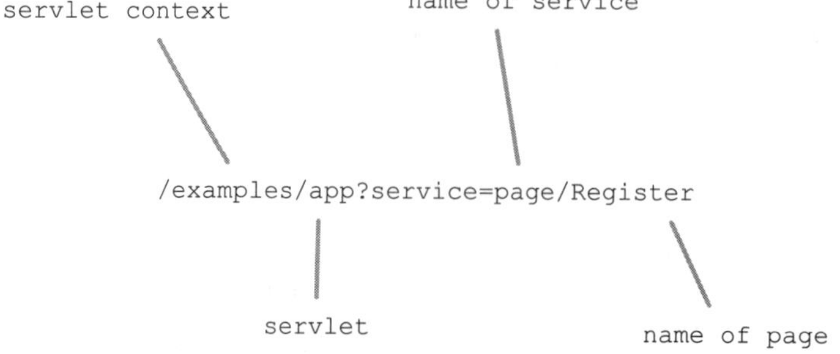

Figure 7.7 Page service URL construction. The service query parameter identifies the service (page) and the name of the page to render (Register).

Unlike the home service, which is entirely implicit, the page service has to encode into its URLs two things: that it is the page service, and which page is to render the response. All engine services use a pair of standard query parameters for encoding this kind of information: `service` and `sp`.

- `service` is used to encode the name of the service, plus any additional context values needed by the service. Multiple values are separated by slashes.
- `sp` is a string that encodes a `service` parameter. The page service doesn't use this query parameter, but other services do (such as the direct service).

Figure 7.7 shows how an application URL might appear within the HTML of a rendered page. Tapestry generates absolute URLs; application URLs always start with a leading slash and identify the servlet context as well as the application servlet. Reserved characters, such as the ampersand, will be properly converted into HTML entities (such as the `&` in figure 7.9).

The service query parameter starts with the name of the service, page. The page service has some additional context: the name of the page you want to render. This is also part of the service query parameter. Some services may have four or five additional context values beyond the name of the service, each value separated by a forward slash.

When the page service is invoked to service a request, it uses the context value as the name of the page to activate and render the response. Other than that, the sequence is the same as in figure 7.5, including invoking the page's `validate()` method to perform security checks.

7.4.5 Linking to listener methods with the direct service

The direct service is the true workhorse of Tapestry. The vast majority of links and forms make use of this service. It is used to trigger an action defined by a component, either a DirectLink or a Form. A DirectLink component will notify its listener immediately (as described in chapter 2), whereas a Form component will perform a rewind to process the form submission and then notify its listener (as described in chapter 3).

Checking for a stale session

One aspect of bridging the stateless HTTP protocol to stateful application development is that the server has to guess when the user has finished using the application. After some period of inactivity, the `HttpSession` is invalidated. Once it's invalidated, any attributes stored in the session are discarded. The server (or cluster of servers) will no longer have any knowledge of the client, or any server-side state for the client.

Complications can occur if a user steps away from his or her computer for a period of time and then returns and attempts to continue work. In many cases, links and forms don't rely on server-side state, so it is irrelevant whether the state has been lost between the time the page was rendered and the new request.

In those cases where server-side state is relevant, the framework can validate that the session still exists. This validation is implemented by the direct service, which optionally checks for stale sessions. The direct service records into the URL it generates (when a page renders) whether the application was stateful at the time the URL was created. When the URL is later processed, the direct service can check to see if the session still exists or if it has timed out. This shifts the responsibility for checking for stale sessions away from you and onto the framework—all you have to do is inform Tapestry whether the link or form in question requires a valid session.

Both the DirectLink and Form components include a `stateful` parameter that defaults to `false`. Setting it to `true` enables the stale session check. If the session has been invalidated and the component is stateful, then the user is sent to the StaleSession page. Figure 7.8 shows the default StaleSession page.[2]

Figure 7.9 shows how the direct service encodes information into the application URL. The direct service has several service context values: the stateful flag, the name of the page, and the component ID path within the page.

A stateful flag indicates whether the application was stateful at the time the link was generated. If the value is 1, then the session validation check will take place when the URL is triggered. Also included in the service parameter value is the name of the page containing the component, as well as the ID path of the

[2] It is possible to override this page in an application, by creating a page in the application named StaleSession.

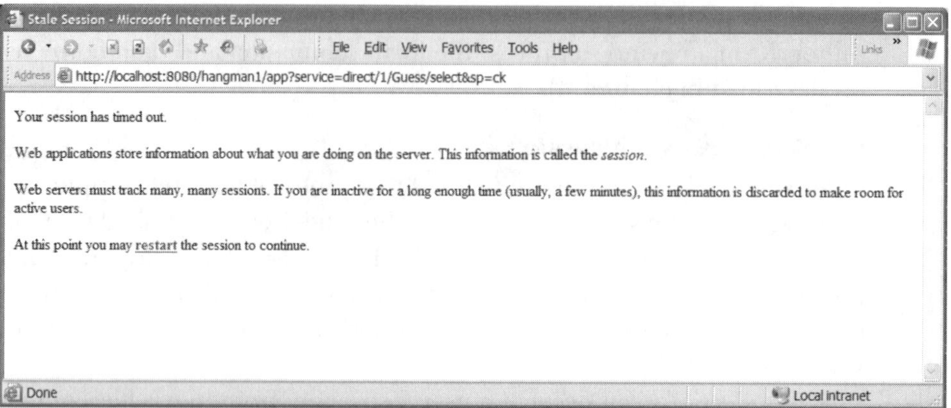

Figure 7.8 The default StaleSession page, presented when a stateful request is sent after the server-side session has expired. This page can be easily overridden.

component. In this example, the component "select" on the page "Guess" is referenced. If the component was contained within another component (which is quite often the case), then the component ID path would be a series of IDs separated by periods.

This URL is an example of a link from the Hangman application in chapter 2, and it uses a single service parameter to identify which letter the user is guessing. The `sp` query parameter is used for this purpose. The value, `cu`, is an encoding of the type (*c* is for `Character`; other types have their own prefix) and the value, the letter *u*.

Don't be concerned by all this talk of encodings, URLs, and query parameters. Short of creating your own engine services, you will almost never have to be

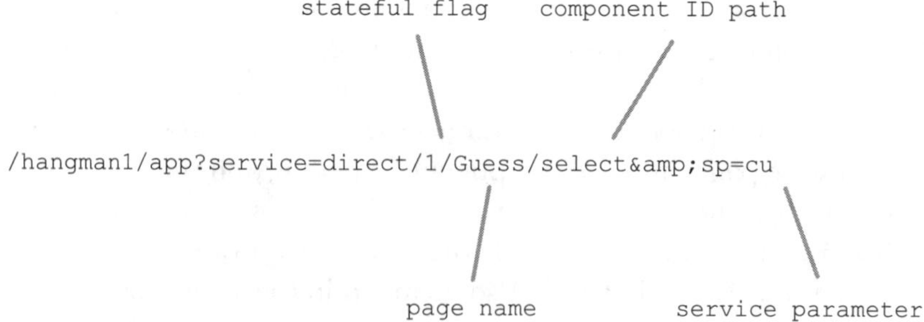

Figure 7.9 The direct service URL identifies the page and component and allows for application-specific service parameters.

concerned with these issues. What's more important are the exact steps taken by the direct service when processing a request.

Processing a request with the direct service

Figure 7.10 shows the processing the direct service performs for a request. This is important, because the order in which the operations take place can be critical. For example, the `validate()` check occurs very early (as part of the call to the

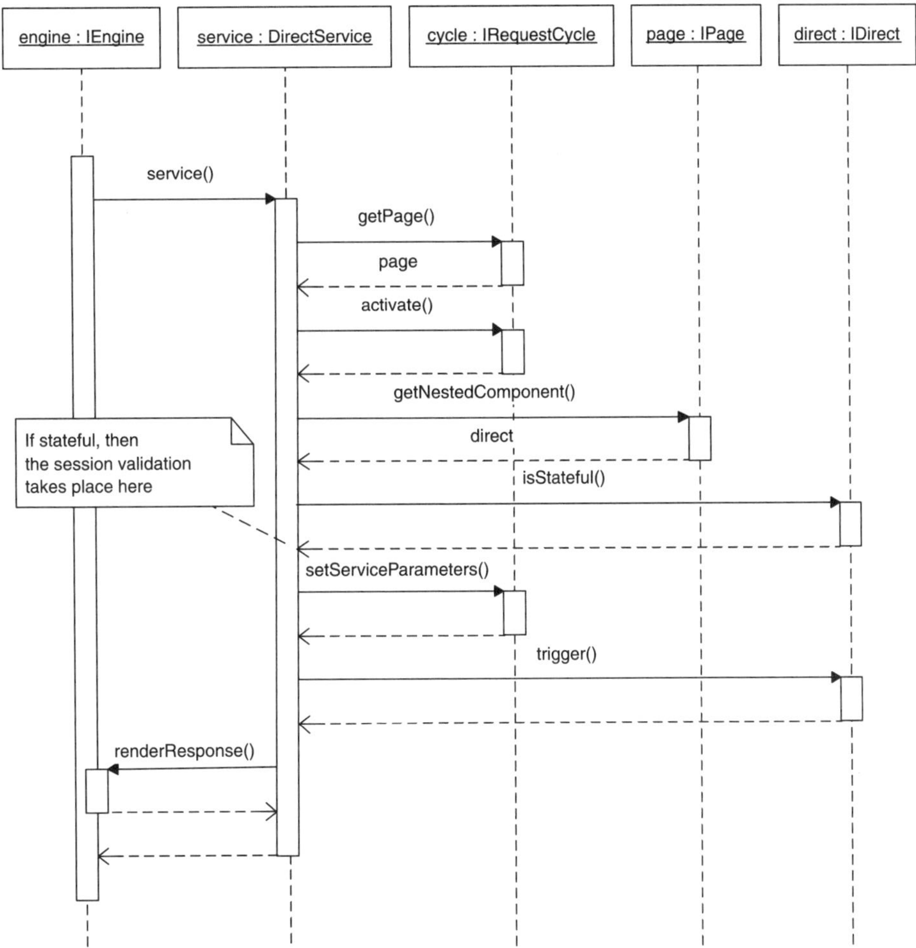

Figure 7.10 The direct service gets the component, which implements the `IDirect` interface, and invokes the `trigger()` method on it before rendering a response. The `trigger()` method invokes the component's listener method (not shown).

`activate()` method), and won't have access to the service parameters. The stateful check occurs after `validate()`.

Like the page service, the direct service begins by getting the page (as provided in the context). The `validate()` method is invoked on the page; then the component is located within the page. The component must implement the interface `IDirect` (which is an extension of `IComponent`). This interface is implemented by the Form and DirectLink components. After the optional stale session validation, the service parameters are extracted and stored in the request cycle's `serviceParameters` property, for later access by a listener method. Finally, the `IDirect` method `trigger()` is invoked.

For a DirectLink, the `trigger()` method will result in a listener method being invoked, as shown in figure 7.11.

The direct service doesn't know, or need to know, what the component is. It only needs to know that it implements the `IDirect` interface. Forms also use the direct service and implement the `IDirect` interface. For a Form, some additional steps occur; the exact sequence is shown in figure 7.12.

The key aspect of form processing, as covered in chapter 3, is the rewind phase. When a Form component is triggered by the direct service, it works with the request cycle to perform the rewind. The page render events (the `pageBeginRender()` and `pageEndRender()` methods) occur even when only a form within the

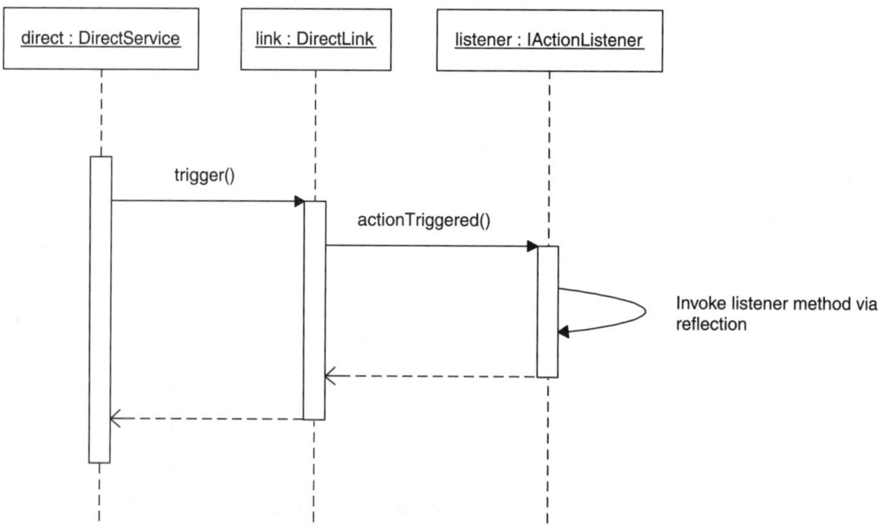

Figure 7.11 The direct service invokes the `trigger()` method on the DirectLink component, which obtains its listener and invokes `actionTriggered()` on it. This results in the listener method being invoked.

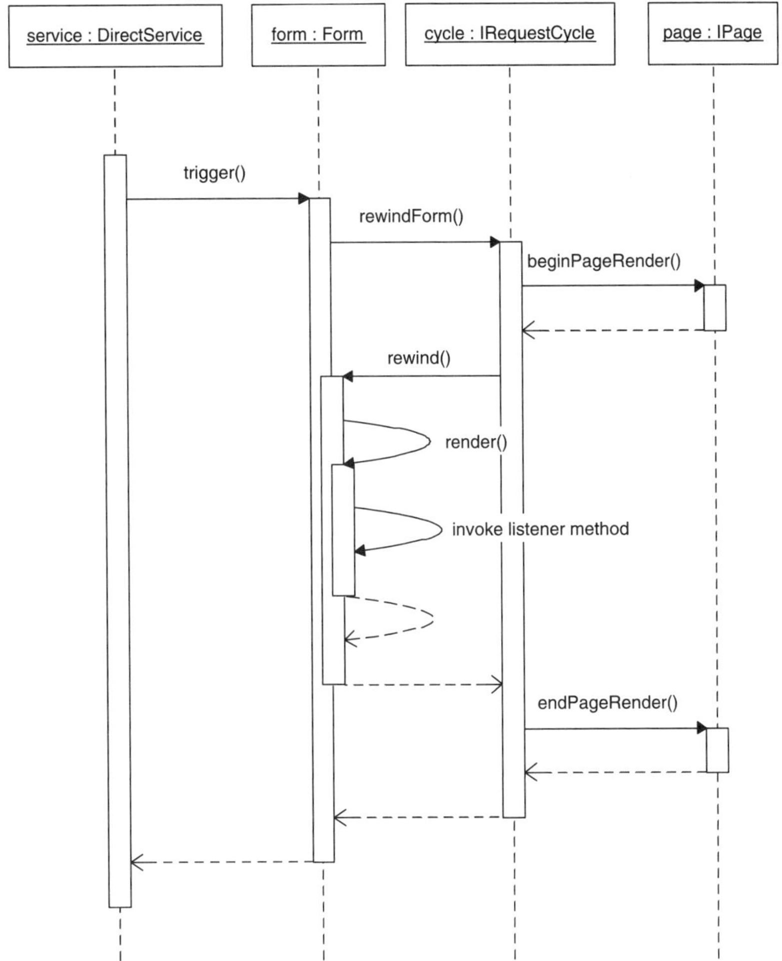

Figure 7.12 Form submission using the direct service. The page is notified before and after the rewind occurs.

page is rewinding. This is very useful; in the examples in chapters 4, 5, and 10, we make use of this to ensure that empty objects exist for form element components to write values to.

The direct service (with its companion component, DirectLink) is useful for creating a link to an operation within a running application. However, the direct service exposes quite a bit about the internal structure of the application inside its URL. Inside the context is not just the page name, but also the component ID, or even a component ID path if the component is contained within another component.

Exposing such construction details of a component is acceptable during the duration of a user's session with the application because the construction of the application will not change mid-session. However, the URLs created by the direct service are not acceptable for long-term storage, such as being recorded as a web browser bookmark. The application URLs generated by the direct service are often stateful and, worse, contain elements (the component ID path) that may change as the application is extended and changed over time.

7.4.6 Creating bookmarkable links using the external service

The external service exists specifically to support URLs that have a long shelf life; it exposes much less of the structure of the application (just the name of the page). The external service represents a step back toward a more JSP-like approach to application development, where certain pages have one specific purpose. Effectively, the external service is a cross between the page and direct services. Like the page service, the context is the name of a page. Like the direct service, service parameters can be passed along in the URL. The processing of the external service is shown in figure 7.13.

For a page to be the target of the external service, it must implement the interface `IExternalPage`, an interface that extends the standard page interface, `IPage`. This interface defines a single method, `activateExternalPage()`, which is invoked by the service after it activates the page. The external service always assumes that requests can operate "cold," without an active session, since the entire point of the service is to create application URLs that can be bookmarked. Chapter 10 includes several examples of using the external service in the context of a real application.

WARNING If you forget to implement the `IExternalPage` interface, you'll get the following error when you click an external link: *Page DatePicker does not implement the IExternalPage interface.*

This service is useful for pages that have a single, specific function. For example, an e-commerce application can use the external service to create links to product catalog pages, and will encode product IDs or SKUs as service parameters.

The ExternalLink component is used to create links to pages using the external service. It has a `page` parameter that specifies the externally addressable page (like a PageLink component), but it also has a `parameters` parameter (like a DirectLink component) used to provide service parameters to the target page.

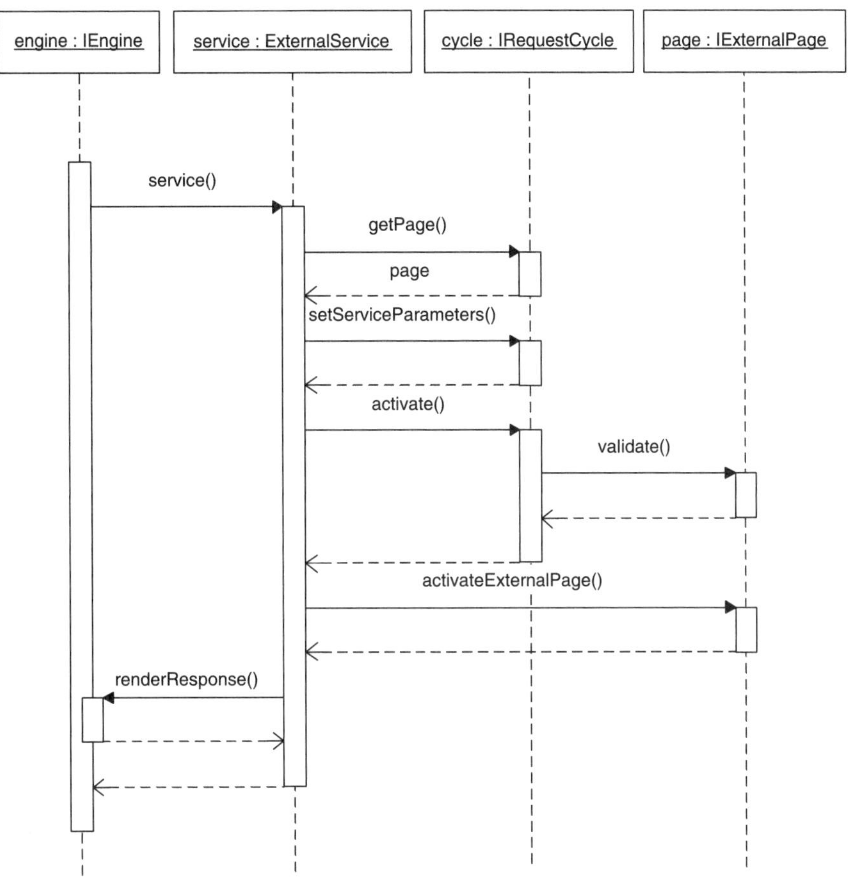

Figure 7.13 The external service validates the page and then invokes the method `activateExternalPage()` before rendering the response.

7.5 Page rendering in detail

The point of any web application is to get HTML into the client web browser where it can be displayed to the user. Perhaps that's too specific; it may not be HTML—it may be some other markup language such as XML, XHTML, or WML (Wireless Markup Language). And the client at the other end may not be a web browser; it could be a cell phone or personal digital assistant (PDA). Although Tapestry is primarily focused on HTML, it is designed to operate in any XML-related markup language.

Rendering in Tapestry is tied to many other subsystems with the framework, including localization and persistent page properties. At the core of rendering in Tapestry is the IRender interface, which declares a single method, render():

```
public void render(IMarkupWriter writer, IRequestCycle cycle);
```

This interface is implemented by any object that wishes to participate in the page-rendering process. As shown back in chapter 1, figure 1.11, IRender is a parent interface of IComponent, so as expected, all components may render. This interface is simple: The writer parameter will be an instance of IMarkupWriter, which can be used to render markup output. The cycle parameter is the request cycle, the object that represents the current request being processed. Through the request cycle, it is possible to obtain an instance of any page in the application, the application engine, and all the objects of the Servlet API.

7.5.1 Using markup writers

The IMarkupWriter interface is similar to the JDK's java.io.PrintWriter class. Although the interface defines a number of overloadings of the print() method for different parameter types, markup writer instances perform extra work before writing output. The input is scanned for reserved character values, which are converted to HTML entities. This means that reserved characters, such as < and &, are converted to their corresponding HTML entities (< and &, respectively). It also means that non-ASCII characters and nonprinting characters are converted to numeric entities.

Once again, you see the simplicity and consistency goals of Tapestry; by using IMarkupWriter, and not simpler interfaces such as PrintWriter or OutputStream, all code throughout the application can easily output safe HTML (HTML that will display properly in the user's web browser). In addition, IMarkupWriter has extensions (seen in chapter 5) that streamline the generation of markup output—special methods for outputting elements and attributes, simply and consistently.

We use HTML as an example here. Different implementations of IMarkupWriter exist for different languages, and the list of reserved characters and entities you can use vary. This means that components don't have any special understanding of the content type; that information is isolated inside the markup writer.

These conversions are useful—and very important. They mean that whether you're using components such as Insert or writing output directly within Java code, you don't have to constantly check for invalid characters or explicitly run output strings through filters. The filters are built directly into the markup writer implementation. This affects both usability and security.

End users will never be able to enter input into a form that "breaks" the page. For example, entering HTML markup as part of the example Register page (from chapter 5) is perfectly valid. In figure 7.14, the user includes <font size="+5"> as part of the first name field. In figure 7.15, the ValidField component displays that value as the default for the field. With no special checks inside ValidField, it is the markup writer that scans and corrects the illegal characters. The text is rendered as <form size="+5">, and the end result is that the default value in the field matches the user's actual input.

When the form is corrected and submitted, the output (shown in figure 7.16) continues to conform to the user's expectations. The input provided is accepted

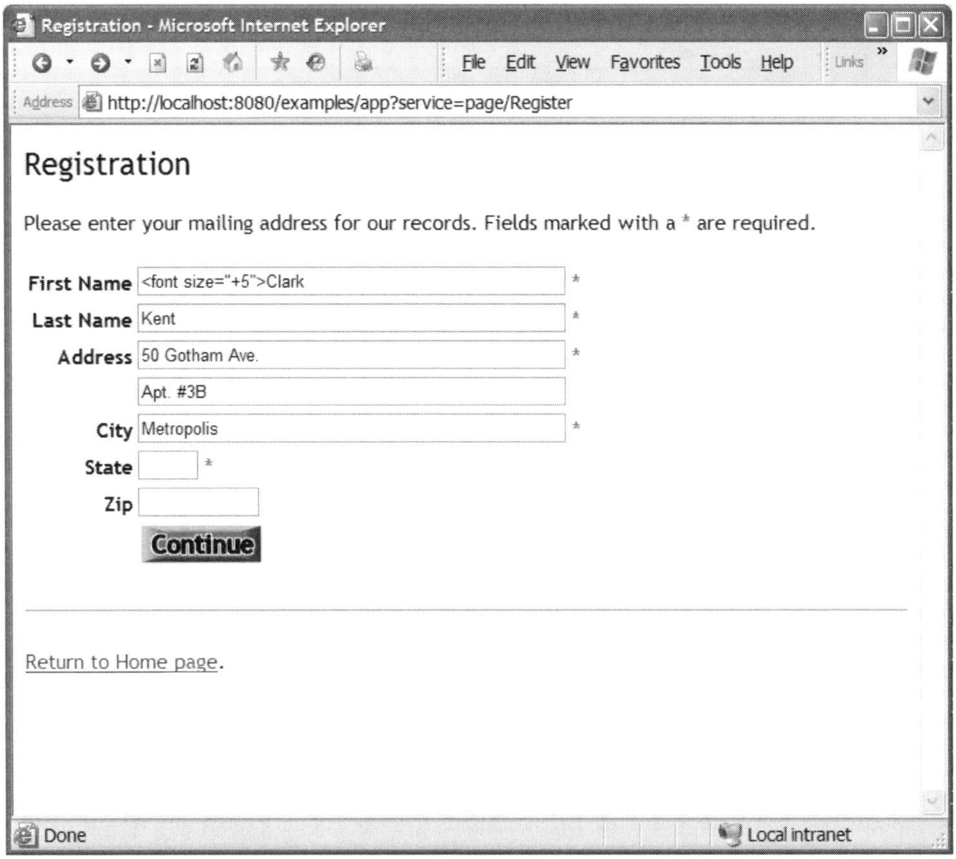

Figure 7.14 Entering HTML markup into a TextField could be a problem.

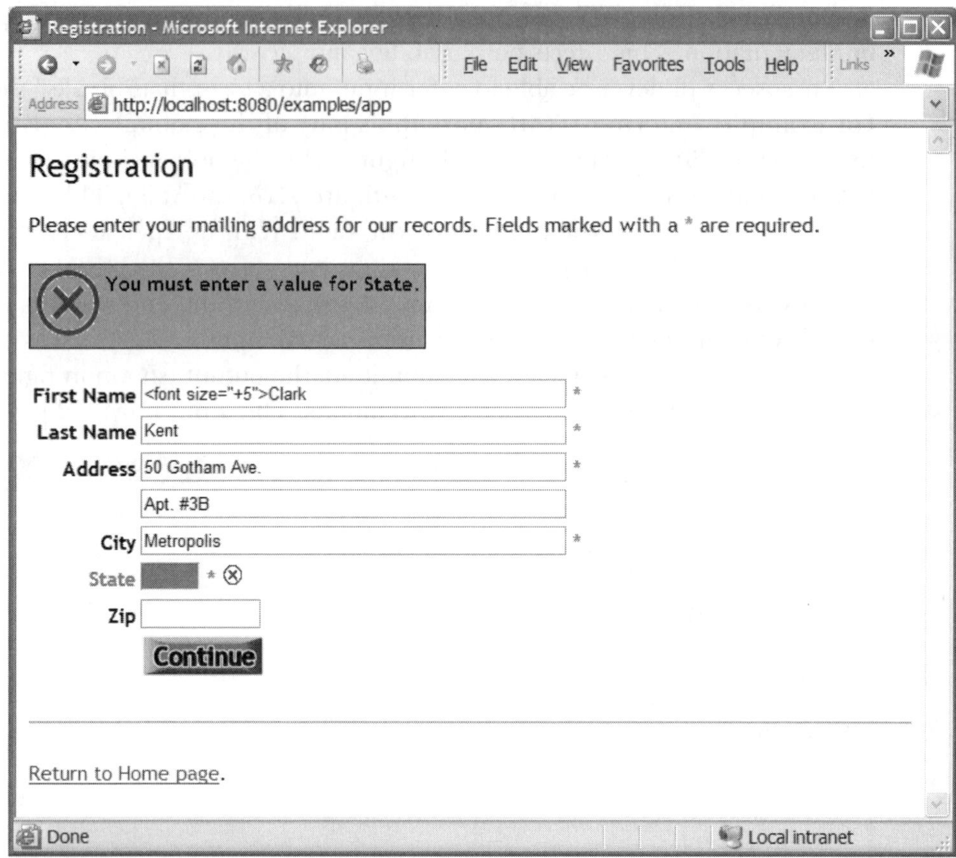

Figure 7.15 The markup writer used by Tapestry components, including ValidField, properly escapes invalid characters that are HTML entities.

and displayed as the output, regardless of the fact that the user entered characters with a specific meaning to HTML. Again, the Insert component used to display the first name can rely on the markup writer to perform the necessary filtering of HTML characters into HTML entities. If this filtering was not present, the unwanted HTML tag would not appear, and the formatting of the rest of the page would be affected, as shown in figure 7.17.

Security can also be affected when user input is reproduced without filtering. A known exploit used on many online forums is to enter malicious JavaScript into a text area of a form, including a `<script>` element. When another user reads the "message," the `<script>` tag and malicious JavaScript are executed within that user's web browser. Because of the filtering inside Tapestry, this

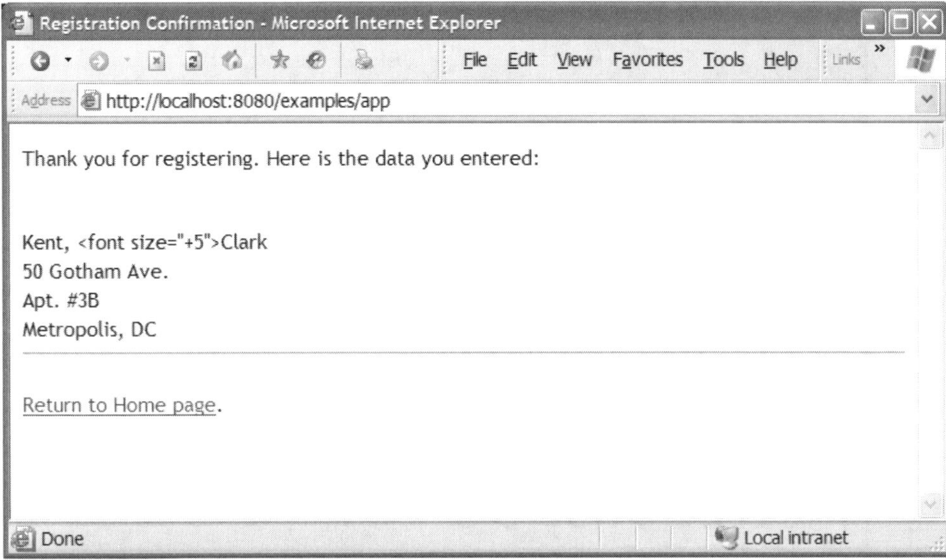

Figure 7.16 All components get the filter benefit automatically, so users see as output the input they provided, even though it contains markup.

exploit is not possible; the <script> element entered by the malicious user would be output as <script>, which would be displayed by the web browser and not executed.

7.5.2 *Going beyond HTML*

Much of this book focuses on HTML, but of course the World Wide Web is more than HTML. Web applications that don't use HTML but instead use WML (Wireless Markup Language), XML, or XHTML are becoming increasingly useful.

Tapestry is well suited to any kind of HTML or XML style markup. The nature of any output produced by the framework is controlled by the markup writer implementation used and by templates of any pages and components.

Tapestry does not validate its page and component templates; that is, it does not require that the templates conform to any Document Type Definition (DTD), the way an XML parser would. In fact, the Tapestry template parser is designed around compatibility with poorly formatted HTML; it is completely accepting of unquoted attributes and unclosed elements.

The Tapestry template parser finds all the components within the template by looking for tags with the `jwcid` attribute. It matches start tags to end tags and checks that the nesting of dynamic tags is valid. Any text, whether markup

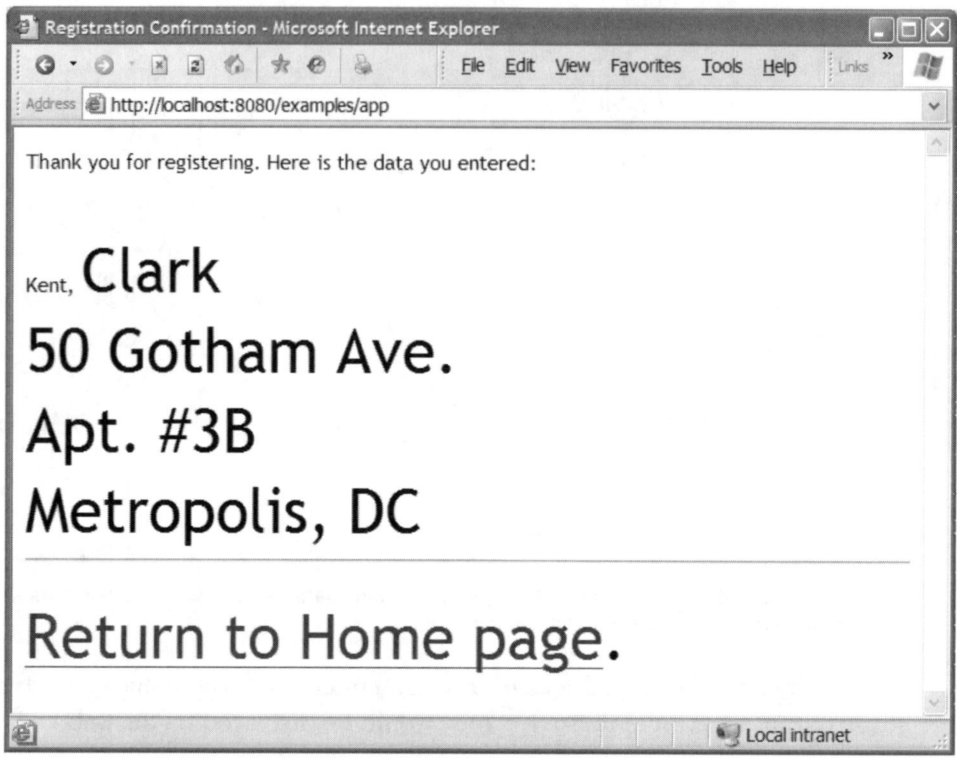

Figure 7.17 Without filtering, the way many non-Tapestry applications execute, the user's input succeeds in mangling the output of the page, causing text to appear large.

or not, that isn't part of a dynamic component tag is treated as static, literal text. This static text will be passed through the client web browser uninterpreted and unchanged. Therefore, in order to generate valid XML, WML, or XHTML pages, the first step is to ensure that the templates used are themselves valid.

The markup writer implementation provided with Tapestry outputs markup that is compatible with XML, WML, or XHTML. In other words, the markup writer properly escapes reserved entities, quotes attributes, and balances start tags with end tags.

One responsibility for a markup writer is to implement a method, `getContentType()`, which returns the Multipurpose Internet Mail Extensions (MIME) type for any content generated with the writer. The only significant difference between a page that renders HTML and one that renders XML or WML is the implementation of this method. The default markup writer generates HTML and returns a content type of `text/html; charset=UTF-8`. The default page class, `BasePage`, implements only a single method, `getResponseWriter()`, which instantiates and returns an `HTMLWriter` instance.

7.5.3 Understanding the page-rendering sequence

As you've seen, once an engine service is ready to render a response, it invokes the engine method `renderReponse()`. Figure 7.18 details exactly what happens inside this method.

The key methods invoked on the page are `getResponseWriter()` and `renderPage()`. As described in the previous section, a page indicates what kind of content type it generated by creating an appropriate instance of `IMarkupWriter`. `IMarkupWriter` provides access to the MIME content type it produces with its `getContentType()` method. This value will be used with the `HttpServletResponse` method `setContentType()`.

Rendering a page involves an interaction with the Tapestry persistent page property subsystem. Once a render begins, it is no longer possible to make changes to persistent page properties (page properties whose values persist between requests). Tapestry gives the page one last chance to make changes to persistent page properties inside the `beginResponse()` method. After that, it invokes the request cycle method `commitPageChanges()`, which notifies the page recorders (which are responsible for managing persistent page properties) that they should save any outstanding changes. More details on persistent page properties are coming later in this chapter.

Finally, after all of this maneuvering and setup, the `render()` method is invoked. The page will begin rendering the contents of its template, recursively rendering any enclosed components along the way.

7.5.4 Using page-rendering events

Sometimes a component (or other object) just needs to know when the page is about to start rendering, or when it has finished rendering. This is commonly required to set properties of objects that will be used during the render, but only just in time, as if the page is actually going to render.

These notifications are made available through an event listener interface: `PageRenderListener`. This interface include two methods: `pageBeginRender()` and `pageEndRender()`.

The `pageBeginRender()` method will be invoked just before the page's `beginResponse()` method. The method is invoked before the page's recorder is committed, while it is still able to change persistent page properties. The

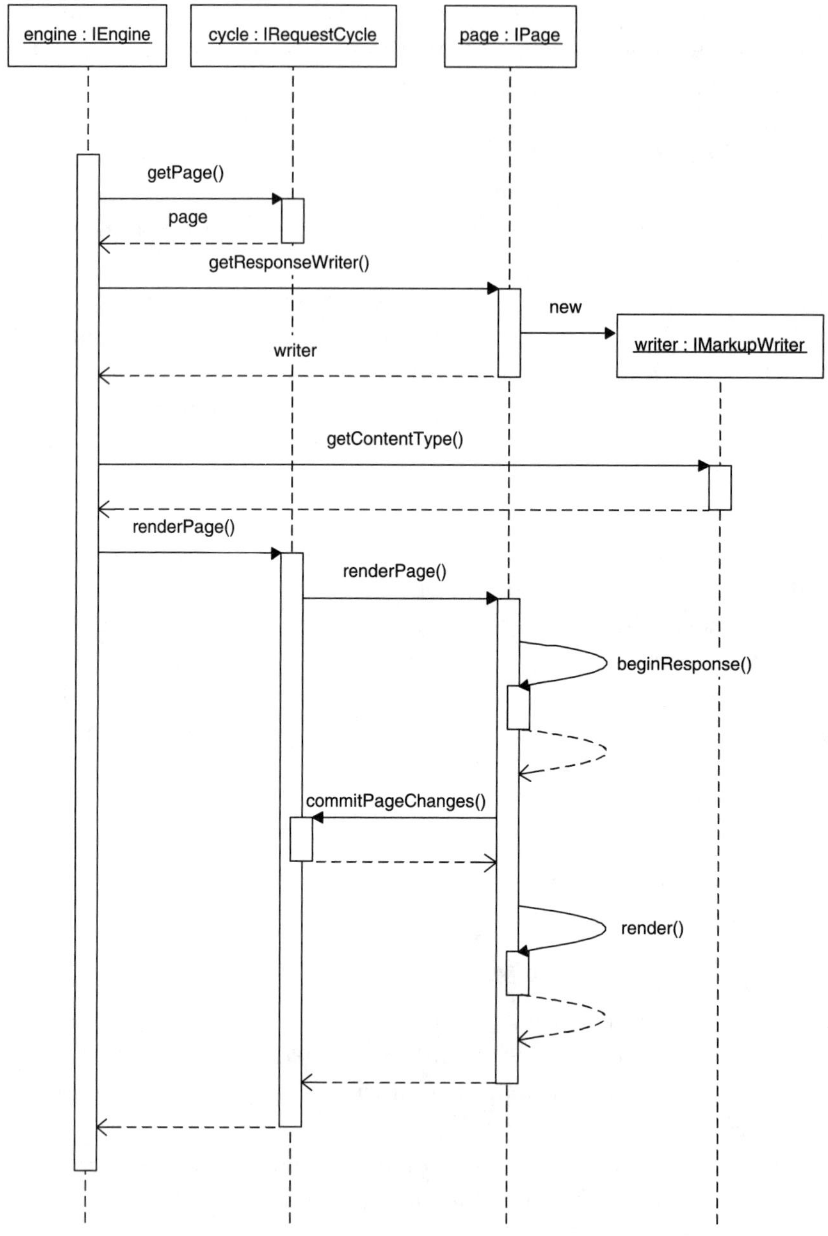

Figure 7.18 The engine's `renderResponse()` method. The page is responsible for creating the markup writer that it, and all components it contains, will use when rendering. The page's `render()` method will render the page and all components it contains, recursively.

`pageBeginRender()` method will also be invoked before a Form component within the page rewinds (as discussed in chapter 3).

The `pageEndRender()` method will be invoked after the page finishes rendering, even if an exception is thrown while the page is rendering. It is also invoked after a Form component finishes rewinding.

The `IPage` interface includes methods for adding and removing listeners: `addPageRenderListener()` and `removePageRenderListener()`.

As a convenience, if a component implements the `PageRenderListener` interface, it will automatically be added as a listener to the page that contains it. Pages may also implement the interface, in which case they will invoke the event methods on themselves. This automatic registration allows for a consistent approach between pages and components for performing initializations just before the page renders.

7.6 Loading and pooling pages

The single thing that allows Tapestry to operate so effectively is that Tapestry applications are built from stateful JavaBeans instead of stateless servlets. This bridging from the stateless world of HTTP and servlets to the stateful world of JavaBeans (pages and components are JavaBeans, as are most domain objects) is both necessary to how Tapestry operates as well as expensive. It is expensive because a page instance is a complex entity to create. Constructing a page instance requires a shopping list of work:

- The page's specification must be located and parsed.
- A subclass of the page may be dynamically created.
- The page is instantiated.
- Each component of the page must also be located, parsed, extended, and instantiated.
- The page's template is read and applied to the page.
- Components with templates also must find their templates, and then parse and apply them.

All told, a single page may contain dozens or more components and hundreds of supporting objects to represent portions of the template, parameter bindings, assets, helper beans, and so forth. Despite the fact that specifications and templates are read once and cached for later use, a significant amount of processing is necessary just to assemble all of these bits and pieces into a functioning page instance that can respond to requests or render a response. Pages are a scarce commodity that should be used and reused, and not be fruitlessly discarded at the end of a single request.

However, creating one instance of a page is not enough either. Because pages (and the components and objects contained within a page) are stateful, they can only be used by one thread, processing one request, for one user. A servlet, with no client-specific internal state, can service any number of simultaneous requests in parallel threads. A page must only be used by a single thread.

As mentioned earlier, the issues that arise when using stateful pages are similar to the issues that arise when using database connections. You can't afford to reserve one database connection for each individual user—you could potentially require thousands of database connections (more than most databases can deal with effectively), even though only a small number will be in use at any one time. However, you can't share database connections haphazardly, because only one thread can use a connection at any one time. The standard, well-documented approach to dealing with these issues is the use of an *object pool* for database connections. The pool contains database connections that are initialized and ready for use. Code that accesses the database may borrow a connection from the pool for a short period and then return the connection to the pool as soon as possible. In some cases, if no connection is available, a new one will be created, on the fly.

Tapestry adopts this same pattern for pages. As a particular page is needed, it is obtained from a central page pool. If the pool contains no such page (either because this is the first request involving the page, or because all page instances created thus far are already in use by other threads), then a new page instance is created (along with all of its components, templates, parameter bindings, and other objects). If a usable page is in the pool, it is removed for the duration of the request.

7.6.1 Retrieving pages from the pool

Once an application is up and running and has processed a few requests, chances are good that most requests can be satisfied with pages that are already stored in the page pool. Figure 7.19 shows how the `IRequestCycle` method `getPage()` obtains and readies a page instance when it is needed by a listener or service. Once a page is obtained in this way, it is cached by the request cycle object for the duration of the request. Future calls to `getPage()` with the same page name return the same instance.[3]

[3] This is a slight simplification. The actual key involves the page name and the desired locale. This is covered in detail in section 7.9.2.

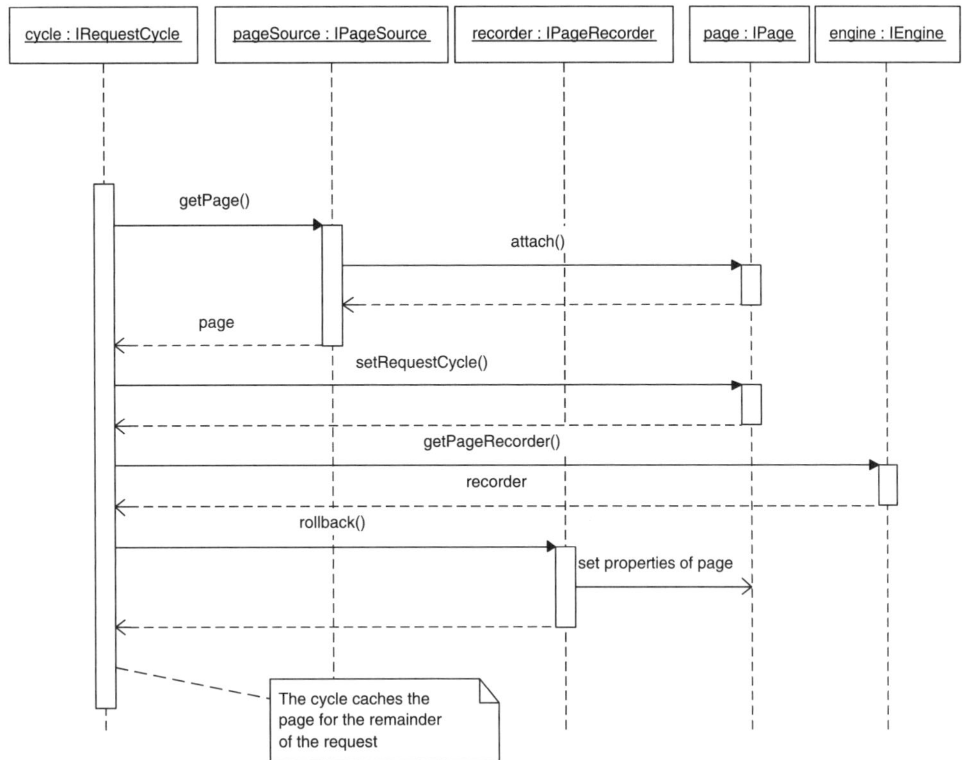

Figure 7.19 The `getPage()` method of the request cycle. The request cycle goes to the page source for a ready page instance. The instance is removed from the page pool and attached to the engine and to the request. The page's recorder will roll back any persistent page properties to their prior values.

The request cycle uses the page source to obtain fresh page instances. The *page source* is a pool for pages, which has the ability to instantiate a fresh page instance if none is available in the pool. Pages are attached to the application's engine via the `attach()` method and returned to the request cycle.

The request cycle then gets the page recorder for the page from the engine. The *page recorder* is an object that is used to track changes to persistent page properties for the page. Persistent page properties are properties of pages (or components within the page) that persist between request cycles. As a persistent page property is changed, the new value is recorded into the `HttpSession` for later use (more information on persistent page properties is available later in this chapter).

This is another fundamental aspect of Tapestry: A page's persistent state, specific to an individual user, is entirely separate from any instance of the page. This is important; it allows us to have our cake and eat it, too—that is, to have a complex object graph without paying the expense of serializing the entire graph to track changes in the state of objects within the graph.

Java developers are accustomed to thinking that the best way to store the state of any object is to make the object serializable. Doing this for Tapestry pages and components would be terribly wasteful. The tiny handful of persistent properties associated with a page (and its components) are vastly outnumbered by the large number of supporting objects, most of which should be shared between page instances. Serializing and deserializing an entire page not only would be a time-consuming and expensive operation, but also would lead to duplication of common objects that would otherwise be shared.

Tapestry instead concentrates on storing just the persistent page properties, the few properties that need to be stored in the `HttpSession` and restored in a later request. The page recorder object is hooked into pages via a simple notification system, described later in this chapter. The page recorder observes changes to the persistent properties and safely stores the values in the `HttpSession` as named attributes. This approach allows for efficient tracking of changes to persistent page properties, because individual properties are stored as individual `HttpSession` attributes. Without the division between page instances and persistent page state, Tapestry couldn't make any claim to efficiency; with it, Tapestry can manage complex server-side state simply and effectively.

7.6.2 Creating new page instances

Figure 7.19 covers only the case where a page instance is ready and waiting to be attached to the request. What happens when there isn't a ready page instance? In that case, the page source will create a new instance, using an instance of `IPageLoader`, as shown in figure 7.20.

The page loader starts by instantiating an instance of the page's Java class. Actually, the class that is instantiated will likely be a generated subclass containing the additional fields and methods for any properties specified in the page's specification. In any case, first the Java page class is instantiated, and then initial properties of the page are set, including the page's name. The page is then attached to the engine. Next is a recursive process, where each component in the page is instantiated in a like manner.

As each component is created, the page loader invokes its `finishLoad()` method. Components that inherit from the `BaseComponent` class will load their templates at this time. Components that contain implicit components in their template will fire off a new round of component instantiation and loading.

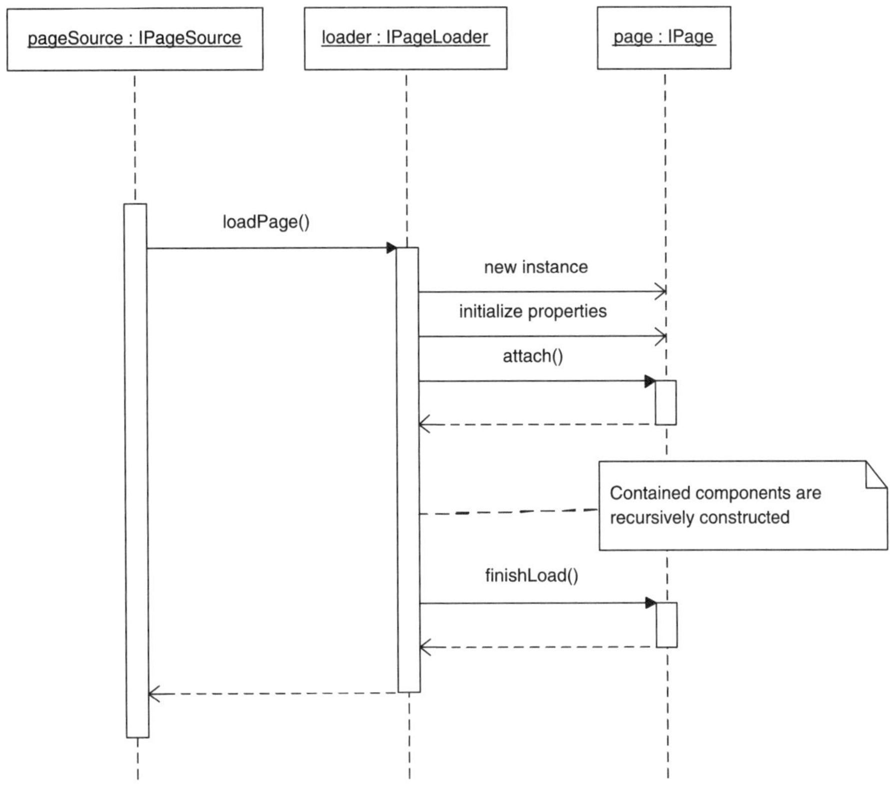

Figure 7.20 The page loader's `getPage()` method, showing the steps when no pooled page is available. The page loader creates a new instance of the page and attaches it to the engine. The page loader recursively instantiates the components of the page. When all components have been created, it invokes `finishLoad()` on the page.

Finally, after the entire tree of components rooted at the page is instantiated and configured, the page's `finishLoad()` method is invoked.

One additional operation that occurs in `finishLoad()` is automatic event registration. When a component implements any of the page event interfaces (`PageRenderListener`, `PageDetachListener`, or `PageValidateListener`), it will automatically be registered with the page as a listener of that type. A page that implements one of these interfaces will be registered with itself as a listener.

For both pages and components, the `finishLoad()` method is a good place to do any final initializations that can't be expressed in the page or component specification. Often these initializations involve other components contained with the page. Once the page's `finishLoad()` method completes, the fully initialized and configured page is returned to the request cycle and, from there, to the service or listener method that originally requested an instance of the page.

TIP Override `finishLoad()` (in pages or components) to perform final initializations when a page instance is first created.

As a final note, the `finishLoad()` method has two versions:

```
public void finishLoad(
  IRequestCycle cycle,
  IPageLoader loader,
  IComponentSpecification specification);
protected void finishLoad();
```

The first version, the public method with three parameters, is defined in the `IComponent` interface. If this method is overridden, the super class implementation must be invoked first.[4] The protected version of the method (which takes no parameters) is a convenience, declared in the class `AbstractComponent` and invoked from the public `finishLoad()` method. The implementation provided by `AbstractComponent` is empty and thus doesn't have to be invoked by a subclass that overrides it.

TIP Always override the protected `finishLoad()` method (the one with no parameters), unless you specifically need access to one of the parameters in the public `finishLoad()` method; it's too easy to forget to invoke the super class implementation of the public method.

7.6.3 Returning pages to the pool

The flip side of page loading occurs at the end of the request, after the response has been sent to the client. At this point, the pages that have been attached to the request must be returned to the pool. More than that, it is necessary that all the properties of the page (both persistent and transient) be reset to pristine values, ready for use by some later request (for another user in another session). Leaving property values in place is a dangerous proposition: The same page instance used by one user in one request will be used by another user in a completely different request. If the first user left his or her credit card number or password or home phone number in a property and that property is not cleared

[4] Failure to invoke the super class implementation will prevent the page or component's template from being loaded, as well as cause other side effects.

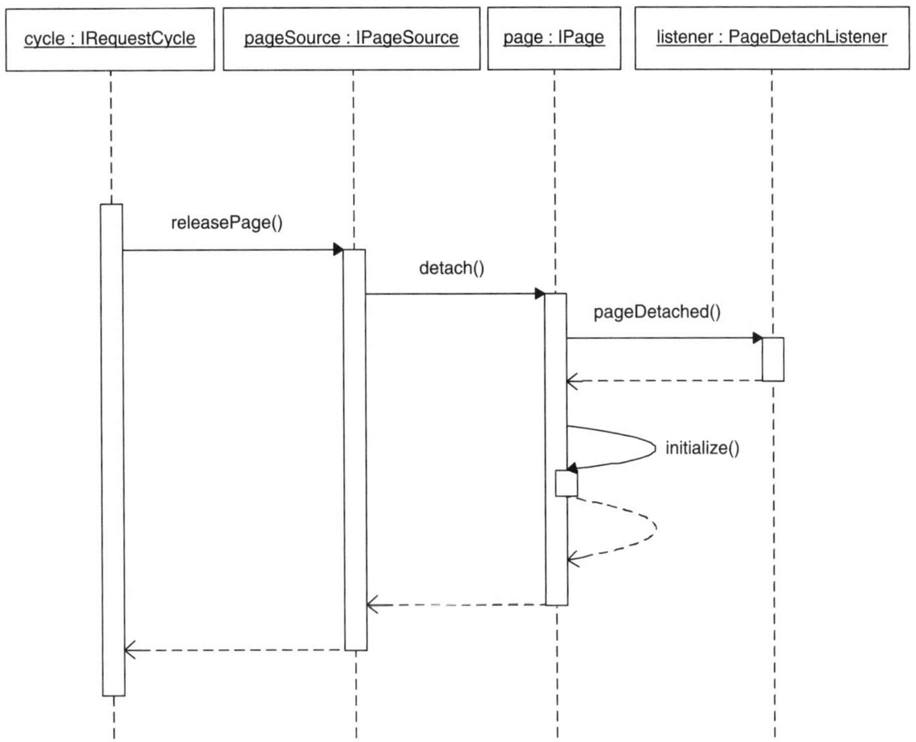

Figure 7.21 The request cycle's `cleanup()` method. At the end of the request, each page is released and stored to the page source's pool. The `detach()` method notifies any listeners, and then invokes `initialize()`. Finally, the page's `visit`, `engine`, and `requestCycle` properties are reset to null.

out, then the next user along may see those values. Figure 7.21 shows the cleanup sequence.

The page method `detach()` is responsible for cleaning up the page before it is stored in the pool for later reuse. The first step is to notify any `PageDetachListeners` that are registered with the page. Following that, the `initialize()` method is invoked. This method is designed to be overridden in subclasses for this exact purpose: reinitializing any properties. After `initialize()`, the page's `visit`, `engine`, and `requestCycle` properties are set to null. The page should now be devoid of any changes specific to the user or to the request; the `initialize()` method should have reset all such properties, assuming the developers did their work.

CAUTION An application should *never* store a reference to a page or component persistently (in the `Visit` object, or as a persistent page property). Pages should always be self-contained, with only references to other objects and components within the same page. Instead, the name of the page should be stored and resolved using the request cycle object. A utility class, `ComponentAddress`, exists for this purpose. Storing a page reference will result in one of two unwanted outcomes: Either the page instance will be illegally accessed while it is in the pool and in an uninitialized state, or the page instance will be accessed by multiple threads. Both of these scenarios will cause confusing behavior and unpredictable runtime exceptions.

Having to be concerned with either the `detach()` or `initialize()` method is something of a throwback to earlier releases of Tapestry; release 2.3 (the release prior to 3.0) and earlier did not have the `<property-specification>` element in page and component specifications. Not only were you responsible for creating the fields and accessor methods, but you were also expected to implement the `initialize()` method to clean up the page at the end of the request cycle. Most applications will not have to be concerned with page cleanup, as long as they use the `<property-specification>` element for all their persistent and transient properties.

TIP Use the `PageDetachListener` interface to perform any cleanups. Implementing the interface ensures that the page will invoke the `pageDetached()` event method; that way, you won't have to worry about invoking super class implementations of methods.

7.7 Using persistent page properties

An important aspect of Tapestry is maintaining the illusion that HTTP is a stateful protocol, and that the user has sole access to the page instances. To the user, it appears as if the web page in the browser is directly connected to specific objects in the server. This is truly an illusion—especially when the application is deployed into a server cluster, since each request may potentially be processed by a different server, using completely different page instances housed in a completely different JVM.

This same illusion applies to your view of the application as a developer. You should be able to code a Tapestry application in the same way you would code a stand-alone application: with the expectation that the object instances continue to exist from instant to instant. You shouldn't have to worry about where objects "go" after your page renders, or after your listener method is executed.

Persistent page properties are the key aspect of maintaining this illusion. Each request is serviced by an equivalent page instance, not the same one, and persistent page properties ensure that equivalence. The persistent properties will be the same from one request to the next, for as long as the `HttpSession` is active.

Despite the name, persistent page properties have nothing to do with database persistence. These properties are not stored in a database for long-term access; they are only available for the duration of the `HttpSession`. Once the session expires or is invalidated, the persistent properties are lost.

A persistent property is no more than a property whose value is stored as an `HttpSession` attribute. When a persistent property changes, the page recorder observes the change and records the new value for later use. Figure 7.22 shows how property changes are propagated from the page to the page's recorder.

A persistent property is only saved persistently as a side effect of invoking the setter method (which, in turn, invokes the static `fireObservedChange()` method of the Tapestry utility class). Refer back to figure 7.13; it identifies a scenario where the value stored in an `HttpSession` attribute is not properly replicated. A similar problem exists with persistent page properties when the property values

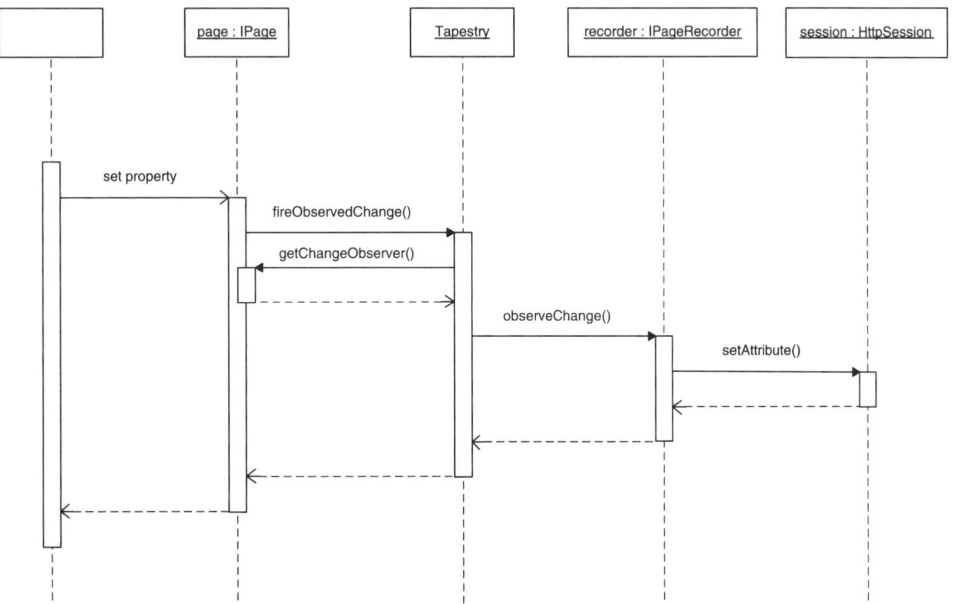

Figure 7.22 The implementation of a setter method for a persistent property will invoke to the static `fireObservedChange()` method, which notifies the page's recorder. The page recorder then constructs a key and stores the value as an `HttpSession` attribute.

themselves are mutable. If, after invoking the accessor method, the property value is changed, the same lack of synchronization can occur. As a rule of thumb, you should be careful not to change the internal state of any mutable object after invoking such an accessor method; otherwise, you will be opening yourself up to a painful class of bugs when you enable clustering for your application.

Despite the name, persistent properties are not limited to the page. Any component may have persistent properties. The mechanism used is the same, regardless. Component properties are specific to the page that ultimately contains the component; if the same component is used in two different pages, then each component will store its individual persistent property as a different `HttpSession` attribute. This makes sense from Tapestry's point of view; these are different instances of the same component type, not different references to the same component.

Although it is possible to implement persistent properties yourself, there's no reason to do so. Tapestry is fully capable of creating the fields, accessor methods, notifications, and cleanups necessary to support a persistent property on a page or a component, using the `<property-specification>` element in a page or component specification. Appendix D includes complete details about the use and attributes of the `<property-specification>` element.

7.8 Using specified properties

A page or component specification may declare entirely new properties for the page (or component) class. You've seen this in previous chapters, where we created several properties in the ToDo application to hold individual `ToDoItems` and a list of items.

Tapestry will create an enhanced subclass to support the specified properties. For components, it may create a subclass even if there are no declared properties, to help support any component parameters. In any case, the enhanced subclass will include new fields and accessor methods. If the property is declared to be persistent, then the setter method will properly invoke the `fireObservedChange()` method, as outlined in the previous section.

Declared properties, both persistent and transient, may also have an initial value. The initial value is either the value of the `initial-value` attribute of the `<property-specification>` element or, if there is no such attribute, the body of the `<property-specification>` element. The initial value is an OGNL expression.

The expression is evaluated just once, after the page's (or component's) `finishLoad()` method is invoked. The value for the expression is used to set the property, but it is also saved and used later to update the property when the page is detached from the request, before being stored back into the page pool for later reuse.

If no initial value is provided for the property, then the framework will *read* the property after invoking the `finishLoad()` method. Again, this value is retained and used to update the property when the page is detached. This means that, even for declared properties, it is possible to set an initial value from the `finishLoad()` method.

7.9 Localizing Tapestry applications

Localization is the difficult process of creating an application that is translated appropriately for the user. This means that one user of the application in Boston may see a different version of the application than a user in Venice. Localization of an application starts with simple issues, such as translating text into the proper language, but also encompasses many other potential differences. This may be represented in small changes, such as the exact way numbers and dates are formatted, or in large changes, such as the color and layout of entire web pages. The Java Runtime Environment (JRE) provides a considerable amount of support for localizing of applications; Tapestry includes well-integrated approaches for leveraging that support.

Localization of web applications is often an afterthought. Getting web applications working in a single language, typically U.S. English, is daunting enough that localizing the application is often slipped into "phase 2." For an application with broad-ranging appeal, such as a news site, an e-commerce site, or an advertising site, internationalization is a must from the start.

In Tapestry, localization involves two aspects: tracking the desired language for a particular user and presenting the user interface in that language.[5] Often, the term *locale* is used instead of *language*. Locale is a more precise term than language; it refers not only to a particular language, but also to how that language is used in a particular geographic location. For example, English is a language, but there are differences between American English and British English, such as the spelling of some words (*color* versus *colour*, for example). This is resolved by having (in this case) three different locales to represent English: `en`, `en_US`, and `en_GB`.

---

[5] Localization is often referred to as "l10n" (l, 10 letters, and an n).

7.9.1 Using Java localization

In a traditional Java application, the JRE supplies most of the support for handling localization. The first step is to remove hard-coded message strings from Java code and store them into properties files. A resource bundle is a collection of such message strings that may be accessed by developer-defined keys.

To handle multiple languages, multiple properties files are used. The base properties file has a name that ends in *.properties*; for example, Messages.properties. Additional properties files have the same name, but with a locale name suffix inserted before the .properties extension. These additional files provide overrides of the keys and values in the base properties file. When you are building up a dictionary of keys and localized values, several of these files can be involved. The rule is always that more specific values override less specific values. Figure 7.23 shows how individual properties are mixed, matched, and overridden to form localized resource bundles.

The localization for `en_US` uses just the default values for the two keys: `Hello` and `color`. For the `en_GB` localization, the value for the color key is overridden to `colour` (the British spelling). For the `fr` localization, both keys are overridden.

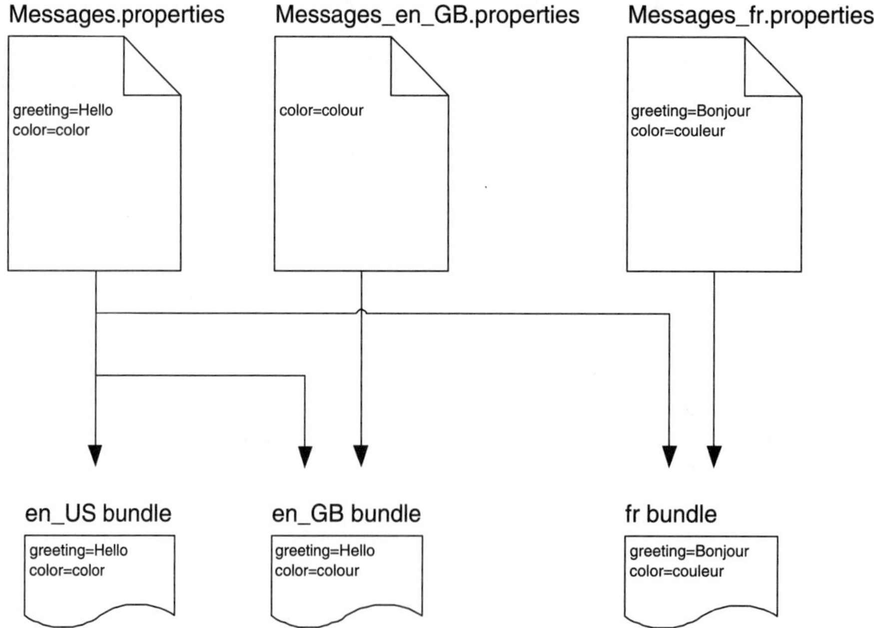

Figure 7.23 Keys and values in the main properties file are merged with, and overwritten by, values from the more specific properties files.

So, all of this allows *strings* to be localized. The next step is to get those strings used in a web application. Other frameworks, those that use JavaServer Pages, include JSP tag libraries for accessing a resource bundle and extracting strings from it. The JSP tags take the place of literal text, with terrible results. The resulting JSP is not even remotely previewable in an HTML editor; it barely looks like HTML. The loss of literal text in the JSP has an awful impact on developers. Those little snippets of text act like signposts, helping you to locate the right form, or the right link, or the right image within a page. Stripping them out makes every change an agonizing search for the right spot within the page.

As you'll see, Tapestry takes a more pragmatic and less intrusive approach.

7.9.2 Using Tapestry's localization features

Tapestry applications allow for localization of both text and images. Localized strings can be easily referenced in the HTML template, both for inclusion as part of the static portion of the page and as values bound to component parameters. Images (or really, any kind of asset) are also automatically localized. Figure 7.24 shows a sequence of pages demonstrating how Tapestry application localization operates.

After the user selects a new locale (labeled more generally as a *Language* in the user interface), the confirmation page is displayed. From there, the user returns to the original page, but the text, graphics, and even the selections within the drop-down list have changed to reflect the new localization of the application.

Creating a localized HTML template

Listing 7.1 contains the HTML template for the L10N (Localization) page. It demonstrates two different ways to use localized text in a template: as a value bound to a component parameter and as a literal value within the template.

Listing 7.1 L10N.html: HTML template for the L10N page

```
<html jwcid="@Shell" title="message:title">    <-❶
<body jwcid="@Body">

<h1><span key="title"/></h1>

<span key="blurb">Descriptive text.</span>    <-❷

<form jwcid="@Form" listener="ognl:listeners.formSubmit">

<span key="language-label">Language</span>:    <-❸
<select jwcid="@PropertySelection"
  value="ognl:engine.locale"
  model="ognl:localeModel"/>

<p/>
```

```
<input type="image"
  src="images/L10N/Change.png"
  jwcid="@ImageSubmit"
  image="ognl:assets.change"
  alt="message:change-label"/>     <-4
</form>

<p><a href="#"
    jwcid="@PageLink"
    page="Home"><span key="return-to-home">Return     5
to Home page</span></a>.
</p>
</body>
</html>
```

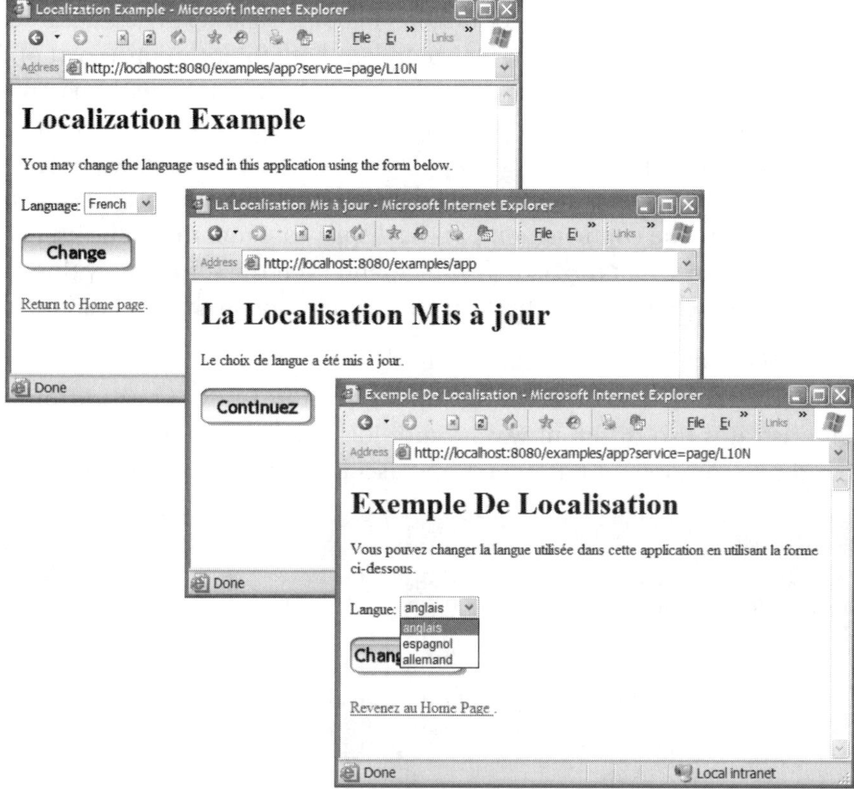

Figure 7.24 The user selects a language from the drop-down list and is presented with a confirmation page in the new language. Returning to the original page shows changes to text, including the window title bar, as well as images, and even changes to the contents of the drop-down list.

❶ The `title` parameter is bound to the localized message for the key `title`.
❷ The `<span>` element is replaced by the localized message for the key `blurb`.
❸ The `<span>` element is replaced by the localized message for the key `language-label`.
❹ The `alt` informal parameter is bound to the localized message for the key `change-label`.
❺ The `<span>` element is replaced by the localized message for the key `return-to-home`.

A localized string component parameter is used in the very first line of the template:

```
<html jwcid="@Shell" title="message:title">
```

Just as the `ognl:` prefix is used to identify a parameter that is actually an OGNL expression, the `message:` prefix is used to identify a parameter that is a localized message key. The `title` parameter of the Shell component will be bound to a specific message string, found by looking up the key `title` in the localized messages for the page.

NOTE Components include a `getMessage()` method for accessing localized messages for the component. It is possible to replace `message:title` with `ognl:getMessage("title")` to achieve the same result, though the `message:` prefix is more efficient, since the framework will know that the value obtained this way is invariant (for the OGNL expression, it must keep reevaluating the expression on each use). The `getMessage()` method, as part of an OGNL expression, can be used when the localized message must be combined with other, nonlocalized text to form a parameter value.

These localized messages are stored in a set of properties files for the page. The properties files are stored in the WEB-INF folder of the web application, alongside the page specification. This example application can be localized in the default language (U.S. English) as well as French, Spanish, and German; therefore, there are four properties files, named L10N.properties, L10N_fr.properties, L10N_es.properties, and L10N_de.properties. The first file, L10N.properties, contains the default language values:

```
title=Localization Example
blurb=You may change the language used in this application using \
the form below.
language-label=Language
change-label=Change
return-to-home=Return to Home page
```

The other files contain the translations of the values appropriate for the locale. For example, the French localization, L10N_fr.properties, contains

```
title=Exemple De Localisation
blurb=Vous pouvez changer la langue utilisée dans \
cette application en utilisant la forme ci-dessous.
language-label=Langue
change-label=Changez
return-to-home=Revenez au Home Page
```

Having many small message properties files has advantages over more common approaches that use a single centralized message properties file employed throughout the entire application. With a single large file, keys often have to be prefixed to identify which page within an application they belong to. In Tapestry, short keys are acceptable because each message properties file is used by only one page or component.

As can be seen in the template, localized message references can be used as both formal parameters (the `title` parameter of the Shell component) or informal parameters (the `alt` parameter of the ImageSubmit component).

A second use for localized messages is to create a localized literal string within the template, not as a parameter to a component. The instructional text at the top of the page ("You may change the language ...") is an example of the kind of literal template text that should be localized. It's given the localization key `blurb` and included in the rendered page by using a specialized `<span>` element:

```
<span key="blurb">Descriptive text.</span>
```

As with a component, the body of the `<span>` element is always removed and replaced with the localized message defined by the `key` attribute. Having text in the body is, once again, useful when previewing the template in an HTML editor, even if the text is a meaningless placeholder. This localized literal construct isn't a component, but it behaves virtually the same as an Insert component:

```
<span jwcid="@Insert" value="message:blurb">Descriptive text.</span>
```

There are two differences between a localized literal string and an Insert component:

- The element must be `<span>` (though case does not matter).
- Additional attributes are always simple literals, even if they have an `ognl:` prefix.

Like an Insert component, the `<span>` tag is rendered only if there are additional parameters. This is useful when the `<span>` tag references a CSS style. Any unsafe characters in the localized string (characters such as `<` and `&`) will be converted to HTML entities, as described in section 7.5.1. This can be defeated, if desired, by specifying the value `true` for the attribute `raw`. This is recognized by Tapestry and disables the use of HTML entity filtering, allowing you to place HTML markup directly in the properties file.

Accessing messages in Java code

Frequently, you will need to make use of localized messages inside your own code, rather than in a template or specification. You might be constructing a specialized error message, or a detailed window title. The `AbstractComponent` base class provides several convenience methods for easily assembling such messages.

The `getMessage()` method takes a string key parameter. The return value is the localized message string for that key, from the component's messages. If no such message string exists, the key is returned in modified form: uppercase and enclosed in brackets. This allows your application to continue operating even with missing message strings, but makes it very noticeable that there's a problem to be addressed.

Frequently, you will want to assemble a message from pieces. This is accomplished using the `format()` method. This method takes a string key and one or more arguments (the method is overloaded to take one, two, three, or an array of arguments). For example, your component's message properties file may contain the following message:

```
overdue-reminder=This task was due on {0}.
```

The `{0}` is a placeholder for the first argument (arguments are numbered starting with 0). You can include any number of arguments. At runtime, you will combine the message format with additional localized messages and strings. For example, the following method returns a localized warning message if the `currentDate` property is later than the `dueDate` property:

```
public String getTaskWarning()
{
  Date dueDate = getDueDate();
  if (getCurrentDate().compareTo(dueDate) > 0)
  {
    DateFormat format =
      DateFormat.getDateInstance(DateFormat.SHORT, getLocale());

    String dueDateString = format.format(dueDate);

    return format("overdue-reminder", dueDateString);
  }

  return null;
}
```

Tapestry uses the Java class `java.text.MessageFormat` to perform formatting. Because of this, the previous example could be rewritten to take advantage of more complicated `MessageFormat` patterns than simple argument substitution. `MessageFormat` can automatically apply different kinds of formatters, if you tell it the types of arguments. The message format string can be rewritten to indicate the type and format of the argument:

```
overdue-reminder=This task was due on {0,date,short}.
```

Putting this pattern information into the message string removes the need to obtain the localized `DateFormat` instance (instead, `MessageFormat` takes care of this). The `getTaskWarning()` method can then be reduced to

```
public String getTaskWarning()
{
  Date dueDate = getDueDate();
  if (getCurrentDate().compareTo(dueDate) > 0)
    return format("overdue-reminder", dueDate);

  return null;
}
```

Using localized messages in this way is ultimately even easier than putting together nonlocalized messages as Java code. The awkward natural language portion is isolated into a properties file, and the Java code is streamlined to just a call to the `format()` method, rather than a potentially long series of string concatenations. There's that Tapestry vision again: Creating uniform, localized messages is easier than the quick-and-dirty approach.

Localizing images

Very often, images used in a page contain text that must be localized. In this example, the ImageSubmit component uses a localized image. In figure 7.24, the image is initially the word *Change*, but when the page is later redisplayed in French, the button is labeled *Changez*. Since this is an image, it involves more than just a change in a message: There are two (or more) versions of the same button, and Tapestry must create a reference to the correct version when rendering the page's HTML.

Tapestry accomplishes this by using an asset to represent the image. You first saw assets in chapter 2, when we used this feature to map from logical names for images to specific files in the web application's context folder. That is just one aspect of assets; another is related to localization. Each asset defined in the page specification may be matched against multiple files, named with the

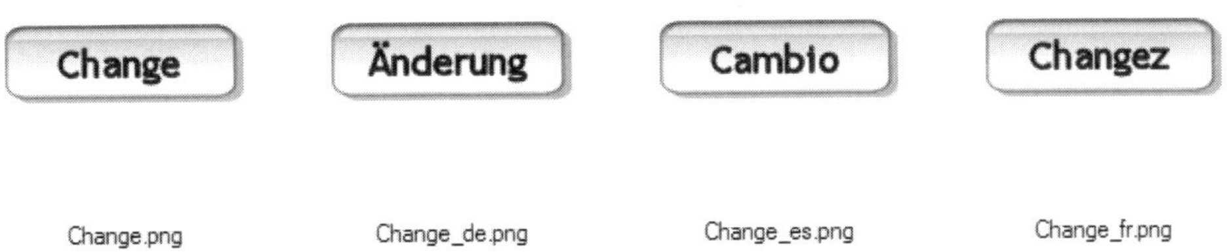

Figure 7.25 A single asset may be mapped to different files, each providing the correctly translated text.

message strings properties files. Figure 7.25 shows the four different files for the change asset.

At runtime, the page's locale is used by the asset to determine the correct URL to include in the rendered page. When there isn't a match on locale (for instance, if the locale was somehow changed to Hutu), then the best default (the file Change.png) is used.

Editing the engine's locale

Changing the locale for an application is as simple as changing the engine's `locale` property. The default value for the engine locale is the server's locale, which is often U.S. English. When the locale is changed, an HTTP cookie is recorded in the client web browser so that, in future sessions, the newly selected locale will be the default.

The engine's locale is used for a single purpose: when obtaining a page instance from the pool (or when creating a fresh page instance). Page instances are stored in the pool using a key; that key incorporates both the name of the page and the locale of the page. This shows up in figure 7.19, where the `IRequestCycle` invokes the `getPage()` method on the page source. The page source takes into account the engine's current locale when finding or creating a page instance to attach to the request.

This all means that whenever a page is first accessed during a request, the locale for the page will match the engine's locale. So, if the engine is set to locale `fr`, the page will render in French and will use French page and component templates, French assets, and so forth. Once a page instance is attached to a request, it is used for the duration of that request. Even if the engine's locale is changed to a different value in a listener method, the page instance will *still* be French. There's no way to detach a page instance from the request once it's attached, so there's no way to change the locale of an active page. Therefore, after changing the locale, it is important to load a new page in the new locale.

This shows up in the listener method for the form on the L10N page:

```
public void formSubmit(IRequestCycle cycle)
{
  cycle.activate("L10NResult");
}
```

By the time this listener method is invoked, the engine's instance will already have been changed by the PropertySelection component. Redisplaying the current page (L10N) will, confusingly, show the page in the previous locale. By instead loading, activating, and rendering a new page, the response will be in the correct localization.

Localizing the drop-down list

The drop-down list used to select the new language is also localized, in two ways:

- The labels are localized to the current locale.
- The selectable values omit the current locale.

This is accomplished by creating an `IPropertySelectionModel` implementation for selecting locales. The model is provided by the L10N page, in its Java class:

```
private IPropertySelectionModel _localeModel;

public IPropertySelectionModel getLocaleModel()
{
   if (_localeModel == null)
    _localeModel = new LocaleModel(getLocale());

  return _localeModel;
}
```

The first time this method is invoked, it creates an instance of the model, passing the current locale to the model's constructor. Note that the page is not required to release this cached model instance at the end of the request cycle. This property is not specific to the client in any way; it is specific to the locale. Even if the page did release this model, it would create an identical instance the next time the method is invoked.

The implementation of the model is shown in listing 7.2.

Listing 7.2 LocaleModel.java: property selection model class

```
package examples.l10n;

import java.util.ArrayList;
import java.util.List;
import java.util.Locale;
```

```
import org.apache.tapestry.form.IPropertySelectionModel;

public class LocaleModel implements IPropertySelectionModel
{
  private Locale _activeLocale;
  private List _locales = new ArrayList();

  private static final Locale[] AVAILABLE_LOCALES =
    { Locale.ENGLISH, Locale.FRENCH, new Locale("es"),
      Locale.GERMAN };                                         ❶

  public LocaleModel(Locale activeLocale)
  {
    _activeLocale = activeLocale;


    String activeLanguage = activeLocale.getLanguage();

    for (int i = 0; i < AVAILABLE_LOCALES.length; i++)
    {
      if (AVAILABLE_LOCALES[i].getLanguage().
            equals(activeLanguage))
        continue;                                       ❷

      _locales.add(AVAILABLE_LOCALES[i]);
    }
  }

  public int getOptionCount()
  {
    return _locales.size();      ❸
  }

  public Object getOption(int index)
  {
    return _locales.get(index);
  }

  public String getLabel(int index)
  {
    Locale l = (Locale) _locales.get(index);

    return l.getDisplayLanguage(_activeLocale);      ❹
  }

  public String getValue(int index)
  {
    return Integer.toString(index);      ❺
  }
```

```
    public Object translateValue(String value)
    {
      int index = Integer.parseInt(value);

      return getOption(index);
    }

}
```

❶ This defines the four different locales that may be displayed in the drop-down list.
❷ The active language is removed from the list, leaving just the other three locales.
❸ This should return 3, unless the initial locale is not one of the expected four.
❹ The `Locale` class can create a localized description.
❺ We encode the index into the list of locales as the client-side value.

The model starts with a list of available locales but excludes the current locale (matching on language). The rest of the model is similar to those shown in chapter 4, where the desired locale is encoded as an index number into a list of locales. Locales are self-describing, and the method `getDisplayLanguage()` is perfect for our needs because it provides a localized, user-presentable name for a locale translated into another locale.

Localizing HTML templates

Another option exists for handling localization, one that is applicable to pages that contain a large amount of text and a small number of components. Rather than isolating localized text into properties files and then using localized literals to pull them out, it is possible to provide multiple templates instead.

Tapestry localizes templates in much the same way it localizes assets; it searches for the best match based on the current locale when the page is constructed. It is not a requirement that the different templates differ only in terms of visible text. Different localizations of the template may be considerably different in layout and construction, and may even contain a different number of components. Each localization of a page is independent.[6]

For components that are the same regardless of localization, it is best to use declared components and put the type and parameters of such components into

[6] It is acceptable to vary the implicit components in different localizations of the template. Omitting a declared component from a localization of the template will result in a runtime warning (on the console), not a runtime error, but should still be avoided.

the page specification. Page specifications are not localized; only the templates are. Using declared components instead of implicit components reduces the amount of duplication in the templates—which is a very good thing when you're fixing bugs in the page.

Of course, as the developer, you are free to mix and match solutions. You can certainly use localized literals in concert with localized templates. In addition, you can use components with their own templates, and they, too, can use whatever mixture of localized resources is best for them.

7.10 Summary

In this chapter we've examined some of the problems related to grafting a stateful application on top of a stateless protocol, HTTP. Tapestry uses a variety of techniques to maintain the illusion that the there is a direct connection between the web pages viewed in the client's web browser and specific page objects within the server. It extends this illusion to you, the developer, as well, allowing you to code your pages without concern for all the issues related to page pooling and clustering. The framework imposes only a few modest constraints on you to fit into this system, and provides declared properties to make it easy to conform to those constraints.

Tapestry includes many hooks for extending the behavior of individual pages and components. The `pageValidate()` method allows for simple security checks, and the `finishLoad()` method allows pages and components to perform initializations that can't be expressed in a page or component specification. By understanding how the different major interfaces (`IRequestCycle`, `IEngine`, `IPageSource`, and others) work together, you can replace some or all of them to radically change the behavior of Tapestry.

Integrated into all aspects of Tapestry is the concept of localization. The framework makes localizing an application as simple as providing translations of templates, string properties files, and image asset files.

You've also seen how Tapestry utilizes engine services to bridge between the application and the Servlet API. In the next chapter, you'll see how to combine the ideas from this chapter, and from chapter 6, with a few new ideas in order to create components of even greater complexity and reusability.

8 Advanced techniques

This chapter covers

- Creating new engine services
- Generating dynamic client-side JavaScript
- Integrating Tapestry with JSPs

In previous chapters, we described the basics of creating reusable components and gave you an overview of how Tapestry operates internally. Quite a bit can be accomplished by simply combining existing components and leveraging the existing services of the Tapestry framework, but even more can be done by expanding both the server- and client-side processing of components.

In this chapter, we'll cover three additional advanced Tapestry techniques and illustrate them with practical examples:

- **Defining new engine services**—You can create new engine services to create new kinds of interactions between the client web browser and the server. As an example, we'll create a simple banner ad system.
- **Generating JavaScript dynamically**—Tapestry handles the dynamic generation of client-side JavaScript to allow for significant client-side processing. You'll see how this works by creating a reusable a credit card input field component.
- **Integrating Tapestry with JSPs**—You may not always have the freedom to implement exclusively in Tapestry; fortunately, it's reasonable to mix and match a Tapestry application with a more traditional application implemented using servlets and JSPs.

8.1 Creating new engine services

As we discussed in chapter 7, engine services fill the role of servlets within a Tapestry application. Because Tapestry applications are highly structured (in terms of a component hierarchy within each page), a small number of services are sufficient to implement most functionality.

Most of the engine services (notably the page, direct, and external services) fall into the same mold:

- A page name, and perhaps a component ID, is encoded into the URL.
- The page is loaded, and methods are invoked on the page or component.
- The active page renders a response.

Not all interactions between the client and the server fall into this mold. For example, in chapter 6 we described how components may be packaged with private assets, and how the asset service is involved in exposing those assets, stored on the classpath inside a JAR file, so that they may be accessed by the client web browser. For the asset service, the request cycle doesn't involve pages or components at all but only the path to a classpath resource, which is sent back to the client web browser as a stream of bytes.

New services can be defined easily and are free form. You can create page-oriented services similar to the framework's page and external services as well as component-oriented services similar to the framework's direct service. You can also create entirely new forms of services that don't even send an HTML response, such as the asset service.

To demonstrate how to build these kinds of interactions, let's create a new type of service that does not involve rendering a response page.

8.1.1 Defining a banner ad system

A ubiquitous presence on many high-volume web sites is the *banner ad*. Banner ads are small images that span the top, bottom, or sides of a web page. Clicking a banner ad sends the user to an advertiser's web site. Banner ads are one of the oldest forms of advertising on the Internet. For this example, we've created banners for several popular Java and open-source software web sites. Figure 8.1 shows an example of the demo application in operation. You can try it yourself by opening a web browser to http://localhost:8080/ads/app.

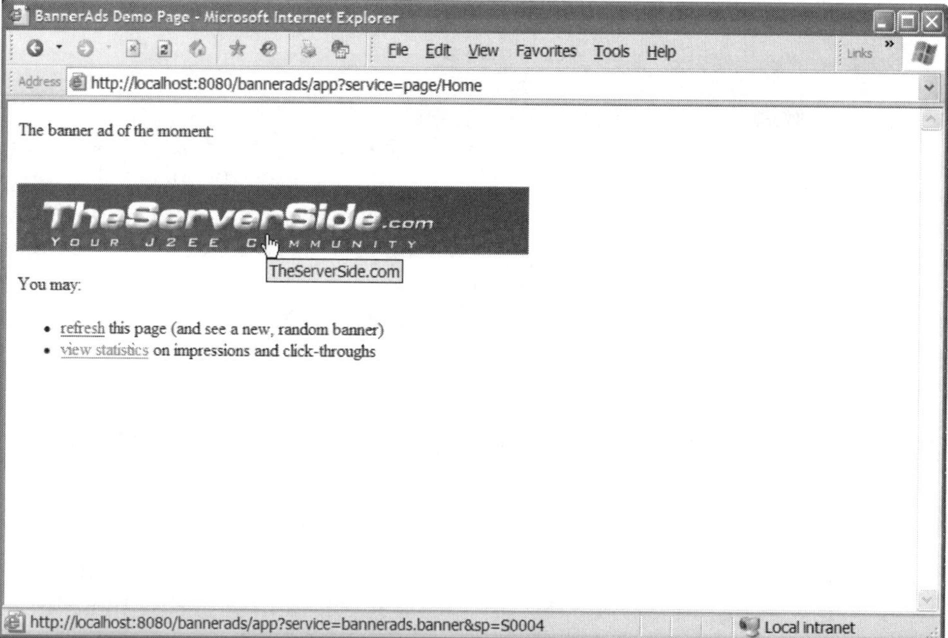

Figure 8.1 The banner ad is selected at random and includes a tooltip. Clicking on the ad opens a new window showing the advertiser's page (but will also record the click-through).

It isn't enough to have the banner ad be a simple link to the target web site. Advertisers pay popular web sites to display advertising banners. They also need to know how often users are enticed into clicking on the ad banner. A banner ad system must track how often a particular banner is displayed (called an *impression*) and how many times users have "clicked through" from the web site serving up the banner ad to the advertiser's web site. The demo application includes a statistics page for viewing this information, as shown in figure 8.2.

A proper banner ad system as a Tapestry component library will need to meet the following requirements:

- Tracks which ads have been displayed
- Tracks which ads have been clicked through
- Easily allows new ads to be defined

We could build a banner ad system using the DirectLink component easily enough, but such a solution would have some problems:

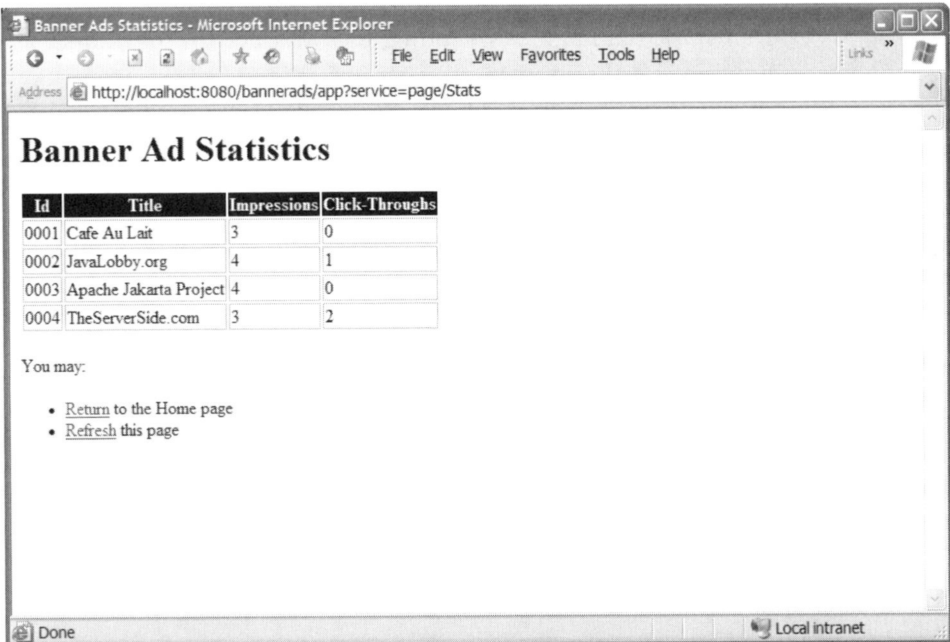

Figure 8.2 The number of impressions and click-throughs for each advertiser is available.

- The link generated by the DirectLink component would not be bookmarkable, since URLs created by the underlying direct service contain details about the structure of the application, which can change over time.
- The link would work only if the page's `PageValidateListeners` do not interfere, which is not acceptable; clicking through a banner ad should operate regardless of anything else on the page.
- A DirectLink would require that a page instance be obtained and persistent page properties be restored. This is unnecessary overhead for a banner ad redirect, which never uses or changes page state.

Basically, servicing a request for a banner ad click-through is quite different from servicing an ordinary component-oriented request. We need to bypass page validation, and instead of activating application logic and responding with a page from the application, we'll always be sending a redirect response to the client web browser. Either of these requirements would lead us to consider creating a new engine service.

To build this system, we'll take the following steps:

1. Define the data model, including the interface for the banner ad and the interface for the source of the banner ads.
2. Use an application extension to access the banner ad data.
3. Implement the BannerAd component.
4. Implement the new banner ad service.
5. Create a library to contain the component and service.

Finally, we'll build a small demonstration application to test the banner ad system.

8.1.2 Defining the data model

The first step is to define a data model for banner ads. This is accomplished in two parts. First, we need an interface to represent an individual banner ad, providing the following read-only properties:

- The URL for the banner ad image
- The width and height of the image
- The URL of advertiser's web site
- A title describing the advertiser
- A unique ID for the banner ad

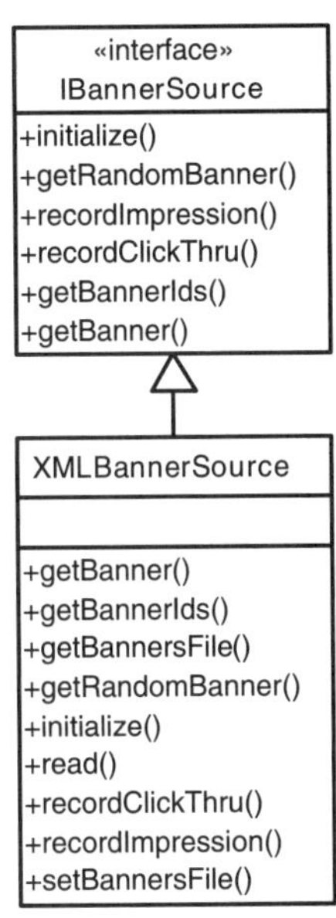

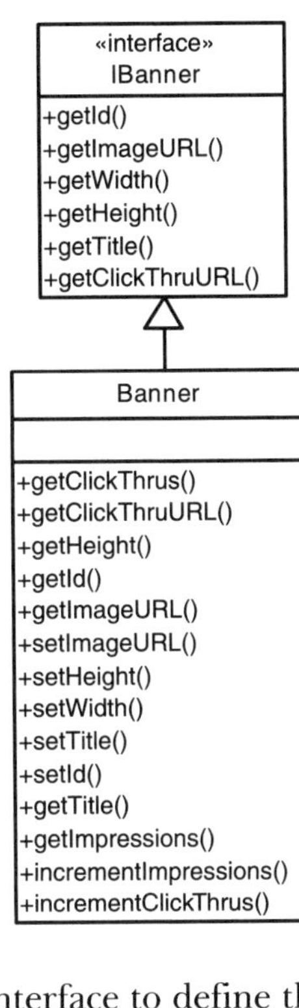

Figure 8.3
Two interfaces define the banners, as well as the source of the banners. The banner source is also responsible for recording impressions and click-throughs.

In addition, we need an interface to define the *source* of the banner ads. Its primary job is to provide a random banner ad for inclusion on a page. A secondary job is to record impressions and click-throughs of specific ads.

Figure 8.3 shows these interfaces, as well as the two implementations.

At runtime, the banner source is used to retrieve a random banner for inclusion on a page (and record the banner as an impression). Later, if the user clicks the banner, the banner source is used to record the click-through, before a redirect response is sent back to the client web browser to redirect the web browser to the advertiser's web site.

The implementations provided, `Banner` and `XMLBannerSource`, are deliberately simple. The `XMLBannerSource` reads an XML file that contains a list of banner ad definitions, which are converted into instances of `Banner`. The `Banner` class is largely a data object, providing access to the properties we've listed. In addition, in this simple implementation, the `Banner` class is used to record the impression and click-through count.

Obviously, a real production system would be more involved. It would more likely operate using a database to define the advertisements, and it would store impressions and click-throughs persistently back into the database. A real system would support various types of banners (such as Java applets, embedded Flash movies, or whatever technology comes next), and the selection of which banner to show to which client wouldn't necessarily be random—there would be a way to target specific ads at particular users.

The first hurdle to clear is coming up with a way to access the banner ad data provided by the `XMLBannerSource` instance.

8.1.3 Accessing the data model as an application extension

As you'll see, two different sections of code need to access the banner ad data. The BannerAd component will have to access the banner source to get a random banner to include on the page. If the user clicks that banner, the banner engine service will be invoked, which will need to again access the banner ad data, in order to get the advertiser's web site URL as well as record the click-through.

The design of this simple banner ad system uses only a single list of potential banner ads, stored as a file within the web application. Ideally, the banner data should be a singleton object, created as needed by the component or by the service. The banner data singleton should be created just once, initialize itself from the banner data file once, and be accessible by any number of simultaneous requests. Tapestry includes a mechanism for just these kinds of singletons: application extensions.

Application extensions are very much like helper beans: They are declared as part of an XML specification, they are instantiated only as needed, and they can have their properties initialized. Unlike helper beans, they are not associated with any single page but with the overall application. Additionally, they are always singletons.

Application extensions are declared in the application specification. The specification for the BannerAd demo application includes the following:

```
<extension name="bannerads.banner-source"
  class="bannerads.library.impl.XMLBannerSource"/>
```

Application extension names are allowed to contain periods and dashes. In order to avoid naming conflicts, prefix the names with a Java package name.

You can retrieve application extensions by their name. The first time an extension is accessed, the Java class for the extension is instantiated and configured. This object is stored for later access as a singleton—the same object will always be returned in any future lookup with the same extension name. This is necessary in our example because both the BannerAd component (described next) and the banner ad engine service (described in section 8.1.5) must access a single, shared instance.

8.1.4 Implementing the BannerAd component

A BannerAd component will render an `<a>` hyperlink element enclosing an `<img>` element. The `href` attribute for the hyperlink will reference the banner ad service, which will record the click-through before sending a client redirect response to the web browser. The `src` attribute for the `<img>` element will be dynamically determined from the underlying `Banner` object.

BannerAd allows informal parameters, which are included as additional parameters for the `<a>` element. This allows the page to specify a CSS class attribute for the component.

The BannerAd component has no template; what HTML it produces is rendered in code. Its component specification, shown in listing 8.1, is also quite short.

Listing 8.1 BannerAd.jwc: specification for the BannerAd component

```
<?xml version="1.0"?>
<!DOCTYPE component-specification PUBLIC
  "-//Apache Software Foundation//Tapestry Specification 3.0//EN"
  "http://jakarta.apache.org/tapestry/dtd/Tapestry_3_0.dtd">

<component-specification
  class="bannerads.library.components.BannerAd"
  allow-body="no"
  allow-informal-parameters="yes">

  <reserved-parameter name="href"/>

</component-specification>
```

The BannerAd component does not allow a body. Although it allows informal parameters, it reserves the `href` parameter, since it will render a value for the `href` attribute in Java code. The specification for the BannerAd component is stored on the classpath as /bannerads/library/BannerAd.jwc. Listing 8.2 shows the `BannerAd` class.

Listing 8.2 BannerAd.java: Java class for the BannerAd component

```
package bannerads.library.components;

import org.apache.tapestry.AbstractComponent;
import org.apache.tapestry.IEngine;
```

```
import org.apache.tapestry.IMarkupWriter;
import org.apache.tapestry.IRequestCycle;
import org.apache.tapestry.engine.IEngineService;
import org.apache.tapestry.engine.ILink;
import org.apache.tapestry.spec.IApplicationSpecification;

import bannerads.library.BannerService;
import bannerads.library.IBanner;
import bannerads.library.IBannerSource;

public class BannerAd extends AbstractComponent
{
  protected void renderComponent(IMarkupWriter writer,
    IRequestCycle cycle)
  {
    if (cycle.isRewinding())
      return;                              Skips render when form rewinds

    IBanner banner = getRandomBanner(cycle);
    IEngineService service =
      cycle.getEngine().getService(BannerService.SERVICE_NAME);

    ILink link = service.getLink(cycle, this,
      new Object[] { banner.getId()});     Constructs link to banner ad service

    writer.begin("a");
    writer.attribute("href", link.getURL());     Converts link object to URL
    renderInformalParameters(writer, cycle);

    writer.beginEmpty("img");
    writer.attribute("src", banner.getImageURL());
    writer.attribute("width", banner.getWidth());
    writer.attribute("height", banner.getHeight());
    writer.attribute("alt", banner.getTitle());
    writer.attribute("border", 0);

    writer.end();
  }

  private IBanner getRandomBanner(IRequestCycle cycle)
  {
    IEngine engine = cycle.getEngine();
    IApplicationSpecification specification =
      engine.getSpecification();
    IBannerSource source =
      (IBannerSource) specification.getExtension(
        IBannerSource.BANNER_SOURCE_EXTENSION_NAME,
        IBannerSource.class);              Obtains banner source application extension

    source.initialize(cycle);              Initializes the banner source
```

```
        IBanner result = source.getRandomBanner();

        source.recordImpression(result.getId());

        return result;
    }
}
```

The renderComponent() method invokes getRandomBanner() to obtain a random instance of IBanner from the banner source. Once it has the banner, the component can then access the banner service and use it to create a link (much like the DirectArea component in chapter 6, but with a different service). The banner service expects a single service parameter: the ID of the banner that is being rendered.

The remainder of the renderComponent() method uses the link object returned from the service, and the banner information provided by the banner source, to generate an <a> hyperlink element enclosing an <img> element. Any informal parameters are rendered as part of the <a> element.

One special case to watch out for when creating components involves forms. When a form is submitted, the Form component will rewind, rerunning the render process for *all* components it encloses—even components that have nothing to do with the form itself, such as BannerAd. It would not be correct to count a form rewind as a new banner impression—so we check the request cycle first thing to see if a form is rewinding, and do no work in that case.

The getRandomBanner() method is also straightforward. The application specification is obtained from the engine instance; the getExtension() method accesses an extension, instantiates it if necessary, and returns the shared instance. In addition, it checks that the extension instance is assignable to the type passed in as the second argument (that is, the method checks that the extension either implements the interface or is a subclass of the indicated class). In this class, the extension must implement the IBannerSource interface.

WARNING Only invoke getExtension() for an extension that is defined in the application extension. If the application specification does not have an <extension> for the given name, then the framework will throw an exception: *No extension named 'bannerads.banner-source' exists in this namespace.* If an extension is optional, then you must use the checkExtension() method to see if a named extension exists.

Obtaining the shared banner source instance is not quite enough: We must ensure that the source is initialized. There's a wide range of possible implementations of the banner source. The example implementation reads an XML file, but you can easily imagine a banner source that works with a database, or an Enterprise Java Bean (EJB), or a Java Messaging Services (JMS) queue, to obtain banners and record impressions and click-throughs. The `initialize()` method is passed the request cycle, which gives the banner source access to the entire Tapestry and Servlet APIs; this should be sufficient for any banner source implementation to initialize itself.

In addition, we must invoke `initialize()` every time we get the banner source, since there's no way to determine if it was created just then or if it was an already-existing instance.

8.1.5 Implementing the banner service

Implementing an engine service is much like implementing a servlet: Engine services are shared instances that must be thread safe (they may be accessed by many threads simultaneously). Unlike a servlet, an engine service is responsible for building the URLs for the requests it may later service. The `getLink()` method builds URLs, and the `service()` method reacts when those same URLs are triggered by a request from the client web browser. Listing 8.3 provides the code for the `BannerService` class.

Listing 8.3 BannerService.java: Java class for the banner service

```
package bannerads.library;

import org.apache.tapestry.IComponent;
import org.apache.tapestry.IRequestCycle;
import org.apache.tapestry.RedirectException;
import org.apache.tapestry.engine.AbstractService;
import org.apache.tapestry.engine.IEngineServiceView;
import org.apache.tapestry.engine.ILink;
import org.apache.tapestry.request.ResponseOutputStream;
import org.apache.tapestry.spec.IApplicationSpecification;

public class BannerService extends AbstractService
{
  public static final String SERVICE_NAME = "bannerads.banner";

  public ILink getLink(IRequestCycle cycle, IComponent component,
    Object[] parameters)
  {
    return constructLink(cycle, SERVICE_NAME,
```

```
      null, parameters, false);
  }

  public void service(
    IEngineServiceView engine,
    IRequestCycle cycle,
    ResponseOutputStream output)
    throws ServletException, IOException
  {
    IApplicationSpecification specification =
      engine.getSpecification();
    IBannerSource source =
      (IBannerSource) specification.getExtension(
        IBannerSource.BANNER_SOURCE_EXTENSION_NAME,
        IBannerSource.class);

    source.initialize(cycle);

    Object[] parameters = getParameters(cycle);

    String bannerId = (String) parameters[0];          Get the banner ID from the URL

    IBanner banner = source.getBanner(bannerId);       Obtain the matching banner
    source.recordClickThru(bannerId);

    throw new RedirectException(                       Send redirect to client
      banner.getClickThruURL());
  }

  public String getName()
  {
    return SERVICE_NAME;
  }

}
```

In Tapestry, application URLs are not represented as strings; they are represented as instances of the interface `ILink`. You can see this in the return value of the `getLink()` method. An `ILink` is a combination of the URL for accessing the application servlet and any query parameters (the `service` and `sp` parameters, generally) that must be passed in the request. This distinction allows the link components (such as DirectLink and PageLink), which use the HTTP `GET` method, to encode the query parameters within the URL directly, but allows the Form component, which uses the HTTP `POST` method, to encode the parameters as hidden form fields.

`AbstractService` provides a `constructLink()` method. The last two parameters are an array of strings (that form the service context) and an array of objects, the service parameters. As you've seen with the page and direct services, the service context can be used to identify a page or a component within a page. Because those concepts are not relevant to this service, we simply pass null.

This service does use a single parameter, the banner ID, which was passed in from the BannerAd component. The last parameter to `constructLink()` is a flag indicating whether the URL should be encoded using `HttpServletRequest.encodeURL()`. The `encodeURL()` method encodes the `HttpSession` ID into the URL, which ensures that the connection between the client web browser and the `HttpSession` on the server is maintained, even when the browser has disabled HTTP cookies (the normal way of communicating the `HttpSession` ID from the client to the server). For most services, the `encode` flag should be true, but this service doesn't require encoding, because triggering a banner ad does not affect any client-specific state that may be stored in the `HttpSession`.

TIP When in doubt about whether to encode or not encode the URL, just pass true and let the URL be encoded. It costs virtually nothing and ensures you won't get any nasty surprises from clients who have disabled HTTP cookies.

Servicing a request

When the user clicks on the banner ad, a new request to the server will be directed at the banner engine service, which will invoke the `service()` method. This method must

- Obtain an instance of the banner source
- Ensure that the source is initialized
- Get the correct banner from the source
- Record the click-through for the banner
- Redirect the client's web browser to the advertiser's web site

Obtaining the banner source and initializing it is the same here as in the BannerAd component. It may appear that there is no need to invoke the `initialize()` method, because the BannerAd will already have initialized the banner source. However, this is not the case; the call `to initialize()` is necessary:

- The URL to the banner service may have been bookmarked by the user, in which case there's no assurance that a BannerAd component has yet executed its `renderComponent()` method and initialized the banner source (the server receiving the request may have restarted in the meantime).

- In a cluster, it is possible that the banner source was initialized within one server but that the banner service request was received by a different server in the cluster.

The ID of the banner was provided as a service parameter; the `getParameters()` method (provided by the `AbstractService` base class) will extract the service parameters from the `sp` query parameter, and convert them from encoded strings back into objects. We can then cast the first parameter back into a string:

```
Object[] parameters = getParameters(cycle);

String bannerId = (String) parameters[0];
```

Armed with the banner ID, we can get the banner instance from the banner source, and record that a click-through for that banner has occurred:

```
IBanner banner = source.getBanner(bannerId);
source.recordClickThru(bannerId);
```

The final step is to send a redirect back to the client web browser. This is accomplished by throwing a `RedirectException`. The `RedirectException` is constructed with the advertiser's web site URL:

```
throw new RedirectException(banner.getClickThruURL());
```

Note that this is a distinct exception from the `PageRedirectException` that may be thrown in a `pageValidate()` event method. `PageRedirectException` is handled internally by Tapestry and simply represents a change in the active page (the page that will render the response). Throwing a `RedirectException` here sends an HTTP redirect back to the client web browser, forcing it to submit a new `GET` request to the indicated URL.

Providing the service name

The last requirement of an engine service is that it knows its own name. The service must implement a `getName()` method to provide this name. This method ensures that the service name declared in the library specification (discussed shortly) matches the name used by the service to create links.

The standard procedure is to define a public static field with the engine service name, which not only ensures consistency but (as in the BannerAd component) makes it easier for other classes to obtain the service instance:

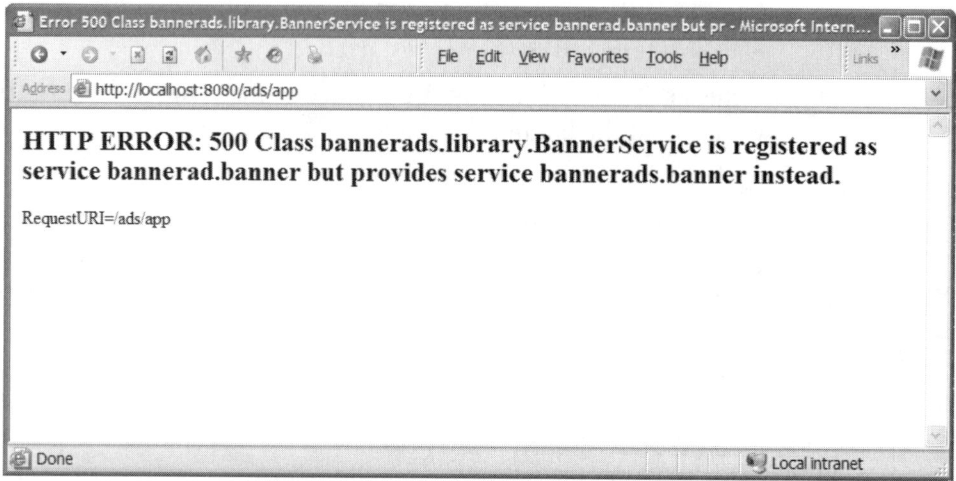

Figure 8.4 Tapestry checks that each engine service matches up against its declared names; if not, it doesn't even try to service the request.

```
public static final String SERVICE_NAME = "bannerads.banner";

public String getName()
{
  return SERVICE_NAME;
}
```

Providing the correct service name is critical to Tapestry. On the first request, it will instantiate all the services and verify that each service has the correct name. On any mismatch, it will abort the request (by throwing a `ServletException`), and the user will see an Error 500 page. Figure 8.4 is an example of what you'll see if there's a typo in your library specification.

At this point, we have the component and matching service, plus the `IBanner` and `IBannerSource` interfaces (and implementations of those interfaces). It's time to package all of this together as a reusable component library.

8.1.6 Creating the library specification

Before we can use this service and component in an application, we must create a library to contain them. The library specification, shown in listing 8.4, defines the service provided with the library. The file is stored in the classpath as /bannerads/library/BannerAds.library.

Listing 8.4 BannerAds.library: specification for the banner ad library

```
<?xml version="1.0"?>
<!DOCTYPE library-specification PUBLIC
  "-//Apache Software Foundation//Tapestry Specification 3.0//EN"
  "http://jakarta.apache.org/tapestry/dtd/Tapestry_3_0.dtd">

<library-specification>

  <service name="bannerads.banner"
    class="bannerads.library.BannerService"/>

</library-specification>
```

Finally, you see how the banner service is plugged into Tapestry: The `<service>` element provides a name for the service and a class to instantiate. As we just discussed, the name must be unique (which is why it is prefixed by a package name), and the actual service instance must know its name, to ensure that it will generate usable URLs. The BannerAd component is part of the library, because its specification file, BannerAd.jwc, is also stored in the /bannerads/library folder.

After packaging the classes, interfaces, and specifications together as a JAR file, we are ready to use this library in an application.

8.1.7 Building a banner ad application

A small demonstration application that makes use of the BannerAds library and the BannerAd component is included with the book examples, and figures 8.1 and 8.2 show this application in operation. You can try it yourself by directing your web browser to http://localhost:8080/ads/app.

Using the library is nearly as simple as the examples in chapter 6. The only extra step is to define an application extension for the banner source. Listing 8.5 shows how the application extension is declared.

Listing 8.5 ads.application: specification for the banner ad demo application

```
<?xml version="1.0"?>
<!DOCTYPE application PUBLIC
  "-//Apache Software Foundation//Tapestry Specification 3.0//EN"
  "http://jakarta.apache.org/tapestry/dtd/Tapestry_3_0.dtd">

<application name="BannerAd demonstration">

  <extension name="bannerads.banner-source"
    class="bannerads.library.impl.XMLBannerSource"/>
```

```
  <library id="banner"
    specification-path="/bannerads/library/BannerAds.library"/>

</application>
```

The extension creates an instance of `XMLBannnerSource`, an implementation of the `IBannerSource` interface that gets its list of ad banners from an XML file stored inside the WEB-INF folder. The file, banners.xml, provides the banner information for four Java and open-source web sites. Listing 8.6 shows the contents of this file.

Listing 8.6 banners.xml: list of banner ads used in the demo application

```
<?xml version="1.0"?>

<banner-ads>
  <banner id="0001" title="Cafe Au Lait"
    width="468" height="82" imageURL="ads/cafeaulait.png"
    clickThruURL="http://www.ibiblio.org/javafaq/"/>

  <banner id="0002" title="JavaLobby.org"
    width="468" height="60"
    imageURL="ads/javalobby.png"
    clickThruURL="http://www.javalobby.org"/>

  <banner id="0003" title="Apache Jakarta Project"
    width="468" height="60"
    imageURL="ads/jakarta.png"
    clickThruURL="http://jakarta.apache.org"/>

  <banner id="0004" title="TheServerSide.com"
    width="468" height="60"
    imageURL="ads/theserverside.png"
    clickThruURL="http://www.theserverside.com"/>
</banner-ads>
```

The BannerAd component is used just on the template of the application's Home page:

```
<a href="#" target="_new" jwcid="@banner:BannerAd">[Banner Ad]</a>
```

And that really is all it takes! Using `target="_new"` directs the client web browser to open the URL in a new window. We've defined a whole new service that handles requests from the client's web browser in an entirely new way but hidden that service behind a component. Despite this component's very special request processing (recording the click-through event and sending a client redirect to a completely different web site), no requirements were forced on the page or on the application containing the page. The BannerAd component can be literally dropped right into a page without concern for how it operates internally, and it can be added to any application merely by providing a banner source in the application specification. This level of automatic integration is a key distinguishing feature of Tapestry, something that is simply not possible when using ordinary servlets and JSPs, or even prevailing frameworks such as Struts.

The banner ad examples illustrate how flexible Tapestry is in terms of server-side request processing. As you'll see in the next section, Tapestry has an equally in-depth approach to client-side scripting.

8.2 Client-side scripting

An unavoidable aspect of a high-quality web application is the use of client-side JavaScript to extend the application directly into the client web browser. Incorporating JavaScript behaviors into the user interface allows for interactions that simply aren't possible using the standard approaches involving links and form submissions. The interface can react to the user without the delay of a new request to the server.

The downside to making use of client-side scripting is that the skills necessary to write functional, cross-browser JavaScript are extremely specialized, bordering on arcane, and not something every developer has accumulated. Using Tapestry unavoidably complicates this further, because Tapestry pages can be so very dynamic.

You've already seen examples of client-side logic in Tapestry. In chapter 4, you saw the DatePicker component, which uses client-side JavaScript to create a pop-up calendar. In chapter 5, you saw that the input validation framework could perform client-side validations before forms were submitted, in addition to performing server-side validations of the submitted form data.

You've also seen the Palette component, in chapter 6, which uses a significant amount of client-side scripting to provide a complicated user interface. In all of these cases, the rendering of HTML also involved the production of customized JavaScript to support the HTML elements. For the validation framework, the JavaScript took the form of `onsubmit` form event handlers that validated user input and displayed alerts if the input was not acceptable. The client-side scripting for the Palette component includes much logic for enabling and disabling buttons and moving selections between the two columns. This is much more than simply including a pre-canned JavaScript file; in each of these cases, it is necessary to create the client-side JavaScript dynamically, using a template, and adapt it to the specific situation it is being used for.

In the case of ValidField components, the exact checks that will occur vary from one field to the next. Beyond general format checks, there is checking for minimum values, maximum values, and so forth. Each of these checks is configured on a case-by-case basis. In addition, the JavaScript generated for a ValidField component must adapt to the element name for the component (which is assigned by the enclosing Form) and to the name of the enclosing Form itself (which is assigned by Tapestry).

In a traditional servlet application, the development process often consists of creating the script and then requiring that the names of the elements on the page (the form, the input field) match. This is certainly simpler—if the usage of the script is well understood and well documented. All too frequently, that isn't the case; JavaScript support is often provided by the HTML designers, who are, naturally enough, the least disciplined team members when it comes to creating code. In addition, it is too easy to create a script that specifically allows *one* field in *one* form to have special behavior, and that is not able to handle multiple fields in multiple forms.

As elsewhere, Tapestry tips this equation on its head. Tapestry uses a special template, a script specification, to create customized JavaScript on demand. Even in the simplest case, the script specification must adapt to the various IDs assigned by the framework. This means that a Tapestry script specification easily adapts to reuse within the same page. The downside is that instead of writing a block of JavaScript, you must write a *template* from which the JavaScript can be dynamically produced at runtime.

The other great benefit of dynamic JavaScript generation is that the creation of the JavaScript is compartmentalized inside specific components. Once again, the component may be dropped into a page and will function properly, client-side JavaScript and all, without any special handling in the page. By using JavaScript-enabled components, you gain all the advantages of a client-side JavaScript without any of the costs!

Creating such a component has a few prerequisites:

- You must know *exactly* what the component should do.
- You must understand how to accomplish that using JavaScript, which includes understanding the client-side Document Object Model (DOM) and the programming differences between various browsers.

- You must understand how Tapestry assigns names and IDs.
- You must understand how to invoke the Tapestry scripting subsystem.

As usual, we'll start with a reasonable example.

8.2.1 Defining the CreditCardField component

Many web applications have some point where they ask for a credit card number. All too often, you are advised on how to enter that number: as all digits, no spaces or dashes. Forcing the user to bend to the needs of the programmer is never a good sign; instead, the interface should resemble figure 8.5. Here, the input is four individual text fields. As you fill one field, the cursor automatically tabs to the next field. When you submit the form, the input is checked for validity (that each of the four fields has exactly four numeric digits).

Let's develop this component in three steps:

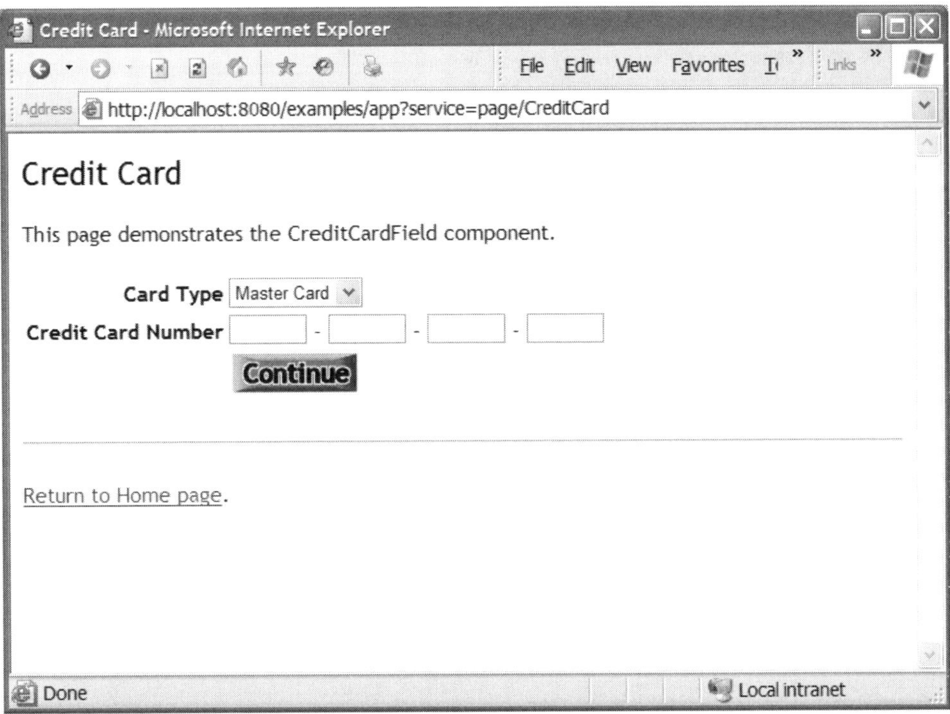

Figure 8.5 The CreditCardField component renders as four separate text fields. It includes client-side scripting to automatically tab to the next field as each field is filled. When the form is submitted, client-side scripting checks that each field consists of exactly four numeric digits.

- We'll create a static HTML mockup, in order to figure out the general form of the client-side JavaScript.
- We'll create a Tapestry script specification, a special-purpose template for creating JavaScript dynamically.
- Finally, we'll create a component that makes use of the script specification when it renders and knows how to obtain the submitted value when the enclosing form is submitted.

Let's start with the HTML mockup, shown in listing 8.7.

Listing 8.7 HTML mockup for the CreditCardField component

```
<html>
<body>
<script>

function onkeyup_cc_field(field, next)
{
  var keycode = window.event.keyCode;

  if (keycode >=  48 && keycode <= 57 && field.value.length == 4)   ❶
  {
    next.focus();
    next.select();
  }
}

function validate_cc_field(field)   ❷
{
  if (! field.value.match(/^\d{4}$/))
  {
    field.focus();
    field.select();
    window.alert(
      "Credit card numbers consist of four groups of " +
      "four numbers.");
    return false;
  }

  return true;
}

function onkeyup_cc$g0 ()   ❸
{
  onkeyup_cc_field(document.f.cc$g0, document.f.cc$g1);
}
```

```
function onkeyup_cc$g1 ()
{
  onkeyup_cc_field(document.f.cc$g1, document.f.cc$g2);
}

function onkeyup_cc$g2 ()
{
  onkeyup_cc_field(document.f.cc$g2, document.f.cc$g3);
}

function validate_cc()     <-❹
{
  return validate_cc_field(document.f.cc$g0) &&
    validate_cc_field(document.f.cc$g1) &&
    validate_cc_field(document.f.cc$g2) &&
    validate_cc_field(document.f.cc$g3);
}


window.onload = function ()     <-❺
{
  document.f.cc$g0.onkeyup = onkeyup_cc$g0;
  document.f.cc$g1.onkeyup = onkeyup_cc$g1;
  document.f.cc$g2.onkeyup = onkeyup_cc$g2;

  document.f.onsubmit = validate_cc;
}
</script>

<form name="f">

Enter credit card number:
<input type="text" name="cc$g0" value="" size="4" maxlength="4"/> -
<input type="text" name="cc$g1" value="" size="4" maxlength="4"/> -
<input type="text" name="cc$g2" value="" size="4" maxlength="4"/> -
<input type="text" name="cc$g3" value="" size="4" maxlength="4"/>

<br/>
<input type="submit"/>

</form>
</body>
<html>
```

❶ When a number is entered and the field is full, the cursor moves to the next field.

❷ This JavaScript function is invoked when the form submits to validate that the field contains exactly four digits.

❸ Each of the first three fields gets its own `onkeyup` event handler.

❹ When the form submits, it invokes the `validate_cc()` function to validate that each of the four fields contains exactly four digits.

❺ When the HTML page finishes loading into the web browser, this anonymous function registers event handlers for the form and fields.

This listing may look somewhat odd, since it's very mechanical in structure. This is to reflect the constraints on generating the JavaScript that occur in a running Tapestry application. The path of least resistance is to attach JavaScript event handlers to objects from within the `window.onload` event handler, rather than as `javascript:` attribute values on the elements themselves. As you'll see, the script for a component is often generated after the component itself renders, when it is too late to provide values for attributes.

In addition, the names assigned to the four text fields reflects some experience concerning how dynamic names may be generated within Tapestry. Here, the `cc` portion of the name will probably be a component ID. The suffix (`g0`, `g1`, etc.) distinguishes the four groups of digits that compose a credit card number (this component is focused on 16-digit credit card numbers, such as used by Master Card and Visa; other credit cards use a different format). Using the dollar sign as a separator is a safe bet: the dollar sign is not allowed in a user-specified component ID, so there's no possibility of a naming conflict.

The operation of the mockup script is simple enough. The `onkeyup` event handlers are triggered as each key is released within the first three fields. If the key entered was a number and that number filled the field, the cursor moves to the next field. When the form submits, the `onsubmit` event handler checks each of the four fields against a regular expression to ensure that they contain exactly four numeric digits.

8.2.2 Working with the Body component

As mentioned in chapter 4, when a page uses dynamic JavaScript, you must use a Body component to generate the HTML `<body>` element. As this chapter demonstrates, it's not always possible to know ahead of time *if* a component will be using the JavaScript features provided by the Body component, so you should always use a Body component, just to be safe.

A principal function of the Body component is to support and organize the generation of dynamic JavaScript throughout the page. All the JavaScript created by all components throughout the page is organized into a single HTML `<script>` block, which is placed just inside the HTML `<body>` element, as shown in figure 8.6.

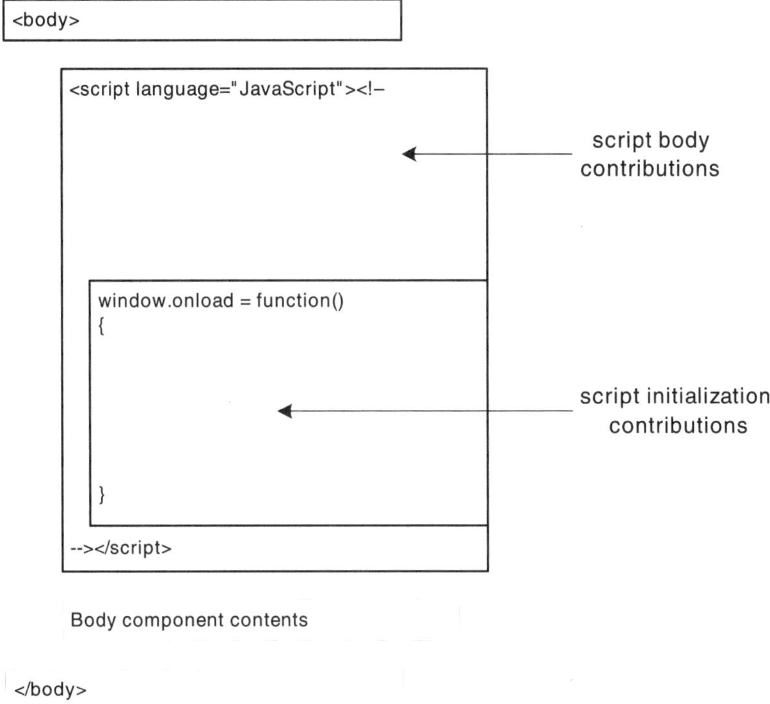

Figure 8.6 The Body component organizes all the JavaScript for the page into a single block, just inside the `<body>` tag. Any component enclosed by the Body may contribute to the script body or script initialization.

Notice that the scripting block goes first even though what goes into the scripting block is determined by rendering the body of the Body component. The Body component *buffers* the output of the components it encloses. As each component renders, it has a chance to ask the Body component to contribute some text to the script body or script initialization.

Once rendering is complete, the Body component can render out the `<script>` block, then the buffered output from its body and then, finally, the end tag. This approach—buffering the output of enclosed components to affect how the enclosing component renders—is a powerful technique used throughout Tapestry.

8.2.3 Creating the Tapestry script specification

Creating the Tapestry script specification and the component would normally occur in parallel; they are both dependent on each other. For this example, we'll show you how to convert the static JavaScript from the mockup into a dynamic script specification. At runtime, the XML script specification will be parsed into an executable script.

When a script is executed, it accomplishes three things:

- Input symbols are combined and manipulated to create new symbols. For example, the component's element ID may be used as the basis of a JavaScript event handler function name.
- A contribution to the page's script body block is made. This is typically JavaScript event handler functions.
- A contribution to the page's script initialization block is made. This is typically setup code that connects client-side DOM objects to the JavaScript event handler functions.

Listing 8.8 shows the script specification used by the CreditCardField component. Large sections of it are similar to the static HTML from listing 8.7. The remainder involves customizing each usage of the script to the particulars of the page where it is used and the component that uses it.

Listing 8.8 CreditCardField.script: script specification used by the component

```
<?xml version="1.0"?>
<!DOCTYPE script PUBLIC
  "-//Apache Software Foundation//Tapestry Script Specification
  ➥ 3.0//EN"
  "http://jakarta.apache.org/tapestry/dtd/Script_3_0.dtd">

<script>

<input-symbol
  key="creditCardField"
  class="examples.cc.CreditCardField" required="yes"/>     ❶

<input-symbol key="formatMessage"
  class="java.lang.String"                  ❷
  required="yes"/>

<set key="name" expression="creditCardField.name"/>    ❸

<let key="baseName">                              ❹
  document.${creditCardField.form.name}.${name}
</let>

<let key="field0">   ❺
  ${baseName}$g0
</let>
```

```
<let key="field1">
  ${baseName}$g1
</let>

<let key="field2">
  ${baseName}$g2
</let>

<let key="field3">
  ${baseName}$g3
</let>

<let key="formValidateFunction" unique="yes">     ⑥
  validate_${name}
</let>

<body>

<unique>
<![CDATA[
function onkeyup_cc_field(field, next)
{
  var keycode = window.event.keyCode;

  if (keycode >=  48 && keycode <= 57 && field.value.length == 4)
  {
    next.focus();
    next.select();
  }
}

function validate_cc_field(field)                                          ⑦
{
  if (! field.value.match(/^\d{4}$/))
  {
    field.focus();
    field.select();
    window.alert("${formatMessage}");
    return false;
  }

  return true;
}
]]>
</unique>

<![CDATA[

function ${formValidateFunction}()
{
  return validate_cc_field(${field0}) &&
    validate_cc_field(${field1}) &&
```

```
        validate_cc_field(${field2}) &&
        validate_cc_field(${field3});
    }

    ]]>
    </body>

    <initialization>

    ${field0}.onkeyup = function()
    {
      onkeyup_cc_field(${field0}, ${field1});
    }

    ${field1}.onkeyup = function()
    {
      onkeyup_cc_field(${field1}, ${field2});
    }

    ${field2}.onkeyup = function()
    {
      onkeyup_cc_field(${field2}, ${field3});
    }

    </initialization>

    </script>
```

❶ The `<input-symbol>` element is equivalent to a component specification `<parameter>` element. It declares a particular type of symbol to be passed into the script, with a type. The `creditCardField` symbol must be an instance of `CreditCardField`, the Java class for the CreditCardField component.

❷ The `formatMessage` symbol is required and must be a string.

❸ The `<set>` element is used to create a new symbol using an OGNL expression.

❹ The `<let>` element creates a new symbol from a string. Leading and trailing white space is removed. The `${…}` values are interpreted as OGNL expressions; this is how other symbols are referenced.

❺ The component and the script must agree on what each of the four fields is named. The name is based on the field's element ID with `$g0`, `$g1`, `$g2`, or `$g3` appended.

❻ Tapestry can ensure that the new symbol value is unique within the page, which may require appending a suffix to the value.

❼ The contents of a `<unique>` element will be rendered only once per page render, even if the script specification is used multiple times on the same page. The XML `<![CDATA[…]]>` construct is used to work around the `&` characters, which are not normally valid XML.

When the script executes, it takes input symbols (primarily, the CreditCardField component for which the script is being generated), transforms the input symbols into new symbols (such as the field and function names), and generates JavaScript for inclusion in the page. In some cases, the created symbols are useful to, and needed by, the component.

Appendix D includes a complete definition of the script specification DTD.

Defining the input symbols

The script begins by defining two input symbols, which must be provided by the CreditCardComponent when it executes the script. The first symbol, `creditCardField`, is the Java object for the component itself. The second, `formatMessage`, is a message that will be displayed to users if they attempt to enter a credit card number using an invalid format.

Defining input symbols is optional; it simply allows Tapestry to check that required symbols are provided. If a class is specified, then the symbol must be that type, or assignable to that type (it may be the fully qualified name of a class or interface). Again, providing this information to Tapestry allows the framework to perform better error checking.

These symbols, especially `creditCardField`, become the basis for all the other symbols created while the script is executing.

Creating new symbols

New symbols are created using the `<set>` and `<let>` elements. The `<set>` element is used to evaluate an OGNL expression and assign its value as a new symbol. It is a close cousin to the `<binding>` element in a page or component specification. In the CreditCardField script, the name symbol is created by retrieving the `name` property of the `creditCardField` symbol:

```
<set key="name" expression="creditCardField.name"/>
```

If the OGNL expression is long or complicated, then the `expression` attribute can be omitted, and the OGNL expression can be placed in the body of the `<set>` element.

The `<let>` element creates a new symbol, always a string, from its body, but its body can contain both text and specially delimited OGNL expressions.[1] In the script, the `baseName` symbol is created using a `<let>` element:

---

[1] The `<let>` element may also contain several other script elements: `<foreach>` for looping, `<if>` and `<if-not>` for conditionals, and the `<unique>` element we'll cover shortly—but using any of these is quite rare.

```
<let key="baseName">
  document.${creditCardField.form.name}.${name}
</let>
```

This `baseName` symbol is a JavaScript DOM reference to a field. The `${…}` sequences indicate OGNL expressions. The first traverses from the `creditCardField` to the Form component that encloses it and obtains the name assigned to the Form. The second expression references the previously defined name symbol. Ultimately, this symbol is used to build the complete names of the four text fields that form the component. Table 8.1 identifies the remaining symbols created by the script (the Example Value column assumes the Form's name is Form0 and the CreditCardField's name is ccField, though of course the actual names will vary from page to page).

Table 8.1 Symbols created by the script

Symbol	Description	Example Value
`name`	Name assigned to the CreditCardField by the Form	`ccField`
`baseName`	Base value for building client-side DOM references to the four text fields	`document.Form0.ccField`
`field0`	First field's DOM reference	`document.Form0.ccField$g0`
`field1`	Second field's DOM reference	`document.Form0.ccField$g1`
`field2`	Third field's DOM reference	`document.Form0.ccField$g2`
`field3`	Fourth field's DOM reference	`document.Form0.ccField$g3`
`formValidateFunction`	Name of the JavaScript event handler for the containing Form's `onsubmit` event	`validate_ccField`

A few notes:

- The four text fields are given names based on the component. The dollar sign is a good choice for a separator here, since it is not allowed as a part of a component ID—this ensures that there will be no name conflicts, regardless of which component IDs the developer selects.
- The naming of the fields must coordinate with code in the component that writes the HTML for the four text fields and reads the query parameters when the form is submitted.

- The `formValidateFunction` is an output symbol, the name of a JavaScript function. Shortly, you'll see how to hook it into the enclosing form's `onsubmit` event handler.

The `<let>` element that defines the `formValidateFunction` symbol demonstrates another useful feature:

```
<let key="formValidateFunction" unique="yes">
  validate_${name}
</let>
```

It is very important that this function name be unique within the page; if the CreditCardField component is used multiple times, then each usage of the component must have its own validate function. Simply incorporating the component's name into the name of the function is very nearly enough to ensure uniqueness because the name itself is uniquely generated by the form.

To absolutely ensure that the value for the `formValidateFunction` symbol is unique, we've used the `unique` attribute of the `<let>` element. Tapestry ensures that the final symbol value is unique, tacking on a suffix to ensure uniqueness if necessary. This functionality is provided by the Body component that ultimately encloses the CreditCardField; therefore, it doesn't matter which script specification is executed—the uniqueness filter is applied universally.

NOTE The use of the `unique` attribute here is overkill. It is all but impossible for two different CreditCardFields to share the same element ID, because element IDs are related to component IDs, which are always unique within a container (the page or component). Uniqueness issues tend to crop up when a complex component is assembled from simpler components, and the complex component is used multiple times—the Palette component is an example of a complex component that requires uniqueness support to ensure that you can use it faultlessly in all circumstances. Tapestry provides you with the tools to defuse this potential issue painlessly.

TIP Use reasonable names, and incorporate the component ID into the function name. You may have to debug the rendered HTML page, and it will be easier to do so if the function names reflect the component they are related to.

Contributing to the body

The script specification `<body>` element is where the real work begins. This is where the JavaScript event handlers are created. These event handlers will provide two examples of client-side behavior:

- When the user fills one of the component's text fields, the cursor will automatically tab to the next text field.
- When the user submits the form, the text fields will be validated to contain exactly four numeric digits.

The CreditCardField script includes some common utility functions: `onkeyup_cc_field()` and `validate_cc_field()`. These two functions are used by all four text fields created by the component—but potentially, there will be other CreditCardField components on the same page, and they all should share the same utility functions. These utility functions should be contributed into the page's `<script>` block only once.

This situation is similar to the previously described issue concerning unique symbols, and it has a similar solution. The portion of the `<body>` element that should only occur once is itself enclosed in a `<unique>` element:

```
<unique>
<![CDATA[
function onkeyup_cc_field(field, next)
{
  var keycode = window.event.keyCode;

  if (keycode >=  48 && keycode <= 57 && field.value.length == 4)
  {
    next.focus();
    next.select();
  }
}

function validate_cc_field(field)
{
  if (! field.value.match(/^\d{4}$/))
  {
    field.focus();
    field.select();
    window.alert("${formatMessage}");
    return false;
  }

  return true;
}
]]>
</unique>
```

When the <unique> element is encountered, it checks to see if the block it encloses has been contributed yet; if not, the contents of the <unique> element are contributed to the page's <script> block, and the fact that the block has been contributed is recorded. As with the unique symbol generation, this tracking is a responsibility of the Body component, and it applies only to the current request cycle. Whatever is enclosed by the <unique> element will appear just once inside the page's <script> block.

The remainder of the <body> element's content is not enclosed by the <unique> tag and is contributed to the page's <script> block every time the script specification is executed. This is where the form's validate function is created:

```
<![CDATA[

function ${formValidateFunction}()
{
  return validate_cc_field(${field0}) &&
    validate_cc_field(${field1}) &&
    validate_cc_field(${field2}) &&
    validate_cc_field(${field3});
}

]]>
```

This snippet uses a CDATA block to work around the invalid XML characters: the && (logical and) operators that are valid JavaScript but not acceptable in an XML document. As before, we use the ${…} syntax to plug in the symbols created earlier in the script specification.

In the final rendered page, with the expansion of symbols, this block will look something like this:

```
function validate_ccField()
{
  return validate_cc_field(document.Form0.ccField$g0) &&
    validate_cc_field(document.Form0.ccField$g1) &&
    validate_cc_field(document.Form0.ccField$g2) &&
    validate_cc_field(document.Form0.ccField$g3);
}
```

Of course, both the name of the form (Form0) and the name of the component (ccField) will vary.

Wiring event handler methods to client-side objects

The last step is to connect event handler functions to the objects. This poses a minor dilemma: The HTML <script> element containing all the JavaScript for the page is placed just inside the HTML <body> element. The HTML that ultimately defines the objects comes later. Referencing those objects using the DOM before they exist will cause runtime errors inside the client web browser, and your client-side logic will break.

The solution to this is to wait until the page is fully loaded into the client web browser before accessing the objects and connecting up event handlers. That is the function of the `<initialization>` element in the script specification. The JavaScript contributed inside the `<initialization>` element is executed within the `window.onload` event handler, which is invoked only after the page is fully loaded. The script specification includes an `<initialization>` block to "wire up" the handlers by setting the event handlers (such as `onkeyup`) for the fields:

```
<initialization>

${field0}.onkeyup = function()
{
  onkeyup_cc_field(${field0}, ${field1});
}

${field1}.onkeyup = function()
{
  onkeyup_cc_field(${field1}, ${field2});
}

${field2}.onkeyup = function()
{
  onkeyup_cc_field(${field2}, ${field3});
}

</initialization>
```

This wires up the first three (of the four) fields, creating anonymous JavaScript functions that invoke the `onkeyup_cc_field()` function. This function checks to see if the pressed key was a number and if the field is now full, and tabs to the next form field if that's the case. Unfortunately, we can't tab out of the fourth text field, since the CreditCardField doesn't know what the next field is (it will not have even rendered yet at the time the CreditCardField component renders and executes the script specification).

That still leaves the form's submit function, which checks that each of the four fields contains exactly four numeric digits. In theory, we could hook that in here as well:

```
document.${creditCardField.form.name}.onsubmit =
  ${formValidateFunction};
```

That approach would work—as long as the CreditCardField component was the only component within the Form that needed to hook into the Form's onsubmit event handler. There's no way the CreditCardField can know this, however; certainly there could be ValidField components with client-side validation enabled, as well as other custom components, which may render before or after the CreditCardField.

Instead, this problem is solved at the code level as an interaction, in Java code, between the CreditCardField component and the Form component that encloses it. The Form component is prepared to handle the case where multiple components need to hook into the onsubmit event handler. The details of this are covered shortly, along with the code for the CreditCardComponent Java class.

8.2.4 Creating the CreditCardField specification

The CreditCardField component is a form element component; it is intended for use as part of a form. As such, its Java class has some basic responsibilities:

- The class must implement the interface IFormComponent.
- The class must implement a form property of type IForm.
- The class must implement a name property of type string.

The easiest way to accomplish all this is to have the CreditCardField class inherit from the AbstractFormComponent base class, and to specify the two properties (form and name) in the component specification. Inheriting from AbstractFormComponent adds another requirement: implementing a disabled parameter of type boolean.

In addition, the whole point of the CreditCardField component is to allow the user to enter a credit card number and update a domain object property. Although the user interface is in the form of four text fields, each accepting four digits, this is not the best way to represent the credit card number once it's submitted in the form. A single 16-digit string is much more natural. The CreditCardField defines this, as the parameter cardNumber. This is another example of the Model-View-Controller pattern: The Model (the domain object property) represents the credit card number as a single string; the View (the HTML rendered by the component) uses four individual fields. The Controller, the CreditCardField class, is responsible for translating between the two representations.

Listing 8.9 shows how the CreditCardField class specifies its two parameters (cardNumber and disabled) and two properties (form and name).

Listing 8.9 CreditCardField.jwc: specification for the CreditCardField component

```
<?xml version="1.0"?>
<!DOCTYPE component-specification PUBLIC
  "-//Apache Software Foundation//Tapestry Specification 3.0//EN"
  "http://jakarta.apache.org/tapestry/dtd/Tapestry_3_0.dtd">

<component-specification
  class="examples.cc.CreditCardField"
  allow-body="no" allow-informal-parameters="no">

  <parameter
    name="cardNumber"
    type="java.lang.String"
    direction="form"
    required="yes"/>

  <parameter name="disabled" type="boolean" direction="in">
    <description>
    If true, then all four text fields will be disabled.
    </description>
  </parameter>

  <property-specification
    name="form"
    type="org.apache.tapestry.IForm"/>
  <property-specification
    name="name"
    type="java.lang.String"/>

</component-specification>
```

The `cardNumber` parameter uses the value `form` for its `direction` attribute, which makes sense for this purpose, a form element component. The property bound to the `cardNumber` parameter will be updated (from the `cardNumber` property) after the CreditCardComponent rewinds when the enclosing form is submitted. The `disabled` parameter still uses `in` as its `direction` attribute; the `disabled` property will be set from the parameter before the component renders (even during a form rewind).

8.2.5 Creating the CreditCardField component

The `CreditCardField` Java class is shown in listing 8.10. `CreditCardField` extends from `AbstractFormComponent`, a base class used by many different form element components (such as Checkbox and TextField). `AbstractFormComponent` defines two abstract properties, `form` and `name`, which we must implement (by specifying those properties in the component specification). In addition, `CreditCardField` is required to implement a `disabled` parameter.

Listing 8.10 CreditCardField.java: Java class for the CreditCardField component

```
package examples.cc;

import java.util.HashMap;
import java.util.Map;

import org.apache.oro.text.regex.MalformedPatternException;
import org.apache.oro.text.regex.Pattern;
import org.apache.oro.text.regex.Perl5Compiler;
import org.apache.oro.text.regex.Perl5Matcher;
import org.apache.tapestry.ApplicationRuntimeException;
import org.apache.tapestry.IForm;
import org.apache.tapestry.IMarkupWriter;
import org.apache.tapestry.IRequestCycle;
import org.apache.tapestry.IResourceLocation;
import org.apache.tapestry.IScript;
import org.apache.tapestry.engine.IScriptSource;
import org.apache.tapestry.form.AbstractFormComponent;
import org.apache.tapestry.form.FormEventType;
import org.apache.tapestry.html.Body;
import org.apache.tapestry.request.RequestContext;
import org.apache.tapestry.valid.IValidationDelegate;
import org.apache.tapestry.valid.ValidationConstraint;
import org.apache.tapestry.valid.ValidatorException;

public abstract class CreditCardField
  extends AbstractFormComponent
{
  private IScript _script;
  private Pattern _compiledPattern;
  private Perl5Matcher _matcher;

  public abstract void setCardNumber(String cardNumber);
  public abstract String getCardNumber();

  protected void renderComponent(IMarkupWriter writer,
    IRequestCycle cycle)
  {
    IForm form = getForm(cycle);
                                                      ❶
    String name = form.getElementId(this);
    boolean disabled = isDisabled();
    IValidationDelegate delegate = form.getDelegate();    ❷

    if (form.isRewinding())    ❸
    {
```

```
    if (!disabled)
      updateCardNumberFromRequest(name, form, delegate, cycle);

    return;
  }

  if (cycle.isRewinding())
    return;

  String cardNumber[] = extractCardNumber(delegate);     ❹

  delegate.writePrefix(writer, cycle, this, null);     ❺

  for (int i = 0; i < 4; i++)
  {
    if (i > 0)
      writer.print(" - ");

    String fieldName = name + "$g" + i;     ❻

    writer.beginEmpty("input");
    writer.attribute("type", "text");
    writer.attribute("name", fieldName);
    writer.attribute("size", 4);
    writer.attribute("maxlength", 4);
    writer.attribute("value", cardNumber[i]);

    if (disabled)
      writer.attribute("disabled", "disabled");

    delegate.writeAttributes(writer, cycle, this, null);
  }

  delegate.writeSuffix(writer, cycle, this, null);

  if (!disabled)
  {
    if (_script == null)
    {
      IScriptSource source = cycle.getEngine().getScriptSource();
      IResourceLocation specLocation =
        getSpecification().getLocation().getResourceLocation();
      IResourceLocation scriptLocation =
        specLocation.getRelativeLocation(                          ❼
          "CreditCardField.script");

      _script = source.getScript(scriptLocation);
    }

    Body body = Body.get(cycle);
```

```
      Map symbols = new HashMap();
      symbols.put("creditCardField", this);
      symbols.put("formatMessage",
        getMessage("card-number-format"));

      _script.execute(cycle, body, symbols);

      String formValidateFunction =
        (String) symbols.get("formValidateFunction");

      form.addEventHandler(FormEventType.SUBMIT,
        formValidateFunction);
    }
  }

  private void updateCardNumberFromRequest(
    String name,
    IForm form,
    IValidationDelegate delegate,
    IRequestCycle cycle)
  {
    RequestContext context = cycle.getRequestContext();

    StringBuffer buffer = new StringBuffer();

    for (int i = 0; i < 4; i++)
    {
      String value = context.getParameter(name + "$g" + i);

      if (value != null)
      {
        if (value.length() > 4)
          value = value.substring(0, 4);

        buffer.append(value);
      }

      while (buffer.length() < 4 * (i + 1))
        buffer.append(' ');
    }

    String cardNumber = buffer.toString();

    delegate.recordFieldInputValue(cardNumber);

    try
    {
      validate(cardNumber);
      setCardNumber(cardNumber);
    }
    catch (ValidatorException ex)
```

8 9 10 11 12

```
    {
      delegate.record(ex);
    }

  }

  private String[] extractCardNumber(IValidationDelegate delegate)
  {
    String cardNumber =
      delegate.getFieldInputValue();

    if (cardNumber == null)
      cardNumber = getCardNumber();

    if (cardNumber == null)
      return new String[] { "", "", "", "" };

    String[] result = new String[4];
    StringBuffer buffer = new StringBuffer(cardNumber);

    while (buffer.length() < 16)
      buffer.append(' ');

    for (int i = 0; i < 4; i++)
      result[i] = buffer.substring(4 * i, 4 * (i + 1));

    return result;
  }

  private void validate(String cardNumber)
    throws ValidatorException
  {
    if (_compiledPattern == null)
    {
      Perl5Compiler compiler = new Perl5Compiler();
      try
      {
        _compiledPattern = compiler.compile("^\\d{16}$");
      }
      catch (MalformedPatternException ex)
      {
        throw new ApplicationRuntimeException(ex);
      }
    }

    if (_matcher == null)
      _matcher = new Perl5Matcher();

    if (_matcher.matches(cardNumber, _compiledPattern))
      return;
```

⓭

```
        String formatted =
          cardNumber.substring(0, 4)
            + "-"
            + cardNumber.substring(4, 8)
            + "-"
            + cardNumber.substring(8, 12)
            + "-"
            + cardNumber.substring(12);

        throw new ValidatorException(
          format("invalid-card-number", formatted),
          ValidationConstraint.NUMBER_FORMAT);
      }
    }
```

❶ The inherited `getForm()` method locates the enclosing Form component (represented as an instance of the `IForm` interface). From the Form, we obtain the name used for this form control component.

❷ This component integrates into the validation subsystem (from chapter 5) and needs access to the validation delegate, which is provided by the Form component.

❸ When the Form is rewinding, we don't render HTML. Instead, we invoke this method to assemble the 16-digit credit card number from the four query parameters (one for each text field in the rendered form), as well as perform validations.

❹ When rendering, the 16-digit credit card number must be split into four groups of 4 digits.

❺ As with a ValidField component, the validation delegate is allowed to render before and after the text fields are rendered. This allows the validation delegate to write HTML to support any application-specific look and feel.

❻ The names for the individual text fields computed here must match against the JavaScript generated by the script specification.

❼ The script source is used to obtain an executable script. The location of the script is computed relative to the component specification. Because of these extra steps required to obtain the executable script instance, the instance is cached for later use.

❽ Input symbols are provided to the executable script as a `Map`.

❾ The script is executed. It will modify the `symbols` `Map` as it executes. It will also communicate with the Body component to contribute JavaScript to the page's script block.

❿ The `formValidateFunction` symbol is created by the script to store the name of a client-side JavaScript function that must be hooked into the form to validate the fields. The `addEventHandler()` method is used to inform the enclosing Form component about the function.

⓫ The validation delegate can store only a single input string, so the 16-digit credit card number is recorded. If the client has disabled JavaScript, then this value may not be a valid credit card number and will be used when the form renders to present errors.

⓬ As with a ValidField, the input is validated before the final value (a valid 16-digit credit card number) is assigned to the `cardNumber` parameter.

⓭ If the validation delegate has a recorded input value for this component, then use that value (it represents a value provided by the user). Otherwise, obtain the value from the `cardNumber` parameter.

Even though CreditCardField is not a ValidField, it expects the form to have a delegate and will make use of it to report any input errors. This can happen only if the client web browser fails to do its part, probably because the user has explicitly disabled JavaScript. In any case, if invalid data does make it to the server, the component will perform its own validations, but will interact with the validation delegate to visually show that the component (all four fields) is in error. Figure 8.7 shows an example of this.

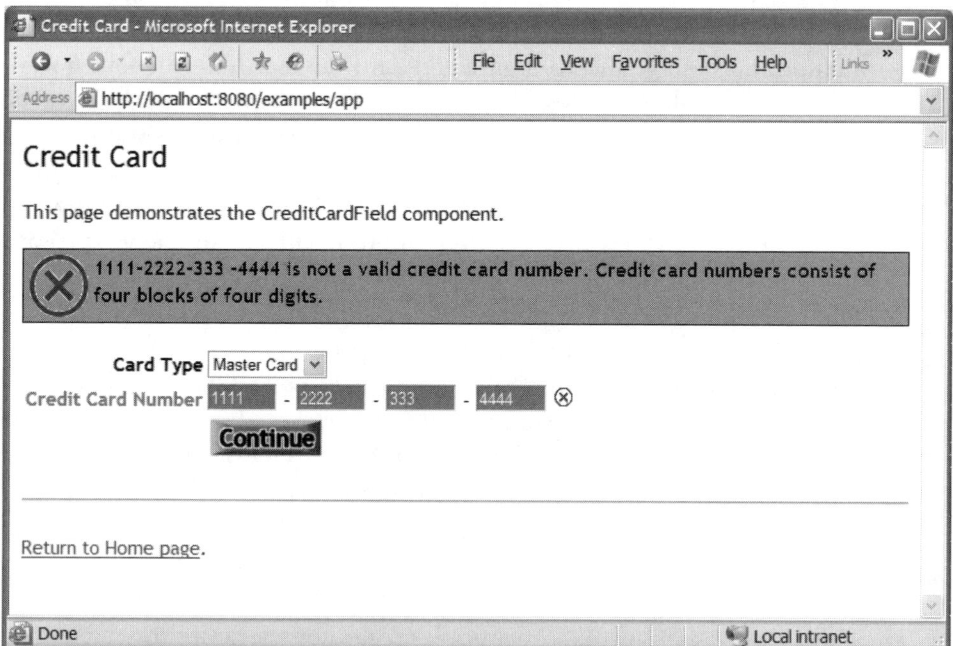

Figure 8.7 The component does its own validations, in case JavaScript is not enabled in the client. The component interacts with the input validation subsystem to adjust the visual display of the fields to reflect that the component is in error.

The CreditCardComponent has a number of responsibilities: It must render the HTML for the four credit card fields as well as the JavaScript that supports the four fields, and it must handle form submissions for the fields. It also translates between the client-side data format (four fields of 4 digits) and the server-side data format (a single 16-digit string).

Rendering the component

Because this is a form element component, the first step in the `renderComponent()` method is to find the enclosing Form component and have the Form provide a name for this element. The `AbstractFormComponent` base class provides most of this functionality:

```
IForm form = getForm(cycle);

String name = form.getElementId(this);
boolean disabled = isDisabled();
IValidationDelegate delegate = form.getDelegate();
```

If the form is rewinding, we extract the credit card number from the query parameters, validate the number, and return:

```
if (form.isRewinding())
{
  if (!disabled)
    updateCardNumberFromRequest(name, form, delegate, cycle);

  return;
}
```

Alternately, if the page as a whole is rewinding but not specifically this form, we can skip the rest. This scenario occurs only when the action service is used:

```
if (cycle.isRewinding())
  return;
```

Next we render the four fields and the dashes that separate them. The first step is to extract the 16-digit credit card number and break it apart into four strings, one for each 4-digit group. We can then render each group as its own text field:

```
String cardNumber[] = extractCardNumber(delegate);

delegate.writePrefix(writer, cycle, this, null);

for (int i = 0; i < 4; i++)
{
  if (i > 0)
    writer.print(" - ");
```

```
    String fieldName = name + "$g" + i;

    writer.beginEmpty("input");
    writer.attribute("type", "text");
    writer.attribute("name", fieldName);
    writer.attribute("size", 4);
    writer.attribute("maxlength", 4);
    writer.attribute("value", cardNumber[i]);

    if (disabled)
      writer.attribute("disabled", "disabled");

    delegate.writeAttributes(writer, cycle, this, null);
  }

  delegate.writeSuffix(writer, cycle, this, null);
```

In addition, we invoke methods on the validation delegate to decorate our fields if they are in error.

Converting the server-side value

The credit card number stored as a server-side property is a 16-digit string, but when rendering the four text fields, four smaller (4-digit) strings are needed. This is handled in the `extractCardNumber()` method.

In addition, another interaction with the input validation subsystem occurs here. When a form is submitted, the validation delegate records the input provided by the user, before the values are converted and validated. If the form is redisplayed (due to an error), the validation delegate is the source of the unconverted values. The validation delegate's `getFieldInputValue()` method is used to gain access to the exact input provided by the user so that the invalid input can be sent back to the user for correction:

```
private String[] extractCardNumber(IValidationDelegate delegate)
{
  String cardNumber = delegate.getFieldInputValue();

  if (cardNumber == null)
    cardNumber = getCardNumber();

  if (cardNumber == null)
    return new String[] { "", "", "", "" };

  String[] result = new String[4];
  StringBuffer buffer = new StringBuffer(cardNumber);

  while (buffer.length() < 16)
    buffer.append(' ');
```

```
    for (int i = 0; i < 4; i++)
      result[i] = buffer.substring(4 * i, 4 * (i + 1));

    return result;
  }
```

So far, we've covered somewhat familiar ground; CreditCardComponent is simply a complicated component. What makes it interesting is what comes next: adding the client-side JavaScript.

Obtaining the script

The final portion of the `renderComponent()` method involves obtaining and executing the script specification. The script specification is stored in the WEB-INF folder alongside the component specification and is named CreditCardField.script. The script specification must be parsed and converted into an executable script: an instance of the `IScript` interface.

Scripts are obtained from the script source, a Tapestry subsystem accessible via the engine. To get a script, we must know the location of its script specification. We are able to build a location relative to the component's specification:

```
Body body = Body.get(cycle);

if (_script == null)
{
  IScriptSource source = cycle.getEngine().getScriptSource();
  IResourceLocation specLocation =
    getSpecification().getLocation().getResourceLocation();
  IResourceLocation scriptLocation =
    specLocation.getRelativeLocation("CreditCardField.script");

  _script = source.getScript(scriptLocation);
}
```

It's likely that the page containing the CreditCardComponent will be used many times, so we cache the `IScript` instance in the `_script` instance variable. The script source also caches parsed script specifications (once it parses a script specification, it doesn't parse it a second time), so all we're saving is the runtime cost of constructing the script specification's location.

Executing the script

To execute the script, we need to get the Body component. The `Body` class includes a static method for accomplishing this:

```
Body body = Body.get(cycle);
```

Next we must create the input symbols that are passed to the script when it executes:

```
Map symbols = new HashMap();
symbols.put("creditCardField", this);
symbols.put("formatMessage", getMessage("card-number-format"));
```

With everything in place, we can now execute the script, which will communicate with the Body component:

```
_script.execute(cycle, body, symbols);
```

The final step is to connect the form's validate function to the Form component. The script will have modified the symbols `Map` passed to it. The `Map` now includes all the symbols created using the `<let>` and `<set>` elements, including the `formValidateFunction` symbol. It is easy enough to extract the value for that symbol, which is the name of the JavaScript function:

```
String formValidateFunction =
  (String) symbols.get("formValidateFunction");

form.addEventHandler(FormEventType.SUBMIT, formValidateFunction);
```

The Form component includes an `addEventHandler()` method that allows the components it encloses to hook into its `onsubmit` event handler. Any number of components may provide the names of JavaScript event handler functions to execute; the Form component will execute each in turn.

Handling form submissions

When the form containing the CreditCardField component is submitted, the CreditCardField is responsible for reading the query parameters submitted as part of the form, assembling the 16-digit card number from the four text fields, validating the card number, and updating the `creditCard` parameter property with the final value.

Most of this logic is present in the `updateCardNumberFromRequest()` method. It makes use of the `RequestContext` object to access the query parameters posted by the form:[2]

```
private void updateCardNumberFromRequest(
  String name,
  IForm form,
  IValidationDelegate delegate,
  IRequestCycle cycle)
{
```

[2] Although you can also get access to the `HttpServletRequest` to read query parameters, it is best to use the `RequestContext` object. Because of the way the Servlet API handles file uploads (as discussed in chapter 4), when a form contains an Upload component, the `HttpServletRequest` object will *not* have access to the query parameters, but the `RequestContext` object will.

```
    RequestContext context = cycle.getRequestContext();

    StringBuffer buffer = new StringBuffer();

    for (int i = 0; i < 4; i++)
    {
      String value = context.getParameter(name + "$g" + i);

      if (value != null)
      {
        if (value.length() > 4)
          value = value.substring(0, 4);

        buffer.append(value);
      }

      while (buffer.length() < 4 * (i + 1))
        buffer.append(' ');
    }

    String cardNumber = buffer.toString();

    delegate.recordFieldInputValue(cardNumber);

    try
    {
      validate(cardNumber);
      setCardNumber(cardNumber);
    }
    catch (ValidatorException ex)
    {
      delegate.record(ex);
    }

  }
```

The method has extra checks on the length and format of the credit card number that duplicate the client-side checks. This is still appropriate, since there is no way to ensure that the client-side validations took place (the client web browser may have JavaScript disabled, or may not even be a web browser).

A key part of the validation subsystem is the `IValidationDelegate`'s `recordFieldInputValue()` method. This is used to record the value of a submitted ValidField before it is converted to a target type and validated. This explains how, when a form is redisplayed with errors, the input provided by the user can be redisplayed as entered; the input "lives" inside the validation delegate until needed to redisplay the form.

Since the CreditCardField should mimic the behavior of a ValidField component, it too must inform the validation delegate about the user's input.

Before updating the `cardNumber` parameter property, the complete credit card number is validated, using the `validate()` method. This method checks that the number consists of 16 digits; if it doesn't, the method formats an error message and throws a `ValidatorException`. The `updateCardNumberFromRequest()` method catches that exception and passes it to the Form's validation delegate.

8.2.6 Using the component

So far, we've shown how to create a complex component, a component that renders a complex mix of HTML and JavaScript. Despite this, the component fits into the overall page's HTML template very simply:

```
<tr>
  <th>
    <span jwcid="@FieldLabel"
      displayName="Credit Card Number"
      field="ognl:components.inputNumber">
      Credit Card Number
    </span>
  </th>
  <td>
    <input type="text"
      jwcid="inputNumber@CreditCardField"
      cardNumber="ognl:cardNumber"
      size="50"/>
  </td>
</tr>
```

As you can see, using the CreditCardField component is no more complex than using a ValidField component. We're using a FieldLabel with the CreditCardField, just as we did in chapter 5. When previewing the page, the component will display as a single, 50-character wide text field (even though in the live application, it renders as four small text fields).

Adding client-side JavaScript support to a component is one of the more complex tasks you will face as a Tapestry developer—but by keeping a clear head about which code (Java or JavaScript) is executed where (on the server or in the client web browser) and when (at page render, within the client, or on form submission), you'll ensure that the entire process is manageable. Tapestry includes the necessary subsystems and hooks to provide you with the flexibility you need to create powerful, reusable components.

Up to this point, we've discussed integrating components with Tapestry engine services and integrating components with dynamically generated JavaScript. Another common task is to integrate a Tapestry application with a non-Tapestry application.

8.3 Integrating with JavaServer Pages

There will be times when you must make a Tapestry application work in concert with a standard servlets-and-JSP application. Most likely, you have an existing application, and you want to transition to a Tapestry implementation but can't do it all in one fell swoop. What you need is a hybrid application, partly written using Tapestry and partly written using servlets and JSPs.

In some cases, JSPs will have links that connect to Tapestry pages, or forms that submit to Tapestry pages. On the flip side, you may have listener methods that use a JSP (or even some other servlet) to render a response. Tapestry supports all of these scenarios.

We'll explore all of these possibilities using the sample application; you can open a web browser to http://localhost:8080/examples/app and select the JSP link under the chapter 8 heading.

8.3.1 Redirecting to a JSP

On the Tapestry side, you may need to use a JSP to render a response. For example, in figure 8.8 a Tapestry page contains two links that invoke the Tapestry application, but the responses are ultimately rendered by a JSP.

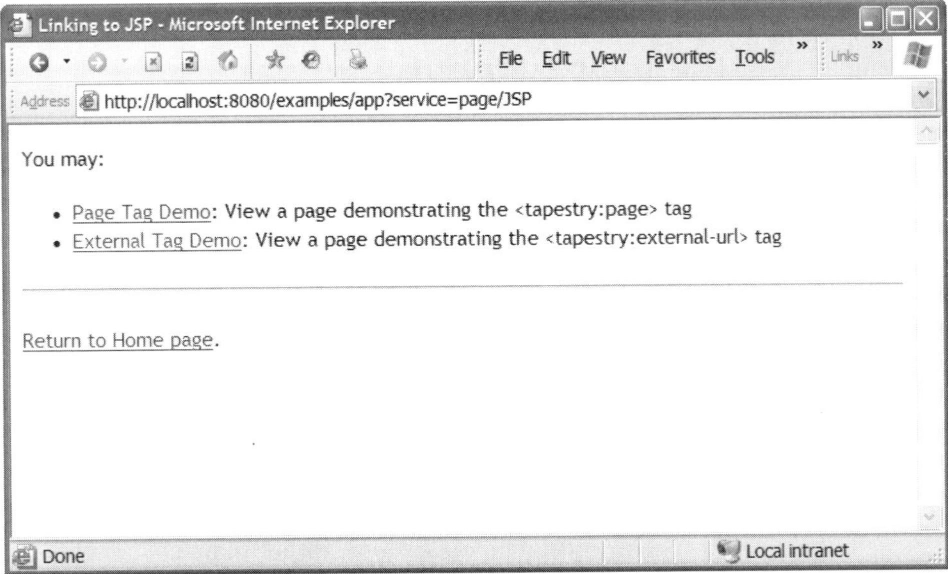

Figure 8.8 The Tapestry page used to redirect to one of the JSPs.

The template for the page is shown in listing 8.11. This page makes use of the Border component to render the top and bottom of the page. It includes two links, using the DirectLink component. Clicking those links invokes listener methods, but the ultimate responses are provided by a pair of JSPs.

Listing 8.11 JSP.html: HTML template for the JSP

```
<span jwcid="@Border" title="Linking to JSP">

You may:
<ul>
  <li><a href="#" jwcid="@DirectLink"
    listener="ognl:listeners.displayPageTagDemo">Page Tag Demo</a>:
    View a page demonstrating the &lt;tapestry:page&gt; tag</li>

  <li><a href="#" jwcid="@DirectLink"
    listener="ognl:listeners.displayExternalTagDemo">External
    Tag Demo</a>:
    View a page demonstrating the &lt;tapestry:external-url&gt;
    tag</li>
</ul>

</span>
```

As you've seen before, normally when a DirectLink component is triggered by a request, the default behavior (after invoking the component's listener method) is to render the page containing the component. Alternately, a different *Tapestry* page may be activated to render the response. As before, with the banner service, we'll use the `RedirectException` to sidestep this ordinary behavior and instead redirect to another URL:

```
public void displayPageTagDemo(IRequestCycle cycle)
{
  throw new RedirectException("PageTagDemo.jsp");
}

public void displayExternalTagDemo(IRequestCycle cycle)
{
  throw new RedirectException("ExternalTagDemo.jsp");
}
```

In this case, we are specifying a local resource rather than a complete URL. Tapestry will not send a redirect to the client web browser (as it did with the banner ads example). Instead, it will instruct the Servlet API to forward the current request to the named resource.[3] In this case, the resource is a JSP, but it could be the path of any servlet, or even a static resource, such as an image or an HTML file.

Relative paths are relative to the servlet. In this case, the two JSPs are in the context root directory, along with the HTML templates. Absolute paths, starting with a leading slash, are relative to the context.

These two examples represent some unnecessary complexity; the HTML template could just as easily include <a href="PageTagDemo.jsp"> and <a href="ExternalTagDemo.jsp">. However, the same technique works in more complicated cases, such as handling a form submission, or when it is necessary to perform some kind of business operation before redirecting to the JSP.

That's the easy side of the equation; the tough side is getting a JSP to call into a Tapestry application.

8.3.2 *Linking JSPs to Tapestry pages*

Linking from a JSP back into the Tapestry application involves creating a link with the correct URL. The application URLs used by Tapestry have a very regular format, as we discussed in chapter 7. For example, a JSP could include a link such as <a href="/app?service=page/Home"> to create a link to the Tapestry Home page. Despite this regularity, hard-coding links in this way is not advisable:

- A static URL like this is not properly encoded;[4] a client that does not support HTTP cookies will lose its HttpSession.
- If the target page is variable, a Java scriptlet will be needed to construct the correct URL.
- If a new release of the framework changes the encoding system used for application URLs, then the JSP will generate invalid URLs (just such a change occurred between releases 2.3 and 3.0).
- If the application has overridden the default engine service implementations (either to encode additional information or to control the format of the URL in an application-specific way), the JSP may not encode the information correctly.

---

[3] Specifically, it obtains the RequestDispatcher object for the resource, and then invokes the forward() method on it.

[4] All application URLs provided to the client web browser should be encoded using the HttpServletResponse method encodeURL(). This method ensures that the HttpSession ID is encoded into the URL when the client doesn't allow cookies. Tapestry services automatically invoke this method as needed.

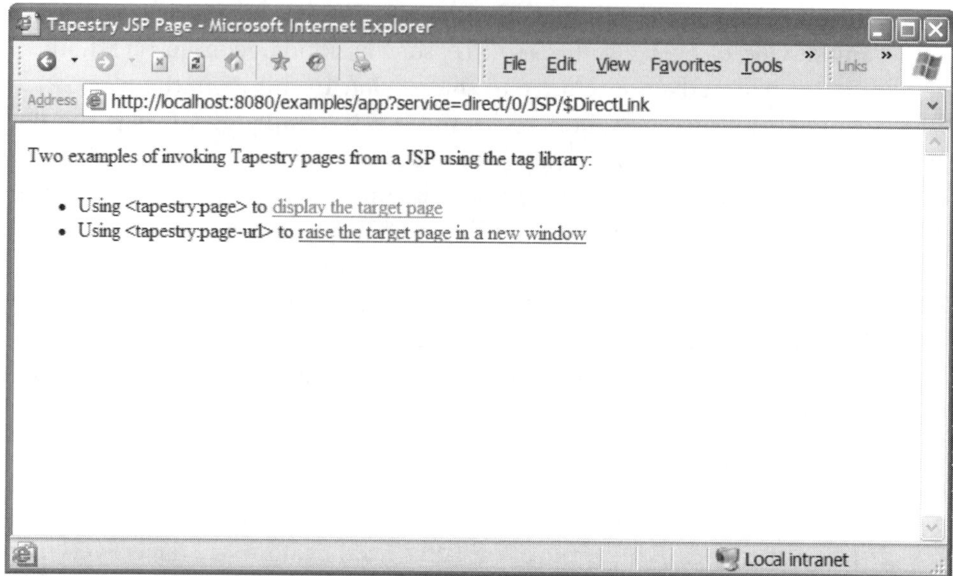

Figure 8.9 The HTML page displayed here was rendered by a JSP and uses the Tapestry tag library to render the two links back into the Tapestry application.

In short, there's no substitute for having a Tapestry engine service construct the URL for that service. That's what the framework does internally, and it is what we want here, even though a JSP is responsible for rendering the response. It isn't possible to drop a Tapestry component into a JSP, but it is possible to make use of a close cousin to a Tapestry component: a custom JSP tag.

The Tapestry framework includes a custom JSP tag library expressly for this purpose. The library allows you to easily create links to pages, leveraging the Tapestry page and external services. Figure 8.9 illustrates a JSP that makes use of two of the tags from the library to create links to pages.

The first custom tag is used to create an `<a>` hyperlink element that links to a particular page. The second tag creates just the URL portion and is incorporated into a client-side script that raises the window into a pop-up window. The source for this page is shown in listing 8.12.

Listing 8.12 PageTagDemo.jsp: JSP using the page and page-url tags

```
<%@ taglib
  uri="http://jakarta.apache.org/tapestry/tld/tapestry_1_0.tld"
  prefix="tapestry" %>
```
❶

```
<html>
<head>
<title>Tapestry JSP Page</title>
</head>
<body>
<script>
<!--

function raiseTarget(targetURL)
{
  var width = 200;
  var height = 200;
  var screenX = Math.floor((screen.width)/2)
    - Math.floor(width/2);
  var screenY = Math.floor((screen.height)/2)
    - Math.floor(height/2) - 20;

  var features =
    "toolbar=no," +
    "scrollbars=no," +
    "status=no," +
    "top=" + screenY  + "," +
    "left=" + screenX + "," +
    "screenX=" + screenX + "," +
    "screenY=" + screenY + "," +
    "width=" + width + "," +
    "height=" + height;

  window.open(targetURL, "TargetPage", features).focus();
}
-->
</script>

Two examples of invoking Tapestry pages from a JSP
using the tag library:

<ul>
  <li>Using &lt;tapestry:page&gt; to
    <tapestry:page page="Target">display the
    target page</tapestry:page>                    ❷
  </li>
  <li>Using &lt;tapestry:page-url&gt; to
    <a href="javascript:raiseTarget(
      '<tapestry:page-url page="Target"/>');">raise the     ❸
    target page in a new window</a>
  </li>
</ul>

</body>
</html>
```

❶ This code declares the use of the Tapestry tag library within this JSP, using the prefix `tapestry:` for the tags provided by the library.

❷ The `tapestry:page` tag is very similar to the PageLink component; it creates a link that will reference a Tapestry page.

❸ The `tapestry:page-url` tag writes out just the URL for a Tapestry page; it is meant for incorporation into JavaScript, as shown here.

Before we use these custom JSP tags, let's see how to declare a tag library for use within a JSP.

Declaring the tag library

Every JSP page that makes use of a tag library must declare the tag library using a JSP `taglib` directive, which is shown at the start of the listing. This declaration identifies the `taglib` in terms of a resource URI (Uniform Resource Identifier) and indicates the prefix to be used within the JSP to reference tags defined by the library. The JSP engine doesn't look for the named resource on the Internet (which is fortunate since it does not exist); the resource URI is just used as a key to indirectly locate the tag library descriptor.

A *tag library descriptor* is an XML file that defines the tags in a library. For each tag, it further defines the parameters allowed for the tag. The descriptor for each tag library used in the application must be included somewhere inside the web application archive.

The web.xml deployment descriptor matches `taglib` resource URIs to tag library descriptors. For the example application, the web.xml deployment descriptor includes the following elements:

```
<taglib>
  <taglib-uri>
    http://jakarta.apache.org/tapestry/tld/tapestry_1_0.tld
  </taglib-uri>
  <taglib-location>
    /WEB-INF/lib/tapestry-3.0.jar
  </taglib-location>
</taglib>
```

This declares the tag library to be packaged as part of the Tapestry framework JAR. The tag library descriptor is stored inside the Tapestry framework JAR as the file META-INF/taglib.tld. For this to work, the Tapestry framework must be stored in the web application archive rather than on the general classpath.

Using the page tag

The most basic of the Tapestry custom JSP tags is the page tag, which is very much like a PageLink component:

```
<tapestry:page page="Target"> . . . </tapestry:page>
```

The tapestry: prefix matches the taglib directive previously discussed (it is often the case that a single JSP makes use of many taglibs, each with its own prefix). Where Tapestry components have parameters, JSP tags have attributes. Table 8.2 lists the attributes for the page tag.

Table 8.2 Attributes for the Tapestry page tag

Attribute	Required	Description
page	Yes	The Tapestry page we want to link to
servlet	No	The path to the Tapestry servlet; defaults to /app
styleClass	No	If specified, becomes the HTML class attribute

JSP tags don't have the equivalent of Tapestry's informal component parameters. Because it is common to want to specify the CSS class for the <a> tag rendered by the page tag, an optional attribute for that purpose, styleClass, is provided.

Sometimes, you don't want the entire <a> tag and just need the application URL generated by the service. On the example page, the second link doesn't directly trigger a request; it invokes a JavaScript function to raise the Target page in a new window. An <a> element is used that incorporates a page-url tag:

```
<a href="javascript:raiseTarget(
  '<tapestry:page-url page="Target"/>');"> . . .</a>
```

Unlike the page tag, which wraps around a portion of the JSP, the page-url tag is empty (much like a Tapestry component that discards its body). The tag is replaced by the application URL for the named page. The page-url tag accepts the same page and servlet attributes as the page tag.

8.3.3 Submitting JSP forms into Tapestry

There are times when a JSP will contain a form that must be processed by Tapestry. It isn't possible to leverage the normal Tapestry form submission mechanism—that's based on a Form component and form element components within a Tapestry page, things that can't exist within a JSP. Instead, the JSP form submission must be processed in the traditional servlets way: by obtaining values for query parameters.

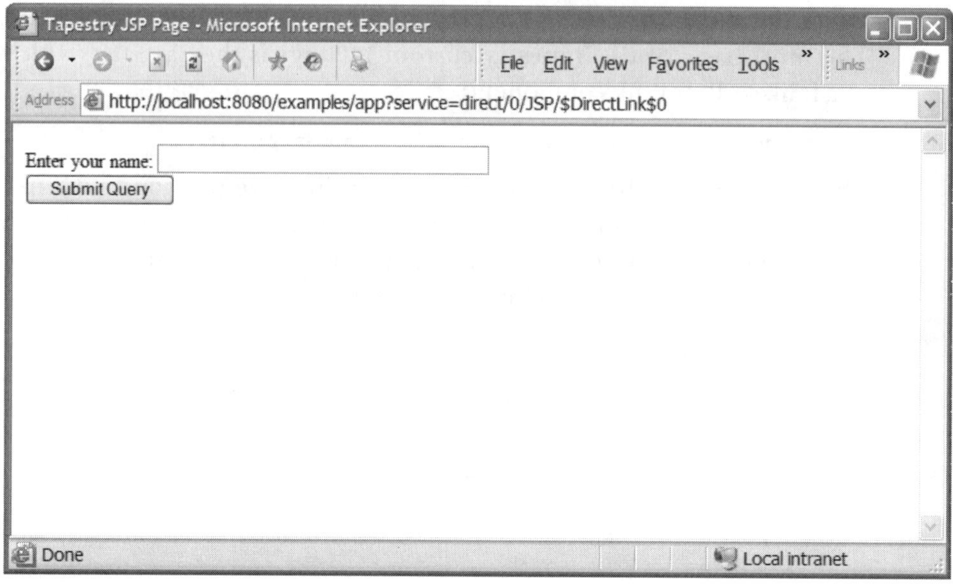

Figure 8.10 A JSP containing a simple form. The form will submit to an external page.

But what can a JSP submit to? As before, the level of granularity is an entire Tapestry page, not a component within the page. How could the JSP know the ID of a component, especially if the component is anonymous? This is where the external service comes in: It provides a hook, in the form of the `activateExternalPage()` method, where we can process the form submission.

Figure 8.10 shows such a page. It contains a simple form into which you can enter a name. The form submits into a Tapestry page that displays the name entered in the JSP-based form.

NOTE Don't be confused by the URL displayed in the address field of figure 8.10. Referring back to chapter 7, you can see that the URL in the window corresponds to clicking some DirectLink within the Tapestry page named JSP (the page shown in figure 8.9). As you've seen, the listener for that component performed a server-side redirect to the JSP (which is named ExternalTagDemo.jsp). Because this was a server-side (not client-side) redirect, the address field still displays the URL used to trigger that DirectLink component.

This JSP builds the `<form>` around a Tapestry application URL provided by an `external-url` tag. The source for the JSP is shown in listing 8.13.

Listing 8.13 ExternalTagDemo.jsp: JSP using the external-url tag

```
<%@ taglib
  uri="http://jakarta.apache.org/tapestry/tld/tapestry_1_0.tld"
  prefix="tapestry" %>

<html>
<head>
<title>Tapestry JSP Page</title>
</head>
<body>

<form
  action="<tapestry:external-url page="JSPForm"/>"
  method="POST">

Enter your name:
<input type="text" name="userName" maxlength="100" size="40"/>
<br/>
<input type="submit"/>

</form>

</body>
</html>
```

The example in listing 8.13 resembles the previous one. It starts with a `taglib` declaration for the Tapestry tag library. The two key points are as follows:

- The action URL for the form is provided by the `external-url` tag.
- The method for the form is `POST`, not `GET`.

Why `POST`? The URL provided by the `external-url` tag includes a query parameter, `service`. When using `GET`, the client web browser can omit this query parameter in favor of the query parameters provided in the form submission. Using the `POST` method, the query parameters in the action and from within the form are properly integrated.

On the flip side, when the form is submitted, the JSPForm Tapestry page is activated. The source for this class is shown in listing 8.14.

Listing 8.14 JSPForm.java: Java class for the JSPForm page

```
package examples;

import org.apache.tapestry.IExternalPage;
import org.apache.tapestry.IRequestCycle;
import org.apache.tapestry.html.BasePage;
```

```
public abstract class JSPForm extends BasePage
  implements IExternalPage
{
  protected abstract void setUserName(String userName);

  public void activateExternalPage(Object[] parameters,
    IRequestCycle cycle)
  {
    String userName =
      cycle.getRequestContext().getParameter("userName");

    setUserName(userName);
  }

}
```

The `activateExternalPage()` method ends up with all the responsibility for processing the form, much like a traditional servlet. Here, the `userName` query parameter is extracted and stored into the matching `userName` page property, where it will be available to the page's HTML template when the page renders.

Using service parameters with the external-url tag

As with the ExternalLink component, it is possible to encode service parameters when using the `external-url` tag. This is one way to pass additional information along with the form submission (the other is to make use of hidden form fields).

Table 8.3 lists the attributes that may be used with the `external-url` tag. The last attribute, `parameters`, is used to specify the service parameters. This value can be either a single string or (by prefixing the string with `ognl:`) an OGNL expression. The OGNL expression is evaluated in the JSP context; it will have access to the `HttpServletRequest` and `HttpSession`, as well as any beans declared in the JSP.

Table 8.3 Attributes used with the `external-url` tag

Attribute	Required	Description
`page`	Yes	The Tapestry page to link to, which must implement the `IExternalPage` interface
`servlet`	No	The path to the Tapestry servlet; defaults to `/app`
`parameters`	No	Used to specify service parameters

A final note: In addition to the `external-url` tag, there is an external tag that generates an `<a>` element, much like the `page` tag. Like the `page` tag, the external tag includes a `styleClass` attribute.

8.4 Summary

In previous chapters, we discussed how to extend the Tapestry framework from within, by using the services and components available with the framework, even to the point of creating new components. That's just scratching the surface of Tapestry. Because of its open-ended, object-oriented structure, the framework has untold avenues for extension. You can bend Tapestry to the needs of your project—even when your project needs new kinds of services, or complex client-side scripting, or even integration into an existing JavaServer Pages application.

So far, the examples and discussions in this book have concerned isolated examples, but that's not how Tapestry is used in real life: It is used to create working applications. Chapters 9 and 10 describe a real-world Tapestry application and demonstrate how the approaches explained in this and the preceding chapters are utilized in a real project.

Part 3

Building complete Tapestry applications

Chapters 9 and 10 focus on the Virtual Library, a Tapestry-driven example J2EE application. Within the context of a complete application, you'll be exposed to many of the design and development issues common to web applications, and you'll see good examples of how to address those issues.

9 Putting it all together

This chapter covers

- The Virtual Library application
- Thinking about application flow
- Limiting access to parts of the application

So far in this book we've focused on individual components or simple isolated examples—but that's not how Tapestry is supposed to be used. New issues arise when you're creating a real working application:

- **Who is the user?**—Most applications have some concept of users and logging in, and some aspects of the application change once the user has been authenticated.
- **Can the user view this page?**—Parts of an application may be accessible only to users who have logged in. Some applications may impose more restrictions, preventing some users from accessing certain pages.
- **How do I know what to display on this page?**—More important, if the page is redisplayed (for example, if the user logs in and is returned to the same page afterward), is there server-side state to determine what to display?

In this chapter, we'll describe the functionality of a demonstration application included in the Tapestry distribution: the Tapestry Virtual Library. In the next chapter, we will implement the application.

9.1 Introducing the Virtual Library

Ever notice all those books lining the shelves of your cubicle, as well as all the cubicles of your neighbors? Ever notice the degree of duplication of books? You might need a book just for a week or two, and so you buy your own copy of it. It might be nice to get a copy from the library, but public libraries are probably not up to date enough with cutting-edge technical books. What if there was a way to find a copy of a book you needed that just happened to be gathering dust on a coworker's shelf? What if there was a way to track where borrowed books are (which makes the books' owners more amenable to lending them out)? That's the Virtual Library, a kind of match-making application for books.

The Virtual Library is an application, built using Tapestry, that implements this idea. It tracks books and the people who own and borrow those books. The Virtual Library includes search capabilities that allow you to find books of interest and records that you've borrowed them. It also includes all the necessary pages for creating and editing a record of your books.

The Tapestry distribution includes the precompiled Enterprise Application Archive (EAR) containing the presentation layer for the Virtual Library, as well as the Enterprise JavaBeans (EJBs) that perform database access.

This chapter takes you on a tour of all the pages in the application, spotlighting interesting challenges related to the functionality on each page. Chapter 10 describes the implementation of the Virtual Library application.

The Tapestry distribution includes all the necessary directions for configuring and starting an instance of the open-source JBoss application server to execute the Virtual Library application. Nearly all the configuration is done automatically using an Ant build script. Once JBoss is up and running, the Virtual Library application may be accessed using the URL http://localhost/.

9.2 Performing searches

After launching the application, you will be presented with the application's search page, shown in figure 9.1. Since you must locate books before you can borrow them, this page is the central focus of the application. The Search page includes a form that allows you to search for books by entering a partial title or author name, the name of the book's owner (using a drop-down list), or the name of a publisher (again, using a drop-down list).

All pages in the Virtual Library include a navigational border that identifies the application and page title along the top, and that provides a navigation menu linking to different parts of the application along the left edge. Initially,

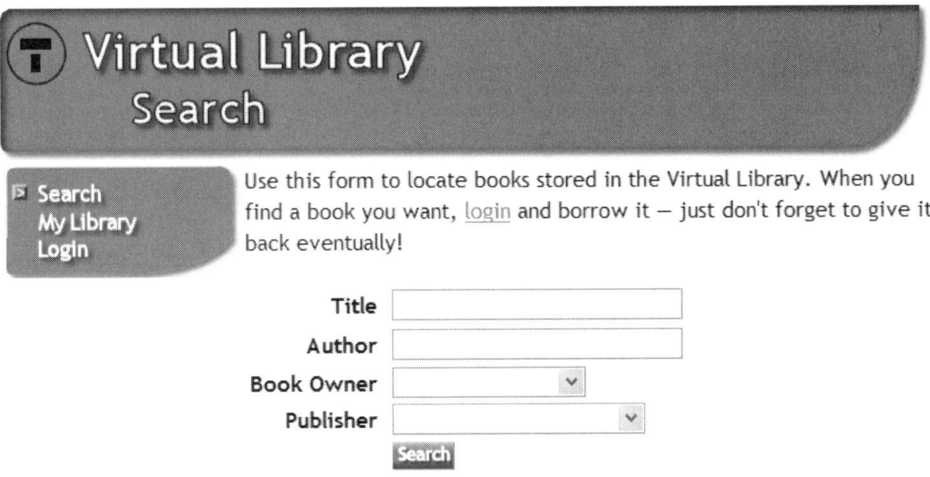

Figure 9.1 The Search page allows books to be located by title, author, owner, or publisher. The navigation menu along the left side expands once you execute the search, or after you log into the application.

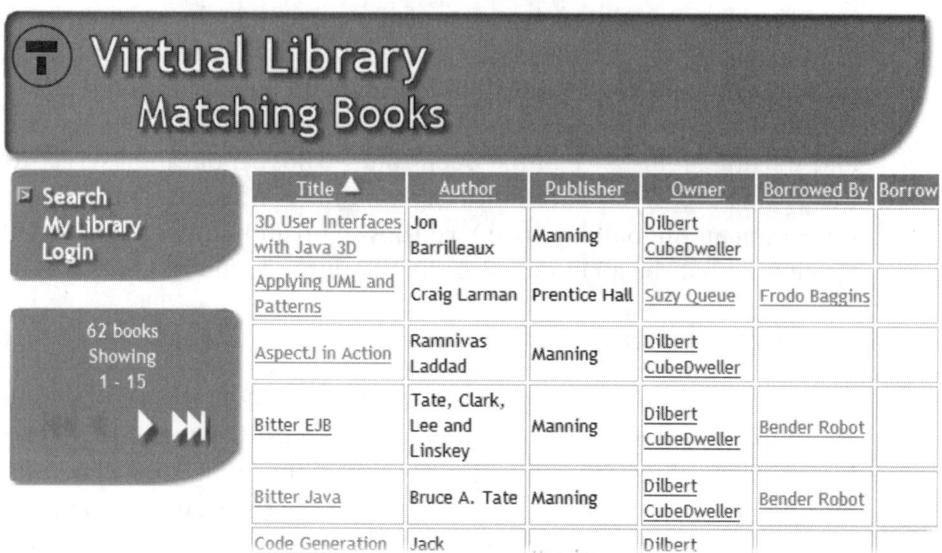

Figure 9.2 Search results listing matching books. Columns may be sorted using the links and icons across the top, and the results may be paged through using the controls along the left edge.

the only selections in the navigation menu are Search, My Library, and Login. Once you log in, more options appear in the navigation menu.

After entering search terms and clicking the Search button, you are presented with a listing of books matching the search criteria (figure 9.2). The Matching Books page presents these results in a table format, complete with navigation options for paging through the results.

The main listing is the title, author, publisher, owner, and current borrower (if any) for each book. Names of books and people are clickable links leading to detail pages about the book or user. Recently added books are marked with a "new" icon. Until you log in, books added in the previous month are marked new; but after you log in, the application knows when your previous visit occurred, and only books added since then are marked new.

The far-right column, Borrow, contains buttons for borrowing books. The column starts empty, since only authenticated users may borrow books. After you log in, icons will appear for books you may borrow—that is, books you aren't already in possession of. In addition, a book owner may mark a book as nonlendable; such a book will appear in the listing, but no borrow icon will ever appear for it.

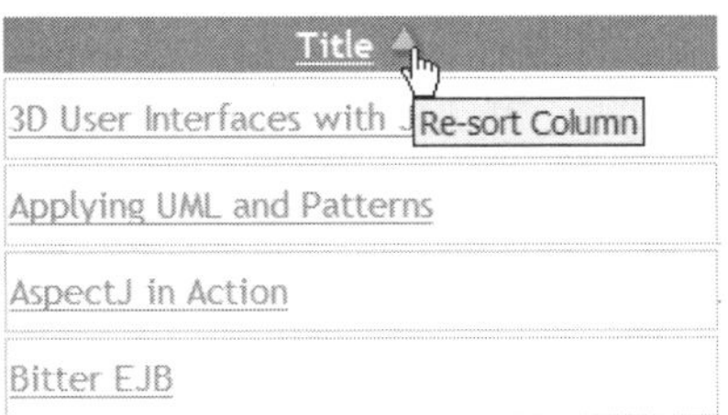

Figure 9.3
Clicking the column name or the sort icon toggles between ascending and descending sort order. Clicking a different column title re-sorts the table on that column instead.

9.2.1 Changing the table sort order

The columns may also be sorted; initially the listing is sorted by book title (in ascending order), which is indicated by the triangle icon in the Title column. Figure 9.3 shows how you may sort columns using either links or visible icons. Clicking on a column title sorts (or re-sorts) the results according to the content within that column.

Many pages in the application display lists of books, much like the Matching Books page. All of these pages allow you to control sort order in the same way.

9.2.2 Paging through the results

Because the book listing may be very large, the Virtual Library pages the results, showing 15 books per page. When a book listing is displayed, a set of page navigation controls appears along the left side, under the navigation menu. Figure 9.4 shows the detail for this portion of the page.

These controls show the total number of books in the listing and the range currently showing. Four buttons control navigation: First, Previous, Next, and Last. The First and Previous buttons are disabled on the first page of the listing, and the Next and Last buttons are disabled on the last page. Disabled buttons are drawn "grayed out" to provide additional feedback to you that it is not appropriate to click the button.

As with sorting, all pages that display lists of books use the same page navigation controls.

Figure 9.4
This control allows navigation through the query results a page at a time (each page showing 15 books), or lets you jump to the first or last page. The buttons on the left are disabled since the first page is showing. The button under the cursor is highlighted.

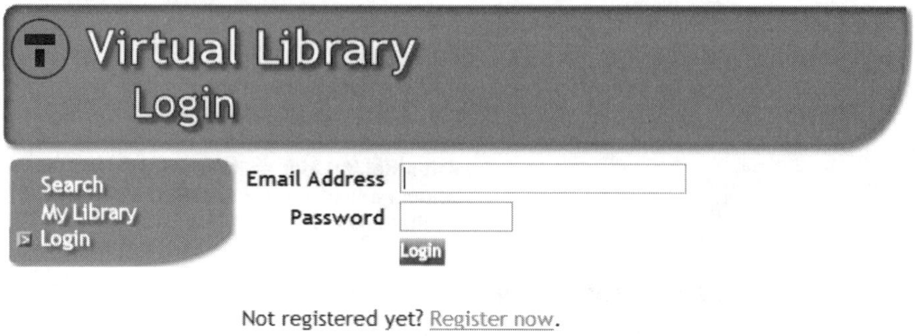

Figure 9.5 The user's email address is used as a login ID. You may also register on the fly. Return users will see their email address filled in automatically and have to enter only their password.

9.3 Logging in and registering

You may log into the Virtual Library from any page by clicking the Login link in the navigation menu. After you log in, you are returned to the page where you started. The My Library link will also allow you to log in but will send you to the My Library page instead.

The Login page, shown in figure 9.5, makes use of the validation subsystem described in chapter 5. Entering an unknown email address or an invalid password redisplays the form with an error message and the invalid fields well marked, as shown in figure 9.6. For security reasons, even if you entered a password, the Password field is redisplayed empty.

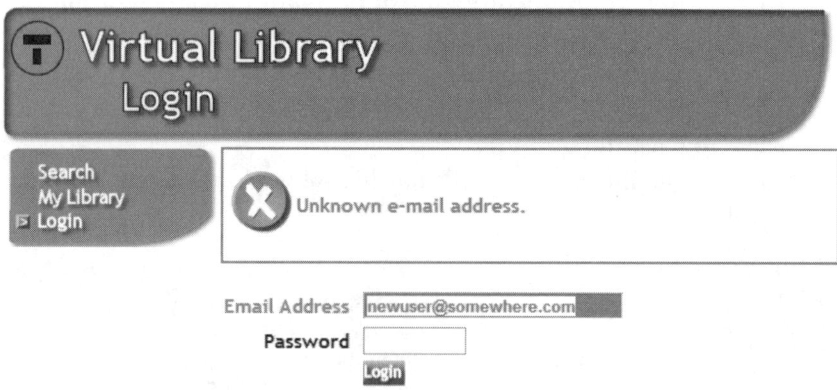

Figure 9.6 The Virtual Library uses the validation subsystem from chapter 5. Errors are clearly displayed and invalid fields marked.

Figure 9.7 New users can register at any time by providing their name, email, and password. The password is entered twice to ensure accuracy.

The sample database that comes with the Virtual Library includes three users: ringbearer@bagend.shire, squeue@bug.org, and dilbert@bigco.com. All three use the same password, *secret*.

New users can register on the fly by clicking the "Register now" link on the Login page. This displays the Register page, shown in figure 9.7.

After logging in or registering, you are returned to the page where you started. Because you are now authenticated, borrow icons will appear for books you can borrow, and additional navigation links are shown, as illustrated in figure 9.8.

9.4 Borrowing books

To borrow a book, click the borrow book icon (it appears in the Matching Book page, and in the View Person and View Book pages we haven't discussed yet). This will update the Virtual Library database, identifying you as the holder of the book. This is your opportunity to stroll over to the owner's cubicle and get the actual, physical book. When borrowing a book, you will be returned to the Search page, and an informational message will be displayed, as shown in figure 9.9.

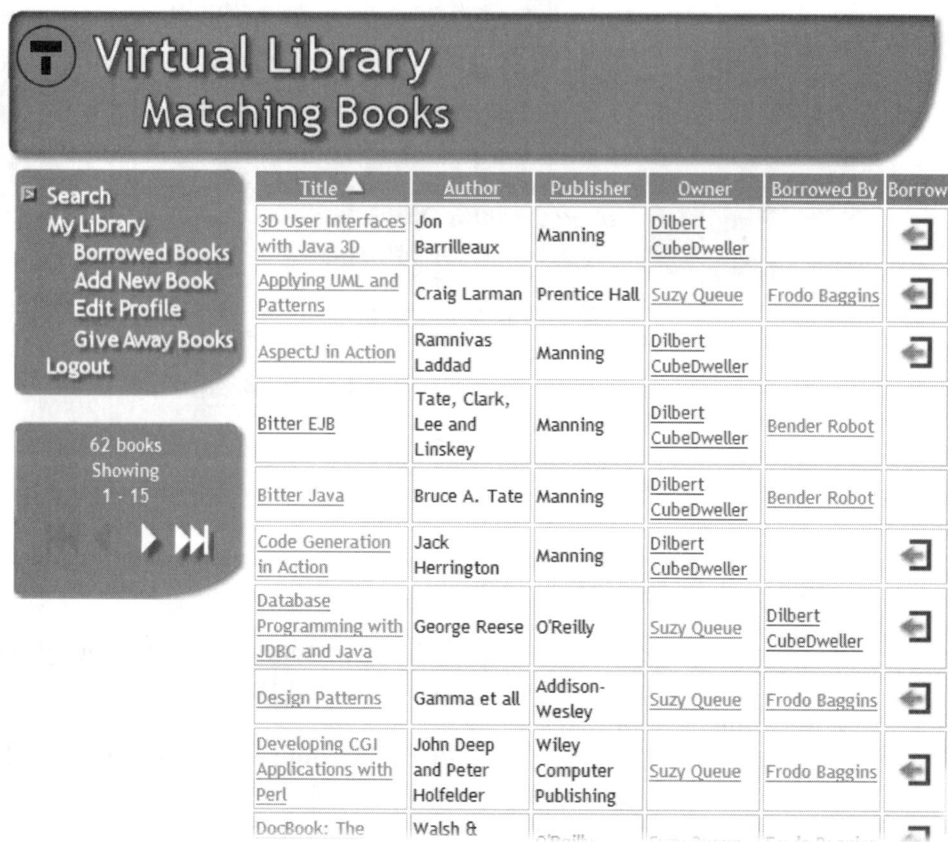

Figure 9.8 After logging in (or registering), you are returned to the original page. You may now borrow books, and you have additional navigation options (listed under My Library).

9.5 Getting details about books and persons

Throughout the application, whenever the name of a book or the name of a person appears, it is displayed as a link. Clicking the link directs you to a details page, showing more information about that book or about that person.

9.5.1 Viewing book details

Figure 9.10 shows an example of the View Book page. The page displays all the information provided by the book's owner, including a long description of the book. The page includes links to the book's owner and the person currently holding the book (which may be the book's owner or another user borrowing the

Figure 9.9 After borrowing a book, you are returned to the Search page, and a reminder appears.

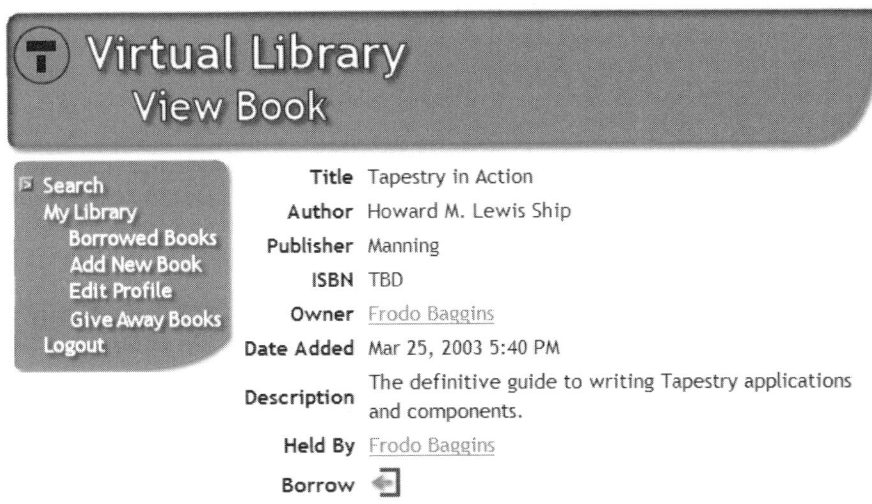

Figure 9.10 Clicking the name of a book displays the details about a book, with an icon for borrowing the book, as well as links to the book's owner and holder.

book). In addition, the View Book page includes a borrow icon (but only if the current user has logged in).

The ability to log into the application on the fly is very handy here. Figure 9.10 shows an example of the View Book page after a user has logged in; it includes a borrow icon. If you were, instead, to launch the Virtual Library and do a search without logging in first, there would be no borrow icon. A poorly designed system would require you to log in and then perform the search again before you could borrow the book. The Virtual Library allows you to log in on the fly and automatically returns you to the page you were viewing before logging in, at which point a single additional click will borrow the book.

9.5.2 Viewing a person

Clicking on a person's name displays the View Person page for that person, which includes a listing of all the books owned by that person (if any). An example of the View Person page is shown in figure 9.11. As elsewhere, the list of books can be paged through or re-sorted, and borrow icons appear for all appropriate books, provided the current user has logged in.

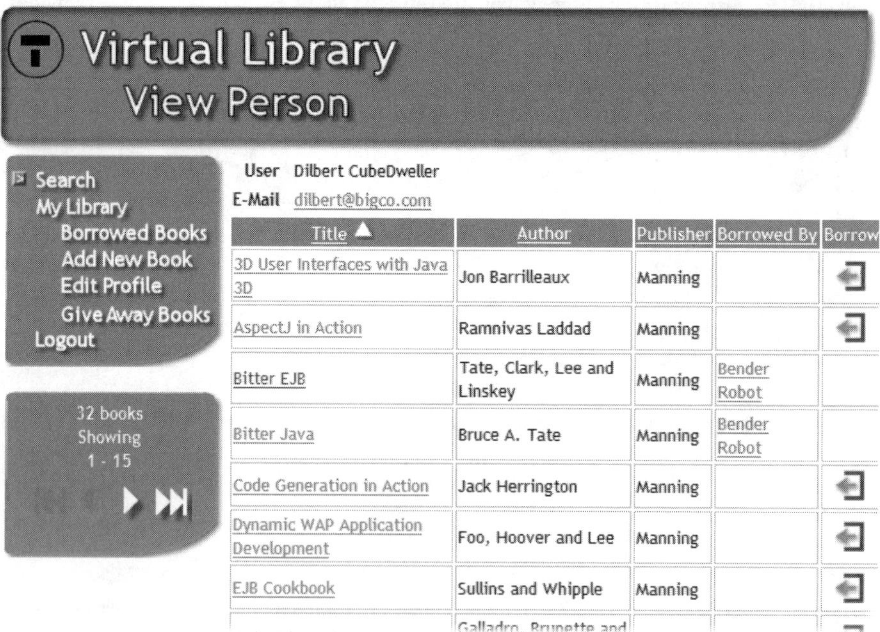

Figure 9.11 The View Person page includes a listing of the books owned by the person, with yet more icons for borrowing books. The book *Bitter Java* may not be borrowed, because Bender Robot is the current user and is currently holding the book.

The borrow icon does not appear unless the user is logged in. Even for a logged-in user, the icon does not appear if the current user is already holding the book, or if the book is not lendable (the owner of a book selects whether books can be borrowed).

9.6 Managing your books

The My Library page is the starting point for managing the books that you own. From the My Library page (and by using the menu items listed below My Library), it is possible to add records for new books, modify existing books' records, and even give books away to other users of the application.

The My Library page (shown in figure 9.12) shows the entire list of books the current user owns, with controls to allow you to edit or delete existing books. It is

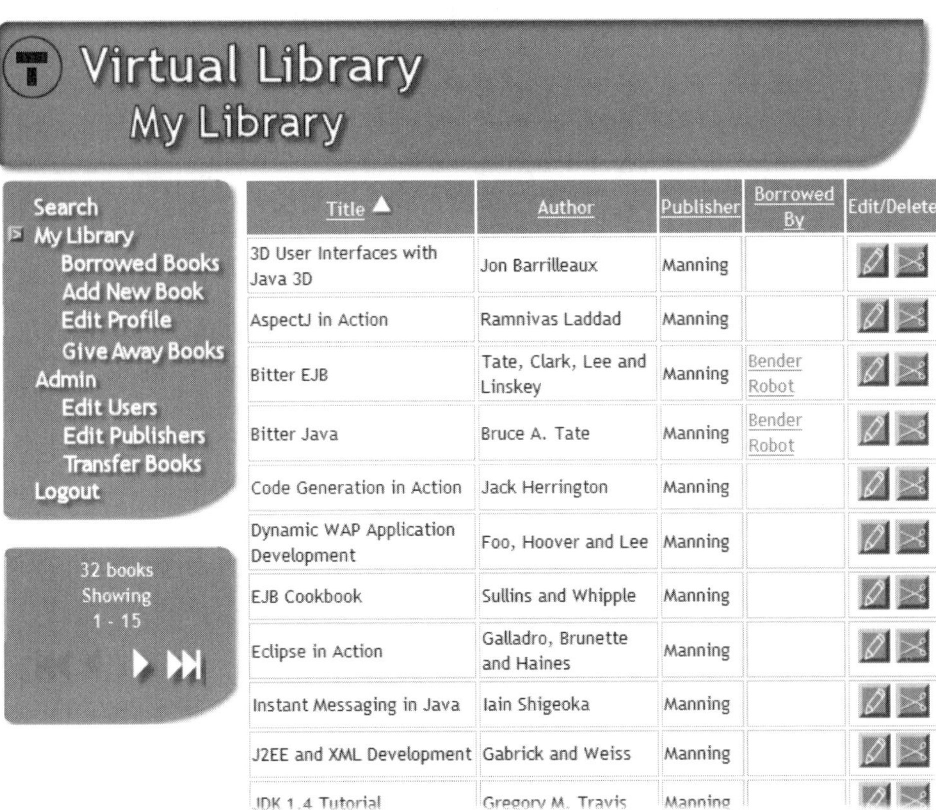

Figure 9.12 This interface is used to edit or delete books owned by the current user.

accessed using the My Library link in the navigation menu. As with other book listings, the My Library page includes navigation controls for paging through the list and lets you change the sort order of the list. Each book has a pair of buttons for editing and deleting the book. Unlike the other pages, the book titles in My Library are not links; this is to remove any ambiguity about what clicking the link would do (would it show the book detail or edit the book?).

9.6.1 Editing a book

Clicking the edit icon for a book in the My Library page allows the details of a book to be edited. The Edit Book page, shown in figure 9.13, is a form allowing you to update the details of the book, including the current borrower of the book.

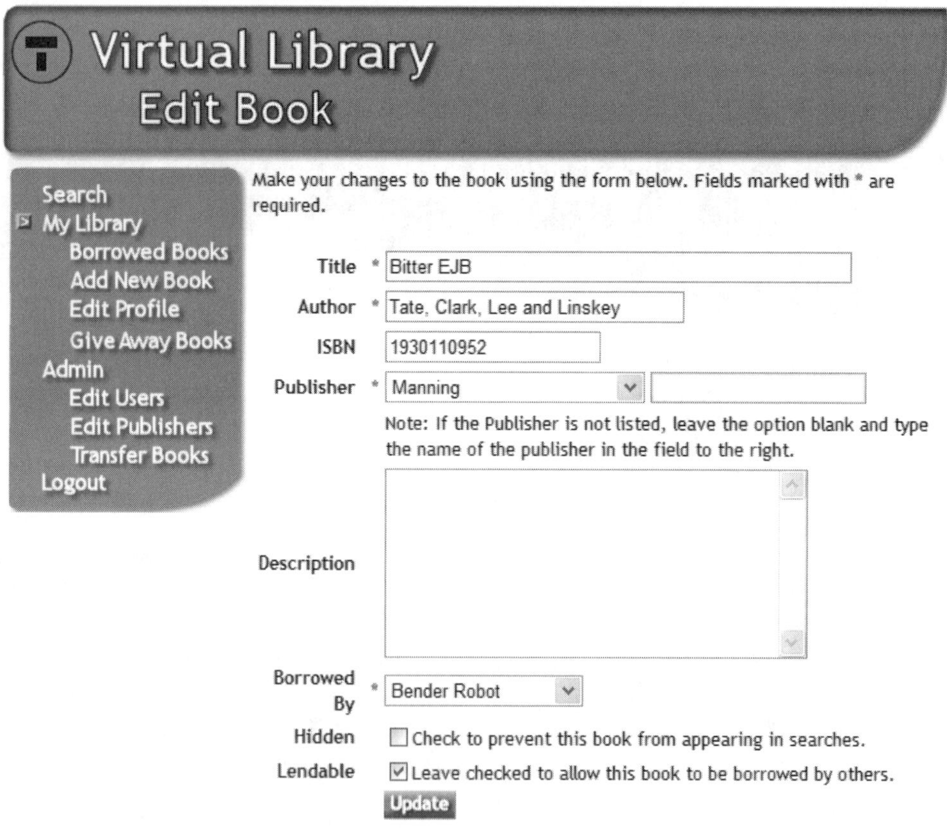

Figure 9.13 Books may be edited, updating all information, including who is currently borrowing the book. Publishers may be selected from a list or entered into the text field (but not both).

An interesting aspect of this page is the Publisher field. You can either select an existing publisher from the drop-down list or leave the drop-down blank and enter the name of a new publisher into the adjacent text field. This input behavior is backed up by client-side JavaScript that enables and disables the text field based on the selection in the drop-down list. The text field is disabled if the drop-down list has a nonblank value selected. Selecting the blank entry in the drop-down list enables the text field and moves the cursor into it.

9.6.2 Deleting a book

Books may be deleted by clicking the delete icon on the My Library page. This results in a confirmation page, shown in figure 9.14.

9.6.3 Returning books

The Borrowed Books menu item shows a listing of all books the logged-in user is currently borrowing, as shown in figure 9.15. From here, you can also return books by clicking the book return icon (in the rightmost column). Like all other pages that show lists of books, the Borrowed Books page includes page navigation controls and the ability to change the sort order of the list.

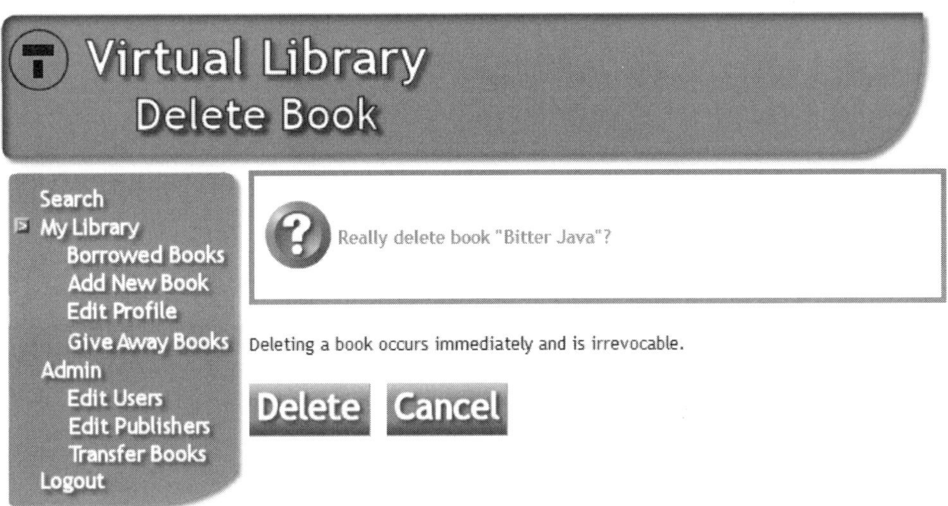

Figure 9.14 Clicking a delete icon on the My Library page displays a confirmation page before the book is actually deleted.

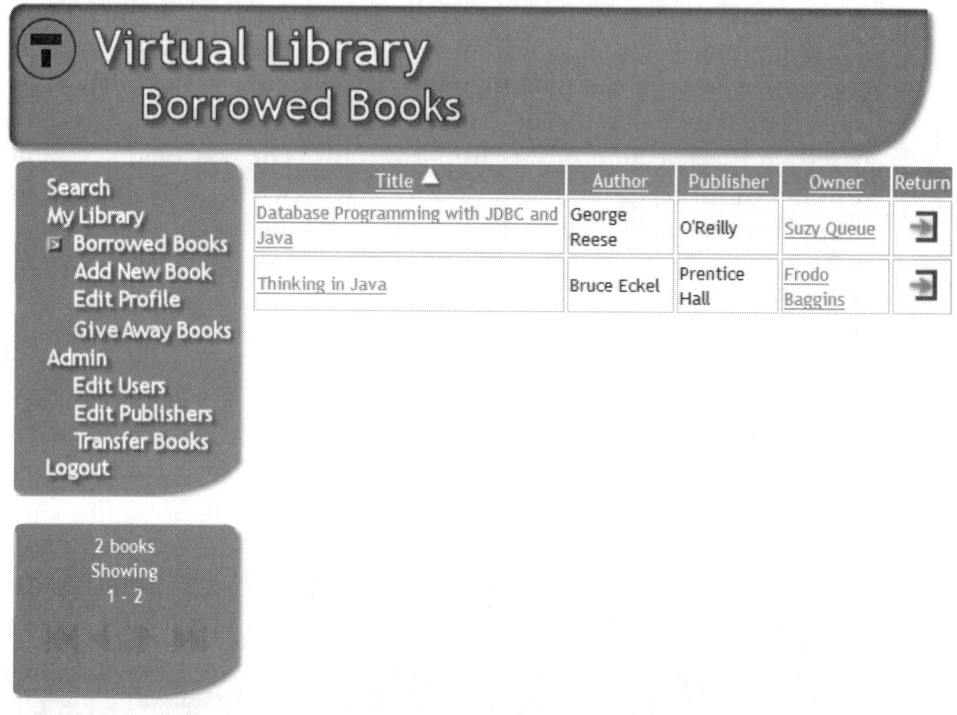

Figure 9.15 The Borrowed Books listing shows all books borrowed by the current user. The return icon in the rightmost column allows books to be returned.

9.6.4 *Adding a new book*

Before there can be books to edit or delete, books must be added. The Add New Book page, accessed via the Add New Book item in the navigation menu, is the means for adding new books. This page is shown in figure 9.16.

As with the Edit Book page, the Publisher drop-down list is exclusive with the adjacent text field.

9.6.5 *Editing your profile*

The Edit Profile page, shown in figure 9.17, is used to edit your name, email address, and password. It is accessed using the Edit Profile item in the navigation menu.

9.6.6 *Giving away books*

Sometimes you'll want to give away books. You may no longer need the book, or you may just be clearing out some shelf space. One way to move ownership of a

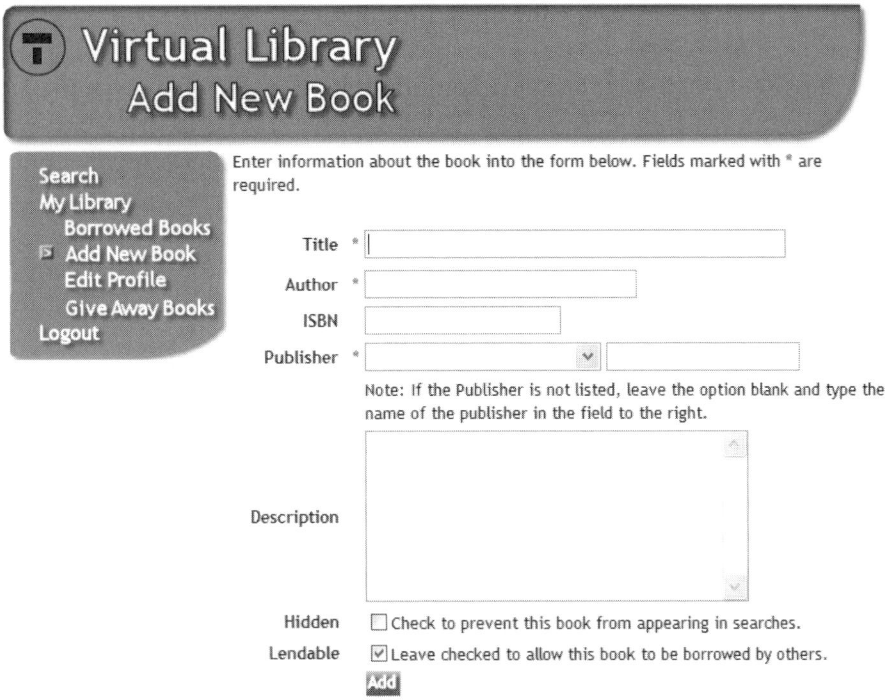

Figure 9.16 Adding a new book is much like editing an existing book, except that the borrower cannot be edited.

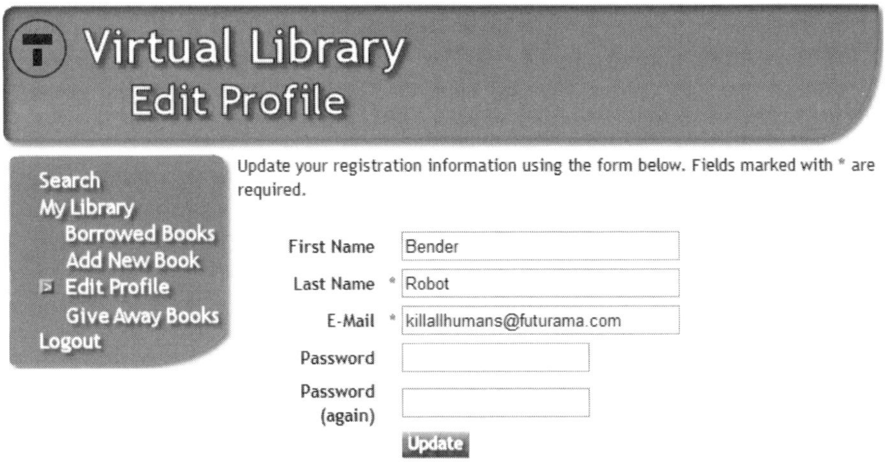

Figure 9.17 The Edit Profile page allows users to update their name, email address, and password.

book is to delete it from your My Library and let the new owner add it to his or her My Library. A better way is simply to shift the ownership of the book without otherwise changing it. This is accomplished using the Give Away Books item on the navigation menu.

The Give Away Books page, shown in figure 9.18, lets you select one or more books and designate a person to give those books to. The ownership of the books is then immediately changed over to the new owner.

Obviously, we're using a Palette component (discussed in chapter 6) to select the books to transfer, but notice how we've customized its configuration. Normally, the column titles are Available (on the left) and Selected (on the right). On this page, the left column is labeled "Books you currently own," and the right column includes a drop-down list for selecting the target person (to transfer books to).

That covers all the pages that may be reached by ordinary users. The next section covers the remaining pages accessible to Virtual Library administrators.

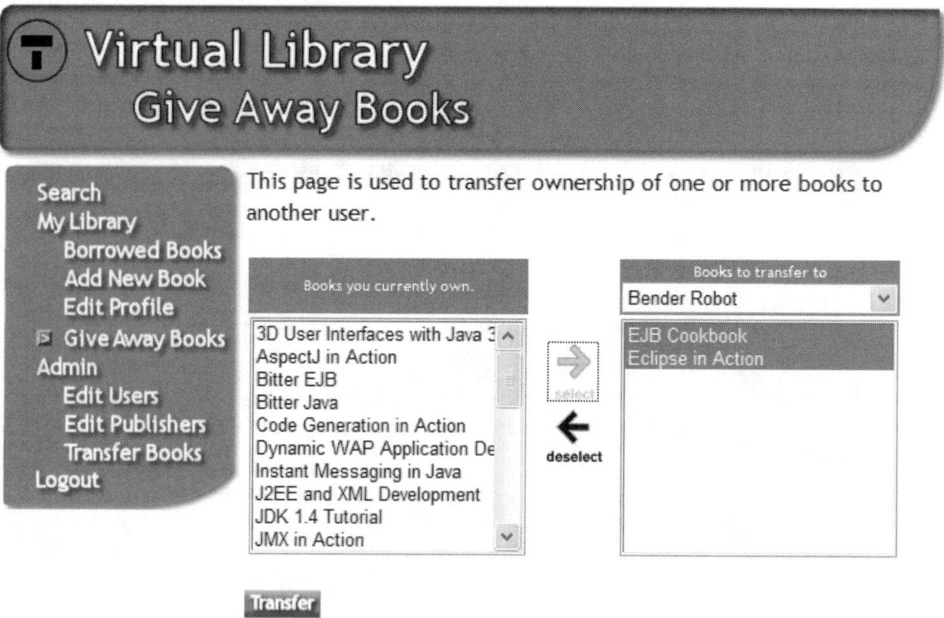

Figure 9.18 The Give Away Books page allows the ownership of books to be changed. A target user is selected, and the Palette component is used to identify which books are to be transferred.

9.7 Administering the Virtual Library

As a demonstration application, the Virtual Library extends past functionality that ordinary users will see. It includes additional functionality needed to administer the application. A less complete application might omit this functionality, forcing administrators to perform these operations directly against the database. Instead, the Virtual Library seamlessly integrates this functionality into the overall application.

The administrative pages are *protected*; if you attempt to access them before logging in (or after your session expires), you will be forced to log in. If you don't have administrative privileges, you'll be returned to the Search page with an error message.

If you do have administrative privileges, you will see additional menu items in the navigational menu. Administrators can

- Delete existing users
- Override passwords for users
- Add or remove administrative privilege for users
- Manage the list of publishers
- Transfer ownership of books between users

Of these, the most common activities relate to managing users, so we'll start there.

9.7.1 Editing users

The chief job of an administrator is to manage the other users of the Virtual Library. This is done through the Edit Users item in the navigation menu, which displays a list of all users in the database (as shown in figure 9.19).

To test the administrative pages, you may log in as user ringbearer@ bagend.shire, using the password *secret*. Three new options will appear in the navigation menu: Edit Users, Edit Publishers, and Transfer Books.

The page allows data about other users to be changed; the current user is omitted from the list. This ensures that administrators do not accidentally delete themselves or remove their own administrator privilege. User names and email addresses cannot be changed, but users can have administrator access granted or revoked, can be locked out of the system entirely, can have their password changed, and can be deleted outright.

When a user is deleted, any books owned by the user are reassigned to the current user, the administrator who performed the deletion. Additionally, any books borrowed by a deleted user are returned to their owners.

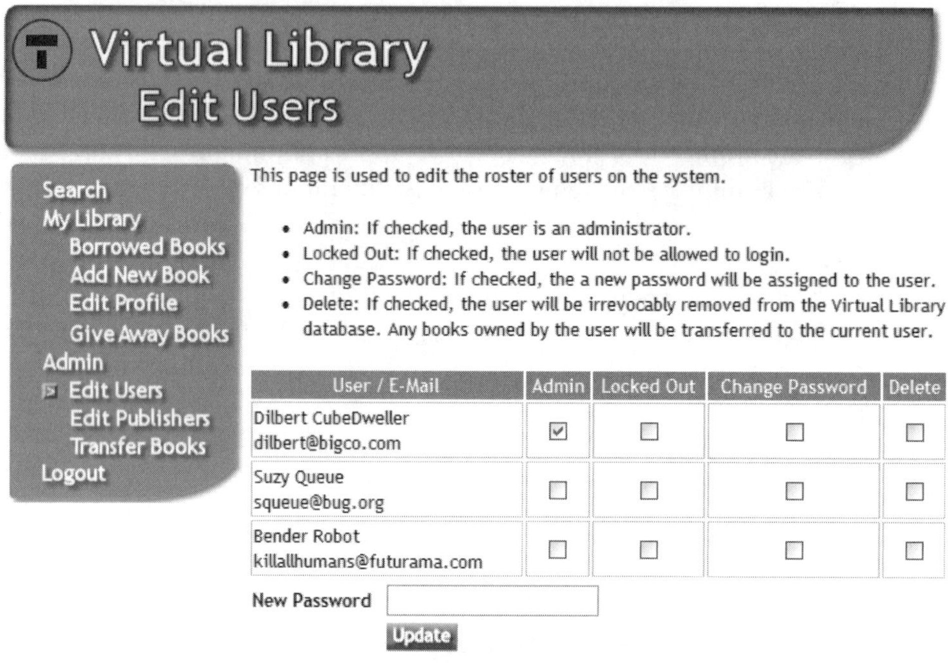

Figure 9.19 The Edit Users page allows an administrator to modify or delete the users in the system. The current user (ringbearer@bagend.shire in this figure) does not appear in the list.

9.7.2 Editing publishers

When users add or edit books, they often select a known publisher for the book from the drop-down list. Users may also create new publishers as needed. Of course, they won't always get it right, and the Edit Publishers page, shown in figure 9.20, allows an administrator to clean things up. The page is accessed using the Edit Publishers item on the navigation menu.

The Edit Publishers page allows all the known publishers to be edited in a single place. In the Virtual Library, a publisher is simply a name (the point is to populate the drop-down list with a reasonable value). The Edit Publishers page enables all the publishers be renamed or deleted in a single operation.

9.7.3 Transferring books

The final operation for administrators is to forcibly transfer book ownership between users. This is much like the Give Away Books page, except the administrator can choose any two users to transfer between. This operation takes the form of a two-page wizard, accessed using the Transfer Books item in the navigation menu. The first page of the wizard is shown in figure 9.21.

Virtual Library
Edit Publishers

Search
My Library
Borrowed Books
Add New Book
Edit Profile
Give Away Books
Admin
Edit Users
Edit Publishers
Transfer Books
Logout

This page allows you to rename and delete publishers.

Publisher	Delete
Addison-Wesley	☐
Computer Science Press	☐
Coriolis	☐
IDG Books	☐
M&T Books	☐
Manning	☐
O'Reilly	☐
Prentice Hall	☐
Wiley Computer Publishing	☐

Update

Figure 9.20 The complete list of publishers is displayed. Publishers may be renamed or deleted outright.

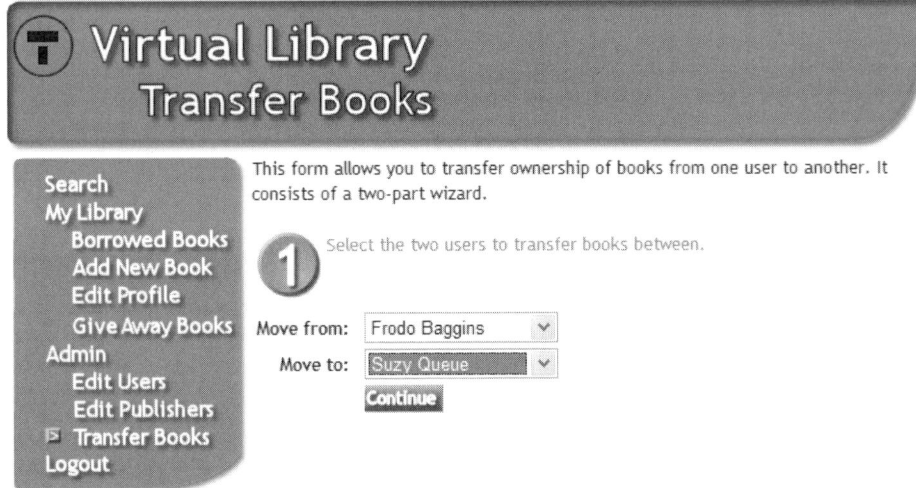

Figure 9.21 The Transfer Books wizard starts by having the adminstrator select the two users to move books between.

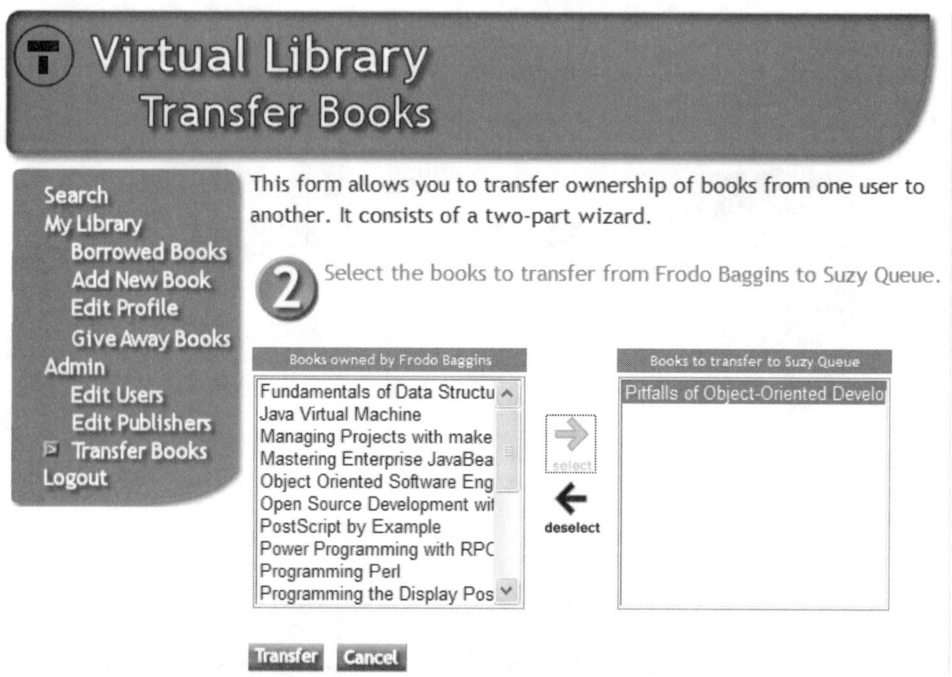

Figure 9.22 After the administrator selects two users, the second step is to choose the books to be transferred to the target user.

The first step is to select the two users to move books between. The source user must own some books. The target user can be anyone but the source user. Once the two users are selected, the second page in the wizard (see figure 9.22) is displayed.

9.8 Summary

The Virtual Library is a small, simple application with only three entities (books, persons, and publishers); even so, you've seen that a proper approach to this application is moderately complex. There's a lot of polish to the application, with features such as on-the-fly login and registration (that remembers where you started) and consistent column sorting and page navigation, and even little features such as rollover buttons. In addition, we've included a suite of administrative pages that will keep the owner of the Virtual Library from having to muck about with the underlying SQL database.

Chapter 10 continues with the Virtual Library, providing details on how each page and component is implemented.

10 Implementing a Tapestry application

This chapter covers

- Dividing the application into layers
- Combining Tapestry with Enterprise JavaBeans
- Authenticating the user
- Adding security checks to pages
- Deploying an enterprise application

In the previous chapter, we described the Virtual Library, a demonstration application included with the Tapestry distribution. We covered quite a bit of functionality, some of which is specific to individual pages, while other functionality is distributed throughout the entire application. In this chapter, we'll get down to the nuts and bolts of implementing the Virtual Library. Along the way, we'll investigate how to best utilize the facilities of Java 2 Enterprise Edition (J2EE) to support the application, and how to best organize our code for robustness and maintainability.

The source code for the Virtual Library is part of the main Tapestry distribution; the code for the Enterprise JavaBeans (EJBs) is in the examples/VlibBeans directory; and the code for the Tapestry portion of the application is in examples/Vlib. Appendix B tells you how to obtain the Tapestry distribution.

10.1 Looking at the application layers

Because it's a J2EE application, the Virtual Library is split into two distinct sections: a presentation layer and an application layer, as shown in figure 10.1. The presentation layer is the user-facing aspect of the application, and is the portion constructed using Tapestry. The application layer consists of the session and entity EJBs that, ultimately, interact with the database.

The application layer for the Virtual Library consists of six EJBs (listed in table 10.1): three entity beans using container-managed persistence, and three session beans. The presentation layer will only access two of those beans: `BookQuery` and `Operations`.

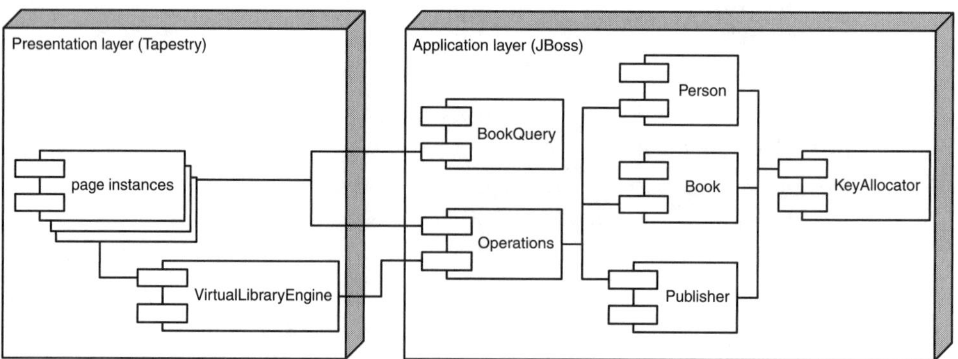

Figure 10.1 The presentation layer, the Tapestry portion of the application, is separate from the application layer.

Table 10.1 EJBs used to manage interactions with the database

Bean	Usage
`Book`	Entity bean for books.
`BookQuery`	Stateful session bean for executing queries about books. Creates and executes dynamic JDBC queries and stores results.
`KeyAllocator`	Stateless session bean; allocates primary keys for entity beans.
`Operations`	Stateless session bean for performing most operations, including creating, reading, and updating entity beans (using value objects).
`Person`	Entity bean for persons (a.k.a. users).
`Publisher`	Entity bean for publishers.

All database access, without exception, occurs in the application layer, as either direct Java Database Connectivity (JDBC) calls in the `Operations`, `BookQuery`, or `KeyAllocator` bean, or as container-managed persistence in the three entity beans. In a production environment, the presentation and application layers will be operating within the same Java Virtual Machine (JVM). Most application servers (including JBoss and WebLogic) will recognize this configuration and have the different objects communicate directly, without utilizing Remote Method Invocation (RMI). RMI is intended for communications between different processes often on different servers, so avoiding that overhead provides a great performance boost.

In a development environment, things are different. During development, the application layer changes far less often than the presentation layer. When was the last time you tweaked an EJB because it "didn't look right"? Here's where the enforced discipline of developing a J2EE application, with real separation between the layers, actually pays off: The application layer can run in one process, just as it would in a production environment, while the presentation layer runs in another process, executing within your IDE. Important advantages to structuring your development environment this way include the following:

- Debugging the presentation layer is much faster and easier than debugging the application server remotely, especially when using an IDE that supports "hot code replace" (changing methods while the application is still running), such as Eclipse.
- The presentation layer may be stopped and restarted in a manner of a few seconds. Even a lightweight application server such as JBoss can take at least a minute, often much longer, to shut down and restart.

- You can work on files directly within your development workspace, without constantly having to repackage and redeploy your web application.
- You will discover early any problems with object serialization (of any value objects that move between the two layers). Operating within a single JVM can mask these problems (since RMI will not be used).

10.2 Organizing EJB access

The Virtual Library makes use of Tapestry features to organize the application sensibly. This organization takes the form of specific responsibilities for the engine, the `Visit` object, and the `Global` object. The `Global` object is similar to the `Visit` object but is shared by all sessions. Figure 10.2 shows how these central objects are stored on the server. The engine and the `Visit` object are stored within the `HttpSession` as attributes; there will be many engine and `Visit` instances, one pair for each concurrent user of the application.

The `Global` object, on the other hand, is global to (and shared by) *all* engine instances, stored as a `ServletContext` attribute. In the Virtual Library, the `Global` object is responsible for performing Java Naming and Directory Interface (JNDI) lookups on behalf of the engine, locating home interfaces for the Operations and BookQuery EJBs. This is an excellent use for the `Global` object, since it can cache references to the EJB home interfaces. JNDI lookups of home interfaces are a notoriously slow operation, so caching the results for quick access is an effective performance enhancement.

As you'll see shortly, locating these lookup operations centrally leads to not only a better-performing application but also a more robust one. Having a single, authoritative location for JNDI lookups means that there will be a single, authoritative approach to handling JNDI lookup errors. It also provides a single place to manage recovery from `RemoteExceptions`. A traditional servlet application can have JNDI lookups and cached home interface references scattered across

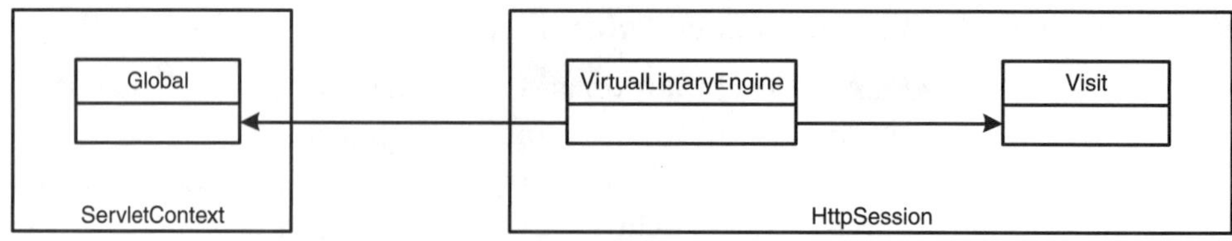

Figure 10.2 The engine is responsible for common EJB operations. The `Visit` object is responsible for authentication. The `Global` object, which is responsible for JNDI lookup, is a singleton, shared by all engines.

many servlets and JSPs, but Tapestry makes it easy to centrally locate these important operations.

10.2.1 Handling authentication

The `Visit` object is responsible for authentication. It simply tracks the ID of the currently logged-in user. This ID is an `Integer`, the primary key type of all three entities used by the Virtual Library (Person, Book, and Publisher). Additionally, the `Visit` object retains the matching instance of `Person`, so that full details about the user (such as name, email address, and administrative privilege) can be made available to the application.

10.2.2 Accessing Enterprise JavaBeans

The majority of interaction between the two layers involves the `Operations` bean. This is a stateless session bean, and it consists of a number of methods for creating, reading, and updating back-end data. The application uses a subclass of the `BaseEngine` class. The subclass has extensions for obtaining a reference to the `Operations` bean's remote interface as needed, as well as implementing several of the most common operations, such as reading a `Person` value object corresponding to a person ID.

As with JNDI lookups in the `Global` object, having operations implemented in the engine centralizes handling of, and recovery from, remote exceptions. This leads to much greater application stability, especially during redeployment of the application. In the code excerpts that follow, you'll see how the engine provides support for retry loops used in every location where remote object access occurs.

10.2.3 Tracking user identity with the Visit object

The specific requirements for the `Visit` object in the Virtual Library are that it track the following:

- Who the logged-in user is (if any)
- The last time the user accessed the system (information used to identify which books are "new")

Listing 10.1 shows how this class is implemented.

Listing 10.1 Visit.java: Java class for the Virtual Library `Visit` object

```
package org.apache.tapestry.vlib;

import java.io.Serializable;
import java.sql.Timestamp;
```

```
import org.apache.tapestry.IRequestCycle;
import org.apache.tapestry.vlib.ejb.Person;

public class Visit implements Serializable
{
  private static final long serialVersionUID =
    8589862098677603655L;
  private transient Person _user;          ❶
  private Integer _userId;
  private Timestamp _lastAccess;

  public Timestamp getLastAccess()
  {
    return _lastAccess;
  }

  public Person getUser(IRequestCycle cycle)
  {
    if (_user != null)
      return _user;

    if (_userId == null)
      return null;

    VirtualLibraryEngine vengine =
      (VirtualLibraryEngine)cycle.getEngine();                ❷

    _user = vengine.readPerson(_userId);

    return _user;
  }

  public Integer getUserId()
  {
    return _userId;
  }

  public void setUser(Person value)
  {
    _lastAccess = null;
    _user = value;
    _userId = null;

    if (_user == null)
      return;

    _userId = _user.getId();

    _lastAccess = _user.getLastAccess();
  }
```

```
    public boolean isUserLoggedIn()
    {
      return _userId != null;
    }

    public boolean isUserLoggedOut()
    {
      return _userId == null;
    }

    public boolean isLoggedInUser(Integer id)
    {
      if (_userId == null)
        return false;

      return _userId.equals(id);
    }

    public void clearCache()
    {
      _user = null;
    }

  }
```

❶ The `_user` instance variable stores the `Person` data object for the logged-in user. Because the field is transient, its value may be lost at any time due to clustering.

❷ Whenever the `_user` variable is null, it can be reacquired from the engine (using the `VirtualLibraryEngine` subclass).

The `Visit` object is stored in the `HttpSession` as a session attribute after most requests. On any request where the `Visit` object is accessed, the framework makes the assumption that the `Visit` has been changed.[1] This triggers the Tapestry `ApplicationServlet` to store the engine (and with it, the `Visit`) in the `HttpSession` at the end of the request, after the response page has been sent back to the client.

In a nonclustered environment, this has little impact because the `HttpSession` is just a glorified `java.util.Map`; storing attributes in the session doesn't trigger any additional behavior. In a clustered environment, the engine and, with it, the `Visit` may be serialized and copied to a backup server within the cluster. It's in

[1] Since the engine doesn't know anything about the `Visit`, it is forced to assume that any access of the `Visit` is a potential change to the `Visit` that must be propagated throughout the application server cluster.

the best interests of general application performance for the `Visit` object to serialize efficiently.[2]

The `Visit` object declares a static `serialVersionUID` constant. Declaring this as a static variable means that the JVM does not have to compute this value at runtime, leading to a modest efficiency improvement. A better improvement is to implement the `java.io.Externalizable` interface (instead of the `java.io.Serializable` interface). This allows you to write more efficient methods to save and restore the state of the object. This is an example of where runtime performance profiling would be used: to see just how much time is being spent serializing the `Visit` object. Based on that data, a decision about the merits of expending effort on serialization of the `Visit` can be made.

The `Visit` object tracks the logged-in user's ID, but also the `Person` object representing the user. The latter is the value object for the Person entity and is needed in the presentation layer to display the user's name or to determine the user's administrative privilege. These user ID and `Person` instances are stored in two separate instance variables. The user's ID is stored persistently, but the `Person` object is stored transiently. This means that the `Person` object, within the `Visit`, does not have to be serialized when the `Visit` is itself serialized, an obvious optimization—but only if the `Person` object can be restored when needed.

This on-demand restoration is handled in the `getUser()` method. Rather than being a pure accessor method (taking no arguments), this method requires that the `IRequestCycle` object be passed in. If the `Person` object has been lost, this method can use the cycle to obtain the `VirtualLibraryEngine` instance for the application, and use the engine to reread the `Person`.

You'll be seeing this pattern in different guises repeatedly: store the minimum persistent state possible and recover the full state only as needed. The Tapestry framework provides the necessary structure for maintaining the minimal state and recovering the full state.

10.2.4 Understanding page inheritance

The inheritance hierarchy for pages is shown in figures 10.3 and 10.4. Figure 10.3 shows interfaces and base classes, and figure 10.4 shows how each page in the Virtual Library inherits from or extends from those interfaces and base classes.

At first glance there is an awfully large number of classes, but this is natural for a Tapestry application: Each page has its own class, even though in most

---

[2] The engine implements the `java.io.Externalizable` interface for efficiency reasons.

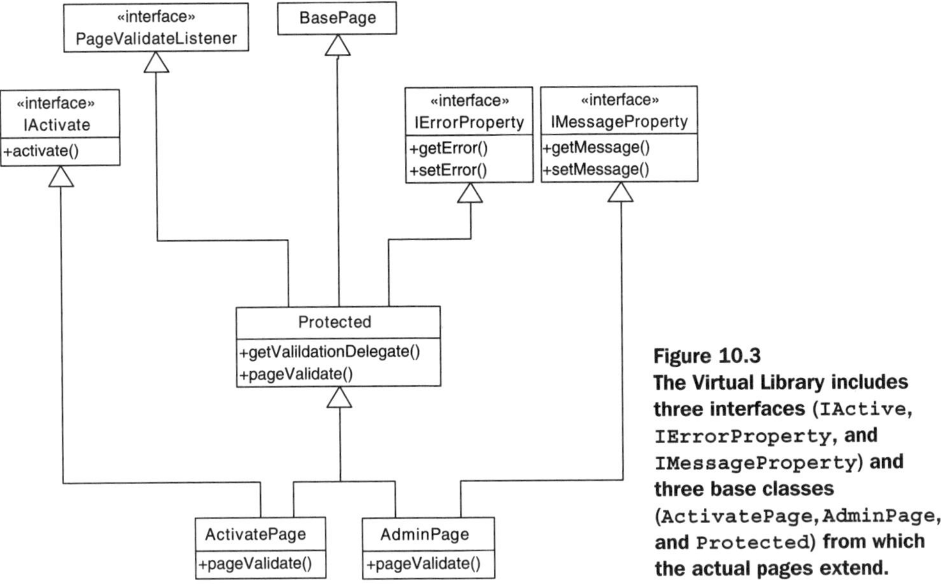

Figure 10.3 The Virtual Library includes three interfaces (`IActive`, `IErrorProperty`, and `IMessageProperty`) and three base classes (`ActivatePage`, `AdminPage`, and `Protected`) from which the actual pages extend.

cases, the class is only a few lines long. The presentation layer accounts for approximately 1,850 lines of code, excluding comments. This is a surprisingly small number of lines, considering the amount of functionality present in the Virtual Library application. The application layer (the EJB implementations and value objects), at about 1,250 lines, is slightly smaller. Of course, a significant portion of the presentation layer is in non-Java artifacts: HTML templates, page specifications, and component specifications.

The Virtual Library includes base classes and interfaces that define additional logic. These classes and interfaces are primarily concerned with preventing unauthorized users from seeing pages, at least until they are authenticated. In addition, the Java classes for the ViewPerson and ViewBook pages implement the `IExternalPage` interface. This is to allow links to persons and books to be stored as bookmarks. Table 10.2 lists the base classes and interfaces used by the application.

Table 10.2 Base classes and interfaces used to define and implement behavior common to many application pages

Class/Interface	Usage
`AdminPage`	Restricts access to the page to users with administrative access.
`Protected`	Restricts access to the page to logged-in users, forcing an on-the-fly login as necessary.

Table 10.2 Base classes and interfaces used to define and implement behavior common to many application pages *(continued)*

Class/Interface	Usage
`IActivate`	Defines a page that needs an extra initialization phase before it initially renders.
`IErrorProperty`	Defines a string property named `error`. Matches a property specification in the page specification.
`IMessageProperty`	Defines a string property named `message`. Matches a property specification in the page specification.

Now that we've established the general framework of the application, we can start to drill down into the pages and components of the Virtual Library.

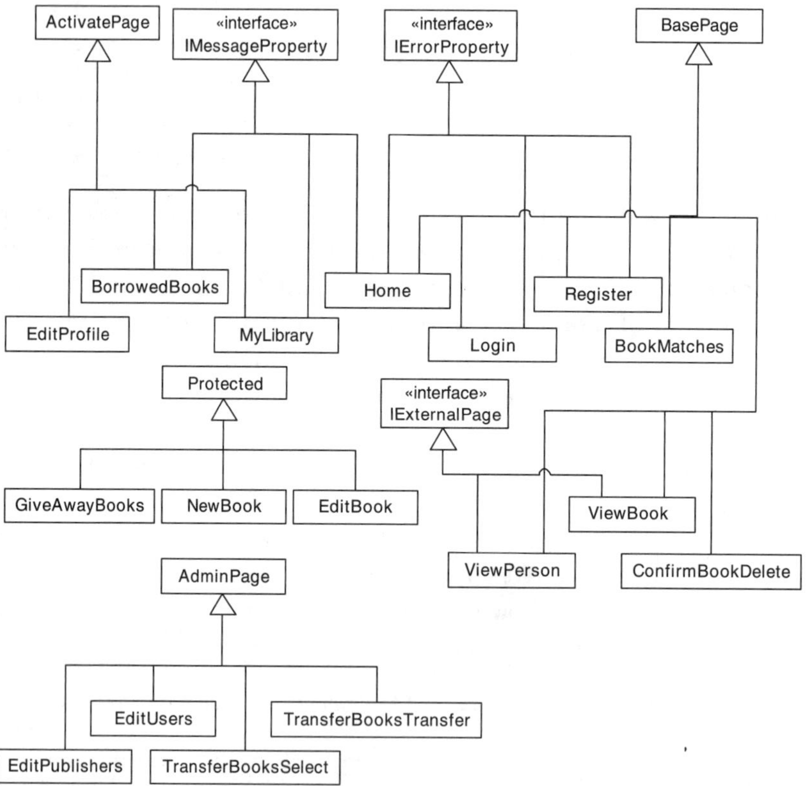

Figure 10.4 The 17 pages of the application extend from framework base classes, such as `BasePage`, or from application-specific base classes, such as `ActivatePage`.

10.3 Implementing the Search page

In the Virtual Library, the page used for searching is the Home page (it is labeled *Search* in the user interface but is the Home page nonetheless). The function of this page is to collect user input (the title, author, and so forth), execute the query, and use the BookMatches page to display the results. The Home page is, in many ways, the simplest page in the application. Refer to figure 9.1 to see what the Home page looks like.

The majority of the template for the Home page (listing 10.2) is the Form component and the `<table>` element used to control its layout. At runtime, the majority of the HTML is produced inside the Border component.

Listing 10.2 Home.html: HTML template for the Home page

```
<html jwcid="$content$">
<body jwcid="@Border">

<p>
Use this form to locate books stored in the Virtual Library.
When you find a book you want,
<a href="#" jwcid="@PageLink" page="Login">login</a> and borrow
it &#151; just don't forget to give it back eventually!
</p>

<span jwcid="@ShowError"/>
<span jwcid="@ShowMessage"/>

<form jwcid="@Form" listener="ognl:listeners.search"
   stateful="ognl:false">
  <table class="form">
    <tr>
      <th>Title</th>
      <td><input type="text" jwcid="inputTitle@TextField"
            value="ognl:title" size="30" maxlength="100"/>
      </td>
    </tr>
    <tr>
      <th>Author</th>
      <td><input type="text" jwcid="inputAuthor@TextField"
            value="ognl:author" size ="30" maxlength="100"/>
      </td>
    </tr>
    <tr>
      <th>Book Owner</th>
      <td><select jwcid="inputOwner@PropertySelection"
            value="ognl:ownerId"
            model="ognl:engine.buildPersonModel(true)"/></td>
```

```
        </tr>
        <tr>
          <th>Publisher</th>
          <td><select jwcid="inputPublisher@PropertySelection"
                value="ognl:publisherId"
                model="ognl:engine.publisherModel"/>
          </td>
        </tr>
        <tr>
          <td></td>
          <td>
            <input type="image" src="images/search.png" width="46"
              height="20" border="0" alt="Search"/>
          </td>
        </tr>
      </table>
    </form>

    </body>
    </html>
```

The Form component for the search form specifies a value of false for the Form's `stateful` parameter. By default, the `stateful` parameter is true, but setting this parameter to false allows the application to recover more gracefully from an expired `HttpSession`. If a user logs into the system and returns to the Home page, and then lets the session expire (by waiting 15 minutes or so) before submitting the search form, the application will still be able to perform the search, even though a new `HttpSession` will be created in the process and the user will no longer be logged in.

Leaving the `stateful` parameter in its default value, true, changes this scenario. When submitting the form after the session expires, Tapestry will recognize that the session is stale and throw a `StaleSessionException`. The `VirtualLibraryEngine` handles the `StaleSessionException` by returning the user to the Home page with a message about being logged out.[3] Although better than displaying the StaleSession page, it is still less than ideal, and is quite easy to avoid. There are times when it is better to leave the `stateful` parameter as true—for example, in forms that require the user to be logged in for the forms to operate.

---

[3] The default behavior in this case is normally to display the StaleSession page; the Virtual Library uses its own subclass of `BaseEngine` and overrides the engine method `handleStaleSessionException()` to instead redirect the user to the Home page with an error message.

10.3.1 Identifying application-specific components

The first thing you'll notice in the Home page template is that there isn't any HTML for the title bar that spans the top of each page, or for the navigation menu that runs down the left side. These common fixtures are entirely produced by the Border component, an application-specific component we'll discuss in a bit. The Border component is referenced in the `<body>` tag of the template.

In fact, all the templates in the application are minimal; they don't make more than a small effort to maintain WYSIWYG preview. The Home page's HTML template is a valid HTML file, but it does not reference a stylesheet. The end result is only a limited ability to preview the application using an HTML editor. Figure 10.5 shows what such a preview looks like.

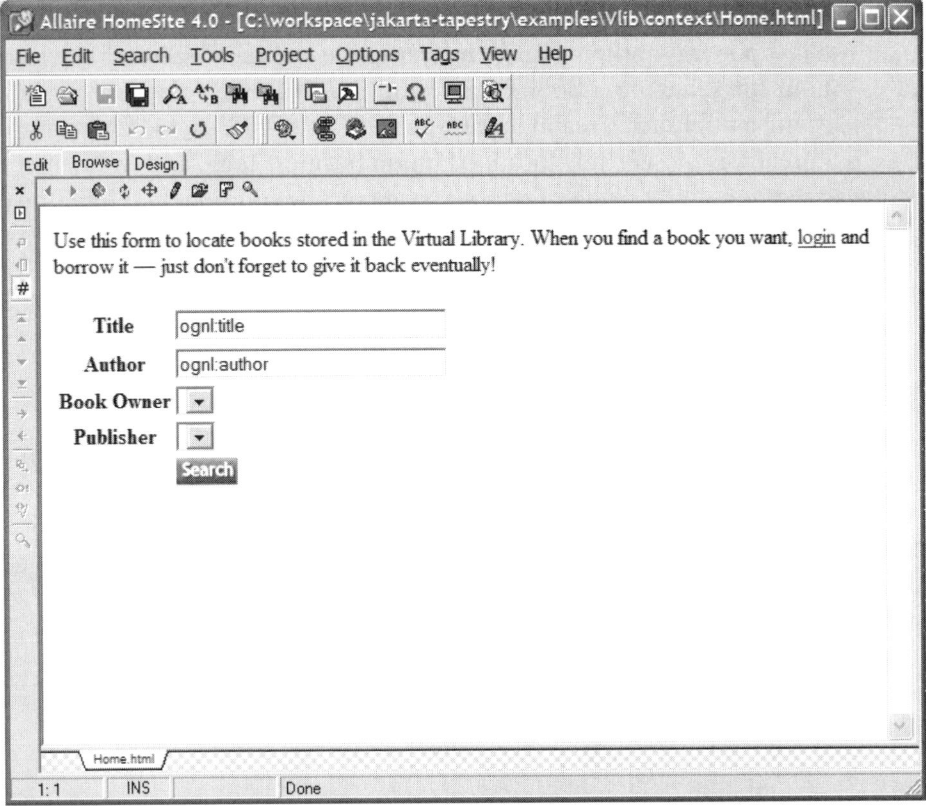

Figure 10.5 Previewing the Home page in a WYSIWYG editor is only a limited success. Navigational borders and stylesheet information are missing. Compare this to figure 9.1, taken from the live application.

Two other application-specific components are used in the template: ShowError and ShowMessage. They are used to display errors or informational messages. Figure 9.6 shows an example of the ShowError component (on the Login page), and figure 9.9 shows an example of the ShowMessage component.

These components don't take any parameters; they expect that the page implements an `error` property (for ShowError) or a `message` property (for ShowMessage). If you refer to figure 10.3, you'll see that there are two interfaces, `IErrorProperty` and `IMessageProperty`. These two interfaces define the accessor methods for the two properties. Java page classes that implement one or both interfaces include matching property specifications for the properties in the pages' specifications.

10.3.2 Referencing the engine

Two components in the template reference the engine: the PropertySelection component for selecting a book owner, and the PropertySelection component for selecting a publisher. Creating a custom subclass of `BaseEngine` for your application is a great way to centrally locate common business logic and utility methods in a way that is easily accessible from any page or any component. Here, the engine is being used to create property selection models for persons and publishers.

The inputOwner component uses the engine to build a model of all the users in the system:

```
<select jwcid="inputOwner@PropertySelection"
  value="ognl:ownerId"
  model="ognl:engine.buildPersonModel(true)"/>
```

The engine's `buildPersonModel()` method invokes the `Operations` bean to obtain this list of persons. It constructs and returns an `IPropertySelectionModel` instance. The argument, specified as true, indicates that an initial empty element should be included in the model. This is necessary in the user interface, because the user may not want to filter results by book owner at all.

Likewise, the inputPublisher component uses the engine to build a model for selecting a publisher:

```
<select jwcid="inputPublisher@PropertySelection"
  value="ognl:publisherId"
  model="ognl:engine.publisherModel"/>
```

Here, the engine provides a simple property that is an `IPropertySelectionModel` of all the publishers currently in the database. This model always includes an empty element (so that the user may choose not to filter by publisher).

10.3.3 Specifying the page class and properties

The meat of the page is the Form and form element components that collect the search terms from the user. Each of these form element components updates a property of the page, a property created at runtime from a `<property-specification>` in the Home page's page specification (see listing 10.3).

Listing 10.3 Home.page: specification for the Home page

```
<?xml version="1.0" encoding="UTF-8"?>
<!DOCTYPE page-specification PUBLIC
  "-//Apache Software Foundation//Tapestry Specification 3.0//EN"
  "http://jakarta.apache.org/tapestry/dtd/Tapestry_3_0.dtd">

<page-specification class="org.apache.tapestry.vlib.pages.Home">

  <property name="page-type" value="Search"/>

  <property-specification name="error"
    type="java.lang.String"/>
  <property-specification name="message"
    type="java.lang.String"/>

  <property-specification name="title"
    type="java.lang.String"/>
  <property-specification name="author"
    type="java.lang.String"/>
  <property-specification name="ownerId"
    type="java.lang.Integer"/>
  <property-specification name="publisherId"
    type="java.lang.Integer"/>

</page-specification>
```

Specifies page type for Border component

Specifies error property for IErrorProperty interface

Specifies message property for IMessageProperty interface

Specifies properties for user input

Part of the page specification is a piece of metadata needed by the Border component. Metadata is extra information that can be attached to a page or component specification. Each metadata property is in the form of a key-value pair (keys and values are strings). This information is read from the specification by the framework and is available to the application at runtime but is not used by Tapestry. Instead, it's used only by the application. Page and component specifications (as well as application and library specifications and many other elements within the specifications) support metadata in the form of `<property>` elements. A specification may have any number of metadata properties, with each value identified by a unique key. In this case, the metadata property is named `page-type`.

This metadata property is read by Border component; this is how it knows which page to display in the title bar and which images to use when displaying the navigation menu. Not all pages need it—just "rule-breakers" like the Home page (which needs to be labeled *Search*). When we discuss the Border component a bit later, you'll see exactly how this metadata property is used.

The rest of the page specification consists of property specifications used on the page. Because this page uses the ShowError component, the class implements the `IErrorProperty` interface, and a `<property-specification>` for the `error` property is included. Likewise, the ShowMessage component requires the `IMessageProperty` interface and a specification for the `message` property.

10.3.4 Performing searches

All of these templates, components, and specifications come together in the Home page's Java class. The class includes abstract accessor methods for the four properties supplied by the form control components (`title`, `author`, `ownerId`, and `publisherId`). The real work of performing a search is done in the BookMatches page. All that's left in the Home page's Java class is the listener method used to link the two pages together. This method, `search()`, is shown in listing 10.4.

Listing 10.4 The search() method of the Home class

```
public void search(IRequestCycle cycle)
{
  BookMatches matches =
    (BookMatches) cycle.getPage("BookMatches");

  MasterQueryParameters parameters =
    new MasterQueryParameters(getTitle(), getAuthor(),
      getOwnerId(), getPublisherId());

  matches.performQuery(parameters, cycle);
}
```

The `search()` method packages up the four search constraints (the title, the author, the owner, and the publisher) as an instance of `MasterQueryParameters`, then invokes the `performQuery()` method on the BookMatches page. `MasterQueryParameters` is simply a class for holding all the parameters for this search. It is easier and more extensible to pass a single object than four separate parameters.

The BookMatches page is responsible for taking it from there. It performs the query and then displays the results.

This basic Tapestry approach should start looking awfully familiar by now: Components on the page read and update properties of the page (often specified in the page's specification), then listener methods read those same properties and act on them, possibly invoking methods on other pages within the application or on other objects entirely.

10.4 Implementing the BookMatches page

The BookMatches page is quite a bit more complex than the Home page. It has to run the query against the database and present the results, complete with support for paging and column sorting. It must know if the user is logged in and support borrowing of books directly from the book listing.

The BookMatches page has four properties related to paging and sorting, identified in table 10.3. All four of these properties are persistent.

Table 10.3 Properties used for displaying a sorted list of books

Property	Type	Description
`bookQuery`	`org.apache.tapestry.vlib.ejb.IBookQuery`	Reference to `BookQuery` stateful session bean (remote interface)
`sortColumn`	`org.apache.tapestry.vlib.ejb.SortColumn`	Enum for defining which column to sort on
`descending`	`boolean`	Flag for ascending vs. descending sort
`queryParameters`	`org.apache.tapestry.vlib.MasterQueryParameters`	Defines constraints on query

The core of this page is the `bookQuery` property, which stores a reference to the remote interface of the `BookQuery` stateful session bean. The `BookQuery` bean performs one of several possible queries against the database, merging together data from the Book, Person, and Publisher entities.

The BookMatches page invokes the `BookQuery` bean's `masterQuery()` method, passing in the query parameters and the desired sort ordering (in terms of a column to sort on and a descending flag). The `BookQuery` bean constructs and executes a JDBC statement for the query, and then caches the complete result in memory, returning just the number of matching books. This result count is passed to the Browser component, which stores the count and computes the number of pages needed to display the results. Figure 10.6 identifies these steps.

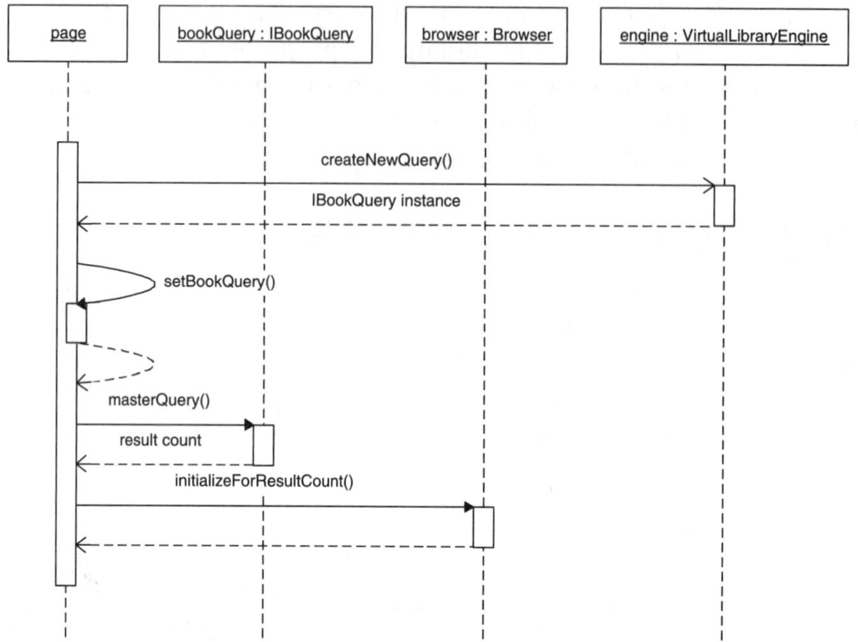

Figure 10.6 The page invokes `masterQuery()` and then informs the Browser component of the number of books.

The Browser component is responsible for handling pagination. It is also responsible for communicating with the `BookQuery` bean in order to obtain a subset of the full results that should be displayed on the current page. We cover this in greater detail shortly.

10.4.1 Handling paging and column sorting

So, what about re-sorting? To re-sort the list of books, the `sortColumn` and/or `descending` properties are updated, and the query is executed again. The `BookQuery` bean will then construct and execute a new JDBC statement and store a new set of results. When the page renders, the Browser component gets a subset of `Book` objects from the new set of cached results stored by the `BookQuery` bean.

At this point we have shown how to start a query, as well as how to handle things when the sort ordering changes, but we don't know how the links and icons appear in the user interface to trigger sort order changes. We also know that the Browser component somehow manages paging, but it isn't clear how the page navigation menu appears (figure 9.4). The answers to these questions are in the page's HTML template (shown in listing 10.5) and specification, and, of course, the answers involve components, methods, and properties.

Listing 10.5 BookMatches.html: HTML template for the BookMatches page

```
<html jwcid="$content$">
<body jwcid="@Border" title="Matching Books"
    browser="ognl:components.browser">

<table class="data">
  <tr>
    <th><span jwcid="sortTitle">Title</span></th>
    <th><span jwcid="sortAuthor">Author</span></th>
    <th><span jwcid="sortPublisher">Publisher</span></th>        ❶
    <th><span jwcid="sortOwner">Owner</span></th>
    <th><span jwcid="sortBorrower">Borrowed By</span></th>
    <th>Borrow</th>
  </tr>
    <tr jwcid="browser@Browser"
      query="ognl:bookQuery"
      value="ognl:currentMatch"                ❷
      listener="ognl:listeners.requery">
      <td><a href="#" jwcid="@BookLink" book="ognl:currentMatch">   ❸
          Swing Second Edition</a>
      </td>
      <td><span jwcid="@Insert" value="ognl:currentMatch.author">
          Robinson and Vorobiev</span>
      </td>
      <td><span jwcid="@Insert"
            value="ognl:currentMatch.publisherName">
          Manning</span>
      </td>
      <td><a jwcid="ownerLink" href="#">Jim Moran</a>
      </td>                                                         ❹
      <td><a jwcid="holderLink" href="#">Howard Lewis Ship</a>
      </td>
      <td class="icon"><a href="#" jwcid="@Borrow"
                       book="ognl:currentMatch">
          <img src="images/checkout.png" alt="Borrow"
             border="0" vspace="2"></a>
      </td>
    </tr>
</table>

</body>
</html>
```

❶ These components allow the columns to be sorted; they are fully declared in the page specification.

❷ The Browser component acts much like a Foreach component.

❸ The BookLink component creates a link to a particular book (the ViewBook page); the link may be bookmarked.

❹ These two components are PersonLink components, which create "bookmarkable" links to particular persons (in the ViewPerson page).

The pieces of the puzzle start falling together here. First we have an answer to the question of how the paging navigation controls appear. On this page, the `browser` parameter of the Border component is used; this appears in the HTML template:

```
<body jwcid="@Border" title="Matching Books"
    browser="ognl:components.browser">
```

Before (in chapter 5), we bound a ValidField component to the `field` parameter of a FieldLabel component; we can here bind a Browser component to the `browser` parameter of the Border component. This is another powerful and useful concept: components as parameters to other components. It allows different components (here the Border and Browser components) to cooperate with each other in a flexible and dynamic fashion.

The Border component's `browser` parameter is optional (remember, the Home page didn't specify a value, since there is no Browser component on the Home page). When the `browser` parameter is not bound to null, the Border component includes the paging navigation controls. Later we'll go into more detail on exactly how the Border and Browser components interact.

Next inside the HTML template are controls for updating the table's sort order. These appear in the header line of the table:

```
<th><span jwcid="sortTitle">Title</span></th>
<th><span jwcid="sortAuthor">Author</span></th>
<th><span jwcid="sortPublisher">Publisher</span></th>
<th><span jwcid="sortOwner">Owner</span></th>
<th><span jwcid="sortBorrower">Borrowed By</span></th>
```

As you can see, very little of the sorting functionality is specified in the template. The page specification will declare the five components (one for each sortable column) that control the sort order, so let's look at the relevant portions of the page specification. First, we define the two persistent properties for controlling the sort order, giving an initial value for the `sortOrder` property (the `descending` property will default to false):

```
<property-specification name="sortColumn"
  type="org.apache.tapestry.vlib.ejb.SortColumn"
  persistent="yes">
    @org.apache.tapestry.vlib.ejb.SortColumn@TITLE
  </property-specification>

<property-specification name="descending"
  type="boolean"
  persistent="yes"/>
```

The `SortColumn` class is an enumeration of the different columns that can be sorted in any of the queries supported by the `BookQuery` bean. Each of the ColumnSorter components will update the page's `sortColumn` property to a different value. The first of these components, used for sorting by title, binds the page's `sortColumn` and `descending` properties. We use the OGNL syntax for referencing a public static field of a class to ensure that the component and the page's Java class agree on names.

The definition of the sortTitle component within the page specification fills in the details of the communication between the component and the containing page:

```
<component id="sortTitle" type="ColumnSorter">
  <binding name="selected" expression="sortColumn"/>
  <binding name="sortColumn">
    @org.apache.tapestry.vlib.ejb.SortColumn@TITLE
  </binding>
  <binding name="descending" expression="descending"/>
  <binding name="listener" expression="listeners.requery"/>
</component>
```

The component type, ColumnSorter, is an application-specific component, just like the Border component. We'll discuss its implementation shortly. The ColumnSorter's `selected` parameter is bound to the `sortColumn` property of the page; this allows the `sortColumn` property to be updated when the ColumnSorter's link is clicked. Likewise, the ColumnSorter will read and update the `descending` property via its own `descending` parameter.

The `sortColumn` parameter of the ColumnSorter is bound to the value used to update the `selected` parameter when the link is clicked (this is a usage pattern similar to the `selected` and `tag` parameters of the Submit component, covered in chapter 3). Each of the components declared in the BookMatches page specification will use a different value for the `sortColumn` parameter, resulting in the page's `sortColumn` property being updated to a different value when the corresponding link is clicked.

Updating the `sortColumn` and `descending` properties does not, of itself, cause any change to the cached data stored within the `BookQuery` bean. It is necessary to force the BookQuery bean to perform a new query, using the updated sort ordering. This is the job of a listener method, as specified using the ColumnSorter's listener parameter. The listener is notified after the sortColumn and descending properties have been changed. The requery() method contains the code that runs the revised query (with the same query parameters but with a new sort ordering) in the BookQuery bean.

The other four columns are configured in the same way, with only the sortColumn parameter changing from one component to the next. In Tapestry page and component specifications, there's a shortcut for handling this kind of duplication within a specification, utilizing the copy-of attribute:

```
<component id="sortAuthor" copy-of="sortTitle">
  <binding name="sortColumn">
    @org.apache.tapestry.vlib.ejb.SortColumn@AUTHOR
  </binding>
</component>

<component id="sortPublisher" copy-of="sortTitle">
  <binding name="sortColumn">
    @org.apache.tapestry.vlib.ejb.SortColumn@PUBLISHER
  </binding>
</component>

<component id="sortOwner" copy-of="sortTitle">
  <binding name="sortColumn">
    @org.apache.tapestry.vlib.ejb.SortColumn@OWNER
  </binding>
</component>

<component id="sortBorrower" copy-of="sortTitle">
  <binding name="sortColumn">
    @org.apache.tapestry.vlib.ejb.SortColumn@HOLDER
  </binding>
</component>
```

Each of the other four components simply copies the component type and parameter bindings of the sortTitle component, then replaces the binding for the sortColumn parameter with a different binding, constructed around a different constant value.

Consider for a moment what we're putting together here; the page has a pair of properties that control the sort order for the book listing, but it doesn't know, and doesn't need to know, how these properties get set. At the same time, the sorting components have an almost independent life within the page: They use the knowledge of the current sort ordering (as expressed in that pair of properties) to decide how to render, and to decide what to do when the links they themselves generate are clicked. When all of this is tied together, the end result is columns that sort within the table—and all of this is completely reusable in other pages that also display a list of books (even when the columns displayed are somewhat different). That's a lot of reuse, so let's see how these other components are themselves used and implemented.

10.4.2 Using the Browser component

The Browser component is used, in the page's HTML template, in much the same way as a Foreach component. It wraps around a block of the template, which is repeatedly rendered:

```
<tr jwcid="browser@Browser"
  query="ognl:bookQuery"
  value="ognl:currentMatch"
  listener="ognl:listeners.requery">
  <td><a href="#" jwcid="@BookLink" book="ognl:currentMatch">
    Swing Second Edition</a>
  </td>
  <td><span jwcid="@Insert"
        value="ognl:currentMatch.author">
    Robinson and Vorobiev</span>
  </td>
  <td><span jwcid="@Insert"
        value="ognl:currentMatch.publisherName">
     Manning</span>
   </td>
   <td><a jwcid="ownerLink" href="#">Jim Moran</a>
   </td>
  <td><a jwcid="holderLink" href="#">Howard Lewis Ship</a>
  </td>
  <td class="icon"><a jwcid="@Borrow"
    book="ognl:currentMatch" href="#">
      <img src="images/checkout.png" alt="Borrow"
        border="0" vspace="2"></a>
  </td>
</tr>
```

The Browser is represented in the template as a `<tr>` element. It has three parameters. The first, `query`, is an instance of `IBookQuery` (the `BookQuery` bean's remote interface) from which a portion of the query result set (the list of books matching the query) can be obtained. This parameter fills a role similar to the Foreach component's `source` parameter.

The `value` parameter is used just like the Foreach component's `value` parameter: The property bound to the `value` parameter is updated just before the body of the Browser is rendered. On the BookMatches page, the `currentMatch` property is bound to the `value` parameter.

The last parameter, `listener`, is used only if there is a `RemoteException` communicating with the query. This could occur if the application server has discarded the `BookQuery` EJB due to lack of use. Whatever the reason, the `listener` parameter is used by the Browser component to request that the BookMatches page perform the query again. The `listener` parameter is connected to the same `requery()` method as the ColumnSorter components.

Three additional application-specific components are used on the page. The BookLink component creates a link to the ViewBook page for a particular Book. This link is built around the title of the book, and the URL for the link may be bookmarked (it makes use of the external service).

The PersonLink component does an equivalent job, creating a link to the ViewPerson page for a particular person. The URL for the link may also be bookmarked.

The last component is the Borrow component, which creates a link and icon for borrowing a book. The Borrow component contains the checks for whether the user is logged in and whether the user is already in possession of the book.

10.4.3 Executing queries and re-queries

Although the components on the page do most of the work, they can't quite do it all. The `BookMatches` class (shown in listing 10.6) is responsible for performing the actual query when the search form (on the Home page) is submitted or when a change in sort ordering occurs.

Listing 10.6 BookMatches.java: Java class for the BookMatches page

```
package org.apache.tapestry.vlib.pages;

import java.rmi.RemoteException;

import org.apache.tapestry.IRequestCycle;
import org.apache.tapestry.html.BasePage;
import org.apache.tapestry.vlib.IMessageProperty;
import org.apache.tapestry.vlib.VirtualLibraryEngine;
import org.apache.tapestry.vlib.components.Browser;
import org.apache.tapestry.vlib.ejb.IBookQuery;
import org.apache.tapestry.vlib.ejb.MasterQueryParameters;
import org.apache.tapestry.vlib.ejb.SortColumn;
import org.apache.tapestry.vlib.ejb.SortOrdering;

public abstract class BookMatches extends BasePage
{
  private Browser _browser;
```

```
public void finishLoad()
{
  _browser = (Browser) getComponent("browser");     <-- Stores reference to
}                                                       Browser component

public abstract IBookQuery getBookQuery();

public abstract void setBookQuery(IBookQuery bookQuery);

public abstract SortColumn getSortColumn();

public abstract boolean isDescending();

public abstract MasterQueryParameters getQueryParameters();

public abstract void setQueryParameters(
  MasterQueryParameters queryParameters);

public void performQuery(
  MasterQueryParameters parameters,
  IRequestCycle cycle)
{
  setQueryParameters(parameters);

  int count = executeQuery();

  if (count == 0)                                        Is invoked by
  {                                                      Home page
    IMessageProperty page =
      (IMessageProperty) cycle.getPage();
    page.setMessage(getMessage("no-matches"));
    return;
  }

  _browser.initializeForResultCount(count);
  cycle.activate(this);
}

public void requery(IRequestCycle cycle)
{
  int count = executeQuery();                            Is invoked when
                                                         sort order or
  if (count != _browser.getResultCount())                direction changes
    _browser.initializeForResultCount(count);
}

private int executeQuery()
{
  VirtualLibraryEngine vengine =
    (VirtualLibraryEngine) getEngine();
```

```
      MasterQueryParameters parameters = getQueryParameters();

      SortOrdering ordering = new SortOrdering(getSortColumn(),
        isDescending());

      int i = 0;
      while (true)
      {
        try
        {
          IBookQuery query = getBookQuery();

          if (query == null)
          {
            query = vengine.createNewQuery();
            setBookQuery(query);
          }

          return query.masterQuery(parameters,
            ordering);
        }
        catch (RemoteException ex)
        {
          vengine.rmiFailure(
            "Remote exception processing query.",
            ex, i++);

          setBookQuery(null);
        }
      }
    }
  }
```

Performs query (with retry loop)

Because the page must invoke methods on the Browser component in several places, a reference to the Browser component is kept in an instance variable, `_browser`. Previously we've said that your code should not store references to pages or components inside persistent page properties, and this requirement still holds. It is acceptable, as in this case, to keep a reference to a component within the *same* page hierarchy, as long as it is not stored persistently. This is just a simple optimization; the value stored in the `_browser` instance variable is the exact value that would be returned by invoking `getComponent("browser")`. This optimization removes the need for the method call and the typecast.

The appropriate place to create such a reference is within an implementation of the `finishLoad()` method. The `finishLoad()` method is invoked after the page has been created and configured, and all components for the page (specified either in the template or in the page specification) have also been instantiated and configured. This means that `finishLoad()` is invoked just once, and long before other methods, such as `render()`, are invoked.

The `performQuery()` method is invoked by the Home page to start a search. The method begins by storing the query parameters into the persistent `queryParameters` property. This property must be persistent because the parameters will be needed later, if a change in sort order occurs, so that the query can be executed with the new sort order.

The `executeQuery()` method executes the query and returns the result count, the number of books that matched the search query parameters. If the count is zero, the user is returned to the Home page with a message that there were no matches. The user can than modify the search parameters and attempt another search.

Normally, there will be at least one matching book. In that case, the Browser is informed of the new result count so that it can calculate the number of pages. Lastly, the current page, the BookMatches page, is activated as the response-rendering page to render the response to the client web browser.

The `requery()` method, invoked as a listener method by the ColumnSorter components, is even simpler. It invokes the `executeQuery()` method to perform the query with the updated sort ordering, then informs the Browser if the result count has changed. When the result count changes, the current page is always reset to 1, so it's best not to invoke the `initializeForPageCount()` method on the Browser instance unless the result count actually does change.

The leaves just the `executeQuery()` method itself. This method first assembles the parameters to the `BookQuery` beans' `masterQuery()` method: the `MasterQueryParameters` instance and a `SortOrdering` instance (built from the `sortColumn` and `descending` page properties).

Next, a reference to the `BookQuery` bean's remote interface is obtained, if needed. Since many pages utilize the `BookQuery` EJB, the code to find and create an instance is centralized in the `VirtualLibraryEngine` class. The method then executes the `masterQuery()` method on the bean and returns the result, the count of matching books.

The only complication is the retry loop, used to ride out any exceptions related to invoking the remote method on the `BookQuery` bean.[4] In the event

[4] In the deployed application, the presentation and application layers are in the same JVM, so `RemoteExceptions` are rare. This retry code is most useful when the layers are separate, which can frequently occur when testing.

of a `RemoteException`, the `VirtualLibraryEngine`'s `rmiFailure()` method is invoked. The attempt index (the variable `i`) is passed in. On the first attempt, the error is logged, and `rmiFailure()` returns, to allow a retry. On the second attempt, an actual failure occurs, and the user will see an exception report page. This approach to `RemoteException` recovery recurs throughout the Virtual Library application.

Also, on a failure, the `BookQuery` bean reference is discarded, forcing a new `BookQuery` bean to be obtained from the engine. This addresses the most likely cause of a `RemoteException`: that the `BookQuery` bean, a stateful session bean, has been discarded by the application server due to lack of use. Invoking methods on a discarded remote reference results in a `RemoteException` that can be rectified by creating a new instance of the EJB.

Here robustness and usability go hand in hand. The user should not need to know that the application uses stateful session beans, or that such beans may be discarded by the application server even as the rest of the application continues to run. Instead, the user will get the results they expect: Clicking on the column titles will re-sort the columns. Building this level of robustness into a Tapestry application takes care and some foresight but is quite manageable. This is one area where the framework's advantages shine: Because all the Java code is inside real Java classes (as opposed to scriptlets inside a JSP), it is possible to write robust, well-organized code. As we continue looking at the other components and objects inside the Virtual Library, you'll see how these individual islands of code work together to form a robust whole.

10.5 Implementing the Browser component

The Browser component is an integral part of several pages in the application: BookMatches, MyLibrary, BorrowedBooks, and ViewPerson. Each of these pages works with its own instance of the `BookQuery` bean to present a list of books. Each one supports paging access to the overall list of books, and each supports sorting by column.

10.5.1 Specifying Browser's parameters

The Browser component is half of the paging navigation equation; it is the half that actively communicates with the `BookQuery` bean, as a part of the page that contains it, and renders a subset of the query results cached by the bean.

Listing 10.7 Browser.jwc: specification for the Browser component

```
<?xml version="1.0" encoding="UTF-8"?>
<!DOCTYPE component-specification PUBLIC
  "-//Apache Software Foundation//Tapestry Specification 3.0//EN"
  "http://jakarta.apache.org/tapestry/dtd/Tapestry_3_0.dtd">

<component-specification
  allow-informal-parameters="yes"
  class="org.apache.tapestry.vlib.components.Browser">

  <parameter name="query"
    required="yes"
    type="org.apache.tapestry.vlib.ejb.IBookQuery"
    direction="auto"/>

  <parameter name="value"
    type="java.lang.Object"
    required="yes"
    direction="auto"/>

  <parameter name="element"
    type="java.lang.String"
    direction="in"/>

  <parameter name="listener"
    type="org.apache.tapestry.IActionListener"
    required="yes"
    direction="auto"/>

  <property-specification name="resultCount"
    type="int"
    persistent="yes"/>
  <property-specification name="currentPage
    type="int"
    persistent="yes"/>
  <property-specification
    name="pageCount" type="int"
    persistent="yes"/>
  <property-specification name="pageResults"
    type="java.lang.Object[]"/>

</component-specification>
```

The component specification for the Browser component, shown in listing 10.7, declares the three parameters we've previously discussed, as well as an additional parameter, `element`, which controls the HTML element that will be used when rendering the component (the default for which is `tr`). The `query`, `value`, and listener parameters all use the auto value for their direction attribute, for reasons we'll cover shortly.

In addition, several properties are declared. The resultCount, pageCount, and currentPage properties are persistent. These properties store the total number of books in the query, the number of pages required to display all the books, and the current page (numbered from 1) within the range of pages.

The final property, pageResults, is not persistent. It is an array of Book objects, the Books to display on the current page. It may not immediately be obvious why this is necessary—it's related to error recovery mixed with persistent page properties.

10.5.2 Getting results from the BookQuery bean

The Browser component must invoke the get() method of the BookQuery bean to obtain the results for the current page, but as we've discussed, the request may fail for a number of reasons. When the request fails, the Browser notifies its listener, which will in all likelihood create a new BookQuery bean instance and update the persistent property used to store the reference to the bean's remote interface.

There's the problem: Updates to persistent properties are not allowed once the rendering of a response has started (this is covered in detail in chapter 7). Therefore, the access to the BookQuery bean must occur *before* the page renders, since it is possible that the persistent property storing the reference to the bean will change.

This is accomplished by having the Browser component implement the PageRenderListener interface. The pageBeginRender() method is invoked before the page starts to render, when it is still allowable to change persistent properties. The page results, obtained from the BookQuery bean, are stored in the pageResults property at this point, as shown in figure 10.7. Later, when the Browser component renders, the results will be ready and waiting in that property.

The pageBeginRender() method includes the same kind of retry loop used by the BookMatches page. In this case, the recovery from a RemoteException accessing the BookQuery bean will invoke the listener method to perform a new query. This will result in a second execution of the loop, and getQuery() will return the new BookQuery bean instance. The results obtained from the BookQuery bean are then stored in the pageResults property.

This method is invoked outside the normal rendering of the component. Therefore, the connected parameter properties that are referenced in the method (query and listener) must specify a direction attribute of auto, not in.

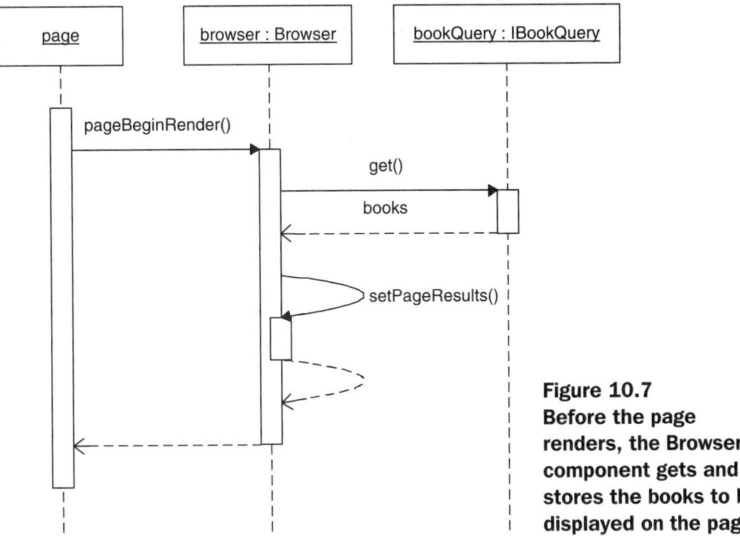

Figure 10.7 Before the page renders, the Browser component gets and stores the books to be displayed on the page.

10.5.3 Rendering the Browser component

All this work in the `pageBeginRender()` method means that the `renderComponent()` method (provided in listing 10.8) is very simple. All it has to do is obtain the array of books as stored in the `pageResults` property and repeatedly render its body, updating its `value` parameter for each `Book` object provided by the `BookQuery` bean.

Listing 10.8 The renderComponent() method of the Browser class

```
protected void renderComponent(IMarkupWriter writer,
  IRequestCycle cycle)
{
  Object[] books = getPageResults();
  int count = Tapestry.size(books);
  String element = getElement();

  for (int i = 0; i < count; i++)
  {
    setValue(books[i]);

    if (element != null)
    {
      writer.begin(element);
      renderInformalParameters(writer, cycle);
    }

    renderBody(writer, cycle);
```

```
    if (element != null)
      writer.end();
  }
}
```

Because the value parameter's direction attribute is auto, each time the property is updated (using the setValue() method), the bound property of the page (the currentMatch property for the BookMatches page) will be updated. The other components on the page read the currentMatch property (or properties nested within it) when rendering.

That covers how the query is created, accessed, and rendered. The next section delves into how the page's sortColumn and descending properties are updated, which is encapsulated inside the ColumnSorter component.

10.6 Implementing the ColumnSorter component

Continuing our tour of the BookMatches page, we'll next visit the ColumnSorter component. This component is responsible for making the column titles on the page clickable links. Clicking a link will sort the selected column in ascending order—unless the column was already the selected column, in which case clicking a link will toggle between ascending and descending order.

In addition, the selected column gets an icon next to the title that indicates whether the column is sorted in ascending order or descending order. The title text comes from the body of the ColumnSorter component.

The ColumnSorter component leverages Tapestry's component-level request dispatching; it's a component that contains components, and these internal components have interactions with the end user that the containing page is completely unaware of!

10.6.1 Creating the ColumnSorter HTML template

The template for the ColumnSorter component (shown in listing 10.9) is primarily an <a> link element wrapped around a RenderBody component. Beyond that, the template includes additional elements that display the sort icon.

Listing 10.9 ColumnSorter.html: HTML template for the ColumnSorter component

```
<a jwcid="link"><span jwcid="@RenderBody"/></a>
<span jwcid="@Conditional" condition="ognl:sortColumn == selected">
<a jwcid="iconLink"><img jwcid="rollover"
    width="17" height="16"
```

```
    alt="Resort Column"/></a>
</span>
```

If the selected `SortColumn` for the page matches the `SortColumn` for this ColumnSorter component, then the second link and the matching icon are also displayed. Using two separate links is necessary only for presentation reasons. If a single link enclosed the RenderBody component, the Conditional component, and the icon, then there would be a visible, underlined space between the page title and the icon.

The specification for the ColumnSorter component defines the two links and introduces a new type of component, Rollover. Rollover is another component provided with the framework. It is a special version of the Image component that must be enclosed by some kind of Tapestry link component (here it is the DirectLink component, but it could be PageLink or ExternalLink). The Rollover component performs mouse rollover effects; that is, the image changes when the user moves the cursor over the image, and changes back when the cursor is moved off it. This provides additional feedback to the user about which elements on the page may be clicked. Rollover components are used throughout the Virtual Library application.

10.6.2 Specifying ColumnSorter parameters

The specification for the component (in listing 10.10) declares all the parameters for the ColumnSorter, as well as the assets used for the sort icon.

Listing 10.10 ColumnSorter.jwc: specification for the ColumnSorter component

```
<?xml version="1.0" encoding="UTF-8"?>
<!DOCTYPE component-specification PUBLIC
  "-//Apache Software Foundation//Tapestry Specification 3.0//EN"
  "http://jakarta.apache.org/tapestry/dtd/Tapestry_3_0.dtd">

<component-specification
  class="org.apache.tapestry.vlib.components.ColumnSorter"
  allow-body="yes" allow-informal-parameters="no">

  <parameter name="selected"
    type="org.apache.tapestry.vlib.ejb.SortColumn"
    required="yes"
    direction="auto"/>
  <parameter name="descending"
    type="boolean"
    required="yes"
```

```
      direction="auto"/>
    <parameter name="sortColumn"
      type="org.apache.tapestry.vlib.ejb.SortColumn"
      required="yes"
      direction="auto"/>
    <parameter name="listener"
      type="org.apache.tapestry.IActionListener"
      required="yes"
      direction="auto"/>

    <component id="link" type="DirectLink">
      <binding name="listener" expression="listeners.handleClick"/>
    </component>

    <component id="iconLink" copy-of="link"/>      <- Copies link as iconLink

    <component id="rollover" type="Rollover">
      <binding name="image">
        descending ? assets.down : assets.up
      </binding>
      <binding name="focus">
        descending ? assets.down_h : assets.up_h
      </binding>
    </component>                                     Defines a Rollover for the icon

    <context-asset name="up" path="images/sort-up.png"/>
    <context-asset name="up_h" path="images/sort-up_h.png"/>
    <context-asset name="down" path="images/sort-down.png"/>
    <context-asset name="down_h" path="images/sort-down_h.png"/>

  </component-specification>
```

A Rollover component has four parameters for specifying image assets to be used with the component. The three common parameters are `image`, `focus`, and `disabled`. The `image` parameter specifies the image the application should normally display and is the only required parameter. The `focus` parameter specifies the image to display when the mouse is moved over the image.[5] The `disabled` parameter specifies the image the application should display when the link enclosing the Rollover component is disabled (in which case the Rollover component does not react to the mouse). A fourth parameter, `blur`, specifies the

[5] This is another example of a less-than-ideal name getting wedged into the framework. Changing the parameter name to something like "mouseOver" would make sense, but that would break too many existing components and applications.

image to use when the mouse is moved out from over the image (there's rarely a reason for this to not be the same as the `image` parameter, so it's usually omitted).

The upshot of this is that it is easy to create clickable image buttons that have dynamic rollover effects. It is simply a matter of defining the necessary assets. The convention used in the Virtual Library is to add an `_h` suffix to the name of an asset to indicate a highlighted version of an image—one appropriate as a mouse-over image (shown here as the `focus` parameter).

The specification declares four image assets: two versions of the up arrow and two of the down arrow. The bindings for the Rollover component dynamically determine which assets to use for the `image` and `focus` parameters based on whether the sort order is ascending or descending. Once again, the use of OGNL expressions allows for a succinct, readable solution to the problem of selecting the correct assets.

10.6.3 Responding to the user

All that's left is a listener method to handle things when either link is clicked. The same listener method, `handleClick()` (in listing 10.11), is invoked by both links.

Listing 10.11 The handleClick() method of the ColumnSorter class

```
public void handleClick(IRequestCycle cycle)
{
  SortColumn selected = getSelected();
  SortColumn sortColumn = getSortColumn();

  if (selected != sortColumn)
  {
    setSelected(sortColumn);
    setDescending(false);
  }
  else
  {
    boolean current = isDescending();
    setDescending(!current);
  }

  IActionListener listener = getListener();
  if (listener == null)
    throw Tapestry.createRequiredParameterException(this,
      "listener");

  listener.actionTriggered(this, cycle);
}
```

The `handleClick()` method first checks to see if the currently selected SortColumn matches the `sortColumn` parameter for this ColumnSorter component. If so, the `descending` parameter is inverted. If it is a non-match, meaning the user has selected as new column as the column to sort, then the `sortColumn` parameter is updated to the correct value, and the `descending` parameter is set to false.

In either case, the listener method is invoked. As you saw in the BookMatches page, the listener method's job is to force the query to be executed again with the updated sort ordering.

The final piece of the Browser puzzle is the browser navigation controls (which are shown in figure 9.4). Presenting these controls on a page demands cooperation between the Browser component and the Border component.

10.7 Implementing the Border component

At this point, we have enough of the pieces of the application to discuss how to construct the Border component. A considerable amount of the look and feel of the application, as well as its functionality, is tied up in this single component. This Border component is responsible for displaying the proper page title (across the top of the page), the main navigation menu on the left (which adjusts to reflect the page and the user), and an optional page navigation menu for pages that use a Browser component (shown in figure 9.4). In fact, the Border component is considerably larger and more complicated than any of the pages that use it.

Most of the Border component's behavior is concerned with the navigation menu. The menu is dynamic in several ways:

- All the images in the menu are rollover buttons, highlighting as the mouse is moved over them.
- The current page is displayed with an alternate image incorporating a small arrow.
- The My Library menu items appear only once the user has logged in.
- Virtual Library application administrators will see three additional menu items.
- The final option in the menu may be Login or Logout depending on whether the user has, in fact, authenticated (logged in or registered).

Despite this highly dynamic nature at runtime, the implementation of the Border component is extremely straightforward. Each menu item consists of a link

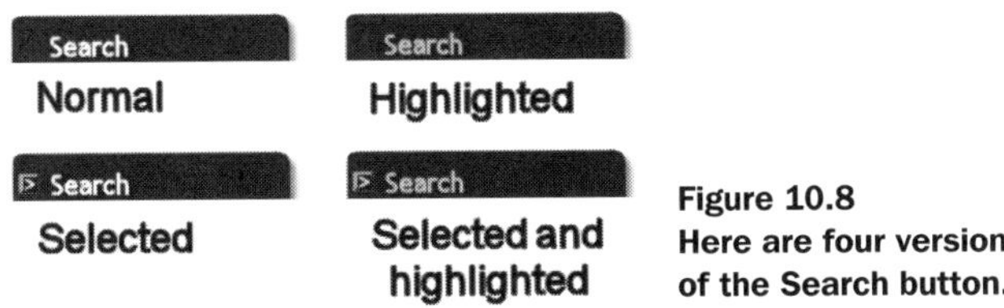

Figure 10.8
Here are four versions of the Search button.

and an image in the HTML template and the specification, plus additional assets for the various button images. For example, the first menu item is the Search link. This link is represented by four images, shown in figure 10.8. One pair of images (either the normal and highlighted, or the selected and selected highlighted) will be used. On a Search-related page (Home, BookMatches, ViewBook, and ViewPerson), the second pair of images will be used. The arrow in the image indicates that the user is in the "Search" section of the application. When other pages render, such as MyLibrary or Login, the first pair of images is used.

In the Border component's HTML template, menu item appears as some form of link component and a Rollover component (both are declared components):

```
<a href="#" jwcid="search"><img
   jwcid="searchRollover" src="images/nav/nav_1x1.png"
   width="178" height="29" border="0" alt="Search"/></a>
```

The Border component's specification includes these two components, along with the four assets for the Search button image:

```
<component id="search" type="PageLink">
  <static-binding name="page" value="Home"/>
</component>

<component id="searchRollover" type="Rollover">
  <binding name="image" expression="searchImage"/>
  <binding name="focus" expression="searchRolloverImage"/>
</component>

<context-asset name="search" path="images/nav/nav_1x1.png"/>
<context-asset name="search_h" path="images/nav-h/nav_1x1.png"/>
<context-asset name="search_s"
  path="images/nav-selected/nav_1x1.png"/>
<context-asset name="search_h_s"
  path="images/nav-selected-h/nav_1x1.png"/>
```

To simplify things, the names of the assets use an `_h` suffix to indicate a highlighted image and an `_s` suffix for the selected image. The Rollover component does not reference the assets directly; instead, it references two properties of the Border component: `searchImage` and `searchRolloverImage`. These properties are computed when the `Border` class, the Java class for the Border component, is instantiated, inside the `finishLoad()` method. Listing 10.12 includes a portion of the Java code for the `Border` class that illustrates this process.

Listing 10.12 Border.java (partial): Java class for the Border component

```
private String _pageType;
private IAsset _titleImage;
private IAsset _searchImage;
private IAsset _searchRolloverImage;

public void finishLoad()
{
  IPage page = getPage();

  String pageName = page.getPageName();

  _pageType = page.getSpecification().
    getProperty("page-type");

  if (_pageType == null)
    _pageType = pageName;

  _titleImage = getAsset("title_" + pageName);

  if (_titleImage == null)
    _titleImage = getAsset("title_" + _pageType);

  if (_titleImage == null)
    throw new ApplicationRuntimeException(
      "Cannot find title image for " + pageName +
      " or " + _pageType + ".",
      this);

  _searchImage = selectImage("Search", "search");
  _searchRolloverImage = selectImage("Search", "search_h");

  . . .
}

private IAsset selectImage(String type, String baseName)
{
  String key = _pageType.equals(type)
    ? baseName + "_s"
    : baseName;

  return getAsset(key);
}
```

Retrieves page-type property from page's specification

Uses page's name as default for page type

Finds normal or selected asset

```
  public IAsset getTitleImage()
  {
    return _titleImage;
  }

  public IAsset getSearchImage()
  {
    return _searchImage;
  }

  public IAsset getSearchRolloverImage()
  {
    return _searchRolloverImage;
  }
```

Provides read-only property referenced in template

The `finishLoad()` method is responsible for adapting the Border component to the page that contains it—this method precalculates a number of properties that are referenced in the component's template and specification. Each page instance will contain its own copy of the Border component—the Border component on the Home page is a completely separate instance from the Border component on the MatchingBooks page, for example. Because Tapestry components are stateful objects, we can precalculate and store the information that will be needed later (when the component renders), which is much more efficient and straightforward than having to calculate all that information on the fly.

The `finishLoad()` method starts by determining the page type for the current page. If the page's specification has a `<property>` for name `page-type`, then that is used as the page type. Otherwise, the page's name is the page type. In most cases, the page type matches the page name, but there are a few rule breakers, such as the Home and BookMatches pages (which define their `page-type` as `Search`).

Next, `finishLoad()` determines the title image to use for the page. If there's an image asset whose name matches the name of the page, then that image is used. Otherwise, the image matching the page type is used.

After that, the `selectImage()` method is used to find the correct image asset to use for the normal and highlighted versions of the Search button. The `selectImage()` method appends an `_s` suffix to the base asset name when the current page type matches the `type` parameter. In the actual class, this continues for each of the many dynamic images used in the navigation menu.

10.7.1 Handling user login

The Border component includes a Login menu item, which allows the user to log into the system (possibly registering on the fly) and, after authenticating, return to the current page. This is useful on pages such as BookMatches, ViewBook, and ViewPerson, since after logging in, the user returns to the same page and is able to borrow a book.

This is accomplished using a DirectLink component and a listener method, `login()`. The source for this method is shown in listing 10.13.

Listing 10.13 The `login()` method of the `Border` class

```
public void login(IRequestCycle cycle)
{
  Visit visit = (Visit) cycle.getEngine().getVisit();

  if (visit != null && visit.isUserLoggedIn())
    return;

  ICallback callback = new PageCallback(getPage().getPageName());
  Login loginPage = (Login) cycle.getPage("Login");
  loginPage.setCallback(callback);
  cycle.activate(loginPage);
}
```

The `login()` listener method checks to see if the user is already logged in. If so, the method returns, and the active page is redisplayed. If the user has not already logged in, the Login page is invoked to allow the user to log in.

The interesting part is how we set up the Login page returns to return to the current page after the user login process is complete. The Login page has a property, `callback`, of the type `ICallback`. `ICallback` is an interface provided with the framework, which exists for just this purpose: to define in an abstract way how to continue after some form of interruption. In this case, the interruption is logging into the application. The interface and a base set of implementations exist specifically to handle common use cases such as logging in, registering, and entering optional addresses into a form. Here, that interruption is authenticating the user, either by logging in or by registering.

The implementation used, `PageCallback`, will activate the named page (invoking the `IRequestCycle` object's `activate()` method), which is what we want in this situation. As you'll see when we cover the Login page in detail, the callback returns users to where they started once they are authenticated.

10.7.2 Linking to MyLibrary

The MyLibrary page displays a list of books owned by the logged-in user. Like the BookMatches page, it must construct and manage a reference to a `BookQuery` bean. Unlike the Home page, which can be rendered at any time, the MyLibrary page must be initialized before it can render.

Two other pages in the application are similar: BorrowedBooks and Edit-Profile. Each has an initialization stage that must occur before the page can be rendered the first time. For the Virtual Library, an interface, `IActivate`, exists for these three pages. This allows all three pages to be treated similarly by the Border component.[6]

At the same time, it is necessary to log the user in, on the fly, before rendering the MyLibrary page. The link to the MyLibrary page is a DirectLink, and the listener method is `viewMyLibrary()`. This listener method simply invokes another method, `activate()`, to do the work (the `Border` class includes other listener methods that invoke `activate()` with different parameters, supporting several other menu items). Both of these methods are shown in listing 10.14.

Listing 10.14 The `viewMyLibrary()` and `activate()` methods of the `Border` class

```
public void viewMyLibrary(IRequestCycle cycle)
{
  activate("MyLibrary", cycle);
}

private void activate(String pageName, IRequestCycle cycle)
{
  IActivate page = (IActivate) cycle.getPage(pageName);

  page.validate(cycle);

  page.activate(cycle);
}
```

The `viewMyLibrary()` and `activate()` methods obtain the MyLibrary page and invoke its `validate()` method. If `validate()` does not throw an exception, then the page's `activate()` method (as defined by the `IActivate` interface) is invoked.

---

6 Another option, which is completely reasonable, would be to create a new type of service for activating such pages. The service could be similar to the page service but also cast the page to `IActivate` and invoke the `activate()` method. If we were to pursue such an approach, we would also create an ActivateLink component.

The MyLibrary class includes an implementation of the activate() method, shown in listing 10.15.

Listing 10.15 The activate() method of the MyLibrary class

```
public void activate(IRequestCycle cycle)
{
  runQuery();

  cycle.activate(this);
}
```

This purpose of this implementation of the activate() method is to execute the query of books owned by the logged-in user (that's primarily what's shown on the MyLibrary page: a listing of books the logged-in user owns) and then set the MyLibrary page as the active page (so that it can render the response). Like the BookMatches page, the MyLibrary page uses its own instance of the BookQuery bean and has its own set of Browser and ColumnSorter components.

The final piece of the puzzle is to force the user to be logged in before activating the MyLibrary page. This comes from ActivatePage, the super class of MyLibrary. ActivatePage is a base implementation of the IActivate interface. ActivatePage also implements the PageValidateListener interface; it includes an implementation of the pageValidate() method that checks whether the user is logged in and, if not, uses the Login page to get the user logged in. Listing 10.16 provides the source code for this method.

Listing 10.16 The pageValidate() method of the ActivatePage class

```
public void pageValidate(PageEvent event)
{
  Visit visit = (Visit) getVisit();

  if (visit != null && visit.isUserLoggedIn())
    return;

  Login login = (Login) getRequestCycle().getPage("Login");

  login.setCallback(new ActivateCallback(this));

  throw new PageRedirectException(login);
}
```

Throwing a `PageRedirectException` forces Tapestry to activate the specified page and use it to render the response, regardless of what the active engine service would normally do. The `ActivateCallback` class implements `ICallback` and is used to invoke `activate()` on a page that implements the `IActivate` interface.

This combination—the listener method in the Border component and the methods in the `MyLibrary` and `ActivatePage` classes—ensures that the MyLibrary page will render only after the user has successfully logged in and that the MyLibrary page will be allowed to initialize properly before being rendered. The same protections also apply to the other (similar) pages, BorrowedBooks and EditProfile.

Before users can access these protected pages, the application must provide a way to authenticate them.

10.8 Authenticating the user

Authentication of the user involves

- Collecting the user's email address and password and validating them against the database

or

- Collecting registration information and registering the user in the database

After login or registration, the process returns the user to the correct page.

As you've seen with the MyLibrary page, the `pageValidate()` method is responsible for both directing the user to the Login page and telling the Login page how to continue after the user is authenticated. The base class `Protected` also implements the `pageValidate()` method (shown in listing 10.17); this method is used by pages such as the NewBook page (whose Java class extends from `Protected`) that are only available to authenticated users but do not require the initialization stage mandated by the `IActivate` interface.

The `Protected` class's implementation of the `pageValidate()` method is similar to the implementation of `pageValidate()` in the `ActivatePage` class, except that the callback is an instance of `PageCallback`, not `ActivateCallback`. Using the `PageCallback` class is appropriate for pages that don't implement the `IActivate` interface.

Listing 10.17 The `pageValidate()` method of the `Protected` class

```
public void pageValidate(PageEvent event)
{
  Visit visit = (Visit) getVisit();
```

```
    if (visit != null && visit.isUserLoggedIn())
      return;

    Login login = (Login) getRequestCycle().getPage("Login");

    login.setCallback(new PageCallback(this));

    throw new PageRedirectException(login);
  }
```

Here again, the `Visit` object is accessed to see if the user has already authenticated. If not, the Login page is rendered, with a callback to return the user to the current page.

10.8.1 Remembering the user

When users launch the application at a later date, the correct email address will be filled out for them and they'll just have to enter a password. This is a natural use for an HTTP cookie. Although Tapestry applications can be coded without referencing the Servlet API, you are not prevented from doing so; the Login page uses portions of the Servlet API to read and set an HTTP cookie that records the identity of the user for later sessions.

The Login page implements the `PageRenderListener` interface so that it may be notified when it is about to render. The `pageBeginRender()` method checks to see if the email address is null and supplies a default value from the HTTP cookie.

The initialization code in listing 10.18 is balanced with code that records the cookie after a successful login, which is shown in listing 10.19 in the next section.

Listing 10.18 The `pageBeginRender()` method of the `Login` class

```
private static final String COOKIE_NAME =
  "org.apache.tapestry.vlib.Login.email";

public void pageBeginRender(PageEvent event)
{
  if (getEmail() == null)
    setEmail(
      getRequestCycle().getRequestContext().
      getCookieValue(COOKIE_NAME));
}
```

10.8.2 Clearing the password field

When a form within a page is submitted and the page redisplayed, normally the TextField and ValidField components within the page redisplay the input that was supplied by the end user. For TextField, the input is stored in a page property when the form is submitted and then read from the same property when the component renders. ValidField does the same, with the extra step of recording user input exactly as supplied by the user. This input will be used if the user makes an error (for instance, entering a string value into a numeric field).

This is not desirable for the password field. On a login form, if the user enters an incorrect password, the password field should be cleared, forcing the user to reenter the correct password from scratch. Because a ValidField component is used to handle the password, an extra step is needed beyond simply setting the page's `password` property to null.

Listing 10.19 The `attemptLogin()` and `loginUser()` methods of the `Login` class

```
public void attemptLogin(IRequestCycle cycle)
{
  String password = getPassword();

  setPassword(null);
  IValidationDelegate delegate =
    getValidationDelegate();

  delegate.setFormComponent(
    (IFormComponent) getComponent("inputPassword"));
  delegate.recordFieldInputValue(null);

  if (delegate.getHasErrors())
    return;

  VirtualLibraryEngine vengine =
    (VirtualLibraryEngine) getEngine();

  int i = 0;
  while (true)
  {
    try
    {
      IOperations operations =
        vengine.getOperations();

      Person person =
        operations.login(getEmail(), password);
```

Clears password field (annotation for `setPassword(null);` through `delegate.recordFieldInputValue(null);`)

Performs login using Operations bean (annotation for `IOperations operations =` through `operations.login(getEmail(), password);`)

```
        loginUser(person, cycle);           <-- Completes login

        break;
      }
      catch (LoginException ex)
      {
        String fieldName =
          ex.isPasswordError()
          ? "inputPassword"
          : "inputEmail";

        setErrorField(fieldName, ex.getMessage());
        return;
      }
      catch (RemoteException ex)
      {
        vengine.rmiFailure(
          "Remote exception validating user.",
          ex, i++);
      }
    }
  }

  public void loginUser(Person person, IRequestCycle cycle)
  throws RemoteException
  {
    String email = person.getEmail();

    Visit visit = (Visit) getVisit();
    visit.setUser(person);                  <-- Stores logged-in user in Visit

    ICallback callback = getCallback();

    if (callback == null)                   Returns to previously active page
      cycle.activate("Home");
    else
      callback.performCallback(cycle);

    IEngine engine = getEngine();           Stores cookie in client's browser
    Cookie cookie = new Cookie(COOKIE_NAME, email);
    cookie.setPath(engine.getServletPath());
    cookie.setMaxAge(ONE_WEEK);

    cycle.getRequestContext().addCookie(cookie);

    engine.forgetPage(getPageName());       <-- Discards persistent properties
  }
```

The validation delegate stores the input value, the exact value supplied by the user, for each ValidField. For the password field to be rendered as empty, it is necessary to override the value supplied by the user with null. This can be seen at the beginning of the `attemptLogin()` method (listing 10.19). Overriding the validation delegate's stored value and setting the page's `password` property to null ensures that if the page is rendered again (for example, if the password is not valid or if the email address is not known), the password field will be empty.

10.8.3 Invoking the login operation

The remainder of the login form's listener obtains a reference to the `Operations` bean and invokes the `login()` method on it. This method may throw a `LoginException` if the email address is unknown or the password is invalid (as a convenience for the presentation layer, this exception includes a flag indicating whether the error should be attributed to the password).

After the user is successfully authenticated, the listener method invokes the `loginUser()` method to finalize the login. This includes using the `callback` property to return to the original page where the user clicked the Login (or My Library) menu item.

After the callback is invoked, the Login page calls the `forgetPage()` method on the engine. This method discards all persistent properties for the page—in this case, the single persistent property, `callback`. Using the `forgetPage()` method is the correct way to fully eliminate persistent state that is no longer necessary. For this application, once the callback is utilized, there's no longer any need to store it.

The `loginUser()` method is public because it is also used by the Register page. After a user registers, the `loginUser()` method is used to store the user's identity in the `Visit` object and invoke the callback, just as if the user already existed and had simply logged in.

We've set the stage now for protecting pages by restricting them to logged-in users, and we've given users the ability to log in or register on the fly. Now let's look at a way to store links to selected pages and data as web browser bookmarks.

10.9 Creating bookmarkable links

Links to both books and persons appear throughout the Virtual Library application. Every book and person listed on the BookMatches, BorrowedBooks, ViewPerson, and ViewBook pages appears as a link to either the ViewBook or ViewPerson page (as appropriate).

These links are "bookmarkable," meaning that they may be saved in a user's bookmark list indefinitely. Bookmarkable links can be created using the external service, and they are expected to be retrieved at a later date—unlike links created with the direct service (using the DirectLink component), which are expected to be used only within a single application session.

Generally, external service links are created using the ExternalLink component. The ExternalLink component will only generate the link itself; by wrapping the ExternalLink inside an application-specific component, it is possible to generate the text inside the link as well.

10.9.1 Creating the BookLink component

The BookLink component creates a link to the ViewBook page. The component has a single parameter, `book`, of the type `Book`. The component's template inserts the `Book`'s title inside a link. It also checks to see whether the book is new; new books are marked with an additional icon. The HTML template for this component is shown in listing 10.20.

Listing 10.20 BookLink.html: HTML template for the BookLink component

```
<a href="#" jwcid="link"><span
  jwcid="@Insert" value="ognl:book.title"/></a>
<span jwcid="@Conditional"
  condition="ognl:newlyAdded"><img src="images/new.png"
    width="27" height="12" border="0" alt="New"></span>
```

The decision on whether a book is "new" is complicated by the fact that the user may not yet be logged in. Normally, only books added since the user's last visit are considered new. If the user hasn't logged in, then anything added in the previous week is considered new. This logic is encapsulated in the `isNewlyAdded()` method (listing 10.21) of the `BookLink` class.

Listing 10.21 The `isNewlyAdded()` method of the `BookLink` class

```
private static final long ONE_WEEK_MILLIS =
  1000l * 60l * 60l * 24l * 7l;

public boolean isNewlyAdded()
{
  IEngine engine = getPage().getEngine();
  Visit visit = (Visit) engine.getVisit();
  Timestamp lastAccess = null;
```

```
    if (visit != null)
      lastAccess = visit.getLastAccess();

    Book book = getBook();

    Timestamp dateAdded = book.getDateAdded();

    if (dateAdded == null)
      return false;

    if (lastAccess == null)
    {
      long now = System.currentTimeMillis();

      return (now - dateAdded.getTime()) <= ONE_WEEK_MILLIS;
    }

    return lastAccess.compareTo(dateAdded) <= 0;
  }
```

The link component passes the `Book`'s ID as a service parameter. This will be enough for the ViewBook page to read the `Book` object when the page is triggered by the URL. The link component is declared in the BookLink's component specification:

```
<component id="link" type="ExternalLink">
  <static-binding name="page" value="ViewBook"/>
  <binding name="parameters" expression="book.id"/>
</component>
```

That covers how to create the link and the text within the link. What happens when the link is clicked by the user? That's the domain of the ViewBook page.

10.9.2 Displaying the Book on the ViewBook page

The ViewBook page is the target of the ExternalLink component contained by the BookLink component. As an external page (ViewBook implements the `IExternalPage` interface, making it compatible with the external service), it implements `activateExternalPage()`, the method invoked by the external service. Listing 10.22 shows the source code for this method.

Listing 10.22 The `activateExternalPage()` method of the `ViewBook` class

```
public void activateExternalPage(Object[] parameters,
    IRequestCycle cycle)
{
```

```
    Integer bookId = (Integer) parameters[0];

    setBookId(bookId);
  }
```

This method's sole responsibility is to extract the ID of the Book entity to view from the service parameters and store the value into the `bookId` page property. When the page renders, the book will be read as needed, using the standard approaches you've seen in prior Virtual Library pages. Listing 10.23 contains the source code for the `pageBeginRender()` and `readBook()` methods.

Listing 10.23 The `pageBeginRender()` and `readBook()` methods of the `ViewBook` class

```
public void pageBeginRender(PageEvent event)
{
  if (getBook() == null)
    readBook();
}

private void readBook()
{
  VirtualLibraryEngine vengine =
    (VirtualLibraryEngine) getEngine();
  Integer bookId = getBookId();

  int i = 0;
  while (true)
  {
    IOperations bean = vengine.getOperations();

    try
    {
      setBook(bean.getBook(bookId));

      return;
    }
    catch (FinderException ex)
    {
      vengine.presentError("Book not found in database.",
        getRequestCycle());
      return;
    }
    catch (RemoteException ex)
    {
      vengine.rmiFailure(
        "Remote exception obtaining information for book #" +
        bookId + ".",
```

```
            ex,
            i++);
        }
    }
}
```

What happens if the user reaches the ViewBook page before logging in, and then clicks the Login menu item? The user will be authenticated using the Login page (and perhaps Register as well) and then will be returned to the ViewBook page using a `PageCallback` object. At this point, the page will be rendered, with the Borrow component enabled.

What's missing in this scenario is which book should be displayed. The `PageCallback` stores only the name of the page to render the response; the `activateExternalPage()` method will not be invoked. For this reason, the `bookId` property is made persistent. This ensures that when the page is rendered again after user authentication, the correct `Book` object is read and displayed.

In the interests of efficiency, and in order to minimize server-side state, only the `bookId` property, not the entire `Book` object (stored in the `book` property), is made persistent. The `book` property can always be restored from the database, as long as the `bookId` is known. This follows the general guideline of storing the minimum persistent state and recovering any additional state as needed.

10.9.3 Creating the PersonLink component

The PersonLink component is slightly more complex than the BookLink component. Instead of passing in a `Person` object, a `Person`'s name and ID are passed in as two separate parameters. This is because the `Person` object is usually not available; instead, the `Book` object includes properties for a book's owner (name and ID) and holder (name and ID). This reflects that the `Book` object, returned by the `BookQuery` bean, is a flattening of information from the Book, Person, and Publisher entities.

In addition, there are places where a PersonLink should be omitted. For example, on the BookMatches page, if the holder matches the owner, the holder is omitted. This is represented as a third parameter, `omit`.

The HTML template for the PersonLink component, shown in listing 10.24, makes use of these three parameters.

Listing 10.24 PersonLink.html: HTML template for the PersonLink component

```
<span jwcid="@Conditional" condition="ognl:! omit">
<a jwcid="link"><span jwcid="@Insert" value="ognl:name">
  Joe User</span></a>
</span>

<span jwcid="@Conditional" condition="ognl:omit">
 
</span>
```

Because the PersonLink component is often used as part of a table (that is, inside a `<td>` element), it is useful to replace the link with a nonbreaking space (the ` ` entity) so that the browser renders the cell containing the PersonLink properly. Different browsers display empty `<td>` elements differently—often the background color or cell borders are omitted for empty table cells. Putting a nonbreaking space inside the `<td>` ensures that the element is never empty.

The specification for the PersonLink component declares all three parameters. The `id` parameter is a connected parameter (its `direction` attribute has the value `in`), but the `id` parameter may not be connected normally; the `IComponent` interface already defines and uses a property named `id` (it stores the component's ID, assigned by the user or by the framework). Therefore, the `id` parameter is connected to a different property, `personId`:

```
<parameter name="id"
  type="java.lang.Integer"
  required="yes"
  direction="in"
  property-name="personId"/>
```

The link component can then reference the `id` parameter via its connected property, `personId`:

```
<component id="link" type="ExternalLink">
  <static-binding name="page" value="ViewPerson"/>
  <binding name="parameters" expression="personId"/>
</component>
```

The other two parameters for the PersonLink component are the `name` parameter (the name to be displayed for the user) and the `omit` parameter (which displays can be used to not display the name or link). The link created references the ViewPerson page.

10.9.4 Displaying the Person

The ViewPerson page displays the properties of the `Person` object, but it also displays the list of books owned by the person. This means that ViewPerson must have the same kind of initialization stage that the MyLibrary page has. It must also have additional components, properties, and Java code to allow the user to control sort order. Because the ViewPerson page is triggered using the external service, it can perform this initialization inside its `activateExternalPage()` method (shown in listing 10.25) rather than implementing the `IActivate` interface (as the MyLibrary page's Java class does).

Listing 10.25 The `activateExternalPage()` method of the `ViewPerson` class

```
public void activateExternalPage(Object[] parameters,
    IRequestCycle cycle)
{
  Integer personId = (Integer) parameters[0];

  setPersonId(personId);

  int count = runQuery();
  _browser.initializeForResultCount(count);
}
```

The method extracts the `id` of the `Person` that should be displayed from the service parameters and stores it in the `personId` property (which, like the `bookId` property of the ViewBook page, is a persistent property). It then invokes `runQuery()` to initialize the query that contains the list of books owned by the `Person`. The `runQuery()` method is shown in listing 10.26.

Listing 10.26 The `runQuery()` method of the `ViewPerson` class

```
private int runQuery()
{
  VirtualLibraryEngine vengine =
    (VirtualLibraryEngine) getEngine();
  Integer personId = getPersonId();
  SortOrdering ordering = new SortOrdering(getSortColumn(),
    isDescending());

  int i = 0;
  while (true)
  {
    IBookQuery query = getQuery();
```

```
        if (query == null)
        {
          query = vengine.createNewQuery();

          setQuery(query);
        }

        try
        {
          return query.ownerQuery(personId, ordering);
        }
        catch (RemoteException ex)
        {
          vengine.rmiFailure("Remote exception for owner query.",
            ex, i++);

          setQuery(null);
        }
      }
    }
```

This code resembles the code you've already seen in the BookMatches and MyLibrary pages. The only significant difference involves which method of the `BookQuery` bean is invoked: in this case, it is the `ownerQuery()` method. Again echoing the ViewBook page, the ViewPerson page initializes the `person` property using the `pageBeginRender()` method (shown in listing 10.27).

Listing 10.27 The `pageBeginRender()` method of the `ViewPerson` class

```
public void pageBeginRender(PageEvent event)
{
  Person person = getPerson();

  if (person == null)
  {
    VirtualLibraryEngine vengine =
      (VirtualLibraryEngine) getEngine();

    person = vengine.readPerson(getPersonId());

    setPerson(person);
  }
}
```

So far, the functionality you've seen has been concerned with presenting data already stored in the database. Many of the remaining pages involve adding or updating data.

10.10 Editing a Book

From the MyLibrary page, it is possible to edit an existing `Book` using one of the icons on the right side of the page. The HTML template for the MyLibrary page includes a link that encloses a Rollover component for the button image:

```
<a jwcid="edit"><img jwcid="editRollover"
  src="images/edit.png" width="25" height="25"
  alt="Edit" border="0"/></a>
```

The edit component is a DirectLink. It invokes the `editBook()` listener method and encodes the `Book`'s `id` as a service parameter:

```
<component id="edit" type="DirectLink">
  <binding name="listener" expression="listeners.editBook"/>
  <binding name="parameters" expression="currentBook.id"/>
</component>
```

Like several other pages, the EditBook page requires an initialization stage before it can render. This initialization involves reading the `Book` to be edited. The `EditBook` class does not implement the `IActivate` interface, even though its needs are similar. The `IActivate` interface doesn't leave any room for specifying the book to edit. The `IActivate` interface is for pages (like MyLibrary) whose initialization does not require any additional parameters.

Instead, the `editBook()` listener method, shown in listing 10.28, invokes a specific method on the `EditBook` class to begin editing the book identified as a service parameter.

Listing 10.28 The `editBook()` method of the `MyLibrary` class

```
public void editBook(IRequestCycle cycle)
{
  Object[] parameters = cycle.getServiceParameters();
  Integer bookId = (Integer) parameters[0];
  EditBook page = (EditBook) cycle.getPage("EditBook");

  page.beginEdit(cycle, bookId);
}
```

The `beginEdit()` method, shown in listing 10.29, stores the `bookId` and reads the book from the database, using the Operations bean. When the user edits an existing book here, or adds a new book (using the NewBook page), the book is stored as a `Map` of attributes and values, rather than as a `Book` instance. The `Book` object is designed only as the output from the `BookQuery` bean. It contains flattened data from the Book, Person, and Publisher entities and is not designed for updates.

Instead, the EditBook page uses a Form component and form control components to edit the values stored in a `Map`. The `Map` is then used to update the Book entity.

Listing 10.29 The `beginEdit()` method of the `EditBook` class

```
public void beginEdit(IRequestCycle cycle, Integer bookId)
{
  setBookId(bookId);

  VirtualLibraryEngine vengine =
    (VirtualLibraryEngine) getEngine();

  int i = 0;
  while (true)
  {
    try
    {
      IOperations operations = vengine.getOperations();

      setAttributes(operations.getBookAttributes(bookId));

      break;
    }
    catch (FinderException ex)
    {
      throw new ApplicationRuntimeException(ex);
    }
    catch (RemoteException ex)
    {
      vengine.rmiFailure(
        "Remote exception setting up page for book #" +
        bookId + ".",
        ex,
        i++);
    }
  }

  cycle.activate(this);
}
```

The `beginEdit()` method uses the `Operations` bean to get the attributes of the `Book` and assigns those attributes to the `attributes` property of the EditBook page, ready to be edited by the form control components on the page. Each of the form control components edits a property within the attributes `Map`. Tapestry (or, really, OGNL) treats `Maps` as if they were JavaBeans, where the properties are the keys of the `Map`. When the page renders, each component will read a property from the attributes `Map` (such as `attributes.title` or `attributes.author`).

What about when the form is submitted? The components will attempt to set properties of the `Map`, but since this is a new request, the `attributes` property will initially be null. The way to address this is to ensure that a non-null `Map` is available when the page renders. This is handled by the page's `pageBeginRender()` method, shown in listing 10.30.

Listing 10.30 The `pageBeginRender()` method of the `EditBook` class

```
public void pageBeginRender(PageEvent event)
{
  if (getAttributes() == null)
    setAttributes(new HashMap());
}
```

The `pageBeginRender()` method is invoked before a page renders, but also before a form within the page rewinds. In either case, this event listener method will ensure that a non-null `Map` is stored in the `attributes` property, ready to be read or updated by the form control components.

10.10.1 Tracking the Book ID

How do we know which book is being edited? When the page is initially rendered, we know the ID of the book (it is stored in the `bookId` property), and we need that piece of information again when the form is submitted. In chapter 4, we discussed scenarios where clicking the browser's back button could
some grief (if the user jumps back to previously
browser's back button). The solution here is to reco
using a Hidden component. This ensures that the for
consistent: The field updates are packaged with the
updated, and there's no possibility of the client and t
which book is being edited. The following code is i
page's HTML template as the first thing within the For

```
<span jwcid="@Hidden" value="ognl:bookId"/>
```

This records the `bookId` property into the form when rendering, and then restores the `bookId` property when the form is submitted. Since the `bookId` property is not used until the form's listener is invoked, the Hidden component can go anywhere on the page, as long as it is enclosed by the Form component.

10.10.2 Generating dynamic JavaScript

The Virtual Library application allows new publishers to be defined on the fly. When adding a new book or editing an existing book, the user has the option of either selecting an existing publisher (from a drop-down list) or providing the name of a new publisher in a text field.

This either-or relationship between the drop-down list and the text field is enforced in the client web browser using client-side JavaScript (and then double-checked on the server, in case the client has JavaScript disabled). The JavaScript consists of client-side event handlers that observe changes to the drop-down list. When the list has a nonblank value selected, the text field is disabled. When the user selects the empty option in the drop-down list, the text field is enabled, and the cursor is moved to the text field. As discussed in chapter 8, JavaScript in Tapestry is complicated by the fact that the framework assigns the names of forms and form control elements, and this requires a specialized template, the script specification, to dynamically create JavaScript customized to the names assigned by the framework.

The EditBook page includes a Script component for creating the JavaScript. A Script component is another framework component, whose goal is to provide an easy way to add dynamic JavaScript to a page without our having to resort to overriding the `renderComponent()` method (as we did in chapter 8). The script is passed the two components (informal parameters to the Script component become input symbols to the script specification), as well as the relative (to the page specification) location of the script specification. Although the Script component appears in the HTML template, it does not produce any HTML—it works with the Body component to add JavaScript to the page.

The Script component is configured in the EditBook page's HTML template to execute the Publisher.script specification:

```
<span jwcid="@Script" script="Publisher.script"
  select="ognl:components.inputPublisher"
  field="ognl:components.inputPublisherName"/>
```

The Script component reads and executes the Publisher.script file (which is stored in the WEB-INF folder with the page specification). The two informal parameters, `select` and `field`, are passed to the executable script as input symbols. The script specification is shown in listing 10.31.

Listing 10.31 Publisher.script: script specification used by the EditBook page

```
<?xml version="1.0"?>
<!DOCTYPE script PUBLIC
  "-//Apache Software Foundation//Tapestry Script Specification
  ➥ 3.0//EN"
  "http://jakarta.apache.org/tapestry/dtd/Script_3_0.dtd">

<script>
<input-symbol key="select"
  class="org.apache.tapestry.form.PropertySelection"
  required="yes"/>
<input-symbol key="field"
  class="org.apache.tapestry.form.AbstractTextField"
  required="yes"/>

<let key="formObject">
  document.${select.form.name}
</let>

<let key="selectObject">
  ${formObject}.${select.name}
</let>

<let key="fieldObject">
  ${formObject}.${field.name}
</let>

<let key="functionName" unique="yes">
  onChange_${select.name}
</let>

<body>
function ${functionName}()
{
  var select = ${selectObject};
  var field = ${fieldObject};

  if (select.selectedIndex == 0)
  {
    field.disabled = false;
    field.focus();
    field.select();
  }
  else
  {
    field.disabled = true;
```

Receives the PropertySelection for the Publisher

Receives the TextField for the Publisher name

Defines name of onchange event handler function

```
      field.blur();
      field.value = "";
    }
  }
  </body>

  <initialization>
  ${selectObject}.onchange = ${functionName};      <-- Connects the handler
                                                       to the select object
  if (${selectObject}.selectedIndex != 0)
    ${fieldObject}.disabled = true;
  </initialization>
  </script>
```

This script specification works by defining new symbols for client-side Document Object Model (DOM) references to the `<form>`, `<select>`, and `<input type="text">` elements (as symbols `formObject`, `selectObject`, and `fieldObject`). It also constructs a unique name for the event-handling function for the `<select>` element.[7]

The event-handling function appears in the `<body>` element of the script specification. The function is invoked when the user has changed the `<select>` element to select the first option, empty, and adjusts the text field accordingly.

In the `<initialization>` element, event-handling functions are connected to client-side objects. The content of the `<initialization>` element is executed once the complete HTML page is loaded into the client web browser. The initialization here sets the `onchange` event handler for the `<select>` element to the event-handling function. It also checks to see if the `<select>` is displaying a non-empty option and disables the text field if so.

This level of indirection may seem unnecessary in this specific case; you could just see what names the framework assigns for the fields and write a script block as static HTML. Doing so would not be a wise idea, however, since a future version of the framework may change the naming conventions for forms and form controls.

As a final note, because JavaScript generation in Tapestry is parameterized, this same script is used in another page: the NewBook page, which also accepts a publisher name from a drop-down list or a text field.

---

[7] The function name will typically be something like `onChange_inputPublisher`. This script isn't reused on the page, so adding `unique="yes"` to the `<let>` is overkill, but not a bad habit to get into.

The EditBook page has one limitation: It isn't possible to change the owner of a book using the page. Instead, a different page (accessible from the menu) is used: the GiveAwayBooks page, which we discuss next.

10.11 Giving books away

The GiveAwayBooks page (figure 9.18) allows a user to transfer the ownership of one or more books to another user within the application. This page is built around a Palette component (to select the books we want to transfer) and a Property-Selection (to select the user we want to transfer books to). What's interesting is that the Palette has been configured to display the PropertySelection in the title area for the right column (normally labeled "Selected").

This is accomplished using another type of component: a Block. A Block component is a way of marking a section of a template so that it can be passed to another component as a parameter. In the GiveAwayBooks template, the form looks like this:

```
<form jwcid="@Form" listener="ognl:listeners.formSubmit">

<select jwcid="selectBooks"/>

<span jwcid="availableTitleBlock@Block">
Books you currently own.
</span>

<span jwcid="selectedTitleBlock@Block">
Books to transfer to <select jwcid="selectTarget"/>
</span>

<br clear="left"/>

<input type="image" src="images/transfer.png" width="56"
  height="20" alt="Transfer"/>

</form>
```

Contains the Palette's available column title

Contains the Palette's selected column title

The selectBooks component is the Palette, and the selectTarget component is the PropertySelection. In the GiveAwayBook page's specification, the select-Books component is configured to replace its default title for the two columns with the Blocks provided in the template:

```
<component id="selectBooks" type="contrib:Palette">
  <binding name="sort">
    @org.apache.tapestry.contrib.palette.SortMode@LABEL
  </binding>
```

```
    <binding name="model" expression="booksModel"/>
    <binding name="selected" expression="selectedBooks"/>
    <binding name="selectedTitleBlock"
      expression="components.selectedTitleBlock"/>
    <binding name="availableTitleBlock"
      expression="components.availableTitleBlock"/>
  </component>
```

The Palette's `availableTitleBlock` and `selectedTitleBlock` parameters are used to replace the default Blocks (which are inside the Palette's own template) with content from the page's template. As this page demonstrates, this content can not only include simple text ("Books you currently own") but can be arbitrarily complex, with a mix of static HTML and other components.

The GiveAwayBooks page is the last page accessible to ordinary users. The remaining pages are restricted to users with administrative privilege. Let's look at the first of these pages, EditPublishers, next.

10.12 Editing the publishers

The EditPublishers page allows a Virtual Library administrator to rename or delete any publishers in the Virtual Library database. This is an important and necessary page, since users may enter publisher names on the fly, and can thus introduce inconsistencies and misspellings.

This page is an example of a Form that loops over a number of domain objects, providing form control elements for editing properties of each of the domain objects. In this case, the domain objects are `Publishers`, and the property we want to edit is the `name` of the `Publisher`. In addition, the form tracks which `Publishers` should be deleted. The Operations bean provides a method for performing all the updates and deletions as a single method invocation.

Chapter 4 discussed the ListEdit component, which is designed for looping over lists of objects within a form. The EditPublishers page demonstrates how to properly use the ListEdit component, how to use the `ListEditMap` utility class, and how to recover from out-of-date submissions (which can happen when the user hits the browser's back button and resubmits a form).

10.12.1 Constructing the EditPublishers template

The template for the EditPublishers page contains a Form component, a ListEdit component (the e component), a TextField for editing the publisher's `name` property, and a Checkbox for marking publishers as deleted. The EditPublishers template is shown in listing 10.32.

Listing 10.32 EditPublishers.html: HTML template for the EditPublishers page

```
<html jwcid="$content$">
<body jwcid="@Border">
<span jwcid="@ShowMessage"/>
<span jwcid="@ShowError"/>
<form jwcid="@Form" listener="ognl:listeners.processForm">
<p>This page allows you to rename and delete publishers.
</p>
<table class="data">
  <tr>
    <th>Publisher</th>
    <th>Delete</th>
    </tr>
    <tr jwcid="listEdit">
      <td class="control">
        <input jwcid="inputName@TextField"
          value="ognl:publisher.name"
          size="40" maxlength="40"/>
      </td>
      <td class="checkbox">
        <input type="checkbox"
          jwcid="delete@Checkbox"
          selected="ognl:listEditMap.deleted"/>
      </td>
    </tr>
    <tr>
      <td class="control">
        <input type="image" src="images/update.png"
          width="52" height="20" alt="Update"/>
      </td>
    </tr>
  </table>
</form>
</body>
</html>
```

Iterates over the available Publishers

Edits current Publisher's name property

Edits listEditMap's deleted property

The checkbox does not edit a property of the `Publisher` object (`Publisher` doesn't have any kind of `deleted` property). Instead, it edits the property `listEditMap.deleted`. As you'll see shortly, the `ListEditMap` object is essential in terms of handling the form submission, including its ability to track the keys of objects that should be deleted.

10.12.2 Declaring properties for the EditPublishers page

The page specification for the EditPublishers page (listing 10.33) declares the standard `message` and `error` properties. It also declares a `publisher` property (which stores the current `Publisher` instance inside the loop) and a `listEditMap` property, used in concert with the ListEdit component to convert between publisher IDs and `Publisher` objects and to track which publishers should be deleted. The ListEdit component was previously discussed in chapter 4, and the EditPublishers page is a perfect example of how to make use of it.

Listing 10.33 EditPublishers.page: specification for the EditPublishers page

```
<?xml version="1.0" encoding="UTF-8"?>
<!DOCTYPE page-specification PUBLIC
  "-//Apache Software Foundation//Tapestry Specification 3.0//EN"
  "http://jakarta.apache.org/tapestry/dtd/Tapestry_3_0.dtd">

<page-specification
  class="org.apache.tapestry.vlib.pages.admin.EditPublishers">

  <property-specification name="listEditMap"
    type="org.apache.tapestry.form.ListEditMap"/>
  <property-specification name="message" type="java.lang.String"/>
  <property-specification name="error" type="java.lang.String"/>

  <property-specification name="publisher"
    type="org.apache.tapestry.vlib.ejb.Publisher"/>

  <component id="listEdit" type="ListEdit">
    <binding name="source" expression="listEditMap.keys"/>
    <binding name="value" expression="listEditMap.key"/>
    <static-binding name="element" value="tr"/>
    <binding name="listener"
      expression="listeners.synchronizePublisher"/>
  </component>

</page-specification>
```

The ListEdit component sets the `key` property of the `ListEditMap` instance on each iteration. It is up to the `synchronizePublisher()` listener method (which is invoked by the ListEdit component on each pass through its loop) to convert this to a `Publisher`. Listing 10.34 shows the `synchronizePublisher()` method.

Listing 10.34 The `synchronizePublisher()` method of the `EditPublishers` class

```
public void synchronizePublisher(IRequestCycle cycle)
{
  ListEditMap map = getListEditMap();
  Publisher publisher = (Publisher) map.getValue();
```

```
    if (publisher == null)
    {
      setError(getMessage("out-of-date"));
      throw new PageRedirectException(this);
    }

    setPublisher(publisher);
  }
```

When the form is submitted, a new `ListEditMap` instance will be created from the data stored in the database at that time. If other users have been editing publishers, the data in the new `ListEditMap` may not precisely match the data in the `ListEditMap` used when the page was rendered. The ListEdit component will pull the publisher IDs from the form submission, but it will still plug each successive publisher ID into the `Map`'s `key` property, and it will still invoke the ListEdit's listener method to synchronize the `publisher` property.

If two users are both deleting Publishers at the same time, then the second user's form submission will include publisher IDs that were deleted by the first user. In that case, the `ListEditMap` instance will return null from its `getValue()` method for that publisher ID. That's why the `synchronizePublisher()` method includes a null check—null indicates that just such a race condition has occurred and that the user is out of date. Throwing a `PageRedirectException` aborts the form rewind and renders the EditPublishers page again.

10.12.3 Creating the ListEditMap

A `ListEditMap` instance is created whenever the page renders. As usual, this is accomplished using the `PageRenderListener` interface. Listing 10.35 contains the short `pageBeginRender()` method, as well as the longer `readPublishers()` method.

Listing 10.35 The `pageBeginRender()` method of the `EditPublishers` class

```
public void pageBeginRender(PageEvent event)
{
  readPublishers();
}

private void readPublishers()
{
  VirtualLibraryEngine vengine =
    (VirtualLibraryEngine) getEngine();
  Publisher[] publishers = null;
```

```
    int i = 0;
    while (true)
    {
      try
      {
        IOperations operations = vengine.getOperations();

        publishers = operations.getPublishers();

        break;
      }
      catch (RemoteException ex)
      {
        vengine.rmiFailure(getMessage("read-failure"), ex, i++);
      }
    }

    ListEditMap map = new ListEditMap();
    int count = Tapestry.size(publishers);

    for (i = 0; i < count; i++)
      map.add(publishers[i].getId(), publishers[i]);

    setListEditMap(map);
  }
```

The `readPublishers()` method uses the `Operations` bean to get the list of publishers, sorted in alphabetical order. It uses this list to construct the `ListEditMap` instance, which is stored in the `listEditMap` property of the page.

A `ListEditMap` instance remembers the order in which keys are added to it. The `keys` property, used by the ListEdit component as the source of values when rendering, will return the keys in this order. The publishers are displayed in ascending alphabetical order because the `Operations` bean's `getPublishers()` method returns them in that order, and that is the order in which they are added to the `ListEditMap`.

The `ListEditMap`'s `getValue()` method doesn't require a parameter to indicate which value to get. The ListEdit component will have already updated the `key` property of the `ListEditMap` for this pass through its loop—that is, the key used by the `getValue()` method. The listener method obtains this value and casts it to type `Publisher`.

10.12.4 Updating the publishers

When the form is submitted, the `ListEditMap` instance is re-created from current data stored in the database (the `pageBeginRender()` method is invoked before the form rewinds as well as before the page renders). As the form is rewound, the `Publisher` objects are updated, and any deleted publishers are tracked.

Inside the form's `processForm()` listener method (provided in listing 10.36), the updates are organized. The `ListEditMap`'s `getValues()` method returns all the values (in this case, `Publisher` objects) that are *not* deleted. The `getDeletedKeys()` method returns the IDs of all the deleted publishers. Care must be taken because the `ListEditMap` returns null from `getDeletedKeys()` when no publishers have been marked for deletion.

Listing 10.36 The `processForm()` method of the `EditPublishers` class

```
public void processForm(IRequestCycle cycle)
{
  if (isInError())
    return;

  ListEditMap map = getListEditMap();
  List updateList = map.getValues();
  List deletedIds = map.getDeletedKeys();

  Publisher[] updated = (Publisher[])
    updateList.toArray(new Publisher[updateList.size()]);

  Integer[] deleted =
    deletedIds == null
      ? null
      : (Integer[])
          deletedIds.toArray(new Integer[deletedIds.size()]);

  VirtualLibraryEngine vengine =
    (VirtualLibraryEngine) getEngine();

  int i = 0;
  while (true)
  {
    try
    {
      IOperations operations = vengine.getOperations();

      operations.updatePublishers(updated, deleted);

      break;
    }
    catch (FinderException ex)
```

```
        {
          throw new ApplicationRuntimeException(ex);
        }
        catch (RemoveException ex)
        {
          throw new ApplicationRuntimeException(ex);
        }
        catch (RemoteException ex)
        {
          vengine.rmiFailure(getMessage("update-failure"), ex, i++);
        }
      }

    vengine.clearCache();
  }
```

After the values and deleted IDs are extracted and converted to arrays, the `Operations` EJB is again used to perform the update as a single operation. After the normal retry logic, the final step is to have the engine clear any cached information it might have (the engine caches a list of publishers).

The same techniques used by the EditPublishers page are expanded for use on the EditUsers page.

10.13 Editing the list of users

Like the EditPublishers page, the EditUsers page is accessible only to administrators. It allows the current user to edit select aspects of the other users: granting or revoking administrative privilege, locking or unlocking users, changing users' passwords, or deleting users outright.

As with deleting publishers (on the EditPublishers page), tracking which users will have their password changed is a function of the `ListEditMap` rather than an attribute of the `Person` object. This requires a subclass of `ListEditMap`.

The EditUsers page's HTML template contains the same kind of loop, built around a ListEdit component, as the EditPublishers page. The checkbox for the reset password column is bound to the `ListEditMap`'s `resetPassword` property:

```
<tr jwcid="listEdit">
  <td><span jwcid="@Insert"
        value="ognl:user.naturalName">Joe User</span>
    <br>
    <span jwcid="@Insert"
      value="ognl:user.email">foo@bar.com</span>
  </td>
```

```
  <td class="checkbox">
    <input type="checkbox"
      jwcid="inputAdmin@Checkbox"
      selected="ognl:user.admin"/>
  </td>
  <td class="checkbox">
    <input type="checkbox"
      jwcid="inputLockedOut@Checkbox"
      selected="ognl:user.lockedOut"/>
  </td>
  <td class="checkbox">
    <input type="checkbox"
      jwcid="inputResetPassword@Checkbox"
      selected="ognl:listEditMap.resetPassword"/>
  </td>
  <td class="checkbox">
    <input type="checkbox"
      jwcid="inputDelete@Checkbox"
      selected="ognl:listEditMap.deleted"/>
  </td>
</tr>
```

10.13.1 Creating the ListEditMap subclass

The purpose of the `UserListEditMap` is to extend `ListEditMap` to also track a set of keys identifying which `Person` values should have their passwords reset. This involves creating a `Set` to track those keys and making use of methods provided by the `ListEditMap` super class to use that `Set`. `ListEditMap` is designed specifically to support this kind of extension, so the final class (listing 10.37) is quite succinct.

Listing 10.37 UserListEditMap.java: `ListEditMap` subclass used on the EditUsers page

```
package org.apache.tapestry.vlib.pages.admin;

import java.util.List;
import java.util.Set;

import org.apache.tapestry.form.ListEditMap;

public class UserListEditMap extends ListEditMap
{
  private Set _resetPasswordKeys;

  public List getResetPasswordKeys()
  {
    return convertSetToList(_resetPasswordKeys);
  }
```

```
    public boolean getResetPassword()
    {
      return checkSet(_resetPasswordKeys);
    }

    public void setResetPassword(boolean resetPassword)
    {
      _resetPasswordKeys =
        updateSet(_resetPasswordKeys, resetPassword);
    }

  }
```

The `ListEditMap` class provides three protected methods to be leveraged by subclasses: `checkSet()`, `updateSet()`, and `convertSetToList()`. The `checkSet()` method checks a `Set` to see if it contains the current key. It automatically returns false if the `Set` is null.

The `updateSet()` method updates a `Set`, adding or removing the current key based on the `boolean` parameter. It may seem odd that the method takes a `Set` as a parameter and returns the same `Set` as a result. This is because the `Set` passed in may be null. In that case, `updateSet()` will create a new instance of `Set` and return it. This slight twist of the code allows the `Set` to be created only if it is needed.

Finally, the `convertSetToList()` method converts a `Set` (possibly null) to a `List`. It can return null if the set is null or empty. The order of elements in the returned `List` is not defined. In this case, `List` is returned because access to the values inside a `List` is more efficient than with a `Collection`. With a `List`, it is possible to get each element using the `get()` method (passing in an index). With a `Collection`, it is possible to access all elements only with the use of an `Iterator`.

10.13.2 Handling the form submission

When the form is submitted, the `UserListEditMap` instance is used to get the updated users, as well as the list of deleted user IDs and the list of user IDs whose password will be reset. Listing 10.38 contains the `updateUsers()` listener method and a utility method, `toArray()`, used to convert a `Collection` to an array of objects.

Listing 10.38 The `updateUsers()` and `toArray()` methods of the `EditUsers` class

```
public void updateUsers(IRequestCycle cycle)
{
  if (isInError())
    return;

  Visit visit = (Visit) getVisit();
  VirtualLibraryEngine vengine =
    (VirtualLibraryEngine) cycle.getEngine();

  UserListEditMap map = getListEditMap();

  List updatedUsers = map.getValues();
  Person[]updates = (Person[])
    updatedUsers.toArray(
      new Person[updatedUsers.size()]);

  Integer[] resetPasswordUserIds =
    toArray(map.getResetPasswordKeys());
  Integer[] deletedUserIds =
    toArray(map.getDeletedKeys());

  String password = getPassword();
  setPassword(null);

  if (Tapestry.isBlank(password) &&
      Tapestry.size(resetPasswordUserIds) != 0)
  {
    setErrorField("inputPassword", getMessage("need-password"));
    return;
  }

  Integer adminId = visit.getUserId();

  int i = 0;
  while (true)
  {
    try
    {
      IOperations operations = vengine.getOperations();

      operations.updatePersons(
        updates,
        resetPasswordUserIds,
        password,
        deletedUserIds,
        adminId);
      break;
    }
    catch (RemoteException ex)
```

Skips update if validation errors

Gets Person objects to update

Gets IDs of Persons to reset passwords

Gets IDs of Persons to delete

Gets and clears password field

Performs all updates and deletes

```
      {
        vengine.rmiFailure(getString("update-failure"), ex, i++);
      }
      catch (RemoveException ex)
      {
        throw new ApplicationRuntimeException(ex);
      }
      catch (FinderException ex)
      {
        throw new ApplicationRuntimeException(ex);
      }
    }

    setMessage(getMessage("users-updated"));
  }

  private Integer[] toArray(Collection c)
  {
    int count = Tapestry.size(c);

    if (count == 0)
      return null;

    return (Integer[]) c.toArray(new Integer[count]);
  }
```

With that, we've covered all the key pages and the components in the application—but that's not quite the entire application. We still need to define the web deployment descriptor, and there a few interesting deployment issues there.

10.14 Creating the web deployment descriptor

A common desire for web applications is that the URL be short and succinct; this is as much for marketing reasons as for technical reasons, and is perfectly valid. Users should just need to know the domain name, such as http://www.amazon.com or http://www.slashdot.org, in order to launch the application. Tapestry applications, however, require a reference to the application servlet, so the URL for launching a Tapestry application has an extra term—for example: http://www.myserver.com/app. Let's see how to avoid that unwanted part, /app, at the end.

When using a JSP application, it is possible to specify a JSP as the "welcome page." The servlet container is responsible for recognizing a "bare" URL (a URL that references a folder, not a particular JSP) and will send a redirect response to the client, which results in a new request for the welcome page JSP. When Servlet

API 2.4 becomes widely available, it will be possible to perform this same kind of redirection to a servlet.

In the meantime, Tapestry makes use of a feature of the 2.3 Servlet API:[8] Servlet filters. A filter is "plugged into" the request-processing pipeline within the servlet container. The `RedirectFilter` class provided with the framework intercepts the initial request for the bare URL and sends a client redirect response, forwarding the client to the application servlet.

To make use of this feature, we must declare the filter in the web.xml deployment descriptor, much as we define the Tapestry application servlet. This is shown in listing 10.39. Because filters are part of the Servlet 2.3 API, we must use the `<!DOCTYPE>` for the 2.3 API (in previous examples, we used the 2.2 DOCTYPE).

Listing 10.39 web.xml: deployment descriptor for the Virtual Library application

```
<?xml version="1.0"?>
<!DOCTYPE web-app PUBLIC
  "-//Sun Microsystems, Inc.//DTD Web Application 2.3//EN"
  "http://java.sun.com/dtd/web-app_2_3.dtd">
<web-app>
  <display-name>Tapestry Virtual Library Demo</display-name>

  <filter>
    <filter-name>redirect</filter-name>
    <filter-class>
      org.apache.tapestry.RedirectFilter
    </filter-class>
  </filter>

  <filter-mapping>
    <filter-name>redirect</filter-name>
    <url-pattern>/</url-pattern>
  </filter-mapping>

  <servlet>
    <servlet-name>vlib</servlet-name>
    <servlet-class>
      org.apache.tapestry.ApplicationServlet
    </servlet-class>
    <load-on-startup>0</load-on-startup>
  </servlet>

  <servlet-mapping>
    <servlet-name>vlib</servlet-name>
```

Defines the redirect filter

Maps the redirect filter to bare URL

8 Other than this, Tapestry uses only features of the Servlet 2.2 API, for maximum portability to the many application servers in use even today.

```
    <url-pattern>/app</url-pattern>
  </servlet-mapping>

  <session-config>
    <session-timeout>15</session-timeout>
  </session-config>

</web-app>
```

That shortens the launch URL for the application from http://www.myserver.com/vlib/app down to http://www.myserver.com/vlib. Ideally, the launch URL should be just http://www.myserver.com. Going that extra step takes two different forms, depending on how the application is deployed.

10.14.1 Deploying web applications as root

When you're deploying an individual web application, the name of the WAR file becomes the name of the prefix. So, a web application named demo.war would be deployed as http://www.myserver.com/demo. Most servlet containers, including Jakarta Tomcat, follow a convention that a web application named ROOT.war is deployed without a prefix, as http://www.myserver.com/. Combining such a deployment with the filter described earlier allows us to reach that ideal, minimal-launch URL: http://www.myserver.com.

10.14.2 Deploying an enterprise application as root

The Virtual Library does not deploy as a simple web application; it is deployed as an enterprise application. An enterprise application is another level above a web application and bundles together one or more web applications with any number of other libraries, including EJB modules.

In the case of the Virtual Library, the vlib.war web application is combined with the vlibbeans.jar EJB module to form the vlib.ear enterprise application. vlibbeans.jar and vlib.war are built separately and then combined to form the final application. These two modules are included inside the enterprise application archive (which is another version of a JAR file, with a different extension, .ear).

Just as a web application has a web.xml deployment descriptor and an EJB module has an ejb-jar.xml deployment descriptor, an enterprise application has an application.xml deployment descriptor. The descriptor for the Virtual Library enterprise application is shown in listing 10.40.

Listing 10.40 application.xml: enterprise application deployment descriptor for the Virtual Library application

```
<?xml version="1.0" encoding="UTF-8"?>
<!DOCTYPE application PUBLIC
  "-//Sun Microsystems, Inc.//DTD J2EE Application 1.2//EN"
  "http://java.sun.com/j2ee/dtds/application_1_2.dtd">
<application>
  <display-name>Virtual Library Application</display-name>
  <module>
    <ejb>vlibbeans.jar</ejb>
  </module>
  <module>
    <web>
      <web-uri>vlib.war</web-uri>
      <context-root>/</context-root>
    </web>
  </module>
</application>
```

The application deployment descriptor identifies how to deploy the two modules packaged within the enterprise application archive, identifying one as an EJB module and the other as a web application. The critical part in this discussion is the `<context-root>` element. This element gives us absolute control over the URL prefix used to identify the web application; the name of the web application archive is no longer relevant.

For our purposes, we deploy the web application as / rather than /vlib. The end result is that the application will launch with the URL http://www.myserver.com, which is what we want.

10.15 Wrapping it all up

Every application contains a unique set of challenges driven by the need to know who the user is, what the user is doing, and what data is stored on the server (as persistent page properties) or in the client (as service parameters or hidden form fields). Tapestry provides a clean, object-oriented approach to meeting all these challenges.

You've seen that it is possible, in a rather small amount of code, to create a complex, robust, usable application. Tapestry provides the necessary hooks, in the form of page lifecycle events, to fill in any gaps in functionality that the framework can't provide. All of these techniques can be expanded and adapted to new applications with new challenges.

In the space of these few chapters, you've seen how Tapestry simplifies and improves web application development in everything from a simple word game to an entire J2EE application. Tapestry accomplishes quite a bit from just a few basic building blocks:

- Tapestry's component object model allows the framework to manage the lifecycle of pages and components and facilitates the ability to address a particular page or component within a URL.
- Expressing the relationships and interactions within the framework in terms of JavaBean properties eliminates the impedance between different parts of the application—especially between the components provided by the framework and the domain objects specific to your application.
- Dividing an application into self-contained pages and achieving reuse through the creation of components leads to more functionality and fewer bugs, and requires less code.
- Embracing a separation of concerns by dividing pages (and components) into Java classes, HTML templates, and specifications mirrors the Model-View-Controller pattern and enables developers to work together easily.

This book has given you the tools to understand how to create your own custom Tapestry applications. You are well on your way to thinking in terms of components: reusing existing components or creating your own (with an eye toward reusing them). This book, and these examples, are just the start of the Tapestry world, which begins at the Tapestry home page: http://jakarta.apache.org/tapestry/. Tapestry is built around a thriving, world-spanning community of users and volunteers, which translates to a wealth of support and examples.

Using Tapestry, you are freed from the most troublesome and taxing concerns of developing web applications. Now you can concentrate on the *real* challenges: unrealistic project schedules, difficult clients, the changing technology landscape, and all the other realities of twenty-first century software development.

"OK, folks, we don't get much of a break, the client is really breathing down our necks for phase two, and we've got a lot of work to do." As usual, you tune out for a bit and start visualizing the changes; the new registration wizard is twisted, may be time to refine those workflow components you've been prototyping ... you'll need a component to raise that new pop-up window ... and you'll have to whip something together for that Flash animation. You frown. The new functionality is going to break the fragile links into the client's back-end systems. Again. More quality time with their IT department. Why couldn't it all be as simple and straightforward as the web interface?

A Getting involved with Tapestry

One of the great aspects of any open-source project is just how easy it is to get started and, potentially, guide the evolution of the project. The starting point for participation is the Tapestry home page at http://jakarta.apache.org/tapestry/ and the two mailing lists, tapestry-user@jakarta.apache.org (where you'll find discussions on how to use Tapestry) and tapestry-dev@jakarta.apache.org (which focuses on ways to improve the framework). Instructions for subscribing to the mailing lists are available on the Tapestry home page.

Tapestry has benefited immensely from the ideas brought up for discussion in the mailing lists. For example, line-precise error reporting evolved from a strong suggestion (really more of a complaint) by a new user who had difficultly working backward from runtime errors to mistakes in the XML specifications. That simple request led to significant improvement to the framework.

Here's another example: Through Tapestry release 2.3, there was no concept of an implicit component; that came out of a discussion involving Marc Fleury (the volatile lead of the JBoss application server project). Again, a major enhancement to the framework came out of direct discussions with the framework's end users. In many more cases, extensions to individual components or to APIs were a result of end-user feedback.

If you want to go beyond making suggestions to actually supplying code, there is a path for this as well. Tapestry is an Apache Jakarta project and is organized along the Apache meritocracy guidelines—which means all decisions are made out in the open, on the mailing lists, and are based on open votes. There are no barriers to entry, beyond an ability to communicate, a willingness to work with the Tapestry team, and, of course, the ability to produce high-quality code. Several current members of the Tapestry team came up through the ranks by mentoring new users on the mailing lists and eventually submitting code patches, before being voted in as Tapestry committers.

A.1 Tacos—the Tapestry component repository

As you saw in chapters 6 and 8, Tapestry has sophisticated support for component libraries. Creating, packaging, and using a Tapestry component library is quite simple, and Tacos, the Tapestry Component Archive project, is a source for these libraries. Tacos is a SourceForge project located at http://sf.net/projects/tacos/. At the time of this writing, Tacos is in a formative stage, but plans are in progress to make it the second epicenter for Tapestry development (after the Tapestry home page at Jakarta) and a source for Tapestry components, sample applications, and application skeletons.

A.2 What's coming next in Tapestry?

Tapestry is an ongoing project at Jakarta. At the time of this writing, Tapestry 3.0 is deep into its beta period, but advanced users have helped the team identify a number of areas deserving of attention in the next full release.

By the time this book is published, work will be well under way on release 3.1 of Tapestry. The community is very active, and there is a constant drive to improve the framework—a continuous search for ways to extend the power of Tapestry and, at the same time, reduce even further the time and effort involved in creating Tapestry applications.

A.2.1 Improving application testability

Development and testing go hand in hand. If you want to complete a project on time, your best bet is to take the time to develop tests for your code in parallel with the code itself. Some developers, those who embrace the Extreme Programming philosophies, go further: They write the tests first and then create code to make the tests pass.

This seems like a paradox: If you are under the gun, struggling to meet an aggressive development schedule, writing tests seems like a luxury you can't afford. That's a terrible misconception. The minutes you may spend creating a test suite are a small price to pay compared with the hours you can waste tracking down bugs deployed into the bowels of an application server. Think about it—inside a unit-test suite, you have a simple, predictable environment where it is easy and natural to use the debugger. Running your test suite should be as simple as hitting the Test button in your IDE.

Finding a bug inside your application server is much more complicated; you have to deal with debugging a remote process, with building and deploying the application, and with filtering through all of the application server overhead. In short, it's a long and complicated cycle, adding minutes or more to each iteration of your test cycle.

As we've often said, *when you write tests, you find bugs*. Those bugs will eventually come to light in integration testing of the application, long after you've forgotten the minute details of how your code works—which will further multiply the time and effort needed to find and fix the bugs. The only solution is to create tests early.

By dividing up your code carefully, you can test portions of your application outside the Tapestry framework; for example, back in chapter 2, the `Game` and `WordSource` classes could be tested easily using their own unit-test suites. These classes were carefully coded to have no dependencies on Tapestry or on any other user interface.

Unfortunately, the majority of a Tapestry application requires the active involvement of the Tapestry framework to be tested. Not only do most of the component classes fail to work in isolation, but many of them are abstract classes that can't even be instantiated, much less tested. Tapestry applications can only be tested with the Tapestry framework.

The testing story for Tapestry applications is less than ideal:

- Obtain a testing tool, such as Mercury Interactive's LoadRunner, Minq Software's PureLoad, or OpenSTA.[1]
- Set up a test environment for the tool: an application server and any back-end database or other external dependencies.
- Build the application and deploy it to the application server.
- Use the tool to execute the tests.
- Analyze the results.

That's not a bad scenario for performing load and performance testing, but it is not appropriate for day-to-day (or even minute-to-minute) functional testing. As a developer, you want to hit that Test button to run your application through its paces to prove you haven't broken anything, and you don't want to wait long. You want to use the same build-and-test strategy you'd use for a noninteractive or nonweb application.

A number of extensions to the JUnit framework are available for merging unit testing with web application testing. You'll find these listed at http://www.junit.org/news/extension/web/index.htm. All of these extensions require a running web server or application server to execute against; the excellent open-source servlet container Jetty (http://jetty.mortbay.com) is easily embeddable for testing purposes.

Internally, Tapestry includes an extensive test suite in excess of 400 tests. A significant number of these tests are based on executing small applications inside a simulated servlet container. These tests execute several hundred simulated HTTP requests in the space of a few seconds.

A focus for Tapestry release 3.1 will be to improve, generalize, and document the internal test suite, converting it into a part of the Tapestry framework proper.

---

[1] Information about web site testing software is available online at www.extremetech.com/article2/0,3973,1154892,00.asp, http://www.aptest.com/resources.html#web-func, and elsewhere.

This will provide a starting point for you to build a test suite for your own application, allowing you to perform constant, pervasive testing without the complexity and overhead of running a servlet container or application server.

A.2.2 Offline content generation

There's no question that static content can be served up by a web server at tremendous speed; static content can be held in memory, cached in multiple locations, and more easily distributed than dynamic content. As soon as the content is dynamic, there is at least an order of magnitude drop-off in speed, and this only gets worse when the application is database driven.

Large content sites, such as Yahoo! and CNN, take the approach of generating static content at frequent intervals (every hour, or even every few minutes). This splits the difference between a fully dynamic, fully personalized web site, and a fast, static web site. Various contributors to the Tapestry development mailing lists have described approaches they have taken to bridge between the static and dynamic approaches. One approach is to keep a Tapestry application running and periodically use scripts (written in Perl or Python) to "scrape" the dynamic content and store it to a static file, accessible via a web server.

For Tapestry to be useful in the very highest top-end applications, the kind visited by thousands of concurrent users, offline content generation is at least as important as application server clustering. Offline content generation will be another key goal in Tapestry 3.1.

A.2.3 Other simplifications and improvements

Part of the fun of developing Tapestry is that there's always something new to be added, refined, or sometimes rethought. Discussions with users on the Tapestry mailing lists (see the next section) can be quite invigorating.

There are at least two additional areas in Tapestry that will receive some attention in release 3.1.

Simplifying parameters

The use of the `<parameter> direction` attribute to describe how Tapestry component parameters are used (covered in chapter 6) is less than ideal. It requires that you, the developer, understand exactly how data moves between a component and its container (whether the container is a page or another component). The idea was to optimize the number of accesses to the binding object so that properties would not be read or updated unnecessarily. These accesses, both reads and writes, rely on Java reflection, which is much slower than ordinary Java method invocation, so optimizations here can be very worthwhile.

With the bytecode enhancement technology introduced in release 3.0, it is quite possible for a much improved version of the `auto` value for the `direction` attribute to be implemented that can accomplish the same, or better, optimizations with even greater efficiency.

Simplifying persistent properties

As you saw in chapter 10, sometimes elaborate measures must be taken to work around the fact that persistent page properties may not be modified once the page begins rendering. Release 3.1 will explore whether these strict rules surrounding persistent page properties may be relaxed.

B Building the examples with Ant

Ant is an open-source build tool for Java that is used in a vast number of open-source and proprietary software projects. Ant is used to automate the steps for building, testing, and deploying Java software. The examples used throughout this book are available in source form from the Manning web site for this book, www.manning.com/lewisship/. This appendix describes how to use Ant to convert that source into applications that run within the Tomcat servlet container.

A complete, indispensable, and definitive guide to Ant is *Java Development with Ant*, by Erik Hatcher and Steve Loughran (Manning, 2002).

B.1 Downloading the software

Building the example applications involves four software packages:

- The Ant tool, which will compile the classes and assemble and deploy the web applications.
- The Tomcat servlet container. Tomcat is the reference implementation of the Java Servlet API.
- The Tapestry framework.
- The *Tapestry in Action* examples

Table B.1 lists the home page for each package (you'll see a download link on the page) and specifies which version you should use.

Table B.1 Packages ued to build the examples

Package	Home page	Version
Ant	http://ant.apache.org	1.5.1
Tomcat	http://jakarta.apache.org/tomcat/	4.1.24
Tapestry	http://jakarta.apache.org/tapestry/	3.0[1]
Tapestry in Action examples	www.manning.com/lewisship/	N/A

B.1.1 Installing Ant

Unpack the Ant distribution (it will be a zip file for Windows, or a .tar.gz file for GNU/Linux or UNIX) to a directory. Ant includes installation directions in the docs/manual/index.html file. The installation process involves updating the

[1] At the time of this writing, Tapestry 3.0 was in a late beta stage. By the time you read this, Tapestry will have reached its final 3.0 release.

system PATH environment variable, adding Ant's bin directory to the list of search directories. The bin directory contains scripts that run Ant. In addition, you will set up an ANT_HOME environment variable to point to the installation location of Ant.

B.1.2 Installing Tomcat

On Windows, Tomcat is easiest to install by downloading as a self-extracting archive (.exe) file, which has an integrated installer. By default, the server is installed in the directory C:/Program Files/Apache Group/Tomcat 4.1. For GNU/Linux and UNIX systems, a .tar.gz file may be extracted instead.

B.1.3 Installing Tapestry

Tapestry is distributed as a zip file for Windows and as a .tar.gz file for GNU/Linux and UNIX. The binary distribution includes the compiled libraries as well as a number of dependencies needed by Tapestry (these are other open source libraries that Tapestry makes use of, such as OGNL).

You should extract the Tapestry distribution to a working directory.

Tapestry includes a README file with additional instructions for configuring its turnkey demos for use with Tomcat or with JBoss.

B.1.4 Installing the examples

Installation of the examples involves two steps. First the archive file, TapestryInActionSource.zip, must be extracted to a working directory.

Second, you must create a file, common/build.properties (listing B.1), within the working directory. This file is referenced by the Ant build script to identify where Tapestry and Tomcat have been installed. Listing B.1 is an example of this file for a Windows installation. The distribution includes a sample file, build.properties.template, which you can edit to match your choice of directories and then rename to build.properties.

Listing B.1 build.properties: configuration file for building the examples

```
tapestry.dist.dir = C:/Tapestry-3.0
tomcat.dir = C:/Program Files/Apache Group/Tomcat 4.1
```

B.2 Building the examples

Now that you've extracted the examples and created the configuration file, Ant can compile and deploy the four web applications directly into Tomcat. Simply execute the command `ant` from the examples distribution directory.

The top-level Ant build file will, by default, build the library, and then build and deploy each of the four web applications.

In addition, a small change to the Tomcat configuration is installed. Its goal is to resolve a naming conflict between the Tapestry examples web application and an example web application distributed as part of Tomcat.

B.3 Running the examples

You should start Tomcat and allow it to fully initialize. On Windows, the installer creates a Start menu group; on other systems, follow the directions in the distribution.

Once Tomcat has initialized and loaded the applications, you may start a web browser and open the URL http://localhost:8080/examples/app. This will display the Home page of the main examples application, which has links to all the pages of the examples application and to the other three applications (both versions of Hangman and the banner ads demo).

B.4 Understanding the examples build system

The examples distribution consists of a number of subprojects, each in its own subfolder, and each with its own Ant build file. These subprojects are shown in table B.2. A master Ant build file, in the distribution directory, links together all the subprojects.

Table B.2 Subprojects in the examples distribution

Name	Type	Description
examples-library	Library	Library containing components described in chapters 7 and 8
examples	Web application	Application containing pages and components from chapters 3–7
hangman1	Web application	Application described in chapter 2
hangman2	Web application	Application described in chapter 6
bannerads	Web application	Application described in chapter 8

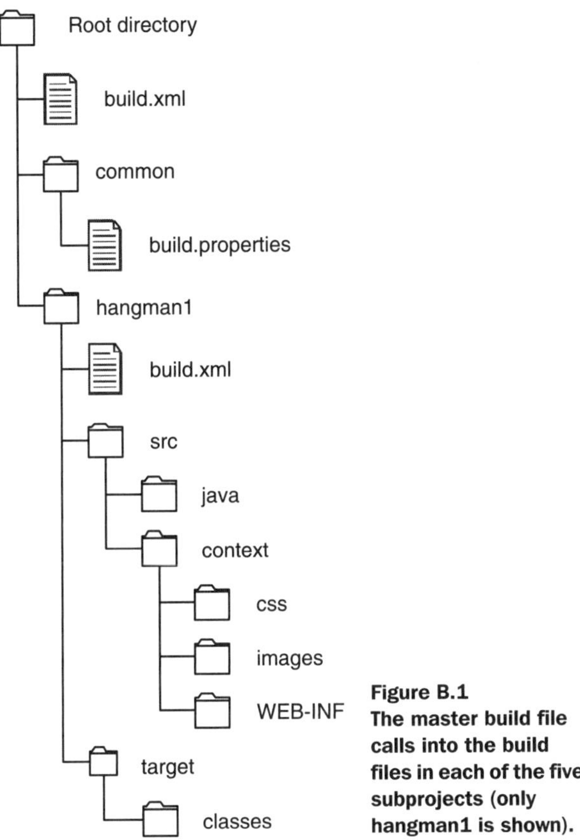

Figure B.1 The master build file calls into the build files in each of the five subprojects (only hangman1 is shown).

The build environment used by the examples is worth taking a look at as a starting point for building your own build environment. The basic layout is shown in figure B.1 (which shows only the hangman1 subproject).

Each file and directory has a specific purpose during the build, as table B.3 shows.

Table B.3 Files and directories for the hangman1 subproject

File	Purpose
build.xml	Master Ant build file for the entire project
common/build.properties	Identifies the location of the Tapestry and Tomcat distributions
hangman1/build.xml	Rules for building just the hangman1 web application
hangman1/src/java	Java code to be compiled
hangman1/target/classes	Compiled Java source code (created as needed)

Table B.3 Files and directories for the hangman1 subproject *(continued)*

File	Purpose
hangman1/context	HTML templates for pages, plus static assets
hangman1/context/WEB-INF	web.xml deployment descriptor, page and component specifications, and so on
hangman1/target/hangman1.war	Completed WAR, including compiled Java code, contents of context, plus all necessary Tapestry libraries and dependencies

In each subproject is a build.xml file used by Ant and an src directory. Ant will create the target directory (which contains all the derived files, such as compiled Java classes) and ultimately create the deployable web application archive within the `target` directory.

Listing B.2 shows the build file for the hangman1 subproject.

Listing B.2 build.xml: Ant build file for the hangman1 subproject

```
<?xml version="1.0"?>
<project name="Tapestry In Action -- Hangman, version 1"
        default="war">

  <property name="project.name" value="hangman1"/>

  <property file="../common/build.properties"/>        <-- Reads configuration file

  <property name="target.dir" value="target"/>

  <property name="src.dir" value="src/java"/>
  <property name="context.dir" value="src/context"/>
  <property name="conf.dir" value="src/conf"/>

  <property name="classes.dir" value="${target.dir}/classes"/>
  <property name="war.file"
          value="${target.dir}/${project.name}.war"/>
                                        Defines symbols for files and folders

  <property name="servlet.jar"
          value="${tomcat.dir}/common/lib/servlet.jar"/>
                                        Defines path to Servlet API library

  <path id="project.class.path">
    <fileset dir="${tapestry.dist.dir}/lib">
      <include name="*.jar"/>
      <include name="ext/*.jar"/>
    </fileset>
    <pathelement location="${servlet.jar}"/>
  </path>
                                        Constructs compile classpath
```

```
  <target name="clean" description="Deletes derived files.">
    <delete dir="${target.dir}" quiet="true"/>
  </target>

  <target name="compile" description="Compile Java classes.">
    <mkdir dir="${classes.dir}"/>
    <javac srcdir="${src.dir}" destdir="${classes.dir}" debug="on"
           classpathref="project.class.path"/>
  </target>

  <target name="war" depends="compile"
          description="Compile all classes and build the WAR.">
    <war warfile="${war.file}"
         webxml="${context.dir}/WEB-INF/web.xml">

      <fileset dir="${context.dir}">
        <exclude name="WEB-INF/web.xml"/>
      </fileset>

      <classes dir="${classes.dir}"/>

      <classes dir="${src.dir}">
        <exclude name="**/*.java"/>
        <exclude name="**/package.html"/>
      </classes>

      <lib dir="${tapestry.dist.dir}/lib">
        <include name="*.jar"/>
      </lib>
      <lib dir="${tapestry.dist.dir}/lib/ext">
        <include name="*.jar"/>
      </lib>
    </war>
  </target>

  <target name="deploy" depends="war"
          description="Deploy the WAR into Tomcat.">
    <property name="deploy.dir" value="${tomcat.dir}/webapps"/>

    <copy file="${war.file}" todir="${deploy.dir}"/>
  </target>
</project>
```

Packages application as WAR file

The compile target is responsible for compiling the Java source code, stored under src/java. The class files are stored under target/classes. The WAR file is created by combining these compiled classes with the image of the web application context, plus any additional artifacts inside the source directory (this includes page and component specifications, HTML templates, script specifications, or other assets). In addition, the Tapestry libraries and dependencies are copied into the WAR so that they will be available at runtime.

The last step is to copy the WAR to the Tomcat webapps directory so that Tomcat can serve the web application.

C Tapestry component reference

This appendix is a quick reference to the basic components provided with the Tapestry framework. A more complete reference, with examples, is provided online and as part of the Tapestry distribution. We cover only the framework components here. The framework includes two other libraries: the Contrib library, which includes recent contributions to the framework (including the Palette component discussed in chapter 6), and a set of WML (Wireless Markup Language) components.

These reference materials briefly identify each component and its primary formal parameters (more obscure parameters are omitted for brevity; the online reference has complete details). In addition, each component can either render or discard its body, and can either accept or reject informal parameters.

ActionLink

The ActionLink component creates an `<a>` hyperlink. When the link is triggered, a listener method is invoked. ActionLink differs from DirectLink in that it uses the action service, not the direct service, to rewind the entire state of the page back to its incarnation when the link was initially rendered. (This is the same technique used by forms to rewind the state of the form submission, as discussed in chapter 3.)

Table C.1 Parameters for the ActionLink component

Parameter name	Type	Direction	Required	Default value	Description
`disabled`	`boolean`	`in`	No	false	If true, the ActionLink doesn't render a tag (but still renders its body).
`listener`	`IActionListener`	`in`	Yes		The listener to be invoked when the link is triggered.

ActionLink renders its body and allows informal parameters.

Any

The Any component is a Tapestry component that can emulate any type of markup tag. It has no formal parameters but allows informal parameters. It is typically used to add simple dynamic output to a normally static tag—for example, to dynamically calculate (using an OGNL expression) the `class` attribute of a `<span>` tag.

Any renders its body and allows informal parameters.

Block

A Block component is used to pass a portion of an HTML template (including static text and components) as a parameter to another component, or even another page. A RenderBlock component is used to make the Block render its contents. Chapter 10 includes an example of this, where a portion of a page's HTML template was passed into a Palette component to provide part of the Palette's user interface.

Block renders its body but forbids informal parameters.

Body

The Body component is responsible for the `<body>` tag of a Tapestry page. As discussed in chapter 8, it is also very much involved in any dynamic JavaScript created by the components within the page.

Body renders its body and allows informal parameters.

Button

The Button component creates an HTML form button element (`<input type="button">`). Form buttons are used exclusively to provide client-side actions (using JavaScript) as part of a form.

Table C.2 Parameters for the Button component

Parameter name	Type	Direction	Required	Default value	Description
`disabled`	`boolean`	`in`	No	false	If true, the button will be disabled—it will not respond to the mouse and will be rendered specially by the browser to indicate this state.
`label`	`string`	`in`	No		The label displayed for the button (this becomes the `value` attribute of the output element).

Checkbox

The Checkbox component is one of the standard form element components. It renders a checkbox (`<input type="checkbox">`) and reads and updates a `boolean` property. The Checkbox component is discussed in detail in chapter 3.

Table C.3 Parameters for the Checkbox component

Parameter name	Type	Direction	Required	Default value	Description
`selected`	`boolean`	`in/out`	Yes		Read when the form is rendered and updated when the form is submitted.
`disabled`	`boolean`	`in`	No	false	If true, the button will be disabled—it will not respond to the mouse and will be rendered specially by the browser to indicate this state.

Checkbox discards its body and allows informal parameters.

Conditional

The Conditional component is used to render a portion of a page only if a certain condition is met.

The Conditional component normally just renders (or skips) its body. If desired, the Conditional may also output an element surrounding its body; in this respect, it operates much as the Any component does.

Table C.4 Parameters for the Conditional component

Parameter name	Type	Direction	Required	Default value	Description
`condition`	`boolean`	`in`	No	false	The body of the Conditional is rendered only if this value is true.
`invert`	`boolean`	`in`	No	false	If true, then the condition is inverted (the body is rendered only if the condition is false).
`element`	`string`	`in`	No		If given, then an element is output around the component's body.

Conditional renders its body and allows informal parameters (which are used only if the `element` attribute is specified).

DatePicker

The DatePicker component is a complex form element component that allows users to select dates using a JavaScript-powered pop-up window.

Table C.5 Parameters for the DatePicker component

Parameter name	Type	Direction	Required	Default value	Description
value	java.util.Date	in/out	Yes		The date property edited by the DatePicker component.
format	string	in	No	dd MMM yyyy	The date format used to display the date.
disabled	boolean	in	No	false	If true, then the date field and calendar pop-up buttons will be disabled.

DatePicker discards its body and forbids informal parameters.

Delegator

The Delegator component is an "escape clause" that allows you to write Java code to render a portion of a page. You provide the Delegator object with a renderable object (implementing the `IRender` interface), and it invokes the `render()` method on the object. Often, the renderable object is an inner class. An example of this is in chapter 4, where Delegator was used to produce formatted, hexadecimal output of an uploaded binary file.

Table C.6 Parameter for the Delegator component

Parameter name	Type	Direction	Required	Default value	Description
delegate	IRender	in	Yes		The object to invoke to render on behalf of the Delegator component

Delegator discards its body and forbids informal parameters.

DirectLink

The DirectLink component is the primary way to create hyperlinks in Tapestry pages; examples of DirectLink appear throughout this book, starting in chapter 2. DirectLinks allow URLs to be created that reference a particular component within a page; in addition, a list of parameters may be encoded into the URL, with the parameter values made available when the link is triggered.

Table C.7 Parameters for the DirectLink component

Parameter name	Type	Direction	Required	Default value	Description
`listener`	`IActionListener`	`in`	Yes		The object (usually a listener method) to be invoked when the user triggers the link.
`parameters`	`many`	`in`	No		Zero or more values to be encoded into the URL and provided to the listener.
`disabled`	`boolean`	`in`	No	false	If true, the DirectLink doesn't render a tag (but still renders its body).
`stateful`	`boolean`	`in`	No	true	If true (the default), then the DirectLink will validate that the `HttpSession` is still active when the link is triggered (if a session was active when the link is rendered).

DirectLink renders its body and accepts informal parameters.

ExceptionDisplay

ExceptionDisplay is a specialized component used by the Tapestry Exception page to display the stack of exceptions. It is useful if you are creating a customized Exception page.[1]

Table C.8 Parameter for the ExceptionDisplay component

Parameter name	Type	Direction	Required	Default value	Description
`exceptions`	`ExceptionDescription[]`	`in`	Yes		The stack of exceptions as generated by the `ExceptionAnalyzer` utility class

ExceptionDisplay discards its body and rejects informal parameters.

[1] Note that the portion of the page that displays the Servlet API is produced by using a `Delegator`, with the `RequestContext` as the delegate. `RequestContext` implements the `IRender` interface, for just this purpose.

ExternalLink

The ExternalLink component creates a link to a page, much like the PageLink component, with two differences: Service parameters may be passed in the URL, and the target page must implement the `IExternalPage` interface (the `activateExternalPage()` method defined by the interface will be invoked). ExternalLink is used to create links that the end user may safely bookmark, because all the necessary information is encoded into the URL.

Table C.9 Parameters for the ExternalLink component

Parameter name	Type	Direction	Required	Default value	Description
`page`	`string`	`in`	Yes		The name of the page to link to, which must implement the `IExternalPage` interface.
`parameters`	`varied`	`in`	No		Any number of additional parameters to be encoded into the URL.
`disabled`	`boolean`	`in`	No	false	If true, the ExternalLink doesn't render a tag (but still renders its body).

ExternalLink renders its body and accepts informal parameters.

FieldLabel

The FieldLabel component is used to display the label for a ValidField component, integrating into the overall form validation subsystem described in chapter 5. The FieldLabel coordinates with the enclosing Form's validation delegate to visually identify fields within the form that contain errors.

Table C.10 Parameters for the FieldLabel component

Parameter name	Type	Direction	Required	Default value	Description
`field`	`form component`	`in`	Yes		The field for which a label should be displayed
`displayName`	`string`	`in`	No		Overrides the display name obtained from the ValidField

FieldLabel renders its body and rejects informal parameters.

Foreach

The Foreach component is used to iterate over a list of values and repeatedly render its body for each value. It can update a property of its container to identify the specific value within the list, or the index within the list. A Foreach component can optionally render a tag around its body, much like the Any component.

Table C.11 Parameters for the Foreach component

Parameter name	Type	Direction	Required	Default value	Description
`source`	`varied`	`in`	No	null	The list of input values, as a `Collection`, `Iterator`, object array, or single object.
`value`	`Object`	`out`	No		Updated before the Foreach renders its body.
`index`	`int`	`out`	No		Updated before the Foreach renders its body.
`element`	`string`	`in`	No		If given, then the Foreach renders a tag (with informal parameters) around its body on each pass through the loop.

Foreach renders its body and accepts informal parameters (which are used only if the `element` parameter is specified).

Form

The Form component is used to create HTML forms within Tapestry pages, as discussed in chapters 3 through 5. The Form component is responsible for orchestrating both the rendering of the form and the processing when the form is submitted. A Form has a listener that is invoked when the Form is submitted, after all the enclosed form control elements have had a chance to update properties from the submission.

Table C.12 Parameters for the Form component

Parameter name	Type	Direction	Required	Default value	Description
`listener`	`IActionListener`	`in`	No		If provided, the listener is notified after the form submission is processed.

Table C.12 Parameters for the Form component *(continued)*

Parameter name	Type	Direction	Required	Default value	Description
delegate	IValidationDelegate	in	No		The validation delegate used by FieldLabel and ValidField components enclosed by the Form.
stateful	boolean	in	No	true	If true and the application is stateful when the form is rendered, then a check occurs that the application is still stateful when the form is submitted.

The Form component renders its body and accepts informal parameters.

Frame

The Frame component is used within a `<frameset>` to identify a Tapestry page to fill a `<frame>`.

Table C.13 Parameter for the Frame component

Parameter name	Type	Direction	Required	Default value	Description
page	string	in	Yes		The name of the page whose content is rendered within the frame

The Frame component discards its body but accepts informal parameters.

GenericLink

The GenericLink component is used to create hyperlinks to arbitrary URLs. It may be used to create links to off-site URLs, but it is most often used in conjunction with client-side JavaScript.

Table C.14 Parameters for the GenericLink component

Parameter name	Type	Direction	Required	Default value	Description
href	string	in	Yes		The target URL for the link.
disabled	boolean	in	No	false	If true, then the GenericLink does not render a tag, just its body.

GenericLink renders its body and accepts informal parameters.

Hidden

The Hidden component is used to record information in an HTML form.

Table C.15 Parameters for the Hidden component

Parameter name	Type	Direction	Required	Default value	Description
`value`	`Object`	`in/out`	Yes		The value to be recorded in the form (and restored when the form is submitted).
`listener`	`IActionListener`	`in`	No		If provided, the listener is notified after the `value` parameter is updated when the form is submitted.
`encode`	`boolean`	`in`	No	true	If true, the value is encoded with its type. If false, the value must be a `String` and is recorded as is.

The Hidden component discards its body and forbids informal parameters.

Image

The Image component is used to render an image as part of a Tapestry page. The source of the image is specified as an asset, which hooks into Tapestry's localization mechanism to ensure that the correct localization of the image is automatically used.

Table C.16 Parameters for the Image component

Parameter name	Type	Direction	Required	Default value	Description
`image`	`IAsset`	`in`	Yes		The image asset to be displayed
`border`	`int`	`in`	No	0	Sets the width of the border displayed around the image

The Image component discards its body and allows informal parameters.

ImageSubmit

The ImageSubmit component is closely related to the Submit component; it is used to display an image that submits a form. When the form is submitted, the ImageSubmit component can update a property of its container to a specific value or invoke a listener method (or both). The Submit and ImageSubmit components are discussed in chapter 3.

Table C.17 Parameters for the ImageSubmit component

Parameter name	Type	Direction	Required	Default value	Description
`image`	`IAsset`	`in`	Yes		The image asset to be displayed.
`disabled`	`boolean`	`in`	No	false	If true, the rendered image will be disabled (it will not respond to the mouse).
`disabledImage`	`IAsset`	`in`	No		An optional image to display instead of the standard image if the component is disabled.
`point`	`java.awt.Point`	`out`	No		The point (x and y coordinates) within the image clicked by the mouse.
`selected`	`Object`	`out`	No		A property updated by the ImageSubmit if it is the cause of the form submission.
`tag`	`Object`	`in`	No		A value used to update the `selected` property when the ImageSubmit is the cause of the form submission.
`listener`	`IActionListener`	`in`	No		A listener invoked by the ImageSubmit when it is the cause of the form submission (after optionally updating the `selected` parameter).

ImageSubmit discards its body and allows informal parameters.

Insert

The Insert component is used to insert some text into a rendered Tapestry page. By default, it escapes out any invalid HTML entities (that is, it converts `&` to `&`, and so on). It may optionally use a `java.text.Format` object to format an object before inserting its value.

Table C.18 Parameters for the Insert component

Parameter name	Type	Direction	Required	Default value	Description
`value`	`Object`	`in`	No		The value to be inserted.
`format`	`java.text.Format`	`in`	No		If specified, then the value is formatted to a string before being inserted.
`raw`	`boolean`	`in`	No	false	If true, then no conversion of HTML entities occurs. This is used when the value to insert is known to contain HTML markup.
`class`	`string`	`in`	No		If specified, then the output text is wrapped in a `<span>` tag, with a `class` attribute set to this value.

The Insert component discards its body and allows informal parameters, which are used only if the `class` parameter is specified.

InsertText

The InsertText component is used to insert a block of text into a Tapestry page; it breaks the text into individual lines and either inserts line breaks between lines or wraps each line as a separate paragraph. This is commonly used to display text that was collected using a TextField.

Table C.19 Parameters for the InsertText component

Parameter name	Type	Direction	Required	Default value	Description
`value`	`string`	`in`	No		The multiline text to be inserted.

Table C.19 Parameters for the InsertText component *(continued)*

Parameter name	Type	Direction	Required	Default value	Description
`mode`	`InsertTextMode`	`in`	No	InsertText-Mode.BREAK	By default, inserts breaks between lines. Use `InsertTextMode.PARAGRAPH` to wrap each line as a paragraph.

InsertText discards its body and forbids informal parameters.

LinkSubmit

The LinkSubmit component is used when you wish to have a hyperlink on a page cause a form to submit. This is useful when using a Rollover component inside the link. LinkSubmit requires client-side JavaScript.

Table C.20 Parameters for the LinkSubmit component

Parameter name	Type	Direction	Required	Default value	Description
`disabled`	`boolean`	`in`	No	false	If true, the LinkSubmit will not render a tag, but will still render its body.
`selected`	`Object`	`out`	No		A property updated by the LinkSubmit when it is the cause of the form submission.
`tag`	`Object`	`in`	No		A value used to update the `selected` property when the LinkSubmit is the cause of the form submission.
`listener`	`IActionListener`	`in`	No		A listener invoked by the LinkSubmit when it is the cause of the form submission (after optionally updating the `selected` parameter).

LinkSubmit renders its body and allows informal parameters.

ListEdit

The ListEdit component is used within a Form to iterate over a list of values in a fashion that is compatible with use within a Form. The ListEdit component records into the Form the values it iterates over during the render (as a number of hidden fields). This ensures that the form submission is processed consistently with the Form's render. ListEdit was covered in detail in chapter 4.

Table C.21 Parameters for the ListEdit component

Parameter name	Type	Direction	Required	Default value	Description
`source`	`varied`	`in`	No	null	The list of values to iterate over, as a `List`, `Iterator`, or object array.
`value`	`Object`	`out`	No		Set by the ListEdit on each pass through the loop.
`index`	`int`	`out`	No		Set by the ListEdit on each pass through the loop.
`listener`	`IActionListener`	`in`	No		Invoked by the ListEdit just after the `value` parameter is set (both when rendering and when rewinding the form).
`element`	`string`	`in`	No		If specified, the ListEdit writes a tag around its body on each pass through the loop.

ListEdit renders its body and accepts informal parameters.

Option

The Option component renders an HTML `<option>` tag. Option components must be enclosed by a Select component. In most cases, it is easier to use a Property-Selection component than to build the equivalent using Select and Option. Select and Option were covered in chapter 3.

Table C.22 Parameters for the Option component

Parameter name	Type	Direction	Required	Default value	Description
`selected`	`boolean`	`in/out`	Yes		Set to true if the option is selected when the form is submitted

Table C.22 Parameters for the Option component *(continued)*

Parameter name	Type	Direction	Required	Default value	Description
`label`	`string`	`in`	No		A string used as the label of the option

Option renders its body (which is another way to specify its label) and accepts informal parameters.

PageLink

The PageLink component is used to create a link to a specific Tapestry page. The indicated page is rendered as the response when the link is clicked.

Table C.23 Parameters for the PageLink component

Parameter name	Type	Direction	Required	Default value	Description
`page`	`string`	`in`	Yes		The name of the page to be rendered.
`disabled`	`boolean`	`in`	No	false	If true, the PageLink component does not render its tag but still renders its body.

PageLink renders its body and accepts informal parameters.

PropertySelection

The PropertySelection component is used to create a drop-down list for selecting a value for a single property. As discussed in chapter 4, PropertySelection uses a model to provide the possible values and the labels for those values.

Table C.24 Parameters for the PropertySelection component

Parameter name	Type	Direction	Required	Default value	Description
`value`	`Object`	`in/out`	Yes		The property to edit; the property is read during render and updated when the form is submitted.
`model`	`IProperty SelectionModel`	`in`	Yes		Used to identify the possible values and associated labels.

Table C.24 Parameters for the PropertySelection component *(continued)*

Parameter name	Type	Direction	Required	Default value	Description
disabled	boolean	in	No	false	If true, the Property-Selection is inactive.
submitOn-Change	boolean	in	No	false	If true, changing the value will cause the enclosing form to submit.

PropertySelection discards its body and allows informal parameters.

Radio

The Radio component creates a radio button within a form. Radio components must be enclosed by a RadioGroup. Radio and RadioGroup were discussed in chapter 3.

Table C.25 Parameters for the Radio component

Parameter name	Type	Direction	Required	Default value	Description
value	Object	in	No		The value is used to determine if the radio button is initially selected (when rendering) and is the value assigned to the `selected` parameter when the form is submitted, if the HTML radio button is selected.
disabled	boolean	in	No	false	If true, the radio button will be disabled and will not respond to the mouse.

Radio discards its body and allows informal parameters.

RadioGroup

The RadioGroup component acts like a container for any number of Radio components. It is responsible for identifying the selected Radio component and updating a property to match the selection. Radio and RadioGroup were discussed in chapter 3.

Table C.26 Parameters for the RadioGroup component

Parameter name	Type	Direction	Required	Default value	Description
`selected`	`Object`	`in/out`	Yes		The property updated when the form is submitted.
`disabled`	`boolean`	`in`	No	false	If true, all Radio components within the group are disabled.

RadioGroup renders its body but rejects informal parameters.

RenderBlock

The RenderBlock component is used to make a Block component renders its body. In effect, a portion of a page may be passed as a parameter to a component. Block and RenderBlock are commonly used to create a tabbed view.

Table C.27 Parameters for the RenderBlock component

Parameter name	Type	Direction	Required	Default value	Description
`block`	`Block`	`in`	No		The Block whose body should be rendered

Block discards its body and allows informal parameters.

RenderBody

The RenderBody component allows a component to insert its body at a prescribed position within its own template. RenderBody takes no parameters and discards its body.

Rollover

The Rollover component is a specialized version of the Image component that is used within some form of link component (DirectLink, ExternalLink, GenericLink, and so on). Rollover can perform mouse rollovers (displaying a different image when the user moves the mouse over the image). In addition, a Rollover component can adjust the image displayed when the enclosing link is disabled.

Table C.28 Parameters for the Rollover component

Parameter name	Type	Direction	Required	Default value	Description
`image`	`IAsset`	`in`	No		The initial image to display.
`focus`	`IAsset`	`in`	No		If given, the image to display when the mouse is moved over the image.
`blur`	`IAsset`	`in`	No		If given, the image to display when the mouse is moved out from over the image. If not specified, the normal image is displayed.
`disabled`	`IAsset`	`in`	No		If given, the image to display instead of the default image if the enclosing link is itself disabled.

Rollover discards its body and allows informal parameters.

Script

The Script component is used to construct client-side JavaScript from a script specification. Informal parameters to the Script are added as additional input symbols. Dynamic script creation was discussed in chapter 8. Script components must be enclosed by a Body component.

Table C.29 Parameters for the Script component

Parameter name	Type	Direction	Required	Default value	Description
`script`	`string`	`in`	Yes		The name of the script specification file
`symbols`	`Map`	`in`	No		If given, provides the base set of input symbols for the script

Script discards its body and allows informal parameters.

Select

A Select component renders an HTML `<select>` element and encloses a number of Option components. In most cases, using a PropertySelection component achieves the same result and is easier; the Select component is most often used when multiple selection is desired. An example of using Select and Option for multiple selection appears in chapter 3.

Table C.30 Parameters for the Select component

Parameter name	Type	Direction	Required	Default value	Description
`multiple`	`boolean`	`in`	No	false	If true, then multiple selection will be allowed.
`disabled`	`boolean`	`in`	No	false	If true, the rendered `<select>` will include the `disabled` attribute.

Select renders its body and allows informal parameters.

ServiceLink

The ServiceLink component is used to render a hyperlink that references a named engine service. This is often used to invoke the restart engine service, but may also be used with custom application services.

Table C.31 Parameters for the ServiceLink component

Parameter name	Type	Direction	Required	Default value	Description
`service`	`string`	`in`	Yes		The name of the engine service.
`parameters`	`varied`	`in`	No		Objects to be encoded into the URL (as with DirectLink).
`disabled`	`boolean`	`in`	No	false	If true, the ServiceLink does not render its tag but still renders its body.

ServiceLink renders its body and accepts informal parameters.

Shell

The Shell component is a convenience for rendering the `<html>` and `<head>` portions of a page. It is particularly useful for adding one or more stylesheets to a page.

Table C.32 Parameters for the Shell component

Parameter name	Type	Direction	Required	Default value	Description
`title`	`string`	`in`	Yes		The title of the page
`stylesheet`	`IAsset`	`in`	No		A single stylesheet to include

Table C.32 Parameters for the Shell component *(continued)*

Parameter name	Type	Direction	Required	Default value	Description
stylesheets	Array or collection of IAsset	in	No		A list of stylesheets to include
refresh	int	in	No		If specified, the time (in seconds) before redisplaying the same page
DTD	string	in	No	-//W3C//DTD HTML 4.0 Transitional//EN	Used to specifying the <!DOCTYPE> of the page
delegate	IRender	in	No		A renderer, used to add content to the <head> element

The Shell component renders its body and forbids informal parameters.

Submit

The Submit component renders a submit button within a form. When the form is submitted due to the rendered button, the Submit component can update a property or invoke a listener method (or both).

Table C.33 Parameters for the Submit component

Parameter name	Type	Direction	Required	Default value	Description
selected	Object	out	No		A property updated by the Submit if it is the cause of the form submission.
tag	Object	in	No		A value used to update the selected property when the Submit is the cause of the form submission.
listener	IActionListener	in	No		A listener invoked by the Submit when it is the cause of the form submission (after optionally updating the selected parameter).

Table C.33 Parameters for the Submit component *(continued)*

Parameter name	Type	Direction	Required	Default value	Description
disabled	boolean	in	No	false	If true, the button will be disabled (it will not respond to the mouse).

Submit discards its body and accepts informal parameters.

TextArea

The TextArea component creates a multiline input field as an HTML `<textarea>` element.

Table C.34 Parameters for the TextArea component

Parameter name	Type	Direction	Required	Default value	Description
value	string	in/out	No		The value to edit, which is read when the TextArea renders and updated when the enclosing form is submitted.
disabled	boolean	in	No	false	If true, the TextArea is disabled and will not update the `value` parameter.

TextArea discards its body and accepts informal parameters.

TextField

The TextField component is used to create an HTML text or password field within a form. TextField is described in detail in chapter 3.

Table C.35 Parameters for the TextField component

Parameter name	Type	Direction	Required	Default value	Description
value	string	in/out	No		The value to edit, which is read when the TextField renders and updated when the enclosing form is submitted.
hidden	boolean	in	No	false	If true, the field is rendered as a password field (which hides the exact text entered by the user).

Table C.35 Parameters for the TextField component *(continued)*

Parameter name	Type	Direction	Required	Default value	Description
`disabled`	`boolean`	`in`	No	false	If true, the field is rendered with a `disabled` attribute, and the component does not update the `value` parameter when the form is submitted.

TextField discards its body and accepts informal parameters.

Upload

The Upload component allows users to upload files from their computer to the server. Upload is a form component and must be enclosed by a Form. Upload is discussed in detail in chapter 4.

Table C.36 Parameters for the Upload component

Parameter name	Type	Direction	Required	Default value	Description
`file`	`IUploadFile`	`out`	Yes		The uploaded file is represented by an instance of `IUploadFile`, assigned to this parameter.
`disabled`	`boolean`	`in`	No	false	If true, the HTML `<input>` element will include a `disabled` attribute.

Upload discards its body and allows informal parameters.

ValidField

The ValidField component is a specialized version of TextField that is integrated into the Tapestry validation subsystem, described in chapter 5. A ValidField is not limited to editing string properties (as TextField is) but can edit any data type, as long as it has an appropriate validator to perform the necessary conversions.

Table C.37 Parameters for the ValidField component

Parameter name	Type	Direction	Required	Default value	Description
`value`	`Object`	`in/out`	Yes		The property to be edited by the ValidField.
`validator`	`IValidator`	`in`	Yes		An object that validates user input and translates between strings and object values.
`displayName`	`string`	`in`	Yes		The name of the field, used in error messages and by the FieldLabel component.
`hidden`	`boolean`	`in`	No	false	If true, the component renders a password field, not a normal text input field.
`disabled`	`boolean`	`in`	No	false	If true, the `<input>` tag will include a `disabled` attribute, and the ValidField will not update the `value` parameter when the form is submitted.

ValidField discards its body and accepts informal parameters.

D

Tapestry specifications

Tapestry applications include five types of specifications: page, component, application, library, and script. All of these specifications are XML documents, validated against a document type definition (DTD). The first four specifications are the primary specifications, and they share a single DTD (but use different document root elements). The script specification uses its own, separate DTD.

D.1 Primary specifications

The primary specifications use the following XML `<!DOCTYPE>`:

```
<!DOCTYPE root element PUBLIC
  "-//Apache Software Foundation//Tapestry Specification 3.0//EN"
  "http://jakarta.apache.org/tapestry/dtd/Tapestry_3_0.dtd">
```

Each type of specification has its own file extension and a specific root element, shown in table D.1.

Table D.1 Tapestry specifications and file extensions

Type	File extension	Root element
application	.application	`<application>`
page	.page	`<page-specification>`
component	.jwc	`<component-specification>`
library	.library	`<library-specification>`

The following sections identify each element, explaining how it's used and listing its attributes and nested elements.

<application>

The `<application>` element is the root element of an application specification. Application specifications are generally optional and are used in only a few situations:

- When a page or component specification is not stored in an expected location
- When the application defines custom engine services
- When the application makes use of a component library (as discussed in chapter 6)
- When the application defines any application extensions (as discussed in chapter 8)

Figure D.1 identifies the elements that may be contained within the `<application>` element. Table D.2 lists the attributes that may be specified.

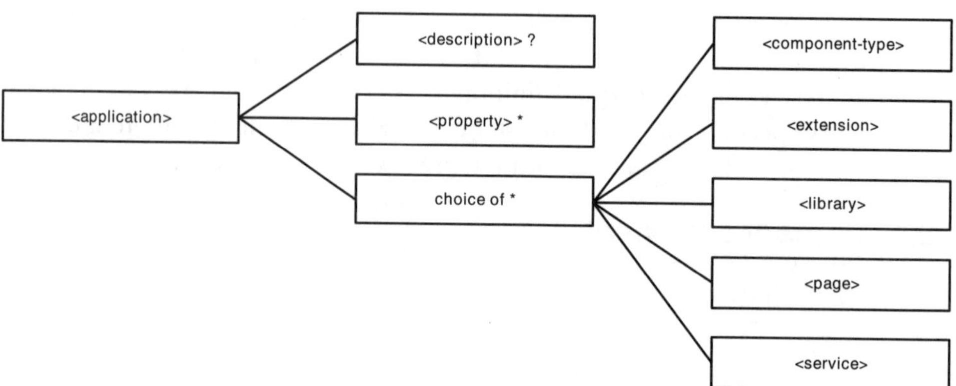

Figure D.1 The `<application>` element is primarily used to override the default rules for locating pages and components, and to specify libraries, extensions, and services.

NOTE These diagrams express the rules for the content of an element. Elements contain a sequence of other elements, with a symbol to indicate how many of that element are allowed (`?` indicates optional, `*` indicates zero or more, `+` indicates at least one). `Choice of` means that exactly one of the listed elements is allowed. Figure D.1 indicates that an `<application>` can contain an optional `<description>`, followed by any number of `<property>` elements, followed by any number of the remaining elements.

Table D.2 Attributes of the `<application>` element

Attribute name	Required?	Description
`engine-class`	No	Name of the class to instantiate as the application engine; if not specified, `BaseEngine` is used.
`name`	No	A user-presentable name for the application, used in some debugging output.

<bean>

The `<bean>` element is used to create a helper bean, a Java bean that provides additional logic to a page. `<bean>` appears inside `<page-specification>` and `<component-specification>`.

Frequently, `<bean>` is used to create the validation delegate and individual validator objects used with the form validation subsystem described in chapter 5. Figure D.2 identifies the elements that may be contained by `<bean>`, and table D.3 lists the attributes for the `<bean>` element.

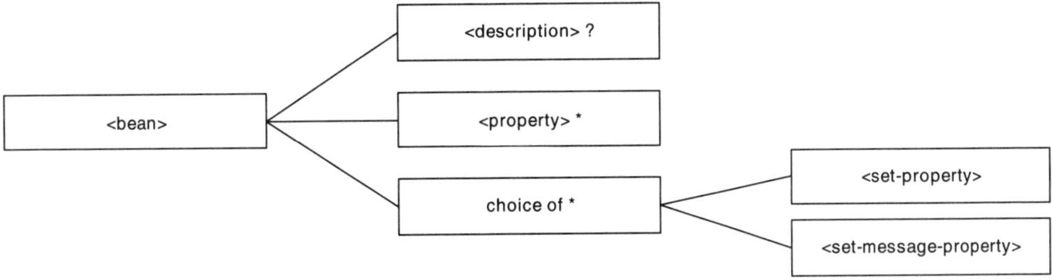

Figure D.2 The `<bean>` element is used to define a helper bean and configure its properties.

Table D.3 Attributes of the `<bean>` element

Attribute name	Required?	Description
`class`	Yes	The Java class to instantiate.
`lifecycle`	No	The lifecycle of the bean: none, request, page, or render. The default is request.
`name`	Yes	The name of the bean, which must be a valid Java identifier.

<binding>

The `<binding>` element appears inside the `<component>` element. It binds a parameter of the component to an OGNL expression. The expression, which is most often simply the name of a property, is evaluated in the context of the containing page or component.

OGNL expressions can be very complex and involve characters, such as single and double quotes, that are awkward to express within an XML attribute. To accommodate such situations, the OGNL expression can be provided as the wrapped character data enclosed by the `<binding>` element.

Table D.4 lists the attributes for the `<binding>` element. `<binding>` may not contain any other elements.

Table D.4 Attributes of the `<binding>` element

Attribute name	Required?	Description
`expression`	No	The OGNL expression. If not specified, the content of the element is used as the expression.
`name`	Yes	The name of the component parameter to bind; this may be either a formal or informal parameter.

<configure>

The `<configure>` element is used within the `<extension>` element to configure one property of the application extension. `<configure>` may not contain other elements. Table D.5 lists the attributes of the `<configure>` element.

Table D.5 Attributes of the `<configure>` element

Attribute name	Required?	Description
`property-name`	Yes	The name of the property of the extension to configure.
`type`	No	The type of the property, which is used to convert the value: `boolean`, `int`, `long`, `double`, or `String`. `String` is the default.
`value`	No	The value to be assigned. If not provided as an attribute, the character data enclosed by the element is used as the value.

<component>

The `<component>` element declares the use of a component within another page or component. It identifies the ID of the component, its type, and the configuration of any of its formal and informal parameters. Figure D.3 identifies the elements that may be enclosed by `<component>`; these are mostly different elements for binding parameters of the component.

In most cases, the `<component>` element defines the type of component. In some cases, it is convenient to copy another component's type and bindings, and optionally extend or override the bindings. This can be accomplished using the `copy-of` attribute instead of the `type` attribute. Table D.6 lists the attributes of the `<component>` element.

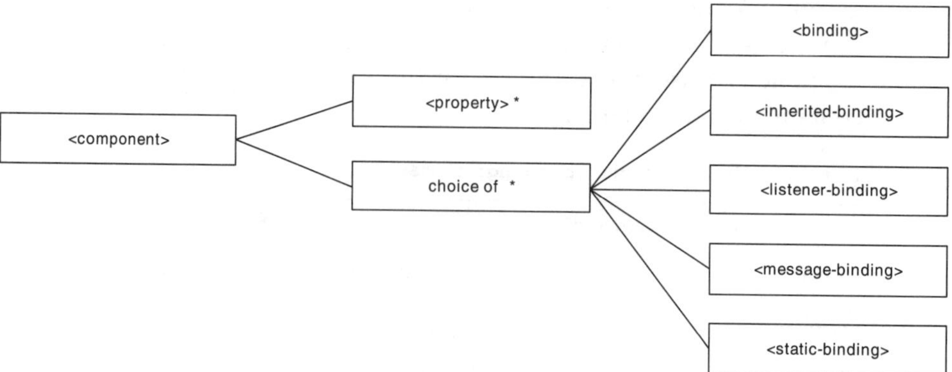

Figure D.3 The `<component>` element primarily contains different types of bindings for the parameters of the component.

Table D.6 Attributes of the `<component>` element

Attribute name	Required?	Description
`copy-of`	No	Identifies another component, already defined in the containing page or component, to use as a template for this component. May not be specified with the `type` attribute.
`id`	Yes	The ID used for the component, which must be unique within the container and must be a valid Java identifier.
`inherit-informal-parameters`	No	If `yes`, then the component inherits informal parameters from its container. The default is `no`.
`type`	No	The type of component to create. The type may include a prefix to identify the library that contains the component. May not be specified with the `copy-of` attribute.

<component-type>

The `<component-type>` element is used within an application specification (`<application>`) or library specification (`<library-specification>`) to define a type of component. Normally, this is not needed; in most cases, putting the component specification (the .jwc file) in the same folder as the application or library specification is sufficient. You use `<component-type>` when the specification file is not stored in the default location.

Keep in mind that `<component-type>` may not contain other elements. Table D.7 lists the attributes for `<component-type>`.

Table D.7 Attributes for the `<component-type>` element

Attribute name	Required?	Description
`specification-path`	Yes	The location, relative to the application or library specification, of the component's specification file
`type`	Yes	The component type to define

<component-specification>

The `<component-specification>` element is the root element of a component specification file (with a .jwc extension). A component specification defines a reusable component, including its formal parameters, and specifies whether it uses or discards its body, as well as embedded components and assets. Figure D.4 shows the elements that may be enclosed by `<component-specification>`.

The `<component-specification>` element's `class` attribute is used to identify the Java class for the component. If the component has formal parameters or

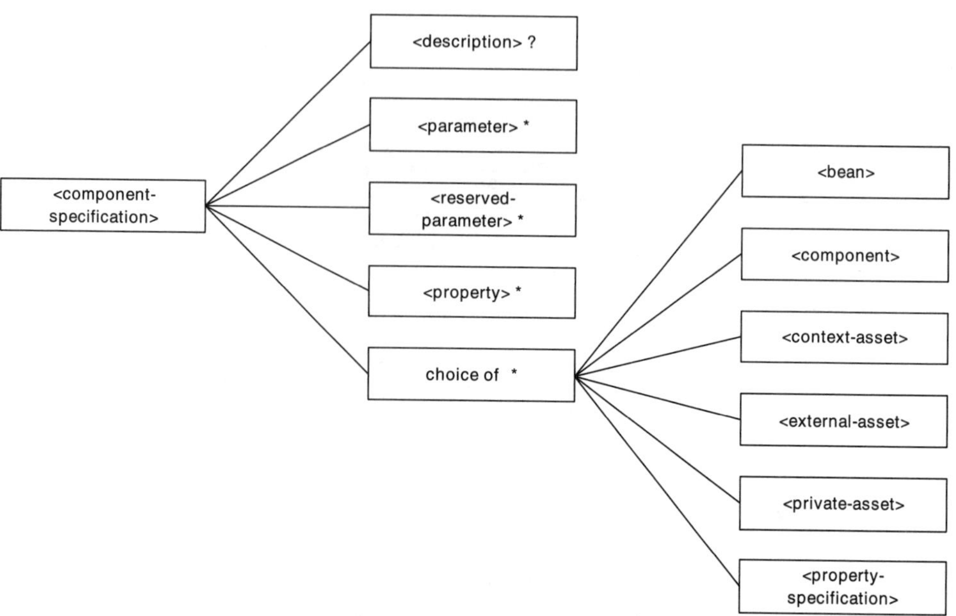

Figure D.4 The `<component-specification>` element defines the parameters, beans, components, and assets used by the component.

any specified properties, then Tapestry will create a subclass to provide the attributes and accessor methods for those properties. Table D.8 lists the attributes for the `<component-specification>` element.

Table D.8 Attributes for the `<component-specification>` element

Attribute name	Required?	Description
`allow-body`	No	If `yes` (the default), then the component keeps its body; if `no`, the component discards its body (and the body may not define components).
`allow-informal-parameters`	No	If `Yes` (the default), then the component will allow informal parameters. If `no`, then informal parameters are not allowed.
`class`	No	The Java class for the component, or `BaseComponent` if not specified. Tapestry will create a subclass to contain specified properties and parameters.

<context-asset>

The `<context-asset>` element is one of three elements used to define assets. (Assets are described in chapters 2 and 6.) Use `<context-asset>` to define an asset stored within your web application context. The element may appear inside `<page-specification>` or `<component-specification>`. The asset path is relative to the web application context root. The `<context-asset>` element may contain the `<property>` element. Table D.9 lists its attributes.

Table D.9 Attributes for the `<context-asset>` element

Attribute name	Required?	Description
`name`	Yes	The name of the asset to define, which must be a valid Java identifier
`path`	Yes	The path of the asset, relative to the context root

<description>

The `<description>` element appears inside many other elements and allows a user-presentable description to be attached to many elements. It is always optional, and the framework does not directly use the description. The descriptive text is the character content enclosed by the `<description>` element. This element may not enclose any other elements.

<extension>

The `<extension>` element is used to create an application extension. Application extensions are similar in intent to helper beans (the `<bean>` element) but are global to the entire application. The `<extension>` element appears inside the `<application>` element (of an application specification), or inside the `<library-specification>` element of a library specification. Figure D.5 shows the elements that may be contained within an `<extension>` element.

The `<extension>` element defines a JavaBean to instantiate. Normally, an extension is instantiated only when first referenced (see the Javadoc for the `ILibrarySpecification` interface). The `immediate` attribute is used to force the extension to be instantiated when the application initializes. Table D.10 lists the attributes of the `<extension>` element.

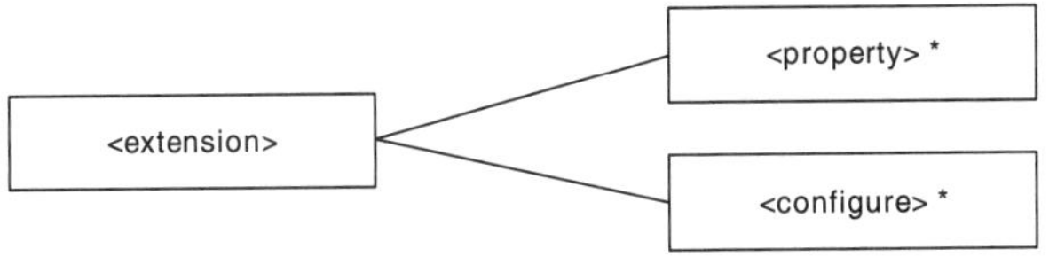

Figure D.5 The `<extension>` element contains metadata (`<property>`) and `<configure>` elements to set the properties of the extension.

Table D.10 Attributes of the `<extension>` element

Attribute name	Required?	Description
`class`	Yes	The name of the Java class to instantiate.
`immediate`	No	If `yes`, then the extension is instantiated and configured at startup; if `no` (the default), then the extension is instantiated lazily, on first reference.
`name`	Yes	The name of the extension, which is usually qualified with a Java package prefix (i.e., org.apache.tapestry.property-source).

<external-asset>

The `<external-asset>` element is one of three used to define assets. (Assets are described in chapters 2 and 6.) The `<external-asset>` element is used to define an asset at an arbitrary URL. External assets are never localized; they are always used as is. This element may appear inside `<page-specification>` or `<component-specification>`, and it may contain the `<property>` element. Its attributes are listed in table D.11.

Table D.11 Attributes of the `<external-asset>` element

Attribute name	Required?	Description
`name`	Yes	The name of the asset to define, which must be a valid Java identifier
`URL`	Yes	The URL of the asset, which is used as is

<inherited-binding>

The `<inherited-binding>` element is used to bind a parameter of a component to a parameter of its container. This element appears inside the `<component>` element and may not contain other elements. Table D.12 lists the attributes for the `<inherited-binding>` element.

Table D.12 Attributes of the `<inherited-binding>` element

Attribute name	Required?	Description
`name`	Yes	The name of the component parameter to bind
`parameter-name`	Yes	The name of the containing component's parameter to bind

<library>

The `<library>` element is used in an application specification (`<application>`) or library specification (`<library-specification>`) to identify a library that may be referenced in the page and component specifications of the application or referencing library. The name provided becomes a prefix on the component type. This is demonstrated in chapters 7 and 8, where the Palette component (from the Tapestry contributions library) is used.

The `<library>` element may not contain other elements. Its attributes are listed in table D.13.

Table D.13 Attributes of the `<library>` element

Attribute name	Required?	Description
`id`	Yes	The ID for the library, which must be a valid Java identifier. The ID is used as a prefix to access the components within the library.
`specification-path`	Yes	The path to the library. If a relative path, then it is relative to the referencing application or library specification; if a complete path (starting with a /), then the specification is expected to be stored on the classpath (i.e., within a JAR file).

<library-specification>

The `<library-specification>` element is the root element of a library specification. It is similar to the `<application>` element, except that library specifications are not optional—a library must have a specification, even if it is empty.

The `<library-specification>` element can contain the same elements as `<application>` (see figure D.1 for a listing). The `<library-specification>` element does not have any attributes.

<listener-binding>

The `<listener-binding>` element allows listeners (for Form, DirectLink, and similar components) to be specified, in the page or component specification, using a scripting language such as Jython. This functionality is targeted at rapid application development and is still experimental. The character content enclosed by the `<listener-binding>` element consists of the script you want to execute. Table D.14 lists the attributes for the `<listener-binding>` element.

The `<listener-binding>` element is based on the open source Bean Scripting Framework (http://jakarta.apache.org/bsf), a runtime environment that supports multiple scripting languages. The default scripting language is Jython (Python

Table D.14 Attributes for the `<listener-binding>` element

Attribute name	Required?	Description
`language`	No	The name of the scripting language used by the script
`name`	Yes	The name of the parameter of the component to bind to the listener

implemented in Java). More information on Jython is available from www.jython.org/. Jython is not distributed with Tapestry, and you must download it separately and include it in the runtime classpath.

<message-binding>

The `<message-binding>` element appears inside a `<component>` element. It is used to bind a parameter of a component to a literal value from the containing component's localized message properties. The `<message-binding>` element may not contain other elements. Table D.15 lists the attributes of this element.

Table D.15 Attributes for the `<message-binding>` element

Attribute name	Required?	Description
`name`	Yes	The name of the component parameter to bind
`key`	Yes	The key used to obtain the localized message

<page>

The `<page>` element is used to define a page, much like a `<component-type>` defines a component. It appears within the `<application>` and `<library-specification>` elements, and is only necessary when the page specification cannot be located by the normal search path.

The `<page>` element may not enclose other elements. The attributes for the `<page>` elements are shown in table D.16.

Table D.16 Attributes for the `<page>` element

Attribute name	Required?	Description
`name`	Yes	The name of the page, which must be a valid Java identifier
`specification-path`	Yes	The location of the page specification, relative to the application or library specification

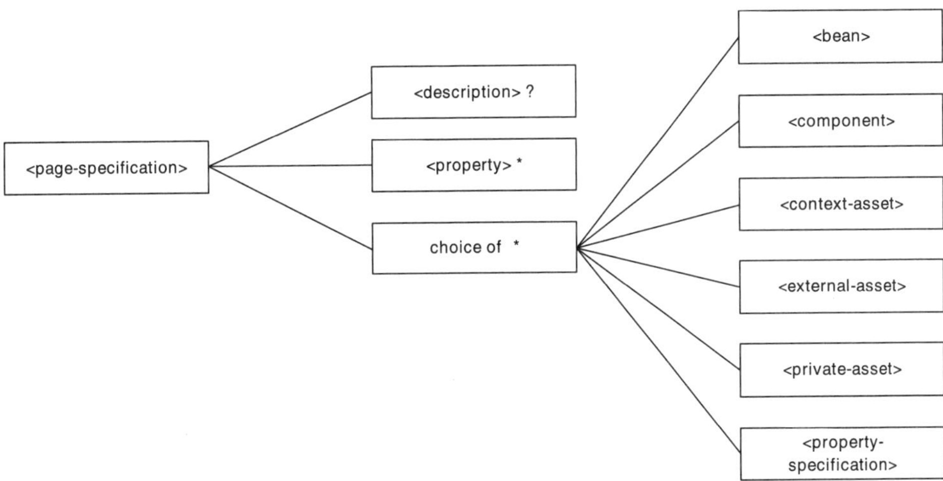

Figure D.6 The `<page-specification>` element is similar to the `<component-specification>` element, with elements related to parameters omitted.

<page-specification>

The `<page-specification>` element is the root element for a Tapestry page specification. Page specifications are similar to component specifications, with those attributes and elements related to parameters removed (pages do not have parameters). The common elements are those that describe embedded components, assets, beans, and properties.

Figure D.6 identifies the elements that may be enclosed within the `<page-specification>` element.

Table D.17 lists the lone attribute for the `<page-specification>` element, `class`. When the `<property-specification>` element is used to define new properties, Tapestry will create a subclass containing the necessary attributes and accessor methods.

Table D.17 Attribute for the `<page-specification>` element

Attribute name	Required?	Description
`class`	no	The page's class, or `BasePage` if not specified

<parameter>

The `<parameter>` element is used to define a formal parameter inside a `<component-specification>`. The `<parameter>` element may contain a `<description>` element, which is used to document the parameter. Table D.18 lists the attributes of the <parameter> element. Components and component parameters are discussed in chapter 6.

Table D.18 Attributes for the <parameter> element

Attribute name	Required?	Description
default-value	No	A default value for the parameter, if not specified, as an OGNL expression.
direction	No	The direction of the parameter, as discussed in chapter 7. The attribute value can be in, form, auto or the default, custom.
name	Yes	The name of the parameter, which must be a valid Java identifier.
property-name	No	If specified, then the property for the parameter will be created with the given name rather than the parameter name. This is used when the parameter name collides with an existing parameter, such as the page parameter on the PageLink component.
required	No	If yes, then the parameter must be bound. If no (the default), then it is acceptable to omit the parameter.
type	No	The name of a Java class or primitive type; this is used when creating a property for the parameter. If not specified, then java.lang.Object is used.

<private-asset>

The <private-asset> is one of three elements used to define assets. (Assets are described in chapters 2 and 6.) The <private-asset> element is used to define an asset stored on the classpath. Typically, such a resource is distributed as part of a JAR containing a component library. The <private-asset> element may appear inside <page-specification> or <component-specification>. The resource path is relative to the specification file. The <private-asset> element may contain the <property> element; its attributes are listed in table D.19.

Table D.19 Attributes for the <private-asset> element

Attribute name	Required?	Description
name	Yes	The name of the asset to define, which must be a valid Java identifier
resource-path	Yes	The path to the asset

<property>

The `<property>` element is used to define metadata about the element which contains it;[1] it is contained by many elements, notably `<application>`, `<component-specification>`, and `<page-specification>`. Tapestry makes only limited use of the `<property>` element (such as to define the `Visit` object's class). Chapter 10 includes an example of an application-specific use of the `<property>` element. Beyond that, this element is provided as a flexible hook to be exploited by future Tapestry tools; for example, it could be used by a Model-Driven Architecture (MDA) tool to facilitate round-trip engineering of a generated Tapestry application.

In any event, the `<property>` element contains no other elements. Table D.20 lists the attributes of this element.

Table D.20 Attributes for the `<property>` element

Attribute name	Required?	Description
`name`	Yes	The name of the metadata property.
`value`	No	The value of the property; if not specified, then the enclosed character data is the value for the property.

<property-specification>

The `<property-specification>` element directs Tapestry to create a new property within the page or component class. Tapestry will create a subclass, adding the necessary attributes and accessor methods (as well as any notifications that are needed).

An OGNL expression may be provided as the initial value for the property; this can be specified as the `initial-value` attribute or as the enclosed character data. The property may be either persistent or transient. Persistent properties are restored at the start of each request cycle, whereas transient properties are reset to the initial value at the end of each request cycle. Table D.21 lists the attributes for the `<property-specification>` element. This element may not enclose other elements.

---

1 In hindsight, the name `<meta>` may have been more appropriate.

Table D.21 Attributes for the `<property-specification>` element

Attribute name	Required?	Description
`initial-value`	No	An OGNL expression used to set the initial value for the property. If omitted, the character data enclosed by the element is used.
`name`	Yes	The name of the property to create.
`persistent`	No	If `yes`, then the value for the property will persist between request cycles. If `no` (the default), the value will be reset to the initial value at the end of each request.
`type`	No	The type of the property: a Java class name or primitive type. If omitted, the default is java.lang.Object.

<reserved-parameter>

The `<reserved-parameter>` element is enclosed by the `<component-specification>` element; it is only used with components that allow informal parameters. Each name specified by a reserved parameter is not allowed as an informal parameter. This is used by components that emit their own HTML attributes to indicate which HTML attributes are reserved to the component. For example, the DirectLink component reserves the `href` parameter, since it generates that parameter in its own implementation.

Each informal parameter is matched, ignoring case, against all reserved names. Informal parameters that match a reserved name or a formal parameter name are discarded.

Table D.22 identifies the sole attribute of the `<reserved-parameter>` element; `<reserved-parameter>` may not contain other elements.

Table D.22 Attribute for the `<reserved-parameter>` element

Attribute name	Required?	Description
`name`	Yes	A name to reserve

<service>

The `<service>` element is used to define a new engine service (as described in chapters 7 and 8). This element may be contained within an application specification (`<application>`) or a library specification (`<library-specification>`). Tapestry starts with a basic set of services; it is possible to override the default implementations of these services or create new services. New services should be given names that avoid conflicts, typically by prefixing the name with a Java package name.

The `<service>` element may not contain other elements. Table D.23 lists its attributes.

Table D.23 Attributes for the `<service>` element

Attribute name	Required?	Description
`class`	Yes	The name of the Java class to instantiate as the service. The class must implement the `IEngineService` interface.
`name`	Yes	The name of the service.

<set-property>

The `<set-property>` element is contained within a `<bean>` element; it is used to set a property of the instantiated bean to a value computed from an OGNL expression. The `<set-property>` element may not contain other elements. Table D.24 lists the attributes for this element.

Table D.24 Attributes for the `<set-property>` element

Attribute name	Required?	Description
`expression`	No	The OGNL expression to set the property to. If not specified, the enclosed content of the element is the source of the expression.
`name`	Yes	The name of the property to set.

<static-binding>

The `<static-binding>` element appears inside the `<component>` element, and it is used to bind a parameter of a component to a static (or literal) value. It may not enclose other elements. Table D.25 lists the attributes for the `<static-binding>` element.

Table D.25 Attributes for the `<static-binding>` element

Attribute name	Required?	Description
`name`	Yes	The name of the component parameter to bind.
`value`	No	The literal value to bind the parameter to. If not specified, the enclosed character content of the element is the literal value.

D.2 Tapestry script specification

Tapestry script specifications are used when generating dynamic JavaScript for a Tapestry page, and are covered in chapter 8. Script specifications consist of five sections:

- Including static JavaScript libraries
- Defining input symbols
- Creating new symbols by combining the input symbols
- Producing the script body
- Producing the script initialization

Figure D.7 shows this structure reflected in the construction of the `<script>` element, the root element of a script specification.

The `<!DOCTYPE>` for a script specification must be

```
<!DOCTYPE script PUBLIC
  "-//Apache Software Foundation//Tapestry Script Specification
➥ 3.0//EN"
  "http://jakarta.apache.org/tapestry/dtd/Script_3_0.dtd">
```

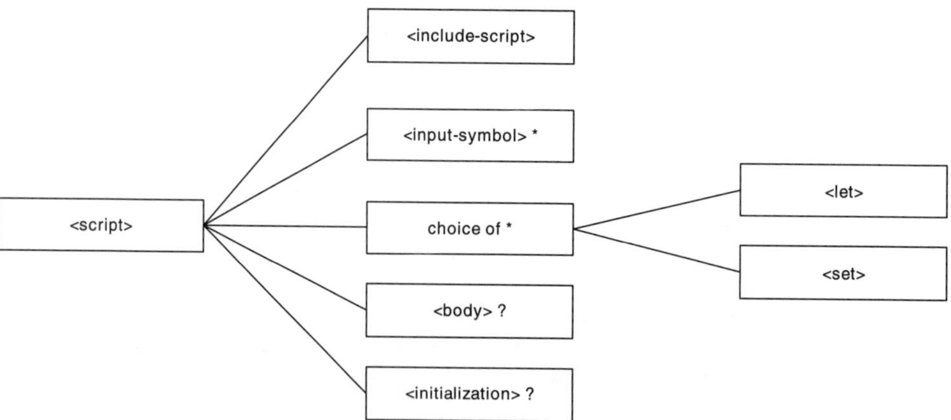

Figure D.7 The `<script>` element is the root element of a Tapestry script specification.

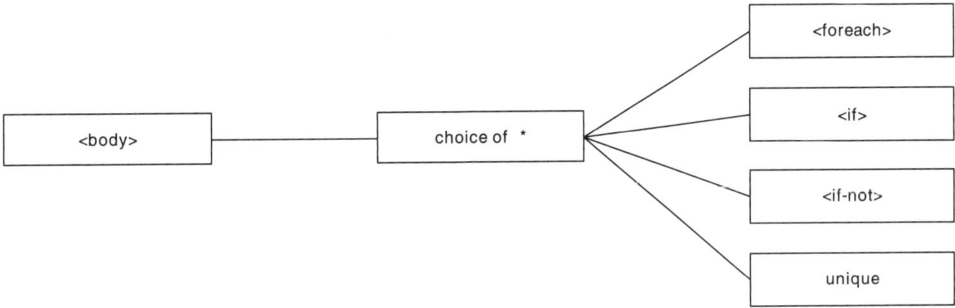

Figure D.8 The <body> element contains text, OGNL expressions, and the other main elements.

<body>

The `<body>` element makes a contribution to the page's main JavaScript block. This element, which takes no attributes, contains a mix of text and elements shown in figure D.8.

Static text is contributed to the JavaScript block as is. Text may also contain expressions, using the Ant-like syntax `${expression}`. See chapter 8 for examples of this.

<foreach>

The `<foreach>` element is analogous to the Foreach component; it iterates over a list of items, rendering its body repeatedly. The `<foreach>` element may contain the exact same content as the `<body>` component (shown in figure D.8).

Like the Foreach component, the `<foreach>` element has attributes for defining the input list, for setting the current item from the list, and for setting the index within the list. These attributes are shown in table D.26.

Table D.26 Attributes of the `<foreach>` element

Attribute name	Required?	Description
`expression`	Yes	The OGNL expression is evaluated to provide the list of items to iterate over; this may be a single object, an array of objects, or a `List` of objects.
`index`	No	If provided, then the index within the loop is stored as a symbol with the provided key.
`key`	Yes	The key used to store the value of the current item from the list.

<if>

The `<if>` element evaluates an expression and renders its body only if the expression evaluates to true. This element may contain the exact same content as the `<body>` component (shown in figure D.8). Table D.27 lists the single attribute of the `<if>` element.

Table D.27 Attribute of the `<if>` element

Attribute name	Required?	Description
`expression`	Yes	The OGNL expression to evaluate

<if-not>

The `<if-not>` element is exactly the same as the `<if>` element, with one exception: It renders its body only if the expression evaluates to false.

<include-script>

The `<include-script>` element is used to include a common JavaScript library as part of the page. Tapestry will ensure that the library will be included only once, regardless of how many times a script specification is executed (or how many script specifications include the same script). This may be useful when you're integrating a third-party JavaScript library into a Tapestry application.

The JavaScript library must be stored on the classpath, typically as part of a JAR file containing a component library. The path can be specified as a relative path, in which case the path is relative to the script specification (this should be used only with script specifications that are stored on the classpath). If the path is absolute (starting with a leading /), then the location is always assumed to be on the classpath, regardless of the location of the script specification.

Table D.28 lists the attribute of the `<include-script>` element.

Table D.28 Attribute of the `<include-script>` element

Attribute name	Required?	Description
`resource-path`	Yes	The path to the library

<initialization>

The `<initialization>` element is exactly the same as the `<body>` element, with one exception: The content of the `<initialization>` element is placed in a JavaScript block that executes only when the page loads. The `<initialization>` content is typically used to connect client-side objects to event handlers (with the event handlers defined within the `<body>` element).

<input-symbol>

The `<input-symbol>` element is used to define an input symbol to a script specification. Defining input symbols is optional but useful; it allows the framework to verify that all required input symbols are specified and that the values passed are of the correct type.

The `<input-symbol>` element may not contain other elements; its attributes are defined in table D.29.

Table D.29 Attributes of the `<input-symbol>` element

Attribute name	Required?	Description
`class`	No	The Java class (or interface) that the symbol value must be assignable to; if not specified, `java.lang.Object` is used.
`key`	Yes	The input symbol to be defined.
`required`	No	If `yes`, then a non-null value must be supplied to the symbol. If `no` (the default), then it is acceptable to omit the symbol.

<let>

The `<let>` element is used to create a new symbol by combining existing symbols. The body of the `<let>` element is evaluated and converted into a string, which is trimmed of leading and trailing whitespace and assigned as a new symbol. The symbol may be further modified to ensure that it is unique throughout the entire page (as discussed in chapter 8).

The `<let>` element contains the same content as the `<body>` element (in figure D.8). Table D.30 lists the attributes of the `<let>` element.

Table D.30 Attributes of the `<let>` element

Attribute name	Required?	Description
`key`	Yes	The key for the new symbol.
`unique`	No	If `yes`, then the value may be modified to ensure that it is unique.

<set>

The `<set>` element is used to create a new symbol by evaluating an OGNL expression. The `<set>` element may not contain any content. The new symbol is not necessarily a text value; it is whatever type results from evaluating the expression. Table D.31 lists the attributes for the `<set>` element.

Table D.31 Attributes of the `<set>` element

Attribute name	Required?	Description
`expression`	Yes	The OGNL expression to evaluate
`key`	Yes	The key for the new symbol

<unique>

The `<unique>` element defines an area within the specification that is evaluated only once per render of the page, regardless of how many times the script specification is executed. This is useful for producing portions of the page's JavaScript block that contains invariant sections. This is similar to including the content of an external JavaScript library (as with the `<include-script>` element) but doing so inline.

The `<unique>` element takes no attributes and allows the same content as the `<body>` element (shown in figure D.8).

index

Symbols

A

N

O

Q

R

S

W

X

Z